1001 WINES
YOU MUST TRY BEFORE YOU DIE

1001 WINES
YOU MUST TRY BEFORE YOU DIE

GENERAL EDITOR NEIL BECKETT

PREFACE BY HUGH JOHNSON

CASSELL
ILLUSTRATED

A Quint**essence** Book

First published in Great Britain in 2008 by Cassell Illustrated
A division of Octopus Publishing Group Limited
Endeavour House, 189 Shaftesbury Avenue
London, WC2H 8JY
www.octopusbooks.co.uk

An Hachette UK Company
www.hachette.co.uk

A CIP catalogue record for this book is available from the British Library

ISBN: 978-1-84403-807-7
QSS.KWIN2

This book was designed and produced by
Quint**essence** Editions Ltd.
The Old Brewery, 6 Blundell Street
London N7 9BH
www.1001beforeyoudie.com

First edition published in 2008
This edition first published in 2014

Update Editor	Ruth Patrick
Update Designer	Dean Martin
Senior Editor	Jodie Gaudet
Editor	Frank Ritter
Editorial Assistant	Andrew Smith
Copy Editor	Rebecca Gee
Art Director	Akihiro Nakayama
Designer	Jon Wainwright
Image Editor	Stuart George
Editorial Director	Jane Laing
Publisher	Mark Fletcher

Color reproduction by Pica Digital Pte Ltd., Singapore
Printed in China by Midas Printing Ltd.

Contents

Preface   6

Introduction   8

Index by region of origin   12

Sparkling wines   **20**

White wines   **122**

Red wines   **410**

Fortified wines   **848**

Glossary   934

Index of producers   938

Index by price   945

Contributors   956

Picture credits   959

Acknowledgments   960

Preface

By Hugh Johnson, wine author

"There are no great wines, only great bottles of wine." It is one of the oldest sayings among wine lovers, and it has to stand at the head of any list defining what should be the treasures of the cellar. It means, of course, that wine is a liquid with a life of its own. From the same barrel can come bottles that are supremely delicious and others that leave only disappointed expectations. At the same time it reflects on the drinker; greatness is a matter of recognition. The finest wines can go unappreciated, and wines of much lesser status can create moments of sublime enjoyment. The wine trade has interests in convincing you and me that quality is something objective and measurable. You and I know that it is no such thing: you love what you love. The only measurable thing, in the final analysis, is price. Price depends on consensus—and that is what the market is for. However, there are many things that move the market that have little to do with quality.

Therefore this book is not called "The 1001 Best Wines in the World." The dimension in which it plays is variety. Wine is a miraculous product. You ferment ripe grapes—and that is it. Which grapes, from where, when, and by whom are all the parameters of difference. Yet with every harvest, all over the world, certain predictable results appear: certain tastes that cannot be patented. They can be imitated—up to a point. But uniqueness is guaranteed; the precise circumstances that produced one wine cannot be reproduced. If they could be reproduced, the whole edifice that is the wine trade, indeed the wine world, would be pointless. Château Lafite cannot make Château Latour: end of story.

When I first met fine wine, nearly fifty years ago, the story did almost end there. The wines worth meeting may have run into a few hundreds, but nowhere close to 1,000. Half a century of progress has had the opposite effect to what many predicted: that all wines would eventually taste the same. Greater knowledge, growing aspirations, new territories, and more money have simply expanded the list of unique experiences wine has to offer. Each generation of practitioners makes its contribution. Very few wines, once established as memorable, drop off the list. We are the fortunate beneficiaries of a world of increasing variety and increasing choice. In the mere thirty-five years since I first did a Puck, girdling the earth in slightly more than forty minutes for my *World Atlas of Wine*, wine geography has set off in directions I never dreamed of.

Much of this expansion has consisted of trying to find new wells of anything adequate to drink. It was not terribly interesting, to me at least, that Australians had found a way of turning water (from the Murray River) into wine. Wines from regions where the grapevine merely acts as a pump for sugary water rarely command attention. What were, and are, always interesting are trials of the vine in marginal places where it is touch and go whether grapes can be persuaded to ripen. Cool climates have been the Holy Grail of New World winemakers through all these years. It is matter for serious pondering that cool climates may be what we will all be searching for in years to come.

The most productive new regions for a list of must-taste wines are either high in latitude, therefore, or high in altitude. Up in the Andes; down near the Cape; northward up the Pacific Coast; southward almost into New Zealand's fiord land; even snuggling up to the Niagara Falls. It is not that grapevines like extremes, it is winemakers who do—and, of course, their highly critical customers.

If today's wine atlas, then, is nearly twice as long as its great-great-grandfather, it is surely unalloyed good news. What do you say when you hear somebody is planting cuttings from Château Lafite in China? Is "Yippee!" the current idiom?

1001 Wines You Must Try Before You Die is a selection that ranges from new discoveries to bottles so outstanding they remain benchmarks after half a century. No one can keep up with all the annual additions to the world's wine list. To be listed here, though, wines must have a record of high quality and, even more important, distinctive character. You may never taste them all, but it is certainly time to start.

Hugh Johnson, March 2008

Introduction
By Neil Beckett, General Editor

A thousand and one wines are at once a thousand too few and a thousand too many. A thousand too few because, as Hugh Johnson has highlighted in his Preface (see pp. 6–7), the fine-wine world is now wider than ever before; it would be easy to come up with at least as many again—many times as many if we reveled in the full range of vintages, which in many cases stretch back a hundred years. A thousand too many because we are in danger of forgetting how much pleasure any one wine can give.

Comparing and contrasting can be as fascinating with wine as with anything else. And where our preference changes with almost every eager sip—now for the Bâtard-Montrachet, now for the Chevalier-Montrachet—so that in the end we have no preference and are aware only of differences in personality, we can almost double our pleasure. But such giddily happy occasions are rare. Even with two wines—still more the three, four, five, or six that may be competing for our favor at extravagant fine-wine dinners nowadays—the danger is that one of the wines will emerge "the winner." The others, sadly and unfairly, will be the losers. How apt the French saying, "the best is the enemy of the good." So do not let the other thousand wines here blind you to the one you have, or might have, in your glass. (Reducing this risk is one of the many reasons for not having scores.)

To talk even of one wine is too general. As Hugh again rightly reminds us, "there are no great wines, only great bottles of wine"—another French saying, and probably the most profound thing that has ever been said or written on the subject. That is not only because different bottles of the same wine will be different in chemical or physical terms. What appears to be the same Champagne may have been disgorged at several different times, some releases having much longer on lees than others, and therefore tasting very different. Many older wines (Bordeaux, Burgundy, and classic fortified wines right up to the 1970s) may have been bottled at different places as well as at different times. Then, of course, there is the cork: even where it is free of the TCA (Trichloroanisole) taint that can spoil the wine, the amount of oxygen it lets in will vary widely. The effect of this will depend in turn on the conditions to which the wine is exposed during transport and storage (above all on the temperature). So the fact is that even bottles from the same case can differ in objective, verifiable ways.

They differ even more in subjective ways, for there is always what we bring (or do not bring) to the party—appetite, enthusiasm, experience, expertise, health, humor, receptiveness, sympathy . . . If we have a cold, or are down, or too hungry, or too rushed, or too tired, or cannot abide the

In this book the following abbreviations are used:

ABV	Alcohol by volume
AG	Auslese Goldkapsel
ALG	Auslese lange Goldkapsel
BA	Beerenauslese
C.	Cabernet
Ch.	Château
DC	Deuxième Cru
Dom.	Domaine
GC	Grand Cru
LBV	Late Bottled Vintage
NV	Non-Vintage
P.	Pinot
PC	Premier Cru
S.	Sauvignon
SGN	Sélection de Grains Nobles
ST	Spätlese Trocken
T.	Touriga
TBA	Trockenbeerenauslese
VORS	Very Old Rare Sherry
VOS	Very Old Sherry
VT	Vendange Tardive
VV	Vieilles Vignes

$	under £10
$ $	£10-20
$ $ $	£21-50
$ $ $ $	£51-100
$ $ $ $ $	£101 and more

guest opposite, or are unable to smell anything other than his aftershave or her perfume, then the wine will not taste half as special as it might on another more conducive occasion. The atmospheric pressure, the humidity, the temperature of both the room and the wine, the time of day, the glass, the food, the previous wine, the water, the wine waiter, whether the wine has been decanted and for how long—all these and other variables make sure that the same wine will never taste exactly the same twice.

And that is what is best about the "only great bottles" dictum: it captures the existential thrill of wine. Unlike many of the other worthwhile subjects in our 1001 series—albums, books, movies, buildings, paintings, classical recordings—wine has to be destroyed to be enjoyed. For some, its fleeting nature reduces its value. For others of us, its immediacy is part of its magic. The North Star may be reassuring, helping us to know where we are; but a shooting star is far more spellbinding, reminding us of where we are going. It may be there only briefly, but it may live a lifetime in the memory. It may be transient, but it may be transcendental too.

Coming back to earth, and to this book: For all the profound wisdom of "only great bottles," every bottle is a bottle *of something*. And although many of the greatest wines in this book are non-vintage (some of the very finest Champagnes, Madeiras, Ports, and Sherries, for example), most are vintage—largely or wholly the product of a single year, which is shown on the label. Vintages can vary widely in quality and in style: the 1945 may still be superb, and may remain so for many years, while the 1946 (or the 1956, for that matter) may be undrinkable. Prices vary widely as well, of course: the 1945 may be many times the price of the 1946 (though the difference may not always reflect the difference in quality, and confidence tricks, fads, fashion, reputation, rarity, and scarcity may all be relevant, too).

To say that vintages vary is not to say that there may not be equally good vintages of the same wine. The current obsession with what is supposed to be "the great vintage"—2000, 2003, 2005 in Bordeaux, for instance—is not always in the best interest of the wine lover. The differences from one year to the next, which mean that there is a new wine every vintage, are part of the rich variety of wine. And now more than ever, most vintages have their own worthwhile story to tell.

There has always been a reason for specifying the "great" vintages in this book (which should be clear in each case), but the reason will vary. Often it will be an acknowledged classic, a particularly special vintage for the wine;

in keeping with the aspirational nature of this series, if one could drink only one vintage of this wine, this would be it. Here is its essence, its fullest expression. Alternatively, especially where quality is consistently high, and where we could have chosen any one of many vintages, it may be because it is historic in some way—the first or the last—or because there is an unusual story to tell. Other times, it will deliberately not be one of the very best vintages—which may, after all, be unrepresentative; instead it will be a very good, maybe more recent, more typical vintage. Other times, it will deliberately be a lesser year, to show how good the top wines can be even then, when they may also be particularly good value, too. Sometimes other vintages well worth seeking out for one reason or another are specified in the text. But where this is not the case, it may normally be supposed that most other vintages of the wine will still be well worth a try. The producer is almost always more important than the vintage.

Just as we have not always gone for the "best" vintages, so we have not always gone for the "best" wines. Although all of the most famous producers are here, and many of the most famous wines, including the *crème de la crème*, this is not meant to be a list of the 1001 "greatest" wines—which would have involved a far narrower range and multiple vintages of the same wine. We have resisted the temptation to have more than one wine from the same producer where the only difference would have been the vintage. This has been hardest and most invidious, perhaps, for the Bordeaux châteaux: which Lafite, Latour, or Yquem vintage is so much better than all the rest? Where a producer offers several outstanding wines, however, we have occasionally included two or more, though seldom the full range, which in Burgundy or Germany, for example, might easily run to ten or more wines in a single vintage. We have not always gone for what is normally regarded as the "top" wines, either: We may have opted for a premier cru rather than a grand cru; for a regular bottling rather than a reserve or special cuvée; for an Auslese rather than a Trockenbeerenauslese (again for reasons that should normally be obvious from the text).

If this is not a list of the greatest wines, still less is it a list of favorite wines (though most of ours are included). Occasionally we have chosen a wine because it is controversial, a love-it-or-hate-it wine (Château Pavie 2003, for instance), and the only way for you to settle the debate in your own mind is to try the wine. If you love it, so much the better; if you hate it, at least you will know and can avoid wasting money on a case. Very occasionally we have included a wine because it is an historic brand or has been highly influential in some way (Blue Nun, for example). Nobody is going to claim that this is a great wine, but it is interesting in other ways, and most wine lovers should try it at least once—if only to determine why they might turn up their noses.

Although few of us can get through 1001 of anything, we hope that you will buy and try as many of these wines as you can. All of them, however old or rare (even the 1795 Barbeito Terrantez), can still be bought—even if only at auction or online and for a pretty price. All of them, however old, should still be at least pleasant to taste (providing they are in good condition), and none have been chosen only for their antique or curiosity value. Most of the younger wines should be approachable now, but still have at least a few years ahead of them. We have tried to indicate a drinking window for every wine, though the ideal moment will vary with taste.

But this is meant to be much more than another buyer's guide, of which there are already too many. Many wine magazines, and most wine columns in newspapers, also offer little more than shopping lists. Instead, this book treats wine as a product that has the potential not only to give great pleasure, but to express, in a special way, particular people, places, and times. While the book should be of service to those whom Terry Theise pities as "pragmatic hedonists," it should be of still greater value to those whose pleasure is enriched by what they know about what they taste.

Even with wines we may never taste, there should still be sufficient intrinsic interest to make reading about them worthwhile. I want to know about Mount Everest and K2 even though I may never see them, still less scale them. Similarly, absorbing the culture of wine means knowing its high points, not only because it helps to put the rest in perspective.

A great wine is the result of attention to 1001 details from grape to glass. The details of viticulture and winemaking are not here for their own sake but to help explain why the wine is as it is. If there is reference to altitude, soil type, or yield, to *dosage*, *élevage,* or yeast, then it is because these determine in some way the smell and taste of the wine.

As with any such selection, even one running to 1001, there are gaps that may seem inexplicable to some. We will all be conscious of producers, wines, vintages, even whole countries or regions that are not represented. But filling the gaps should be almost as much fun as filling the glass. All of us who have been involved with this book hope that it will introduce you to wines that will please, or tease, or thrill, and that one way or another will be worth not only drinking but reading and talking about as well.

Index by region of origin

ARGENTINA
Calchaquí Valley
Yacochuya de Michel Rolland 844
Mendoza
Achával Ferrer 416
Alta Vista 418
Altos Las Hormigas 419
Catena Alta 481
Clos de Los Siete 494
Terrazas/Cheval Blanc 804
Patagonia, Río Negro Valley
Noemía de Patagonia 702

AUSTRALIA
New South Wales
Clonakilla 493
Hunter Valley
Brokenwood 465
De Bortoli 181
Lake's Folly 269
McWilliam's 282
Tyrrell's 389
South Australia
Adelaide Hills
Shaw + Smith 362
Barossa Valley
Greenock Creek 578
Lehmann, Peter 637
Melton, Charles 666
Penfolds 724–5, 726, 906
Ringland, Chris 760
Rockford 762
St. Hallett 772
Torbreck 810
Turkey Flat 822
Yalumba 404, 844
Clare Valley
Barry, Jim 440
Grosset 219
Mount Horrocks 302
Wendouree 838
Coonawarra
Balnaves 439
Katnook Estate 602
Majella 648

Parker 714
Wynn's 842
Eden Ridge
Mountadam 305
Eden Valley
Henschke 593
McLaren Vale
Battle of Bosworth 442
Coriole Lloyd 506
D'Arenberg 517
Hardys 584
Wrattonbully
Tapanappa Whalebone 794
Tasmania
Domaine A 522
Victoria
Beechworth
Giaconda 213, 564
Gippsland
Bass Phillip 441
Goulburn Valley
Tahbilk 374
Grampians
Mount Langi Ghiran 691
Heathcote
Jasper Hill 598
Wild Duck Creek 841
Mornington Peninsula
Stonier Estate 367, 788
Nagambie Lakes
Mitchelton 300
Traeger, David 384
Rutherglen
Chambers 860
Morris Wines 894–5
Stanton & Killeen 920
Western Victoria
Seppelt Great Western 112
Yarra Valley
Chandon, Domaine 40
Coldstream Hills 498
Mount Mary 691
Yarra Yering 845
Western Australia
Great Southern
Howard Park 237
Margaret River
Cullen 512
Leeuwin Estate 271

Moss Wood 687
Pierro 324
Vasse Felix 829

AUSTRIA
Burgenland
Moric 683
Tschida, Angerhof 387
Neusiedlersee
Kracher 256
Opitz, Willi 704
Umathum 823
Neusiedlersee-Hügelland
Feiler-Artinger 198
Prieler 742
Schröck, Heidi 359
Lower Austria
Kamptal
Bründlmayer 149
Hiedler 235
Loimer 277
Schloss Gobelsburg 355
Kremstal
Nigl 311
Salomon-Undhof 351
Thermenregion
Stadlmann, Johann 364
Wachau
Freie Weingärtner Wachau 212
Hirtzberger 236
Knoll 253
Nikolaihof 311
Pichler, F.X. 320
Prager 328
Weinviertel
Pfaffl, R & A 320
Styria
Polz, E & W 327

BRAZIL
Rio Grande do Sul
Cave Geisse 60

CANADA
British Columbia
Inniskillin 240
Mission Hill 300

CHILE
Aconcagua
Casablanca, Viña 476
Matetic 659

Central Valley
Viñedos Orgánicos
Emiliana 836
Colchagua Valley, Apalta
Casa Lapostolle 475
Maipo Valley
Antiyal 424
Concha y Toro 501, 502
Cousiño Macul, Viña 511
El Principal, Viña 538
Haras de Pirque, Viña 583
Santa Rita, Viña 776
Santa Cruz, Colchagua
Montes 676–7

CROATIA
Peljesac
Grgic, Miljenko 578

ENGLAND
Hampshire
Coates & Seely 42
West Sussex
Nyetimber 95

FRANCE
Alsace
Blanck, Paul 136
Bott Geyl, Domaine 144
Deiss, Domaine Marcel 182
Hugel 239
Josmeyer 244
Kreydenweiss, Marc 258
Muré, René 307, 696
Ostertag, André 315
Rolly-Gassmann 344
Schlumberger 359
Weinbach, Domaine 400
Zind-Humbrecht, Dom.
406, 408
Beaujolais
Duboeuf, Georges 530
Moulin-à-Vent, Château du 688
Villa Ponciago 835
Bordeaux
Côtes de Bourg
Falfas, Château 544
Roc de Cambes, Château 761
Côtes de Castillon
Domaine de l'A 522
Graves
Clos Floridène 169

Haut-Médoc
Sociando-Mallet, Château 784
Listrac
Fourcas-Hosten, Château 553
Margaux
Angludet, Château d' 420
Brane-Cantenac, Château 462
Durfort-Vivens, Château 536
Giscours, Château 566
Margaux, Château 289, 651
Palmer, Château 710
Rauzan-Ségla, Château 754
Montagne St.-Emilion
Montaiguillon, Château 675
Moulis
Poujeaux, Château 740
Pauillac
Grand-Puy-Lacoste, Château 574
Lafite Rothschild, Château 617
Latour, Château 626
Lynch-Bages, Château 647
Mouton Rothschild, Château 693
Pichon-Longueville, Châteaux 735
Pontet-Canet, Château 740
Pessac-Léognan
Brown, Château 465
Carmes-Haut-Brion, Les 473
Chevalier Blanc, Domaine de 162
Chevalier, Domaine de 488
Haut-Bailly, Château 588
Haut-Brion, Château 230, 590
La Louvière, Château 260
La Mission-Haut-Brion 615
Laville Haut-Brion, Château 270
Malartic-Lagravière, Château 284
Pape-Clément, Château 712
Smith-Haut-Lafitte, Château 363
Pomerol
Bon Pasteur, Château Le 452
Conseillante, Château La 502
Eglise-Clinet, Château L' 536
Evangile, Château L' 540
Gazin, Château 561
Hosanna, Château 596
Lafleur, Château 618
La Fleur-Pétrus, Château 611
Latour-à-Pomerol, Château 628
Le Pin 631
Petit-Village, Château 729
Pétrus 730

Providence, Château La 745
Trotanoy, Château 820
Vieux Château Certan 834
Premières Côtes de Bordeaux
Lezongars, L'Enclos de Château 642
St.-Emilion
Angélus, Château 419
Ausone, Château 436
Beauséjour Duffau-Lagarrosse 443
Beau-Séjour Bécot, Château 444
Bélair-Monange, Château 446
Berliquet, Château 447
Canon, Château 469
Canon-La-Gaffelière, Château 471
Cheval Blanc, Château 487
Clos de l'Oratoire 493
Figeac, Château 550
La Dominique, Château 611
La Gomerie, Château 613
La Mondotte 615
Le Dôme 628
Magdelaine, Château 648
Pavie, Château 718
Pavie-Macquin, Château 720
Tertre-Roteboeuf, Château 807
Troplong-Mondot, Château 818
Valandraud, Château 824
St.-Estèphe
Calon-Ségur, Château 468
Cos d'Estournel, Château 509
Haut-Marbuzet, Château 592
Montrose, Château 682
Pez, Château de 732
St.-Julien
Branaire-Ducru, Château 462
Ducru-Beaucaillou, Château 532
Gruaud-Larose, Château 581
Lagrange, Château 621
Léoville-Barton, Château 638
Léoville-Las Cases, Château 640
Léoville-Poyferré, Château 640
Talbot, Château 792
Sauternes
Climens, Château 166
Coutet, Château 174
Doisy-Daëne, Château 185
Fargues, Château de 197
Filhot, Château 204
Gilette, Château 214
Guiraud, Château 220
La Rame, Château 263

Lafaurie-Peyraguey, Château 266
Malle, Château de 284
Nairac, Château 308
Rabaud-Promis, Château 332
Rayne-Vigneau, Château 335
Riessec, Château 341
Suduiraut, Château 368, 370
Tour Blanche, Château La 382
Yquem, Château d' 404

Burgundy
Chablis
Dauvissat, René & Vincent 180
Droin, Domaine 188
Fèvre, Domaine William 202
Laroche, Domaine 270
Long-Depaquit, Domaine 277
Raveneau, Domaine 335
Côte Chalonnaise
Auvenay, Domaine d' 129
Chamirey, Château de 483
Jacqueson, Domaine 243
Villaine, Domaine A. et P. de 394
Côte de Beaune
Angerville, Dom. Marquis d' 420
Armand, Domaine du Comte 430
Boillot, Domaine Jean-Marc 138
Bonneau du Martray, Dom. 141
Bouchard Père et Fils 146
Carillon, Domaine 154
Coche-Dury, Domaine 172
Darviot-Perrin, Domaine 180
Drouhin, Domaine Joseph 189
Jobard, Domaine François 244
Lafarge, Domaine Michel 617
Lafon, Domaine des Comtes 268, 269, 618
Leflaive, Domaine 273
Montille, Domaine Hubert de 680
Ramonet, Domaine 334
Rollin, Domaine 763
Romanée-Conti, Dom. de la 347
Roulot, Domaine Guy 347
Sauzet, Domaine Etienne 352
Vogüé, Dom. Comte Georges de 397
Côte de Nuits
Bachelet, Domaine Denis 438
Barthod, Domaine Ghislaine 441
Bouchard Père & Fils 458
Cathiard, Domaine Sylvain 482
Clos de Tart 494
Drouhin, Domaine Joseph 525

Dugat, Domaine Claude 534
Dugat-Pÿ, Domaine 534
Dujac, Domaine 535
Engel, Domaine René 539
Esmonin, Domaine Sylvie 540
Faiveley, Domaine 544
Fourrier, Domaine 553
Gouges, Domaine Henri 569
Grivot, Domaine Jean 579
Gros, Domaine Anne 579
Jayer, Domaine Henri 599
Lamarche, Domaine 623
Lambrays, Domaine des 624
Leroy, Domaine 642
Liger-Belair, Dom. du Comte 274, 644
Maume, Domaine 660
Méo-Camuzet, Domaine 669
Mugnier, Domaine J.-F. 695
Pataille, Domaine Sylvain 716
Ponsot, Domaine 327, 739
Rémy, Domaine Louis 759
Romanée-Conti, Dom. de la 765–6
Roumier, Domaine Georges 767
Rousseau, Domaine Armand 768
Mâconnais
Fuissé, Château de 212
Guffens-Heynen, Domaine 220
Lafon, Héritiers du Comte 268
Thévenet, Jean 378
Verget, Maison 392

Champagne
Billecart-Salmon 28
Bollinger 32, 35
Bouchard, Cédric 35
Dom Pérignon 52, 54
Gosset 68
Gratien, Alfred 70
Heidsieck, Charles 71
Henriot 72
Lassaigne, Jacques 86
Laurent-Perrier 88
Michel, Bruno 90
Côte des Bar
Drappier 59
Mathieu, Serge 89
Moutard 91
Côte des Blancs
Agrapart 22
Cazals, Claude 40

Dampierre, Comte Audoin de 45
De Sousa 47
Delamotte 48
Diebolt-Vallois 51
Gimonnet, Pierre 62
Krug 81
Larmandier-Bernier 86
Lilbert-Fils 88
Mumm 92
Perrier-Jouët 96
Peters, Pierre 98
Pol Roger 101
Pommery 103
Roederer, Louis 108
Salon 111
Selosse, Jacques 112
Taittinger 114
Veuve Fourny 120
Montagne de Reims
Billiot, Henri 28
Cattier 38
Deutz 51
Dom Ruinart 56, 57
Egly-Ouriet 59
Giraud, Henri 64
Jacquesson 77
Krug 78, 82, 83
Philipponnat 98
Prévost, Jérôme 104
Vilmart 120
Vallée de la Marne
Beaumont des Crayères 24
Billecart-Salmon 26
Brun, Roger 36
Collard, René 45
De Meric 47
Pouillon, Roger 103
Tarlant 117
Veuve Clicquot 118

Jura/Savoy
Arlay, Château d' 129
Dupasquier, Domaine 193
Ganevat, Jean-François 213
Grange des Pères 576
Idylle, Domaine de l' 239
Labet, Domaine 264
Macle, Jean 280
Prieuré de St.-Jean de Bébian 743
Puffeney, Jacques 329
Quenard, André et Michel 330
Tissot, André & Mireille 379

Languedoc-Roussillon
Borie de Maurel 457
Gauby, Domaine 559
La Rectorie, Domaine de 886
Le Soula 271
Mas Amiel 891
Mas Blanc 892
Mas de Daumas Gassac 654
Matassa, Domaine 293
Négly, Château de la 698
Prieuré St.-Christophe, Dom. 743
Tour Vieille, Domaine La 813

Loire
Anjou-Saumur
Baudouin, Domaine Patrick 134
Baumard, Domaine des 134
Clos de la Coulée de Serrant 169
Gratien & Meyer 71
Langlois Château 84
Pithon, Domaine Jo 326
Central Vineyards
Bourgeois, Domaine Henri 148
Cotat François 174
Crochet, Lucien 176
Meín, Viña 294
Mellot, Alphonse 294
Pellé, Domaine Henry 317
Pinard, Vincent 324
Pays Nantais
Ecu, Domaine de l' 194
Pierre-Bise, Château 323
Touraine
Champalou, Didier et
    Catherine 157
Chidaine, Domaine François 162
Clos Naudin, Domaine du 170
Clos du Tue-Boeuf Touraine 170
Couly-Dutheil 510
Druet, Pierre-Jacques 525
Huet, Domaine 72, 237
Marionnet, Henri 289
Taille aux Loups, Dom. de la
    114, 376

Provence
Bandol
Tempier, Domaine 800
Bouches du Rhône
Trévallon, Domaine de 814
Palette
Simone, Château 782

Rhône
Northern
Chapoutier, Domaine 158–9, 486
Chave, Domaine J.-L. 161, 487
Clape, Domaine Auguste 492
Dard et Ribo 517
Graillot, Alain 573
Grillet, Château 216
Guigal 582
Jaboulet Aîné, Paul 597
Perret, André 319
Rostaing, René 766
Sorrel, Marc 786
Texier, Eric 807
Vernay, Georges 393
Verset, Noël 834
Southern
Beaucastel, Château de 135, 442
Bonneau, Henri 454
Cayron, Domaine du 483
Chapoutier, M. 486
Clos des Papes 495
Gourt de Mautens, Domaine 214
Mordorée, Domaine de la 683
Rayas, Château 758
Vieux Télégraphe, Dom. du 835

Southwest
Cahors
Cèdre, Château du 484
Lagrézette, Château 621
Gaillac
Plageoles, Robert & Bernard 326
Jurançon
Cauhapé, Domaine 155
Clos Uroulat 171
Madiran
Montus, Château 682
Monbazillac
Tirecul La Gravière, Château 379

GEORGIA
Kakheti
Alaverdi Monastery 416

GERMANY
Ahr
Meyer-Näkel 670
Franken
Sauer 351
Mosel-Saar-Ruwer
Busch, Clemens 151

Christoffel 164
Grans-Fassian 215
Haag, Fritz 224
Heymann-Löwenstein 235
Hövel, Weingut von 236
Karthäuserhof 246
Kesselstatt, Reichsgraf von 249
Loosen, Dr. 279
Maximin Grünhauser 293
Müller, Egon 306
Prüm, J.J. 328–9
Richter, Max Ferd. 341
Schaefer, Willi 352
Schloss Lieser 356
Selbach-Oster 360
Vollenweider 397
Volxem, Weingut van 390
Zilliken 406
Nahe
Diel, Schlossgut 182
Dönnhoff, Hermann 188
Emrich-Schönleber 197
Pfalz
Bassermann-Jordan,
    Dr. von 132
Buhl, Reichsrat von 150
Bürklin-Wolf, Dr. 150
Christmann 163
Koehler-Ruprecht, Weingut 254
Müller-Catoir 306
Rebholz 336
Rheingau
Breuer, Georg 148
Staatsweingüter Kloster
    Eberbach 253
Staatsweingüter Kloster
    Eberbach Assmannhäuser 606
Künstler, Franz 260
Schloss Vollrads 356
Weil, Robert 398
Rheinhessen
Blue Nun 136
Gunderloch 224
Heyl zu Herrnsheim,
    Freiherr 233
Keller, Weingut 249
Sekthaus Raumland 106
Wittmann, Weingut 402

GREECE
Gaia 557
Gerovassiliou 562

HUNGARY
Tokaj
Disznókő 185
Gróf Dégenfeld 219
Hétsőlő 233
Királyudvar 250
Oremus 314
Royal Tokaji Wine
Co. 348
Szepsy 372

INDIA
Sahyadri Valley
Omar Khayyam 95

ITALY
Abruzzo
Valentini 389, 826
Alto Adige
Abbazia di Novacella 125
Mayr, Josephus 662
Niedrist, Ignaz 700
Basilicata
Fucci, Elena 556
Paternoster 717
Campania
Colli di Lapio 173
Cuomo, Marisa 176
Ferrara, Benito 201
Feudi di San Gregorio 202
Mastroberardino 659
Molettieri, Salvatore 672
Montevetrano 679
Emilia Romagna
Castelluccio 480
Medici Ermete 90
Zerbina, Fattoria 846
Friuli Venezia Giulia
Collio
Borgo del Tiglio 143
Colle Duga 172
Gravner, Josko 216
Schiopetto 355
Colli Orientali del Friuli
Felluga, Livio 198
Le Due Terre 629
Miani 296, 670
Isonzo
Vie di Romans 393
Lazio
Castel de Paolis 154
Fiorano 206

Lombardy
Franciacorta
Bellavista 24
Cà del Bosco 36
Cavalleri 38
Valtellina
Negri, Nino 699
Marche
Bucci 149
La Monacesca 263
Piedmont
Asti
Braida 460
Coppo 506
La Morandina 84
Langhe
Accornero 414
Altare, Elio 418
Azelia 438
Ca'Viola 468
Cascina Corte 476
Cavallotto 482
Clerico, Domenico 492
Conterno, Giacomo 504
Conterno Fantino 505
Correggia, Matteo 507
Dogliotti, Romano 52
Gaja 558
Giacosa, Bruno 564
Grasso, Elio 576
Grasso, Silvio 577
La Spinetta 616
Malvirà 89, 286, 649
Marcarini 649
Mascarello, Bartolo 656
Mascarello, Giuseppe 656
Moccagatta 671
Nada, Fiorenzo 698
Oberto, Andrea 703
Paitin 707
Parusso 716
Pelissero, Giorgio 723
Produttori del Barbaresco 745
Rinaldi, Giuseppe 760
Sandrone, Luciano 775
Scavino, Paolo 778
Vajra, Azienda Agricola
G.D. 824
Vigneti Massa 394
Voerzio, Roberto 838
Puglia
Candido 469

Sardinia
Capichera 153
Còntini, Attilio 173
Romangia
Dettori, Azienda Agricola 520
Santadi
Santadi 777
Serdiana-Cagliari
Argiolas 429
Sicily
COS 508
Palari Faro 710
Tasca d'Almerita 796
Marsala
De Bartoli 181, 864
Florio 872
Pellegrino, Carlo 904
Mount Etna
Tenuta delle Terre Nere 802
Pantelleria
Donnafugata 186
Murana, Salvatore 307
Trentino Alto Adige
Ferrari, Giulio 60
Foradori 552
Tenuta San Leonardo 803
Terlano, Cantina di 377
Tuscany
Carnasciale, Podere Il 473
Castello dei Rampolla 477
Fontodi 552
Isole e Olena 596
Petrolo 729
Tenuta Sette Ponti 804
Vecchie Terre di Montefili 829
Bolgheri
Antinori 422, 423
Ca'Marcanda 467
Castello del Terriccio 479
Grattamacco 577
Le Macchiole 629
Satta, Michele 778
Tenuta dell'Ornellaia 801
Tenuta San Guido 803
Carmignano
Capezzana, Villa di 472
Piaggia 734
Castagneto Carducci-Maremma
Tua Rita 822
Chianti
Castello di Ama 480

Fattoria La Massa 548
Fèlsina Berardenga 548
Montevertine 679
Querciabella, Agricola 747
Colline Lucchesi
Tenuta di Valgiano 802
Massa Marittima
Moris Farms 684
Montalcino
Argiano 429
Banfi 439
Biondi Santi 448
Costanti, Andrea 509
Pacenti, Siro 706
Pieve di Santa Restituta 737
Podere 738
Salvioni 774
Soldera 784
Montepulciano
Avignonesi 131
Boscarelli 458
Poliziano 739
Valdipiatta 826
San Gimignano
Cesani, Vincenzo 155
Sant'Angelo in Colle
Lisini 644
Umbria
Montefalco
Caprai, Arnaldo 473
Veneto
Breganze
Maculan 282
Illasi
Dal Forno, Romano 516
Quintarelli 752
Serafini e Vidotto 780
Soave
Anselmi, Roberto 126
Inama, Stefana 240
Nardello, Daniele 308
Pieropan 323
Tamellini 376
Valdobbiadene
Adami 22
Bisol 30
Col Vetoraz 44
Valpolicella
Allegrini 417
Bussola, Tommaso 467

JAPAN
Katsunuma
Grace Winery 215

LEBANON
Bekaa Valley
Kefraya, Château 604
Ksara, Château 608
Musar, Château 696

LUXEMBOURG
Moselle Luxembourgeoise
Duhr, Mme. Aly, et Fils 193

NEW ZEALAND
Auckland
Kumeu
Kumeu River 258
Waiheke Island
Goldwater 569
Stonyridge 791
Te Motu 800
Central Otago
Felton Road 549
Mount Difficulty 688
Peregrine 319
Rippon 761
Gisborne
Millton Vineyard 298
Hawke's Bay
Craggy Range 511
Te Mata 798
Trinity Hill 816
Marlborough
Framingham 211
Fromm Winery 556
Herzog 595
Isabel 242
Jackson Estate 243
Montana Deutz Marlborough 91
Seresin 362
Martinborough
Ata Rangi 432
Dry River 190, 526
Nelson
Neudorf 309

PORTUGAL
Alentejo
Cortes de Cima 508
Herdade de Cartuxa 593
Herdade de Mouchão 594

Herdade do Esporão 594
Quinta do Mouro 749
Bairrada
Bussaco Palace Hotel 151, 466
Filipa Pato 717
Pato, Luís 718
Quinta das Bágeiras 106
Dão
Quinta dos Roques 750
Douro
Barca Velha 440
Chryseia 491
Cockburn's 862
Croft 863
Delaforce 864
Dow's 868
Duas Quintas 528
Fonseca 875
Graham's 881, 882
Niepoort 310, 700, 702, 895, 896
Quinta do Côtto 748
Quinta do Noval 898, 900
Quinta do Portal 908
Quinta do Vale Meão 749
Ramos Pinto 913
Rosa, Quinta de la 914
Sandeman 918
Smith Woodhouse 920
Taylor's 922, 924
Vesúvio, Quinta do 931
Warre's 931
Madeira
Barbeito 853–4
Blandy's 857
Cossart Gordon 862, 863
Leacock's 887
Setúbal
Fonseca, José Maria da 875
Minho
Soalheiro 364

SLOVENIA
Kozana
Kogl Estate 256
Simčič, Edi 363

SOUTH AFRICA
Boberg
KWV 886
Cape Point
Cape Point Vineyards 153

Coastal Region
A. A. Badenhorst Family
Wines 131
Boekenhoutskloof 450
Constantia
Klein Constantia 252
Steenberg 367
Durbanville
GS 581
Elgin
Cluver, Paul 171
Oak Valley 313
Franschhoek
Chamonix 157
Simonsberg-Stellenbosch
Kanonkop 601
Stellenbosch
Anwilka/Klein Constantia 427
Bredell's 858
De Trafford 518
Els, Ernie 539
Le Riche 632
Meerlust 664
Rudera 350
Rust en Vrede 771
Rustenberg 771
Thelema 808
Vergelegen 392, 832
Swartland
Mullineux Family
Wines 695
Sadie Family 350, 772
Testalonga 378
Walker Bay
Bouchard-Finlayson 460
Hamilton Russell Vineyards 226
Western Cape
Alheit Vineyards 125
Fable Mountain Vineyards 542
Solms-Delta 786

SPAIN
Alicante
Gutiérrez de la Vega 883
Mendoza, E. 668
Andalusia
Calvente 152
Aragón
Calatayud
San Alejandro 774
Campo de Borja
Borsao 457

Basque Country
Bizkaiko Txakolina
Itsasmendi 242
Bierzo
Palacios, Descendientes de J. 709
Tares, Dominio de 796
Valtuille 828
Castilla y León
Mauro 660
Castilla-La Mancha
La Mancha
Casa Gualda 475
Más Que Vinos 655
Manchuela
Finca Sandoval 551
Méntrida
Canopy 471
Montes de Toledo
Marqués de Griñón 652
Catalonia
Penedès
Can Ràfols dels Caus 152
Castillo de Perelada 481
Colet–Navazos 44
Torres 813
Montsant
Capçanes, Celler de 472
Venus 832
Priorat
Clos Erasmus 495
Clos Mogador 496
Costers del Siurana 510
Mas Doix 654
Mas Martinet 655
Palacios, Alvaro 709
Vall Llach 828
Sant Sadurní d'Anoia
Codorníu, Jaume 42
Gramona 70
Origan, L' 96
Raventós i Blanc 108
Torelló, Agustí 117
Sot 787
Yecla
Castaño 477
Galicia
Rías Baixas
Ferreiro, Do 201
Fillaboa 207
Lusco do Miño 280

Palacio de Fefiñanes 316
Pazo de Señoras 317
Ribeiro
Mein, Viña 294
Rojo, Emilio 343
Valdeorras
Guitián 222
Jerez de la Frontera
Bodegas Tradición 857
El Maestro Sierra 871
Garvey 876
González Byass 878
Hidalgo, Emilio 884
Luque, M. Gil 887
Marqués del Real Tesoro 891
Navazos Niepoort 309
Paternina 903
Rey Fernando de Castilla 913
Sánchez Romate 917
Valdespino 926, 927, 928
Williams & Humbert 932
Jumilla
Olivares Dulce 902
Lanzarote
El Grifo 871
Majorca
Ànima Negra 422
Málaga
Ordoñez, Jorge & Co 313
Rodríguez, Telmo 343
Montilla-Moriles
Aguilar de la Frontera
Toro Albalá 926
Montilla
Alvear 851
Pérez Barquero 906
Murchia
Casa Castillo 474
El Nido 538
Finca Luzón 550
Navarra
Chivite 163
Guelbenzu 582
El Puerto de Santa María
Gutiérrez Colosía 882
Osborne 902, 903
Ribera del Duero
Aalto, Bodegas 412
Atauta, Dominio de 434
Hacienda Monasterio 583
Moro, Emilio 687
Pagos de los Capellanes 706

Pesquera, Tinto 726
Pingus, Dominio del 737
Sastre, Viña 777
Silos, Cillar de 782
Vega Sicilia 830
Yerro, Alonso del 845

Rioja
Allende 417
Artadi 430
Contador 504
Contino 505
CVNE 178, 514
Izadi, Viña 597
La Rioja Alta 616
López de Heredia 279, 646
Marqués de Murrieta 290, 652
Marqués de Riscal 653
Martínez-Bujanda 653
Mendoza, Abel 668
Muga 693
Remelluri 338
Remirez de Ganuza 758
Roda, Bodegas 763
San Vicente 775

Rueda
Belondrade y Lurton 135
Ossian 314
Palacio de Bornos 315

Sanlúcar de Barrameda
Argüeso 851
Barbadillo 853
Delgado Zuleta 866
Equipo Navazos 872
Hidalgo-La Gitana 885
Lustau 888
Péres Marín 908
Romero, Pedro 914
Sánchez Ayala 917

Toro
Gago Pago La Jara 557
Maurodos 661
Pintia 738
Vega de Toro 830

Valdeorras
Palacios, Rafa 316

Valencia
Roure, Celler del 767

SWITZERLAND
Germanier, Jean-René 561
Mercier, Denis 669

UKRAINE
Massandra Collection 894

UNITED STATES
California
Livermore Valley
  Cellars, Kalin 247
Madera County
  Quady 910
Napa Valley
  Araujo Estate Wines 427
  Beaulieu Vineyard 443
  Beringer 447
  Chappellet 486
  Chimney Rock 491
  Colgin Cellars 501
  Corison 507
  Dalla Valle 516
  Diamond Creek Vineyards 520
  Dominus 523
  Duckhorn Vineyards 532
  Dunn Vineyards 535
  Far Niente 546
  Freemark Abbey 554
  Frog's Leap 554
  Grace Family Vineyards 570
  Harlan Estate 586
  Heitz Wine Cellars 592
  Jade Mountain 598
  La Jota Vineyard Company 613
  Mayacamas 661
  Mondavi, Robert 301, 672
  Montelena, Château 159, 675
  Newton Vineyards 310
  Niebaum-Coppola Estate 699
  Opus One 704
  Pahlmeyer 707
  Phelps, Joseph 734
  Quintessa 752
  Ramey Hyde Vineyard 334
  Schram, J. 111
  Screaming Eagle 779
  Shafer 780
  Stag's Leap Wine Cellars 787
  Stony Hill 368
  Thackrey, Sean 808
  Turley Wine Cellars 823
Santa Barbara
  Au Bon Climat 434
  Fiddlehead 549
  Ojai Vineyard 703
  Qupé 753
Santa Clara County
  Ridge 759
Santa Cruz

Bonny Doon 141, 143, 456
Bruce, David 466
Mount Eden 301
Santa Rita Hills
Sanford 776
Santa Ynez Valley
Qupé 330
Sonoma County / Sonoma Valley
  Arnot-Roberts 126
  Dutton Goldfield 194
  Flowers 208, 551
  Gloria Ferrer 66
  Hanzell 228
  Hirsch Vineyards 595
  Iron Horse 74
  Kistler 252
  Landmark 624
  Littorai Wines 646
  Marcassin 286
  Marimar Torres Estate 380
  Michael, Peter, Winery 296, 671
  Peay Vineyards 723
  Pride Mountain 742
  Radio-Coteau 753
  Ravenswood 756
  Rochioli, J. 762
  Seghesio 779
  Swan, Joseph 791
  Williams Selyem 841

New York
Finger Lakes
  Frank, Dr. Konstantin 211
Long Island
  Channing Daughters 158
  Lenz 273
  Macari Vineyard 647

Oregon
Willamette Valley
  Beaux Frères 446
  Drouhin, Domaine 523
  Eyrie Vineyards 542

Washington State
Columbia Valley
  Chateau Ste. Michelle 161
  K Vintners 599
  L'Ecole No. 41 634
  Leonetti Cellars 637
  Quilceda Creek 748
Yakima Valley
  DeLille Cellars 518

URUGUAY
Carrau, Bodegas 474

CHAMPAG

KRU

A REIMS - FRAN

BRUT

GRANDE CUV

PRODUIT DE FRANCE - PRODUCE OF FR

12%vol

ÉLABORÉ PAR KRUG S.A. REIMS, FRANC

E

G

E

750 ml

Sparkling*Wines*

Adami *Prosecco di Valdobbiadene Bosco di Gica Brut* NV

Origin Italy, Veneto, Valdobbiadene
Style Sparkling dry white wine, 11% ABV
Grapes Prosecco 97%, Chardonnay 3%

In 1920, Abele Adami, grandfather of the present owners, purchased a beautiful vineyard from the Count Balbi Valier. This marked the birth of the Adami estate and its great Proseccos. It appears that the Prosecco grape was originally from the Trieste province, in the far northeast of Italy, on the border with Slovenia, where it is locally called Glera. Nevertheless, it was in the Treviso province that this grape was best understood, producing the beautiful, thirst-quenching, uncomplicatedly fruity wine beloved by so many people.

The Adami Bosco di Gica is produced almost exclusively from Prosecco grapes: A tiny percentage of Chardonnay is used to give more depth to the final blend. Do not be fooled by the Champagne-shaped bottle into thinking that Prosecco is a wine for celebrations or important toasts. The real role of this wine is to give you a small, everyday treat. Open it to welcome unexpected friends, or discover its versatility by matching it with a Parma ham and melon platter—this combination is guaranteed to get you hooked on the wine, and there is no doubt that you will soon be back for more. **AS**

Drink: current release within 1-2 years

Agrapart *L'Avizoise* 2002

Origin France, Champagne, Côte des Blancs
Style Sparkling dry white wine, 12% ABV
Grape Chardonnay

The brothers Pascal and Fabrice Agrapart own 23.5 acres (9.5 ha) of quite exceptional vineyards, mainly in the grands crus of Oger, Cramant, Oiry, and Avize—Chardonnay country par excellence. All efforts are made to express fully their fabulous terroirs in the glass. The Agraparts' painstaking methods of vineyard care include plowing between the rows with a horse to enrich the biological life of the soils. One of their cuvées—Vénus—is even named after the beautiful white mare that does this work in the Avize *lieu-dit* Les Fosses. Agrapart Champagnes are the result of precise vinifications of this and other *lieux-dits*, the use of indigenous yeasts, and long aging on the lees in large oak casks whose size and relative age (eight years on average) prevent overtly oaky flavors.

L'Avizoise is the brothers' best-known Champagne, a pure Avize from Les Robards vineyard, whose rich clay elements give the wine great staying power. Yet the chief virtues of this 2002 are its ripeness, lacelike elegance, and harmony—traits typical of this very great vintage and which put it on a par with supreme years like 1982. **ME**

Drink: to 2020

Agrapart Champagne undergoes its secondary fermentation.

Beaumont des Crayères
Fleur de Prestige 1996

Origin France, Champagne, Vallée de la Marne
Style Sparkling dry white wine, 12% ABV
Grapes Chardonnay 50%, P. Noir 40%, P. Meunier 10%

Beaumont des Crayères is the sonorous brand name for the respected *bijou* Champagne cooperative of Mardeuil, near Epernay. The 247 members cultivate 235 acres (95 ha) of fine vineyards, mainly on the sunny slopes of Cumières and Mardeuil: These premiers crus are renowned for bright, fruit-laden Pinot Noir and refined Pinot Meunier.

Since 1987, Beaumont's *chef de cave,* Jean-Paul Bertus, has created elegant, opulent Champagnes—notably the Fleur de Prestige, the least expensive of Beaumont's vintage range. The Fleur 1996 is the grand apéritif *par excellence*, combining exhilarating acidity and tender ripeness. The presence of Chardonnay shows in the bright-green flashes among the deep-gold colors; the bubbles are lacelike, persistent yet gentle; aromas of spring flowers mingle with the hedgerow fragrances of hawthorn and honeysuckle. As the wine warms, the bouquet embraces pear, peach, and fresh hazelnut. The finish has a splendid mass of lemony freshness.

For regular drinking, Beaumont's non-vintage Grande Réserve is a fine example of how good Meunier-led Champagne can be. **ME**

🍸🍸🍸 **Drink: to 2020**

Bellavista
Gran Cuvée Brut 1999

Origin Italy, Lombardy, Franciacorta
Style Sparkling dry white wine, 12.5% ABV
Grapes Chardonnay 72%, Pinot Noir 28%

The Bellavista estate was created in 1976, when Vittorio Moretti decided to transform a small family-owned *azienda agricola* into what is today a world-class wine estate. He was helped by Mattia Vezzola, the winemaker, who received the Best Italian Winemaker Award in 2004. Vezzola has a restrained and very elegant touch with his wines—a personality and a style that is easily recognizable, even in his entry-level cuvées.

A wine like the Gran Cuvée Brut 1999 makes you see what all the excitement is about. The wines that made it into the final blend were fermented in new oak barrels. After blending and the second fermentation in bottle, the wine was left on its lees for thirty-six months. The result is a wine that has a pale, straw-yellow color with bright greenish tinges. The bubbles are very fine, and the mousse is dense and harmonious. On the nose, it wins you over with a bouquet of fruity Chardonnay notes and more mature bread and fresh yeast notes. It gently fills the mouth with its vibrant freshness, while the soft bubbles seem to sustain the palate, carrying the flavors through a remarkably long finish. **AS**

🍸🍸🍸 **Drink: to 2019**

One of several decoratively carved barrel ends at the Bellavista winery. ➡

Billecart-Salmon
Clos St.-Hilaire 1996

Origin France, Champagne, Vallée de la Marne
Style Sparkling dry white wine, 12% ABV
Grape Pinot Noir

This prestigious small Champagne house has always been innovative, and the latest addition to its range is its most exciting new venture yet. Brothers François and Antoine Rolland-Billecart are proud of their house's reputation for balance, elegance, and finesse, but wanted to show that they could produce richer, more structured wines as well. Clos St.-Hilaire affords the exhilarating proof.

The 2.4-acre (0.97 ha) Clos St.-Hilaire, close to the Billecart-Salmon winery in Mareuil-sur-Aÿ and named after the patron saint of the village, has long been recognized as a special site. First planted with Pinot Noir in 1964, it was used for twenty-five years to produce red wine for rosé. Although its easterly exposure would normally be considered less than ideal, its proximity to the village, its own walls, and its deep, rich soil result in rich, ripe wines. Concentration is increased by restricting the yield, and only the *coeur de cuvée* (the best part of the press run) is used.

The 1995 was a brilliant debut, but the 1996 is more spectacular still. Disgorged after ten years, it received an Extra Brut dosage of 4.5 g/l, to soften slightly the severity of this scintillating vintage. For François Billecart-Salmon it is the greatest Champagne ever produced by the house. Along with Bollinger's Vieilles Vignes Françaises, Jacquesson's Vauzelle Termes, and Philipponnat's Clos des Goisses, this Blanc de Noirs may be celebrated as the ultimate expression of a rare and special style. **NB**
🥂🥂🥂🥂🥂 **Drink: to 2025+**

Billecart-Salmon has made Champagne for almost 200 years. ➡

LLECART

le **CHAMPAGNE**
qui franchit les siècles

HERVÉ
MORVAN

Billecart-Salmon

Cuvée Nicolas François Billecart 1982

Origin France, Champagne
Style Sparkling dry white white, 12% ABV
Grapes Pinot Noir 60%, Chardonnay 40%

Rather than being Billecart-Salmon's greatest ever vintage, 1982 represents the greatest vintage of Billecart's modern era. This era can be defined by the introduction of double *débourbage* and a very long and cool first fermentation, which can detrimentally affect the autolysis and create bland amylic aromas such as peardrops and bubblegum. In practice, however, these processes have led to a high degree of finesse. Another innovation was replacing large vats with sixty-odd small vats, which, unusually, allows Billecart to vinify on a plot-by-plot basis.

The person responsible for these changes was James Coffinet, the *chef de cave* between 1976 and 1985 (after which he made equally great Champagnes at Pol Roger until his retirement in 1999). Coffinet was a brilliant winemaker, but he liked Champagne so much that he tended to walk into things. Painfully thin, with a trademarked bandaged head, he looked more like a shell-shocked soldier than a winemaker, but as the exquisitely balanced Billecart-Salmon 1982 Cuvée Nicolas François demonstrates unquestionably, he was one of Champagne's greatest maestros. **TS**

⊗ ⊗⊗⊗ Drink: to 2020

Henri Billiot & Fils

Cuvée Laetitia NV

Origin France, Champagne, Montagne de Reims
Style Sparkling dry white wine, 12.5% ABV
Grapes Pinot Noir, Chardonnay

Serge Billiot's 13.5-acre (5.5 ha) domaine is one of Champagne's treasures. Owning only grand cru land in the commune of Ambonnay, he makes about 3,700 cases of remarkable wine each year. Ambonnay is known for sumptuous, creamy Champagnes, but Billiot's complex, focused wines seem to elevate the palate on a column of pure energy.

Cuvée Laetitia is a true Tête de Cuvée, inaugurated in 1967 with the birth of Billiot's daughter (for whom it is named); by 2000 it had grown to eleven vintages. The wine is in effect a solera, which is freshened when base wines of sufficient quality are available. Recent bottlings of Laetitia have seemed to contain more Chardonnay.

Years ago, Laetitia was a leviathan of vinosity, fathomless, and sometimes inscrutable, requiring thirty minutes or more in the glass. These days it is superficially more "modern": There is more spice, more flavors of greengage and scents of hawthorn, and low notes of scallops and saffron. You can taste the cherry-tomato, strawberry, and forest-floor signatures of Ambonnay, and experience the vitality and density of Billiot's own style. **TT**

⊗⊗⊗⊗ Drink: current release for up to 7 years

A Reims stained-glass window pays tribute to Champagne makers. ➡

HOMMAGE de LA CORPORATION du CHAMPAGNE et des INDUSTRIES ANNEXÉS

REIMS

Bisol *Cartizze Prosecco* 2005

Origin Italy, Veneto, Valdobbiadene
Style Sparkling dry white wine, 11.5% ABV
Grape Prosecco

Italy has not traditionally been associated with the production of first-rank sparkling wines. The Asti of Piedmont has its die-hard fans, but for anything drier one had to look to Prosecco. Here, wines with the kind of vulgar fruit character often connoted as tutti-frutti were cheaply and cheerfully produced.

In the 1990s, however, Prosecco began to move up in the world as a result of wholesale rethinking of its vinification procedures, more stringent demarcation of appropriate vineyard land, and the quality-led approach of producers such as Bisol.

The family-run Bisol winery has been making wine in this area since the mid-sixteenth century and owns all the vineyards that supply its wines. Its Cartizze bottling bears eloquent witness to the revolution. Grown on crumbly, stony soil—effectively the cru district of Prosecco where the grapes ripen surprisingly slowly (harvests typically start only in mid-October)—it is made by the Charmat, or tank, method. The wines do not announce a vintage on the front label, but are the product of single harvests nonetheless.

This Bisol Cartizze Prosecco is invitingly aromatic, with subtle almond and pear fragrances. On the palate, its gentle mousse is complemented by crisp but ripe acidity, lightish alcohol (11.5 percent), and a firm, substantial finish. Its 25 g/l of sugar lends it a not quite demi-sec softness. It is the kind of sparkler that would stand up to food, perhaps a first course of seared scallops. **SW**

⊖⊖ Drink: current release within 1–2 years

FURTHER RECOMMENDATIONS
Other wines from the same producer
Crede • Desiderio Colmei • Desiderio Jeio Garnéi • Valdobbiadene Vigneti del Fol
More Prosecco producers
Carpenè Malvolti • Adami Adriano • Fratelli Bartolin

An ancient *castello* overlooks Prosecco vines near Valdobbiadene. ◗

Bollinger *R.D.* 1996

Origin France, Champagne
Style Sparkling dry white wine, 12% ABV
Grapes Pinot Noir 70%, Chardonnay 30%

R.D. (Recently Disgorged) Champagne is a concept unique to Bollinger. Other houses very occasionally disgorge an exceptional wine quite late in its maturity, but none does it with quite the élan that this aristocratic firm has employed since 1952. Before it becomes an R.D., the wine is a Grande Année—Bollinger's prestigious Vintage Champagne—but one that matures over a far longer period, anything from eight to twenty years, sometimes more. During this time, R.D. develops subtle, multifaceted aromas, as well as creating a unique vinous style that is Bollinger's expression of great Pinot Noir, but it minds its manners in the company of elegant Chardonnay, which represents just under one-third of the blend.

The weather during 1996 was extraordinary: a crisp, dry winter, with little frost; budding in a hot mid-April, lack of rain and high temperatures recalling 1976; a difficult flowering of Chardonnay in June; a very hot summer until mid-August, then rain; a changeable September, with low nighttime temperatures; and a harvest under cloudless, sunny skies. The result is a rare combination of high natural sugar and acidity. Released as Grande Année, the 1996 showed remarkable verve and bounce, allied to deep wells of Pinot-led fruit. In its R.D. incarnation, that vigor remains, though the nose has developed secondary complexities of dark chocolate and spice; in the mouth, the flavors confirm the aromas, with a burgeoning vinosity, silky texture, and very long finish. This R.D. is still evolving and improving. **ME**
😊😊😊😊😊 Drink: to 2025+

FURTHER RECOMMENDATIONS		
Other great vintages		
1966 · 1981 · 1982 · 1985 · 1988 · 1990 · 1997		
More wines from the same producer		
Spécial Cuvée (NV) · 2003 by Bollinger · Grande Année *Grande Année Rosé · Vieilles Vignes Françaises*		

The splendid headquarters of Champagne Bollinger in Aÿ. ➡

Bollinger *Vieilles Vignes Françaises Blanc de Noirs* 1996

Origin France, Champagne
Style Sparkling dry white wine, 12% ABV
Grape Pinot Noir

This is the beast of Bollinger, the wine that bred the lie that all Blanc de Noirs are big. (Most other Blanc de Noirs have a typical Champagne structure, and some can even be relatively light in weight.) There are two mutually dependent reasons why Vieilles Vignes Françaises is so big: The fact that the grapes are grown on ungrafted vines, and the inflexibility of Champagne's bureaucracy. Thanks to the bureaucrats, this Blanc de Blancs has always been produced from overripe grapes, resulting in a super-concentrated Champagne of extraordinary quality.

Until 2005, Vieilles Vignes Françaises was made from three tiny plots of ungrafted wines: Chaudes Terres (actually in Bollinger's back garden in Aÿ), Clos St.-Jacques (a walled garden, also in Aÿ, but on the western outskirts), and Croix Rouge (on a corner just outside Bouzy, on the road to Louvois). In 2004, however, the vines in Croix Rouge were decimated by phylloxera, so from 2005 Vieilles Vignes Françaises will be a *monocru*. It is difficult to single out one vintage that you should drink before you die, but the 1996 is as massive as they come—intensely flavored, and probably able to last longer than most. **TS**
🔒🔒🔒🔒🔒 **Drink: to 2025**

Cédric Bouchard *Le Creux d'Enfer 2009*

Origin France, Champagne, Aube
Style Sparkling dry rosé wine, 12% ABV
Grape Pinot Noir

Cédric Bouchard has only been making wine since 2000, but already he is one of the leading vignerons of Champagne. Moreover, his wines challenge much of the aesthetic logic that one associates with the region. In a region of blends, where the flavors of lees-aging and work in the cellar are prized, his wines shine in their transparent relationship with the vineyard. Each bottling is from a single variety, a single vineyard, and a single harvest. There is no wood, no chaptalization, no cold-stabilization, no filtration or fining, and absolutely no *dosage*.

The rosé that Bouchard makes from Le Creux d'Enfer is his rarest wine and also the greatest expression of his meticulous ideals. From a mere three rows of expertly tended Pinot Noir in a west-facing vineyard of Kimmeridgian soils, this is a rosé of awesome vinosity, richness, and complexity. Production is reserved for the most successful years and hovers somewhere between 370 and 500 bottles. Crushed by foot and macerated for forty-two hours, the 2009 reflects the warmth of the vintage in its burnished concentration, but remains deftly poised and elegant. **FP**
🔒🔒🔒🔒🔒 **Drink: to 2035**

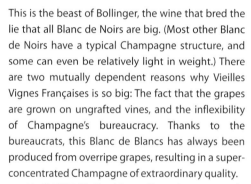

◀ Bollinger Champagne ages in the winery cellars at Aÿ.

Roger Brun
Grand Cru Aÿ La Pelle 2008

Origin France, Champagne, Grande Vallée de la Marne
Style Sparkling dry white wine, 12.5% ABV
Grape Pinot Noir

Ever since the seventeenth century, the Bruns have had a visceral attachment to the bourg and vineyards of Aÿ, where sparkling Champagne was first made almost exclusively from Pinot Noir. This wine comes from a single plot on the central hillside close to the town cemetery—an unbeatable location.

The present incumbent Philippe Brun's medium-sized domaine rises through rich and rounded entry-level Bruts and a full-blooded rosé to this star of the range, which is one of Champagne's finest blancs de noirs. At a tasting in 2011, La Pelle 2000 was open and ready with attractive autolytic development; the 2002 had captivating opulence but a compensating freshness that preempted any corpulence. The 2004 was all elegance, poise, precision, and, for Brun, a certain delicacy. The 2005 was big and butch but lacked the distinction of a really good year; by contrast, the 2006 was a real charmer of bountiful fruit balanced by a propelling vigor. The 2008 is maybe the best so far: less the golden richness of 2002, more an absolutely classic dry style, pervaded with minerals and a deep, elegant acidity that will make it a keeper for many years to come. **ME**
🍾🍾🍾 Drink: to 2030

Cà del Bosco
Cuvée Annamaria Clementi 1996

Origin Italy, Lombardy, Franciacorta
Style Sparkling dry white wine, 12.5% ABV
Grapes Chardonnay 60%, P. Blanc 20%, P. Noir 20%

Annamaria Clementi is the prestige cuvée that takes its name from the mother of Maurizio Zanella, the founder of Cà del Bosco. Equally sentimentally, the name of the estate refers to Annamaria Clementi's move into a large "house in the woods" (Cà del Bosco) in Franciacorta in 1965. It was at this time that Zanella fell in love with the area and decided to commence wine production there. The official version states that "after studying at the Faculty of Enology in Bordeaux, Maurizio Zanella decided to start producing Traditional Method sparkling wines"—although the first vintage of his Annamaria Clementi was 1979 and he studied in Bordeaux in 1980.

With every sip, this cuvée testifies to the huge potential of the area. In the 1996 wine—an intense straw-yellow color with golden hues—is the background to a fine and very persistent mousse. The nose is well defined and mesmerizing. The initial fruity notes (citrus fruits and pears) open into floral scents rounded off by a delicate yeastiness and a touch of vanilla. The perfect synergy between the acidity and mousse seems to suffuse the palate with flavor and to sustain it there for several minutes. **AS**
🍾🍾🍾🍾 Drink: to 2017+

Chardonnay vines in Cà del Bosco's Breda vineyard at Passirano. ➜

Cattier
Clos du Moulin NV

Origin France, Champagne, Montagne de Reims
Style Sparkling dry white wine, 12% ABV
Grapes Pinot Noir 50%, Chardonnay 50%

Cavalleri
Brut Satèn Blanc de Blancs 2006

Origin Italy, Lombardia, Franciacorta
Style Sparkling dry white wine, 12.5% ABV
Grape Chardonnay

The charming, flower-decked village of Chigny-les-Roses has been home to the Cattier family since the eighteenth century. Beneath their house are some of the deepest cellars in Champagne: Dug on three levels to a depth of 100 feet (30 m), they feature a series of magnificent vaults designed in the Gothic, Renaissance, and Roman styles.

The Champagnes produced here live up to their surroundings, none more so than the wine from the Clos du Moulin. The Champagne from this plot is always a blend comprising three good vintages. The current release is composed of 1996, 1998, and 1999 from Pinot Noir and Chardonnay in roughly equal proportions. The straw color is flecked with green; the aromas are relatively mature, with biscuity notes. In the mouth, this Champagne is still a teenager—tight, with a lot in reserve. After ten minutes' contact with air, however, the Pinot Noir finally makes its presence known, richly filling the palate.

More recently, Cattier has also introduced to the market an excellent Blanc de Noirs, which is full of exuberant flavors of red fruits and possesses a swaggering and joyful character. **ME**

🙂🙂🙂🙂 Drink: current release for up to 5 years

The Cavalleri estate's first vintage (for still wines) was 1905, when Italy's production was cheap and not particularly cheerful. Fortunes changed, however, in 1967 when the region gained DOC status, and with it recognition for its unique combination of soil and climate. The glacial moraines that spill into northern Lombardy are ideal for the vine; the deep, gravel soils are both free draining and poor in organic material. Cool nights and breezy days, thanks to the nearby Alps, preserve acidity at the ideal level for the production of high-quality sparkling wines.

The estate's grapes are hand-harvested and hand-sorted before pressing. The minimum aging on the lees for non-vintage Franciacorta DOCG is eighteen months, but the Satèn, made exclusively from Chardonnay and only in the finest vintages, is aged for no fewer than thirty months. Satèn, a style that stipulates a maximum of 18 g/l added sugar for the second fermentation, produces a delicate mousse similar to that in French *crémant*. Cavalleri Satèn is both subtle and succulent, with Chardonnay's citrus lift balanced by the toasty complexity found only in great sparkling wines. **MP**

🙂🙂🙂 Drink: current release within 3–5 years

Sediment collects on the caps of bottles in the Cavalleri cellar. ➜

Claude Cazals
Clos Cazals 1996

Origin France, Champagne, Côte de Blancs
Style Sparkling dry white wine, 12.5% ABV
Grape Chardonnay

The all-Chardonnay domaine of Claude Cazals, founded in 1897 by Ernest Cazals, a cooper from the south of France, extends over 22 acres (9 ha) of the Côte des Blancs, mostly in grands crus Le Mesnil and Oger, but also in premiers crus Vertus and Villeneuve-Renneville. The biggest and brightest in this cluster of diamonds is the 9-acre (3.7 ha) Clos Cazals in Oger, which surrounds the family home—one of the reasons why insecticides have never been used. Some of the vines were planted as long ago as 1947, and on average the natural alcohol levels are one degree higher than from the other parcels. A rigorous selection from these *vieilles vignes*, pressed in traditional Coquard presses, is bottled as Clos Cazals—a mere 2,000 bottles even in good years.

Although Clos Cazals had its debut vintage only in 1995, it is already, thanks to its distinguished origin and meticulous production, one of the very greatest wines of the region. The first three vintages—namely 1995, 1996, and 1997—were all beautifully balanced, dense, elegant, fine, mineral, rich, ripe, and scintillating. Every successive release should be equally well worth seeking out. **NB**
❸❸❸ Drink: to 2020

Domaine Chandon
Green Point NV

Origin Australia, Victoria, Yarra Valley
Style Sparkling dry white wine, 12.5% ABV
Grapes Chardonnay, Pinot Noir, Pinot Meunier

Moët & Chandon has been at the forefront of European producers investing in New World wines, but these are not simply wines made by the Champagne giant in its overseas holdings. They are wines largely made by indigenous practitioners, in which the parent company happens to have a stake.

In Green Point, the flagship sparkler of Australia's Domaine Chandon, made by the trailblazing Dr. Tony Jordan, we have an eloquent case in point. Made by the traditional method, the non-vintage blend contains up to 30 percent reserve wines from older vintages to fill out the palate, adding depth and authority to its elegant, Chardonnay-sharpened finesse. The reserve wines are housed in a kind of solera system, including batches of both Pinot and Chardonnay, some of them aged in oak.

A range of vintage cuvées is also made, but—as in Champagne itself—a sparkling-wine producer must stand or fall on the quality of its leading brand. The pedigree of Green Point shines through its painstaking *assemblage* each year, and is reflected in the fact that the wines will continue to develop in the bottle for over a year or so after release. **SW**
❸❸ Drink: current release within 3 years

Domaine Chandon's modern tasting room at Green Point in Victoria. ▰

Coates & Seely
Rosé NV

Origin England, Hampshire
Style Sparkling dry rosé wine, 12% ABV
Grapes Pinot Noir, Chardonnay

In 2006, Christian Seely and Nicholas Coates founded an English sparkling wine estate in the North Downs of East Hampshire, where the soils come closest in England to those of Cramant and Avize in Champagne's fabled Côte des Blancs.

From initial holdings of 20 acres (8 ha), Coates & Seely's vineyards now extend to nearly 60 acres (24 ha) of Pinot Noir, Chardonnay, and Pinot Meunier in the choicest sites, notably Meon Valley. The winery is equipped with the best modern tools—the Bucher press, stainless-steel vats, the concrete oval egg fementer, and traditional oak casks—and the team of highly qualified winemakers works to express the special character of the classic Champenois grapes.

The Rosé, first made in 2009, has won fine notices: A limpid ruby, it abounds in witty Pinot fruitiness, reminiscent of strawberries, and hedgerow red berries that add a touch of tart tension; there is also a lovely, lemony side-act that suggests fine Chardonnay playing its part. English sparkling wine is sometimes hyped by well-meaning patriots, but this one with class, elegance, and refinement will certainly give the Champenois a run for their money. **ME**

🍷🍷🍷 Drink: to 2018

Jaume Codorníu
Brut NV

Origin Spain, Penedès, Sant Sadurní d'Anoia
Style Sparkling dry white wine, 11.5% ABV
Grapes Chardonnay, Macabeo, Parellada

The names Cava and Codorníu go together. Indeed, the story of Codorníu is the story of Cava: Spain's most famous sparkling wine style was created in 1872, using the *méthode traditionnelle*, by Josep Raventós, then head of the Codorníu winery. His descendants still make Cava and run the company today. The winery itself is a masterpiece of Modernist Catalan architecture, originally designed by Josep María Puig i Cadafalch in 1898, and now a national monument. It has some of the world's most extensive cellars—in excess of 15 miles (24 km) on five underground levels.

Jaume Codorníu Brut is a Cava aged for a long time on its lees. Half is Chardonnay, while the rest is made up of the traditional Cava grapes—Macabeo and Parellada. The wine is golden yellow in color with some green reflections and offers good intensity on the nose, with roasted sesame seed notes up front, and tropical fruit, yeast, and mineral notes in the background. Medium-bodied, it has bright acidity, lively fruit, and a remarkable finish. A special edition, made only with Chardonnay and Parellada, was released in magnum for the winery's 450th anniversary. **LG**

🍷🍷 Drink: current release within 3 years

Codorníu vineyards in hills near Monestir de Poblet. ➡

Col Vetoraz
Prosecco Extra Dry NV

Origin Italy, Veneto, Valdobbiadene
Style Sparkling dry white wine, 11.5% ABV
Grape Prosecco

The Col Vetoraz cellar is situated right in the heart of Proseccoshire, in Santo Stefano di Valdobbiadene. This area, in the province of Treviso (north of Venice), is renowned for producing what seems to be Italy's compulsory aperitif—Prosecco, a perfect example of a great wine for uncomplicated drinking. Smile, pop the cork, be merry.

Prosecco is one of the few wines in Italy named after a grape variety, but in fact Prosecco is often blended with other varieties in the final wine. Its most common companion is Verdiso, together with Perera and Boschera, but small quantities of Pinot Blanc and Chardonnay may also find their way into the mix. The second fermentation of the wine is carried out by the Charmat (or tank) method, greatly reducing the time between the production and the sale of the wine. The point of this is to preserve the primary aromas, which is what Prosecco is all about.

This Extra Dry version of Col Vetoraz, with a touch more sugar than you would expect in a sparkling wine, offers the delicate freshness of pears and peaches, the hint of sweet, ripe fruit framed by the slightly off-dry palate and creamy mousse. **AS**

🚫 **Drink: current release within 2 years**

Colet–Navazos
Extra Brut 2010

Origin Spain, Penedès, Pacs del Penedès
Style Sparkling dry white wine, 12.5 % ABV
Grape Xarel.lo

There are some intriguing structural similarities between the biologically aged wines of Andalusia and Champagne. Both are grown on white, chalky soils and make use of relatively neutral base wines that gain character through their respective complex biological processes of aging under *flor* and secondary fermentation in bottle. Curiosity about these similarities prompted an initial contact between Equipo Navazos and Sergi Colet that predated even the first private release of wine under the Equipo Navazos label, and by 2006 there was a serious project in progress to investigate making Palomino-based sparkling wines in Andalusia with an element of biological aging.

That project is ongoing, but in the meantime Colet–Navazos has settled upon the production of sparkling wines in the Penedès DO with a secondary fermentation in bottle, but receiving an Andalusian slant from the wine used in place of the *liqueur d'expédition*. The 2010 Extra Brut is the fourth vintage of this wine and the first to be 100 percent Xarel.lo, sourced from a single Colet vineyard from the hills in the higher part of the appellation. **FP**

🚫🚫🚫 **Drink: on release and for up to ten years**

René Collard
Cuvée Réservée Brut 1969

Origin France, Champagne, Vallée de la Marne
Style Sparkling dry white wine, 12% ABV
Grape Pinot Meunier

Comte Audoin de Dampierre
Family Reserve GC Blanc de Blancs 1996

Origin France, Champagne, Côte des Blancs
Style Sparkling dry white wine, 12% ABV
Grape Chardonnay

René Collard succeeded in 1943 to the domaine that his father established, and for more than fifty years persisted with traditional viticulture and winemaking: He used no herbicides, insecticides, or pesticides. Fermentation was in large oak vats, the malolactic was blocked, and only after maturation in 158-gallon (600-liter) *demi-muids* for several years was the wine bottled. The wines were then given extensive further aging on lees in chalk cellars. Even when a wine was finally released, a high proportion of the stock was reserved.

Disgorged once a year, these wonderful old wines have mellowed to the point where they require no sweetening *dosage*, being topped up with the same wine. At almost forty years of age, the 1969 still had great finesse and freshness on the nose, and a fine streak of acidity to cut the honeyed richness of the palate. Subsequent vintages share this well-nigh perfect harmony and integrity, and René's last wine, the poignantly named Cuvée Ultime Brut Nature (a blend of the excellent 1988, 1990, and 1993 vintages), is an equally fitting testimony to an influential, principled, and talented winemaker. **NB**
☻☻☻ Drink: to 2019+

Comte Audoin de Dampierre is an aristocratic, mildly eccentric Champenois, whose family connections in the region go back more than 700 years. Living up to his proud family motto—*Sans peur et sans reproche* (Without fear and above reproach)—he buys only grand and premier cru fruit, making no apology for the correspondingly high prices of his wines.

Among those who can afford the wines are ambassadors around the world, as well as the occasional monarch, president, and prime minister. But although forty-two ambassadors cannot be wrong, and the Cuvée des Ambassadeurs NV is a fine Chardonnay/Pinot Noir blend, the count has good taste too—his Family Reserve Blanc de Blancs is, not surprisingly, the top wine.

This Blanc de Blancs is sourced exclusively from Grands Crus Avize (50 percent), Le Mesnil-sur-Oger (40 percent), and Cramant (10 percent). Fermented in stainless-steel tanks, it reflects its distinguished origins. The exquisite 1996 has a super-fine mousse, silky texture, and scintillating finish. The wine comes with a label designed in the nineteenth century and a cork that is hand-tied to the bottle with twine. **NB**
☻☻☻ Drink: to 2021

De Meric
Cuvée Catherine NV

Origin France, Champagne, Vallée de la Marne
Style Sparkling dry white wine, 12% ABV
Grapes Pinot Noir 60%, Chardonnay 40%

The small Aÿ-based Champagne house of De Meric has undergone a radical transformation in recent years. In 1997 the brand was sold by Christian Besserat to a small group of eight Champagne-loving U.S., French, and German investors, headed by Daniel Ginsburg. The new president of De Meric acquired his passion for old Champagne after tasting the 1961 Vintage of René Collard, who became the "spiritual father" of the new venture.

The house buys in grapes (not *vins clairs*) from twelve growers. Only the cuvée is used, at least 60 percent of the wines are fermented and matured in old Burgundy barriques, the malolactic fermentation is blocked, and the lees are stirred. *Dosage* is low, and added as rectified concentrated grape must (a popular solution for those without large stocks of reserve wines for the liqueur).

The most remarkable wines produced under the old regime are the rare Cuvées Catherine, for which the selection is so rigorous that production has been only 10,000 to 20,000 bottles per decade. These are 100 percent Aÿ Grand Cru, 60 percent Pinot Noir, and 40 percent Chardonnay, and have generally been blends of two great consecutive vintages. The 1995/1996 cuvée is an exquisitely poised wine that combines supremely well the best qualities of the twin varieties and vintages. The previous release was the magnificent 1988/1989, which may be slightly less fine but is richer still. The single vintage 1999 marked a new departure, being the first wine to be 100 percent fermented in wood. **NB**
☺☺☺ **Drink: current release for 20+ years**

De Sousa
Cuvée des Caudalies NV

Origin France, Champagne, Côte des Blancs
Style Sparkling dry white wine, 12% ABV
Grape Chardonnay

Based in the grand cru village of Avize, this is now one of the most exciting growers in Champagne, thanks to the ambition and determination of third-generation proprietor Erick de Sousa. A graduate of the *lycée viticole* in Avize, he returned to run the property in 1986. His inheritance was impressive—an estate now of 321 acres (8.5 ha), with holdings in six grands crus in the Côte des Blancs and Montagne de Reims, and more than 6 acres (2.5 ha) of very old vines, now vinified separately.

An admirer of Bollinger and Krug, Erick introduced small wooden barrels to the winery. He has converted his estate to biodynamic cultivation, ferments with indigenous yeasts, and puts all of the wines through malolactic fermentation. Autolysis influence is promoted through *poignettage*—an old term relating to the wrists used to shake the bottles and stir up the lees, a practice once common in Avize but now rare because of the time it takes.

At the top of an excellent range is the prestige Cuvée des Caudalies, the descriptive name coming from *caudalies* or seconds, referring to the length of the finish. This is normally NV, and is 100 percent Avize Chardonnay from vines at least fifty years old, fermented without chaptalization in wood, and aged in a "solera" started in 1996. Dense, intensely fruity, ripe, and richly silky, it certainly lives up to its name. In exceptional years—maybe two or three a decade—there is a Vintage version, where the blend and the treatment vary with the year, but where the quality is consistently very high. **NB**
☺☺☺ **Drink: current release for 10+ years**

◀ Vineyards demarcate the edge of the village of Aÿ.

Delamotte *Blanc de Blancs* 1985

Origin France, Champagne, Côte des Blancs
Style Sparkling dry white wine, 12% ABV
Grape Chardonnay

Founded in 1760, this intimate little Champagne house with a big reputation among connoisseurs has no finer standard-bearer than this magnificent expression of great Chardonnay in the intense 1985 vintage. The harvest that year was small because of frost damage earlier in the spring, but the weather at picking time was perfect. Even more remarkably, the finished Champagne, now well past its twentieth birthday, is still very fresh. The color is youthful, vital green tints among the gold; the mousse is super-fine, so discreet as to be barely perceptible to the eye but reassuringly invigorating on the palate; the nose is vivacious, precise yet with the multitoned notes of white flowers yielding to more mature sensations of apricots and peaches; the palate has everything—delicacy, honeyed richness, yet with that freshness that pervades the wine. Ideally, you need to drink this very great Champagne with a loved one over a two-hour period, to let its complexities unfold.

The secret of such exceptional wine is the outstanding quality of the grapes. And, being based in Le Mesnil, Delamotte has peerless sources of supply from the grands crus of Oger, Cramant, and Mesnil themselves. The 1999 is a fine successor to the 1985, with a special flavor of *sousbois* (undergrowth), particularly wild mushrooms. Visitors to the Côte des Blancs can judge for themselves by trying a Delamotte Vintage, and maybe fresh monkfish cooked by Cédric Boulhaut, the chef-patron of Le Mesnil restaurant in the village. **ME**
🌕🌕🌕 **Drink: to 2020**

FURTHER RECOMMENDATIONS		
Other great vintages		
1982 • 1996 • 1999		
More Blanc de Blancs		
Cazals Clos Cazals • Gosset Celebris Blanc de Blancs		
Krug Clos du Mesnil • Pol Roger Blanc de Chardonnay		

A 1900 advertisement depicts Champagne's ice-breaking properties. ➡

Deutz

Cuvée William Deutz 1996

Origin France, Champagne
Style Sparkling dry white wine, 12% ABV
Grapes P. Noir 55%, Chardonnay 35%, P. Meunier 10%

Diebolt-Vallois

Fleur de Passion 1996

Origin France, Champagne, Côte des Blancs
Style Sparkling dry white wine, 12% ABV
Grape Chardonnay

William Deutz is one of the greatest Champagnes of the intense 1996 vintage, yet it remains subtle and refined—something that is eminently in keeping with Deutz's just reputation for being the most discreet of the Grandes Maisons. The image of this old Aÿ firm—founded in 1838 by German immigrants William Deutz and Pierre-Hubert Geldermann—is the antithesis of "bling, bling."

The Deutz approach shows in this prestige cuvée, which, perhaps more than any other of the "greats," is simply a very fine wine with gossamer-fine bubbles. The color is brilliant gold, the very 1996 nose powerful and complex but with that gentle Deutz touch, leading with primary aromas of hedgerow fruits, flowers, and even a touch of mint.

On the palate, the wine has a strong personality, though its assertiveness is checked by a classy finish, which brings out the loveliest of orchard fruit flavors. Interestingly, there is 10 percent Meunier in the blend. The wine is exquisitely pure and will live for decades. It would be fascinating to compare the 1996 in another year or two with the 1990, which is its only real rival in recent vintages. **ME**

🍷🍷🍷🍷 Drink: to 2025+

A jolly, well-nourished vigneron with a taste for fine antiques, Jacques Diebolt has a sure talent for making particularly refined and pretty Champagnes that belie his comfortable frame. It helps, of course, that his 25-acre (10 ha) family domaine is home to some of the very best vineyard plots in the hilltop village of Cramant—the raciest grand cru of the Côte des Blancs.

Jacques's lightness of touch is well illustrated by this, his finest wine in a great vintage. The Passion 1996 is an *assemblage* of barrel-fermented wines from such top Cramant vineyard sites as Bouzons, Grosmont, and Goutte d'Or. The oak is seamlessly integrated in the finished Champagne, which has lost none of its fresh purity after a decade in bottle.

The color is vivid straw-yellow, reflecting the ripeness of the year, and the bubbles are fine and persistent; scents of citrus fruit mingle with hints of the mineral-rich earth from which the wine came. The mouthfeel is crisp and incisive, enhanced by a generous fullness of white orchard fruit flavors—truly a masterly Blanc de Blancs, at once complex, subtly powerful, yet ethereal. **ME**

🍷🍷🍷🍷 Drink: to 2025+

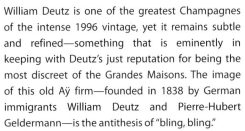

Gentlemen and their lady escorts enjoy Champagne refreshment.

Romano Dogliotti
Moscato d'Asti La Galeisa 2013

Origin Italy, Piedmont, Langhe
Style Sparkling dry white wine, 5.5% ABV
Grapes Moscato Bianco, Muscat Blanc à Petits Grains

Dom Pérignon
1998

Origin France, Champagne
Style Sparkling dry white wine, 12% ABV
Grapes Pinot Noir 50%, Chardonnay 50%

In the years following World War II, when Redento Dogliotti first started making Moscato from the grapes of his high, steep vineyards in Castiglione Tinella, he was reviving a tradition that had all but died out. His Moscato (Muscat) did not bring the renown he hoped for, but he did pass his enthusiasm on to his son Romano, who now, with the help of sons Alessandro, Sergio, and Marco, produces a highly respected Moscato d'Asti: La Galeisa. For this delicious wine, Dogliotti hand-harvests grapes from just 7 acres (3 ha) of sandy, calcareous, south-facing slopes. Grapes are fermented in an autoclave and the fermentation is arrested at around 5% ABV, when the carbon dioxide pressure is still low. Such low pressure allows the wine to have a normal cork, fully inserted into the bottle, with no mushroom top.

La Galeisa typically has a fine mousse of tiny bubbles, with an elegant citrus fruit and sage nose. The palate opens sweet, lightly frothing, but often finishes with an attractive bitter twist. 2013 was a good vintage, but this is not a wine that should be kept: Moscato is best drunk at the height of freshness, and is all the more precious for that. **SB**
🍷 **Drink: current release within 1 or 2 years**

It is a mug's game to chart the maturing pattern and eventual ranking of any vintage of Dom Pérignon—the daddy of all prestige cuvées—too early in its life. For this is preeminently Champagne that shows its full splendor only after a period of fifteen or twenty years, due to the deliberately reductive winemaking (no wood) and the intricate blending from the same top-flight vineyards. But at the risk of putting one's neck on the block, DP 1998 may well be the dark horse of recent years, and could yet outrun such fulsomely praised vintages as 1996.

The 1998 vintage is unusual in that record temperatures in August of that year were followed by exceptionally high rainfall in early September; but the sun soon put its hat on again, and the result is a very fine Champagne. The wine has a floral nose touched with fresh almonds and spices and a complement of lightly toasted brioche; then there is that satiny middle palate, which is the steady signature of this brilliantly assembled Champagne at its best. The coup de grâce is the finish, which is very persistent with just an undertone of lemony tartness. Sublime. **ME**
🍷🍷🍷🍷 **Drink: to 2030+**

The signature of Dom Pérignon, in the Abbey of Hautvillers museum. ➡

18. auril 1691

Dom Irenée Richard
prieur

L. pierre perignon

Dom Pérignon *Rosé* 1990

Origin France, Champagne
Style Sparkling dry rosé wine, 12% ABV
Grapes Pinot Noir, Chardonnay

The Cuvée Rosé is very much in the Dom Pérignon style—particularly in terms of its intensity without heaviness on the palate and its creamy texture. Yet at the same time, this Rosé is an alternative expression of that famous style. Without vitiating the structure or complexity of Dom Pérignon, the composition and balance of the pink blend are palpably different—the main difference being the stronger presence of Pinot Noir.

The 1990 growing season was almost perfect. After a very mild winter and an early flowering, that year's summer was hot and particularly sunny. To improve matters still further, a lucky spell of rain just before the harvest prevented heat stress and also helped to maintain a respectable level of acidity.

The color of the DP Rosé is a coppery gold with orange tints; aromas of fresh gingerbread and cashew nuts mingle with candied orange peel. The wine is full and caresses the palate; its sensuous texture is at once solid and rich, yet with that characteristic trait of suppleness and elegance that is the essential Dom Pérignon—always with something in reserve. And the long, precise finish is nothing short of faultless. It is as well to remember, though, that the composition and construction of Dom Pérignon Rosé is certainly not set in stone. Without doubt, it is as great a wine as the 1990, but it reveals yet another expression of the style—the Rosé 1982 is rather more ethereal than the 1990, with Chardonnay for once dominant. **ME**

🍷🍷🍷🍷🍷 Drink: to 2020+

FURTHER RECOMMENDATIONS
Other great vintages
1982 • 1985 • 1996 • 1999 • 2002
More Rosé Champagnes
Billecart-Salmon Cuvée Elisabeth Salmon
Cristal • Deutz Cuvée William Deutz • Dom Ruinart

A statue commemorates the famous Dom Pérignon. ➔

Dom Ruinart 1990

Origin France, Champagne
Style Sparkling dry white wine, 12% ABV
Grape Chardonnay

The 1990 vintage in Champagne had the potential for greatness from the start. It was a very warm summer, with a record 2,100 hours of sunshine. Fortunately, the grapes did not suffer heat stress, as rain arrived at just the right moments, so, for vigilant growers, there was a decent level of acidity. Conditions were nothing short of perfect for making a sumptuous Dom Ruinart, the all-Chardonnay prestige cuvée of Champagne's oldest firm.

Yet this is Blanc de Blancs with a difference, for Ruinart has always used a sizable percentage of Chardonnay from its Montagne de Reims home villages of Sillery and Puissieulx. These Montagne crus give wines that are richer and rounder than those from the great growths of the Côte des Blancs. When the Montagne and Côte Chardonnays are deftly blended—as they were by cellar master Jean-François Barot, who made this 1990—you have something very special.

Disgorged in 2002, everything has knit together as the Champagne approaches its eighteenth birthday: a golden color, a nose at once sensuously ripe yet mineral, and a broad, luxurious mouthfeel—richer and silkier than the still adolescent 1996—with a glorious vanillalike end note.

Needless to say, the opulence of the 1990 makes it a gastronomic natural for special occasions. It would make an exciting partner for fresh foie gras, perhaps, or—most sensationally of all—with white *tartuffi* in the ultimate risotto. Bon appetit. **ME**

🌢🌢🌢🌢🌢 **Drink: to 2020**

FURTHER RECOMMENDATIONS
Other great vintages
1975 · 1982 · 1985 · 1988 · 1996 · 2002
More Ruinart wines
R de Ruinart · Ruinart Blanc de Blancs Ruinart Brut Rosé

Dom Ruinart *Rosé* 1988

Origin France, Champagne
Style Sparkling dry rosé wine, 12% ABV
Grapes Chardonnay 87%, Pinot Noir 13%

The Dom Ruinart Rosé 1988 may be the finest pink Champagne on the market, and certainly gives the lie to the myth that Rosé Champagne is an ephemeral fizz to be drunk young. It is made from the same Chardonnay grands crus as the Blanc de Blancs, but with 17 percent Bouzy Rouge added in the 1988.

This is a Champagne vintage for Champagne makers and connoisseurs—a classic, well-balanced year, firmer, drier, less showy than the 1990, but just as fine. Of exquisite salmon hue with copper lights, the 1988 has an extraordinary bouquet, freshly vegetal, and Burgundian in its sensual appeal. With its high Chardonnay content, the palate is elegant, of course, but it also has a wonderful complexity associated more with Pinot Noir—close your eyes and, if it were not for the bubbles, you might be drinking something stylishly racy from Volnay.

The exoticism and spice of this beautifully aged but still vital Rosé makes it a versatile partner for a wide repertoire of dishes, both classic and Asian: air-dried beef, Prosciutto di San Daniele, baby lobster with vanilla sauce, rack of new season veal, Cantonese duck, Epoisse cheese—the list is endless.

For the visitor, the Reims premises, restored to their eighteenth-century style, ooze tradition. The firm's Gallo-Roman chalk cellars (known as *crayères*) are the finest in the city, classified as a national monument. For many years, the cellars have been the venue for the Trophée Ruinart, an international competition to find Europe's best sommelier. **ME**
😌😌😌😌😌 Drink: to 2025+

FURTHER RECOMMENDATIONS
Other great vintages
1982 • 1985 • 1990 • 1996
More 1988 wines
Dom Pérignon Oenothèque • Gosset Celebris • Henriot Cuvée des Enchanteleurs • Jacquesson Signature • Krug

Drappier
Grande Sendrée 1996

Origin France, Champagne, Côte des Bar
Style Sparkling dry white wine, 12% ABV
Grapes Pinot Noir 55%, Chardonnay 45%

Grande Sendrée is the prestige cuvée of Drappier, leading independent Champagne house of the Aube, based in Urville, whose Champagne style is for full-on Pinot Noir flavors tempered by good Chardonnay. In the 1850s, there was a great fire on the village slopes, reducing trees and bushes to cinders. Afterwards, the Drappiers planted a vineyard here, which became known as les Cendrées (French for "cinders"). However, it was not until 1974 that Michel Drappier made his first cuvée of Grande Sendrée (the "C" having been replaced by an "S" due to an error) when the title of the vineyard was registered. Today, it is one of the finest wines in Champagne.

Always made with a slight majority of top-flight Pinot Noir over Chardonnay, it almost invariably comes from wines of real structure and finesse, needing time to show themselves. The 1996 is both an exceptional Champagne and an exception to the classic style of harmonious, silky greats like the 1990 and 1995. Of deep gold hue with copper tones, it still bounces with vigorous acidity, yet is super-ripe and mature. This is certainly not a Champagne that could ever be called boring. **ME**
🍷🍷🍷🍷 **Drink: to 2021**

Egly-Ouriet *Les Crayères*
Blanc de Noirs Vieilles Vignes NV

Origin France, Champagne, Montagne de Reims
Style Sparkling dry white wine, 12.5% ABV
Grape Pinot Noir

Francis Egly of Ambonnay makes perhaps the finest Blanc de Noirs in Champagne. The wine comes from old Pinot Noir vines planted in 1947. The deep earth of this exceptional terroir holds chalk from the top soil to the bedrock dozen of yards below—indeed, this *lieu-dit* is known as *Les Crayères* ("chalk pits") and the vine is firmly rooted in it, giving the wine voluptuous red fruits flavors balanced by a subtle minerality. The result: fullness, power, and elegance. A wine for the finest table, it is a perfect partner for feathered game like partridge or marvelous with aged Comté or Tomme de Savoie cheese.

Although Crayères does not carry a vintage label, it is always the wine of a single harvest. A number of the first years of the twenty-first century have been intriguing: the great, opulent 2002; the precise, scintillating 2004; the punchy, foursquare 2005; the hedonistic charmer that is 2006; and for future drinking well into the 2020s, the classically dry 2008 and the intense, fabulous 2012 (the best yet). Egly's peerless plot always delivers an arresting wine, however, as much due to the chalk-wrapped vines below as to the changing skies above. **ME**
🍷🍷🍷🍷 **Drink: to 2020+**

Giulio Ferrari
Riserva del Fondatore 1989

Origin Italy, Trentino, Trento
Style Sparkling dry white wine, 12.5% ABV
Grape Chardonnay

Cave Geisse
Terroir Nature 2009

Origin Brazil, Pinto Bandeira, Rio Grande do Sul
Style Sparkling dry white wine, 12.5% ABV
Grapes Chardonnay, Pinot Noir

The Giulio Ferrari Riserva del Fondatore, arguably the best Italian spumante, has been produced by the Lunelli family since 1971. The wine is named for Giulio Ferrari, who founded and ran "G. Ferrari & Cie—Trento, Autriche" (Trento was once part of the Austro–Hungarian Empire) from 1902 to 1952 when, after considerable haggling, he finally sold to Bruno Lunelli. All Ferrari insisted on was a staggeringly high price and the right to work in the cellars for the rest of his life. He died in 1965, aged eighty-six.

Ferrari was a meticulous man, and his rigorous attention to detail, together with a painstaking desire for perfection, helped make this spumante the marvel it is today. The Chardonnay grapes used in its production are descendants of those Ferrari himself introduced to the region, apparently smuggling them in from Epernay in Champagne. The 1989 vintage is a great one. Its mature nose offers aromas of peanut butter and freshly baked croissants, along with fresher notes of lavender and Seville orange. On the palate it is lively and vibrant, despite its considerable weight, thanks to the acidity and minerality that sustain it through a long, focused finish. **AS**
😊😊😊😊 **Drink: to 2019**

Mario Geisse is a pioneer of the flourishing sparkling wine industry in Brazil. In 1976, he moved from his native Chile to run Moët & Chandon do Brasil, before setting up his own estate, Cave Geisse. The vineyards belong to the wine-growing region of Vale da Montanha, the higher altitude ensuring enough sun to ripen the fruit and cool nights to preserve the acidity necessary for making fine sparkling wines.

The wines are made by the *méthode traditionnelle* from a 50–50 blend of Chardonnay and Pinot Noir. The grapes are hand-picked and the bottles of fermenting wines resting on their lees are turned by hand. Although no sweet *liqueur d'expédition* is added to the bottle fermentation, a good balance is achieved between the acidity and the fruit flavors.

In 2009, the Terroir Nature cuvée had a production of 7,600 bottles. It has a light, golden color, and is filled with aromas of bread and yeast, with notes of apple and pear. It is mouth-filling with a fine, gentle mousse, fresh acidity, and generous, ripe orchard fruit. It has a pleasingly mild, bitter finish and good length. **BS**
😊😊😊 **Drink: to 2017**

The high-altitude vineyards at Cave Geisse provide ideal growing conditions for sparkling wines. ➡

Pierre Gimonnet *Millésime de Collection Blanc de Blancs* 1996

Origin France, Champagne, Côte des Blancs
Style Sparkling dry white wine, 12.5% ABV
Grape Chardonnay

Didier Gimonnet, like many Champagne growers, produces a *Tête de Cuvée* from his best lots, oldest vineyards, and/or finest parcels. As he is a member of the so-called Club Trésors de Champagne, these bottlings are known as Spécial Club and are produced in appropriate vintages, among which 1996 was especially great. The same wine is also bottled in magnum for later release, under the name Vintage Collection, and we are thus allowed to see the difference that bottle size makes in a Champagne's aging curve. Magnums, it should be said, are for the drinker who is not in a hurry.

Gimonnet's 62 acres (25 ha) are concentrated in the northern half of the Côtes des Blancs, mostly in the premier cru village of Cuis and the grand cru villages of Cramant and Chouilly. The 1996 was 45 percent Cramant (forty- to eighty-year-old vines), 25 percent Chouilly, and 30 percent Cuis. Didier believes an entirely grand cru wine would be too heavy and would lack the elegance and freshness he seeks. "For me, we must have concentration, but also balance, elegance, and harmony," he says.

Although the wine, at ten years old, has been forbiddingly austere as it makes its leisurely way to the pinnacles ahead, Gimonnet believes in it. "A great wine is a mineral wine at the beginning, not a fruity wine," he says. This 1996 is considerably more approachable from bottle, but the magnum seems to create electro-magnetic activity on your palate—enough to interfere with airport security devices. **TT**
🜚🜚🜚🜚 Drink: to 2025

FURTHER RECOMMENDATIONS		
Other great vintages		
1975 • 1982 • 1985 • 1988 • 1990 • 1999 • 2002 • 2004		
More Pierre Gimonnet wines		
Special Club Millésime Premier Cru 1996		
Millésime de Collection 1995 • Premier Cru Sans Année		

The church at Cuis, in the limestone-rich Côte des Blancs. ➡

Henri Giraud *Aÿ Grand Cru Fût de Chêne* 1996

Origin France, Champagne, Montagne de Reims
Style Sparkling dry white wine, 12% ABV
Grapes Pinot Noir 70%, Chardonnay 30%

Fût de Chêne (Oak Cask) features prominently on the label of this original Grand Cru Aÿ Champagne—and with good reason—for Claude Giraud is almost certainly the producer who has thought most deeply and originally about the use of oak in modern Champagne making. He is in a privileged position—his family has been making wine in Aÿ since the seventeenth century, and today he owns thirty parcels of vines in fourteen *lieux-dits* perfectly located in the commune's best hillsides and valleys.

With such great grapes to hand, it is natural that Claude should be committed to oak. Going back to first principles, Claude did a lot of research into the type of oak that would best suit both the power and the finesse of Aÿ Champagne. He finally alighted on oak from the Argonne forest near Ste.-Ménehould, one and a half hour's drive southeast of Aÿ. This local wood is both gentle and flattering, but it virtually disappeared from the Marne for decades.

This is among the best 1996s. Its deep gold-light amber color reflects the Champagne's power and partnership with oak; the nose is taking on the complexities of evolution, vanilla tones melding with vinosity and a touch of the oxidative *rancio* in Sherry; the palate is a mighty mouthful, the high acidity and huge fruit still circling each other warily but being gradually brought together by the oak. Yet this is not a long-term wine, because for all its magnificence this is not a classic Champagne of textbook balance: It is a great wine of exception. **ME**
ʘʘʘʘʘ **Drink: to 2018+**

FURTHER RECOMMENDATIONS
Other great vintages
1993 • 1995 • 1998
More producers using wood
Bollinger • Alfred Gratien • Krug • Jérôme Prévost
Roederer • Jacques Selosse • Tarlant

A moment of excitement created by Champagne's explosive force. ➜

Gloria Ferrer *Royal Cuvée* 2000

Origin USA, California, Sonoma
Style Sparkling dry white wine, 12% ABV
Grapes Pinot Noir 65%, Chardonnay 35%

Many Californian producers were caught out by the 1980s phylloxera epidemic. Gloria Ferrer, owned by Cava producer Freixenet, was planted with a single clone each of Chardonnay and Pinot Noir. Fortunately, their wine-growing team, led by Mike Crumly and Bob Iantosca, carried out clonal trials for sparkling wine in 1986, visiting Champagne to find suitable Chardonnay and Pinot Noir clones. Three fairly obscure clones (Colmar 538, UCD 32, PN 927) form the base of their prestige cuvées, including the vintage-dated Royal Cuvée. Made from estate fruit, the soft, free-run juice receives a cool, stainless-steel fermentation in order to retain the delicate fruit aromatics. The number of base wines in the Royal Cuvée blend has increased steadily over the years, reaching seventeen for its 2000 vintage.

For sparkling wine producers, 2000 was ideal—an uneventful flowering, a cool July, and relatively cool conditions through October delayed harvest. Although some red producers never got their grapes phenolically ripe before they began to raisin, the long ripening period allowed grapes designed for sparkling wine to develop complex aromatics while retaining brisk acidities. Typical of the Royal Cuvée, the 2000 exhibits ripe fruit, complex floral notes, vibrant acidity, and a capacity for aging. "Fit for a king" is one way of characterizing this prestige cuvée, as its inaugural vintage was first served to King Juan Carlos I and Queen Sophia of Spain during their 1987 California visit. **LGr**

🍷🍷 **Drink:** to 2018

FURTHER RECOMMENDATIONS
Other great vintages
1994 • 1995 • 1996 • 1997
More Gloria Ferrer wines
Blanc de Blancs • Blanc de Noirs
Carneros Cuvée • Sonoma Brut

Mustard plants flower among the vines at Gloria Ferrer. ➽

Gosset
Celebris 1988

Origin France, Champagne
Style Sparkling dry white wine, 12% ABV
Grapes Chardonnay 70%, Pinot Noir 30%

Dating its origins to 1584, Aÿ-based Gosset is arguably the oldest Champagne house, bought by the Cointreau family in 1994 after over 400 years of Gosset ownership, and ably overseen by Béatrice Cointreau until 2007. The grapes have been expertly managed since 1983 by Aÿ-born *chef de cave* Jean-Pierre Mareigner, whom Tom Stevenson includes in his list of the forty greatest ever winemakers in Champagne. The malolactic fermentation is always arrested here, which contributes to the great longevity of the wines and the penetrating, powerful house style. Most cuvées offered by the house are fermented partly in wood, including the outstanding prestige cuvée, Celebris.

The Chardonnay and Pinot Noir grapes for Celebris are sourced exclusively from between seven and nine grands crus, and the wine is made only in exceptional years. The 1988 was a dazzling (and still scintillating) debut. (Only 18,000 bottles were produced, though the only succeeding vintages—1990, 1995, 1998, 2000, and 2002—were produced in slightly larger volumes.) For a prestige cuvée of this quality, the wines represent excellent value. **NB**
🍷🍷🍷🍷 Drink: to 2020+

Gosset *Cuvée Celebris*
Blanc de Blancs Extra Brut NV

Origin France, Champagne
Style Sparkling dry white wine, 12% ABV
Grape Chardonnay

Gosset first extended its prestige cuvée range with the 1998 Celebris Rosé. But *chef de cave* Jean-Pierre Mareigner had been working on an all-Chardonnay cuvée since the mid-1990s, reserving some 4,000 bottles each vintage. The end result has been well worth the wait. The initial release is a blend of Chardonnays from eleven different crus, most in the Côte des Blancs, including Grands Crus Avize, Chouilly, Cramant, Le Mesnil-sur-Oger, and Oger, and Premiers Crus Cuis, Grauves, Vertus, and Villeneuve-Renneville (all 95 percent on the *échelle des crus*). It is also blended from four different vintages: 1995, 1996, 1998, and 1999. True to house style, the base wines did not undergo malolactic fermentation, and some were fermented in wood.

The first release is an impressive, individual wine, at once in its first and second childhood. It was brave to release this prestige cuvée as an NV blend, defying the supposition that vintage wines are always superior, but it has surely resulted in a more complex and distinctive wine, one that Gosset's executive director, Odilon de Varine, describes fairly as "our own unique interpretation of Chardonnay." **NB**
🍷🍷🍷🍷 Drink: to 2020+

Harvesting time on the Côte des Blancs. ➡

Gramona

III Lustros Gran Reserva 2001

Origin Spain, Penedès, Sant Sadurní d'Anoia
Style Sparkling dry white wine, 11.5% ABV
Grapes Xarel-lo, Macabeo

The world of Cava is dominated by large companies producing a substantial number of bottles; but there are also a number of small family-owned wineries making quality wine that is well worth seeking out. Gramona, founded in 1921, is one of these.

Gramona works 62 acres (25 ha) of vineyards used, not only for Cava, but also for a range of still wines and rarities such as Icewine, which is produced with the help of carbonic snow. III Lustros was born at the end of the 1930s, after the Spanish Civil War. The intention was to make a Cava that would be aged in the cellar for about fifteen years. The word *lustro* in Spanish means half a decade, so it was aged for three *lustros*—hence the name.

Today, the market has changed radically, and so has the wine. III Lustros is now aged for five or six years, but this is still a very long time compared to most Cavas. Its percentage of Xarel-lo—the grape considered better for long aging—is high, complemented by 30 percent Macabeo. It is a Brut Nature (no sweetening *dosage* is added), and Gramona insists on closing the bottles with cork during the second fermentation. **LG**

🥂🥂 **Drink: current release**

Alfred Gratien

1998

Origin France, Champagne
Style Sparkling dry white wine, 12% ABV
Grapes Chardonnay, Pinot Noir, Pinot Meunier

This highly individualistic Champagne house was founded in 1867 by Alfred Gratien, a sparkling-wine maker from Saumur. The house is now owned by Henkell, the mighty *Sekt* producer. Wisely, the German giant has been happy to leave their Gratien baby in the safe and tender care of the Jaeger family, cellar masters here over three generations.

The Champagne making is splendidly traditional throughout the range. From the utterly reliable NV Brut (shipped to the Wine Society in Britain without a break since 1906) right up to the exquisite prestige Cuvée Paradis, all the wines are vinified in oak barrels. Malolactic fermentation is avoided to ensure that the Champagnes live long, distinguished lives.

This will certainly be the case with this Gratien 1998 Vintage, a year of much more substance than the preceding charming '97. This younger wine is a brilliant, shimmering gold. The aromas are already expressive and developed, with notes of grilled bread and brioche. The mouthfeel is beautifully crisp, fresh, and precise, but with great depth of both citrus and stone fruit flavors that will develop gradually for several more years. Bravo! **ME**

🥂🥂🥂🥂 **Drink: to 2020+**

Gratien & Meyer
Cuvée Flamme Brut NV

Origin France, Loire, Saumur
Style Sparkling dry white wine, 12% ABV
Grapes Chenin Blanc, C. Franc, Chardonnay

Charles Heidsieck
Brut Réserve NV

Origin France, Champagne
Style Sparkling dry white wine, 12% ABV
Grapes P. Noir 55%, Chardonnay 30%, P. Meunier 15%

Alfred Gratien was a man who saw the big picture, in 1864 founding houses in both Saumur on the Loire and Epernay in Champagne. The Saumur firm has always been the firm's main concern, and today remains one of the quality leaders of Loire *mousseux*, made appropriately in a veritable temple on the banks of the great river. The grapes for the Cuvée Flamme, a classic mix of Chenin and Cabernet Franc, with a little Chardonnay, are grown on the white limestone soil called *tuffeau*, endemic to Saumur, and give the sparkling wines a distinctive and refined flavor. The *tuffeau* soil also retains the sun's heat during the day and warms the vines at night. This is a crucial factor in the quality of the wine.

Cuvée Flamme has a vital pale gold color, while the *cordon* of the mousse is steady, regular, and elegant. The wine's aromas are both profound and pretty, the dominant scents being those of springtime woodland flowers. Outside Champagne, Flamme is one of the very few sparkling wines to come near to the taste of the real thing, with its delicate, mineral fruitiness combined with a depth of complex, mature flavors. **ME**

🥂🥂🥂 **Drink: current release within 3 years**

This wine is simply one of the finest non-vintage Champagnes, its precepts and composition an enduring legacy of the late Daniel Thibault, Charles Heidsieck's winemaker and, for many observers, the greatest Champagne blender of his day.

Why, at its launch in the mid-1990s, did this non-vintage Champagne have a year specified on the label? Daniel believed that connoisseurs should have full information about the age of the blend in order to gauge its maturity. The term *Mis en Cave* effectively means "bottling date," and the base wine is bottled in the spring or summer after the preceding harvest.

After Daniel's premature death in 2004, the technical information, including the bottling date, was transferred to a back label, to prevent confusion on the part of the consumer. Yet, in the cellar, Daniel's innovative wine concept lives on under his friend and winemaking successor, Régis Camus. In this 2008 bottling, the wine is precise and pure: Exquisitely balanced orchard and citrus fruits meld seamlessly, with a voluptuous texture that comes from extended aging under a clamped cork; maturity brings aromas of vanilla and controlled yeasty autolysis. **ME**

🥂🥂🥂 **Drink: current release for up to 10 years**

Henriot
Cuvée des Enchanteleurs 1988

Origin France, Champagne
Style Sparkling dry white wine, 12% ABV
Grapes Chardonnay 55%, Pinot Noir 45%

Domaine Huet
Vouvray Brut 1959

Origin France, Loire, Touraine
Style Sparkling dry white wine, 12% ABV
Grape Chenin Blanc

Joseph Henriot is one of the most influential men in Champagne, a complex character who is both a fervent guardian of quality and a wheeler-dealer of extreme agility. His abiding passion is Chardonnay, and it is Chardonnay that drives his greatest wine, the Cuvée des Enchanteleurs.

Made only in exceptional years, this is a particularly long-lived Champagne that ideally should not be touched until it is thirteen years old, and often tastes better at twenty. The great crus of the Côte des Blancs are the heart of the blend, with equally fine growths from the Montagne de Reims usually playing a supporting role.

The 1990 Enchanteleurs has been much lauded, but the 1988 beats it by a short head, simply because the older wine is one of the most magnificent Champagnes made in the last fifty years. The color is star-bright yellow gold, with more green highlights than the 1990; the bouquet is arresting and very complex, minerality its hallmark, but also with slowly evolving notes of butter and hazelnut; the palate defies description, every component of fruit, terroir, vinosity, and length of flavor in perfect harmony. **ME**
🍷🍷🍷🍷 Drink: to 2020+

For anybody convinced that no other sparkling wine can match the excitement of mature vintage Champagne, this gently sparkling Vouvray Brut will be a revelation. Gaston Huet, who took over the family estate in Vouvray in 1938, did more than anyone to preserve the reputation of this famous village, of which he served as mayor from 1947 to 1989 (two of the greatest vintages of the century).

The original Huet vineyard, Le Haut Lieu (later supplemented by Le Mont and Clos du Bourg), was probably the source for this superb wine. As with most other Huet sparkling wines of the time, it was made *pétillant* (at three bars of pressure, lightly sparkling) rather than *mousseux* (at six bars, fully sparkling). A good bottle still has a definite sparkle; and this, together with the classic Chenin acidity and minerality, helps keep the wine fresh, despite its mellow richness. Deep gold, it has a captivating autumnal nose of apples, honey, and pastry, and a glorious mouthful of ripe, silken fruit. Of the two 1959 Huet Pétillants, the Brut may have the edge over the Demi-Sec thanks to better definition and extension on the finish. **NB**
🍷🍷🍷🍷 Drink: now to 2019

Noël Pinguet, winemaker at Domaine Huet for more than thirty years before his resignation in 2012. ➔

Iron Horse *Vrais Amis* 2001

Origin USA, Sonoma County, Green Valley
Style Sparkling dry white wine, 13% ABV
Grapes Pinot Noir 70%, Chardonnay 30%

Sparkling wines have toasted countless friendships, but few are products of friendships. Vrais Amis was originally conceived as a joint cuvée between two close friends, Barry Sterling of Iron Horse and the late Bernard de Nonancourt of Champagne Laurent-Perrier. Once Sterling bought Laurent-Perrier's share of Iron Horse in 1998, the Pinot Noir, originally designated for the project, was recognized to produce spectacular still wine. So the plan faded, until another close friend of Sterling, Chicago chef Charlie Trotter, requested an exclusive cuvée to complement Trotter's innovative cuisine.

Sterling bought the Iron Horse Vineyard property from Rodney Strong in the mid-1970s, intending to produce Chardonnay and Pinot Noir. Conditions in the Green Valley, however, also argued for sparkling wine production. The winery does produce still wines, but it is the complex sparkling wines that ground Iron Horse's fine reputation.

The Vrais Amis is a variation on the traditional Iron Horse Brut Vintage. As in all Iron Horse sparkling wines, malolactic fermentation is blocked to maintain a vibrant acidity. It is aged a minimum of five years on the lees and disgorged by hand; what distinguishes the Vrais Amis is an all-Chardonnay *liqueur d'exposition*—a nod to de Nonancourt, who always viewed Iron Horse's Chardonnay, with its distinctive Green Valley character, as its finest wine. With its fine structure and complex flavors, the Vrais Amis mirrors the bonds it celebrates. **LGr**

❾❾ **Drink: to 2017+**

FURTHER RECOMMENDATIONS
Other great vintages
1992 • 1993 • 1994 • 1995 • 2002
More Iron Horse sparkling wines
Classic Vintage Brut • Joy
Russian Cuvée • Wedding Cuvée

Iron Horse vineyards amid conifers in Sonoma's Green Valley. ➲

Jacquesson
Cuvée 730 NV

Origin France, Champagne
Style Sparkling dry white wine, 12% ABV
Grapes Chardonnay 48%, P. Noir 32%, P. Meunier 20%

Of all the great names in Champagne, Jacquesson now stands apart from the pack in its approach to the craft of blending a dry, non-vintage cuvée. Jean-Hervé Chiquet, co-owner with his brother Laurent, explains, "In the late 1990s we became aware that the fundamental principle of making a classic Brut Non-Vintage in a consistent style was limiting our possibilities of improving the wine." The Chiquets decided, with effect from the 2000 harvest, to prize excellence over consistency by crafting wines that reflected the main vintage in the blend, rather than replicating the even flavors of traditional blends.

This Cuvée 730, being the 730th cuvée blended by the house since its foundation in 1798, is based on the splendid 2002 vintage. Gloriously ripe Pinot Noir, although accounting for only one-third of this cuvée, pervades its profound, vinous flavor. The cleverness of the blending, in a wine with satisfactory but not excessive acidity (often the sign of greatness in Champagne) is the compensating high level of Chardonnay, which contributes bounce and crispness. The Cuvée 730 was fermented mainly in large oak tuns and never filtered. **ME**

🥂🥂🥂 **Drink: to 2015+**

Jacquesson *Grand Cru*
Vauzelle Terme 2004

Origin France, Champagne, Grande Vallée de la Marne
Style Sparkling dry white wine, 12% ABV
Grape Pinot Noir

Vauzelle Terme is the smallest of Jacquesson's great vineyards: 0.75 acres (0.3 ha) lying halfway up a south-facing hillside, close to an inlet of the Marne Canal, providing protection against springtime frost. The soil is calcareous (with clay content), and has been formed by alluvial deposits rich in burrstone pebbles. A bedrock of chalk facilitates swift drainage. All this makes the vineyard, above the River Marne, a privileged site for the great black grape.

The 2004 was vinified in *demi-muid* large casks. Beforehand, no sulfur dioxide was added at the time of pressing and the wine naturally went through malolactic fermentation in cask, extra richness of flavor being encouraged by weekly *bâtonnage* (stirring) of the fine lees. The crop was one of the largest ever recorded, yet due to very moderate yields and careful husbandry of the vines, this 2004 has an amplitude and burgeoning vinosity beyond the precision and delicacy that generally marked this vintage. Lustrous gold tints mingle with buttercup yellow, peach, and a touch of cherry. It has a suave but lively mouthfeel, and the controlled effects of oak bring spices and oxidative expression. **ME**

🥂🥂🥂🥂🥂 **Drink: to 2024**

◀ A dramatic 1930s Jacquesson advertisement by A. Cometti.

Krug *Clos d'Ambonnay* 1995

Origin France, Champagne, Montagne de Reims
Style Sparkling dry white wine, 12% ABV
Grape Pinot Noir

Twenty-one years after the debut of Clos du Mesnil 1979 in 1986, Clos d'Ambonnay 1995 was revealed in 2007, having remained a secret until Henri, Rémi, and Olivier Krug welcomed the first few fortunate visitors to the tiny walled vineyard on the edge of this Montagne de Reims grand cru.

As early as the 1880s, founder Paul Krug I identified Ambonnay and Le Mesnil-sur-Oger as ideal sources of Pinot Noir and Chardonnay respectively, and they have played an important part in Krug Grande Cuvée ever since. The Krugs bought Clos d'Ambonnay in the mid-1990s and, although they made experimental cuvées for nearly ten years, they thought that the 1995 vintage was the first "to express the quintessence" of this special terroir.

A flat "garden plot" of 1.69 acres (0.7 ha)—one-third the size of Clos du Mesnil—Clos d'Ambonnay represents what Rémi Krug calls "individuality in the extreme." The character of the wine from this chalky, shallow soil is indeed highly individual. The bouquet of the 1995 boasts remarkable complexity and purity (a classic Krug paradox), as well as a distinctive, earthy, very noble savagery; anise, almond croissant, candied fruits, white flowers, and acacia honey turn eventually to dried apricots and licorice. On the palate, the wine is dense and intense, but also elegant, harmonious, and richly silky (the Krugs praise Ambonnay as the Château Margaux of Champagne). There is extraordinary race for a warm vintage, and extraordinary, even length. **NB**
🍾🍾🍾🍾 **Drink: to 2020+**

FURTHER RECOMMENDATIONS
Other vintages likely to be released
1996 • 2000 • 2002 • 2004
More single-vineyard Champagnes
Billecart-Salmon Clos St. Hilaire • Cattier Clos du Moulin
Cazals Clos Cazals • Philipponnat Clos des Goisses

A barrel is spun forward along its edge at the Krug winery. ➜

Krug
Clos du Mesnil 1979

Origin France, Champagne, Côte des Blancs
Style Sparkling dry white wine, 12% ABV
Grape Chardonnay

Grand Cru Le Mesnil-sur-Oger is one village capable of producing wines that can stand alone in all their mineral splendor. Nestling at its heart is the enclosed Clos du Mesnil vineyard (one of only nine officially recognized *clos* in Champagne), whose easterly exposure, gentle slope, and high walls help secure an extra degree of ripeness. At just 4.5 acres (1.8 ha), the most famous vineyard in Champagne is the same size as the world's most famous vineyard: Romanée-Conti. In both cases, the combination of exceptional quality and extreme rarity results in very high prices: Until recently Clos du Mesnil was the most expensive Champagne on release, the 1995 and 1996 starting at $1,000 (£492, €726) per bottle.

The Clos dates back to 1698, but Krug acquired its holding here only in 1971, when it replanted. The first Krug Clos du Mesnil was the 1979, released in 1988 and ranked by Champagne expert Tom Stevenson as one of the three greatest Champagnes of the past thirty years. The wine has been released in just twelve other vintages—1980, 1982, 1983, 1985, 1986, 1988, 1989, 1990, 1992, 1995, 1996, and 2000. Like all Krug's wines, it is fermented in small barrels of aged Argonne oak and undergoes no malolactic fermentation—factors that contribute to its complexity, identity, and longevity. With a bracing minerality and penetrating purity in their youth, these thrilling wines develop aromas and flavors of acacia honey, apricots, *fleurs blanches*, coffee, vanilla, and walnuts with age. **NB**
🍷🍷🍷🍷🍷 **Drink: to 2019+**

◀ White paint is used to mark a cask in the Krug barrel room

Krug *Collection* 1981

Origin France, Champagne
Style Sparkling dry white wine, 12% ABV
Grapes Pinot Noir, Chardonnay, Pinot Meunier

When stored in perfect condition, Krug's Vintage Champagnes mature gracefully for decades, revealing new and intriguing facets of their personality. One key to their long life is Krug's first fermentation in small oak casks. This strengthens the infant wine's resistance to oxidation, encouraging a slow, lengthy evolution while ensuring that the wine stays vibrant. After fifteen or twenty years, Krug vintages enter a "second life"—the balance of their taste shifts as individual flavors become more intense, at which point they are ready to be re-released from the Krug cellars as Krug Collection, representing the last bottles available of an exceptional past vintage.

The 1981 is one such year. A mild, wet winter was followed by sharp frosts in April; then a long, sunny summer led up to a very small harvest in October. Brisk and incisive when young, this Krug Collection has evolved into a Champagne of great maturity, balancing power and finesse. Luminous gold, it unleashes aromas of white truffles, sweet spices, toast, ripe apple, and candied lemon, rounding out into mellow flavors of apricot and honey. Extremely long on the palate, the lasting impression is one of elegance and vigor. Subtlety and substance in a glass.

Did gastronome Paul Levy have the Collection 1981 in mind when he said: "Krug is the Champagne that God gives his angels when they have been especially good"? Maybe, though it could also have been the 1979, the 1976, or almost any of the others, back to the legendary 1928. *Quelle collection.* **ME**
〇〇〇〇〇 Drink: to 2020+

FURTHER RECOMMENDATIONS
Other great vintages
1964 • 1966 • 1969 • 1971 • 1973 • 1975 • 1976 • 1979
More 1981 Champagnes
Bollinger Vieilles Vignes Françaises
Cristal • Taittinger Comtes de Champagne

Krug *Grande Cuvée* NV

Origin France, Champagne
Style Sparkling dry white wine, 12% ABV
Grapes Pinot Noir, Chardonnay, Pinot Meunier

For many connoisseurs, Krug is simply the *ne plus ultra*, the greatest name in Champagne, Grande Cuvée the lodestar of the blender's art. It is made from all three Champagne grapes—the democratic Meunier playing a supporting role to the more aristocratic Pinot Noir and Chardonnay—in an intricate assembly of up to forty wines from a dozen vintages. Grande Cuvée is first fermented in small oak barrels of varying ages (from one to twenty years old), then passes immediately into stainless-steel tanks so the optimal freshness may be preserved.

Since this family firm became part of the Moët family of Champagnes in 2004, the financial resources of this huge group have contributed "greater power to our motor," in the words of the late Henri Krug, long the head winemaker and celebrated custodian of the Krug style. In 2007, the group made a major investment at Krug, installing forty state-of-the-art tanks, each one divided into two compartments, thereby allowing for the separate maturation of small parcels of the finest wines in the interests of complete traceability and perfectionist winemaking.

Aged for six years before release, this is a wine of vital green-gold, vital first aromas of citrus fruits preceding those of hazelnut, butter, and honey—grand Chardonnay. The mouthfeel is opulent yet refined and fine-drawn, the little red fruits of great Pinot Noir melding with palate-filling Meunier tones of baked bread and spices. The finish is long and multifaceted, like a peacock's tail. **ME**
🝔🝔🝔🝔 **Drink: on release or age for 10+ years**

FURTHER RECOMMENDATIONS
Other great Krug Champagnes
Krug Collection • Krug Rosé • Krug Vintage
More Non-Vintage Champagnes
Billiot Cuvée Laetitia • De Meric Cuvée Catherine
De Sousa Cuvée des Caudalies • Selosse Substance

La Morandina
Moscato d'Asti 2013

Origin Italy, Piedmont, Asti
Style Sparkling sweet white wine, 5.5% ABV
Grape Moscato

Having labored long under the shadow of its frothier cousin Asti, it is time for Moscato d'Asti to step into the spotlight. The wine is only lightly *pétillant*, unlike Asti, and the purity of its Moscato fruit—tasting like sweet, fresh-picked grapes—hardly ever disappoints. Moscato d'Asti is the perfect choice for a long, hot summer afternoon, with its low alcohol and bracing, scintillant fruitiness.

The Morando brothers, Giulio and Paolo, have taken their estate to new heights in recent times. Parts of the cellar may still be the original construction of the early nineteenth century, but the thinking is flawlessly modern. Since 1988, the grapes for the Moscato d'Asti have been grown in the commune of Castiglione Tinella, not far from the town of Asti itself, where 35 acres (14 ha) of plantings on limestone soils bring out the aromatic beauty inherent to great Moscato. Although La Morandina is a vintage-dated wine, there is remarkable year-to-year consistency. This is a wine that needs to be caught in its first flush of youth.

There is a wealth of lustrous grapey freshness in the bouquet, backed up by a little of the sugared almond quality that sweeter Moscato takes on. In the mouth, the sappy, refreshing character of the wine beautifully balances its gentle, peachy sweetness. The fizz prickles and teases without dominating the mouthfeel, and there are extraordinary herbal hints of mint and even fresh basil. The wine finishes freshly and cleanly, leaving the palate ready for a further mouthful at the earliest opportunity. **SW**

🍷🍷 **Drink: current release within 2 years**

Langlois Château
Crémant de Loire Brut NV

Origin France, Loire, Anjou
Style Sparkling dry white wine, 12.5% ABV
Grapes Chenin Blanc, Chardonnay, Cabernet Franc

Chenin Blanc, with its deep reserves of sap (what the French call *sève*) and acidity, is the great white grape of the Loire. It is the motor that allows the splendid dessert wines of Anjou such as Bonnezeaux, Quarts de Chaume, and Vouvray to live for decades in great vintages. It is also an ideal grape for making sparkling wine, particularly when partnered by Chardonnay. And in François-Régis de Fougeroux, Langlois Château has a star winemaker who has brought its range of sparkling wines to the top rank of the Crémant de Loire appellation. Born in Angers in 1974, François-Régis took a biology degree before military service as a cavalry officer at Saumur. He then worked in a vineyard next to his father's farm before going to Australia as an assistant winemaker at Petaluma, where he learned much from Brian Croser. On his return to France, he joined Langlois Château as production manager.

This entry-level Crémant de Loire Brut is a delight. Fresh and vital, with a fine *mousse*, the nose has a nice touch of bready maturity; The palate is dominated by the waxy, lemony flavor of Chenin, supported by the race of Chardonnay, and a little punch from the white juice of Cabernet Franc. The Crémant Réserve is of exactly the same composition as the Brut, but with more time on the lees (three years plus). It has more developed, secondary flavors—a wine for food or after-dinner reflection. The Langlois Crémant Rosé is pure Cabernet Franc, strawberries in a glass, and a great partner for the local *rillettes*, charcuterie, or a barbecued steak. **ME**

🍷🍷🍷 **Drink: current release within 3 years**

A 1940s French poster associates Champagne with high society. ➠

Larmandier-Bernier *VV de Cramant GC Extra Brut* 1999

Origin France, Champagne, Côte des Blancs
Style Sparkling dry white wine, 12.5% ABV
Grape Chardonnay

Jacques Lassaigne *Les Vignes de Montgueux Blanc de Blancs* NV

Origin France, Champagne, Aube
Style Sparkling dry white wine, 12.5% ABV
Grape Chardonnay

Ten years ago Larmandier belonged to the Club Trésors de Champagne, and their top cuvée was the Spécial Club, which generally hailed from the oldest vineyards in Vertus. The old-vines Cramant existed as a separate cuvée, but it has since become not only Larmandier's top wine but also one of the great Blanc de Blancs of Champagne.

Larmandier began a program of *bâtonnage* (stirring the lees) in his still wines prior to the second fermentation, and the wines have great stuffing and authority. The practice is not without controversy—detractors claim to miss a pristine clarity of fruit.

Cramant Champagne usually comes from two parcels, one nearly forty and the other nearly seventy years old. Cramant's vineyards vary in steepness and exposure, but in general these are the most Riesling-like of Champagnes, with nuances of jade-oolong and other green teas, lime zest, tarragon, Stayman-apple, and mineral. As with nearly all small-production cult Champagnes, the old-vines Cramant is released before it is fully ready, but the drinker who ages it will be rewarded with one of Champagne's most profound wines. **TT**
❸❸❸❸ **Drink: 10–20 years after the vintage**

Planted on steep south-facing slopes almost entirely to Chardonnay, the vineyards of Montgueux catch the sun from morning to dusk; their golden wine, known affectionately as the "Montrachet" of Champagne, is sought after by the chefs de caves of Reims and Epernay as an eminently ripe factor in their blends. Geologically, the hill of Montgueux is an extension of the fabled Côte des Blancs, Montgueux's soils of Turonian chalk shaping an incisive minerality to balance the wine's succulent fruitiness.

For the seductive taste of pure Montgueux, Jacques Lassaigne is the best producer. In 1999, Lassaigne's son Emmanuel took over at the 11-acre (4.5-ha) domaine and follows the best of organic and sustainable principles. Though his finest plot, Cotet, produces the most complex wine, and another, La Colline Inspirée, produces a sumptuous oak-fermented cuvée, his entry-level non-vintage Les Vignes de Montgueux delivers top quality at a reasonable price. A blend of three vintages—recently 2008, 2007, and 2004—the wine is a model amalgam of citrus, mango, and passion fruit; the touch of 2004 adds elegance and precision. **ME**
❸❸❸ **Drink: to 2020**

The vineyards on the hill of Montgueux overlook the historic city of Troyes. ➡

Laurent-Perrier
Grand Siècle La Cuvée NV

Origin France, Champagne
Style Sparkling dry white wine, 12% ABV
Grapes Chardonnay 55%, Pinot Noir 45%

Resistance war hero and long the head of Laurent-Perrier, the late Bernard de Nonancourt is a courageous pacesetter. In the 1950s, he dreamed of creating a prestige cuvée that would be very different from those of the great houses of Reims and Epernay. Rejecting the traditional choice of a vintage-dated wine, he preferred a blend of three great years that would be consistent in style and quality.

Since its launch in 1957, La Cuvée has shown an admirable balance of Pinot Noir and Chardonnay, often with a light majority of the great white grape. Over ten years later, my notes speak of "lustrous straw gold with green reflections: Chardonnay dominates on entry with aromas of lily, brioche, and toasted almond. Lemony, elegant flavors are the keynotes, buttressed by the quiet power of Pinot Noir."

Like all sensible people, de Nonancourt and his team did not always practice what they preached. Just occasionally, for example, they produce Grand Siècle as a single-vintage wine in an outstanding year. The 1985 *exceptionellement millésimé* is a majestic wine that features super-concentrated Pinot Noir in the driving seat. **ME**

🥂🥂🥂🥂 Drink: upon release for 10+ years

Lilbert-Fils
Cramant Grand Cru Brut Perle NV

Origin France, Champagne, Côte des Blancs
Style Sparkling dry white wine, 12% ABV
Grape Chardonnay

The Lilbert family has owned vines in Cramant since 1746, and has been winning gold medals at the Epernay Fair since as long ago as 1907.

The family's Cramant holdings are in some of the most distinguished *lieux-dits*, where the average age of the vines is more than forty years. Fermentation is conducted with cultured yeast in stainless steel, to reduce the risk of off-aromas or flavors that would detract from the crystalline purity sought here. The malolactic is encouraged, and the wines spend at least twenty-four to thirty months on their lees.

The Brut Perle is the most unusual wine in this compact range, and one of the few from the village to preserve a precious, previously popular style—Crémant de Cramant. Originally, *crémant* designated a "creamy" Champagne at lower than normal pressure, but the term had to be surrendered to the producers of other French sparkling wines when they agreed to stop using the term *méthode champenoise*. This beautifully elegant Lilbert version is brisk, chalky, and floral on the nose, but with a gentle, silky smooth vinosity on the palate, the better to reveal its terroir transparency. **NB**

🥂🥂 Drink: on release and for up to 5 years

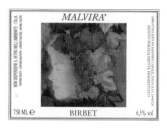

Malvirà
Birbét Brachetto NV

Origin Italy, Piedmont, Roero
Style Sparkling sweet red wine, 6.5% ABV
Grape Brachetto

The Malvirà estate is located in the small town of Canova, on the left bank of the River Tanaro. This area of Roero is just across the river from the more famous Langhe, home to Barolo and Barbaresco, and the soil here is of more recent formation than that in the Langhe, allowing for steeper hills than on the other side of the river. Malvirà was founded in 1974, but the Damonte family, which still owns the winery, has produced wine for more than 200 years.

Birbét Brachetto's alcohol level is deliberately left below the legal minimum for "wine," and so is regarded (and labeled) as "partially fermented grape must"—although it is far more satisfying than many other sweet wines. The first fermentation takes place in stainless-steel vats, the second in pressurized tanks. The bottling of the wine normally happens in three different batches in the months of November, February, and May, to ensure that the wine is as fresh as possible. Much of the beauty of this Brachetto lies in its primary aromas, powerfully reminiscent of roses and strawberries, which would fade with bottle aging. On the palate it is light, refreshing, and dangerously easy to drink. **AS**

🥂 **Drink: current release within 2 years**

Serge Mathieu *Cuvée Tradition*
Blanc de Noirs Brut NV

Origin France, Champagne, Côte des Bar
Style Sparkling dry white wine, 12% ABV
Grape Pinot Noir

A pure Pinot Noir cuvée from the richer limestone soils of Southern Champagne that provides excellent value. Serge Mathieu's top-drawer domaine at Avirey-Lingey is managed by his daughter Isabelle and her husband, Michel Jacob—a fine non-interventionist winemaker, a scrupulous, eco-friendly guardian of the 27-acre (11 ha) estate, and a pragmatist who stops just short of believing in the faith of biodynamism. The vineyard is mainly planted with Pinot Noir, with some excellent Chardonnay. There is no wood in the cellar, so the purity of the grape and the character of the terroir emerge unoaked.

This Blanc de Noirs is a striking burnished gold, almost bronze, in color; the aromas of ripe cherrylike Pinot melding with meat, spices, and leather lead on to a grand palate-filling mouthfeel uncannily like a mini Bollinger (Grande Année, not Special Cuvée!). Yet the most lasting impression is of finesse, balance, and the lightest of touches in the winemaking—all for under $30 (£15, €22) a bottle retail.

Michel also makes the refined Brut Sélect Tête de Cuvée, in which Chardonnay adds a delicate racy balance to the punch of Aubois Pinot Noir. **ME**

🥂🥂 **Drink: upon release for 5+ years**

Medici Ermete
Lambrusco Reggiano Concerto 2013

Origin Italy, Emilia-Romagna
Style Sparkling dry red wine, 11.5% ABV
Grape Lambrusco

Lambrusco is often bad-mouthed both in Italy and abroad. Its unfortunate reputation comes from the fact that production of this wine is controlled by huge cooperatives of grape growers, which are paid by the ton regardless of the quality of the grapes. The lax production laws did the rest.

The Medici Ermete estate was the first, back in the mid-1980s, to take real pride in the production of Lambrusco. Back then they decided to grow their own grapes for their top wines, while continuing to buy in grapes from cooperatives for the rest. The difference this made was dramatic: The press noticed right away, as did the market and other producers, who began to follow their example. The Medicis increased the density of the vines to 1,620 per acre (rather than the traditional 650), and reduced yields to 5.4 tons per acre (rather than the 13 tons permitted under the DOC regulations). They also changed the training and trellising systems from long, high-trained shoots (to facilitate mechanization) to proper spur-pruned cordons.

Lambrusco Reggiano Concerto is a wine to change people's opinion about this much-maligned DOC. When poured it develops a beautiful, pale-pink mousse that is the image of happiness itself. The nose is of summer berries, but it possesses a delicate floral appeal as well. On the palate, it is dry, packed with summer-fruit flavors, with a cleansing acidity and a reasonably long finish. Its place is at the dinner table, where it perfectly matches Italian salami and robust, meaty pasta dishes. **AS**

🕑 **Drink: recent vintages within 2 years**

Bruno Michel
Cuvée Blanche NV

Origin France, Champagne
Style Sparkling dry white wine, 12% ABV
Grapes Pinot Meunier 53%, Chardonnay 47%

This is an exciting, small house that has been created almost from nothing by the application, passion, and vision of its current owners. Bruno Michel's father owned vines but did not produce wine. After graduating with a degree in microbiology, Bruno became a nurseryman, but from 1982 started to buy and rent vines. He and his wife Cathérine now cultivate some forty-three different parcels over 37 acres (15 ha) from the small village of Pierry.

The Michels adopted organic viticulture in 1999, and are gradually converting to biodynamics. Since 1994 they have used Burgundy barriques, purchased from one of the most prestigious producers in the Côte de Beaune, for the first fermentation, making possible the separate treatment of all the different parcels. The fate of each barrel is decided by blind tasting rather than by the origin of the wine. Indigenous yeasts are used for some lots, *bâtonnage* is practiced where it will add beneficial richness, and the malolactic proceeds as it will. All of the wines spend at least three years *sur lattes*.

Bruno wants his Cuvée Blanche to be much more than an average NV *cuvée de base*; even here he wants to produce something "a little original." Fermentation partly in wood, and the blend of two varieties from different villages and vintages, result in a complexity that is exceptional for such an affordable, entry-level wine. The nose has great allure and interest, at once exotic, floral, and mineral, while the palate is fine and flourishing. **AS**

🕑 **Drink: current release for up to 5 years**

Montana Deutz Marlborough Cuvée *Blanc de Blancs* 2003

Origin New Zealand, Marlborough
Style Sparkling dry white wine, 12% ABV
Grape Chardonnay

Montana Wines (now Pernod Ricard NZ) formed a partnership with Champagne Deutz in 1988 to help them exploit New Zealand's potential for making premium sparkling wine. Three wines are produced: the basic Deutz Marlborough Cuvée, Deutz Marlborough Cuvée Blanc de Blancs, and Deutz Marlborough Cuvée Pinot Noir Cuvée. By far the best of these is the Blanc de Blancs.

The majority of the Chardonnay grapes used in the blend are grown in Pernod Ricard's own Renwick Estate vineyard on the southern side of the Wairau Valley, where heavier soils produce wines of greater elegance and finesse. Mendoza is the favored clone because it gives more concentrated flavors than other clones grown in Marlborough.

Deutz Marlborough Cuvée Blanc de Blancs is made only in very good vintages—only seven since 1994. The grapes are hand-picked when they are ripe but not overtly fruity and have a good level of acidity. They are whole bunch-pressed in a Champagne press to extract high-quality juice with minimum tannin extraction. Various components are assessed and blended to achieve optimal quality rather than a consistent house style. The wine then spends three to five years in bottle.

The 2003 is a fine, tight wine with explosive bubbles and appealing lime, mineral, toast, and roasted hazelnut flavors. Already accessible, it has good cellaring potential thanks to its impressive flavor purity and backbone of fine acidity. Always an impressive wine, this is the best yet. **BC**

⊖⊖ **Drink: recent vintages within 2 years**

Moutard Cuvée *aux 6 Cépages* NV

Origin France, Champagne, Côte des Bar
Style Sparkling dry white wine, 12% ABV
Grapes Chardonnay, P. Noir, P. Meunier, Others

If anyone is responsible for the revival among some of the new generation of growers in the Champagne region, it is Lucien Moutard, who revived the Arbanne grape in his vineyards as far back as 1952. The fact that cuvée after cuvée of Moutard's Arbane [sic] Vieille Vigne was not very good is beside the point. The important thing is that he bothered to resurrect an historical variety that was notoriously difficult to cultivate. Quite frankly, it was not just the Arbane Vieille Vigne that was not good. Very few Champagne Moutard products were grabbing the headlines until relatively recently.

This producer's true strength has always been not its Champagnes but its spirits. The Diligents have been artisanal distillers since the nineteenth century, and this experience shows through in the entire range, from the excellent Marc de Champagne Blanc and Vieux Marc de Champagne to the beguiling fruit brandies, particularly the Eaux-de-vie de Poire William and Eaux-de-vie de Framboise. The Champagnes, however, perennially lacked anything like the same level of excitement.

Until, that is, the Cuvée aux 6 Cépages was launched with the 2000 vintage. Fermented in two-year-old Burgundian barriques, sealed with corks rather than crown caps for the second fermentation, and lightly *dosé* (6 g/l), this Champagne is very soft and smooth, and its critical acclaim seems to have had an invigorating effect on the rest of the range, nearly all of which are much fresher and more interesting than they used to be. **TS**

⊖⊖⊖ **Drink: current release for up to 5 years**

Mumm
De Cramant NV

Origin France, Champagne, Côte des Blancs
Style Sparkling dry white wine, 12% ABV
Grape Chardonnay

Mumm is a rare pure Chardonnay Champagne, set apart from most vintage-dated Blanc de Blancs in its production, presentation, and state of maturity. This fine-drawn *demi-mousse* or *crémant* (a Champagne bottled at low pressure) was called Crémant de Cramant when first created for GH Mumm in 1882. At that time, this special wine was delivered by messenger to friends of the house in a plain bottle with a business card turned down at the right-hand corner. This inheritance lives on in the current label and nineteenth-century bottle design.

It is composed solely of grand cru Chardonnay grapes from Cramant. To preserve its dynamism and freshness, the wine is aged for only two years, and so according to French wine law cannot carry a vintage label. It is always, however, from a single year.

The final blend is bottled at 4.5 atmospheres of pressure, giving a delicate, refined wine with tiny bubbles. The color is pale yellow with silvery lights; the bouquet suggests white flowers and fresh citrus fruit; the mouthfeel is crisp yet kind, with tastes of lime and grapefruit. The finish is focused, subtle, and rather long for such a fine-drawn Champagne. **ME**

❸❸❸ **Drink: upon release and up to 3 years**

Mumm
Cuvée R. Lalou 1998

Origin France, Champagne
Style Sparkling dry white wine, 12% ABV
Grapes Pinot Noir 55%, Chardonnay 45%

The first vintage of Cuvée R. Lalou is this 1998. It succeeded Mumm's famous Cuvée René Lalou, and took three *chefs de caves* to craft: Pierre Harang, Dominique Demarville, and Didier Mariotti. Harang took over from André Carré, who was primarily responsible for destroying Mumm's reputation with the wines he made between 1982 and 1991 (marketed between 1985 and 1999). Unbeknown to their employers, Harang and Demarville developed a future terroir-based prestige cuvée, the vineyards and stocks for which they hid in the computer system as GC, short for Grand Cru. When Harang retired, Demarville took over, and the project was legitimized. Didier Mariotti fine-tuned the *dosage*.

The result is complete and harmonious, with a slowly unfolding mousse of tiny bubbles, floral notes including acacia on the nose, black grapes dominating the front and middle palate, and citrus fruits shifting into walnut complexity toward the finish, with minerality on the aftertaste. Cuvée R. Lalou is long, linear, and intense, rather than rich, requiring time and/or the right accompaniment of food to show its true potential. **TS**

❸❸❸❸ **Drink: to 2018+**

Bins await bottles of Cuvée R. Lalou in a dedicated Mumm cellar. ➡

Nyetimber *Tillington*
Single Vineyard 2009

Origin U.K., West Sussex
Style Sparkling dry white wine, 12% ABV
Grapes Pinot Noir, Chardonnay

When American couple Stuart and Sandy Moss established this vineyard in 1988, they had been told by German-trained British consultants that Chardonnay and Pinot Noir grapes could not be grown in England's cold and wet climate. The Mosses, however, had tunnel vision and ended up proving the so-called experts wrong. Not only that, but their maiden wine, the Premier Cuvée Blanc de Blancs 1992, won a raft of awards, as did follow-up vintages, and Nyetimber became the U.K.'s first world-class wine.

The Mosses sold the Grade I-listed Nyetimber to songwriter Andy Hill in 2001. Unfortunately Hill's marriage broke up and in 2006 he sold Nyetimber to the present owner, Eric Heerema, a Dutch entrepreneur, for a reputed $12.5 million (£7.5 m).

A wine lover and Anglophile, Heerema has taken Nyetimber on to even greater heights, expanding its vineyards from 34½ to 395 acres (14 to 160 ha) spread over eight locations in two counties, and employing the talented Cherie Spriggs as winemaker. From one of the new locations, Tillington, Spriggs has produced one of the U.K.'s greatest ever sparkling wines, Nyetimber Tillington Single Vineyard 2009. A blend of 79 percent Pinot Noir and 21 percent Chardonnay, it is the expansive fruit of the Pinot Noir that dominates, unsurprisingly. It is already a class act, but it will take a decade or more for its central core of intensity to show its true potential. It is sold at the price of some prestige cuvée Champagnes—but it will not disappoint. **TS**

🍷🍷🍷🍷 **Drink: to 2025+**

Omar Khayyam
NV

Origin India, Sahyadri Valley
Style Sparkling dry white wine, 12.5% ABV
Grapes Chardonnay, Pinot Noir, Ugni Blanc

Named after the Persian poet Omar Khayyam, whose *Rubaiyat* collection of poems contains many references to wine, this Indian traditional-method sparkler surprises many people with its quality. Mumbai millionaire Shamrao Chougule, whose company constructed turnkey engineering plants, fell in love with Champagne during trips to Europe and wanted to make quality sparkling wine in India. His wine, known in the West as Omar Khayyam, and in India as Marquise de Pompadour, has been made from 1988 at his Chateau Indage winery. The winery was originally developed by a young French enologist, Raphael Brisbois, who was dispatched to India in the 1980s by Champagne house Piper-Heidsieck, following a request by Chougule.

The vineyard has expanded to 600 acres (243 ha) on hillsides in the Sahyadri Valley, east of Mumbai, and production is now overseen by Indian-born winemaker Abhay Kewadkar. Some 40 percent of Indage's production is exported to Europe—including France. The wine is also sold in the United States, Canada, and Japan (although the reference to "Champagne India" on the label in some markets annoys the Champenois).

Both Omar Khayyam and Marquise de Pompadour are made from the classic Chardonnay and Pinot Noir grapes used to produce Champagne, but there is also some Ugni Blanc (also used for Cognac) in the blend. Omar Khayyam is matured for three years before release, whereas Marquise de Pompadour is on the market after two years. **SG**

🍷🍷 **Drink: current release within 2 years**

L'Origan
L'O Cava Brut Nature NV

Origin Spain, Penedès, Sant Sadurní d'Anoia
Style Sparkling dry white wine, 12% ABV
Grapes Xarel-lo, Macabeu, Parellada, Chardonnay

Perrier-Jouët
La Belle Epoque 1995

Origin France, Champagne
Style Sparkling dry white wine, 12.5% ABV
Grapes Chardonnay 50%, P. Noir 45%, P. Meunier 5%

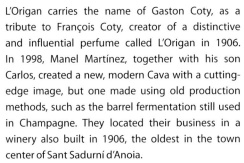

L'Origan carries the name of Gaston Coty, as a tribute to François Coty, creator of a distinctive and influential perfume called L'Origan in 1906. In 1998, Manel Martínez, together with his son Carlos, created a new, modern Cava with a cutting-edge image, but one made using old production methods, such as the barrel fermentation still used in Champagne. They located their business in a winery also built in 1906, the oldest in the town center of Sant Sadurní d'Anoia.

The initial release was this non-vintage Blanc de Blancs Brut Nature, a blend of the local Xarel-lo and Macabeu complemented by Chardonnay, partly fermented in oak barrels and aged for thirty months. The Brut Nature has a most unusual nose of great personality, continually changing in the glass. Closed initially, it slowly reveals notes of star anise and lime flower tea, together with yeast and toast, turning to hay and straw, and finishing with medicinal and balsamic touches. Medium-bodied in the mouth, fresh, and with fine bubbles, it has white fruit, aniseed, and toast, with the medicinal and balsamic notes reappearing on the long finish. **LG**

🍷🍷 **Drink: current release within 1–2 years**

Launched in 1970 in a Paris nightclub to celebrate the seventieth birthday of U.S. jazz musician Duke Ellington, La Belle Epoque—its name conjuring up images of 1890s Paris— was an immediate success.

The 1995 (a Chardonnay year par excellence) is an especially fine expression of Belle Epoque, the white grapes for this vintage coming largely from the firm's superb vineyards in the grands crus of Cramant and Avize. These Chardonnays lead the blend (50 percent); great Pinot Noir from Mailly, Verzy, and Aÿ (45 percent) is also an important element, creating a union of Montagne de Reims styles; and there is a touch, too, of superior Meunier from Dizy.

The Champagne is now *à point*, the main impression one of freshness and purity, showing in the still-green hints amid the gold, and an evolving aroma of white peaches with a note of toast. As air gets to the wine, this delicate, ethereal style is made more complex by buttery baker's flavors, particularly brioche; and the *soupçon* of Meunier adds a palate-filling roundness that works beautifully with the sustained power of Pinot Noir. A great 1995, and the first vintage of cellar master Hervé Deschamps. **ME**

🍷🍷🍷🍷 **Drink: to 2020+**

Perrier-Jouët Champagne features on a Belle Epoque menu card. ▶

RESERVE CUVEE
PERRIER-JOUET&Cⁱᵉ
EPERNAY

MENU

DEVAMBEZ, GR.

Pierre Peters *Cuvée Speciale*
Grand Cru Blanc de Blancs 1996

Origin France, Champagne, Côte des Blancs
Style Sparkling dry white wine, 12% ABV
Grape Chardonnay

This is quickly becoming a cult Champagne from an excellent small domaine. Peters' NV and ordinary Vintage wines are blends from vineyards in other Côte des Blancs communes; but the Cuvée Speciale is a *monocru,* a single-site wine from seventy-two-year old Mesnil vines in a vineyard called Les Chetillons.

Peters himself calls the wine "mineral," but vintages such as 1996 can show notes he refers to as "vegetal." There is little literature delineating the flavors of Chardonnays from the string of grand cru communes comprising the Côte des Blancs. That said, this writer's impression of Mesnil is that of a brisk, jasmine-scented lemon pudding strained through chalk. Oger and Avize are more incisive, appley, lead-pencilly. Cramant is more green tea and lime. Mesnil is a gesture of chalky authority.

Seekers of the "Champagne experience" might be nonplussed by the sheer vinosity of Peters' Cuvée Speciale. In firm vintages such as 1996 (and 1990) the wine assumes the identity of grand cru Chablis with bubbles. It begs for decades of age in which to unfold its buttery, saffrony depths. But it is certainly among the iconic Chardonnay Champagnes. **TT**
⊖⊖⊖⊖ **Drink: 10–30 years after the vintage**

Philipponnat
Clos des Goisses 2002

Origin France, Champagne, Montagne de Reims
Style Sparkling dry white wine, 13% ABV
Grapes Chardonnay, Pinot Noir

It seems lamentable that this amazing 13.5-acre (5.5 ha) vineyard cannot be classified as grand cru, but the village to which it belongs—Mareuil-sur-Aÿ—is a mere premier cru (of 99 percent). Clos des Goisses rises steeply over the houses of Mareuil, facing due south, and is planted 70 percent with Pinot Noir and 30 percent with Chardonnay. For years this singular wine was the ultimate insider's secret in Champagne. But these days Clos des Goisses is the name one cites to demonstrate one's credentials as a true Champagne aficionado.

Clos des Goisses is anti-varietal. It is close to impossible to delineate its components of Pinot Noir and Chardonnay as signatures. What makes this wine tick is its sturdiness, masculinity, and profoundly chalky minerality. It both defines the genre of great Champagne and stands somewhat apart from it; not as fruity as Cristal, not as briny and nutty as Krug.

Clos des Goisses is perhaps the preeminently important Champagne, the one you really must seek out because you will not entirely understand it. This is a searching wine, capable of arousing not only your admiration but also your curiosity. **TT**
⊖⊖⊖⊖⊖ **Drink: to 25 years after the vintage**

Birds flock above the steep slope of Philipponnat's Clos des Goisses. ➨

CHAMPAGNE POL ROGE

Pol Roger
Blanc de Blancs 1999

Origin France, Champagne
Style Sparkling dry white wine, 12% ABV
Grape Chardonnay

Pol Roger Blanc de Blancs is an insanely delicious, classy, and ridiculously undervalued Champagne—though it is a paradoxical beast. Since Pol Roger Champagnes are renowned for their longevity, and Chardonnay is the longest-lived of Champagne's grape varieties, it would not be unreasonable to expect a pure Chardonnay Pol Roger to have the greatest aging potential of all. Yet it has the shortest. All vintages of this cuvée are so sumptuous and creamy when first released that there is little point in aging them, although they will develop nicely for a further three to five years in your cellar. Even when not moved from Pol Roger's own cellars, this wine rarely has a greater lifespan than twenty to twenty-five years. If you want a Champagne guaranteed to last fifty years or more, buy Pol Roger Vintage, but if you want an instant and mesmerizing hit, open a bottle of Blanc de Blancs.

The 1998 was one of the greatest recent vintages of this cuvée, yet the 1999 (made in the first year of Dominique Petit, Krug's former *chef de caves*) is even classier, which is no mean achievement considering that 1998 was the better vintage. **TS**

⑤⑤⑤ **Drink: to 2018**

Pol Roger
Cuvée Sir Winston Churchill 1975

Origin France, Champagne
Style Sparkling dry white wine, 12% ABV
Grapes Pinot Noir, Chardonnay

The first vintage of the greatest prestige cuvée of modern times, the 1975 was produced only in magnums and launched in 1984. In accepting this honor on behalf of her late father, Lady Soames commented on Churchill's legendary consumption of Champagne Pol Roger: "I saw him many times the better for it, but never the worse."

All Pol Roger will say about its composition is that it is a Pinot-dominated Champagne produced exclusively from those villages Pol Roger had access to for Churchill's favorite vintages. However, it is probably safe to say that Cuvée Sir Winston Churchill is 80 percent Pinot Noir and 20 percent Chardonnay, although during Churchill's lifetime, the Champenois failed to mention that more than half their vineyards consisted of Pinot Meunier. Putting all speculation to one side, Cuvée Sir Winston Churchill must have 80 percent black grapes.

This wine has become very rich, with the fruit intensifying and gaining more of a Christmas cake complexity and finesse than broad toasty maturity, though there are some very fine toasted notes. A lingering and undoubtedly great Champagne. **TS**

⑤⑤⑤⑤ **Drink: to 2025**

◄ Gaspar Camps portrays Pol Roger as the ultimate lifestyle accessory.

Pommery
Cuvée Louise 1990

Origin France, Champagne
Style Sparkling dry white wine, 12% ABV
Grapes Chardonnay 60%, Pinot Noir 40%

Jeanne Alexandrine Louise Pommery was widowed in 1858, leaving her with two children, one of whom—Louise—was still a baby. The then Pommery house was occupied by the Prussian governor of Rheims during the Franco–Prussian war (1870–71), but afterward Madame Pommery began to rebuild her business. She enlarged the cellars by purchasing 148 acres (60 ha) of land for that purpose, and also bought 741 acres (300 ha) of prime vineyards.

Pommery's prestige wine is named in honor of Madame Pommery and her youngest daughter. Cuvée Louise is made only in exceptional years from a selection of vineyards in grands crus Avize, Aÿ, and Cramant. Based mainly on Chardonnay, it is a lighter style of Vintage Champagne, but capable of aging for many years.

At a masterclass hosted by Pommery's *chef de cave* Thierry Gasco in London in April 2006, a magnum of 1990 had a lovely amber-gold color, fading to a watery rim, with a marvelously toasty, complex nose of brioche, caramel, and coffee. Full and concentrated, it was not tart, thanks to the ripeness of the 1990 vintage. **SG**

🍷🍷🍷🍷 Drink: to 2020+

Roger Pouillon
Cuvée de Réserve Brut NV

Origin France, Champagne, Vallée de la Marne
Style Sparkling dry white wine, 12% ABV
Grapes P. Noir 80%, Chardonnay 15%, P. Meunier 5%

Although the Pouillon family has grown grapes for generations, it is only within the past three that it has bottled wine under its own name. Under Fabrice Pouillon, grandson of Roger, who started working for the house in 1998 at the age of twenty-two, the domaine has grown and quality has risen.

Based in Mareuil-sur-Aÿ, the domaine also owns vines in the grands crus Le Mesnil-sur-Oger and Aÿ, as well as in several premier cru villages—some 37 acres (15 ha) in total. In his vineyards Fabrice practices what he calls *une culture artisinale raisonnée*, which includes organic pesticides, grassing over, and plowing, although since 2003 he has also performed organic and biodynamic trials. All of the wines go through malolactic, *bâtonnage* is performed on the wooded wines, and cane sugar is used in a liqueur of NV Brut for the *dosage*.

The Cuvée de Réserve Brut NV is exceptionally good of its type. Honeyed, ripe, and rounded, it is very full with dried fruit richness; heaviness is prevented thanks to perfectly pitched acidity. The resounding finish attests its overall quality, and the wine represents outstanding value. **NB**

🍷🍷 Drink: current release within 5 years

◄ A 1902 Art Nouveau-styled poster promotes Champagne Pommery.

Jérôme Prévost *La Closerie Cuvée Les Béguines* NV

Origin France, Champagne, Montagne de Reims
Style Sparkling dry white wine, 12.5%
Grape Pinot Meunier

CHAMPAGNE
La Closerie
BRUT NATURE
12.5%vol/75cl

Jérôme Prévost is in many ways the most individual Champagne grower-producer of them all, as well as one of the bravest, most committed, original, and poetic (read his back label). He works by himself, makes only one wine, always from a single year, and always from a single variety—Pinot Meunier. That may not sound so remarkable, but La Closerie Cuvée Les Béguines is an extremely interesting wine.

Prévost, a child of the late 1960s, took over his family's 5.4 acres (2.2 ha) of vines at Gueux, on the Montagne de Reims, at the age of twenty-one. After selling his grapes to others, he started making his own wine when celebrated fellow-grower Anselme Selosse made space for him in his winery from 1998 to 2001. Attempting to get the best out of his vines, planted in the 1960s, he plows and uses biodynamic preparations. He ferments in wood (mostly barriques) and, standing conventional wisdom on its head, prefers the wine to have extended contact with lees from indigenous yeast in barrel, rather than with lees from selected yeast in bottle. Because of their richness and ripeness, they have only a very light *dosage*, leaving them Extra Brut.

Prévost says that "Pinot Meunier is like a child: it has interesting things to say, but you need to encourage it to say them." He offers it all the encouragement it needs, and it responds with massively complex, concentrated, exotic wines. Like René Collard in Reuil, he produces not only a great Pinot Meunier, but a great Champagne. **NB**

Drink: current release within 4–10 years

FURTHER RECOMMENDATIONS

Other great Pinot Meunier Champagnes

René Collard • Egly-Ouriet Les Vignes de Vrigny

More wood-fermented Champagnes

Bollinger • De Sousa • Alfred Gratien • Krug
Jacques Selosse • Tarlant

Pinot Meunier is the sole variety used for this cuvée.

Quinta das Bágeiras
Espumante Grande Reserva 2004

Origin Portugal, Bairrada
Style Sparkling dry white wine, 13.6% ABV
Grapes Maria Gomes (60%), Bical (40%)

Portugal's Bairrada region holds the distinction of producing the country's first *méthode traditionnelle* sparkling wine. It was made in 1890, precisely 101 years before Quinta das Bágeiras released its maiden Espumante Grande Reserva (in 1991). Made exclusively from estate-grown fruit and with zero *dosage*, the artisanal handcrafted sparkling wines of Quinta das Bágeiras bear little resemblance to the majority of fizz from the region.

Fourth-generation grower Mário Sérgio Alves Nuno founded the Quinta das Bágeiras label in 1989 and was the first member of his family to produce sparkling wines, which account for 60 percent of the 70-acre (28-ha) estate's production. However the flagship Espumante Grande Reserva is made only in those years when nature conspires to produce grapes high in both acidity and sugar. It is sourced predominantly from old vines grown on chalky clay soils. Disgorged and labeled by hand after five years' aging on the lees (a Grande Reserva must spend a minimum of three years on lees), this is a complex, rich, toasty wine with a vinous, creamy mouthfeel and deceptive undertow of mineral acidity. **SA**

🍷🍷🍷 **Drink: to 2025**

Sekthaus Raumland
MonRose Brut 2004

Origin Germany, Rheinhessen
Style Sparkling dry white wine, 12.5% ABV
Grapes Pinot Noir, Pinot Meunier, Chardonnay

Volker Raumland is Germany's leading Sekt producer in terms of quality. Raumland started in the early 1980s as a consultant and Sekt producer with mobile filling equipment. Today he is responsible for some of the finest Sekts in Germany, from Rebholz to Wehrheim, and others. On calcareous soils he cultivates his own Pinot Noir, Pinot Meunier, Pinot Blanc, Chardonnay, and Riesling vineyards on a total eco-certified area of 24¾ acres (10 ha), which gives an annual production of 600,000 bottles of Sekt.

Raumland's Sekts have a maximum 12.5 percent ABV, with most having only 12 percent or even less. However, it is the fragmented pressing that makes Raumland Sekt so Champenois: only the cuvée is used, which gives a pure wine with high acidity and low phenolics. The most impressive and delicate Sekt is the extremely rare 2004 MonRose, a blend of partly barrel-fermented Pinot Noir, Pinot Meunier, and Chardonnay that spent ten years on its lees after the second fermentation in bottle. It is a very fine and elegant Sekt of impressive freshness and complexity. The finish is long, but the wine seems to be feather-light because of its delicate mousse. **SR**

🍷🍷🍷🍷 **Drink: to 2020+**

The chalky soils of Raumland's vineyards are perfect for producing delicate sparkling wines. ▶

Raventós i Blanc *Gran Reserva de la Finca Brut Nature* 2003

Origin Spain, Penedès, Sant Sadurní d'Anoia
Style Sparkling dry white wine, 12% ABV
Grapes Macabeo, Xarel-lo, Parellada, Others

This firm includes in its name that of Josep Raventós, the legendary member of the Codorníu family who controversially introduced the "Champagne method" to Penedès in 1872, and who produced the first quality Spanish sparkling wine. The firm is the brainchild of another great character in the history of Catalan Cava, Josep Maria Raventós i Blanc, who decided to devote his life to winemaking in 1986.

Near the entrance to the winery's cellars, opposite the buildings designed by the great modern architect Puig i Cadafalch, stands the majestic old oak that appears in the house logo. The vineyards and cellars comprise one of the most impressive estates in Penedès, boasting some 250 acres (100 ha) of vineyards planted mostly to the traditional Cava varieties—Macabeo, Xarel-lo, and Parellada. These constitute 85 percent of the blend for the Gran Reserva de la Finca Brut Nature 2003, the balance being Chardonnay and Pinot Noir.

Given its modest price, this sparkler strikes a rare balance between complexity and freshness: It is fruity, complex, creamy, polished, and elegant. This is a Cava with greater than usual longevity. **JB**
🍷🍷 Drink: 2018+

Louis Roederer *Cristal* 1990

Origin France, Champagne
Style Sparkling dry white wine, 12% ABV
Grapes Pinot Noir 63%, Chardonnay 37%

This excellent Cristal vintage was used for the millennium cuvée wine that was bottled into 6-liter Methuselah, each equivalent to eight standard-sized bottles. In commemoration of the millennium, only 2,000 were produced, each individually numbered. There is an apocryphal story that a container-load of these was accidentally destroyed, making the wine even more scarce. These Methuselah have acquired iconic status and become the ultimate "bling" wine that no self-respecting rapper or Russian millionaire can live without. In London in April 2007, there were scurrilous reports of a "shoot-out" between English, German, and Russian revelers in Movida nightclub, involving Jéroboams of Cristal rather than guns.

As for the wine itself, in 1990 the larger bottles received a slightly higher *dosage* than standard, so the wine is a bit sweeter than usual. At a comparative tasting of Cristal 1990 from Methuselah and magnum held in London in 2005, the magnum was, at least for some tasters, superior. Although smaller formats might contain better wine, by mid-2007 1990 Methuselah were fetching more than $16,000 (£8,000; €11,000) each at auction. **SG**
🍷🍷🍷🍷 Drink: to 2020+

Théophile Roederer is now Louis Roederer's second label. ➡

Salon

1996

Origin France, Champagne, Côte des Blancs
Style Sparkling dry white wine, 12% ABV
Grape Chardonnay

Salon is a legend, a story of perfectionism. It is always a Blanc de Blancs from Grand Cru Le Mesnil, always vintage-dated, and it is only released when the *chef de cave* thinks the wine is worthy of its awesome reputation. Salon uses only grapes from forty-year-old vines and the fruit is picked and sorted by hand. It is a wine produced only in the very best years.

The 1996 is certainly one of the greatest vintages of Salon. Everything went right that year and at vintage time the Chardonnay was fully ripe, but unusually was rich in sugar and acids, which are the two seeds of greatness.

The wine has a very pale yellow color with hints of green, at once star-bright, crystalline, and lively. The nose is wonderfully complex, the first scents of green apple ceding to lemon and grapefruit; then, after further brief contact with air, richer tones of pear and kiwi emerge. In the mouth, Salon 1996 is a big boy, virile and muscular, yet with a latent richness and subtlety of character that will slowly unfold over the next twenty, even thirty, years. Old-timers compare this vintage with the 1928. Salon in top years like these is indeed a legend. **ME**
🍾🍾🍾🍾 Drink: to 2025+

J. Schram

2000

Origin USA, California, Calistoga
Style Sparkling dry white wine, 12.6% ABV
Grapes Chardonnay 80%, Pinot Noir 20%

"The stirring sunlight, and the growing vines, and the vats and bottles in the cavern, made a pleasant music for the mind," wrote Robert Louis Stevenson in *The Silverado Squatters* after he visited Jacob Schram's Diamond Mountain property in 1880. However, the estate was dilapidated when Jack and Jamie Davies purchased it in 1965. They revived Schramsberg Vineyards to produce arguably the finest sparkling wines in the United States. J. Schram, their Chardonnay-based Tête de Cuvée (first vintage 1987), pays tribute to the German barber from Calistoga who first prepared the property.

The definitive factor for the team, led by Hugh Davies and Craig Roemer, is cool climate sites close to the Pacific. The wine is aged on lees for nearly six years in hillside caves dug by Jacob Schram's Chinese laborers. In 2000, a mild spring led into a cool and foggy summer, which allowed the Chardonnay to retain its acidity and develop more concentrated, lifted aromas. With more persistence and density on the palate than earlier vintages, the 2000 J. Schram bursts with dynamic tangerine, green apple, and brioche flavors, leading to a minerally finish. **LGr**
🍾🍾🍾 Drink: to 2018

◀ Salon bottles are "riddled" to dislodge the deposit from fermentation.

Jacques Selosse
Cuvée Substance NV

Origin France, Champagne, Côte des Blancs
Style Sparkling dry white wine, 12.5% ABV
Grape Chardonnay

Anselme Selosse, head of this iconic family domaine in grand cru Avize, is an original who has brought the hand-made approach of white Burgundy-making to the larger scale, blend-oriented world of Champagne. So his are big, bold expressions of grand cru Chardonnay, best seen in his renowned Cuvée Substance, which tastes like no other Champagne, more like a wine of intense vinosity. Substance is pure Avize, a particularity of its *assemblage* being that the reserve wines are introduced on a solera system: One-third of the reserve wines is drawn off and replaced by wine from the most recent vintage, so creating a perpetual reserve of increasing complexity.

The color of Substance is bronze/gold verging on amber. The nose is extraordinary, with scents of the sap of a vine that has pushed its roots deep into the earth; there are secondary sensations of spices and the savory tang of the finest Sherry. The mouthfeel is all embracing and, boy, is it substantial—one great Champagne that can take on smoked fish, tapas, and any strong flavors from the Mediterranean. **ME**

◉◉◉◉ Drink: upon release for 10+ years

Seppelt Great Western
Show Sparkling Shiraz 2004

Origin Australia, Western Victoria
Style Sparkling dry red wine, 13.5% ABV
Grape Shiraz

Sparkling Shiraz is an esoteric speciality unique to Australia. Made from old vine Shiraz by the "traditional" sparkling wine method, it is matured in large oak casks for one year before undergoing its second fermentation in bottle. It is then kept on its lees for as long as nine to ten years before disgorgement, whereafter it gains great complexity with extended bottle maturation prior to release. The style, which dates back more than 100 years, is complex, massive, and capable of long life.

The Seppelt story began with Joseph Ernst Seppelt, a wealthy chemist and snuff manufacturer, who migrated from Germany to the Barossa Valley with his family in 1851. He established the property now known as Seppeltsfield in the Barossa Valley, but it was only in 1918, with the purchase of vineyards and cellars in the gold rush town of Great Western in Victoria, that Seppelt became involved in the production of sparkling wine.

Even fully mature, the Show Sparkling Shiraz still drinks superbly, showing cassis together with overtones of pepper and spice, as well as earthy, leathery notes from the extended bottle aging. **SB**

◉◉◉ Drink: upon release for up to 20 years

Seppelt owns cellars that were excavated in the nineteenth century. ➡

Domaine de la Taille aux Loups *Triple Zéro* NV

Origin France, Loire Valley, Montlouis-sur-Loire
Style Sparkling dry white wine, 12.5% ABV
Grape Chenin Blanc

Jacky Blot was a négociant before he started making his own wine in 1988. Domaine de la Taille aux Loups produces exceptional still wines—from dry to sweet—on both sides of the River Loire, east of Tours, but the *pétillant* Montlouis is his cult cuvée. Triple Zéro, with its black velveteen label, is at home in the coolest Parisienne wine shops and bars.

There is zero chaptalization, zero *liqueur de tirage*, and zero *dosage*. On the three occasions in the winemaking process where Blot might add sugar, he doesn't, so the wine is bone dry. Triple Zéro was born in 1993, of Blot's desire to make an organic sparkling wine, but as he didn't have organic sugar he didn't add any at all. Instead, the wine is fermented very slowly in old oak barrels and is bottled before the first fermentation has finished. It is then topped up with the same wine rather than *liqueur d'expédition*.

Triple Zéro is a beautifully pure expression of Chenin Blanc. Made from vines more than fifty years old, it possesses wonderful complexity, with a floral nose of cow parsley, and rich bruised apple on the palate. It is a perfect aperitif: extremely refreshing and brilliantly bracing. **EL**

🥂🥂 **Drink: on release for up to 20 years**

Taittinger *Comtes de Champagne* 1990

Origin France, Champagne, Côte des Blancs
Style Sparkling dry white wine, 12% ABV
Grape Chardonnay

The Taittinger family has always loved Chardonnay. Comtes de Champagne, the house's top cuvée, is an impressively consistent all-Chardonnay Champagne entirely sourced from grapes from the grands crus of Avize, Cramant, Chouilly, and Le Mesnil on the Côte des Blancs. Made only in exceptional years, the wine is fermented in tank, then 5 percent of it is aged in oak casks for four months. After malolactic fermentation and the *prise de mousse*, the Champagne is matured on its lees for four years before disgorging the sediment.

The 1990 has a reassuring pale gold-green color, hinting at the vigor to come; the mousse is fine and swirling; the aromas are delicate, with subtle nuances of wood, yet there is an underlying depth. The palate is racy, lean, and long, with maturing flavors of candied lemon and lime, enhanced by a certain nuttiness endemic to great Chardonnay.

Overall, this is a classically elegant Comtes de Champagne, still with years ahead of it. Due to its purity and restraint, it is a very grand aperitif, but would also complement to perfection a plain grilled Dover sole or steamed lobster. **ME**

🥂🥂🥂🥂 **Drink: to 2020+**

A graffito by a soldier sheltering from bombing in a Taittinger cellar. ➡

Tarlant
Cuvée Louis NV

Origin France, Champagne, Vallée de la Marne
Style Sparkling dry white wine, 12% ABV
Grapes Chardonnay 50%, Pinot Noir 50%

Agustí Torelló
Kripta 2007

Origin Spain, Penedès, Sant Sadurní d'Anoia
Style Sparkling dry white wine, 11.5% ABV
Grapes Macabeo, Xarel-lo, Parellada

The Tarlant family, based in the small village of Oeuilly, have been vignerons from father to son since 1687, as their labels proudly remind us, and have been bottling their own wine since the 1920s. The current head of the family, Jean-Mary, has served on the technical committee of the Conseil Interprofessionnel des Vins de Champagne, and as president of the Institut Technique Viticole.

Jean-Mary and his son Benoît now own some 32 acres (13 ha) of vines, most in Oeuilly but also in other villages. Sensitive to their very varied terroirs, they produce several single-vineyard varietal wines as well as the original single-vineyard prestige Cuvée Louis. This superb wine, entirely fermented in wood, is a Chardonnay/Pinot Noir blend from vines planted in the 1960s in their oldest vineyard, Les Crayons.

The back labels are excellent, clearly stating the date of both bottling and disgorgement. The 1995/1994 blend, bottled in 1996 and disgorged seven years later, was magnificent at around twelve years old, with mature, Krug-like complexity, intensity, and thrill. Subsequent releases are also well worth cellaring for a special occasion. **NB**
🝫🝫🝫 **Drink: current release for 10+ years**

This family business, located in the outskirts of Sant Sadurní d'Anoia, was founded in the 1950s by Agustí Torelló Mata, and is now managed by his four sons. Their grapes are mostly grown on their 69-acre (28 ha) estate; the rest come from growers who subscribe to their strict vineyard practices.

All the sparkling wines are produced using the three traditional white varieties of Cava, with the red variety Trepat exclusively destined for their sparkling rosé. Each variety is grown in a specific location and plays a specific role in the final blend: Macabeo, grown in the coastal area of Garraf, provides finesse and elegance; Xarel-lo, from the low Penedès at 656 feet (200 m) above sea level, adds body and structure; while Parellada, from the Alt Penedès at 1,640 feet (500 m), supplies acidity and freshness.

Kripta is original not least for its Rafael Bartolozzi-designed bottle, in the shape of an amphora, as well as for its long aging period of over four years. This maturity, anchored in excellent fruit, gives a delicate creaminess, fine bubbles, and a complex nose of almonds, brioche, and toast. The palate is rich and savory, with toasty echoes. **JB**
🝫🝫🝫 **Drink: recent vintages for up to 10 years**

◀ A hillside vineyard turns gold in the Vallée de la Marne.

Veuve Clicquot
La Grande Dame 1990

Origin France, Champagne
Style Sparkling dry white wine, 12% ABV
Grapes Pinot Noir 61%, Chardonnay 39%

La Grande Dame is unquestionably one of the finest Champagne prestige cuvées, although it does not have quite as high a profile as some of its corporate brothers. No matter: La Grande Dame is for the quiet wine connoisseur, its style a splendid balancing act of richness and finesse, reflecting the sure tastes of its creators, Joseph Henriot and Jacques Péters.

The third of three consecutive great vintages, the 1990 growing season commenced quickly; flowering time was colder than usual, but in July summer appeared and continued through August, recording the highest number of sunshine hours for thirty years. These impeccable conditions were enhanced by rain at the right moment.

Of pretty gold color with green reflections, the wine has fine, delicate bubbles. The nose has terrific finesse and complexity: white flowers and fruits at first, then a touch of softness, and notes of candy complemented by light, roasted tones of hazelnut and almond. In the mouth, great richness and pleasant roundness dominate, while balance is retained by a light, creamy aspect. The end flavor—lingering, fresh, and noble—is exceptional. **ME**

🍷🍷🍷🍷🍷 **Drink: to 2020**

Veuve Clicquot
La Grande Dame Rosé 1989

Origin France, Champagne
Style Sparkling dry rosé wine, 12% ABV
Grapes Pinot Noir 60%, Chardonnay 40%

Throughout France, 1989 was the year of great heat. The Clicquot vineyard managers and winemakers, though, were well up to the mark, their talent realized in this now superbly mature prestige rosé.

Its name refers to Barbe-Nicole Clicquot who took over her husband's vineyards on his death in 1805. Pink Grande Dame is a classically constituted Clicquot Champagne, dominated by black grapes but with an emphasis on finesse. The *assemblage* for Grand Dame here is about 60 percent Pinot Noir from the great vineyards of Aÿ, Verzenay, Ambonnay, and Bouzy, balanced by around 40 percent grand cru Chardonnay from Avize, Oger, and Le Mesnil. A key to its special quality is the excellent red wine added to the blend from Clicquot's top site—Les Censières—in the heart of Bouzy.

The 1989 has a fine, warm color, gold-red with a touch of brick at the rim; the nose is, of course, powerful, with exotic aromas of black fig, dates, and soft spices, particularly vanilla. In the mouth, the warmth of the sun pervades the wine: voluptuous, sensuous, evolved for sure, but still in good shape around its twenty-fifth anniversary. **ME**

🍷🍷🍷🍷🍷 **Drink: to 2019**

An 1859 portrait of Widow Clicquot (1777–1866), by Leon Cogniet. ➜

Veuve Fourny *Cuvée du Clos Faubourg Notre Dame* 1996

Origin France, Champagne, Côte des Blancs
Style Sparkling dry white wine, 12% ABV
Grape Chardonnay

Although less well known than some of the other *veuves* (widows) in Champagne, this small family house can hold its head high in terms of the authenticity, originality, and quality of its wines. Established in 1856, the house is now run by Madame Monique Fourny and her two able sons Charles-Henry and Emmanuel.

Based in the premier cru village of Vertus, the domaine owns some forty parcels of vines across 30 acres (12 ha) of the Côte des Blancs. Many of the vines are old, having been planted in the 1960s and '70s, and all are carefully supervised. Several aspects of the winemaking reflect skills Emmanuel acquired in Burgundy, such as fermentation in Burgundy barriques with *bâtonnage*.

At the top of the range are two superb wines. One, Cuvée R, an NV blend, is an homage to late husband and father Roger, made like his own early wines from three varieties. The other, a Blanc de Blancs, Cuvée du Clos Faubourg Notre Dame, is even more remarkable. It comes from one of only nine officially recognized *clos* in Champagne—a mere third of an acre (0.13 ha)—planted with Chardonnay vines in the 1950s. The barriques in which it is fermented are generally newer than used for the Cuvée R, but it is also fermented with indigenous yeasts, lees-stirred, put through malolactic, and bottled unfiltered. It is made as a Vintage wine in great years such as 1996. Fine and persistent as well as rich and seductive, it deserves to be one of the most recherché wines in Champagne. **NB**
🍷🍷🍷 **Drink: to 2018+**

Vilmart *Coeur de Cuvée* 1996

Origin France, Champagne, Montagne de Reims
Style Sparkling dry white wine, 12% ABV
Grapes Chardonnay 80%, Pinot Noir 20%

Vilmart is based at Rilly-la-Montagne, in the heart of the northern Montagne de Reims. The most unusual thing about most of its wines, including this one, is their high proportion of Chardonnay, in this case 80 percent. If Vilmart were located on the eastern Montagne de Reims, this would be more the rule than the exception, but both the northern and southern slopes here are predominantly Pinot Noir.

The most important factor affecting the quality of Vilmart Champagne is the exceptionally high standard of viticulture applied to its vineyards. Among the earliest to go organic (in 1968), then biodynamic (in the 1980s), Vilmart reverted to *viticulteur raisonnée* in 1998. These immaculate vineyards are grassed between the vines, severely pruned, and receive minimal fertilizing with organic manure only. The low yields that result account for the intense, ripe flavors that burst out of the glass, but it is the oak that most consumers notice first. While it is true that the vintages of the late 1980s and early 1990s were over-oaked, with the 1996 Coeur de Cuvée Vilmart turned the corner in its development of barrique-fermentation techniques.

The 1996 Coeur de Cuvée sold out in a flash, and there is no stock left at Vilmart, not even library stock. However, the heavily oaked vintages, such as the 1992 and 1993 Coeur de Cuvée, are sublime when in magnum after twelve years or so, albeit in a Montrachet, sometimes Corton-Charlemagne, sort of way. Unfortunately (and incredibly) Vilmart did not produce any magnums of this wine in 1996. **TS**
🍷🍷🍷🍷 **Drink: to 2030+**

A Vilmart window of Israelites carrying grapes from the Promised Land. ➡

MARGARET R

CHARDONN

2005

PIERR

Vintaged at Caves Road Wil

Margaret River region of

750

ml

WINE OF AUSTRAL

FROM MARGARET RI

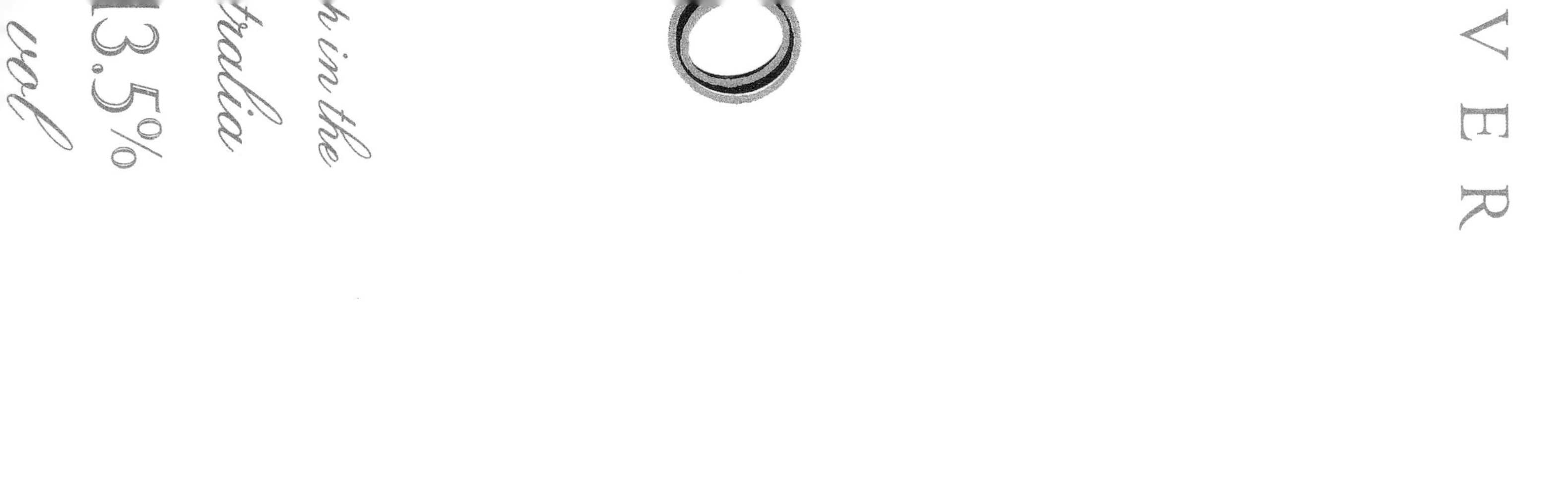

VER

h in the

tralia

3.5%

vol

White_Wines_

Abbazia di Novacella

Praepositus Kerner 2002

Alheit Vineyards

Cartology 2012

Origin Italy, Alto Adige, Valle Isarco
Style Dry white wine, 13.5% ABV
Grape Kerner

Origin South Africa, Western Cape
Style Dry white wine, 14% ABV
Grapes Chenin Blanc 86%, Sémillon 14%

Founded in 1142, the Abbazia di Novacella was a shelter for pilgrims traveling to the Holy Land and an important cultural center, renowned throughout Europe. Today the Abbazia (still run by monks) has been transformed into a modern conference center that boasts state-of-the-art technology, a restaurant, and accommodation. Luckily, the winery has also survived, producing wines mostly from local (Germanic) grape varieties, and the quality standards are among the highest anywhere.

The Praepositus Kerner 2002 will put Kerner on your list of favorite grapes. The grapes were obtained from selected vineyards at altitudes of 2,130 to 2,300 feet (650–931 m). The soil is mainly sandy and very rich in pebbles, which ensures excellent drainage. The harvest took place toward the end of October and, unlike almost everywhere else in Italy, here 2002 was almost an ideal vintage. The vinification and maturation of the wine was carried out in stainless steel. Expect, partly as a result, great purity and vibrancy of flavors, complexity that will improve with bottle age, remarkable structure, and reasonable longevity. **AS**

🜨🜨 **Drink: recent vintages for up to 10 years**

Young husband-and-wife team Chris and Suzaan Alheit are besotted with old vines (in South Africa that usually means anything more than thirty-five years) and with expressing terroir.

All the grapes in Cartology are from carefully sought, mature, dryland-farmed bushvines (different proportions in each vintages). The 2012 Cartology derives from one particularly old block of Sémillon in Franschhoek, and Chenin Blanc from hillside vineyards as far apart as Skurfberg in the Olifants River region, Kasteelberg and Perdeberg in the Swartland, and Bottelary in Stellenbosch. Vinification happens (with no yeast inoculation, additives or acidification; maturation is in old barriques) in rented cellar space in the Hemel-en-Aarde area.

The maiden vintage of Cartology—2011—brought immediate international recognition to the Alheits, and the 2012 is arguably even finer. Already complex in its youth, it should mature well, given the serenely taut poise of its balance and the concentration of the fruit. There's texture and form, subtly sweet citrus and stone-fruit with earthy and saline elements, and a lingering finish. **TJ**

🜨🜨🜨 **Drink: to 2022**

▣ The Abbazia di Novacella, flanked by its Kerner vineyards.

Roberto Anselmi *I Capitelli*
Veneto Passito Bianco 2001

Origin Italy, Veneto, Soave
Style Sweet white wine, 12.5% ABV
Grape Garganega

Roberto Anselmi came to wine via motor racing, and it is fair to say he has driven something like a Ferrari through the placid world of Veneto winemaking in recent years. In the 1980s, he took over the family estate established by his father in 1948. Although entitled to one of Italy's DOCs in Soave, where he makes three dry whites and a *recioto*-method dessert wine, he now labels his wines "IGT Veneto."

Why such recalcitrance? Because, feels Anselmi, Soave is for the time being a name so taken in vain, so traduced by the quality of the tasteless quaffing stuff the DOC turns out by the tanker load, that he fears being tainted by association.

The grapes from I Capitelli vineyard, which go into the sweet wine, are treated in classic *passito* fashion, being laid out to dry on bamboo mats after the harvest, so that as they gradually dry in the air currents, the sugars, acidity, and flavors correspondingly intensify. Guyot vine-training, not widely practiced in Soave, significantly lowers the grape yield, assisting concentration. Fermenting in French oak adds further spicy aromatic character.

I Capitelli is a deep golden color in youth, and throws out notes of acacia honey, candied lemon, and roasted cashews. On the palate, it is striking for the exquisite balance of peachy sweetness and structured, even slightly astringent, acidity. This combination makes it a surefire keeper, and in the luscious 2001 vintage all its elements are in symbiotic harmony. Drunk with one of Italy's creamy blue cheeses, it is a celestial match. **SW**
🥂🥂🥂 **Drink: to 2020+**

Arnot-Roberts *Ribolla Gialla*
Vare Vineyard "A" 2012

Origin USA, California, Healdsburg
Style Dry white wine, 11.5% ABV
Grape Ribolla Gialla

Formed in 2001 by childhood friends Duncan Arnot Meyers and Nathan Roberts, the Arnot-Roberts brand quickly distinguished itself through the finesse and ingenuity of its wines. The 4,000 annual cases are divided into over a dozen different wines, sourced from carefully selected sites throughout Northern California. In the cellar, the fruit is handled with restraint; only native yeast and bacteria are employed, and many of the wines are aged in oak barrels that are personally crafted by Nathan Roberts, a second-generation cooper.

The grape varieties used range from Cabernet Sauvignon, Pinot Noir, and Chardonnay to more esoteric varieties such as Trousseau and Touriga Nacional. But perhaps their most exciting wine comes from an improbable patch of Ribolla Gialla, planted in the Vare Vineyard at the foot of Mount Veeder. For the most recent vintages, the friends obtained a thick-walled clay amphora in which they ferment and age half the wine (the amphora bottling is stamped with an "A"). The grapes are harvested on the early side, at around 19 Brix, and then left on their skins inside the amphora for two months before being pressed and put to rest in neutral French barrels for nine months.

The 2012 Ribolla Gialla Vare Vineyard "A" offers both tension and breadth, as well as aromas of quince, lemongrass, and white peach. The skin contact imbues the wine with a warm golden hue as well as appreciable tannin. The intensity of structure implies age-ability, but that theory is as-yet unproven. **KW**
🥂🥂🥂 **Drink: to 2020+**

Different varieties of grape growing in the vineyards at Arnot-Roberts. ➲

Château d'Arlay
Côtes du Jura Vin Jaune 1999

Origin France, Jura, Côtes du Jura
Style Dry white wine, 13.5% ABV
Grape Savagnin

Domaine d'Auvenay
Chevalier-Montrachet GC 2002

Origin France, Burgundy, Côte de Beaune
Style Dry white wine, 13% ABV
Grape Chardonnay

You can see them for miles—the ruined ramparts of the old château running around the top of a little hill, with vineyards on the slopes below. The modern (eighteenth-century) château of Comte Alain de Laguiche is at the base of the hill, just above the village of Arlay, on the western fringes of the Jura. It was the count's father who first gained a fine reputation for Château d'Arlay Vin Jaune. There are seams of the famous marl here, but the soil is mainly limestone. Around 8.5 acres (3.5 ha) of Savagnin are grown in two quite different plots.

Château d'Arlay makes the wine quite traditionally, and bottles each January after the requisite six years and three months. Normally at least four vintages are available to taste at the château, and what is most remarkable is the intensity of flavor each vintage shows. The 1999 is spectacular, and de Laguiche considers it "classic Château d'Arlay." It has the tremendous structure needed for long aging, coupled with intense crystallized fruit, mushroom, and even tobacco flavors. Somehow it manages to be both elegant and rich at the same time. **WL**
🜃🜃🜃 **Drink: to 2025+**

Mme. Lalou Bize-Leroy is the proprietor, with her shareholders, of both Domaine Leroy, based in Vosne-Romanée, and the *négociant* firm of Maison Leroy, based in Auxey-Duresses. Together with her sister she owns half of the Domaine de la Romanée-Conti. As if this were not enough, she has also built up, piece by piece over the past twenty or more years, a private estate of her own. There is not very much—a total of less than 10 acres (4 ha). But this estate includes Mazis-Chambertin, Bonnes-Mares, Criots-Bâtard-Montrachet, and Chevalier-Montrachet, in the case of the latter enough to make two and a half casks. She bought this parcel from the Chartron domaine in Puligny-Montrachet in the early 1990s. It lies in the Demoiselles, just upslope from the northern wall of Le Montrachet.

Yields in the Leroy estates are cut to the quick. Others might make a third as much more. But the gain is in the concentration of the wine. This 2002 has the power only seen elsewhere in a Montrachet. It is full-bodied, currently youthful, if not austere. It is dry but rich, profound, multi-dimensional, aristocratic, and magnificent. **CC**
🜃🜃🜃🜃 **Drink: to 2035+**

◄ Sheltered eighteenth-century buildings of Château d'Arlay.

Avignonesi *Occhio di Pernice Vin Santo di Montepulciano* 1995

Origin Italy, Tuscany, Montepulciano
Style Sweet rosé wine, 16% ABV
Grape Prugnolo Gentile

A. A. Badenhorst Family Wines *White Blend* 2010

Origin South Africa, Coastal Region
Style Dry white wine, 14.3% ABV
Grapes Chenin Blanc, Roussanne, and 10 others

Occhio di Pernice ("Eye of the Partridge," so called because of its pinkish hue) is the generic name for Vin Santo made exclusively from red grapes, though this special sweet wine category is mostly white. For many years, Avignonesi was the only producer of the wine, which it first released in 1974.

Made from 100 percent Prugnolo Gentile, the local clone of Sangiovese found in Montepulciano, the wine is made from the best grapes that have been dried on cane mats for at least six months in a process known as *appassimento*, when they lose at least 70 percent of their original liquid. The resulting must, slowly pressed drop by drop, has an almost oil-like consistency that is rich in both sugar and alcohol. The dense nectar is then put into small oak barrels called *caratelli* that are sealed for ten years.

According to Burton Anderson, Avignonesi's Occhio di Pernice "may be Italy's most cherished sweet wine." Highly polished, with a luscious texture, it has a complex bouquet redolent of dried fruit, figs, and spices, reminiscent of aged Cognac. Rich flavors and sweetness are balanced with bracing tannins and an extraordinary length. **KO**
🥂🥂🥂🥂🥂 Drink: to 2020+

In his mid-thirties, Adi Badenhorst abandoned a prestigious winemaking job in Stellenbosch for the excitement of joining the winemaking revolution in the Swartland. Together with his cousin Hein, he bought Kalmoesfontein, a neglected wine farm on the Paardeberg slopes, where old vineyards were the prime attraction. Much effort later, the cellar—unused for over seventy years—has been restored, and equipped with wooden *foudres* supplementing the old concrete fermenters.

The Swartland's treasure is old-vine Chenin Blanc, and it's at the core of this blend, with Roussanne also prominent. The mix can vary, depending on the vintage and what "amazing parcels of fruit" Adi finds; it usually draws on up to ten other varieties. Fermentation occurs in old casks, and there's six to eight months maturation in concrete before the wine goes into bottles with their delightfully quirky labels.

There is power in the wine, and ripeness, but the natural acidity keeps it fresh. There is also volume, a lovely texture, and complexity of aroma and flavor, even in youth. The fruit is supported to a long finish by a firm structure, with a little phenolic grip. **TJ**
🥂🥂 Drink: to 2020+

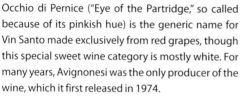

🖼 Grapes dry on cane mats, to be used for Avignonesi white Vin Santo.

Dr. von Bassermann-Jordan *Forster Pechstein Riesling* 2005

Origin Germany, Pfalz
Style Dry white wine, 13% ABV
Grape Riesling

The small village of Forst, with its famous vineyards, is considered the superstar of the Mittelhaardt region in the heart of the Palatinate. Here the perfect microclimate meets valuable vineyard soil, which is unique because of its basalt rock deposits. And nowhere can the mineralogical anomaly of the Forst terroir be better studied than Pechstein, whose name recalls the black stones of volcanic origin (*Pechstein* is German for pitch stone).

About thirty-eight million years ago, when the collapse of the Rhine Rift valley occurred, the earth's crust became brittle and liquid magma from deep inside the earth was able to ascend in some places and solidify into basalt on the surface. In Forst there is a small deposit, around 2,100 feet (640 m) long and 600 feet (182 m) wide, the only one on the slopes of the Mittelhaardt. Beside the basalt veins in Pechstein's soil, the basalt rocks visible on the surface today were brought to the vineyard by human hands in former centuries. These rocks were extracted from a cold lava dome on the edge of the Palatinate Forest.

Pechstein's unique mineral composition can be tasted in the wines of the top winery, Dr. von Bassermann-Jordan, which has 200 years of experience. The aroma of the Pechstein Riesling is reminiscent of candied citrus fruits and also, for some, the hot smoky flavors of the basalt rock. The wines have a prominent backbone, and even as dry wines they have extraordinary aging potential. **FK**

💲💲 **Drink: to 2020**

FURTHER RECOMMENDATIONS
Other great vintages
2002 • 2004
More wines from the same producer
Deidesheimer Hohenmorgen and Kalkofen
Ruppertsberger Reiterpfad • Forster Kirchenstück

The label pays tribute to the Roman Emperor Probus (232–282). ➡

Weingut Geheimer Rat
Dr. von Bassermann-Jordan
D-67146 Deidesheim

Pfalz

2005

Pechstein

Forst

Dom. Patrick Baudouin *Après Minuit Coteaux du Layon* 1997

Origin France, Loire, Anjou
Style Sweet white wine, 6.29% ABV
Grape Chenin Blanc

Patrick Baudouin, a former trade unionist, took over the estate created by his great-grandparents, Maria and Louis Juby, in 1990. Within a decade, this passionate vigneron established a reputation for flamboyantly sweet, characterful wines that have played no small part in reviving the fortunes of the previously down-and-out Coteaux du Layon region.

Après Minuit is an iconoclastic wine that contravenes the appellation laws by reason of its low degree of alcohol and high level of residual sugar. For Baudouin, a healthy respect for the domaine's aged Chenin Blanc vines and terroir count for much more than the appellation rules, which have encouraged less conscientious vignerons to prop up alcohol levels by adding sugar.

In 1997, a dream vintage, Après Minuit was made from the second *tri* (picking), which had a potential alcohol of 28.4 degrees and took around a year to ferment. With 373 g/l of residual sugar, it shows an exceptional richness and concentration of citrus and orchard fruits and, as its name suggests, should be enjoyed in an atmosphere of mellow contemplation and camaraderie. **SA**

🍷🍷🍷 **Drink: to 2030**

Domaine des Baumard *Quarts-de-Chaume* 1990

Origin France, Loire, Anjou
Style Sweet white wine, 12.5% ABV
Grape Chenin Blanc

In 1957 Jean Baumard acquired 15 acres (6 ha) in Quarts-de-Chaume. The name is of medieval origin. When the monks of the Abbey of Ronceray in Angers rented vines in the village of Chaume, payment took the form of the finest quarter of their crop; this invariably came from the Quarts-de-Chaume. The area was granted its own subappellation in 1954.

The wines exhibit tremendous purity and structure with an unmistakable *nervosité*, especially in benchmark vintages like 1990. In this classic Layon vintage, a hot, dry summer was followed by a warm September and October; regular morning mists produced the ideal conditions for botrytis, which affected around 80 percent of the crop.

At Baumard, only overripe or botrytized Chenin Blanc grapes are hand-harvested, typically in three *tris* (selective pickings), then swiftly transported to the winery in shallow boxes to keep grapes intact and avoid oxidation. Domaine Baumard has used a pneumatic press since 1966, and this, together with temperature-controlled fermentation in stainless steel tanks, accounts for Baumard's freshness and very pure expression of fruit and terroir. **SA**

🍷🍷🍷 **Drink: recent vintages for up to 25 years**

Ch. de Beaucastel *Châteauneuf-du-Pape Roussanne VV* 1997

Belondrade y Lurton *Rueda* 2004

Origin France, Southern Rhône
Style Dry white wine, 13.5% ABV
Grape Roussanne

Origin Spain, Rueda
Style Dry white wine, 14% ABV
Grape Verdejo

For some decades the Perrin family of Beaucastel has produced one of the finest and most consistent red wines of Châteauneuf-du-Pape. But they also make one of the most remarkable white wines of the entire Midi—the Vieilles Vignes, produced from a parcel of Roussanne that is more than sixty-five years old. In order not to overwhelm the wine with oaky aromas and flavors, half the wine is fermented in tanks, the balance in one-year-old barrels.

White Châteauneuf is something of a mystery. Grown in a very hot region and inevitably low in acidity, it is nonetheless capable of aging. Often it is delicious young, then goes through a dumb phase between four and eight years of age, before blossoming anew. Vintages such as 1987, which are not outstanding for red Châteauneuf, are often best for the white wine. The Roussanne Vieilles Vignes here is no exception, and the 1997 is a wonderful example. There is very rich fruit on the nose, with hints of apricot and even quince, while the texture is sumptuous and rich in glycerol. Though plump, full-bodied, and concentrated, it is not a heavy wine and has surprising length of flavor. **SBr**

🍷🍷🍷🍷 **Drink: to 2017**

Didier Belondrade is a Frenchman in love with Spain and, when he traveled to Castilla, he fell in love also with the white Verdejo grape, responsible for the wines of Rueda. When the first vintage of Belondrade y Lurton 1994 was released, it amounted to revolution on the Spanish white wine scene. Most Rueda wines were produced in a fresh and fruity style for early consumption; but here we had a Rueda in the style of a great white Burgundy.

The 2004 vintage was a good one in the region, and the wines of Belondrade show more balance and better integrated wood with each harvest. The color is pale yellow and, when young, the nose shows the influence of the oak, together with the typical Verdejo descriptors—fresh hay and apple—as well as some orange rind and a touch of balsamic. On the palate, the wine is creamy but fresh, with well-balanced acidity, good length, and a slightly bitter twist on the end finish. The wines age well, in the style of a *village* Burgundy, developing some notes of wet wool and showing a calcareous minerality that is more noticeable once the wood has been completely integrated. **LG**

🍷🍷 **Drink: recent vintages for up to 8 years**

Paul Blanck *Schlossberg Grand Cru Riesling* 2002

Origin France, Alsace
Style Dry white wine, 12% ABV
Grape Riesling

Blue Nun
2005

Origin Germany, Rheinhessen
Style Off-dry white wine, 9.5% ABV
Grapes Müller-Thurgau 70%, Riesling 30%

In 1975, Schlossberg was the very first Alsace grand cru to be delimited, and Marcel Blanck was the driving force behind this achievement. The Blancks can trace their viticultural roots back to 1610, but it was not until the second half of the twentieth century that this winery began to evolve into its present dynamic form. Today, operations are in the hands of Frédéric and Philippe Blanck. The 89-acre (36 ha) estate includes grands crus Furstentum, Mambourg, Schlossberg, Sommerberg, and Wineck-Schlossberg, and *lieux-dits* Altenbourg, Grafreben, Patergarten, and Rosenbourg.

The Blancks produce up to sixty different wines each year, but their signature wine is Schlossberg Grand Cru Riesling. This classified vineyard stretches to just over 198 acres (80 ha), and is split between the villages of Kaysersberg and Kientzheim—literally split (separated from the rest of the grand cru) at its northeastern extremity. The slopes are south- and southeast facing, much of them terraced. The soil is coarse, alluvial, clayey sand, rich in minerals, over a granitic bedrock. In a rare combination, the 2002 has both minerality and delicious richness. **TS**

❂❂❂ Drink: to 2022

The Blue Nun Liebfraumilch brand was launched in 1921 by H. Sichel Söhne, with a label designed as a consumer-friendly alternative to the then characteristic German wine labels with Gothic script and complicated names. The "nun" is an allusion to Liebfraumilch's origins as a single-vineyard wine called Liebfrauenstift, which was next to a church.

After several years of declining sales, the German family firm Langguth bought Sichel in 1996. Langguth upgraded the wine from a Liebfraumilch—a catch-all name covering huge tracts of Germany and for which wines need not contain Riesling—to a superior Qualitätswein, meaning that the grapes must come from a designated region (in Blue Nun's case, Rheinhessen). Blue Nun now contains a minimum of 30 percent Riesling in the blend, and the wine is made in a noticeably drier style, with residual sugar reduced from 42 g/l to 28 g/l.

Blue Nun might still be tainted by associations with all things tacky, but it is a triumph of marketing and rebranding, and is all things to all people. Langguth says the wine is "versatile enough to go with most foods. And great to drink on its own." **SG**

❂ Drink: current release within 3 years

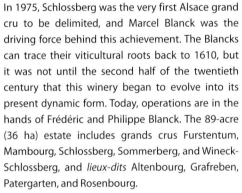

Liebfraumilch originally came from this church vineyard in Worms. ➦

Dom. Jean-Marc Boillot *Puligny-Montrachet PC La Truffière* 2002

Origin France, Burgundy, Côte de Beaune
Style Dry white wine, 13.5% ABV
Grape Chardonnay

When the renowned Etienne Sauzet estate released some of its vineyard land in the 1980s, it was Jean-Marc Boillot, grandson of the original Etienne Sauzet, and formerly winemaker (and son of a winemaker) at Olivier Leflaive, who carried it off.

Puligny-Montrachet is not short of premiers crus, not all of which are worth the high prices they command. J.-M. Boillot's wines strive for greatness, but in a leaner, more classical style than the big, fat, oaky idiom at which much Burgundian Chardonnay now aims. The wines have a pure, mineral core and, although they are certainly given an *élevage* in *barrique*, the oak is judiciously, even sparingly, applied. There is a steely nervosity to them in their youth, reflecting the concentrated juices from which they are born, but with age they take on a rounder profile, with a strong sense of terroirs.

La Truffière is one of the better known Puligny premiers crus, one of the smallest and highest, being even farther up the Mont-Rachet slope than the great Chevalier-Montrachet grand cru. The 2002 vintage produced great white Burgundies that were probably the best wines since the 1996s. Boillot's 2002 La Truffière has intense pear and lemon scents, with just the faintest lick of melted butter. On the palate, it is elegant, chic, but sternly focused, too, with brilliant acid balance to the peach-toned fruit. At three years old, the finish was substantial but still coiled tight, needing time to open out in the bottle. **SW**
🍷🍷🍷🍷 **Drink: to 2017+**

Rows of newly planted vines near Puligny-Montrachet. ➔

Dom. Bonneau du Martray
Corton-Charlemagne GC 1992

Origin France, Burgundy, Côte de Beaune
Style Dry white wine, 13% ABV
Grape Chardonnay

Bonny Doon
Le Cigare Blanc 2009

Origin USA, California, Santa Cruz
Style Dry white wine, 13.5% ABV
Grapes Roussanne 73%, Grenache Blanc 27%

An architect by training, Jean-Charles le Bault de la Morinière inherited the family property at Bonneau du Martray in 1994. The domaine has one continuous holding of 23.5 acres (9.5 ha) on the Pernand side of the great Corton hill, which corresponds to the site owned by the ninth-century Emperor Charlemagne, who gave his name to the white wine made from grapes grown here. It is the only Burgundy domaine, other than the Domaine de la Romanée-Conti, that sells only grands crus (the other being red Corton).

The 1992 white Burgundy vintage was much hyped at the time, with high levels of ripeness producing full-bodied wines, although acidity levels were generally on the low side. John Kapon of New York wine retailer and auction house Acker Merrall & Condit tasted a bottle of Bonneau du Martray 1992 in March 2007, noting that it "had a honeyed, sweet nose that reminded me of buttered, brown sugared bacon . . . still round and tasty." Although piercingly pure and fresh when young, the wine becomes rich and nutty with bottle age, developing aromas of honey, toffee, and caramel, but still with the telltale mineral undertow. **SG**

🍷🍷🍷🍷 Drink: to 2017+

The white blends of the northern and southern Rhône are not among the most conspicuously lauded of French white wines. Too often, they have a lumpish quality, a stone-dry, inelegant weightiness that does not give much away aromatically, or appear to do anything interesting if aged in bottle. Trust Randall Grahm to rewrite the book.

In the Cigare Blanc, the stark minerality of Roussanne is used to form the backbone of the wine, while the proportion of Grenache Blanc adds an unexpected dimension of softening aromatic fruit and spice. There is a waft of white peach in the wine and a scattering of honeysuckle, together with a subtle hint of saffron. Significantly, the 2004 vintage produced a notably successful wine, almost certainly as a result of its higher than usual proportion of the Grenache Blanc. In previous vintages, it has been as low as 3 percent—why not let it allow the wine to sing thus more often?

Low yields contribute to the wine's extraordinary textural concentration—there is a viscous, clinging mouthfeel, buoyed up by 13.5 percent alcohol, that can divide opinion. **SW**

🍷🍷🍷 Drink: recent vintages for up to 6 years

◀ Corton-Charlemagne ages in Bonneau du Martray's cellars.

Bonny Doon
Muscat Vin de Glacière 2012

Origin USA, California, Santa Cruz
Style Sweet white wine, 11.5% ABV
Grape Muscat

Borgo del Tiglio
Malvasia Selezione 2002

Origin Italy, Friuli Venezia Giulia, Collio
Style Dry white wine, 13% ABV
Grape Malvasia Istriana

In 1986, Randall Grahm of Bonny Doon branched out into Icewine. The European antecedent, Germany's Eiswein, is one of the great, theoretically inimitable styles of sweet wine, produced from grapes that are left to hang and shrivel, and then freeze, on the vines in winter. In California the answer to Icewine production is cryoextraction, in which bunches of grapes are thrown into a deep freezer (*glacière* in French). The technique has been applied over the years to Gewürztraminer and even Grenache, but it is the Muscat that takes the palm. Various clones of Muscat go into the wine—principally Muscat Canelli, but in recent years Orange Muscat and the Greco and Giallo offshoots have been included.

Spangled fruit streamers come surging forth from the glass. These are tangerine, preserved lemon, pineapple, and sugared grapefruit, borne aloft by an array of sweet spices such as cinnamon and ginger, and sprinkled with crystallized petals of orange blossom and jasmine. The wine is clingingly intense in texture, possessed of a multilayered richness for which the word "decadent," too often pressed into service, seems fully merited. **SW**
☻☻☻ **Drink: to 2020+**

The Collio is a small, hilly stretch of land in the northeast of Italy, on the border with Slovenia. It is widely appreciated as one of the best areas for the production of white wines in Italy. The soil is characterized by marl and sandstone.

The Borgo del Tiglio estate was founded in 1981 by Nicola Manferrari, who studied pharmacy. When producing his wines, Manferrari is as meticulous as any pharmacist: The oak, acidity, and alcohol are always perfectly proportioned, and the pleasure of drinking these wines easily repays the effort expended in finding them. The total production of the estate is around 3,300 cases per year.

Malvasia Istriana is a grape variety that is frequently and unfairly overlooked, even in the Collio scheme of things, but this Malvasia Selezione 2002 is a salutary reminder of its worth. The concentrated aromas of apples and white flowers are inviting and irresistible. On the palate, the wine is intense, perfectly balanced, and even more complex than on the nose, with soft fruit and an almost savory acidity that helps ensure the longevity of this revelatory wine. **AS**
☻☻☻ **Drink: to 2017+**

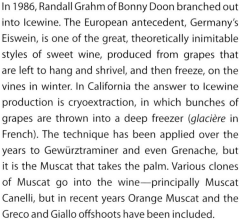

◄ Bien Nacido vineyard, one source of grapes used by Bonny Doon.

Dom. Bott Geyl *Sonnenglanz*
GC Tokay Pinot Gris VT 2001

Origin France, Alsace
Style Sweet white wine, 13.5%ABV
Grape Pinot Gris

Jean-Christophe Bott's first task upon succeeding his father Edouard in 1992 was to prune the vines to cut yields by 35 percent; he also rubbed out any excess buds growing on them after the risk of spring frosts had passed. He then ensured that the hand-picked grapes arrived at the winery intact as whole bunches. The aim was to achieve the "soft and subtle pressing" that gives Bott-Geyl wines their clarity.

In 2001, Jean-Christophe picked the Pinot Gris in his main grand cru site, the Sonnenglanz in Beblenheim, starting around October 15, intending to make two wines. The first grapes picked were destined originally for a Séléction de Grains Nobles (SGN) because they were nobly rotten. Between October 25 and 30, the remaining grapes were picked, destined for a separate Vendanges Tardives or "late harvest" bottling. The Vendanges Tardives grapes were fermented partly in tank, but those for the SGN were fermented in new oak barrels.

After tasting both wines, Jean-Christophe said, "While both were extremely good, I wanted to make an exceptional wine, and I achieved this by combining the two together." The wine has a smoky character from the nobly rotten grapes, with notes of truffles from the late harvested ones, and a combination of the defining characteristics of the 2001 season—full-body from a hot summer, concentration from low yields and the fine late fall weather, and lively acidity from early fall rain. **MW**
ⓢⓢⓢ **Drink: to 2030**

The foliage of Alsace vineyards turns gold with the onset of fall. ➡

Bouchard Père et Fils *Corton-Charlemagne Grand Cru* 1999

Origin France, Burgundy, Côte de Beaune
Style Dry white wine, 13.5% ABV
Grape Chardonnay

The family firm of Bouchard was established in 1731. After being handed down through successive generations of the family, it moved into its home in the Château de Beaune in 1810. The house was acquired by Henriot, makers of fine, Chardonnay-dominated Champagnes, in 1995. The portfolio incorporates 30 acres (12 ha) of grand cru vineyard land in various appellations, with a 7.5-acre (3 ha) holding in Corton-Charlemagne among the jewels in the crown. This is a domaine-bottled wine that possesses all the concentration, elegance, and firepower one expects from wines of its ilk. Early harvesting is a Bouchard philosophy maintained by the current owners, the aim being to freeze-frame a certain freshness in the acidity that will help the wine to weather prolonged aging in barrel and bottle. Separate passes through the vineyard are made at harvesting, with each lot vinified distinctly, prior to blending and maturing for six months in new oak, and then another year or so in older wood.

The 1999 vintage produced superbly well-balanced wines. This Corton-Charlemagne has the mixture of buttery baked apple and faint farmyard aromas typical of the cru, with a palate that is hugely weighty, rich, and authoritative, its lush, vanillin oak counterpointed by a fruit acidity reminiscent of pineapple. The density of structure indicates that this was never a wine intended for early consumption. In an ideal world, it would be drunk lightly chilled with a *poulet de Bresse* cooked in tarragon and cream. **SW**
🙂🙂🙂🙂 **Drink: to 2019+**

FURTHER RECOMMENDATIONS
Other great vintages
1992 • 1995 • 1996 • 1997 • 2000 • 2002 • 2005 • 2009
More producers of Corton-Charlemagne
Bonneau du Martray • Coche-Dury • Michel Juillot
Olivier Leflaive • Jacques Prieur • Rollin

A wealth of top-class Burgundy rests in Bouchard's ancient cellars. ➦

Domaine Henri Bourgeois
Sancerre d'Antan 2010

Origin France, Loire, Sancerre
Style Dry white wine, 12.5% ABV
Grape Sauvignon Blanc

The winery at Domaine Henri Bourgeois stands at the top of Chavignol, with a stunning vista of vines spreading out from its windows. Jean-Marie Bourgeois, when pressed, admits to owning half of the vineyards rolling away to the horizon, but he is underestimating. Monsieur is the big cheese in Chavignol, and is just being genuinely modest. To start our tasting he gets out two bottles, but keeps his own council while I sniff and slurp. The wines are overtly varietal—a Sauvignon Blanc and then a Pinot Noir. I ask which parcel they are from, expecting a gesture outside. "Marlborough, New Zealand," he responds, "from my property there called Clos Henri."

Domaine Henri Bourgeois makes around 550,000 bottles a year, and Clos Henri a further 120,000. Sancerre d'Antan accounts for only 6,000 to 10,000 per year. The d'Antan is from 100 percent flint soil. The terroir is obvious from the mineral note on the nose. The palate has a unique mixture of flinty, crisp flavors rounded out with a flavor of toasted sultana bread richly spread with butter. This is Sauvignon Blanc at its most opulent, traveling beyond terroir and into the sublime. **KA**

🍷🍷 **Drink: recent vintages for up to 9 years**

Georg Breuer *Rüdesheimer Berg*
Schlossberg Riesling Trocken 2002

Origin Germany, Rheingau
Style Dry white wine, 12.5% ABV
Grape Riesling

Bernhard Breuer's life work was the rediscovery and renaissance of the concept of terroir in Germany, and he worked untiringly to transform his top-quality dry Rieslings into grand cru wines of the Rheingau. His highest priority was the uniqueness of his vineyards, and this philosophy can nowhere be more persuasively tasted than in his Riesling from the Rüdesheimer Berg Schlossberg— long regarded as a modern classic of German wine culture. The soil of this steep vineyard (primarily of slate and quartz) produces wine that is expressive, exquisitely tangy, and mineral-rich, with superb length and longevity. Though rather closed in its youth, Breuer's Schlossberg blooms into great complexity.

Bernhard Breuer died in 2004, at just fifty-seven years of age. His legacy is a long line of outstanding, world-renowned Rieslings and, above all, the Schlossberg 2002. In 2005, Michael Broadbent MW pronounced: "The finest German Riesling Trocken I've ever drunk. . . . An aroma so outpointing, so celestial, and a flavor of such subtlety and length that one wondered how such grapes could be grown, such wine made." **FK**

🍷🍷🍷 **Drink: to 2017+**

Bründlmayer *Zöbinger Heiligenstein Riesling Alte Reben* 2002

Origin Austria, Kamptal
Style Dry white wine, 13.5% ABV
Grape Riesling

The Heiligenstein is the Kamptal's preeminent place for Riesling. With its rare flora, fauna, and geology, this rock was known for centuries by the monks who farmed it as "Hell's Stone" (Höllenstein).

For years, Willi Bründlmayer watched the ancient plantings being tended by an octogenarian who arrived on a bicycle. When the visits ceased, Bründlmayer became concerned for both vines and owner. A son-in-law had promised to attend the vines, but had no time for it. Bründlmayer agreed to handle everything, and the owner died believing that his daughter's husband was in charge.

Bründlmayer's Heiligenstein Alte Reben series began in 1991. Intermittent autumn rain in 2002 presented challenges, but this site proved its mettle with a Riesling of riveting clarity and dynamic flavor interplay. Wafting buddleia and lemon blossom; almost wanton profusion of citrus, berry, pit, and tropical fruits; ineffable, subtly sizzling minerality—all of these Heiligenstein-typical traits were gracefully choreographed in 2002, though nowadays powerfully rich Heiligenstein Riesling of up to 15 percent alcohol is not uncommon. **DS**

🟢🟢 **Drink: to 2017+**

Bucci *Verdicchio dei Castelli di Jesi Riserva Villa Bucci* 2003

Origin Italy, Marche
Style Dry white wine, 14% ABV
Grape Verdicchio

The Riserva Villa Bucci is produced only in very good vintages. The grapes come from vines planted in the 1960s, and after fermentation the wine is matured in large oak vats. The DOC law requires the Verdicchio dei Castelli di Jesi Riserva to be aged for at least twenty-five months before release; for the Villa Bucci, the maturation lasts for at least eighteen months in vat, then a further twelve months in bottle.

The recommendation is to decant the wine some ten to fifteen minutes before serving "to stretch its legs." It is also important not to serve it too cold, in order not to compromise its complexity. This is especially true of older vintages, because this Verdicchio is able to age gracefully for many years, developing alluring aromas of aromatic herbs.

The 2003 has a long life ahead. It has a bright straw-yellow color with emerald-green highlights. The nose abounds with notes of ripe peaches, citrus fruits, and freshly baked biscuits, whereas on the palate it seems to focus more on its nutty side, enlivened by fresher balsamic and citrus peel tones. The length of flavor is remarkable, as is the ease with which the bottle disappears. **AS**

🟢🟢 **Drink: to 2020+**

Reichsrat von Buhl
Forster Ungeheuer Riesling ST 2002

Origin Germany, Pfalz
Style Dry white wine, 12.5% ABV
Grape Riesling

The Ungeheuer vineyard of Forst became world famous in the nineteenth century, above all because of the wines from the Buhl estate which, back then, were counted among the best white wines in the world. German Chancellor Otto von Bismarck (1815–98) called it his favorite wine and named the then-owner, Franz Armand Buhl, his "personal friend and comrade-in-arms."

Sandy loam and clay soils, streaked with limestone rubble and basalt rock, distinguish the soil structure of the Ungeheuer and guarantee a high mineral extract in the wines. Moreover, in the late afternoon a "hair dryer" wind regularly blows through the area, sucking the dampness out of the vineyard and enabling the harvest of very ripe but healthy grapes. This makes for wines with particularly expressive, inviting fruit flavors and juicy textures. But not only are the dry wines from this site outstanding; in many years sweet wines of an almost royal nature can also be produced here. So it is fitting that the British Queen Elizabeth the Queen Mother enjoyed an Ungeheuer Beerenauslese from the Buhl vineyard on her hundredth birthday in 2000. **FK**
🕑🕑 **Drink: to 2017+**

Dr. Bürklin-Wolf *Forster*
Kirchenstück Riesling Trocken 2002

Origin Germany, Pfalz
Style Dry white wine, 13.5% ABV
Grape Riesling

Sometimes described as the "Montrachet of the Palatinate," the Kirchenstück vineyard occupies a prime position covering only 8.9 acres (3.6 ha). No other terroir in the Palatinate yields such a luscious yet elegant Riesling. Thick layers of clay and sand are permeated by basalt and limestone debris. The nearby church and knee-high wall surrounding the vineyard make for a unique microclimate.

And no producer is better able to transform the potential of this site into such an overwhelming wine monument as Dr. Bürklin-Wolf. This, the largest private German winery, owns only thirteen rows of vines at the heart of the Kirchenstück, yet the Riesling produced here has been among the few cult dry wines of this variety for several years. Bürklin-Wolf's Kirchenstück 2002 was acclaimed by the *Gault Millau Weinguide* as one of the best dry Rieslings ever made in Germany. The wine unifies forceful depth with beguiling elegance, and aromatic richness with brilliance and finesse. The Wagneresque final chord on the finish seems to go on forever and leaves many tasters speechless. A wine that demands and rewards time, in both bottle and glass. **FK**
🕑🕑🕑 **Drink: to 2020+**

Clemens Busch *Pündericher Marienburg Riesling TBA* 2001

Origin Germany, Mosel-Saar-Ruwer
Style Sweet white wine, 6% ABV
Grape Riesling

Bussaco Palace Hotel
Buçaco Branco Reservado 2001

Origin Portugal, Luso
Style Dry white wine, 13% ABV
Grapes Encruzado, Maria Gomes, Bical

Producing wine described by Berlin-based wine journalist Stuart Pigott as "Wagneresque Mosel wine to be exalted!" the enterprise, run since 1985 by Clemens and Rita Busch, is considered to be an insider's tip on the Mosel. The ecologically run estate yields equally outstanding dry and sweet Rieslings. The international breakthrough, however, was managed with extremely rare noble sweet wines.

It was the Riesling TBA 2001 that thrilled experts. In this year, there was only a relatively small amount of adequately dried botrytis grapes available until mid-November, meaning a TBA could only be produced after an extremely strict selection of individual berries. However, the tiny amount of must contained an almost unbelievably high amount of acid. Today, this brilliant acid structure cuts through the baroque, creamy sweetness with surgical precision, lending the TBA a fascinating balance as well as an almost endless life expectancy. This is a wine to which Pigott, without any hesitation, gave the perfect 100 points: "Anybody who would like to taste the universe's ultimate material density is in the right place here." **FK**
〇〇〇〇〇 Drink: to 2060+

Conceived as "a cathedral of wine" by its founder, Alexandre de Almeida, the Bussaco Palace Hotel's atmospheric cellar is home to over 60,000 bottles, dating back to the 1920s (when the wines were first made). To all intents and purposes, the wines are exclusive to the Almeida hotel group, whose wine lists uniquely feature select back vintages.

Buçaco Branco Reservado is a blend of Encruzado from Dão with Maria Gomes and Bical from Bairrada, and the grapes are fermented separately at low temperatures. Until 2000, the wine was aged in traditional large barrels (*toneis*) made of Brazilian oak, mahogany, and Bussaco oak or chestnut. These days, it is aged in new 79-gallon (300-liter) French oak barrels for twelve months. They are released with three years' bottle age, at which point this firmly structured, flinty wine remains youthful. A tight citric backbone gives line and length, steeling Buçaco Branco Reservado for the long haul (easily twenty to thirty years). Over time, its citrus and white peach fruit slowly gives way to complex tertiary, sometimes pungently vegetal nuances, including peach tea, resin, nuts, honey, and lanolin. **SA**
〇〇〇〇 Drink: to 2030

Calvente *Guindalera Vendimia Seleccionada Moscatel* 2006

Origin Spain, Andalusia, Granada
Style Dry white wine, 12.5% ABV
Grape Moscatel (Muscat)

Can Ràfols dels Caus *Vinya La Calma* 2000

Origin Spain, Catalonia, Penedès
Style Dry white wine, 13% ABV
Grape Chenin Blanc

While most new winemaking projects in Andalusia are focused on concentrated red wines aged in new oak, this wine has deeper roots in Andalusian tradition, which has been based for three centuries on three white varieties—Palomino Fino, Pedro Ximénez, and Moscatel (Muscat).

Some 200 years ago, Simón de Rojas Clemente identified Moscatel as the dominant variety on the Almuñécar ridge. Here, planted on unbelievably steep hills, grow the thirty- to sixty-year-old vines owned and lovingly nurtured by Horacio Calvente. The vines literally hang over the Mediterranean, as if suspended from balconies, at 1,968 to 2,296 feet (600–700 m) above sea level; hence the day–night temperature contrasts that lead to optimum ripening while preserving natural acidity.

In the first decade of this century, 2002 and 2006 have been the best vintages. The wine has powerful and focused fruit expression, both on the nose, where varietal aromas speak loud and clear, and on the palate, where a most harmonious balance is crowned on the finish by the characteristic bitterness of dry-fermented Moscatel. **JB**

⊖ Drink: recent vintages for up to 3 years

Can Ràfols dels Caus is the property of Carlos Esteva, a real pioneer and visionary in the Spanish wine trade. The property of 1,100 acres (445 ha) was acquired by his family in the 1940s. Nowadays, 120 of the acres (48 ha) are under vine, most of them around twenty years old, but some as old as sixty. In the 1980s, Esteva paid special attention to the reds, unusual in Penedès at that time, whereas now he has developed some interesting whites when everybody else seems to be concentrating on the reds.

The soil is very rich in chalk with some clay, a characteristic of the Garraf region. The property is divided into many small plots with different orientation, soil composition, and grape varieties, harvested, fermented, and matured separately. La Calma, the vineyard where the Chenin Blanc was planted in the late 1970s, has a calcareous soil rich in seashell fossils, and is sited at the top of a hill.

The La Calma 2000, the only Chenin Blanc in Spain, is deep gold in color. It has a distinctive, fine aroma, with white peach, quince, star anise, and dried fruit and wood notes. Medium-bodied, it has high acidity, plenty of glycerin, and a long finish. **LG**

⊖⊖ Drink: recent vintages for up to 10 years

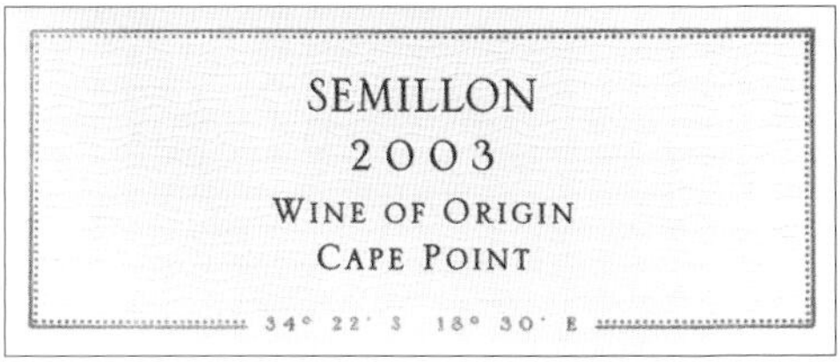

Cape Point Vineyards *Semillon* 2003

Origin South Africa, Cape Point
Style Dry white wine, 13.7% ABV
Grapes Sémillon 85%, Sauvignon Blanc 15%

The days are long past since Sémillon constituted most of the Cape vineyard—days when no grapes at all were grown this far down the rocky Cape Peninsula, beyond Constantia. Cape Point Vineyards is the sole winery in the Wine of Origin district that shares its name. The first vines were planted only in 1996 by businessman Sybrand van der Spuy.

The less than 3 acres (1.2 ha) given to Sémillon are proving to be, as Cape Point's winemaker Duncan Savage claims, "a great site." But Savage is alertly sensitive to what the vineyard offers: In 2003 only 30 percent of the wine was fermented in oak, to preserve the green, pyrazine notes he valued. There was no bottling at all in 2004, then the riper 2005 vintage saw half the wine into wood, emphasizing a tangerine character, with a little Sauvignon adding verve to what is effectively a Graves/Pessac-style wine. (There was a little more made in 2005, but this is likely to remain a small-production wine.)

The wines are austere in youth, with cool-climate minerality; by mid-2007, the 2003 was evolving from its early herbaceousness, gaining complexity and adding asparagus, earth, and herby notes. **TJ**

Drink: to 2018

Capichera *Vermentino di Gallura Vendemmia Tardiva* 2003

Origin Italy, Sardinia
Style Dry white wine, 14% ABV
Grape Vermentino

The Capichera estate is near the village of Arzachena, in the extreme northeast of Sardinia. The soil of this side of the island is very barren, characterized by the presence of granite rock and sand. The Agnedda family, owner of the Capichera estate, has been involved in wine production for nearly 100 years, but until the 1970s it was only for the family's own consumption. The 1980 vintage was the first Capichera Vermentino to hit the shelves, and the difference between this and the other Vermentinos was instantly noticed. This wine was more concentrated, more fragrant, and more complex. In 1990 brothers Fabrizio and Mario Agnedda released their first Vermentino Vendemmia Tardiva, a dry wine made from late harvested grapes.

The Vendemmia Tardiva 2003 is a wine of impressive concentration, yet it manages to be both elegant and suave. On the nose it shows a honeyed and floral character, refreshed by a welcome citrus undertone. On the palate, it is soft and caressing, very densely textured and velvety, with hints of flowers, citrus fruits, honey, and Mediterranean bush. The finish is long and finely focused. **AS**

Drink: recent vintages for up to 10 years

Domaine Carillon *Bienvenues-Bâtard-Montrachet GC* 2002

Origin France, Burgundy, Côte de Beaune
Style Dry white wine, 13% ABV
Grape Chardonnay

Bow your head as you enter the Carillon cellar and you will see, on the lintel, the date 1632. The Carillons have been making wine in Puligny-Montrachet, father and son, since at least as far back as this; even earlier, according to some records. This is a very fine estate, one of the top white wine properties in the world. There is no chi-chi, no gallivanting off to be at every wine manifestation from Tokyo to Los Angeles, nothing "mediatic," just a firm family concentration on getting the very best out of their vines.

There are a mere 30 acres (12 ha) and twelve wines, a typical Burgundian breakdown. Most is simple (though not simple in any pejorative sense) Puligny-Montrachet: a village wine reared in double-sized barrels. There are various premiers crus: Combettes, Perrières, Champ-Canet, Champ-Gain, and Referts. Jacques Carillon, today the man in charge, is thin and fifty-ish, a tenor, not a bass.

But the jewel of the cellar, and the only grand cru, is the Bienvenues-Bâtard-Montrachet. There is about 0.27 of an acre (0.11 ha) of this: about two and a half barrels, perhaps 750 bottles a year. Like all great white Burgundy, it is vinified in its barrel, hardly touched thereafter, apart from one racking, and bottled after eighteen months. Recent white Burgundy vintages have been good, but the best is the magnificent 2002. It is rich, full, and concentrated, but magnificently stylish, steely, and mineral underneath. There is a complexity and a dimension that, alongside the wine's reserve, is a promise that it will continue to improve. **CC**
🙂🙂🙂🙂 Drink: to 2020

Castel de Paolis *Muffa Nobile* 2005

Origin Italy, Lazio, Castelli Romani
Style Sweet white wine, 13.5% ABV
Grapes Sémillon 80%, Sauvignon Blanc 20%

Castel de Paolis exemplifies the huge potential of the area of the Castelli Romani, once famous for the production of Frascati, and then somewhat neglected for precisely the same reason. When Frascati was highly regarded throughout the world, it was not the wine that people drank between the 1960s and the 1980s. Before phylloxera struck (which was right after World War II in this area), the grapes used were Malvasia Laziale, Bellone, Bombino, and Cacchione; afterward, the highly productive Malvasia di Candia and Trebbiano took their place.

In 1985 Giulio Santarelli, owner of Castel de Paolis, was talked into experimenting with traditional local grape varieties by Professor Attilio Scienza, one of the most authoritative experts in his field. They began uprooting the neutral Malvasia di Candia and Trebbiano and replanting the historic varieties, changing the face of Frascati once again, but this time for the better. Santarelli and Scienza also experimented with international grape varieties, which led to the creation of Muffa Nobile.

The Sémillon and the Sauvignon Blanc are completely affected by *Botrytis cinerea* (noble rot). The wine has a pale amber color, and on the nose shows the textbook aromas of botrytized wines: clear, soft, and intense notes of dried fruits, honey, and nuts. On the palate it is intense, with a soft and sweet attack, balanced and sustained by the alcohol and the acidity. Muffa Nobile would be at its best paired with honey-based desserts, such as baclava, or with pungent mature or blue cheeses. **AS**
🙂🙂 Drink: to 2020

Domaine Cauhapé
Quintessence du Petit Manseng 2010

Origin France, Southwest, Jurançon
Style Sweet white wine, 12% ABV
Grape Petit Manseng

In large part, Jurançon, on the slopes of the Pyrenees, is airy pastureland or forest. Suddenly, though, you find a protected south-facing slope of stony clay where the sun can linger and the warm *foehn* wind from Spain teases Petit Manseng grapes toward desiccation over the length of a languid autumn. The result is one of the world's greatest dessert wine locations. Botrytis plays no role in Jurançon; *passerillage* (raisining) is all.

Henri Ramonteu is a wine grower prepared to harry his grapes into the arms of winter before harvesting them. The fruit for this wine was picked in the second half of December over three or four harvesting sorties. The wine is barrel-fermented and aged for two years in new oak.

The virtues of Petit Manseng include a fruit spectrum quite different from those of most of its French peers, with notes of pineapple, mango, and banana striking an exotic, subtropical pose. At the same time, the variety's magnificent acidity provides spellbinding, almost Rieslingesque balance. For truly late-harvested wines like this one, concentration and sugar levels soar, yet the wines retain the aromatic power so evident in earlier picked examples. The choice of new oak might, in a lesser wine, be an aesthetic error; here it adds an extra layer of richness and sensuality. Ramonteu produces a wide range of wines from his 99-acre (40 ha) estate, including Folie de Janvier, made from frozen grapes. The Quintessence, though, is not only Domaine Cauhapé's benchmark but the region's, too. **AJ**

😔😔😔 Drink: 2020+

Vincenzo Cesani *Vernaccia*
di San Gimignano Sanice 2012

Origin Italy, Tuscany
Style Dry white wine, 13% ABV
Grape Vernaccia di San Gimignano

In the 1950s, at the time when Italians were abandoning the countryside and moving to the big cities in the north, the Cesani family moved from the Marches to Tuscany in pursuit of a more "natural" way of life. Vincenzo Cesani believes that you can trust nature to look after you, if you just take the trouble to look after it. Today Vincenzo Cesani and his family trust nature more than ever: In his beautiful farmhouse, a few miles north of San Gimignano, he also produces excellent olive oil and saffron.

Vernaccia di San Gimignano is a grape variety whose origins are still obscure, but whose wines were, as Jancis Robinson MW says, "already known in the shops of medieval London as Vernage." The Sanice from Vincenzo Cesani is an example that easily explains why this DOC enjoyed so much success in the past. The grapes from the southeast-facing vineyards, at an altitude of 980 feet (299 m), are hand-harvested in the last week of September. After picking they are pressed and the juice is fermented in glass-lined cement vats. After the fermentation, the wine is left to mature in new French oak barriques for eight months, then bottled in June. Before it is released for sale, the wine undergoes a further three months of bottle age.

The wine shows a straw-yellow color with golden hues, and a nose that is broad, soft, and suggestive of sweet golden apples and yellow flowers. The oak is never dominant: It shows gently only on the palate, with a light vanilla aroma that accompanies the refreshing, slightly bitter finish. **AS**

😔😔 Drink: to 2019

Chamonix
Chardonnay Reserve 2005

Origin South Africa, Franschhoek
Style Dry white wine, 13.6% ABV
Grape Chardonnay

Didier et Catherine Champalou
Vouvray Cuvée CC Moelleux 1989

Origin France, Loire, Touraine
Style Sweet white wine, 12% ABV
Grape Chenin Blanc

The Chamonix farm has unirrigated vineyards on the slopes of the Franschhoek Valley, providing poorer soils and altitudes crucial to the wines' quality. The spectacularly beautiful area was settled, in the late seventeenth century, by French Huguenot refugees; town and valley became known in Dutch as Franschhoek (French Corner).

Chamonix (more recently named) was part of La Cotte, the first farm granted to the Huguenots, in 1688. It is now owned by German businessman Chris Hellinger and his wife, Sonja. Although Chamonix grapes are reputed to be the last harvested in the area, this relates to the vineyards' comparative coolness rather than to extreme ripeness: In fact, a classical approach has always dominated winemaking here, and alcohol levels are moderate.

When the Reserve 2005 won Gottfried Mocke the Diners Club Winemaker of the Year 2006 title, judges noted aromas and flavors ranging from oatmeal to gentle tropical and citrus fruit. Fresh and full, they added, with a firm acidic backbone; sweet, spicy oak in soft support. But it is the mineral core that is of the essence. **TJ**

🜨🜨 Drink: to 2017+

A steady stream of Vouvrays in all styles has flowed forth since the Champalous established their domaine in 1984: wines of understated intensity, filling out the often bony frame of Chenin with some appetizing, creamy flesh.

The wonder of such a sustained performance is that Chenin is such a tantrum-prone variety. In the wrong vintages, its physiological ripeness can be borderline. In the right ones, it can just hang until half gone to noble rot—then the resulting wines can give the cream of Sauternes a run for their money. 1989 was of the latter stamp. It produced wines of legendary concentration, unctuously filling every corner of the palate, and set fair for a ripe old age.

Champalou's sweet wines are known as CC, with the richer bottling these days bearing the description "Trie de Vendange" to denote that it is the product of painstaking berry selection. What we find in the wine are layers of dried apricots slathered in cream, nectarines and peaches pushing through to a prolonged finish, but all pointed up with the glinting flash of mineral-pure, lemony acidity—an object lesson in perfect balance. **SW**

🜨🜨🜨🜨 Drink: to 2030+

◧ Chamonix's winery lies in the Western Cape wine-growing region.

White wines | 157

Channing Daughters
Tocai Friulano 2006

Origin USA, New York, Long Island
Style Dry white wine, 12.5% ABV
Grape Tocai Friulano

Domaine Chapoutier
Ermitage L'Ermite Blanc 1999

Origin France, Northern Rhône, Hermitage
Style Dry white wine, 15% ABV
Grape Marsanne

James Christopher Tracy, winemaker at Channing Daughters winery since 2002, uses his palate and creativity to design a multiplicity of micro-cuvées (most run to only fifty to 300 cases). Like a chef conceiving a dish, he composes his wines to reveal textures and complexities in a harmonious whole.

With its temperate, humid, maritime climate, Long Island is "not a region for the timid," Tracy notes. The 2006 vintage was fairly typical: Grown on what pass for slopes on Long Island's sandy, loamy East End, the Tocai is picked in one pass to capture different nuances of aroma and flavor. Some lots exhibit green and herbal characters; others, citrus and mineral; still others, tropical fruit notes.

Tracy fermented the 2006 fruit in six stainless-steel barrels, two one-year-old Slovenian oak hogsheads, and four older French oak barriques; each adds different characteristics. The hand-harvested fruit was whole cluster-pressed, handled minimally, and gravity bottled to retain Tocai's lifted perfume of flowers, citrus, almond, and wet stones that bursts on the palate with exotic spices, quinine, and a lightly oily, mineral underpinning. **LGr**

🥂🥂 **Drink: current vintage within 1–2 years**

Terroir is at the heart of Michel Chapoutier's winemaking and it is the reason he began, in the late 1980s, to release a range of wines from individual plots of vineyard. L'Ermite, of which this is the first vintage, is at the top of the Hermitage hill, close to the chapel, where old Marsanne vines grow on the decomposed granite known as gore.

When he took over the winery, Michel resolved to bring about a revolution. His father had let things slide quality-wise and Michel, determined that that would change, turned over much of the estate to biodynamism. His neighbors, by and large, thought him mad. "Botrytis comes from an excess of nitrogen and potassium in the soil," he asserted, somewhat controversially, on one occasion. "Because we use no chemicals, we have no botrytis."

There is no disputing, however, his devotion to terroir expression in his wines, nor the quality of those wines at their best. L'Ermite Blanc is all apples and tropical fruit in cream in its youth, with a touch of herbs and plenty of minerality. The 1999, with some maturity, is showing rich, fleshy notes of honey and nuts, and endless complexity. **MR**

🥂🥂🥂🥂🥂 **Drink: to 2030**

Domaine Chapoutier
Ermitage Vin de Paille 1999

Origin France, Northern Rhône, Hermitage
Style Sweet white wine, 14.5% ABV
Grape Marsanne

When Michel Chapoutier and his brother Marc took over the family estate in the late 1980s, they decided to make radical changes. One of their innovations was this Vin de Paille, a new idea that, they say, was merely reviving an old tradition, since the technique has its roots in Hermitage. It is also found, of course, in many other regions.

The principle is straightforward. The grape bunches must be healthy, with no botrytis. They are brought indoors to dry for two months; after this they are fermented, and the concentration of their sugar content is such that the finished wine has just over 100 g/l of residual sugar.

With 14.5 percent alcohol, this is a fairly weighty wine with great concentration, but also exemplary balance. There is quince fruit there, and apples, and a touch of something tropical; it is nutty and creamy, too, with honey and tremendous complexity. It is a wine of seduction, perhaps a *vino di meditazione*, though its weight means that it can deal with some fairly rich desserts. The 1999 is all dried apricots, delicate in spite of its weight, with fresh acidity. It is the color of satinwood, and is utterly addictive. **MR**

🍷🍷🍷🍷 **Drink: to 2020**

Chateau Montelena
Chardonnay 2004

Origin USA, California, Napa Valley
Style Dry white wine, 13.5% ABV
Grape Chardonnay

The legend of Chateau Montelena begins with the most important story in New World winemaking—the so-called Judgement of Paris in the summer of 1976. British wine importer Steven Spurrier set up a rigorously controlled blind tasting to compare France's finest wines with new bottlings from California. Spurrier's tasting panel—an all-star team of French connoisseurs—worked their way through four white Burgundies and six California Chardonnays. When the votes were counted, and the bottles revealed, the Chateau Montelena '73 came out on top, followed by a Meursault-Charmes '73, and then two other California wines, a Chalone 1974 from Monterey County and a Spring Mountain 1973. Overnight, the myth that French wines could never be matched was forever shattered.

To this day, Chateau Montelena remains an elegant and restrained expression of the form: Aged in a low percentage of new oak and never put through malolactic fermentation, this wine carries the hallmark wood and butter elements of California Chardonnay far in the background, emphasizing instead a distinctive crispness and minerality. **DD**

🍷🍷🍷 **Drink: to 2019**

Chateau Ste. Michelle
Eroica Riesling 2005

Origin USA, Washington State, Columbia Valley
Style Dry white wine, 12.5% ABV
Grape Riesling

It was Ernst Loosen's love of Pinot Noir that drew him to the Pacific Northwest. On one of these visits, Loosen heard that Chateau Ste. Michelle of Washington State was scouting for European partners for joint winemaking ventures. After a detour to Chateau Ste. Michelle's headquarters, the concept for Eroica was born. Named after Beethoven's magisterial Third Symphony, the wine itself embodies Old World and New World philosophies in counterpoint.

Since its inaugural 1999 vintage, Eroica has become more refined in style. It is always a blend of grapes from different vineyard sites. Crushing and destemming is avoided so as not to lose any freshness; similarly, the fermentation is cool and slow, capturing pure, vibrant Riesling character. The 2005 shows the greatest intensity of any Eroica bottling to date: The vineyards from the cooler Yakima Valley at the blend's core had a shy crop in 2005, but this came at no cost to delicacy. 2005 is also the first vintage with grapes from the Evergreen Vineyard, offering a delicate, white peach character alongside the zingy citrus and mineral notes. **LGr**
🍷🍷 **Drink: to 2017+**

Domaine J.-L. Chave
Hermitage Blanc 1990

Origin France, Northern Rhône, Hermitage
Style Dry white wine, 13% ABV
Grapes Marsanne 80%, Roussanne 20%

The Chave line stretches back to 1481: In no other classic French wine region can a family claim such a long and close link to the vine. The spectacular hill of Hermitage is a 321-acre (130 ha) vineyard largely devoted to red grapes. White Hermitage is produced in very small quantities.

Nonetheless, it has always had a fine reputation. By the late nineteenth century, white Hermitage vied with Hock and Mosel as the most prized of white wines. Chave's white Hermitage grapes are spread across four different plots, with some 100-year-old Marsanne in the Péléat *climat* providing a rich but not heavy spine for the finished wine. Late picking contributes to the rich gold color of the wine, and natural yeasts are used.

In 1990 Chave produced probably its best-ever white wine, and one of the greatest of all white Rhône wines. Awarded a maximum six stars by John Livingstone-Learmonth in his book, *The Wines of the Northern Rhône*, it is a wine of astonishing richness and balance, with flavors of dried fruits, apricot, honey, and spice. Despite its low acidity, Hermitage Blanc can age well for twenty or more years. **SG**
🍷🍷🍷🍷 **Drink: to 2020**

◪ Bottles of Eroica are filled at Chateau Ste. Michelle's winery.

Domaine de Chevalier
1989

Domaine François Chidaine
Montlouis-sur-Loire Les Lys 2003

Origin France, Bordeaux, Pessac-Léognan
Style Dry white wine, 12.5% ABV
Grapes Sauvignon Blanc 70%, Sémillon 30%

Origin France, Loire, Touraine
Style Sweet white wine, 12.5% ABV
Grape Chenin Blanc

Together with Haut-Brion and Laville Haut-Brion, Domaine de Chevalier produces the finest dry white wine of Bordeaux. Although Sauvignon-based, it is a wine of remarkable longevity. For over a century the domaine was owned by the Ricard family, but in 1983 they were obliged to sell, and the new owner was Olivier Bernard, the scion of a distilling family.

Only 12 acres (5 ha) are planted with white grapes, so production is limited—even more so because any substandard fruit is eliminated. There is no skin contact, and the wine is barrel-fermented, mostly with indigenous yeasts, then aged for up to eighteen months. Chevalier's vineyards are chilly and prone to frost; this gives the white wines a racy edge, and a minerality that supports the ripe fruit.

Although a hot and precocious year, 1989 was a great vintage at Chevalier. When the wine was young the aromas were very oaky, but now fruit, especially apricots and peaches, dominates the nose. This wine has remarkable power and concentration, and the earthy extract gives it a tremendous mineral bite as well as a very long finish. Although now mature, the wine shows no sign of peaking. **SBr**
🍷🍷🍷🍷 **Drink: to 2019+**

François Chidaine worked with his father Yves before striking out on his own in 1989, single-handedly tending 12 acres (5 ha) in Montlouis-sur-Loire. Since joined by his wife Manuéla and cousin Nicolas Martin, he has expanded the domaine substantially, to 50 acres (20 ha) in Montlouis-sur-Loire and 25 acres (10 ha) in Vouvray.

The domaine works some of the most coveted vineyards that overlook the Loire River, and has been farmed organically since 1990, and biodynamically since 1999. In the winery, long, natural fermentations in old oak yield wines that are intensely mineral, rich, and long, and range from dry to lusciously sweet, depending on vintage and parcel of origin.

Les Lys, a *moelleux*, is made only in exceptional vintages, such as 2003, from *tris* (select harvests) of botrytized grapes. In 2003, this vinous nectar (with 160 g/l of residual sugar) was crafted from a blend of four parcels of old vines clustered around the village of Husseau: Clos du Volagré, Clos du Breuil, Clos Renard, and Les Epinais. It is possessed of great length, balance, and an underlying minerality, which bodes well for the cellar. **SA**
🍷🍷 **Drink: to 2020**

Chivite *Blanco Fermentado en Barrica Colección 125* 2003

Origin Spain, Navarra
Style Dry white wine, 13.5% ABV
Grape Chardonnay

Christmann *Königsbacher Idig Riesling Grosses Gewächs* 2001

Origin Germany, Pfalz
Style Dry white wine, 13.5% ABV
Grape Riesling

Bodegas Julián Chivite is the best known winery in Navarra, in the north of Spain, between Rioja and the Basque country. The origin of the family as grape growers in the region dates from 1647, but the current winery and company was created in 1860. The top-of-the-range Colección 125 was launched to celebrate their 125th anniversary. Originally a red, it is now available in red, white, and sweet versions.

The white is 100 percent Chardonnay, a well-oaked, barrel-aged white made in the Burgundian style, fermented in Allier barrels where it was aged for a further ten months on its lees. The 2003 was voted "best white wine" in January 2007 at the fifth edition of Madrid Fusión, the Madrid gastronomy congress that brings together the best cooks from the world. Bright yellow in color with some green reflections, this is one of Spain's most prestigious and serious white wines. The complex aroma combines lactic and citric notes, yellow fruit, nuts, and toasted sesame seeds, with chalky notes and barrel-derived scents of toast, vanilla, smoke, and butter. Ample and long in the mouth, it delivers all the flavors promised by the nose. **LG**

🥂🥂🥂 **Drink: recent vintages for up to 10 years**

There are few vineyards in Germany renowned for both outstanding white and red wines. The greatest is the 47-acre (19 ha) Idig vineyard near Königsbach in the Mittelhaardt region at the heart of the Palatinate, which might be likened in this respect to Corton in Burgundy. Also comparable to Corton is the soil at Idig, marked by limestone clay with a high percentage of rocks. Alongside elegant, silky Pinot Noirs, remarkable Rieslings grow here and rank among the richest wines of this variety in Germany.

The modern fame of this location is inextricably linked to the Christmann family from Neustadt-Gimmeldingen, which owns about 17 acres (7 ha) at the core of Idig. The affable Steffen Christmann has for years created one of Germany's most impressive dry white wines, a Riesling that combines an almost baroque apricot and melon fruit flavor with the full body, depth, power, and silky texture reminiscent of fine white Burgundy. To do the mineral richness and sheer scale of the Idig 2001 justice, this wine should be decanted in advance, then drunk from balloon glasses. Unusually, its richness and vinosity make it a perfect partner for dishes with cream sauces. **FK**

🥂🥂🥂 **Drink: to 2019**

Christoffel *Ürziger*
Würzgarten Riesling Auslese 2004

Origin Germany, Mosel-Saar-Ruwer
Style Sweet white wine, 8% ABV
Grape Riesling

"This," Hans-Leo Christoffel is fond of saying when savoring any recent Riesling Kabinett that bears his label, "is what we used to call a good Auslese," so spoiled has one become by an uninterrupted spate of ripeness that began in 1988. When it comes to a "three star" Auslese, then—a wine nowadays bottled every year—one is approaching (at least on paper) the Trockenbeerenauslese of an earlier era. And yet, for all its ennobled richness, this wine possesses a fresh juiciness: a clarity, lift, delicacy, and lack of superficial sweetness that belie its analysis. Honey, citrus, but above all strawberries sign themselves Würzgarten, a unique melange of loam and red slate.

Thanks to his U.S. importer, Christoffel's wines—which for fifty years have represented what is best in Mosel Riesling—were long better known Stateside than in Germany. Belated local recognition came with his 1997s, at a time when Germans were rediscovering "sweet" Riesling. In 2000 Christoffel was diagnosed with a heart problem and advised to quit his vineyards. It looked as if this great collection of old vines would go on the block.

But a deal was struck with Ürzig's most influential proprietor—Robert Eymael of the Mönchhof. Eymael leased the vines with long-term options, and took on Christoffel as consultant. The wines from Christoffel's properties are vinified and bottled under his supervision, while those of the Mönchhof preserve their own distinctive style. **DS**
🔊🔊🔊 **Drink: to 2025**

Vines on the banks of the Moselle benefit from reflected sunlight. ➜

Château Climens 2001

Origin France, Bordeaux, Barsac
Style Sweet white wine, 14% ABV
Grape Sémillon

Wines have been made at Climens since the seventeenth century. In those days, it produced red wines as well as white but, with the classification of 1855, it was included as a premier cru for sweet wines. Of the five communes that make up Sauternes, Barsac was the only other entitled to append its name to the property, and Climens enjoys the best of both worlds.

Climens is uncannily capable of producing great wines in vintages that others have written off: the 2001 being a spectacular case in point. Covering 72 acres (29 ha), the property is among a small band that grows only Sémillon, bravely putting all its eggs in one basket in a region where blending is both a birthright and an insurance policy. Sandy, gravelly soils on a limestone base contribute a breathtaking mineral quality to the Sémillon. The harvest is carried out in successive waves, gathering only properly rotted berries in each pass.

Climens believes in the enriching powers of new oak, and up to two-thirds of its wood is renewed each year. Eighteen months' aging in barrel adds layers of creamy vanilla to the sweet fruit. The burnished deep golden-yellow robe offers up wildly decadent scents of honey, dried apricots, and figs. It spreads candied orange and floral honey over the palate, cloaked in clean, scented vanillin, underpinned by the sturdy structure of full-blown botrytis. The freshness of the acidity is miraculous, particularly in a wine that eschews Sauvignon. **SW**
☻☻☻☻☻ **Drink: to 2070+**

FURTHER RECOMMENDATIONS
Other great vintages
1989 • 1990 • 1991 • 1997 • 2003 • 2004 • 2005 • 2007
More producers of Barsac
Château Coutet • Château Doisy-Daëne
Château Doisy-Védrines • Château Nairac

Vineyards in Barsac tend to be flatter than in neighboring Sauternes. ➔

Clos de la Coulée de Serrant
Savennières 2002

Clos Floridène
2004

Origin France, Loire, Anjou
Style Dry white wine, 13% ABV
Grape Chenin Blanc

Origin France, Bordeaux, Graves
Style Dry white wine, 13% ABV
Grapes Sémillon 50%, S. Blanc 40%, Muscadelle 10%

Before returning to his family's Coulée de Serrant estate to help his mother, by that time a widow, in 1976, Nicolas Joly went back to school, studying enology in Bordeaux for two years, before returning to take direct control of the vineyards. In 1981, Joly discovered a book on biodynamic agriculture by the Austrian philosopher Rudolf Steiner and found it a life-changing experience. Within four years, Coulée de Serrant was run on biodynamic principles; Joly remains a vocal advocate of biodynamic viticulture.

Cistercian monks planted the 17-acre (7 ha) Clos de la Coulée de Serrant vineyard in 1130. Although it is a single property in Savennières, it has its own appellation. The 2002 vintage is straw-gold in color, with an opulent, honeyed nose. It looks and smells as though it will be sweet, and it certainly tastes botrytized, with good length, but it is actually dry. The wines can remain fresh and develop for up to a week after opening.

Clos de la Coulée de Serrant can be outstanding, but Joly's winemaking is notoriously inconsistent. He sometimes makes average wine in good vintages, but he can also excel in mediocre years. **SG**

🍷🍷🍷 **Drink: to 2017+**

Denis Dubourdieu is one of the most renowned enologists in Bordeaux. He is also a proprietor, and looks after his father's properties of Doisy-Daëne and Cantegril, as well as estates, such as Château Reynon, that belong to the family of his wife, Florence. Probably the most interesting of these ventures is the Graves estate Clos Floridène, owned jointly by him and his wife. These days the large Graves region is in the shadow of the Pessac-Léognan appellation in the northern Graves. With Clos Floridène, Dubourdieu shows the quality possible, especially with white wines, in the southern Graves.

The 75-acre (30 ha) vineyard was bought and renovated in 1982; Dubourdieu planted Sauvignon Blanc but retained the old Sémillon vines. Lying between Pujols and Illats, this is a cool area and the grapes ripen late. No new oak is used for the Sauvignon, but the Sémillon is aged in about 30 percent new wood. The 2004 is a substantial wine, with peach and lanolin aromas, considerable weight on the palate, and fine length. More forward than some other vintages of Floridène, it still has enough density and extract to age interestingly. **SBr**

🍷🍷 **Drink: to 2019**

◧ Bottles from Nicolas Joly's estate bear his distinctive seahorse crest.

Domaine du Clos Naudin
Vouvray Goutte d'Or 1990

Origin France, Loire, Touraine
Style Sweet white wine, 12.5% ABV
Grape Chenin Blanc

Clos du Tue-Boeuf Touraine
Le Brin de Chèvre 2010

Origin France, Loire, Touraine
Style Dry white wine, 12.5% ABV
Grape Menu Pineau

Philippe Foreau is the third generation of the Foreau family to produce Vouvray from this iconic domaine, purchased by his grandfather in 1923. The appellation's wines are arguably more vintage specific than any other, ranging in style from bone dry to lusciously sweet owing to the Loire's northerly, marginal climate. However, the Domaine du Clos Naudin's reputation rests on the apparent ease with which it produces mineral, concentrated, racy wines of consummate balance year in, year out.

The Domaine du Clos Naudin's 28 acres (11.5 ha) of hillside vineyard are propitiously located mid-slope, facing south-southeast-southwest on flinty, clay soils known locally as Perruches. The vines are farmed using organic methods.

Made from super-ripe, botrytized grapes harvested at more than 27 percent potential alcohol, Vouvray Goutte d'Or 1990 represents the pinnacle of achievement in an exceptional vintage. With more than 200 g/l of residual sugar, its suave texture is akin to liquid caramel. Nonetheless, Vouvray Goutte d'Or 1990 retains great freshness—a tour de force that will bring pleasure for many years to come. **SA**
🝔🝔🝔 **Drink: to 2050**

Although the Loire has become known principally for its Sauvignon Blanc, Chenin Blanc, and Cabernet Franc, the Puzelat brothers of Cheverny prefer to work from a broader varietal palette. Each of the classic trio is grown in their 26 acres (10.5 ha) of vineyards in the Cheverny and Touraine appellations, but they also have Pinot Noir, Gamay, Chardonnay, Côt (a.k.a. Malbec), Pinot Gris, and, in the case of this dry white wine, the local Menu Pineau (a.k.a. Arbois).

The brothers inherited this vinous diversity from their father, and the family has winemaking roots in the region going back to the fifteenth century, but it is their sensitive, natural winemaking style that has propelled this estate—and the ancient *lieu-dit* in Cheverny from which it takes its name—to the forefront of the Loire avant garde. For Le Brin de Chèvre—which roughly translates as "the stranded goat"—the grapes are grown in the family's vineyards in Touraine. A rare example of Menu Pineau vinified on its own, the wine is characterized by its purity of white fruit, the blossomlike delicacy of its aroma, and the clarity of its squeezed lemon acidity that is best in its first flush of youth. **DW**
🝔🝔 **Drink: recent vintages within 5 years**

Weisser Riesling
Noble Late Harvest

Clos Uroulat
Jurançon Cuvée Marie 2010

Origin France, Southwest, Jurançon
Style Dry white wine, 12.5% ABV
Grapes Manseng 90%, Petit Courbu 10%

The Uroulat estate was purchased in 1985 by Charles and Marie Hours, and has been extended fourfold since then. The investment has paid handsome dividends. High-density plantings, high training, and low yields maximize concentration in the fruit, which is thereby enabled to show its dazzling colors. Petit Manseng is reserved for the late-harvest wine that has always been traditional in Jurançon, but its fatter cousin—alongside a *soupçon* of the indigenous Petit Courbu—make up the blend for a divertingly aromatic dry wine.

Cuvée Marie spends up to eleven months in barrel, only a small proportion of which (barely more than 10 percent) is new. It bursts forth with pineapple fruit, mixed in with the sharper influences of green apple and pear, but then a beguiling waft of smoke from the barrel coils up. On the palate, the wine is full, immensely expressive, with a core of steely, citrussy acidity running through the generous tropical fruit. Notes of licorice, cinnamon, and cream emerge on the finish. Hugely attractive when young, its acid structure nonetheless fits it for developing through a few years' bottle age. **SW**

🚫🚫 **Drink: recent vintages for up to 5 years**

Paul Cluver *Noble Late*
Harvest Weisser Riesling 2011

Origin South Africa, Elgin
Style Sweet white wine, 13% ABV
Grape Riesling

In addition to unfashionability and having few suitable terroirs, Riesling in South Africa suffered until 2010 from local officialdom's deference to big business in reserving the great variety's name for an inferior grape; for local consumption, the real thing must be prefixed by Weisser or Rhine. As to climate, Elgin—formerly apple country, now increasingly turned to by wine growers seeking the advantages of the high, cool, mountain-ringed plateau, with its proximity to the sea—is proving itself apt.

The Paul Cluver cellar was the first in the modern appellation, the estate among its largest and oldest. Cool, moist, southerly winds ensure that the Riesling vineyard reliably gets botrytis, and this Noble Late Harvest (the legislated local name for the richest botrytized dessert wines) is made most years.

The style is somewhere between the Germanic (no wooding) and French (higher alcohol). Thrilling tensions electrify sumptuous fruit, sweetness, and nervy acid; honeyed botrytis augments the notes of peach and pepper. Lovely in youth, its potential is untested, but the structure and fruit suggest it should see out more than a decade. **TJ**

🚫🚫 **Drink: to 2021**

Domaine Coche-Dury
Corton-Charlemagne GC 1998

Origin France, Burgundy, Côte de Beaune
Style Dry white wine, 13.5% ABV
Grape Chardonnay

Jean-François Coche is not particularly welcoming to visitors, and he can be slapdash in providing information about his vineyards and wines. Demand for his wines far outstrips supply: He has no need for new importers or new press contacts, and his wines already fetch very high prices. He would rather spend his time either tending his 25 acres (10 ha) of vines or monitoring his wines in the cellar.

Most of the vineyards of this estate are simple village sites, although Coche does have some Meursault Perrières and, since 2003, Genevrières. However, he has no wish to expand his holdings, so if he acquires a choice parcel of vines, he sells off some lesser parcels to maintain the domaine's current size. Although based in Meursault, his best-known wine is his Corton-Charlemagne, yet he cultivates only 0.75 acres (0.3 ha) and production is limited to about 1,200 bottles. It is aged in barrel for about twenty months, with the proportion of new oak varying according to instinct and the vintage.

The scarcity and quality of Coche's Corton-Charlemagne means that it sells for exceedingly high prices. It is possible to obtain Corton-Charlemagne of superlative quality at a fraction of the price, but Coche enjoys a fanatical following and makes the most of it. His is a wine that demands some years in bottle to show at its best. The 1998 is superb, with aromas that are both mineral and floral. On the palate there is remarkable density and power, a creamy texture that steers well clear of heaviness, and a long, nutty finish. **SBr**

ⓈⓈⓈⓈ **Drink: to 2025**

Colle Duga
Tocai Friulano 2009

Origin Italy, Friuli Venezia Giulia, Collio
Style Dry white wine, 13.5% ABV
Grape Tocai

Italy very nearly missed out on having Colle Duga's Tocai Friulano in its vinicultural repertoire. When Colle Duga's founder, Giuseppe Princic, was born in 1898, the land on which the winery is now situated in Cormons fell within Austria's borders. It was only as a result of the largely unpopular redrawing of national confines in 1947 that the larger territory was claimed by the old Italian regime, only to pass to Yugoslavia and finally to Slovenia in 1991, when it gained its independence. Colle Duga's 17 acres (7 ha), divided into four parcels, now sit right on the Italian border, so qualifies as Friulano.

Giuseppe's grandson Damian now owns Colle Duga, having inherited the vineyard from his father Luciano in 1970. Together with his wife Monica and their two children, Damian ensures that every stage of the wine's production continues to be very much a Princic family affair. Damian produces an average of 30,000 to 40,000 bottles of high quality wine per year, as certified by the Centro Mobile di Imbottigliamento in Pozzuolo del Friuli.

The Tocai Friulano is their flagship wine, although the estate's Pinot Grigio and Chardonnay (of "honorary autochtony") are also noteworthy in their own right. In character, Colle Duga Tocai is a wine that embodies summertime in the country it so nearly did not belong to. It is straw-colored, fresh, but rounded, with slightly bitter almond aromas that blend with the refreshing taste of hay, herbs, flowers, and the faintest hint of paraffin. It comes as no surprise that it has won a number of awards. **HL**

ⓈⓈ **Drink: current release for up to 5 years**

Colli di Lapio
Fiano di Avellino 2004

Origin Italy, Campania, Irpinia
Style Dry white wine, 13% ABV
Grape Fiano

Clelia Romano and her family are behind one of the most exciting estates in southern Italy. The first vintage that Colli di Lapio released was 1994, and ever since then Clelia's wine has been the ideal image of a serious, maybe even somewhat austere, but surely uncompromising Fiano di Avellino. Clelia is a determined person; not many producers would have worked six harvests with traditional presses and very little other equipment, let alone produced such beautiful wines in that way. It was only in 1999 that a modern pneumatic press and proper bottling equipment were bought.

The Fiano di Avellino DOCG wines need at least six months after release to give of their best, and the splendid example produced by Clelia Romano is no exception, gaining even finer balance and definition after the first year. The 2004 vintage is a perfect case in point. The grapes were harvested in mid-October and immediately pressed. The must was fermented in stainless steel vats, then left on its fine lees for another six months before the bottling.

Fiano aspires to both elegance and complexity, and the 2004 from Colli di Lapio amply demonstrates the full potential of this variety. The wine has an intense citrus and mineral nose. On the palate it has a lightly creamy texture, balanced by a very fresh attack, a rich yet vivid mid-palate, and an almost savory, nutty finish. This is definitely a wine to trust. And if you resist the temptation to drink it young, it will repay your patience with an extra degree of depth and complexity over time. **AS**

🍷🍷 **Drink: 2019+**

Attilio Còntini
Antico Gregori NV

Origin Italy, Sardinia
Style Dry white wine, 18% ABV
Grape Vernaccia di Oristano

The Attilio Còntini winery is in the village of Cabras, in the province of Oristano on the west side of Sardinia. The main aim of the Còntini estate, today run by the sons and nephews of Attilio, is to enhance the qualities of the local grape varieties, such as Vernaccia di Oristano and Cannonau (elsewhere known as Grenache).

Vernaccia di Oristano is a white grape that found an ideal environment in the lower River Tirso valley, thanks to the particular climate and to the soil. The soil is mainly sandy and quite barren, and is known locally as Gregori, while Antico means "ancient." And ancient it is, as part of the wine contained in every bottle dates back to the beginning of its solera, in the first years of the twentieth century.

The wines that go into the Antico Gregori are carefully selected from among the best Vernaccias of the estate. They are left to age in small oak and chestnut barrels that are filled to only 80 percent of their capacity. The empty space between the surface of the wine and the wood, together with the environment of the cellar, favors the formation of a layer of yeast (*flor*), which at once protects the wine and contributes to the character of the blend.

This wine is not easy to understand. It has a gorgeous deep amber color, a deliberately oxidized character, and intense notes of oily hazelnuts and almonds. On the palate, it shows beautifully defined layers of bitter honey, caramel, toffee, and coffee, like small pearls on a precious bracelet held together by an acidic thread. **AS**

🍷🍷🍷 **Drink: current release for up to 30 years**

François Cotat
Sancerre La Grande Côte 1983

Origin France, Loire, Sancerre
Style Dry white wine, 13% ABV
Grape Sauvignon Blanc

The Cotat family bottled its first Sancerre in the 1920s. In their prime La Grande Côte vineyard, grape pickers habitually slid down vine rows sitting on cushions provided by the Cotats for the pickers' safety (and the Cotats's own amusement).

Sauvignon vines are here grafted onto its ideal rootstock partner, 3309C, which promotes steady flavor ripening even in Sancerre's notoriously fickle autumn climate for those brave enough to wait; and the Cotats's Sancerre grapes were habitually the last to be harvested. 3309C also directs Sauvignon's notably abundant energy into roots deep enough to find the most complex mineral flavors. The Cotats preserve the ripeness and complexity of their grapes by pressing them slowly in a wooden press to avoid Sauvignon's tendency to bitterness, and by using wild rather than laboratory yeasts for fermentation.

The Cotats's nonconformity saw their allegedly "atypical" wines banned from being labeled "Sancerre"—though happily not in 1983, their signature vintage of the 1980s, reticent for its first decade in bottle, gently expressive during its second, and glowingly mineral by the third. **MW**
☉☉☉ **Drink: to 2018**

Château Coutet
Sauternes 1988

Origin France, Bordeaux, Barsac
Style Sweet white, 14% ABV
Grapes Sémillon 75%, S. Blanc 23%, Muscadelle 2%

A thirteenth-century tower at Coutet testifies to the antiquity of this property, and it was already well known as a wine estate by the seventeenth century. In 1977 it was sold to an Alsatian family called Baly, who continue to take a keen interest in the wine.

The vineyards, almost 99 acres (40 ha), lie around the château in a single parcel that has been unchanged since 1855; although the soils are varied, they are typical of the limestone plateau of the finest sectors of Barsac. The average age of the vines is some thirty-five years, and the young vines are not used for Coutet. The winemaking is entirely traditional, with pressing in vertical presses, barrel fermentation, and aging in a proportion of new oak that was around 50 percent in the 1990s but is now closer to 100 percent.

Coutet is an undemonstrative wine with the elegant reticence of a fine Barsac. Yet it does not lack richness or staying power, and vintages from the 1920s remain fresh and even youthful. The 1988 wine has lovely citrus and apricot aromas, and a richness on the palate cut by a tangy acidity and leading to a spicy, persistent finish. **SBr**
☉☉☉ **Drink: to 2018+**

Vertical wine presses, installed in the 1920s, are still used at Coutet. ➔

Lucien Crochet
Sancerre Cuvée Prestige 2002

Origin France, Loire, Sancerre
Style Dry white wine, 13% ABV
Grape Sauvignon Blanc

As recently as the 1960s, Sancerre had no sort of reputation either outside or within France. Sauvignon of the eastern Loire made the sort of crisp, dry white that was good for drinking with simple, rustic country cooking, chunky pâtés, and freshwater fish. All very refreshing, but you would not number it among the ranks of the exalted.

The establishment of Sancerre as a wine of note dates from a sudden obsession with it among Parisian commentators. Its expression of Sauvignon Blanc was seen to be, from the best sites, so purely, austerely flinty, steely, hard, and unyielding that it was hard to mistake it for anything else. And indeed, when on song, it cries shame on those who still resist numbering this variety among the top division.

The Lucien Crochet estate is the happy product of a marriage of the Crochet family with that of the Picards, whose roots in the appellation reach back to the eighteenth century. Crochet's Cuvée Prestige is sourced from an old plot of low-yielding, gnarled vinestock. About 10 percent of each vintage is fermented in barrel, which does not turn the wine inaptly into anything other than its steely Sauvignon self, but serves to emphasize the note of fugitive smokiness that Sancerre often derives from its soils. In 2002, this sector of the Loire had a rather better vintage than much of the rest of France. The Sauvignon ripened well, and the result is a wine that combines almost indecently rich, peach and apricot fruit with the diamondlike core of disciplined acidity that will help such a concentrated wine to age. **SW**

Ⓢ Ⓢ Ⓢ **Drink: to 2017**

Marisa Cuomo *Costa d'Amalfi*
Furore Bianco Fiorduva 2011

Origin Italy, Campania, Amalfi Coast
Style Dry white wine, 13.5% ABV
Grapes Ripoli 40%, Fenile 30%, Ginestra 30%

Fiorduva is an "extreme" wine. The terraced vineyards that face the Mediterranean Sea on this beautiful stretch of coastline have been forcefully established on the inhospitable sides of its high and steep cliffs, and working them takes exceptional dedication and passion. Fiorduva belongs not only to the Costa d'Amalfi DOC, recognized in 1995, but also to one of its three tiny subzones, Furore, which has relatively restrictive DOC regulations.

The vineyards are planted at a density of 2,430 plants per acre, at an altitude that ranges from 660 to 1,640 feet (200–500 m) above sea level, trained with a special locally developed pergola system that allows them to grow on the steepest surfaces. Needless to say, in these vineyards even the simplest operation needs to be done by hand. The grapes used for Fiorduva must be very ripe and harvested toward the end of October, so that they enjoy the long southern Italian summer with direct sunlight, but also the light that is reflected back off the sea. The cool night breeze is essential for the preservation of the acidity and the aromas.

After harvest, the grapes are softly pressed. The free-run juice is allowed to settle, then fermented in barriques for three months. The wine that results from all this hard work rewards the imbiber with a full, golden-yellow color, and aromas of mangoes, ripe apricots, and yellow flowers. On the palate, the wine is dry, very full-bodied, and densely textured, while somehow managing to be elegant and fine at the same time. **AS**

Ⓢ Ⓢ Ⓢ **Drink: recent vintages for up to 10 years**

A pergola supports Fenile grapes at Marisa Cuomo's Furore vineyard. ➋

CVNE *Corona Reserva Blanco Semi Dulce* 1939

Origin Spain, Rioja
Style Off-dry white wine, 12.5% ABV
Grape Viura

Although the Spanish Civil War was declared by Franco to be at an end after the surrender of the Republicans on April 1, 1939, Spain was still in pandemonium by the autumn. In the Rioja region, harvesting was at the back of people's minds, and thus many grapes were left hanging on the vine, becoming affected by botrytis, until somebody could pick them. This Corona Reserva is probably made from botrytis-affected Viura, with some Malvasia and Macabeo, although nobody seems to know (or care). It was left aging in wooden casks for more than thirty years until it was "rediscovered" in the early 1970s and finally bottled, with only 1,000 or so bottles produced.

The beautiful golden amber color of this wine immediately suggests "sweet," though *semi dulce*—as declared on the label—turns out to be an accurate description. The nose displays very complex, honeyed, nutty, burned aromas, not unlike those of an Amontillado Sherry, though there is also a faint hint of oxidation, too. At more than sixty-five years of age, this wine retains searing acidity, which suggests that it is probably a bit sweeter than *semi dulce*—though with all that acidity, the impression is indeed of an off-dry palate. The length is astonishing, lingering like Don Quixote's dreams of Dulcinea. Such combined sweetness, acidity, and oxidation is an acquired taste, but this is surely one of Spain's greatest white wines. Corona Reserva is still made by CVNE, albeit released only in 50-cl bottles. **SG**

🜚🜚🜚🜚 **Drink: to 2019**

FURTHER RECOMMENDATIONS
Other great white Rioja vintages
1922 • 1934 • 1952 • 1955 • 1958 • 1964 • 1982
More wines from the same producer
Imperial Gran Reserva Rioja, Monopole Rioja Blanco, Viña Real Gran Reserva Rioja, Reserva Contino

Isolated hills topped by churches are characteristic of the Rioja region. ➡

Dom. Darviot-Perrin *Chassagne-Montrachet PC Blanchots-Dessus* 2002

Origin France, Burgundy, Côte de Beaune
Style Dry white wine, 13% ABV
Grape Chardonnay

Dom. René & Vincent Dauvissat *Chablis GC Les Clos* 1996

Origin France, Burgundy, Chablis
Style Dry white wine, 13% ABV
Grape Chardonnay

At the southern end of Montrachet there is a fault in the rock. A mere 8 feet (2.5 m) lower down lies the 3.26-acre (1.32 ha) *climat* of Les Blanchots-Dessus. This is about as close as you can get with the Chardonnay grape without being grand cru. Among the leading proprietors here are the Darviot-Perrins, a husband-and-wife team based in Monthélie.

Most of the land has been inherited through Geneviève Darviot (*née* Perrin), and the holdings that she and Didier Darviot now exploit have been increased over the years. Papa Perrin rented out much of his estate on a sharecropping basis as he grew older, but this has ended and use of the vines has reverted to the Darviot-Perrins. They have bottled wine under their own name only since 1989, which explains why they are relatively little known.

Darviot learned much from his father-in-law, a talented grower and winemaker, and makes wines that are minerally very pure. They can be a little austere in their youth, needing time to come round. This 2002 is probably his best yet, the most concentrated and most elegant, and will improve while on its plateau for at least another decade. **CC**
❻❻❻❻ **Drink: to 2020**

This estate is considered by many to be the highest-achieving in Chablis. Established in the 1920s by Robert Dauvissat, the estate comprises 27 acres (11 ha), embracing a pair of grands crus (Les Clos and Les Preuses) and three premiers crus (Sêchet, La Forest, and Vaillons). Meagre yields result in wines that are truly expressive of their provenance. The core of the wines is chalky-dry and mineral-pure, and they age in the bottle with all the stately grace one looks for in great Chablis.

The 4.25 acres (1.7 ha) of Les Clos owned by the estate were planted in 1960. The vineyard sits, like the other grands crus, on Kimmeridgian limestone-marl soils, a little to the northeast of the village of Chablis itself. The 1996 vintage produced the best wines in Chablis since 1990. Their concentration is awe-inspiring, and the best, as here, display a miraculous balance of disciplined acidity with layers of opulent fruit. The oak lends a touch of cinnamon spice to the ripe, appley core of this wine, while the first flush of maturity brings out the excitingly pungent, buttered-leek character that makes mature Chablis so appetizing. **SW**
❻❻❻❻ **Drink: to 2018+**

De Bartoli
Grappoli del Grillo 2009

Origin Italy, Sicily, Marsala
Style Dry white wine, 13% ABV
Grape Grillo

For centuries, Grillo has been in thrall to cheap Marsala, a fortified wine destined for cooking as much as for drinking. Marco De Bartoli, having proven that he could make exceptional unfortified "Marsala," expressive of his patch of Sicily rather than of an impersonal winery, wanted a greater challenge. In 1990, he set out to make a still white wine from what most considered a workhorse variety, and the result was Grappoli del Grillo.

Closer to Bodrum than to Brussels, the De Bartoli vineyards are often swept by a North African scirroco. In this milieu, one might expect Grappoli del Grillo to evoke the Mediterranean, but this wine defies all boundaries. It has a purity, electric acidity, and complexity often associated with noble grapes of fêted Northern European provenances. At a landmark tasting of Italian white wines at *The World of Fine Wine* magazine, the panelists were unanimous that it left the other wines in its wake. It was savory, nutty, Sherry-like, salty, volatile, sappy, aromatic, perfumed, audacious, peachy, smoky, and remarkably balanced and coherent. A great wine, then, but one possessing an enigma that only certain great wines achieve. **AE**
◑◑ **Drink: to 2017+**

De Bortoli
Noble One 1982

Origin Australia, New South Wales, Hunter Valley
Style Sweet white wine, 13% ABV
Grape Sémillon

Darren De Bortoli was still at Roseworthy Agricultural College when he decided to experiment at his family's winery with botrytis-affected grapes after the 1982 Australian vintage. There was a surplus of Sémillon grapes that year, and many had been infected by botrytis. The wine created an immediate sensation, winning many trophies and medals, both in Australia and overseas, and is still made today.

As its faux Château d'Yquem label implies, Noble One is made in the image of the classic French sweet wine Sauternes, though there are differences. Top Sauternes typically spends two years in oak barrels, but Noble One is matured in barrel for a maximum of twelve months. Since 2002, a portion of unoaked wine has been added to the final blend, to give greater freshness. In Sauternes, the wine is usually a blend of Sémillon and Sauvignon Blanc, but only Sémillon is used for Noble One.

Noble One has intense honeyed apricot aromas, with a luscious and richly viscous palate, but always balanced by crisp and clean acidity. And it is always tooth-rottingly sweet. It is the only dessert wine in Langton's Classification of Australian Wines. **SG**
◑◑◑◑ **Drink: to 2017+**

Domaine Marcel Deiss
Altenberg de Bergheim 2002

Origin France, Alsace
Style Off-dry white wine, 11.5% ABV
Grapes Riesling, Gewürztraminer, Pinot Gris

Established after World War II, Domaine Marcel Deiss currently consists of 64 acres (26 ha) spread over numerous sites. After a number of years working organically, Deiss went biodynamic in 1998.

Deiss believes strongly in terroir and, although varietal wines are the rule in Alsace, he makes field blends of different varieties from the top vineyard sites in accordance with an older tradition. In the winery, the grapes are pressed slowly using whole bunches. Because no nitrogen is put on to the vines, fermentation can take anything between three weeks and a year to complete. At the end the wine is cooled and a little sulfur dioxide is added.

The Altenberg de Bergheim 2002, Deiss's top wine, is predominantly Riesling but with Gewürztraminer and Pinot Gris from Grand Cru Altenberg. A remarkable expression of this site, it combines a high level of residual sugar (100 g/l) with incredible minerality and high acidity. It finishes off-dry, but because of the acidity tastes less sweet than the level of sugar would suggest. The profundity of this wine vindicates the terroir-driven approach that Deiss is taking. **JG**

🍷🍷🍷 Drink: to 2020+

Schlossgut Diel *Dorsheimer*
Goldloch Riesling Spätlese 2006

Origin Germany, Nahe
Style Off-dry white wine, 9% ABV
Grape Riesling

Of Armin Diel's three grands crus—Goldloch, Burgberg, and Pittermännchen—Goldloch is his personal favorite. "All of us Mosel lovers prefer the Pittermännchen," he says, "but Goldloch has no equivalent." And he is right: Goldloch is resplendently rococo in its waves of juicy summer fruits, yet there is also a baroque spine of firmness and a structural logic that prevents the wines from collapsing beneath their seductiveness.

Goldloch is also the pick of the three crus in its ability to shine in various styles. Some of the greatest dry German Rieslings ever made have been Diel's recent Grosses Gewächs from Goldloch, and even the lightest Kabinett wines from classic vintages like 1997, 2002, and 2004 are fetching and curvaceous.

The Spätlese 2006 is a very great German Riesling, with a deliciously old-school touch from aging in a not entirely neutral cask. Suffice to say, drinkers will find as many fruit nuances as they care to search for, but wines like this are not about the number of associations we can string together. They are about the swoon and the silence that arrive in the presence of earthly perfection. **TT**

🍷🍷🍷 Drink: 2016–2026

Bold lettering on a rendered wall announces the grand cru vineyard. ⏎

Disznókő

Tokaji Aszú 6 Puttonyos 1999

Origin Hungary, Tokaj
Style Sweet white wine, 12% ABV
Grapes Furmint, Hárslevelű

Disznókő means "Rock of the Wild Boar." The rock lies next to an odd Tuscan temple at the summit of the domaine. The estate was already a classed growth in the list drawn up by Mátyás Bél in 1730. The French insurance giant Axa bought the land around the famous Sárga Borház (Yellow Wine House) in 1992.

Unlike many Tokaj estates, Disznókő is just one 240-acre (100 ha) block. The soil is a mixture of rhyolite and tufa. Until recently, the 6 Puttonyos wine was the gold standard at Disznókő, but a few years ago the decision was taken to sell Kapi as a separate cru, so that it is now undersold and overtrumped.

The wines are released when they are three years old. The most frequently aired criticism of the wines is that they look to France and are too reminiscent of Sauternes. The 1999 was the best 6 Puttonyos wine made at Disznókő since 1993. It had 170 g/l of residual sugar, and 12 g/l acidity. The wine has a little whiff of white truffles and tastes of pineapple and apricots. The slightest hint of frost in the nostrils points to a late-picked vintage. It has beautiful length and structure, to some extent due to a high proportion of Hárslevelű. **GM**

🎗🎗🎗🎗 **Drink: to 2020+**

Château Doisy-Daëne

2001

Origin France, Bordeaux, Barsac
Style Sweet white wine, 14% ABV
Grape Sémillon

Doisy-Daëne is owned by the Dubourdieu family. Son Denis, the winemaker, has been one of the leaders of the quality upheaval that began to overtake dry white Bordeaux from the late 1980s onward, and this excellent Barsac demonstrates his pitch-perfect proficiency with Sauternes, too.

The vineyard encompasses around 37 acres (15 ha) of sandy, clay soil on the region's limestone bedrock. Up to half a dozen passes through the vineyard are typical for the sake of premium selection, and the resulting syrup-sweet juice is given a slow fermentation, followed by three months in barrel during the winter (in new oak), before a further year's maturation in vat. This reduces the amount of sulfur dioxide needed at bottling.

The benchmark profile of Doisy-Daëne is thus a lighter style of Barsac. In the 2001 vintage, however, it is, in common with its neighbors, a sensational wine that will take decades of aging in its stride. There is an oiliness to the texture, allied to magical aromas and flavors of juicy apricots, lime zest, and honey-roasted cashews, kept in disciplinary check by balancing and bracing pineapley acids. **SW**

🎗🎗🎗 **Drink: to 2050+**

◀ Disnókő commissioned this famous garage for its vineyard tractors.

Donnafugata

Ben Ryé 2005

Origin Italy, Sicily, Pantelleria
Style Sweet white wine, 14.5% ABV
Grape Zibibbo

The Donnafugata winery was founded in 1983, long before the days of the Sicilian and the Italian wine renaissance. The prime movers were Giacomo and Gabriella Rallo, using grapes only from vineyards in Contessa Entellina. A few years later the Rallos extended their venture to the island of Pantelleria, halfway between Sicily and the African continent. On this small, windswept island they bought a vineyard planted with Zibibbo, a clone of the Muscat grape, and trained it in the bush system, pruned very short. The vines are actually planted in holes dug in the earth, and each is protected by a small, drystone wall, to shelter it from the fierce, constant winds. These Zibibbo grapes are what the Rallos use to produce Ben Ryé, which in Arabic means "son of the wind."

The grapes come from eleven different plots on the island, all harvested separately and at different times. Some of the grapes are left to dry for four to five weeks, and the rest are used fresh. The resulting blend is a wine that has all the opulent richness of the island's sun yet manages to retain a surprising freshness. The color is a rich amber gold, and the nose is enthralling, with heady notes of dried apricots, honey, and Mediterranean bush, followed by hints of mushrooms and dried herbs. On the palate, it seems to linger for minutes, showing for all its length a perfect balance between body, sweetness, and acidity. **AS**
🍷🍷 **Drink: to 2025+**

Vines grow near Pantelleria's volcanic lake, the Mirror of Venus. ➡

Hermann Dönnhoff
Oberhäuser Brücke Riesling AG 2003

Origin Germany, Nahe
Style Sweet white wine, 8% ABV
Grape Riesling

Domaine Droin
Chablis Grand Cru Les Clos 2005

Origin France, Burgundy, Chablis
Style Dry white wine, 13.5% ABV
Grape Chardonnay

In 1931, Hermann Dönnhoff bought this small site on the so-called Luitpoldbrücke, the bridge that connected the former Bavarian Oberhausen with the former Prussian Niederhausen over the Nahe River, and he planted Riesling vines here. Very early on, the outstanding potential of this vineyard for growing delicately sweet wines was recognized. At only 2.7 acres (1.1 ha), Oberhäuser Brücke is the smallest officially registered single vineyard in Germany.

Thanks to its sheltered position on the river banks, it enjoys an early flowering and the long, slow ripening that is ideal for top-quality Riesling. The special soil formation, a gray slate subsoil covered with loess clay, guarantees an adequate supply of water even in dry years. In warm autumns, the moisture coming from the Nahe creates perfect conditions for the development of noble rot, whereas the shelter of the valley often makes superb Icewines possible as well. In 2003, however, a brilliant, crystal-clear, and densely interwoven Riesling Auslese was produced here. This gold-capped wine is counted among the most sought-after German wines of this exceptional vintage. **FK**
◯◯◯◯◯ Drink: to 2025

The seven grand cru *climats* of Chablis occupy just 3 percent of the total surface planted in the zone. Les Clos is probably the most highly esteemed and is often the weightiest of them all, with great richness but also a raciness that keeps it from being leaden.

Jean-Paul Droin cultivates 60 acres (24 ha) and made his name in the 1980s with exceptionally concentrated and powerful wines. They were quite controversial thanks to the use of a high proportion of new oak, especially for his grands crus. Since the early 2000s, his son, Benoit, has moderated the oak by aging half the cru wines in tank, while the remainder are aged in about 15 percent new oak.

The 2005 is a brilliant wine and an exemplary Les Clos. There is a stoniness on the nose that probably derives from the heavy limestone content of the soil, as well as richness and spiciness, qualities also reflected on the palate. Here there is genuine power and weight, but all in perfect harmony with a racy acidity that gives tremendous persistence of flavor. As a young wine it is surprisingly accessible for Les Clos, but its structure and balance surely guarantee it a long and interesting life. **SBr**
◯◯◯ Drink: to 2020

Joseph Drouhin
Beaune PC Clos des Mouches 1999

Origin France, Burgundy, Côte de Beaune
Style Dry white wine, 13.5% ABV
Grape Chardonnay

Much of the Beaune vineyard is owned by the Beaune *négoces*. The firm of Joseph Drouhin started to buy up land after World War I—in the 1920s prices were very depressed and many small landholdings had lost their menfolk. The first land Maurice Drouhin, son of the original Joseph, bought was a 34-acre (13.7 ha) parcel of Beaune, Clos des Mouches, designated premier cru in 1936. The vineyard lies upslope at the southern end of the commune, on the Pommard border.

Such is the renown of the wine that many people believe this to be a Drouhin monopoly, but there are at least four other proprietors in the same vineyard. However, the Drouhins have just over 50 percent of the land. The Chardonnay is planted upslope, where the soil is shallow, simply limestone debris over limestone rock. On the richer terrain further down is Pinot Noir, in much greater quantities. White Beaunes are quite different from Meursaults or other more classic white Burgundies. They have a spice, and a different sort of weight. Drouhin's Clos des Mouches is the best there is, and this full, luscious, plump 1999 is a most successful example. **CC**

🥂🥂🥂🥂 Drink: to 2019

Joseph Drouhin/Marquis de Laguiche *Montrachet GC* 2002

Origin France, Burgundy, Côte de Beaune
Style Dry white wine, 13% ABV
Grape Chardonnay

Montrachet is the greatest Chardonnay vineyard in the world. This 20-acre (8 ha) *climat* straddles the communes of Puligny and Chassagne, and the largest section belongs to the Marquis de Laguiche family. At 5.09 acres (2.06 ha), it represents over a quarter of the grand cru. Since 1947 the wine has been made by Maison Joseph Drouhin.

What is so special about Montrachet? Aspect and drainage, say the locals. But there is also active limestone—less so than in Chevalier above, but more so than in Bâtard below. There is some clay—more than in Chevalier, less than in Bâtard. There is chromium for effective fruit-setting; zinc for reducing the acidity and increasing the sugar richness; cobalt, speeding up the maturity; iron, of course; magnesium and lead; and even silver.

Drouhin are expert wine-makers. A troop of harvesters with a profound knowledge of the vines can be wheeled in at exactly the correct time, after which the wine is very largely allowed to make itself. The 2002 is a wine awe-inspiringly perfect from start to finish. It is full-bodied, concentrated, rich, profound, and elegant: Chardonnay at its best. **CC**

🥂🥂🥂🥂🥂 Drink: 2030+

Dry River *Pinot Gris* 2010

Origin New Zealand, Martinborough
Style Dry white wine, 14% ABV
Grape Pinot Gris

PINOT GRIS

2010

DRY RIVER

Martinborough

No.3436

WINE OF NEW ZEALAND
D R WINES LTD, PURUATANGA RD, MARTIN...

Having acquired a taste for fine wine while studying at Oxford University in the 1970s, Neil McCallum returned to his homeland and in 1979 planted a vineyard a few miles from Dyerville in a very dry and free-draining area now called the Martinborough Terrace. Other Martinborough pioneers planted Chardonnay, Cabernet Sauvignon, and Pinot Noir, but McCallum had fond memories of great wines from Alsace that he had drunk, and planted Gewürztraminer, Riesling, and Pinot Gris.

First made in 1986, Dry River remains the benchmark New Zealand Pinot Gris, and the only wine of that country that is able to stand alongside the finest examples from Alsace and northeast Italy. Although often high in alcohol (up to 14 percent), it has intense, lush (and completely unoaked) flavors, supported by a remarkable balancing act of sugar and acid. The very crisp acidity is perfectly matched by the slight sweetness of the wine, giving the impression of dryness. The plump fruit and strong acidic backbone mean that the wine can be aged for up to ten years.

McCallum partly attributes the excellence of his wine to the clone of Pinot Gris that he grows, which was originally imported into New Zealand by the Mission in 1886 and produces small crops of tiny bunches with very small berries. This is an example of his meticulous attention to detail in the vineyard and winery, and among the reasons why Dry River is arguably New Zealand's finest producer. **SG**

ᎾᎾᎾ **Drink: recent vintages for up to 10 years**

FURTHER RECOMMENDATIONS
Other great vintages
1999 · 2000 · 2001 · 2002 · 2003 · 2005 · 2008
More wines from the same producer
Chardonnay Amaranth · Gewürztraminer · Pinot Noir
Late-Harvest Riesling · Syrah · Sauvignon Blanc

Vineyards on the Martinborough Terrace benefit from gravelly terrain. ➡

Mme. Aly Duhr et Fils
Ahn Palmberg Riesling 2005

Origin Luxembourg, Moselle Luxembourgeoise
Style Dry white wine, 12.5% ABV
Grape Riesling

Domaine Dupasquier
Marestel Roussette de Savoie 2004

Origin France, Savoy
Style Dry white wine, 13% ABV
Grape Altesse

The history of this family-owned estate dates from 1872. The 20.5 acres (8.3 ha) of vines are planted on the best hills of Ahn, Wormeldange, Machtum, Grevenmacher, and Mertert. The wines range from the Aly Duhr Grand Premier Cru Riesling, crisp, lean, and refreshing, to the Monsalvat Vin de Table de Luxembourg, the winery's "white Burgundy."

Aly Duhr's Palmberg vineyard enjoys a southern exposition in the Moselle Luxembourgeoise. The soil is chalky limestone, which may explain the beautiful minerality in the Riesling grown here. At the same time, Palmberg is known for its almost Mediterranean climate, and is home to insects and plants, such as orchids, that are normally found only in more southerly regions.

The Palmberg Riesling 2005 is a bright golden color. On the nose are deep aromas of ripe apricot and sweet honey, whereas on the palate the wine is very elegant and fresh, with crisp but delicate acidity and good length. An aromatic, dry Riesling, the wine has a slightly oily texture that makes it beautiful to enjoy in its youth, but it also has the potential to age for at least ten to twelve years. **CK**

🚫🚫 **Drink: to 2017+**

Domaine Dupasquier's cellars are in the hamlet of Aimavigne, part of the commune of Jongieux, which lies beneath an impressive mountain, le Mont Charvin. From Dupasquier's backyard you can walk straight up into Jongieux's most famous vineyard, Marestel, a *cru* designated exclusively for Roussette de Savoie wines from the Altesse grape.

Here, Altesse produces wines naturally high in sugar and acidity. Noël Dupasquier's vines are up to 100 years old, and he picks late when the grapes are overripe, usually with noble rot, as mist is a regular feature in this mountain bowl. In recent years potential alcohol of 13 percent has been easily reached, the slow fermentation often continuing in meticulously maintained old *foudres* until January.

The 2004 Marestel is built for very long aging. The nose is stony and citrussy at first, with a white peach character evolving over time. Dry and full-bodied, it has a nervy, applelike acidity (though there is a partial malolactic), and some spice leading to a mineral character on the finish. A classic partner for the local lake fish Omble Chevalier, or Féra, it also matches mature Beaufort cheese perfectly. **WL**

🚫 **Drink: to 2025**

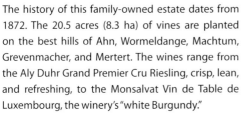

◀ The Moselle is part of Luxembourg's eastern border with Germany.

Dutton Goldfield
Rued Vineyard Chardonnay 2005

Origin USA, California, Sonoma Valley
Style Dry white wine, 13.5% ABV
Grape Chardonnay

Warren Dutton broke ground in the 1960s, planting Chardonnay and Pinot Noir in areas believed to be too cold for quality wine growing. Today the Dutton Ranch includes more than sixty different parcels in the Russian River Valley; the Rued Vineyard, planted to Chardonnay in 1969, is an east-facing hillside in the middle of the Green Valley. Dutton planted here an offshoot of an old Wente clone, which produces exotic and distinctive high-toned fruit characteristics, along with a rich mouthfeel. Now Warren's son Steve and his partner/winemaker Dan Goldfield produce single-vineyard wines that convey the distinctive qualities of each site. The two men have worked together since 1990 (Dutton-Goldfield was founded in 1998).

Dan picks to retain a firm fruit/acid balance, and ferments in French oak barrels where the wines undergo 100 percent malolactic to round out the wine. Supple on the palate, the Rued Vineyard Chardonnay 2005 has succulent yellow fruit and floral notes, with well-integrated oak and a surreptitious structure supporting length and persistence on the palate. **LGr**

🍷🍷 **Drink: to 2017**

Dom. de l'Ecu *Muscadet S. & M.*
Expression d'Orthogneiss 2010

Origin France, Loire, Nantais
Style Dry white wine, 12% ABV
Grape Melon de Bourgogne

Muscadet is one of France's most maligned white wines, enduring the combination of a trickily wet and heavy terroir in the western Loire Valley and a supposedly dull grape, Melon de Bourgogne. In the hands of Guy Bossard, however, the wines deliver both the capacity to age and terroir-driven, mineral-rich flavors. Possibly this is because Bossard plows his oldest vines by horse instead of using soil-compacting tractors, to allow the vine roots a fuller expression; or because Bossard's biodynamic beliefs mean he prunes and picks according to cosmic and earthly rhythms and sprays his vines with teas infused with herbs, minerals, and animal manures. The wine is Demeter-certified biodynamic.

In 2002 Bossard stopped making a blend called Hermine d'Or from his best plots, and instead made three terroir-based cuvées named after their respective soil types—Granite, Gneiss, and Orthogneiss. Of these, the Orthogneiss, named after a granite that formed from the earth's molten core, is the most expressive, if you can wait upward of five years for its flavors of dried fruit and bitter almond to unfold into mineral notes of wet stone. **MW**

🍷🍷 **Drink: recent vintages for up to 8 years**

Visitors to Domaine de l'Ecu are met by this charming grape harvester. ➡

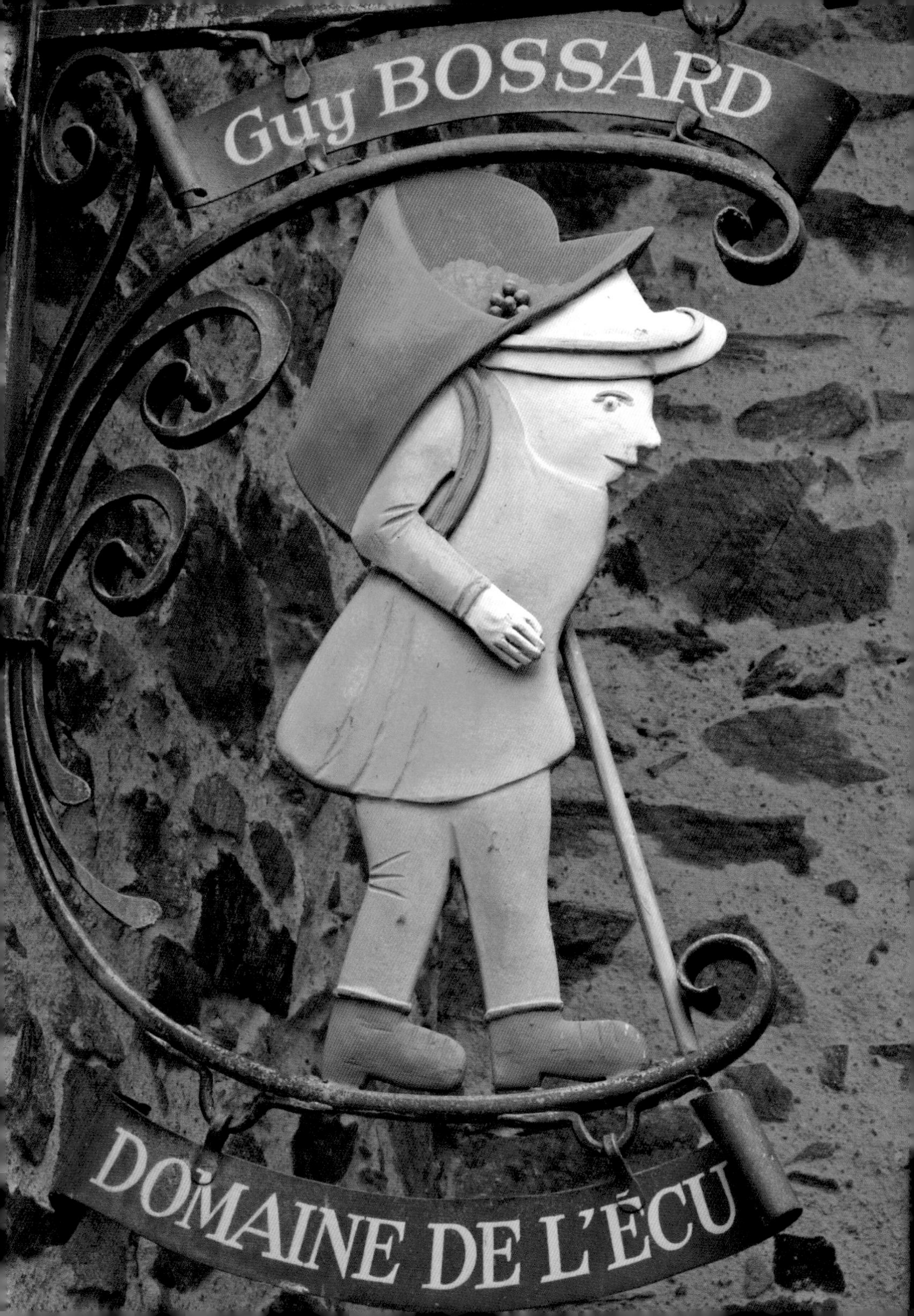
Guy BOSSARD
DOMAINE DE L'ÉCU

Emrich-Schönleber *Monzinger Halenberg Riesling Eiswein* 2002

Origin Germany, Nahe
Style Sweet white wine, 7% ABV
Grape Riesling

Château de Fargues 1997

Origin France, Bordeaux, Sauternes
Style Sweet white wine, 13.5% ABV
Grapes Sémillon 80%, Sauvignon Blanc 20%

Monzinger wine has enjoyed an outstanding reputation in the Nahe growing area for centuries. In the eighteenth century, the Rheinische Antiquarius (a detailed description of the Rhine and its tributaries) told of 500 bottles of wine from this village that were shipped to East India. The captain brought three of the bottles back home with him, and even though the wine had crossed the equator four times, it was said still to be of pristine quality.

More recently, the Icewines of this region have also gained an exalted reputation. It became clear that the vineyards on the upper reaches of the River Nahe, which drains into the Rhine valley, are predestined to produce this special type of wine. The reason is that the ripening of the grapes occurs roughly eight to ten days later than in the Rhine Rift, and therefore in cooler temperatures.

The 2002 vintage has achieved an almost ethereal, transcendental finesse. The *Gault Millau Wine Guide* awarded it the highest possible mark of 100 points and raved: "A magnificent firework of tropical fruits . . . crystal-clear like glacial water, perfection, not to be outdone." **FK**

❸❸❸❸❸ Drink: to 2040+

With just 30 acres (12 ha) of vineyards next to a ruined castle and a typical production of only 1,000 cases per vintage, this Lur-Saluces-owned Sauternes estate is all too rarely seen. As with its big brother, Yquem, immense care is taken throughout the winemaking process, including fermentation and maturation in 100 percent new oak. Often the yield is lower than that of Yquem. The wine is luscious and elegant, but very different from Yquem—the vineyards lie on heavier soil, with more clay. They are prone to frost, and there is a high failure rate.

Only fifteen barrels, or 4,500 bottles, were made in 1997. The lovely golden color precedes a toasty and grapey nose of pronounced noble rot character. Rich and honeyed, with good acidity, though perhaps lacking the "cut" of truly great years like 1989 or 1990. Excellent balance and concentration, finishing clean and very long. Although unclassified, and sometimes cruelly dubbed "the poor man's Yquem," de Fargues can be more expensive than Premier Cru Classé Sauternes such as Rieussec. On this performance, it more than justifies its price, which is usually one-third that of Yquem. **SG**

❸❸❸❸❸ Drink: to 2020+

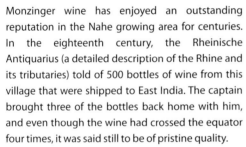

◀ The steep Monzinger Halenberg vineyard is the smallest in the area.

Feiler-Artinger
Ruster Ausbruch Pinot Cuvée 2004

Origin Austria, Burgenland, Neusiedlersee-Hügelland
Style Sweet white wine, 11.5% ABV
Grapes Pinot Blanc 75%, Pinot Gris 25%

The village of Rust became a free city in 1681 thanks to the purchasing power of its botrytized Ausbruch (Aszú), harvested along the western shores of the Neusiedlersee. Meanwhile, at the other end of the Hungarian kingdom, Tokaji Aszú was also being born.

Today, a welter of baroque houses testifies to Rust's former wealth, and none more opulently or colorfully than that of the family Feiler. The Feilers have been known for a century as town fathers and sometimes mayors of Rust, but fame as vintners did not come for any of today's Rust growers until the 1980s. Hans Feiler was among the first to reach that status. Son Kurt now takes the lead, and red wine from Blaufränkisch and the Bordeaux varieties shares center stage with Ausbruch.

In certain vintages, an Ausbruch is essayed from members of the Pinot family (occasionally including that Austrian native, Neuburger). Like most Feiler-Artinger Ausbrüche, the Pinot Cuvée 2004 is fermented in largely new French barriques. Its caramel, butterscotch, nut brittle, and tropical fruit notes one might find in great Sauternes. But here we have a wine of modest alcohol, harboring a vibrant, juicy seam of fresh pit fruits and citrus, baroque in its sensuality and intricacy, intensely sweet, and yet uplifting and refreshing.

Picking in this vintage of variable weather could not take place until November, and then with marvelous concentration and a vibrant core of acids, but at the price of tiny yields. Find the time to savor this "slow wine," solo and sans souci. **DS**

🍷🍷🍷 **Drink: to 2020**

Livio Felluga
Picolit 2007

Origin Italy, Friuli
Style Sweet white wine, 13.5% ABV
Grape Picolit

The Felluga story started in Istria, now in Croatia, but then still part of the Austro-Hungarian Empire. In 1920, Giovanni Felluga was dispatched to manage the family's wine interests in Grado, the seaside resort of the Hapsburg aristocracy. The estate's beautiful wine label that portrays Friuli's hills was created in 1956. Today, the Livio Felluga estate has 360 hillside acres (146 ha) under vine. Annual production averages 650,000 bottles, which are exported all over the world.

Picolit is a Felluga specialty and one of the few genuinely Friulano varieties, with probably less than 74 acres (30 ha) planted in total in Friuli. It is only since 1750, thanks to the writings of the teetotal Count Fabio Asquini, that there is any accurate documentation of Picolit's origins. Some estates base their production of Picolit on these notes. The wine was fashionable and sought-after in the eighteenth century, and Asquini exported 100,000 bottles to courts all over Europe.

The peculiarity of this odd, delicate vine is the small, or *piccoli*, fertilization of its flowers, called "floral abortion" by some. This means that only a few, very concentrated berries ripen in each bunch. Grapes are harvested late in October and then left to dry and raisin on mats before pressing. Although sweet, it is not luscious, and its natural acidity prevents the sweetness from becoming cloying. Although it can be drunk with fruit or desserts, Picolit is best enjoyed as a *vino da meditazione*, a wine to be sipped on its own. **SG**

🍷🍷🍷🍷 **Drink: to 2019+**

The Picolit label follows the traditional Livio Felluga map design. ➡

Livio Felluga®

Picolit

Ciseriis
Sedilis
Chialininis
Romeais
Ramanddo
Nimis
Attimis
Platischis
Qualso
Savorgnano
Ravosa
Gugliano
Torreano
Orsaria
B. Vida
Cividale del Friuli
Spessa
Oleis
R. Bernarda
Buttrio
R. di Manzano
Rosazzo
Vidnale

2005

Benito Ferrara
Greco di Tufo Vigna Cicogna 2005

Origin Italy, Campania, Irpinia
Style Dry white wine, 13.5% ABV
Grape Greco di Tufo

This is one of the great southern Italian wines, full of character, originality, and guts. The Benito Ferrara estate—founded in 1880 in the small town of Tufo and run today by Gabriella Ferrara—is one of the very few that takes the trouble to showcase Greco di Tufo, by producing a single-vineyard bottling from the exceptional Cru Vigna Cicogna.

The grapes are harvested at full ripeness and, after pressing, the free-run juice is left to ferment for about one month in temperature-controlled stainless steel vats. After a brief stay in the vats, the wine is bottled and given a further six months of aging prior to its release onto the market.

Something that most Italian aficionados overlook is that the best white wines from Irpinia (especially those made from Greco and Fiano) seem to perform much better in the glass after twelve to fifteen months of bottle age. Before that, these wines seem to go through a "dumb" phase, during which they are nicely textured on the palate but not very expressive on the nose. Those who are lucky enough to possess these wines are well advised to allow them the bottle age they require.

The Vigna Cicogna 2005 has a deep straw-yellow color that might scare many people off at first. Ditch your suspicions and put your nose into the glass—a delicately floral welcoming note is only the prologue to a feast of ripe peaches and Mediterranean herbs. On the palate the wine is full yet soft and velvety, maybe slightly more powerful than elegant, but nevertheless richly satisfying. **AS**

🥂🥂 **Drink: to 2017+**

Do Ferreiro
Cepas Vellas Albariño 2010

Origin Spain, Galicia, Rías Baixas
Style Dry white wine, 13% ABV
Grape Albariño

Bodega Gerardo Méndez Lázaro, located in the Salnés Valley, produces the wines "of the blacksmith" (*do ferreiro* in Galician). They now rank among the most authentic in the Rías Baixas DO, alongside Fillaboa Selección Finca Monte Alto, Pazo de Señorans Selección de Añada, and Lusco do Miño Pazo Piñeiro. The regular cuvée (the plain Do Ferreiro Albariño label) comes from younger vines, averaging ten years of age, planted in vineyards recovered from hills once invaded by eucalyptus trees. The top cuvée, Do Ferreiro Cepas Vellas Albariño, is produced from a pre-phylloxera vineyard planted several generations ago. The house estimates that the vineyard is at least 200 years old.

Gerardo Méndez, owner and maker of these wines, says that his late grandmother (who died aged ninety-eight) told him that her own grandmother was familiar with the vineyard just as it appears today. These *cepas vellas* (old vines) are located in a plot of 5 acres (2 ha) near the family home. Anyone skeptical of their alleged age should make the trip to the beautiful Val do Salnés and see them for themselves. In the flesh, as it were, their reported age seems entirely credible.

The *cepas vellas* wine is aged on its lees for ten months in stainless steel vats, and released onto the market two years after the vintage date. Year in, year out, this is one of the great Albariños, difficult to find but released at very reasonable prices. It is another great affordable Spanish wine for those lucky or clever enough to find it. **JB**

🥂🥂 **Drink: recent vintages for up to 6 years**

◧ The town of Montefalcione overlooks the Benito Ferrara vines.

Feudi di San Gregorio
Fiano di Avellino 2012

Origin Italy, Campania, Irpinia
Style Dry white wine, 13.5% ABV
Grape Fiano

William Fèvre *Chablis GC*
Bougros Côte Bouguerots 2002

Origin France, Burgundy, Chablis
Style Dry white wine, 13% ABV
Grape Chardonnay

Below Avellino and the Naples–Bari *autostrada*, the Campanian region of Irpinia suffers earthquakes and broken roads. Yet optimism is being generated in this harsh place by Feudi di San Gregorio, a showpiece estate of contemporary viti-viniculture.

Feudi's most visibly successful wine is a dry white of character made from the Fiano grape. Throughout the south, this variety is winning medals at international trade competitions. But Fiano di Avellino is special because of ideal growing conditions. The geographical configuration of the area encourages a system of winds, good annual rainfall, and a special mesoclimate that differentiates it from other regions of Campania. Another boon is that the soil in the subzones of Candida, Parolise, and Sorbo Serpice is predominantly a volcanic clay.

In most vintages, the wine will typically have a pale, straw-yellow color and elegant scents of white fruits and flowers, ceding to mineral notes and an impression of resin, with a hint of honey. The wine has real presence in the mouth: full, structured, and harmonious, with a finale of ripe yellow orchard fruits such as pear and peach. **ME**

🍷🍷🍷 **Drink: recent vintages for up to 8 years**

The William Fèvre domaine is the most important in Chablis, not in total surface area, but in its possession of top vineyards: land in nearly all the grands crus and many of the best premiers crus. In 1998 William Fèvre sold the company, which is also a major *négociant*, to Henriot Champagne, along with a long lease on the 148-acre (60 ha) vineyard.

William Fèvre wines were concentrated, classy, and age-worthy. But those who associate Chablis with something pure, flinty, and austere criticized the Fèvre wines for being too oaky. Winemaker Didier Seguier, since his arrival under the new regime, has tamed this tendency, and the William Fèvre wines are now pleasing the Chablis purists.

The Clos des Bougerots lies in the best section of the grand cru Bougros. Most of Bougros, the most westerly of the great growths, faces more to the southwest than the southeast: the Côte does not. Normally a Bougros would not be as fine as a Valmur, a Vaudésir, or a Les Clos. But here we have a wine comparable with the very finest the area can produce. This 2002 is full, mineral, racy, and profound: everything a top Chablis should be. **CC**

🍷🍷🍷🍷 **Drink: to 2017+**

The distinctive William Fèvre trefoil insignia. ➡

Château Filhot 1990

Origin France, Bordeaux, Sauternes
Style Sweet white wine, 13.5% ABV
Grapes Sémillon 60%, S. Blanc 36%, Muscadelle 4%

Filhot, fringing the pine forests of the Landes, is the most southerly estate in Sauternes, and also one of the largest. The Filhot family established the vineyards in the early eighteenth century, and then built the handsome, spacious château, though the flanking pavilions date from the 1840s.

The Filhots perished under the guillotine in 1794 but the property was returned to the family subsequently. A Filhot heiress married the owner of Yquem in 1807, and he managed Château Filhot, expanding both the vineyards and the buildings. But later in the century the estate was increasingly neglected, and in 1935 the Marquis de Lur-Saluces sold Filhot to his sister, from whom the present owner, Comte Henri de Vaucelles, is descended.

The vineyards are cooler than most others in Sauternes, which may also explain why the wine sometimes lacks richness. The great vintages of the past, such as 1945, demonstrate the potential of the property, but the wines of the 1970s and 1980s, which were never barrel-aged, were disappointing.

Comte Henri's son Gabriel is now running Filhot, and the wines are cleaner and more concentrated, though still not fulfilling their potential. On the other hand, they are among the cheapest of the classified growths. The 1990 is one of the best Filhots of recent years, with aromas of stone fruits and pineapple; although it is not especially intense, it is stylish and does not lack length. Even better is the Crème de Tête bottling from 1990. **SBr**

🄢🄢🄢 **Drink: to 2020**

FURTHER RECOMMENDATIONS

Other great vintages

1976 • 1983 • 1989 • 1997 • 2001 • 2003 • 2007 • 2009

More Sauternes producers

Guiraud • Lafaurie-Peyraguey • Rieussec
Suduiraut • Yquem

Château Filhot, amid parkland landscaped by Louis-Bernard Fischer. ➡

Fillaboa
Seléccion Finca Monte Alto 2011

Origin Spain, Galicia, Rías Baixas
Style Dry white wine, 12.5% ABV
Grape Albariño

This house was founded as Granja Fillaboa in 1986, even before the creation of the DO Rías Baixas, of which it is therefore a founding member. The estate is a beautiful and comparatively large one (the largest in Pontevedra), located on the right bank of the River Miño, in Salvaterra. The winery was family-owned and managed for a long time, before its recent acquisition in 2000 by the Masaveu group. Of the more than 124 acres (50 ha) in production, Fillaboa Selección Finca Monte Alto comes from a small parcel of exceptional quality, planted in 1988.

One of the best examples of the longevity of top-quality Albariños, the wine normally undergoes phases of fruit freshness and aromatic intensity: There are still citrus, pear, aniseed, and herbal notes, but age also provides greater complexity, mineral emphasis, and overall balance. With bottle age, the ideal food and wine pairings change. While young, these wines suit the fresh flavors of simply cooked shellfish and white fish. After a few years in bottle, however, the wines shine with richer fish dishes. Any loss in aromatic exuberance is compensated by the gain in complexity and structure. **JB**

⊖⊖ **Drink: recent vintages for up to 7 years**

Fiorano
Sémillon Vino da Tavola 1978

Origin Italy, Lazio
Style Dry white wine, 11% ABV
Grape Sémillon

Described by Burton Anderson as "a secret shared by a few," the rare cult wines known as Fiorano continue to dazzle the lucky collectors who can get their hands on the last remaining bottles.

Alberico Boncompagni Ludovisi, Prince of Venosa, inherited the Fiorano estate in 1946 and planted local Malvasia along with French varieties, an unprecedented decision at the time; he also engaged the services of leading enologist Tancredi Biondi Santi. The wines were virtually unknown until the early 1960s, when the late Luigi Veronelli, attracted by the perfect vineyards on the Appia Antica outside Rome, eventually secured an invitation from the prince to taste the wines.

Veronelli would later compare the red Bordeaux blend with the great Sassicaia, but it was the 100 percent Sémillon, a variety that has never done particularly well in Italy, that most astounded Veronelli. Older Sémillon vintages continue to amaze with their shockingly youthful color, remarkable freshness, and seemingly infinite aging potential. The 1978 has a rich floral bouquet, with a lively, mineral-rich palate and incredible length. **KO**

⊖⊖⊖⊖ **Drink: to 2018**

◧ Vines are supported by low pergolas amid pine forest in Galicia.

Flowers *Camp Meeting Ridge Chardonnay* 2005

Origin USA, California, Sonoma Coast
Style Dry white wine, 14.2% ABV
Grape Chardonnay

In 1989 successful wholesale nursery owners Walt and Joan Flowers responded to a small advertisement in *Wine Spectator* and discovered Camp Meeting Ridge, an area not planted to vines but, as they discovered, with a temperate clime suitable for Chardonnay and Pinot Noir. Camp Meeting Ridge lies less than 2 miles (4 km) from the Pacific Ocean, on one of several ridges defining the area. The ranch has at least six marine and volcanic soil types. Another coastal ridge to the west protects the vineyard, allowing just enough Pacific Ocean fog and sea breeze to cool the vines.

The vines, old Wente and Dijon clonal selections, grow on west-facing blocks, planted at elevations of 1,150 to 1,375 feet (350–420 m). The core of the cuvée comes from Block 6, a steep, rugged, and rocky terrain on which the vines naturally have poor vigor, yielding grapes with tremendous concentration, length, and minerality.

Since 1997 the wines have been produced at the couple's own gravity-flow winery. Their fruit is hand-sorted and whole-cluster pressed. Fermentation is conducted with indigenous yeasts; there is regular *bâtonnage* until the malolactic fermentation finishes in the spring after the vintage. With poor weather during flowering, the tiny 2005 crop basked in fine weather to produce wines of tremendous concentration and layers of rich flavor, lifted by aromas of jasmine, honeysuckle, and lemon. **LGr**
⊖⊖⊖ **Drink: to 2017+**

Bird netting protects vines below Camp Meeting Ridge. ➡

Framingham
Select Riesling 2007

Origin New Zealand, Marlborough
Style Sweet white wine, 8% ABV
Grape Riesling

This is the best of a new breed of low-alcohol "German-style" Rieslings now becoming popular in New Zealand. The alcohol level of the 2007 is a modest 8 percent, with a sweetness level of 70 g/l of residual sugar, or in German terms, Auslese (select harvest). The wine demonstrates that Germany and Austria cannot afford to feel complacent about the quality of their Riesling, just as New Zealand should not feel smug about its Sauvignon Blanc.

Select Riesling is winemaker Dr. Andrew Hedley's flagship wine. It is a no-holds-barred wine that receives the first harvest from pampered vines. The second cut goes to Framingham Dry Riesling, with the best of the balance to Classic Riesling, while any botrytized component is used to make Framingham Noble Riesling. All are excellent wines, but Select Riesling thoroughly deserves its flagship status.

Select Riesling is a powerful wine with strong mineral, citrus, and white rose flavors. The wine has an ethereal texture and a wonderful balance of sweetness against acidity that creates an exquisite tension. The Select was first produced in 2003 and has been made every vintage since. A recent vertical tasting of every vintage clearly demonstrated the wine's excellent cellaring potential. Bottle age appears to amplify the wine's citrus fruit flavors, while at the same time introducing an element of honeycomb, suggesting a botrytis influence—even though no botrytis was detected when the oldest wine was tasted on first release. A screwcap closure helps to maintain fruit purity. **BC**
🡢🡢 **Drink: to 2017+**

Dr. Konstantin Frank/Vinifera
Wine Cellars *Dry Riesling* 2006

Origin USA, New York, Finger Lakes
Style Dry white wine, 12% ABV
Grape Riesling

Dr. Frank's Dry Riesling originates from the slaty slopes near the glacial Keuka and Seneca Lakes, where a mix of clay and limestone was deposited with slate and shale. Lakes make winemaking possible in cold upstate New York, where the average winter temperature is 22°F (–6°C). But growing Vinifera was a challenge, until Dr. Frank persuaded Charles Fournier, then Gold Seal president, that the key lay in finding winter-tolerant rootstocks.

Frank had emigrated from Ukraine, where he had taught viticulture and was familiar with cold-climate wine production on the banks of the Dniepr. In the 1950s he and Fournier searched for rootstocks in the Atlantic Northeast until, in a Quebec convent garden, they found what they were looking for: vines that survived to bear fruit even after frigid winters. After years of trials, grafting Chardonnay, Riesling, and Gewürztraminer on to these rootstocks, Frank could claim victory when, after a cold snap sent temperatures to –25°F (–32°C), his vines survived to bear fruit when others did not. Frank moved on to establish his own winery in 1962, with a focus on Riesling in its multiple manifestations.

The Dr. Frank Dry Riesling is always crystalline and pure, with long, cool fermentations for as long as six weeks to preserve the floral, green apple, pear, citrus, and quince characters in the fruit. The fermentation is arrested just short of dryness to balance the high acidity, provide juicy texture, and reveal the ripe fruitiness wrapped around a subtle mineral filigree. **LGr**
🡢 **Drink: to 2018+**

🡢 A grape crusher/destemmer in operation at Framingham.

Freie Weingärtner Wachau

Achleiten G. Veltliner Smaragd 2005

Origin Austria, Wachau
Style Dry white wine, 14% ABV
Grape Grüner Veltliner

Château de Fuissé

Le Clos 2005

Origin France, Burgundy, Mâconnais
Style Dry white wine, 13% ABV
Grape Chardonnay

The nearly 700 members of the Freie Weingärtner own close to half the acreage of Austria's most prestigious growing region. The steep, feldspar-rich gneiss and mica-schist slopes along the Danube at Weissenkirchen have been terraced since at least the early Middle Ages. They share with such nearby vineyards as Loibenberg and Kellerberg consistent excellence even in difficult years, and an equally prodigious capacity for success with either Grüner Veltliner or Riesling. The cool summer and early autumn of 2005 were capped by a sunny October and early November. Stringent selectivity to stem rot and botrytis characterized the Riesling harvest, while Grüner Veltliner boasted rude good health.

The Freie Weingärtner's results in Achleiten could scarcely be more typical of that site: Flowers, white peach, and subtle but distinctive mineral notes inform a wine whose richness and subtly creamy texture in no way preclude a delicate interplay of elements, seen through a lens of fruit nearly as clear as that of Mosel Riesling. But there is also the telltale, tactile "bite"—a certain peppery pungency—of Grüner Veltliner. **DS**

🚫🚫 **Drink: to 2019**

For many enthusiasts for white Burgundy, interest diminishes rapidly in any wine coming from points beyond the southern extremity of the Côte d'Or at Santenay. However, one grower has distinguished this area for longer than any other—Jean-Jacques Vincent at Château de Fuissé. As well as producing wines from estate-grown fruit, the Vincent family has also, since 1985, operated a business based on a mixture of estate-grown fruit and purchased musts under the J. J. Vincent Selection label, producing a range of Mâconnais wines as well as Beaujolais.

The Le Clos bottling is produced from a single walled plot of 5.7 acres (2.3 ha), on clay and limestone soils, situated next to the château. The harvest in 2005, after a fine summer, started on September 17 and finished on September 28. After fermentation and a full malolactic (blocked in some vintages), the wine spends nine months in two- to five-year-old oak. The wine shows floral and stone-fruit aromas, with a palate possessing those same characteristics together with apple and apricot flavors. The wine is balanced by refreshing acidity and has a pleasing finish of moderate length. **JW**

🚫🚫🚫 **Drink: to 2019**

Jean-François Ganevat *Les Grands Teppes Vieilles Vignes* 2011

Origin France, Jura
Style Dry white wine, 12.5% ABV
Grape Chardonnay

The Jura is deservedly fashionable now, but was long one of the most underappreciated fine-wine regions of France. Although there are several Jura producers of magnificent Chardonnays, none enjoys the cult status of Jean-François Ganevat, whose family's roots as vignerons stretch back to 1650. He studied and worked in Burgundy for a few years before returning to take over the family's 21-acre (8.5-ha) domaine in 1998. He practices biodynamic viticulture, destems his grapes by hand, ferments with indigenous yeast, matures in barriques or *demi-muids*, and adds only a tiny amount of sulfur dioxide, if that, at bottling, instead keeping the wine on its lees for at least two years and topping up the barrels.

Ganevat offers between thirty-five and forty cuvées—including six Chardonnays—most from very old vines with tiny yields. A particularly fascinating one is the Grands Teppes, from vines planted in 1919 in red marl. It has bright fall aromas of apple and quince with lightly peppery and saline notes, then on the palate it is effortlessly grand, fleshy, and rich, but far from heavy or sluggish, thanks to its scintillating acidity, precision, tension, and soaring finish. **NB**

ⓈⓈⓈ **Drink: to 2020+**

Giaconda *Chardonnay* 2002

Origin Australia, Victoria, Beechworth
Style Dry white wine, 14% ABV
Grape Chardonnay

While still working for Brown Brothers, Rick Kinzbrunner figured that the Beechworth area would produce good wine, so he planted there. Beechworth is famous for its wealthy gold-mining past, and the soils are granite-based. The estate Chardonnay vines are on a very quartzy patch. Kinzbrunner produced his first Cabernet Sauvignon in 1984 and his first Chardonnay in 1985. He has progressively relocated his Chardonnay plantings to cooler, south-facing slopes in an effort to protect the delicacy of the wine, which had been evolving into a more opulent style. In hot years it can be a little too big and fat, with alcohol warming the finish.

The 2002 is one of the richest but also most complex Giaconda Chardonnays, from a cool summer that produced fine dry whites throughout eastern Australia. The preserved peach and apricot aromas of the young wine have developed into roast hazelnut, wheatmeal, butter, and poached stone-fruit aromas. Intense, mouth-filling, rich, and lingering on the palate, it has a touch of alcohol warmth to the finish. At its best from 2008, but should drink well for six to ten more years. **HH**

ⓈⓈⓈ **Drink: to 2018**

Château Gilette
Crème de Tête 1955

Origin France, Bordeaux, Sauternes
Style Sweet white wine, ABV not available
Grapes Sémillon 94%, S. Blanc 4%, Muscadelle 2%

Just outside the village of Preignac, and languishing outside the Sauternes classification, Gilette is one of the most extraordinary names in that area, indeed in all Bordeaux. Planted on sandy soils, with a stony, clay base, the vineyard extends just short of 9 acres (3.6 ha). The flagship wine, the Crème de Tête, is only made in the exceptional vintages. Rather than spending a year or two in cask, it sits in small concrete tanks for two decades. This prolonged maturation is in the interests of affording the wines a more complex maturity than could be achieved by aging them in bottle.

Vintage conditions do not get much better than those provided in 1955, the climate favoring both quality and volume. Harvesting began on September 21, continuing into October, as bunch after bunch was rigorously inspected and stripped of only the most rotted material. The wine was finally bottled twenty-six years later, in 1981. The color has now deepened to tawny; the bouquet is still creamy and rich. On the palate, the wine still has something of its crackly lemon acidity, with gentle caramelized botrytis and a muscular, triumphant finish. **SW**
☺☺☺☺☺ Drink: to 2020+

Domaine Gourt de Mautens
Rasteau Blanc 1998

Origin France, Southern Rhône
Style Dry white wine, 13% ABV
Grapes Grenache Blanc, Bourboulenc, Others

Jerôme Bressy hit the wine headlines when he managed to make some super-concentrated red and (more unusually) white wines in the relatively unpromising southern Rhône appellation of Rasteau. They were made on the garage principle of very low yields and super-concentration.

Bressy has 30 acres (12 ha) and fills about 25,000 bottles. The wines are ECOCERT organic certified. Like his Châteauneuf role models, Henri Bonneau and the late Jacques Reynaud, Bressy decided to cut his yields to less than half those allowed by the AOC. His red Rasteau (largely Grenache with the usual Châteauneuf garnish) has been compared to dry Port (from 2004 he has been making a Rasteau *vin doux naturel*, even closer to Port). Rasteau whites are incredibly rare; his white is even pricier than his red.

Bressy has largely abandoned small oak in favor of tuns, and leaves the wine in wood for ten to twelve months. In the 1998 white, critics have detected a taste of glue and the smell of warm straw, while pointing to its deep, developed color. Others have admired its floral notes, the smell of acacia blossoms, its weight, and well-integrated oak. **GM**
☺☺☺ Drink: to 2018

Grace Winery
Koshu Kayagatake 2012

Origin Japan, Katsunuma
Style Dry white wine, 11.5% ABV
Grape Koshu

Grans-Fassian
Leiwener Riesling Eiswein 2004

Origin Germany, Mosel-Saar-Ruwer
Style Sweet white wine, 6.5% ABV
Grape Riesling

Japanese winemaking started in the late nineteenth century, but Koshu, the signature native grape variety of Japan, was first cultivated more than a thousand years ago. The origin of this purplish-pink grape was the European wine grape *Vitis vinifera*, born in the Caucasus in Asia Minor. It came to Japan via the Silk Road through China, but has only very recently come to international attention, especially since its official recognition by the Organisation Internationale de la Vigne et du Vin in 2010.

Grace Winery was established in 1923 in Katsunuma. This family-owned winery believes good wines come from grapes that bear the character of the place, and their Koshu grapes are grown in the region's mountainous area, giving wines with more concentration and minerality.

The Kayagatake has white-flower aromas, layers of citrus-fruit flavors, and a hint of white-pepper spiciness. The racy acidity and subtle sweetness harmonize perfectly, while a touch of bitterness from the Koshu skin contributes a welcome definition and twist to the finish. Perfect with white fish, shellfish, sashimi, sushi, and tempura. **KS**

🍷🍷 Drink: to 2017+

In 2004, nearly the whole of Riesling-growing Germany was blessed on a single night four days before Christmas with a bumper crop of frozen grapes. For Gerhard Grans, they came from the Leiwener Laurentiuslay, a terraced wall of gray slate whose fruit he generally reserves for a dry wine. The Laurentiuslay is one of many Mosel vineyards of exceptional potential. Still, there has never been a Riesling from that site like this 2004 Eiswein.

An ominous smokiness and prickling in the nostrils are classic signatures of this frozen genre, here present to the point where one begins to twitch. Thick and viscous in the mouth, this elixir has a superficial resemblance to vanilla icing shot through with fresh juice of lemon, again a not uncommon manifestation of youthful Eiswein. Quince and yellow plum preserves remind one of many a Laurentiuslay Riesling of more "normal" stature. With such a cutting, finishing penetration, tasters who still have tonsils may fear for them. Yes, this is a wine of excess, but not without refinement. Tasted today it will make you gasp. Your descendants will find it less audacious, but no less amazing. **DS**

🍷🍷🍷🍷 Drink: to 2035+

Josko Gravner
Breg 1999

Origin Italy, Friuli
Style Dry white wine, 14% ABV
Grapes S. Blanc, Chardonnay, P. Grigio, Riesling Italico

Genius or heretic? Josko Gravner polarizes opinion like no other Italian winemaker. Friulano wines are typically made in an ultra-clean, aromatic style—indeed, Gravner himself was among the pioneers of this style. But in 1998, Gravner started trialing a method of winemaking that used both large Slavonian oak barrels and amphorae. There was a rumor that one of the containers cracked and he lost all his Ribolla Gialla wine. But since 2001, he has used only various sizes of clay amphorae from Georgia (where winemaking has been traced back 4,000 years) for the fermentation and subsequent maceration of his three wines—the two whites, Ribolla and Breg, and the red Rosso Gravner. The estate's 44 acres (18 ha) of vineyards are near Gorizia, in the eastern-most part of the Collio wine zone.

Gravner's oxidative, tannic style of white wine is absolute anathema to those who enjoy freshness and cleanness in their wine—which is almost everybody. In a 2005 *World of Fine Wine* tasting of top Italian whites, Alison Buchanan called Breg 1999 (the penultimate vintage of its "old" style) "strange"; Alex Hunt thought that the wine was "off-puttingly acrid. Its other characters and qualities are unable to stand up and be counted"; and Nicolas Belfrage MW declared, "It takes some thinking about." Since 2001, the wine has become even more challenging. Whatever one thinks of his wines, the reclusive Gravner is an iconoclast, challenging both winemaking orthodoxy and the consumer. **SG**
🌓🌓🌓 **Drink: to 2020**

Château Grillet
Cuvée Renaissance 1969

Origin France, Northern Rhône
Style Dry white wine, 13% ABV
Grape Viognier

Château Grillet is one of France's most incongruous single appellations. Acquired in 2011 by François-Henri Pinault, also the owner of Château Latour, it is a ledged amphitheater, with the château itself standing to one side. Given the historically lowly status of the Rhône Valley in France's wine hierarchy, it is surprising that such a noble appellation exists at all—let alone one for a white wine made from the Viognier grape.

The nearly 10-acre (25 ha) vineyard stands across the River Rhône from factories and industrial plants that have been rivals for the employment of vineyard workers from the 1920s onward. The estate has known troubled times, with the Neyret-Gachet family struggling to keep it going when the wine was difficult to sell in the 1970s and 1980s. Quality has varied over the past fifty years, with a glorious run in the 1960s, a patchy time in the 1970s, and ignoble moments in the 1980s and 1990s. A post-2000 revival saw investment in new cellar equipment and a change of winemaking consultant. In the 1960s and early 1970s, the top wine, the Cuvée Renaissance, was singled out for separate bottling.

There were just 1,730 bottles of the remarkable 1969 Cuvée Renaissance. This is a wine that merits patient cellaring, for it is much more reserved than its neighbor Condrieu. Perhaps the granite and mica soil plays a part in giving it a certain steely nature when young. Over time the wine develops floral and damp wool aromas, and pear and apricot flavors, with some spice attached to the fruits and often a clear, mineral tang on the finish. **JL-L**
🌓🌓🌓🌓 **Drink: to 2019+**

Château Grillet clings to the hillside, surrounded by its vines. ➡

Gróf Dégenfeld
Tokaji Aszú 6 Puttonyos 1999

Origin Hungary, Tokaj
Style Sweet white wine, 10% ABV
Grape Furmint

The story of Gróf (count) Dégenfeld is of one of the rare but significant revivals of an aristocratic estate in the former Eastern Bloc after the Iron Curtain fell in 1989. The Dégenfelds were a German-Hungarian family who made top-quality Tokay in the nineteenth century. Naturally the estate was sequestered by the communists after 1945. Now the 240-acre (100 ha) estate is owned by the German businessman Thomas Lindner, who is married to Countess Marie, the daughter of Gróf Sándor Dégenfeld-Schönfeld. Lindner provided the funds for the development of his father-in-law's family estate in 1996.

The 6 Puttonyos 1999 has a residual sugar of 173 g/l and an acidity of 11 g/l. It was grown in the estate's vineyards north of Tarcal. The soils contain loess and *nyirok*—a weathered, volcanic, claylike soil typical of the Zemplén Hills. The wine is full gold with amber lights. There are hints of leather and walnut on the nose, and a redolence of honey and almond; on the palate it is reminiscent of plum, greengage, yellow peach, and apricot; it has a pretty length, ending with an impression of creamy walnut, huge fruit and structure, and excellent balance. **GM**

🕓🕓🕓🕓 **Drink: to 2019+**

Grosset
Watervale Riesling 2006

Origin Australia, South Australia, Clare Valley
Style Dry white wine, 13% ABV
Grape Riesling

Grosset Watervale Riesling is a single-vineyard wine from the high-altitude Springvale Vineyard. Jeffrey Grosset is the acknowledged master of Australian Riesling. "Making Riesling is the purest form of winemaking," he says, "because the winemaker is very restricted in what can be done. No oak, no malolactic, and usually no lees contact or grape skin contact is employed. A disciplined approach is needed to retain the inherent fruit characters and expression of the individual vineyard site."

This wine epitomizes the classic Clare Valley style with its restraint, pure fruit, and mouthwatering palate. Polish Hill, his other single-vineyard Riesling, might have more structure and intensity (and command a higher price), but Watervale is richer and more generous. On the nose, it is floral, with lime and lemon aromas. The palate is delicate yet intense, with powerful, focused citrus flavors, underscored by mineral notes. As usual, the Watervale 2006 is tightly structured, has impressive weight, some plumpness, and zippy acidity on a long, fine, dry finish. It can be drunk young and fresh, or aged for ten or more years for further complexity. **SG**

🕓🕓 **Drink: to 2018+**

🔲 This restaurant is part of the Dégenfeld Palais on Tokaj's main square.

Domaine Guffens-Heynen
Pouilly-Fuissé La Roche 2002

Origin France, Burgundy, Mâconnais
Style Dry white wine, 13% ABV
Grape Chardonnay

In 1980 a Belgian couple, Jean-Marie and Maine Guffens-Heynen, made their first vintage in the Mâconnais. At his original estate of 2.5 acres (1 ha) of vines in the splendid rocky soils of Vergisson, Jean-Marie continues to make a classic Pouilly-Fuissé that is one of the models for the renaissance of the appellation, his little vineyard vying for press plaudits with big estates such as Château de Fuissé and Château de Beauregard. The Guffens' approach to winemaking is traditional, *la façon de grand-père*, allowing the wine to make itself.

The Vergisson soil is very shallow (if it exists at all), the vine going straight into the limestone rock. This Cuvée La Roche has an exceptional depth of mineral flavors, helped on by the exceptional class of the 2002 vintage. Here in the Mâconnais, it was always a potentially great but challenging year; a warm summer interspersed with showers required a precisely timed harvest date, with picking by hand at Jean-Marie's insistence. Gravity feeding of the must and minimal handling in the cellar have resulted in a wine of majestic austerity in balance with the honeyed, lemony flavors of Chardonnay. **ME**

❸❸❸ **Drink: to 2017+**

Château Guiraud
2005

Origin France, Bordeaux, Sauternes
Style Sweet white wine, 13.5% ABV
Grapes Sémillon 65%, Sauvignon Blanc 35%

In 1981 this large property, the only first growth in the Sauternes commune other than Yquem, was bought by Frank Narby, an Egyptian-Canadian shipowner. Frank's son Hamilton then took control and boldly announced that he would be challenging the supremacy of Yquem. He may not have succeeded, but he certainly transformed Guiraud into a worthy first growth. The involvement of the Narby family waxed and waned over the years, and in 2006 the winemaker Xavier Planty and a consortium made a successful bid for the estate.

Guiraud has a higher proportion of Sauvignon Blanc than most Sauternes estates, but Planty values the smoky character it gives to the wine, though he does not go along with other winemakers who like to pick Sauvignon early to give the wine freshness. Indeed, if there is a criticism one can make of Guiraud it is that it can lack some verve and freshness. The wine, aged in at least 50 percent new oak for up to twenty-four months, is rich and structured, and often with pronounced botrytis character. The 2005 is peachy and voluptuous, with a velvety texture, and it also has complexity and length. **SBr**

❸❸❸ **Drink: to 2035**

Guiraud went by the name of Bayle until the eighteenth century. ➥

Guitián
Valdeorras Godello 2011

Origin Spain, Galicia, Valdeorras
Style Dry white wine, 12.5% ABV
Grape Godello

Godello is a white grape grown in Galicia, in the northwest of Spain, and also in Portugal, where it is known as Gouveio. It is found mainly in the appellation Valdeorras, in the province of Orense, and in the Bierzo and Ribeira Sacra. It was the Guitián family who, in the mid-1990s, elevated it to a higher plane with their superb wines, produced with the help of José Hidalgo and Ana Martín.

La Tapada estate, where 22 acres (9 ha) of grapes have been grown since 1985, is at 1,800 feet (548 m) above sea level. Its soil is rich in slate, with gentle, south-facing slopes. It has a special mesoclimate, with both Atlantic and Continental influences, and the wines transmit a strong sense of terroir. The first vintage was 1992, fermented with wild yeast in stainless steel and without malolactic fermentation.

Guitián was one of the first producers to convince Spanish consumers that whites can actually improve with a few years in bottle. The wine is mid-golden yellow in color, with green reflections. Godello is a very aromatic grape, and this unoaked version brings out all the potential of the fruit. It has a fine, complex, and perfumed nose of marked personality, with mustard, apricot, and elegant bay leaf notes, fennel and grapefruit, musk, and mineral notes of flint and gunpowder. In the mouth it is medium-bodied, well delineated, elegant, pure, and refreshing, lifted by a fine acidity and sustained by intense flavors through a very long finish. **LG**
Ⓢ Drink: recent vintages for up to 5 years

Vineyards in fall with the village of Larouco in the background. ➡

Gunderloch *Nackenheimer Rothenberg Riesling AG* 2001

Origin Germany, Rheinhessen
Style Sweet white wine, 10% ABV
Grape Riesling

Fritz Haag *Brauneberger Juffer-Sonnenuhr Riesling ALG #15* 2002

Origin Germany, Mosel-Saar-Ruwer
Style Sweet white wine, 7% ABV
Grape Riesling

This leading winery in Nackenheim was founded in 1890 by the Mainz banker Carl Gunderloch. Agnes and Fritz Hasselbach have developed a style that interprets the classic characteristics of German white wine in a new way: intense mineral richness, an unusual harmony despite the marked acidity, and deep fruit flavors thanks to advanced grape ripeness. Fritz Hasselbach stresses: "To me, the most important aspect is bringing out the terroir in the best possible way. I know that our site is the greatest treasure that we have, and I feel obligated to bring this treasure to new life every year."

He is most consistently successful in the top Rothenberg site. This vineyard slopes directly down to the Rhine and points to the southeast. The Riesling vines here were planted in the mid-1970s, have roots up to 164 feet (50 m) long, and are exposed to the sun for most of the day, while the river's water surface serves as a giant sun reflector. The red clay slate soil warms quickly and stores enough warmth in late autumn to give the grapes a lush ripeness. The resulting wines exhibit a distinctive aroma, high extract, and good structure. **FK**

🍷🍷🍷🍷 **Drink: to 2020**

The original name of the Fritz Haag winery, the Dusemonder Hof, recalls the original name of the village, which changed to Brauneberg from Dusemond in 1925. Until then, the name Brauneberg applied only to the vine-growing hillside on the opposite banks of the Mosel, on which the world-famous Juffer site is located. The core of the Juffer is marked by an old sundial, which gave the Sonnenuhr parcel its name. With its steep, south-southeast facing slope and stony clay slate soil, the Juffer-Sonnenuhr has always ranked among the best white wine vineyards in the world, and is equaled in the Mosel only by Wehlener Sonnenuhr and Bernkasteler Doctor. The Rieslings grown here combine the mineral richness of the slate soil with the fruity, elegant expression of high ripeness.

For decades, Auslese wines from Wilhelm Haag have served as exemplary expressions of this site. They ally intoxicating aromatic richness with a silky texture and immense length, while at the same time displaying an almost ethereal weightlessness and subtlety. With the Auslese Lange Goldkapsel #15 2002, this magical tension is almost tangible. **FK**

🍷🍷🍷🍷 **Drink: to 2030+**

The Juffer-Sonnenuhr vineyard, looking across the Mosel to Brauneberg. ➡

Hamilton Russell Vineyards *Chardonnay* 2006

Origin South Africa, Walker Bay
Style Dry white wine, 13% ABV
Grape Chardonnay

For a few decades from 1975, the Hamilton-Russells were almost the only spokespeople for terroir in South Africa. In this and in many other ways, their leadership has been significant. The property in the comparatively southerly and cool Hemel-en-Aarde (Heaven and Earth) Valley was selected precisely to be potentially suitable for both great grapes of the Côte d'Or, Pinot Noir and Chardonnay. The vines are cooled by breezes from the sea, only 2 miles (3 km) distant. Efforts to express both origin and variety, alongside the highest possible technical quality, have been painstakingly pursued—despite substantial bureaucratic problems in the highly regulated early years.

Others have built reputations on the basis of the work of these pioneers, but Hamilton Russell Vineyards has grown and remains undoubtedly in the forefront. For Pierre Crisol of Gault Millau, for example, both the Pinot Noir and Chardonnay "stand unrivaled among the best of the New World."

This Chardonnay has helped the increasing international appreciation for the subtlety, naturally poised acidity, and longevity of the best South African white wines. From the best vintages, it has proved an ability not only to maintain its fruit and its freshness, but also to mature gracefully. Subtly oaked (but needing a few years for harmonious integration), the wine is silky, with an elegantly forceful structure and fresh acidity, showing its fruit above a cool, pebbly minerality. **TJ**

🄢🄢🄢 **Drink: to 2018**

FURTHER RECOMMENDATIONS
Other great vintages
2001 • 2003
More South African Chardonnays
Bouchard Finlayson • Chamonix • Glen Carlou • Meerlust Newton Johnson • Vergelegen

Grapes are harvested at a Hamilton Russell vineyard near Hermanus. ➋

Hanzell *Chardonnay* 2003

Origin USA, California, Sonoma Valley
Style Dry white wine, 14.5% ABV
Grape Chardonnay

Founded fifty years ago by a wealthy former U.S. ambassador, James Zellerbach, Hanzell was one of the earliest Californian boutique wineries. The original winery, now a museum, was based, rather freely, on Clos Vougeot, and from the start Zellerbach focused on Burgundian varieties. Hanzell was a pioneer, in California, of barrel fermentation and of aging wines in small French oak barrels. After Zellerbach's death in 1963, his widow sold the estate, and today it is owned by Alexander de Brye. Brad Webb was the initial and most innovative winemaker, installing square, steel fermentation tanks that were revolutionary in 1956. From 1973 to 2001, Bob Sessions was at the helm, defining and refining the oaky Hanzell style.

Most of the Chardonnay vines were replanted two decades ago, though a small block from the 1950s lives on. Yields are nonetheless extremely low because the selection planted here has extremely small berries, which may help to explain the wine's concentration of flavor and remarkable longevity. Only a small proportion of the must is barrel-fermented and then the wine is aged for about twelve months in 30 percent new French oak. The 2003, with its rich, honeyed, toasty aromas, could be mistaken for a Meursault, especially since the wine's fullness of body is cut by a fine thread of acidity; the alcohol is high, as is usually the case with Hanzell Chardonnay, but it is not detectable on the palate, and the wine finishes long. **SBr**

🌣🌣🌣 **Drink: to 2018+**

FURTHER RECOMMENDATIONS
Other great vintages
1994 • 1995 • 1996 • 1997 • 1998 • 1999 • 2002 • 2004
More Californian Chardonnays
Sutton-Coldfield • Flowers • Kistler • Marcassin *Newton • Stony Hill*

Vines grow close to the Hanzell winery in Sonoma County. ➡

Château Haut-Brion
Blanc 1998

Origin France, Bordeaux, Pessac-Léognan
Style Dry white wine, 13.5% ABV
Grapes Sémillon 55%, Sauvignon Blanc 45%

This great property has long produced a small quantity of magisterial white wine from 7 acres (3 ha) of white grapes on parcels of deep gravel soil with clay subsoil. The yields for the Sauvignon Blanc are very low, because the vines suffer from a malady called eutypiose, but the Sémillon gives a larger crop. The microclimate here is precocious, as the estate is within the city, and Haut-Brion is often the first estate in Bordeaux to pick its white grapes.

At whatever point the grapes are picked, they are always fully ripe with natural alcohols, often between 13 and 14 percent. The must is fermented in new Allier barrels, and aged for about twelve months. Haut-Brion used to be aged entirely in new oak, but these days the proportion is closer to 45 percent. There is little lees stirring, because the wine shows sufficient fat and richness without it.

In the 1980s, the wine, although magnificent, had very pronounced oak aromas and flavors that today strike most wine lovers as excessive, but the oak influence has definitely moderated, giving the wine better balance and a more overt fruitiness. 1998 was a great year for red wines in Pessac-Léognan, and at Haut-Brion for white, too. The aromas are rich, oaky, and spicy, and the palate is similar; it is a wine of enormous concentration and chewy extract. As is often the case with Haut-Brion, the Sauvignon is not easily detectable thanks to the ripeness of the fruit. **SBr**

ϾϾϾϾϾ **Drink: to 2020**

Haut-Brion has long been among Bordeaux's finest châteaux. ➡

Hétszőlő
Tokaji Aszú 6 Puttonyos 1999

Origin Hungary, Tokaj
Style Sweet white wine, 10.7% ABV
Grape Furmint

Freiherr Heyl zu Herrnsheim
Niersteiner Pettental Riesling A 2001

Origin Germany, Rheinhessen
Style Sweet white wine, 9.5% ABV
Grape Riesling

The name of this top Tokay estate commemorates the seven Garai brothers, members of a family of local grandees who acquired the land in 1502. The two vineyards are called the Nagy and Kisgarai, or the big and small Garais. Today the company has some 120 acres (50 ha) of the best vines in Tokay, on the south-facing slopes of Mount Tokaj itself at an altitude of around 1,000 feet (304 m). It is an almost perfect vineyard location, reminiscent of the great hill of Corton in Burgundy. The company also owns the historic Rákóczi cellars in the center of Tokaj.

The wines are grown on loess soils with granite subsoils, and are characterized as light and fruity and relatively low in acidity. The 6 Puttonyos 1999 has 157 g/l residual sugar and an acidity of 9.7 g/l, which cannot be said to be negligible. The wine is pale gold with a bouquet of honey and rice pudding and a hint of fleshy, white, cooked pears and peaches; the fruit is cooling on the palate and the taste appears muted at first before rising in a slow crescendo. The wine is not huge but it is above all endearing, and leaves a pleasant, peachy impression in its wake. It is best enjoyed with foie gras or a rich dessert. **GM**
🅂🅂🅂🅂 Drink: to 2019+

The so-called Rheinfront, between Nackenheim and Worms, where the vineyards slope east toward the river, yields a completely different quality of wine than the wide lowlands away from the water. The excellent potential of this region is concentrated in particular in the Roter Hang (Red Slope), between Nierstein and Nackenheim, to which the reddish clay slate soil gives its name. Heyl zu Herrnsheim owns only about 8.6 acres (3.5 ha) of the 75-acre (30 ha) Pettental vineyard. Nevertheless, this estate has always been considered the leading interpreter of this terroir. In addition, the winery has been a pioneer of organic viticulture in Germany.

The Auslese 2001 from the Pettental vineyard is an excellent example. Somewhat riper and more richly structured than comparable wines from the neighboring Rheingau, this wine beguiles with its exotic fruit and teases with its fine floral notes. Despite this accessibility, all Pettental wines possess remarkable longevity, gaining complexity but never losing the almost oily, spicy character from the clay slate soil. At the winery, this wine is served with fresh fruit, particularly with ripe strawberries. **FK**
🅂🅂 Drink: to 2020

🖃 A hygrometer indicates the high humidity in a Tokaj wine cellar.

Heymann-Löwenstein *Riesling*
Von Blauem Schiefer TBA 2002

Origin Germany, Mosel-Saar-Ruwer
Style Sweet white wine, 7% ABV
Grape Riesling

Hiedler
Riesling Gaisberg 2004

Origin Austria, Kamptal
Style Dry white wine, 12.5% ABV
Grape Riesling

Reinhard Löwenstein, once a revolutionary who started with almost nothing and produced only utterly dry wines, now also makes noble sweet Rieslings of sublime quality. His vineyards are perched on the steep slopes near the confluence of the Mosel and the Rhine in Koblenz; this is what Germans call the Terrassenmosel. The impossibly steep terraced vineyards appear stuck like swallows' nests to the rock cliffs well above the river valley below. Many of the vineyards were classified as grands crus by the Prussians who were in control of the region at the time of Napoleon.

Von Blauem Schiefer means "blue slate" in German, and denotes the predominant soil in the finest vineyards, which provides the wine with its salty minerality and cool elegance. This TBA 2002 is the most luxuriant wine that the estate has ever produced. Although Löwenstein cares little for chemical analysis, the 17.5 g/l of acidity and 334 g/l of residual sugar are quite unusual. He prefers, instead, to talk about the inner harmony and complexity that gives the wine—only 40 gallons (152 liters) were produced—international status. **JP**
🌣🌣🌣🌣🌣 **Drink: to 2050**

Ludwig Hiedler is among the several vintners in whose cellars the virtues of Heiligenstein can be compared with those of Gaisberg. The complexity of weathered gneiss and mica-schist relatively rich in clay and humus is mirrored in a Riesling with more spice and herbal pungency, but no less mineral in character than Heiligenstein, here evincing wet stone, saline, and pungent orelike impressions.

The 2004 began life in a completely rebuilt cellar, and Hiedler wanted to slow down his fermentations, rely on ambient yeasts, drastically lower sulfur levels, bottle late, and in general take some chances. "Fall was nearly perpetually humid and foggy," he reports, and in the end it was his latest-ever harvest, and he trimmed out half of each cluster on the vine.

A byproduct of Hiedler's approach and the vintage's character was moody wines. During their stay in cask, depending on the week in question, Gaisberg or Heiligenstein (or both) were unforthcoming. There was also botrytis—hard for any Austrian grower to avoid in 2004—but sometimes the most amazing wines appear in a challenging vintage, as this wine proves. **DS**
🌣🌣 **Drink: to 2017+**

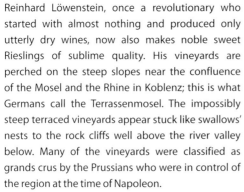

◪ Fresh Riesling vine leaves start into life in a Winningen vineyard.

Hirtzberger
Singerriedel Riesling Smaragd 1999

Origin Austria, Wachau
Style Dry white wine, 13.5% ABV
Grape Riesling

It rained in the Wachau at the beginning of November 1999, but when Franz Hirtzberger finished picking on December 1, he had more than 800 cases of Singerriedel Riesling Smaragd to show for his labor, raising the bar for a new breed of Austrian white wine to an unprecedented level.

Franz Hirtzberger is one of the seminal figures in a new generation of Austrian winemakers. His winery, located above the village of Spitz, lies on the Danube at the western end of the Wachau. Rising directly behind, the Singerriedel vineyard forms an amphitheater covering almost 25 acres (10 ha), of which the estate owns about one-third.

Still brilliant in form, the 1999 shows ripe, smoky, tropical fruit flavors, exotic spice and indelible mineral tones that reflect the gneiss, slate, and iron content of the soil. Although production exceeded the average, Austrian wines such as this are in short supply on the world market. Given demand, it sold out quickly and is seldom available at auction. The enthusiast's best hope today is to find a few bottles of the recently released 2006, which is among the finest vintages ever produced from the vineyard. **JP**

☻☻☻ Drink: to 2019

Weingut von Hövel *Oberemmeler*
Hütte Riesling ALG 2002

Origin Germany, Mosel-Saar-Ruwer
Style Sweet white wine, 8% ABV
Grape Riesling

The von Hövel estate has close historical ties to the well-known Trier abbey of St. Maximin. This abbey, one of the oldest in Western Europe, had a significant impact on the viniculture of the Mosel, Saar, and Ruwer from the Middle Ages to the beginning of the nineteenth century. After secularization, the estate of the monastery's Benedictine monks at Oberemmel was acquired by Emmerich Grach. In 1917, Grach's granddaughter married Balduin von Hövel, whose name the winery has borne ever since.

Although the winery also possesses land in the famous Scharzhofberg vineyard, the Oberemmeler Hütte site of 12.6 acres (5.1 ha), a *monopole* holding of von Hövel, is considered to be the real gem of this estate. Wines grow here that rank among the most intricate and subtle in this Anbaugebiet.

This balance shows itself superbly in the Auslese Lange Goldkapsel (long gold capsule) 2002. The wine, harvested on December 11, with 130° Oechsle, is flanked by a steely acidity (10.3 percent) typical of the Saar; the fruit flavors are marked by the distinctive mineral richness of the finely weathered blue Devonian slate soil. **FK**

☻☻☻☻☻ Drink: to 2025

Howard Park
Riesling 2006

Origin Australia, Western Australia, Great Southern
Style Dry white wine, 13% ABV
Grape Riesling

Domaine Huet
Le Haut Lieu Moelleux 1924

Origin France, Loire, Touraine
Style Medium sweet white wine, 10% ABV
Grape Chenin Blanc

Howard Park has dual residence in Western Australia, with wineries in both Margaret River and the Great Southern. It is the leader in wine quality in the latter, and is also significant in size. The estate's flagship wine is its Riesling, first released in 1986, which has achieved benchmark status. Howard Park's Riesling revealed to the rest of Australia the quality of this grape variety from the Great Southern, and showed that the region is a serious challenger to the supremacy of Clare and Eden Valley Riesling.

The Great Southern is a huge area, but five subzones—Albany, Denmark, Mount Barker, Frankland, and the Porongurups—have already been identified as having particular characteristics. Howard Park's grapes are sourced from the cool climate Mount Barker and Porongurups districts.

Made in small quantities, this Riesling has classic strong lemon and citrus flavors, and a pronounced streak of acidity. But there is a generosity and elegance of flavor, while still being austere, that suggests Western Australia, and the Great Southern. The wine can age well for up to twenty years. Dry, mineral, and super-fresh, it is a classic of its kind. **SG**

🍷🍷 **Drink: recent releases for up to 20 years**

Of all white wines, Chenin Blanc and Riesling share the top prize for longevity and stylistic variety. And among Chenin Blancs, none are longer-lived or more varied than the Vouvrays of Domaine Huet, for many France's top white wine estate. Older wines such as this are still released from Huet's private reserve.

The wines from Le Haut Lieu (as the name suggests, one of the highest points in the appellation, but south-facing) are normally more precocious than those from Huet's other two sites—Le Mont and Clos du Bourg. But from its deep, heavy clay-over-limestone soils come Moelleux wines easily capable of lasting a hundred years or more.

The 1921 Le Haut Lieu Moelleux may be from the best vintage of the decade, on a par with the famous Yquem of that year, but the 1924 is equally exhilarating, and even those who know Huet's wines well may be decades out if asked to date the wine blind. A brilliant gold, less deep than its age would suggest, it is astonishingly fresh and intense on both nose and palate, with perfectly poised acacia honey and citrus notes and incredible depth and length. A completely captivating and thrilling wine. **NB**

🍷🍷🍷🍷🍷 **Drink: to 2025+**

Hugel *Riesling* *Sélection de Grains Nobles* 1976

Domaine de l'Idylle *Vin de Savoie Cuvée Orangerie* 2012

Origin France, Alsace
Style Sweet white wine, 12.5% ABV
Grape Riesling

Origin France, Savoie
Style Dry white wine, 11.5% ABV
Grape Jacquère

The family firm of Hugel, one of the biggest players on the Alsace scene for many generations, is approaching its fourth century. When conditions permit, Alsace is capable of producing botrytized wines that are the equal of anything from Sauternes. The styles, of course, are entirely different to Sauternes, and different to each other, too.

The 1976 vintage was one of the legends of the later twentieth century, turning out wines of majestic concentration in the Alsace heartlands. The present wine is simply given the name of its variety and style, whereas it could technically be designated Grand Cru Schoenenbourg, in that all the grapes were sourced from the vertiginously steep patch of land so honored.

At thirty years old, the wine was still ebulliently alive. Deep golden-yellow in color, it offers up the classic mature Riesling aromas of petrol and honey, but backed up by a wealth of dried apricot and peach fruit. On the palate, its balance of botrytic fat, acidity, and relatively gentle alcohol (12.5 percent) have kept it fresh and vital through the decades, and should keep it going for a long time yet. **SW**

ⓈⓈⓈⓈⓈ **Drink: to 2025+**

On steep slopes against a backdrop of spectacular Alpine scenery, the remote, isolated eastern region of Savoie produces wines that are quite unlike anything else in France. The varieties are different: Roussette (a.k.a. Altesse) and Jacquère for whites; Mondeuse (although you also find Gamay and Pinot Noir) for reds. The styles they produce are different too: feather-light, crisp dry whites; and juicy, peppery, refreshing reds. As the cross on the labels suggests, vins de Savoie are more aligned with nearby Switzerland to the east than the Rhône to the west.

Based in the village of Cruet in the Isère Valley, the Tiollier family is one of Savoie's most established and consistent names, with brothers Philippe and François today managing around 50 acres (20 ha) in a series of precipitous plots at their aptly named Domaine de l'Idylle. The Jacquère, a vigorous variety that can run to blandness if left unchecked, is in their hands crafted into a delicate but racy white that is best consumed in the two years after vintage. Subtly floral with white fruit and red apple, it is distinguished by a flowing freshness that it is almost impossible to resist, comparing to a cool Alpine stream. **DW**

Ⓢ **Drink: current release within 2 years**

🔲 Hugel wines may be purchased at their premises in central Riquewihr.

Stefano Inama *Vulcaia*
Fumé Sauvignon Blanc 2012

Origin Italy, Veneto, Soave
Style Dry white wine, 13% ABV
Grape Sauvignon Blanc

In 1992, Stefano Inama took the reins of the Inama estate, which had been founded by his father some thirty years earlier. Located in the heart of the Soave Classico, Inama has developed an enviable portfolio of wines, ranging from a crisp, flavorful Soave Classico made, as with all Soaves, from the Garganega grape, to more exotic wines such as this striking Sauvignon Blanc. There is also a stunning red wine, Bradisismo, a blend of Cabernet Sauvignon and Carmenère grown on a special terroir. Because of this use of nonauthorized varieties, many of these wines are labeled as IGT (Indicazione Geografica Tipica) Veneto rather than DOC Soave.

Sauvignon Blanc has become a specialty of Inama and was first planted on the slopes of Monte Foscarino in 1986 by Stefano's father, Giuseppe. Two wines are made, both bearing the name Vulcaia, from twenty-year-old Sauvignon vines grown on a Geneva double curtain trellis, with 4,500 vines per hectare and yields of 60 hectoliters per hectare. The first wine is matured in stainless steel, but the Vulcaia Fumé is fermented and aged in small oak barrels, half of which are new. Both are impressive wines, but it is the Fumé that stands out, simply because this is such an intense, crazy wine—the marriage of ripe Sauvignon with oak works surprisingly well.

The wine has a remarkably complex, powerful nose with herby, toasty notes. The palate is rich, with intense herby complexity and a dense texture. Bold and luxuriant, this is remarkable stuff that enthusiasts celebrate as brilliantly different. **JG**
◉◉ Drink: recent vintages for up to 10 years

Inniskillin *Okanagan Valley*
Vidal Icewine 2003

Origin Canada, British Columbia, Okanagan Valley
Style Sweet white wine, 10% ABV
Grape Vidal

Canada is a major producer of Icewine, making considerably more than any other country, thanks to consistent weather conditions. Frigid autumn or winter temperatures are the rule rather than the exception. The grapes are protected from bird and wind damage by netting the vines until the harvest begins in December or January. Fully frozen grapes are often picked individually, frequently during the middle of the night, and careful pressing results in only a small quantity of pure juice going into the fermentation tanks, since all other moisture is discarded as ice. The result is intensely sweet and concentrated wine. Regulations are strict: Artificial freezing is prohibited, and minimum sugar levels are set at a very high level.

A number of different grape varieties are used for Icewine in Canada, including Riesling, Vidal, and the German crossing Ehrenfelser. Riesling Icewines have a unique intensity, but Canada is probably better known for its Vidal Icewines, because the grape variety is rarely encountered elsewhere. Vidal, a French hybrid, has a thick skin that resists botrytis, an advantage here because botrytis infection can detract from the pure, racy flavors of a fine Icewine.

The Inniskillin 2003 from the Okanagan Valley, harvested in early January 2004, has fresh and complex aromas of apple, apricot, and candied lemon. As well as high acidity on the palate, it has a sleek, creamy texture and a long, tangy finish. Inniskillin also produces an oak-aged version, and a unique if bizarre sparkling Icewine. **SBr**
◉◉◉◉ Drink: to 2020

Picking Vidal grapes for Icewine at an Inniskillin vineyard. ➡

Isabel
Sauvignon Blanc 2013

Origin New Zealand, Marlborough
Style Dry white wine, 13% ABV
Grape Sauvignon Blanc

Isabel Estate Vineyard was established in 1982 by Michael Tiller, then an airline pilot with Air New Zealand, and his wife Robyn. Prior to the 1994 vintage, Isabel Estate operated successfully as a contract grape-growing vineyard, supplying some of Marlborough's leading wine producers, including Cloudy Bay, with much sought-after premium fruit. But the high quality of the grapes encouraged the Tillers to produce and market their own wine. At its best, Isabel Estate is arguably the finest Sauvignon Blanc made in New Zealand, and is the only wine to seriously challenge Cloudy Bay's preeminence.

About 10 percent of the blend is barrel-fermented and some use is made of malolactic fermentation and indigenous yeasts. There is certainly the classic Marlborough flavor of capsicum here, but this is overlaid by rounded, rich fruit that lingers in a long and detailed finish. This Marlborough Sauvignon is very dry compared to some other examples. Isabel is a classy, elegant wine that has the ability to age well for several years but, like most Marlborough Sauvignons, it is best drunk young and fresh. **SG**

🝕🝕 **Drink: recent vintages for up to 5 years**

Itsasmendi
Txakolí 2012

Origin Spain, Basque Country, Bizkaiko Txakolina
Style Dry white wine, 12% ABV
Grapes Hondarrabi Zuri, Riesling, Sauvignon Blanc

Txakolí is the white wine from the Basque Country, from Bilbao and San Sebastián. There are two separate Denominaciós d'Origens (DOs)—Bizkaiko Txakolina and Getariako Txakolina—one for each province, but the wine is very similar: a spritzy, low-alcohol, fresh, herbal, and floral white made with the local grape Hondarrabi Zuri.

Bodegas Itsasmendi was founded in 1995, in Guernica, a village made famous by Picasso and his painting about the Spanish Civil War. Consultant enologist Ana Martín pushed the winery to plant some experimental Riesling and Sauvignon Blanc, with the aim of extending the lifespan of the wine and making a different wine, with more body.

Also made are 4,000 half-bottles of a sweet Itsasmendi, harvested one or one and a half months later than normal, with 13 percent alcohol and 80 to 100 g/l of residual sugar. In 2006 more was made because it was an excellent vintage. The regular cuvée, made with Hondarrabi Zuri and a touch of Riesling and Sauvignon, is delicious most years. Very light in color, and showing herbal and floral notes on the nose, the wine has vibrant acidity. **LG**

🝕 **Drink: recent vintages within 1 year**

Jackson Estate
Sauvignon Blanc 2010

Origin New Zealand, Marlborough
Style Dry white wine, 13% ABV
Grape Sauvignon Blanc

Domaine Jacqueson *Bouzeron*
"Les Cordères" Aligoté 2012

Origin France, Burgundy, Côte Chalonnaise
Style Dry white wine, 12.5% ABV
Grape Aligoté

Hardly any varietal wine in the world that can lay claim to a French antecedent has departed so far, and so productively, from its model. There are fruit-filled Sancerres, to be sure, even Pays d'Oc Sauvignons that have the authentic taste of green melon, but nothing approaches the tumbling basketful of runny-ripe, juicy fruit that great Sauvignon from Marlborough delivers. With so many good producers, few stand out, but Jackson is an exception. This estate represents the coming together of two families—the Stichburys and the Jacksons—who had been working land around the Wairau River for more than a century and a half.

The 2006 vintage is still being talked about in Marlborough. It was what the French call *précoce*—the dry, warm growing conditions leading to a harvest in the last week of March, fully one month earlier than normal. In the glass, the wine was all the more dynamically fruit-possessed, with a bouquet of melon, red pepper, passion fruit, and black currant juice scents. The palate is normally scintillant with diamond-bright fruit, checked by perfectly judged, ripe, sappy acids; the finish is vividly prolonged. **SW**

🛇🛇 Drink: recent vintages within 2 years

Many wine drinkers believe that all great white Burgundy is made from the well-known variety Chardonnay. But that has never been the case. Before the phylloxera crisis of the late nineteenth century, there was a broader range of white grapes, including Aligoté, to which parts of what are now grand cru vineyards, such as Corton-Charlemagne, were planted. The stronghold of the variety is now the village of Bouzeron in the Côte Chalonnaise.

Paul and Marie Jacqueson, a father-and-daughter team, produce two excellent Rully premiers crus from Chardonnay (Grésigny and La Pucelle), but this Aligoté is also a gem, and outstanding value. Like most of the best wines from the variety, it is made from the strain known as Aligoté Doré, and from very old, well-situated vines planted in 1937. These distinguished origins, naturally low yields, and careful vinification, including *élevage* in oak (very little new), add complexity, intensity, and suavity to a wine that can otherwise be simple, tart, and thin. This radiant wine is far more than a curiosity: gloriously golden, rich, and ripe, it charms with its generosity and, like all great white Burgundy, thrills with its minerality. **NB**

🛇🛇 Drink: recent vintages within three years

Domaine François Jobard
Meursault PC Poruzot 1990

Origin France, Burgundy, Côte de Beaune
Style Dry white wine, 13% ABV
Grape Chardonnay

Josmeyer
Grand Cru Hengst Riesling 1996

Origin France, Alsace
Style Dry white wine, 13% ABV
Grape Riesling

François Jobard has been making wine at his family domaine in Meursault since 1957. He is famed for his meticulous care of his vineyards—he is always the last to finish pruning, not through sloth or even slowness, but because of his perfectionism.

In the cellar, the grapes are pressed and the juice is sent to barrel without any clarification, which contributes significantly to the taste and texture of Jobard wines in bottle. Fermentation happens slowly and steadily, with the wines being racked at the end of their first summer and only bottled the following summer—a longer barrel aging than almost anybody else today for white Burgundy.

The Les Poruzots vineyard comprises 28 acres (11 ha) in total, of which François Jobard possesses 1.9 acres (0.8 ha) in the upper and better part, east-facing on a steepish slope with little topsoil. His 1990 today has taken on a pale gold color, with a slight biscuity aspect to the bouquet. The palate shows a fine, fresh, citrus fruit, reminiscent of bergamot lemons, competing with the thickness of texture that characterizes all Jobard wines. These two strands make a fascinating counterpoint. **JM**

❂❂❂❂ **Drink: to 2020**

The Josmeyer estate (the name is a contraction of Joseph Meyer) was founded in 1854 by Aloyse Meyer. Today it is an agglomeration of 63 acres (25 ha) of vineyards and varieties, mainly around Wintzenheim and Turckheim, but including a *soupçon* of the Brand grand cru and a slightly more expansive 5 acres (2 ha) of Hengst. One of the larger of the grands crus, Hengst enjoys a south-southeast exposure, and is composed of marl and limestone, a mix that produces big, strapping wines.

Conditions delivered something of a roller-coaster ride in 1996. They led to grapes with appreciably higher acidity than normal, a positive asset for a variety like Riesling, when combined, as here, with concentrated muscle-bulk and flavor intensity. The wine seems clenched shut at first, but gradually opens up with floral tones, lime and peachstone aromas. In the mouth, it has great depth and intricacy, and is shot through with brittle, crackling acids, contributing to precisely the mineral-pure mouthfeel that Alsace Riesling should be all about. Its acid structure is such that the wine will hold well into its second decade. **SW**

❂❂❂ **Drink: to 2018**

The wrought-iron sign outside Josmeyer's Wintzenheim premises. ➡

Kalin Cellars
Semillon 1994

Origin USA, California, Livermore Valley
Style Dry white wine, 13.5% ABV
Grapes Sémillon 75%, Sauvignon Blanc 25%

Microbiologists by profession, Terry and Frances Leighton founded Kalin Winery in 1977, devoting it to artisanal production of a limited number of wines, all from specific vineyard sites, all treated to long periods of bottle age. One of the most singular offerings is their Sémillon, from the Wente Estate Vineyard, near Livermore; the vines, planted in the 1880s, were originally Château d'Yquem cuttings.

Perhaps ironically, the Leightons' intensely scientific approach elicits artistry in the wines. Over the years, they have experimented with thousands of yeasts, seeking strains that develop secondary metabolites that add to the texture of their wines, and strains that will not contribute to the creation of hydrogen sulfide—an important factor given the reductive character of their winemaking. The yeasts selected reproduce poorly, leading to very long fermentations (ten months for the Sémillon) that the Leightons believe give more interesting characters.

Kalin Cellars Semillon is a rich wine with tremendous fruit concentration. Its intense, ripe fruit core is amplified by overtones of spice and honey, and undertones of nuttiness and minerality. **LGr**
⊖⊖ Drink: to 2019+

Karthäuserhof *Eitelsbacher*
Karthäuserhofberg Riesling ALG 2002

Origin Germany, Mosel-Saar-Ruwer
Style Sweet white wine, 9% ABV
Grape Riesling

Although they grow only a few hundred yards from the mouth of the Mosel, the wines of the Karthäuserhofberg are excellent examples of the sovereignty of the particular terroir in the Ruwer Valley. It is the exotic fruit aroma in the bouquet, bringing cassis, passion fruit, peach, and raspberry to mind, that is so typical of Rieslings in the area.

This estate's vineyard is especially noteworthy for the high iron content of the soil. The mineral-rich soil makes the Karthäuserhofberg wines unique. However, the current owner, Christoph Tyrell, also attaches great importance to a healthy humus content. The fertilization of the soil is done primarily with horse and other natural manures.

Thanks to all this, the famous Ausleses from this estate shine with a highly complex fruit flavor and mineral richness, as well as possessing a subtle density and tightly woven inner thickness. In years such as 2002—in which the superb balance, one of the classic qualities of top German Rieslings, shapes the vintage character to an even greater extent than normal—the Ausleses from this vineyard can be counted among the finest German wines. **FK**
⊖⊖⊖ Drink: to 2025

Karthäuserhof wines age in optimum conditions underground. ➡

VINVM

9.

DELECTAT ET

LAETIFICAT

COR HOMINVM

Weingut Keller
Riesling Trocken G Max 2001

Origin Germany, Rheinhessen
Style Dry white wine, 13% ABV
Grape Riesling

Reichsgraf von Kesselstatt
Josephshöfer Riesling AG 2002

Origin Germany, Mosel-Saar-Ruwer
Style Sweet white wine, 7.5% ABV
Grape Riesling

In 2002, Klaus-Peter Keller formally took over the reins of the family estate in Dalsheim. Since graduating from Geisenheim, Klaus-Peter has added excellent sites to the family's holdings, and taken great pains to allow each its individual expression.

Although their noble late-harvest wines have long been sublime, the estate's dry Rieslings have gained enormously in depth, finesse, and stature over the past decade. In 2004, the estate made what the *Gault Millau Wine Guide* considered to be the finest collection of wines in Germany. Although the trio of single vineyards—Hubacker, Kirchspiel, and Morstein—is often among the finest dozen dry Rieslings bottled in Germany in any given year, the G Max is the wine that has garnered the most international attention, not only for its price, but also for its aging potential. The Kirchspiel is more seductive early on, then the Morstein slowly emerges, only to be trumped in time by the G Max.

When first conceived in 2000, G Max contained a high percentage of Hubacker. Today Klaus-Peter prefers not to identify its origin. This is a blend of his finest vineyards with the best aging potential. **JP**

🍸🍸🍸🍸 Drink: to 2018+

That the noble sweet wines of the Mosel enjoy an undisputed worldwide reputation these days can be traced back to the Josephshof estate, not far from Bernkastell. In fact, the production of Auslese from grapes infected with botrytis (Ausbruch) was first introduced successfully to the Mosel at this winery.

The Josephshöfer vineyard is located between Wehlener Sonnenuhr and Graacher Domprobst, and is legally part of the village of Graach, but has always been released without this name on the label. The south-facing escarpment, with a gradient of up to 60 percent, has a gray Devonian-slate weathered soil with a high percentage of fine earth—a relatively heavy soil for the Mosel area. Full-bodied, spicy wines with great aging potential grow here.

The superb Goldkapsel Auslese from 2002 is a textbook example of this site's style. The wine has a rich apricot and gooseberry scent, complemented by a hint of lemon balm. A thick and compact taste with a fine fruit fullness that wins over the tongue and palate. Fruity sweetness in perfect harmony with brilliant acids and mineral richness; "endless" in taste and with enormous potential. **FK**

🍸🍸🍸🍸 Drink: to 2025

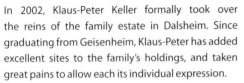

A historic German wine press is displayed at Eberbach, near Dalsheim.

Királyudvar

Furmint 2002

Origin Hungary, Tokaj
Style Off-dry white wine, 13% ABV
Grape Furmint

Királyudvar began in 1998 as a joint venture between the patriarch of Tokay, István Szepsy, and the Filipino Anthony Hwang, though the latter became sole owner in 2007. Hwang is a physician and wine enthusiast and is also the owner of Domaine Huet in the Loire valley. The wines are made at the "royal court" or *királyudvar*, the former depot for the wines destined to be served to the Habsburgs. Although production was overseen by Szepsy, Zoltán Demeter has always made the wine.

Furmint is known as the mainstay of the sweet wines of Tokay, though many of them contain Hárslevelű and some also have a dash of yellow Muscat. A few people vinify it dry or off-dry, like Szepsy. In general, such wines will be used as base wines for the Aszú, the Tokay winemaker's pride and joy. Szepsy's Furmint is just that; in good years the wine will be quite sweet, as it is a reflection of the sunny vintage. When it is worth its salt, the Furmint will have around 25 g/l of residual sugar. Furmint can have searing acidity, which makes it wonderful for sweet wines but can end up unbalancing a dry one.

This Furmint comes from a 10-acre (4 ha) plot in the Urágya (bed of God) vineyard in Mád, where the soil is red clay. (There is also a 2002 Furmint from the Lapis vineyard.) The wine is off-dry, very rich, and honeyed. It has an alluring playfulness that conceals considerable power. A marvelous aperitif, it is also a good match for quite spicy, Asian dishes. **GM**
🍷🍷 **Drink: to 2017+**

Királyudvar in Tarcal, with a signpost pointing to other wineries. ➡

Kistler
Kistler Vineyard Chardonnay 2005

Origin USA, California, Sonoma Valley
Style Dry white wine, 14% ABV
Grape Chardonnay

Klein Constantia
Vin de Constance 1986

Origin South Africa, Constantia
Style Sweet white wine, 13.7% ABV
Grape Muscat de Frontignan

Even nonbelievers in California Chardonnay have found themselves converted to the cause by Kistler wines. Steve Kistler and Mark Bixler produce wines that, for their devotees, represent the quintessence of California Chardonnay: aromatic richness, with concentrated, ripe fruit and toasty oak characters.

Kistler is best known for the many cuvées it makes from purchased grapes, all from cool sites in Napa and Sonoma. But it also has its own Kistler vineyard, which it founded in 1979 after several years of hunting for a cool site. High in the Mayacamas Mountains, 2,000 feet (610 m) above the valley floor, the partners planted budwood from ungrafted vines from the Mount Eden/Martin Ray vineyards, themselves located in the Santa Cruz Mountains.

Now producing several cuvées of Chardonnay and Pinot Noir, Kistler is no longer a small winery, but its cult status remains firm. Notwithstanding the increased production, the wines remain hard to find without a place on the mailing list. The cool 2005 vintage, with no heat spikes, produced wines with an extraordinary level of vibrancy, concentration, and length, even by the high Kistler standard. **LGr**

😊😊😊😊 **Drink: to 2017+**

Austen, Dickens, and Baudelaire all referred to Constantia wine in their writings. Vin de Constance became a long-lost myth, but in 1986 a new wine was made and packaged in a modern version of a hand-blown, eighteenth-century bottle. Duggie Jooste bought the farm, then derelict, in 1980. Although the accounts of the Dutch colony in southern Africa offered some detail, he relied on educated guesswork to determine the best plantings and winemaking techniques for the wine.

Botrytis was first recorded in the Cape in the early twentieth century, so Vin de Constance clearly resembled Tokaji in its natural sweet style, rather than the noble rot wines of Sauternes and Germany. (No botrytis is involved with the modern Vin de Constance.) The twentieth-century examples hover around 100 g/l of sugar, with alcohol levels touching 14 percent. Eighteenth-century samples, yielding more than 15 percent ABV, suggest that the wines were "fortified" for the sea voyage to Europe. Michael Fridjhon noted, "An amplitude of spice, Muscat, and pimento; phenolic notes on the palate, firm acidity still evident; textured not viscous." **SG**

😊😊😊😊 **Drink: to 2020**

Staatsweingüter Kloster Eberbach *Steinberger Riesling* 1920

Origin Germany, Rheingau
Style Dry white wine, ABV not available
Grape Riesling

Knoll *Kellerberg Riesling Smaragd* 2001

Origin Austria, Wachau
Style Dry white wine, 14.5% ABV
Grape Riesling

In the year 1136 Cistercian monks from Clairvaux in Burgundy founded the now famous Eberbach monastery in the Rheingau. An early property register shows that sixteen Morgen vineyards were in their possession by 1178—the ancient plot of land known today as Steinberg. Its impressive surrounding wall, about 2 miles (3 km) long and similar to a Burgundian *clos*, is unique in Germany.

One of the best dry wines ever produced here is the 1920 Riesling. The grapes were harvested when very ripe, at 112° Oechsle, but with an immense acidity of 15 percent. Swede Andreas Larsson, World's Best Sommelier 2007, wrote of this wine in *The World of Fine Wine* in 2006: "The color is crystal clear with an amber nuance; the nose is very clean and tantalizing, with hints of honey, mandarin, blackcurrants, and minerals. The palate is dry, with a lovely depth and a very distinct acidity imbedded in the lovely mandarin/honey flavors. The aftertaste has hints of minerals and sweet fruit, and the length is close to eternal, absolutely astonishing and utterly complex. Quite transcendental, and my most perfect white wine ever!" **FK**
ⓈⓈⓈⓈ **Drink: to 2020**

The Knoll family has been making wine in Wachau for 200 years. It is headed by Emmerich, who took over from his father in 1975. Knoll wines have been a beacon of quality in this beautiful part of Austria since the 1970s, when Wachau was known only to cycling German tourists. Knoll is a natural winemaker and has no time for the picturesque any more than he has for flashiness and techno-wizardry. He carefully nurtures the grapes on the vine and interferes as little as possible once the wine is in the vat. He uses old wood and a little stainless steel to age the wines from the 26-acre (11 ha) domaine.

The Kellerberg Smaragd is one of the two or three very best Knoll wines. Knoll is rare for an Austrian winemaker in that he does not believe in drinking his wines young, and feels they do not express their real quality before their sixth year. The wines can be austere in their infancy, but they are well worth the wait. The Kellerberg showed a return to form in 2001 after a short bad patch. The wine is both dense and refined, and has a marked mineral character. It is also characterized by a redolence of white blossoms and white peaches. **GM**
ⓈⓈⓈ **Drink: to 2017+**

Koehler-Ruprecht *Kallstadter Saumagen Riesling AT "R"* 2001

Origin Germany, Pfalz
Style Dry white wine, 13.5% ABV
Grape Riesling

More than five years after the 2001 vintage, this wine had still not been released, but had already sold out. Bernd Philippi's "R" series has had a cult following since his first release of the 1990 vintage in 1996.

Beginning in the early 1960s, quality German wine experienced a revolution, of which the seminal force was Hans-Günter Schwarz, cellar master at Müller-Catoir in the Pfalz. Schwarz believed in sparing no effort in the vineyard, whereupon the best thing a cellar master could know "[is] the right time to do nothing." The goal was to preserve primary fruit in all its explosive vitality. That came to denote stainless steel, whole-cluster pressing, and temperature-controlled fermentations.

Philippi respected the style, but to him it was not quite wine as he understood it. Wine was not merely about primary fruit; it was saliently about winelike flavors, which could only arise in the presence of oxygen. Further, Bernd believes that a controlled oxygenation in a wine's first youth actually protects it from negative oxidation later on.

The "R" series constitutes Philippi's best dry Rieslings. They are Pfalz Auslese Trocken Rieslings, with an entire bazaar of exotic spice, and yet they are anchored by Riesling's innate finesse. And Philippi, for all his extravagance, is at heart a classicist; his Rieslings are less Mahler than Beethoven. They are for drinking in winter, singular, capacious, and warm-hearted in character. **TT**

🔵🔵🔵🔵 **Drink: on release, or age 15–20 years**

The pretty courtyard of Weingut Koehler-Ruprecht in Kallstadt. ➡

Kogl Estate
Traminic 2012

Origin Slovenia, Podravje
Style Medium-dry white wine, 12.5% ABV
Grape Traminer

Kracher *TBA No. 11*
Nouvelle Vague Welschriesling 2002

Origin Austria, Burgenland, Neusiedlersee
Style Sweet white wine, 7% ABV
Grape Welschriesling

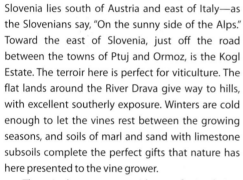

Slovenia lies south of Austria and east of Italy—as the Slovenians say, "On the sunny side of the Alps." Toward the east of Slovenia, just off the road between the towns of Ptuj and Ormoz, is the Kogl Estate. The terroir here is perfect for viticulture. The flat lands around the River Drava give way to hills, with excellent southerly exposure. Winters are cold enough to let the vines rest between the growing seasons, and soils of marl and sand with limestone subsoils complete the perfect gifts that nature has here presented to the vine grower.

There is documentary evidence of wine being made from what is now the Kogl Estate in the middle of the sixteenth century. Today, in the vineyard there is a dedication to the highest quality of viticulture. In the winery, tradition and modern techniques meet to produce some of the best wines of Slovenia.

The Kogl Traminic is a perfect example of the aspirations of this estate. The medium-dry palate is wonderfully balanced by the wine's acidity, allowing the perfumed aroma and purity of fruit from the grape to be enjoyed. This is a perfect wine to drink just by itself or as an aperitif. **GL**

❧❧ **Drink: recent vintages within 1 year**

Alois "Luis" Kracher has become a legend. His dream of making world-class wine from the traditionally impoverished Seewinkel, on the edge of the Neusiedlersee, had more than been fulfilled by the time of his premature death in 2007.

For Kracher, Burgenland's wines lie midway between Sauternes and nobly sweet German Riesling. His annually numbered Trockenbeerenauslesen comprise two groups: those labeled Zwischen den Seen (between the lakes) rendered in tank and never entirely sacrificing fresh fruit essences; and those labeled Nouvelle Vague, vinified in barrel and displaying Sauternes-like opulence.

Welschriesling is no relation of classic Rhine Basin Riesling; it is, under many names, the nearly ubiquitous and generally prosaic grape of central Europe. Yet noble rot—as Kracher showed—can elevate it to extraordinary richness and complexity. No. 11 is the Eszencia-like summit of Kracher's 2002 collection, combining almost gelatinous texture with near weightlessness, and a *mille feuille* of flavors with pure transparency. Kracher's comment was, "I think we picked them at the perfect moment." **DS**

❧❧❧❧ **Drink: to 2025+**

Alois Kracher uses a pipette to draw wine from a barrel. ➋

Marc Kreydenweiss *Kritt*
Les Charmes Gewurztraminer 2002

Origin France, Alsace
Style Dry white wine, 13% ABV
Grape Gewürztraminer

Kumeu River
Maté's Vineyard Chardonnay 2010

Origin New Zealand, Auckland
Style Dry white wine, 13.5% ABV
Grape Chardonnay

The Bas-Rhin, the northern part of the Alsace *vignoble,* stands in the shadow of the more famous Haut-Rhin, which is a shame if you like your Alsace dry and subtle, particularly as expressed in the wines of this great grower in Andlau. Marc Kreydenweiss took over the family vineyards in 1971. A decade later, he decided to make the best possible wines on the basis of terroir, aiming to preserve the wines' traditional finesse while increasing their concentration. In 1989 he went biodynamic.

On the 30 acres (12 ha) of the estate, there are some splendid grand cru sites like Kastelberg and Moenchberg, famous for their Rieslings. However, it is Kritt Les Charmes that is the most unusual. On a gentle, hilly slope, Kritt is not a grand cru, but Marc believes it deserves a single bottling because the soils are extremely rocky and complex.

This Kritt Gewurztraminer 2002 has all the finesse and class of the terroir, with none of the overweight fleshiness of many examples of the grape. The scents of roses, wax, spices, and honey are indubitably Gewurz, yet the palate is *sui generis,* subtle, delicate yet ripe, generous, and expressive. **ME**

⊖⊖⊖ Drink: to 2017+

This extraordinary Chardonnay has probably received more praise from the international wine press than any other New Zealand wine. The 1996 vintage fooled Jancis Robinson MW into thinking it was a mature white Burgundy, and James Halliday rated it as "an outstanding example of the genre."

Maté's Vineyard, christened after founder Maté Brajkovich, was established in 1990. Mendoza-clone Chardonnay vines are planted in moderately heavy clay and loam soils using a split canopy training system to help balance the vigorous site. Winemaker Michael Brajkovich MW uses hand-selected grapes that are whole-bunch-pressed and fermented in oak *pièces* using indigenous yeasts. Brajkovich believes that the yeast cultures endemic in Maté's vineyard contribute toward the unique character of the wine.

The wine normally matures for eleven months, although the oak maturation regime may vary from vintage to vintage. Brajkovich prefers oak to support and enhance the fruit flavors, not compete with them. This powerful, sophisticated, and complex Chardonnay has an appealing mix of mineral, citrus, bran biscuit, and toasted nut flavors. **BC**

⊖⊖⊖ Drink: recent vintages for up to 8 years

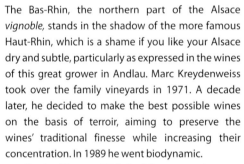

Michael Brajkovich's house overlooks his Maté's Vineyard Chardonnay. ⏎

Franz Künstler *Hochheimer Kirchenstück Riesling Spätlese* 2002

Origin Germany, Rheingau
Style Sweet white wine, 7% ABV
Grape Riesling

As the eastern gate to the Rheingau, Hochheim is known for three outstanding vineyards: Domdechaney, Hölle, and Kirchenstück. Their loess clay soils are shaped by a high percentage of limestone and, with Riesling, this always leads to wonderfully integrated, slightly softened acidity. The wines are beautifully balanced, even in lesser vintages. The good water-retaining capacity of the soil allows slow, even ripening in hot and dry years, giving well-balanced wines in these vintages as well.

No one better understands how to translate the potential of this site than Gunter Künstler. Due to the wine's sublime elegance and finesse, Künstler likes to call Kirchenstück Riesling "the Lafite of Hochheim." His Spätlese 2002 from this vineyard exhibits an exquisitely seductive charm at an early age, but also possesses the potential for a long life. All components of this wine—the delectable fruity aroma, the feminine body, the finest acidity, the feather-light alcohol, and mineral richness—are unified here in an almost dancelike harmony. A wine that, for this writer certainly, almost imperceptibly infatuates and fetters the senses. **FK**

🜚🜚 Drink: to 2017+

Château La Louvière 2004

Origin France, Bordeaux, Pessac-Léognan
Style Dry white wine, 13% ABV
Grapes Sauvignon Blanc 85%, Sémillon 15%

André Lurton bought this splendid property in 1965. Most of the vineyard is planted with red grapes, but there is a significant production of excellent white wine. It is curious that La Louvière, which is probably best known for its white wine, is adjacent to Haut-Bailly, which produces only red wine.

Lurton is an aficionado of Sauvignon Blanc, and this is reflected at La Louvière, where Sémillon is very much in the minority. The wine has been aged in barriques since 1984, and today the proportion of new oak is around 45 percent. The white wine ages remarkably well, and that also applies to the vintages that were aged solely in tank.

The 2004 has forthright but complex aromas of spice, pear drops, and oak, while the palate is full-bodied but vibrant, with ample tangy acidity and a long, solid finish. It is typical of many recent vintages at La Louvière, which have shown greater concentration thanks to more selective harvesting. The practice of pressing whole bunches has brought a suaver texture and immediate accessibility to the wine. There is no reason to think that these vintages will age less well than those of the past. **SBr**

🜚🜚 Drink: to 2020

La Louvière's manor is listed on the Roster of Historic Monuments. ➡

La Monacesca *Verdicchio di Matelica Riserva Mirum* 2004

Château La Rame

Réserve 1990

Origin Italy, Marche
Style Dry white wine, 14% ABV
Grape Verdicchio

Origin France, Bordeaux, Ste.-Croix-du-Mont
Style Sweet white wine, 14.5% ABV
Grapes Sémillon 80%, Sauvignon Blanc 20%

Few Italian whites are cellar-worthy, but Azienda Agricola La Monacesca's Mirum has the necessary stuffing (rich fruit and acidity) for the long haul.

Mirum's fruit is from a 7.5-acre (3 ha), predominantly clay soil vineyard more than 1,312 feet (400 m) above sea level. Harvesting usually takes place in the final two weeks of October, so that the grapes are slightly overripe. No oak is used; the wine spends eighteen months in steel tanks and six in bottle before release two years after the harvest.

For the Mirum 2004, harvesting began on October 25, the same date as the renowned 1993. Incredibly, this already has a deeper color than the 1993. The fresh, very youthful nose has yet to gain its identity, with nothing obvious but the intrinsic Verdicchio character, which is difficult to define. Italian wine expert Michael Palij MW thinks that candied fruit is one sign, but lemon sherbet is also quite distinctive here. Aldo Cifola notes: "Verdicchio is not an aromatic grape, but it is interesting when aged." At 14 percent, the alcohol is on the high side but is carried well. This is a bright, well-focused wine that still shows a lot of promise for the future. **SG**
🔴🔴🔴 **Drink: to 2019+**

La Rame was bought by the parents of the present owner, Yves Armand, in 1956, and Yves himself took over the estate in 1985. Today he is assisted by his son-in-law Olivier Allo. From the outset, Yves Armand was keen on experimentation. Just as importantly, Armand was determined to produce fine wine. In the 1980s the appellation produced mostly mediocre, insipid, lightly sweet wines. As a consequence, Ste.-Croix-du-Mont fetched low prices.

Armand knew there was no future for this style of wine, since the profit margin was minimal. He adopted lower yields and introduced barrique aging and, from 1998, barrel fermentation. He consistently produced wine significantly better than most of his neighbors, and was able to obtain good prices, especially for the barrel-aged Réserve. His use of new oak rarely exceeds 40 percent.

In 1990 the wine was particularly rich, and spent two years in oak. Yet the oak is perfectly integrated into the wine. Its aromas are peachy and sumptuous, with a clear botrytis character; the palate is powerful and concentrated but refreshed by lively acidity, and the finish is remarkably long. **SBr**
🔴🔴 **Drink: to 2020**

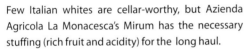

🇮 La Monacesca occupies the site of a tenth-century monastery.

Domaine Labet
Côtes du Jura Vin de Paille 2000

Origin France, Jura, Côtes du Jura
Style Sweet white wine, 14.5% ABV
Grapes Savagnin, Chardonnay, Poulsard

The Labet family are among the most respected vignerons in the section of the Jura region south of Lons le Saunier. On international markets, they are known for their terroir-specific Chardonnays, but locally their Vin Jaune always commands respect and their Vin de Paille enjoys success among those who love the sweeter style. The joy of this wine is that Alain Labet approaches the production, not by any recipe, but rather by selecting different overripe parcels—some before the harvest, some during, and some after. The grape mix can vary dramatically each vintage, and in 2000 included 62 percent Savagnin.

The Labets are unusual in that they dry the grapes in boxes with straw, whereas most have given this up in favor of plastic boxes. The grapes must therefore be super-clean; no trace of rot is permissible. In 2000, the grapes were dried from mid-September into the New Year, being pressed on January 25, 2001. After a slow fermentation, it was aged for nearly three years in old barrels.

The color of this Vin de Paille is amber, with a faint hint of red from the 7 percent Poulsard grapes. The nose is spicy and honeyed, with orange rind notes. Sweeter than many Jura Vin de Paille wines, but with a lovely streak of citrus acidity, it is spicy, long, and fabulously deep in flavor. Matched with foie gras or blue cheese on toast as an aperitif, it also goes superbly well with apricot tart, and, when older, works a treat with dark chocolate desserts. **WL**
🍷🍷🍷 **Drink: to 2030**

Grapes drying on mats of straw to concentrate their juice. ➡

Château Lafaurie-Peyraguey 1983

Origin France, Bordeaux, Sauternes, Bommes
Style Sweet white wine, 14% ABV
Grapes Sémillon 90%, S. Blanc 8%, Muscadelle 2%

In the seventeenth century this splendid 99-acre (40 ha) property was under the same ownership as Château Lafite, but in 1917 it was acquired by the Cordier *négociant* house. In 1996 Cordier sold the property to the Suez Company, which added buildings to facilitate winery operations. Michel Laporte was the estate director from 1963 until 2000, when he was succeeded by his son Yannick.

The vines have an average age of forty years and, when replanting is required, the Laportes select the least productive clones and rootstocks. The vineyards are dispersed, yielding a palette of different wines to work with. This may explain why, even in difficult vintages, Lafaurie often makes exceptional wine. The aim is to pick only fully ripe, botrytized fruit with an average must weight of at least 21 percent, which will result in a wine with around 14 percent alcohol and at least 3.5 ounces (100 g) of residual sugar. Since 2003 a sorting table has been installed at the winery so that the interior of each bunch can be checked for any lurking black rot. The wine is barrel-fermented and aged in one-third new oak for about eighteen months.

The 1983 was delicious when young and remains so. Once citric, the nose now conjures up marmalade, a clear sign of evolution, but the palate is still rich, creamy, and peachy, with attractive acidity and a long, orangey finish. It still retains the vigor that is always a hallmark of this excellent and consistent property. **SBr**
🔴🔴🔴 **Drink: to 2018+**

FURTHER RECOMMENDATIONS
Other great vintages
1986 · 1988 · 1989 · 1990 · 1996 · 1997 · 2001 · 2007
More Sauternes producers
Château Filhot · Château Guiraud
Château Rieussec · Château Suduiraut

A survivor of Lafaurie-Peyraguey production during World War II. ➡

Héritiers du Comte Lafon
Mâcon-Milly-Lamartine 2010

Domaine des Comtes Lafon
Meursault PC Genevrières 1990

Origin France, Burgundy, Mâconnais
Style Dry white wine, 13% ABV
Grape Chardonnay

Origin France, Burgundy, Côte de Beaune
Style Dry white wine, 13.5% ABV
Grape Chardonnay

Many wine collectors were surprised when they heard that Dominique Lafon had ventured beyond his family's estate in Meursault to the more humble Burgundian wine region of Mâcon where, in late August 1999, he purchased the Domaine Janine Emanuel. Of the 20 acres (8 ha) of vineyards, half were spread over two parcels of chalky clay soil near Milly-Lamartine, a small village northwest of Mâcon, which was home to the famous eighteenth-century French poet Alphonse de Lamartine.

Planted entirely to Chardonnay, the same white grape variety used in Meursault, it was a natural extension of his winemaking skills because, before returning to the family estate as winemaker in 1984, Lafon had worked in Mâcon with Becky Wasserman, a wine agent. "I believe there is a great potential here that needs to be exploited," he adds. "In the Côte d'Or, there is very little left to develop."

As in Meursault, he works the vineyards biodynamically and picks by hand. Here, however, he uses larger barrels for fermentation in order to obtain fruitier wines. As Lafon says, "These are not little Meursaults, they are great Mâcons." **JP**

🍷🍷 **Drink: recent vintages for up to 7 years**

Comte Jules Lafon not only invested in holdings in the best Meursault crus—Charmes, Genevrières, and Perrières, as well as Le Montrachet—but also had the wit to purchase prime locations within each cru. Thus the Lafon holding of Genevrières is in the upper part of the vineyard, very close to their parcel of Perrières. The Lafons own 4.2 acres (1.7 ha) of Genevrières, all old vines at the time of the 1990 vintage, the youngest having been planted in 1946. Les Genevrières, whose name derives from the juniper bushes that used to prevail here, comprises 41 acres (16.5 ha) in all, and is noted for its minerality: the light topsoil being laced with small stones derived from the bedrock.

Dominique Lafon was in sole charge when the 1990 was made. He retained the traditional long barrel aging in the domaine's cool, deep cellars in Meursault, but reduced the amount of new oak; indeed the wines are now racked into old wood for their second winter in barrel. The 1990 is a gentle gold in color, with a slightly biscuity nose that soon blows off. There is a magnificent depth of flavor on the palate, with a fresh current of minerality. **JM**

🍷🍷🍷🍷 **Drink: to 2017+**

Domaine des Comtes Lafon
Le Montrachet Grand Cru 1966

Origin France, Burgundy, Côte de Beaune
Style Dry white wine, 13% ABV
Grape Chardonnay

Lake's Folly
Chardonnay 2009

Origin Australia, New South Wales, Hunter Valley
Style Dry white wine, 14% ABV
Grape Chardonnay

This great wine, made by René Lafon, father of the current manager, has a personal story attached to it. I had foraged around the cartons and cobwebs of my godfather, Christopher Lloyd's cellars at Great Dixter, in Sussex, England, for years. Down there one day in 1996, my wife asked: "What's in that little old wooden box there?" "Nothing," I replied. But, undeterred, she looked. "Nothing" turned out to be three bottles of tissue-wrapped Lafon's Le Montrachet 1966, in pristine condition. They had lain undisturbed in that cool cellar for more than twenty-five years.

Christo gave us one bottle that we drank in August 1996. It was a lustrous old gold, with an intense yet very subtle bouquet of honey, roasted nuts, and oatmeal. A wine at once of extraordinary intensity, great finesse, and absolute harmony. Deep, dry yet luscious, gently nutty in flavor, still with a fine, perfectly integrated acidity and a pervasive, delicate, mouth-filling mineral aroma; long, racy, effortlessly contained richness across the palate and with magnificent scented length. Perfect maturity at thirty years; not a trace out of place, a quite astonishing performance. **MS**

ⓢⓢⓢⓢⓢ **Drink: to 2020+**

United States-born surgeon Max Lake established Lake's Folly in the Hunter Valley in 1963, kickstarting the "weekend winemaking" phenomenon of boutique wineries. The first plantings were of Cabernet Sauvignon and Chardonnay, in a region better known for Shiraz and Sémillon. The original "A-frame" winery is commemorated on the label, and the winery has continued to make just two wines, a Cabernet blend and a Chardonnay, using only estate-grown fruit.

As his surgical career came to an end, Max leaped wholeheartedly into the world of wine and food. He also became an obsessive student of the senses, chronicled in his magnificently eccentric and erudite books *Scents and Sensuality* and *Food on the Plate, Wine in the Glass*.

There was a spell in the mid-1900s when the Chardonnay was made with searing acidity levels and was often tainted by cork; but since Peter Fogarty's purchase of the estate in 2000 and the appointment of winemaker Rodney Kempe, there has been an upsurge in quality. The Lake's Folly Chardonnay style now sits on the cusp of lean and fat, making it something of a crowd pleaser. **SG**

ⓢⓢⓢ **Drink: recent vintages for up to 7 years**

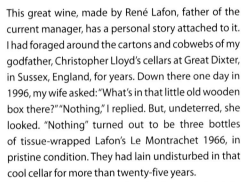

Domaine Laroche
Réserve de l'Obédience 2012

Château Laville Haut-Brion
2004

Origin France, Burgundy, Chablis
Style Dry white wine, 13% ABV
Grape Chardonnay

Origin France, Bordeaux, Pessac-Léognan
Style Dry white wine, 13.5% ABV
Grapes Sémillon 81%, S. Blanc 16%, Muscadelle 3%

As an unaccompanied sonata to a whole symphony stands the Burgundy grand cru to the Bordeaux château: one grape variety, one small vineyard, in clear distinction to the multivarietal blend often from large, widely scattered vineyards. Or at least that's the general rule, which makes this flagship wine a grand cru exceptionnel.

Michel Laroche created the first Réserve de l'Obédience in 1991, and there have been subtle changes over the years, such as more, larger barrels—up to 158 gallons (600 liters), none new—and the selection is even more rigorous—a maximum of 3,000 bottles each vintage. Because of the small size of the 2012 harvest, and the larger barrels, there were "only" thirty-three different blending components this vintage, whereas there have been up to seventy.

If Blanchots—cooler and windier than the other Chablis grands crus, southeast- rather than south-facing—is all about finesse, and if the Laroche style is for elegance, freshness, and fruit, then the talented winemaking team under director Thierry Bellicaud and technical director Grégory Viennois has achieved its twin objectives brilliantly with this wine. **NB**

🍷🍷🍷 Drink: to 2030+

Embedded within the vineyards at La Mission Haut-Brion is a tiny sector that produces the legendary white wine known as Laville Haut-Brion. The varieties are mixed up within the vineyard, and the manager has to flag the vines so the harvesters can tell one from another. The average age of the vines is about fifty years, with the oldest dating from 1934.

Since the property was sold to the Dillons of Haut-Brion in 1983, the Haut-Brion team has maintained the singularity of the wine, which remains differentiated from Haut-Brion Blanc. In the 1990s the wine began to be barrel-fermented, as well as aged in oak for around fifteen months. In the past, Laville was heavily sulfured: Today there is a much lighter hand with the sulfur, but it remains a wine that benefits from aging.

2004 was a highly successful vintage here, and the nose exudes super-ripe fruit, as well as the characteristic spiciness and oakiness that so often mark this wine. The texture is seamless, the fruit ripe but pure, the oak nicely integrated into the wine, and the length exceptional. This is Laville Haut-Brion at the height of its powers and potential. **SBr**

🍷🍷🍷🍷 Drink: to 2025

Le Soula *Vin de Pays des Côtes Catalanes Blanc* 2010

Origin France, Roussillon
Style Dry white wine, 13% ABV
Grapes S. Blanc 35%, Grenache Blanc 35%, Others 30%

Named Le Soula after its principal block of vines, this started as a joint venture between British importer Richards Walford, Eric Laguerre of the eponymous domaine, and Gérard Gauby of Domaine Gauby. The land is farmed organically, as at Gauby's Calce estate.

While visiting another vigneron in the northwest of the region, high up in the Agly valley, Gauby came across two elements that he lacked in Calce: The first was altitude; the second was a soil of decomposed granite washed over with limestone, which imparts a distinctive mineral note to the wine. The combination of altitude and soil has a strong influence on the wine's style. Cooler nights slow down the maturation process, allowing the flavors to develop more fully; the limestone soils help retain acidity and freshness.

Le Soula is a blend of Marsanne, Roussanne, Grenache Blanc, Chenin Blanc, and Vermentino. The ripeness and concentration is hugely impressive—there is a lot of new oak, but this is balanced by the intense and exotic fruit. The refreshing acidic backbone and richly powerful finish suggest that this will age comfortably for several years. **SG**

ʘʘʘʘʘ **Drink: recent releases for up to 10 years**

Leeuwin Estate *Art Series Chardonnay* 2002

Origin Australia, Western Australia, Margaret River
Style Dry white wine, 14.5% ABV
Grape Chardonnay

In 1972, after an extensive search for an area suitable to produce high-quality wines in Australia, U.S. winemaker Robert Mondavi identified the future site of the Leeuwin vineyard. The winery opened in 1978 and released its first commercial vintage in 1979.

Leeuwin Estate has 98 acres (40 ha) of Chardonnay vines divided into ten distinct blocks that are isolated into small parcels at vintage. "Block 20" is always the basis and the backbone of the "Art Series" Chardonnay wine. This represents Leeuwin's most opulent and age-worthy wines, which are identified with paintings commissioned from leading contemporary Australian artists.

Art Series Chardonnay is generally considered to be the finest white wine in Australia, and is one of only two white wines ranked as "Exceptional" in Langton's Classification. The 2002 is very pale green-gold, with oak-derived aromas of coconut and white peach on the nose. The intense and opulent underlying fruit evokes peaches and cream. The style verges on fat, but there is enough acidity to sustain freshness and balance for ten years or more. The finish is extremely rich. **SG**

ʘʘʘʘ **Drink: 2017+**

Domaine Leflaive *Puligny-Montrachet PC Les Pucelles* 2005

Origin France, Burgundy, Côte de Beaune
Style Dry white wine, 13.5% ABV
Grape Chardonnay

There have been Leflaives in Burgundy since 1580 and in Puligny since 1717. Leflaive is surely Puligny's greatest domaine, with holdings in premiers crus Clavoillon, Combettes, Folatières, and Pucelles, along with grands crus Bâtard-Montrachet, Bienvenues-Bâtard-Montrachet, Chevalier-Montrachet, and a tiny slice of Le Montrachet itself.

Les Pucelles, literally "the maidens," ranks with Les Caillerets and Les Demoiselles as among the finest of Puligny's premier cru vineyards. It is adjacent to Bâtard-Montrachet and makes a wine of nearly equal concentration but a little more forward, floral, and lively. The Leflaives possess 7.5 of the 16.7 acres (3 of the 6.8 ha) of this vineyard, and certainly produce the best example of its wines.

In 2005 everything went perfectly for the Domaine Leflaive team, headed by Pierre Morey. A fine, dry, sunny yet not unduly hot growing season continued through to an ideal September. The Puligny-Montrachet Les Pucelles 2005 has a sensational floral nose, with boundless energy. This taut, tightly wound wine of the highest class and persistence will repay years of cellaring. **JM**
🔵🔵🔵🔵🔵 **Drink: to 2020+**

Lenz *Gewürztraminer* 2008

Origin USA, New York, Long Island
Style Dry white wine, 13% ABV
Grape Gewürztraminer

Long Island has only recently begun to emerge as a serious wine region, with a small number of producers moving to cooler climate, white varieties more likely to mature fully, offer aromatic vibrancy, and provide an alternative to Chardonnay. One winery ahead of the curve was Lenz, whose dry Gewürztraminer has always exhibited a distinctive purity of fruit and tensile acidity.

Established in 1978, Lenz is one of the oldest wineries on Long Island, but it did not become truly professional until owner Peter Carroll lured microbiologist-turned-winemaker Eric Fry from the Finger Lakes. His Merlots draw one in with the raspberry fruit and tobacco that distinguishes Long Island's expression of the variety.

To achieve full aromatic ripeness, Fry delays picking, which requires acidification at the crusher; he does it so skillfully that the wine is harmonious and integrated. He uses several different yeast strains to enhance the aromatic complexity; that technique, plus the cool island origins, lead to a crisp and floral wine with classic litchi and spice character, always one of Long Island's best. **LGr**
🔵 **Drink: recent vintages for up to 8 years**

◀ The entrance to the Domaine Leflaive Montrachet parcel.

Domaine du Comte Liger-Belair *Clos des Grandes Vignes* 2012

Origin France, Burgundy, Côte de Nuits
Style Dry white wine, 13.5% ABV
Grape Chardonnay

This distinguished domaine, based in Vosne-Romanée, dates back to the early nineteenth century, and at one time, the family owned an astonishing cluster of vineyards, including in Vosne alone the grands crus La Romanée, La Tâche, and La Grande Rue, as well as several top premier crus. Succession issues meant that most were sold in 1933, and the few that the family retained were rented out. Since 2000, however, the passionate and talented Vicomte Louis-Michel Liger-Belair has been restoring the domaine to its former glory, taking back holdings when leases expired and purchasing or renting others.

The most recent acquisition was the Nuits-St.-Georges premier cru Clos des Grandes Vignes, a monopole of 5½ acres (2.2 ha), which he bought in 2012. It is interesting that ¾ acre (0.35 ha) in the lower part of the vineyard was grafted over to Chardonnay in 2009 by the former owner, though no wine was ever released. Great white wines from the Côte de Nuits are rare, but two come from other Nuits-St.-Georges premier cru monopoles (Domaine de l'Arlot's Clos de l'Arlot and J. F. Mugnier's Clos de la Maréchale).

This is Louis-Michel's first white wine, which he made with very little sulfur dioxide and matured in barrels, of which only one third were new. The wine may well be even better and longer-lived in other vintages, but this is still a very exciting and promising debut: exotic, powerful, and rich on both nose and palate, with an animating energy at the heart of the wine and a long, spiraling finish. **NB**
ΘΘΘΘ Drink: to 2020+

FURTHER RECOMMENDATIONS

Red Nuits-St.-Georges from the same producer

Clos des Grandes Vignes • Aux Cras • Aux Lavières

Other great Côte de Nuits whites

Domaine de la Vougeraie Vougeot Clos Blanc de Vougeot •
Domaine Ponsot Morey-St.-Denis Clos des Monts Luisants

Crates of Liger-Belair stacked and ready to be shipped. ➡

IBAULT LIGER-BELAIR

NUITS-SAINT-GEORGES
CÔTE D'OR

6 Btlles

NUIT

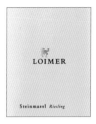

Loimer
Steinmassl Riesling 2004

Origin Austria, Kamptal
Style Dry white wine, 13% ABV
Grape Riesling

The area around the town of Langenlois is singularly blessed with geologically diverse and outstanding terroirs, but another formidable array of vineyards lies to the west of the town, including Loiser Berg and Steinmassl, close to the tiny Loisbach River.

The Steinmassl was once a quarry. A wind-sheltered mass of mica-schist provides a nursery for the late harvesting of strikingly refined Riesling, which needs considerable time on its lees and then in bottle to unfold. Throughout a difficult and protracted harvest, winemaker Fred Loimer was not convinced that his 2004 wines would amount to much, or even merit single-vineyard bottling. But they have blossomed impressively, displaying the fascinating nooks and crannies typical of wines from producers who exercised patience in this tricky and botrytis-tinged year of living dangerously.

Loimer's Steinmassl Riesling 2004 is striking for its combination of creaminess of texture with refreshing clarity and subtle mineral suggestions, as well as for almost red-winelike notes of strawberry and raspberry. Riesling in Loimer's hands, like the 2004 vintage itself, is good for a surprise. **DS**
🍷🍷 **Drink: to 2017+**

Domaine Long-Depaquit
Chablis GC La Moutonne 2002

Origin France, Burgundy, Chablis
Style Dry white wine, 13% ABV
Grape Chardonnay

La Moutonne is a curious *climat* (the Burgundian word for vineyard). It is a grand cru and a monopoly, yet the site straddles two official grands crus. Most lies in an amphitheater that forms the heart of Vaudésir, but part overlaps into neighboring Preuses. In total, the vines cover 5.81 acres (2.35 ha).

In 1791 the vineyard was acquired by Simon Depaquay, as he spelled his name at the time, brother of the former abbot. It remained in the hands of his successors until the firm of Long-Depaquit and its vineyards passed to Albert Bichot, merchants in Beaune, in 1970. The elegant, recently restored château, cellars, offices, and reception rooms of Long-Depaquit can be found in a large park in the center of Chablis, and the set-up is extensive, for the domaine now occupies 153 acres (62 ha).

Chablis should be intense and decidedly steely and minerally; yet, in the case of the grands crus, should possess an inherent richness. The 2002 is a yardstick example. It is firm, cool, and composed; elegant, pure, and balanced. Despite competition from the four other grands crus in the domaine's portfolio, it is clearly the best wine. **CC**
🍷🍷🍷🍷 **Drink: to 2019**

Dr. Loosen *Ürziger Würzgarten*
Riesling Auslese Goldkapsel 2003

Origin Germany, Mosel-Saar-Ruwer
Style Sweet white wine, 8% ABV
Grape Riesling

López de Heredia
Viña Tondonia 1964

Origin Spain, Rioja, Haro
Style Dry white wine, 12% ABV
Grapes Viura, Malvasía

"Opulent, this Auslese has an extra dimension of richness, tanginess, and length. Though concentrated, it's light on its feet and shows intensity to the apricot, lime, and honey flavors," wrote a reviewer in *Wine Spectator* of Ernst Loosen's Goldkapsel Auslese 2003 from the Ürziger Würzgarten. It is an extraordinarily dense wine, harvested on October 24 in that extremely hot year, with a must weight of 106° Oechsle and a relatively mild acidity (for the Mosel) of 7.8 g/l.

Despite the extreme vintage, it is a wine that displays the beguiling signature of its winemaker just as proudly as it does the typicity of the vineyard. One reason for this consistency is that the oldest ungrafted vines of the estate can be found here.

The steep slope of this site (up to 65 percent) has a unique terroir for the Mosel because of the red sandstone and slate soil. The Würzgarten wines can therefore be clearly differentiated from those of other top sites in this region because of the very distinct mineral richness of the scent. And when it comes to playing the score of this terroir, no one does it quite as well as Ernst Loosen. **FK**

🔴🔴🔴 **Drink: to 2025**

The grandes reservas of Bodegas López de Heredia rank among the greatest Spanish whites. Admittedly, they are not easily approachable, since the long aging period in American oak (nine years, in the case of this Gran Reserva 1964) produces elegant oxidative notes that may disconcert novice drinkers.

But this long aging process, preceded by another couple of years in oak vats, and followed by a number of years in bottle, gives the wines an unmistakable profile, where a sharp and well-defined backbone is wrapped and fleshed out by multiple layers of aromas and flavors that in a mythical vintage such as 1964 reach astonishing levels. Other more recent vintages—some showing more sharpness, others more flesh—may one day reach a similarly perfect structure, but so far this 1964 is López de Heredia's greatest white.

After adequate aeration the wine shows itself to be rich, powerful, forward, fresh, with only minor oxidative notes, truly impressive, fragrant with fresh orange scents, a wide array of spices (cinnamon, clove, vanilla), and even petrolly notes, in a harmoniously integrated whole. **JB**

🔴🔴🔴🔴 **Drink: to 2025**

The wine cellar at López de Heredia is nicknamed "the cemetery." ➡

Lusco do Miño
Pazo Piñeiro Albariño 2010

Origin Spain, Galicia, Rías Baixas
Style Dry white wine, 13% ABV
Grape Albariño

Lusco do Miño was founded by the winemaker José Antonio López Domínguez, in partnership with his U.S. importers Stephen Metzler and Almudena de Llaguno. In 2007, however, there was a major reshuffle, and now the major stockholder in the firm is the dynamic Bierzo winery Dominio de Tares.

The best Albariño wines do not merely survive some years in bottle, but actually show at their best in terms of character and structure. Lusco do Miño has placed its two wines among that élite. There is the basic cuvée—under the name Lusco, since the 1996 vintage—which was one of the wines to lead the quality revolution in the DO Rías Baixas in the mid 1990s. The firm has also released this Pazo Piñeiro, named after the estate in Salvaterra do Miño whose 12 acres (5 ha) of Albariño vines, planted in 1970, constitute the main treasure of the house.

Other Albariño bottlings suffer from excessive youth, overproductive vineyards, and abuse of selected yeasts; Pazo Piñeiro shows no sign of these problems. In contrast, it is dry and mineral, fresh and fruity, structured and long, and its virtues become increasingly evident from its third year of life. **JB**

🜂🜂 Drink: recent vintages for up to 5 years

Jean Macle
Château-Chalon 1999

Origin France, Jura, Château-Chalon
Style Dry white wine, 14% ABV
Grape Savagnin

In France, the Château-Chalon appellation, restricted to the production of Vin Jaune, is legendary, and in recent decades Jean Macle's Château-Chalon has been the most sought-after example. Now in his seventies, Jean Macle is convinced that his Château-Chalon should not be drunk sooner than ten years after bottling (in total seventeen years after harvest).

Domaine Macle's 10 acres (4 ha) of Savagnin are farmed, using sustainable methods, on steep, stony marl slopes, partly facing south directly below the village, and partly southeast toward the village of Menétru le Vignoble. Macle maintains that the veil of yeast on the unfilled barrels evens out the differences of terroir. Where the barrels are stocked is key to the aging process, with summer warmth needed to make the yeast work correctly.

The 1999 has the requisite balance of richness, finesse, and high acidity to allow it to age beautifully. As always with Macle's Château-Chalon, the color is a surprisingly pale yellow-gold. The nose is delicate, with green apples and green (wet) walnuts. Bone dry, the acidity builds in the mouth, but with a roundness and spiciness behind giving weight. **WL**

🜂🜂🜂 Drink: 2016–2050+

Château-Chalon overlooks the Baume Les Messieurs valley. ➨

Maculan
Torcolato 2003

Origin Italy, Veneto, Breganze
Style Sweet white wine, 13% ABV
Grapes Vespaiolo, Tocai Friulano, Garganega

McWilliam's *Mount*
Pleasant Lovedale Semillon 2001

Origin Australia, New South Wales, Hunter Valley
Style Dry white wine, 11.5% ABV
Grape Sémillon

Working within the newly created Breganze DOC, Fausto Maculan's wines are instantly recognizable for their uniquely styled and flavored personalities.

Torcolato is the product of three essential processes. First, there may be varying levels of botrytis in the grapes. Second, the grapes are hung on rafters to air-dry for four to five months, then pressed and vinified slowly. The third crucial element is a period of cask-aging in French (Allier) oak for eighteen months. The wine is then held for a further six months before release.

The striking color of the wine is a deep, burnished tawny, even in its youth. Torcolato is explosively fruit-driven, with a riot of tropical flavors (mango, papaya, passion fruit) accompanying the expected peaches, apricots, and honey of *recioto* dessert wines. There is vanilla from the oak, and also a citrus acid edge that recalls the mandarin oranges of Italy. Caramel tones distinguish the wine as it ages in bottle, and the finish gradually changes from fresh fruits to raisins, hazelnuts, and toffee. All these can be seen to great effect in the glorious 2003, a wine that will evolve magisterially. **SW**
⊖⊖⊖ **Drink: to 2025+**

Hunter Valley Semillon is unique, and in the Hunter's poor alluvial soils the grape has found its true home. The original 15 acres (6 ha) of Sémillon in the Lovedale vineyard were planted by the legendary Maurice O'Shea in 1946. The vineyard is now much larger and has several other varieties, but this core of old vines on particularly poor, gravelly sand and silt always supplies the Lovedale wine, which is one of the great classic wines of Australia.

The grapes are hand-picked, crushed, and drained with no skin contact, and the juice cold-settled for up to two weeks, so the juice is ultra-clean before fermentation. Chief winemaker Phillip Ryan believes Hunter Semillon is better than ever, thanks to better viticulture and winemaking. "There's almost a fruit sweetness, though they are bone-dry, because of the mid-palate fruit weight," says Ryan. "There's no reason why people shouldn't be drinking Sémillon young." He now releases a small portion of Lovedale as a young wine. It is still remarkably fresh at six years old, however, with lemon, citrus, and subtle herbal aromas, and a hint of buttered-toasty bottle-age character just starting to emerge. **HH**
⊖⊖ **Drink: to 2021**

Lovedale is one of three plots within the Mount Pleasant vineyard. ➡

Château Malartic-Lagravière

2004

Origin France, Bordeaux, Pessac-Léognan
Style Dry white wine, 13% ABV
Grapes Sauvignon Blanc 80%, Sémillon 20%

One of the eighteenth-century owners of this fine property just outside Léognan was an admiral, which explains the presence of a ship on the label. Malartic-Lagravière passed down to the Marly family, and was run by Jacques Marly from 1947 until his retirement in 1990. He was very devout and saw everything as a divine gift—including the very high yields from his vines. Quality, not surprisingly, was middling.

In 1990 Malartic was bought by the Laurent-Perrier Champagne house, which sold it seven years later to Alfred-Alexandre Bonnie, a Belgian businessman, who poured money into the property, renovating and expanding the vineyards, creating a superb state-of-the-art, gravity-operated winery, and doubling the size of the château.

The vines are planted on deep, well-drained gravel over clay subsoil. Under the Marlys, white Malartic was pure Sauvignon Blanc, but the Bonnies have planted some Sémillon to give the wine more weight and complexity. After harvesting, the grapes are very carefully sorted; then the must is barrel-fermented in about 50 percent new oak. In the 1980s the white wine was often rather hard and charmless, but by 2000 this was one of the best wines of the appellation, mouthwatering and appetizing yet not lacking in substance. The 2004 is especially successful, with its aromas of nettle and passion fruit, and a sophisticated whisper of oak. The palate is plump and concentrated, with ample depth and spice, and excellent, crisp acidity and length. Delicious young, it has the balance to age well. **SBr**
☻☻☻ **Drink: to 2020**

Château de Malle

1996

Origin France, Bordeaux, Sauternes
Style Sweet white wine, 13.5% ABV
Grapes Sémillon 67%, S. Blanc 30%, Muscadelle 3%

Visitors flock to this property by the thousand, but most are there to visit the exquisite seventeenth-century château and park rather than in pursuit of its wines. It has been owned by the Lur-Saluces family since 1702, and was bequeathed to a young Lur-Saluces nephew, Comte Pierre de Bournazel, in 1956. He found the vineyards smitten by the frost of that year, and the buildings in decay. He doggedly repaired the damage, and in 1980 he and his family moved from Paris into the restored château.

Although the property had a good reputation for its Sauternes in the nineteenth century, the wines were fairly mediocre in the 1960s and '70s. In the 1980s Madame de Bournazel, who took over after Bournazel's early death in 1985, invested in improvements in the vineyards. Selection is stern, and no De Malle was bottled in 1992 or 1993.

De Malle is not an especially weighty Sauternes, but it tends to be lush and quite forward, though the good vintages do age well. In the past, the wines were excessively light, elegant but pallid. Today, De Malle has far more richness, but the emphasis is still on accessibility and succulence rather than power. The 1996 vintage was overshadowed by the exceptional 1997s, but it too produced many splendid wines. There are aromas of peach and mango. The wine is aged in about 50 percent new oak, and the oak flavors are quite pronounced. Good acidity balances the concentrated fruit, and the finish is long. Although the wine is sure to age well, it is already giving great pleasure. **SBr**
☻☻☻ **Drink: to 2021+**

The château was built in the seventeenth century by Jacques de Malle. ▸

Malvirà

Roero Arneis Saglietto 2012

Origin Italy, Piedmont, Roero
Style Dry white wine, 13% ABV
Grape Arneis

The Damonte brothers proudly boast two wines in this book—a big achievement for this small winery established in 1974. The restrained elegance and complexity of their wines show how close Roero really is to the much more famous Langhe.

Arneis is the local white grape variety, capable of producing distinctive, crisp wines that are denied the recognition they deserve because of the priority given here to Nebbiolo. Saglietto, the historic vineyard of the Damonte family, lies at an altitude of 750 to 1,000 feet (228–305 m).

The grapes for Saglietto Arneis are pressed straight after picking. Half of the must is fermented and aged for about ten months in French oak casks, whereas the other half ferments in stainless-steel vats. The blending and bottling normally happen in August, and the wine is then given a few more months before it is released.

Roero Arneis Saglietto is a harmonious wine, with a bright straw-yellow color. It is nicely round but crisp, with well-defined notes of apple and pear. The great balance between body and acidity enable it to age gracefully over the medium term. **AS**

⊖⊖ **Drink: recent vintages for up to 8 years**

Marcassin

Chardonnay 2009

Origin USA, California, Sonoma Valley
Style Dry white wine, 14.9% ABV
Grape Chardonnay

Helen Turley had been working steadily but unobtrusively as a winemaker in California from the late 1970s, but it was only during the 1990s that she became the most sought-after winemaker in the state. Her name had become synonymous with the early Peter Michael Chardonnays and the first Zinfandels produced by her brother Larry.

Marcassin is Turley's and her husband John Wetlaufer's own label, limited to small-production, single-vineyard Chardonnay and Pinot Noir. Through Wetlaufer, Turley developed an appreciation of fine Burgundy that has exerted increasing influence on her winemaking. She is meticulous in every detail, both in the vineyard and the winery. The Marcassin vineyard, 2 miles (5 km) from the Pacific Ocean, was planted to her own specifications, with very dense spacing. The soils are very well drained, being composed of gravelly loam over fractured rock of marine, volcanic origin. She maintains that low yields are intrinsic to fine quality, and at her site she is able to harvest fully ripe fruit with firm acidities. Robert Parker, who has never wavered in extolling her virtues, found the 2002 "virtually perfect." **LGr**

⊖⊖⊖ **Drink: recent vintages for up to 10 years**

Turley's dense planting makes the most of Marcassin's 10 acres (4 ha). ▶

MIS EN BOUTEILLE AU CHÂTEAU

PAVILLON BLANC
2001

DU
CHÂTEAU MARGAUX

BORDEAUX
APPELLATION BORDEAUX CONTRÔLÉE
S.C.A. CHÂTEAU MARGAUX PROPRIÉTAIRE À MARGAUX - FRANCE

14,8% vol   75 cl

Vin de pays du jardin de la France
CÉPAGE ROMORANTIN

Provignage

2009

Vigne pré-phylloxérique
Mis en bouteille au domaine de la Charmoise
Henry Marionnet
Vigneron à Soings (Loir-et-Cher) France
PRODUIT DE FRANCE 14 % alc./vol. 750 ml   L 322

Château Margaux
Pavillon Blanc 2001

Origin France, Bordeaux
Style Dry white wine, 14.8% ABV
Grape Sauvignon Blanc

Henry Marionnet
Provignage Romorantin 2009

Origin France, Loire, Touraine
Style Dry white wine, 14% ABV
Grape Romorantin

Although famed above all for its great red wine, Château Margaux also makes a highly regarded white called Pavillon Blanc. On one of the oldest parts of the Margaux estate, there is a 30-acre (12 ha) vineyard planted solely with Sauvignon Blanc. When the Margaux appellation was officially demarcated in 1955, this vineyard was excluded owing to a high risk of spring frost, and so it is bottled as a plain Bordeaux Blanc rather than AOC Margaux.

Unusually for Sauvignon, Pavillon Blanc is barrel-fermented, with a further seven to eight months in barrels. Annual production is usually in the region of 35,000 bottles. Perhaps the greatest vintage of Pavillon Blanc yet made, the 2001 has unsurpassed levels of concentration, complexity, and depth. Long and smooth, with tremendous length, the rich fruit and crisp acidity mask the eye-wateringly high 14.8 percent alcohol. The wine tends to become closed and surly at about two years, but after seven or eight years in bottle it blossoms into one of the finest dry white wines made in Bordeaux. Such a grand wine deserves to be drunk with grand food, such as lobster, scallops, and certain cheeses. **SG**
🍷🍷🍷🍷 Drink: to 2017+

"What do you take me for? A Parisian?" exclaims Henry Marionnet. He is recounting how, in 1998, he was offered a 10-acre (4 ha) parcel of pre-phylloxera vines by an "old peasant" neighbor. It is easy to imagine Marionnet's anticipation, no doubt mixed with skepticism, the first time he saw these ancient plants. If they were genuine, they would be a real treasure trove, perhaps hard to quantify in financial terms, but pure gold for a winemaker with a sense of history. Marionnet called in experts, who declared the vines to be Romorantin. They also accepted, as "probably" true, anecdotal evidence that the vineyard had been planted in 1850 and escaped phylloxera in 1870. So Marionnet bought the parcel and started to vinify Provignage.

The suspicion to which such a poetic tale gives rise is that the charm will lie more in the story than in the wine itself; a kind of liquid historical romance. Not so. Provignage is certainly a characterful wine, but it has a floral, honey aroma, and a rich, viscous, nougat palate, sharply offset by a lean, mineral streak—all of which translates into a highly pleasurable as well as a unique wine. **KA**
🍷🍷🍷🍷 Drink: to 2017+

Château Margaux is often called the "Versailles of the Médoc."

Marqués de Murietta *Castillo Ygay Blanco Gran Reserva* 1962

Origin Spain, Rioja
Style Dry white wine, 12.8% ABV
Grapes Viura 93%, Malvasía 7%

Marqués de Murrieta set the pace not only for classic red Rioja, but also for white. They produce several whites, but Castillo Ygay has always been reserved for only the very best vintages, as for the reds. They have been making and selling traditional oak-aged whites since the company was founded in 1852. And they have remained faithful to their style, resisting the trend for young, fresh, light whites that started over two decades ago when the technology to produce them in this way became widely available to winemakers. They regard their *reserva* whites as a completely different product from those released shortly after the harvest, one that is aimed at a completely different kind of drinker.

The 1962 comes from a special vintage, and the quality of the perfectly ripe grapes, with the traditional vinification methods, has given this wine remarkable longevity. It spent over eighteen years in the company's best old American oak barrels, before nearly five years in bottle. The insides of the barrels were caked with tartrate crystals, helping to protect the wine against oxidation and preserving its color. It was finally bottled in June 1982.

The fashion for young and fruity whites is fading for wine connoisseurs looking for something more profound. Bored with similar, international-style whites, they demand more complex, oak-aged whites with a marked personality. These are the people who appreciate Castillo Ygay whites. **LG**
🥂🥂🥂🥂🥂 **Drink: to 2017+**

Vineyards encircle Logroño, capital of the Rioja region. ➡

matassa.

Domaine Matassa *Blanc Vin de Pays des Côtes Catalanes* 2004

Origin France, Roussillon
Style Dry white wine, 13% ABV
Grapes Grenache Gris 85%, Maccabeu 15%

In 2001, New Zealanders Sam Harrop MW and Tom Lubbe purchased Clos Matassa, a small vineyard high up in the hills of the Coteaux du Fenouillèdes (since reclassified as Côtes Catalanes).

Lubbe had local knowledge: He had been making wine at the celebrated Domaine Gauby and also makes the remarkable Observatory wines in South Africa. Harrop is a consultant winemaker who had previously worked for six years as winemaker and buyer with U.K. retailer Marks & Spencer. In 2003 they purchased twelve further vineyard blocks, including some white vineyards. These vineyards are farmed using biodynamic principles, and the wines are made as naturally as possible.

Although the reds have been impressive, it is the white wine from this young domaine that has really caught the eye of the critics. The 2004 is an exceptional effort. A blend of Grenache Gris and Maccabeu from old vines, it is fermented with indigenous yeasts in *demi-muids*, then aged for eleven months on its fine lees in barrel. It is rich but fresh, with complex flavors and a distinctive minerality. This is a wine that will continue to evolve for many years in bottle. **JG**

⊖⊖ Drink: to 2019

Maximin Grünhauser *Abtsberg Riesling Auslese* 2005

Origin Germany, Mosel-Saar-Ruwer
Style Sweet white wine, 8% ABV
Grape Riesling

The first documented mention of Grünhaus dates back to February 966, when Emperor Otto I presented the Benedictine monastery of St. Maximin in Trier with buildings, vineyards, and estates. Excavations, however, suggest the existence of a vineyard in much earlier Roman times.

In the course of secularization, the property was auctioned off in 1810, and has been in the hands of the von Schubert family since 1822. Of the winery's three *monopole* vineyards the Abtsberg has a central position. The decomposed blue Devonian-slate soil creates bouquet-rich, finely tangy, spicy, full-bodied Rieslings with extremely elegant acidity.

The Auslese 2005 grew in the core area of this vineyard, directly overlooking the residence. This Auslese is demanding and seductive at the same time. It has a thickly woven scent of mango, passion fruit, and peach compote. Initially dense and juicy on the tongue, it is unusually fresh and balanced thanks to the mineral-rich acidity. The exotic fruits create an aftertaste that brings candied lime and papaya to mind. This is an Auslese that resurrects 2,000 years of winemaking history and its terroir with every sip. **FK**

⊖⊖⊖ Drink: to 2020+

◀ Vines trained in the *gobelet* or "bush-vine" style at Domaine Matassa.

Viña Meín
2011

Origin Spain, Galicia, Ribeiro
Style Dry white wine, 12.5% ABV
Grapes Treixadura 85%, Others 15%

Leiro, near Orense in the northeast of Spain, boasts a long tradition of winemaking, derived mainly from the Cistercian monastery of San Clodio. Its monks are responsible for the wine-dedicated atmosphere that impregnates this valley, covered with vineyards all along the River Avia.

While there is a long winemaking tradition in the area, Viña Meín is a young house, founded in the late 1980s, as part of the shift toward quality winemaking in Spain. The vines were all newly planted in parcels totalling 35 acres (14 ha). The dominant variety (around 80 percent) is the local Treixadura, with a ragbag of varieties making up the remaining 20 percent: Godello, Loureira, Torrontés, Albariño, and Lado. The winery includes all these varieties, all estate-grown, in the final blend.

The flagship wine bears the winery name, Viña Meín, and its unoaked version aspires to the purest fruit expression and a tight structure. The best vintages of Viña Meín—2004 or this 2011, for example—combine aromatic intensity (laurel bay, white fruit) and freshness in their youth, with noble maturity after a few years of bottle age. **JB**

🖲 **Drink: recent vintages for up to 6 years**

Alphonse Mellot
Sancerre Cuvée Edmond 2010

Origin France, Loire, Sancerre
Style Dry white wine, 13% ABV
Grape Sauvignon Blanc

The Alphonse Mellot vineyards are based largely around the Domaine La Moussière, a single 86-acre (35 ha) vineyard of Sauvignon Blanc to the south of Sancerre. Located at the heart of the appellation on Kimmeridgian soil, La Moussière contains the classic Sancerre limestone as well as the marls of St.-Doulchard and the chalky soil of Buzançais. La Moussière has been grown according to organic viticulture since the turn of the century and is now cultivated biodynamically.

Cuvée Edmond is produced from a parcel of old La Moussière vines planted between the 1920s and 1960s, with an average yield of 41 hectoliters per hectare. Fermentation takes place at the family's fifteenth-century cellars at Sancerre in new casks for 60 percent of the wine, though oak remains rarely used in the region. Cuvée Edmond is then aged on fine lees for a period that varies according to the year, with ten to fourteen months the norm. Although rich and concentrated for a white Sancerre, some may prefer it young and fresh, and it is an excellent match with shellfish or the local Chavignol cheese. **SG**

🖲🖲🖲 **Drink: to 2017+**

Alphonse Mellot's prestigious Domaine La Moussière vineyard. ➡

Miani
Tocai 1999

Origin Italy, Friuli Venezia Giulia
Style Dry white wine, 12.5% ABV
Grape Tocai Friulano

The 1999 vintage of this wine is one for which we can still legally use the name Tocai. After a European Union ruling, it is still unclear whether the grape will be renamed Friulano, Toccai, or something else, but we should remain philosophical and seek solace in a couple of lines from Shakespeare's *Romeo and Juliet*: "What's in a name? That which we call a rose, by any other name would smell as sweet."

Tocai Friulano has represented Friuli's winemaking industry for centuries. The grape is none other than Sauvignonasse or Sauvignon Vert. Not everyone is convinced that Sauvignon Vert and Sauvignon Blanc are related, but a sniff of recently fermented Tocai Friulano grape juice would convince anyone that they are. After a few weeks the Tocai loses its typical tomato-leaf aroma and moves toward softer, more honeyed tones.

The Tocai Miani 1999 is at the same time the perfect example of a great Tocai Friulano and an untypical example of it. It is untypical because, unlike most Tocai Friulanos, it will age gracefully over the medium to long term. It is perfect because it has all the depth and complexity that one could ever wish for in such a wine. The color is deep yellow with bright golden tinges. The nose is broad and enthralling, with soft notes of golden apple, honey, almonds, hay, white pepper, and other spices— even saffron. The palate is filled in every corner by its buttery sensuality, but do not imagine butter's flavor, rather its smooth texture. The very long, focused finish is unforgettable. **AS**

🍷🍷🍷🍷 **Drink: 2019**

Peter Michael
L'Après-Midi Sauvignon Blanc 2012

Origin USA, California, Sonoma Valley
Style Dry white wine, 14.2% ABV
Grape Sauvignon Blanc

Sir Peter Michael may well be better known in Britain than in the United States, where he pursued a second career as a wine producer. In his earlier life he built up a very successful electronics business, and he also founded the commercial radio station Classic FM. The sale of his business enabled him to purchase a wine estate. After a long search, he settled on the rather obscure Knights Valley, between northern Napa and Sonoma. There he bought a large ranch in 1981, and the first vintage was 1987.

From the outset he focused on highly polished Cabernet, Chardonnay, and Sauvignon Blanc, although the range has subsequently expanded. His team both purchased fruit and developed estate vineyards, many on rocky, volcanic soils up in the mountains behind the winery. Yields are very low, and so, consequently, is the production of many of his cuvées. Initial vintages of the Sauvignon Blanc—given a French name, like most of the Peter Michael wines—were made from Howell Mountain fruit, but since the late 1990s the source has been estate-grown grapes from an elevation of 1,200 feet (366 m). The wine is barrel-fermented with natural yeasts, but little new oak is used.

In good vintages, the wine typically has ripe, appley aromas, enlivened by a discreet spiciness, as is the palate. There is a touch of sweetness on the finish that probably derives from the alcohol level, since there is no residual sugar in the wine. Lively acidity gives good length, and ensures the wine can age over the medium term. **SBr**

🍷🍷🍷 **Drink: to 2020**

Vines are bathed in late afternoon sun on the Peter Michael estate. ➡

Millton Vineyard *Te Arai Vineyard Chenin Blanc* 2002

Origin New Zealand, Gisborne
Style Dry white wine, 12.5% ABV
Grape Chenin Blanc

It is amazing that as recently as the 1980s, New Zealand's most widely planted white grape was Müller Thurgau, the Sauvignon Blanc revolution had only just started, and the industry was tiny. Now the thriving New Zealand white wine scene is dominated by Sauvignon Blanc, with Chardonnay a distant second in terms of profile. Riesling, Pinot Gris, and Gewürztraminer make up the roster of commonly encountered white varieties, which makes this wine, a varietal Chenin Blanc, a bit of a rarity. But it is so good you wonder why more producers have not planted this characterful Loire grape.

Millton Vineyard is just as well known for being a New World pioneer of biodynamics— practiced here for almost twenty-five years—as it is for its wines. The 74-acre (30 ha) estate, located on the banks of the Te Arai River, has been run according to Steiner's biodynamic principles from the outset and was the first in New Zealand to achieve organic certification.

Although good results are obtained here with other grape varieties, it is the Chenin Blanc that has established Millton's reputation. Millton's Chenins typically display crisp fruit in their youth, but age into a mellow roundness. The 2002 is a good vintage and shows the creamy straw notes typical of the variety. There is a rich, rounded texture, with good concentration and minerally acidity. Aging should bring a bit more honey and perhaps some lanolin character. The Milltons reckon their Chenin has the potential to age for fifteen years from release. **JG**

⊘ **Drink: to 2017+**

FURTHER RECOMMENDATIONS
Other great vintages
2000 • 2001 • 2004 • 2005 • 2007
More wines from the same producer
Opou Vineyard Chardonnay and Riesling • Growers Series Gisborne Gewürztraminer and Briant Vineyard Viognier

Sheltered, river-valley Chenin Blanc vineyards at Gisborne. ➡

Mission Hill
S.L.C. Riesling Icewine 2004

Origin Canada, British Columbia, Okanagan Valley
Style Sweet white wine, 10.5% ABV
Grape Riesling

Located approximately 250 miles (400 km) east of Vancouver, Mission Hill was founded by Anthony von Mandl in 1981. Former Montana winemaker John Simes joined the estate in 1992 and remains at the helm. The spectacular winery, which was completed in 2006 after six years of work, was designed by Seattle architect Tom Kundig.

Icewine is produced less frequently in the Okanagan than it is in Ontario (home of renowned Icewine producer Inniskillin), and Mission Hill's S.L.C. (Select Lot Collect) take on Canada's flagship wine is made from Riesling rather than the more commonly used Vidal. Grapes were harvested in January 2005 at 12ºF (-11ºC) at the Naramata Ranch (next to Lake Okanagan) and Mission Hill Road vineyards, from which a mere 476 cases of wine were produced.

S.L.C. Riesling Icewine is intensely sweet, with a whopping 255 g/l of residual sugar, though this is well matched by 12 g/l of total acidity. It feels almost cloying at first, but the acidity is pronounced on the finish, leaving a clean, refreshing aftertaste. With its fine length and intense but elegant fruit, the 2004 is one of John Simes's best Icewines. **SG**

🍷🍷🍷🍷 **Drink: to 2019+**

Mitchelton *Airstrip Marsanne*
Roussanne Viognier 2012

Origin Australia, Victoria, Nagambie Lakes
Style Dry white wine, 14% ABV
Grapes Marsanne 40%, Roussanne 30%, Viognier 30%

In 1967, Melbourne entrepreneur Ross Shelmerdine commissioned wine industry stalwart Colin Preece to find the best site for premium wine grape growing in southeastern Australia. Preece chose an old grazing estate in the Nagambie district of central Victoria. The site's history stretches back to 1836, when the explorer Major Thomas Mitchell crossed the river on his way from Sydney to Melbourne. The riverside town was to have been called Mitchellstown.

The vineyard's first sod was turned in 1969. Don Lewis joined Preece for the estate's first vintage in 1973, and became the winemaker when Preece retired in 1974. That year, Mitchelton's striking winery complex, designed by Ted Ashton, was opened.

Mitchelton's focus is on the Rhône varieties. Marsanne is a specialty of central Victoria, which has the largest plantings outside France. Made in an opulent, slightly oaked style, Airstrip's Marsanne and Roussanne are barrel-fermented in 20 percent new French oak, whereas the Viognier is barrel-fermented in four-year-old French barrels to retain greater fruit expression. It is rare to find blends of all three of these Rhône varieties. **SG**

🍷🍷🍷 **Drink: to 2017**

Robert Mondavi
Fumé Blanc I Block Reserve 1999

Origin USA, California, Napa Valley
Style Dry white wine, 13.5% ABV
Grape Sauvignon Blanc

When Robert Mondavi opened his winery in 1966, the quality of Sauvignon Blanc grown in Napa Valley was less than spectacular. He decided to experiment with the grape, hoping to produce a wine more like the great Pouilly-Fumés and Blanc Fumés he had tasted. Mondavi fermented the juice in stainless-steel tanks after a period of skin contact, and then aged it in new oak barrels.

Mondavi produced a wine so different that some did not believe it was Sauvignon Blanc, so he concluded that he needed a proprietary name to distinguish it from the jug wine associated with the variety. Thus was born, in a simple reversal of the French, Fumé Blanc. Mondavi's greatest Fumé Blanc is the I Block Reserve, exclusively from the To-Kalon vineyard at the Oakville estate. The I Block, planted in 1945 on phylloxera-resistant rootstock, may be the oldest Sauvignon Blanc planting in North America.

The 1999 is still bright, crisp, and focused. The initial, intense attack of fresh citrus fruits continues on the palate, where it blooms with tropical, mineral, and herbal characters, all showing remarkable concentration, persistence, and length. **LGr**
❸❸❸ Drink: to 2020

Mount Eden
Chardonnay 1988

Origin USA, California, Santa Cruz Mountains
Style Dry white wine, 13% ABV
Grape Chardonnay

An irascible and eccentric wine genius, Martin Ray planted his first vineyard on Mount Eden in 1942. The varieties were Pinot Noir, Chardonnay, and later Cabernet Sauvignon. During the 1960s, Ray brought in investors to help him develop more vineyards. However, the partnership soured, and the 1970 vintage was Ray's last from the vines he had planted.

The new owners rechristened the property Mount Eden Vineyards and produced their first vintage in 1972. In 1981 Jeffery Patterson was hired as assistant winemaker. He became head winemaker a year later and has been in charge ever since.

Mount Eden Chardonnay is one of relatively few Californian Chardonnays that ages gracefully. Wine writer Claude Kolm believes that it has more in common with fine white Burgundy than its Californian counterparts, resembling a top Puligny-Montrachet for its minerality and acquiring the austerity of Chablis as it ages. At a vertical tasting back to 1976, Kolm chose the 1988 as his best wine, praising its "great acidity in the mouth, minerality, stoniness, and some apple flavors, and overall electricity, almost like a great Riesling." **SG**
❸❸❸❸ Drink: to 2018+

Mount Horrocks *Cordon Cut Riesling* 2006

Origin Australia, South Australia, Clare Valley
Style Sweet white wine, 12% ABV
Grape Riesling

Mount Horrocks is located in the old railway station of tiny Auburn, a one-pub town at the southern end of the Clare Valley. The Ackland brothers established the Mount Horrocks label in 1981 to process fruit from vineyards that had been planted in 1967, and Jeffrey Grosset was their consultant winemaker for many years. Although he now has his own label, Grosset is still heavily involved with Mount Horrocks—he is the life partner of Stephanie Toole, who purchased the estate in 1993. The pair enjoy a friendly rivalry regarding her winery, yet they delight in each other's success.

Mount Horrocks produces a range of Clare Valley wines, the most notable and unique of which is the Cordon Cut Riesling. "Cordon Cut" refers to a risky process that involves cutting the canes when the grapes are ripe, allowing the remaining fruit to concentrate and raisin naturally on the vine. This results in intense flavor and richness.

The Mount Horrocks Cordon Cut Riesling 2006 is pale yellow-lime in color. Floral Riesling fruit aromas jump out of the glass. In the mouth, the wine is lusciously sweet, without being at all cloying. It displays delicate yet intense fruit flavors of orange and mandarin, with honey, spice, and mineral aromas. The fine, zingy acid balances the fruit intensity. The wine can be enjoyed immediately or cellared for up to a decade. A frost devstated vineyards in the southern Clare Valley in 2006, so cordon cut was made from a vineyard further north for the 2007 vintage. **SG**
ⓈⓈ **Drink: to 2018+**

FURTHER RECOMMENDATIONS
Other great vintages
1996 • 2000 • 2001 • 2002
More wines from the same producer
Watervale Chardonnay • Mount Horrocks Riesling
Mount Horrocks Semillon • Mount Horrocks Shiraz

This Mount Horrocks sales outlet was once an Auburn railway station. ➡

MOUNT HORROCKS WINES

Mountadam
Chardonnay 2006

Origin Australia, South Australia, Eden Ridge
Style Dry white wine, 14% ABV
Grape Chardonnay

If one single type of wine may be said truly to have led the charge of the southern hemisphere wine industries on the European heartlands, it was Australian Chardonnay. The mouth-filling extract, the tropical fruit flavors, and the unabashed layers of sweet-spiced oak were like nothing Europe had ever produced. However, antipodean "Chardie" now has less overt oak on the everyday bottlings, and vineyards are being planted at higher altitudes, making for more European acid-fruit orientation.

The development has been traceable in its finest detail at the Mountadam winery, founded by one of the giants of Australian viticulture, the late David Wynn. Chardonnay for its barrel-aged cuvée comes from the oldest plantings in South Australia, grown on the High Eden Ridge, where cooler daytime temperatures and low yields combine to offer propitious conditions that many would envy.

Mountadam's winemaker is now Con Moshos, once aide-de-camp to Brian Croser in Petaluma days. In 2006, he produced the estate's best Chardonnay for some years, from the array of clones originally planted by David Wynn (one believed to be unique to Mountadam—Marble Hill). Although the wine has the textural density of low-yield must, it is also supremely graceful. There are nectarine, Galia melon, and pear scents and flavors, and the wood adds a subtle note of nutmeg. A substantial, buttered-hazelnut finish speaks volumes. **SW**
🚫🚫🚫 **Drink: recent vintages within 5 years**

◄ *Echium plantagineum* weeds grow among the Mountadam vines.

Egon Müller *Scharzhofberger Riesling Auslese* 1976

Origin Germany, Mosel-Saar-Ruwer
Style Sweet white wine, 8% ABV
Grape Riesling

Müller-Catoir *Mussbacher Eselshaut Rieslaner TBA* 2001

Origin Germany, Pfalz
Style Sweet white wine, 9% ABV
Grape Rieslaner

There is no other winery that can so indisputably be considered the "Elysium of Riesling" as Scharzhof in the Saar Valley, run by the Müller family for five generations. The Rieslings of the associated Scharzhofberg vineyard are among the most sought-after and expensive wines in the world.

Müller's wines almost magically dissolve the conceptual paradox between purity and complexity. From the great 1976 Scharzhof vintage, there is a range of Ausleses that can be differentiated only minimally in their almost transcendental quality, and yet each shows its own remarkable personality thanks to single-vat bottling. In 2006, the Hamburg author Stephan Reinhardt tasted the Auslese No. 32 for *The World of Fine Wine* magazine: "Zesty and multilayered bouquet, with hints of orange tea, cigar, tobacco, and dried apricots. Very stylish, smooth structure, matched by beautifully precise, sweet fruit, layered with honey and cut by brilliant, super-fine acidity. Showing both wonderful concentration and finesse, this is an intense, perfectly balanced, totally irresistible Auslese." According to Reinhardt, these wines clarify rather than cloud the mind. **FK**

🍷🍷🍷🍷🍷 Drink: to 2040+

As the name suggests, Rieslaner is a cross between Silvaner and Riesling. Created in 1921, the Rieslaner ranks today among the rarest grape varieties in Germany: It is cultivated on only around 210 acres (85 ha) of land. As choice Beerenauslese or Trockenbeerenauslese (TBA), Rieslaner can be counted among the world's finest dessert wines.

At the traditional Palatinate estate, Müller-Catoir, Rieslaner has been particularly well cultivated for many decades. The noble sweet wines of this variety are elixirs at Müller-Catoir that exhibit almost unbelievable intensity and nearly explosive fruit flavors combined with intoxicating complexity. You can dive into layer after layer of exotic fruit and fresh citrus aromas.

The TBA of the 1990 vintage was the first German wine to which Robert Parker granted the perfect score of 100 points. The 2001 TBA, however, reached a new height. It was celebrated by *Gault Millau* as "one of the finest wines ever produced in Germany." Only 85 gallons (325 liters) were produced, though—a tiny drop given the worldwide demand for this wine experience. **FK**

🍷🍷🍷🍷🍷 Drink: to 2030+

Salvatore Murana *Passito di Pantelleria Martingana* 2000

Origin Italy, Sicily, Pantelleria
Style Sweet white wine, 15% ABV
Grape Zibibbo

On the sun-scorched, windswept terraces of the tiny island of Pantelleria, the Murana family grows the Zibibbo, a clone of Muscat also known as Muscat of Alessandria. The soil is rocky and of volcanic origin. Each vine has to be planted in a hole dug in the earth and sheltered by a small, drystone wall against the fierce wind. The plants are pruned short and their growth is almost horizontal, to the extent that the vegetation touches the ground. The top of the plant is given the characteristic "bread basket" shape, the fruit grown inside the "basket," still for protection.

Murana owns vineyards in different parts of the island, called Costa, Gadir, Mueggen, Khamma, and Martingana. This last one is in the south of the island, and the vines were planted in 1932. Given their age, the soil, and the climate, these plants produce a tiny crop, which is harvested at two different times. Some of the grapes are dried on stone slabs, and the rest are used freshly picked, to achieve opulence and freshness. The wine exhales the aromas of the island: dried fruits, dates, spices, and coffee. The palate is full and round, and the balance between sweetness and acidity borders on perfection. **AS**

🍸🍸🍸🍸 Drink: to 2028+

René Muré *Vorbourg Grand Cru Clos St.-Landelin Riesling* 2003

Origin France, Alsace
Style Dry white wine, 13.5% ABV
Grape Riesling

The 2003 growing season in Alsace was fraught with challenge for its winemakers. After a precociously mild, sunny March, the night of April 10 brought a severe frost. Then the intense sun of high summer caused excessive dryness and heat stress. René Muré's 37.5-acre (15 ha) Clos St.-Landelin in the grand cru Vorbourg, particularly the south-facing stony soils at the top of the Clos, bore the brunt of the heat; much of the Riesling had its ripening delayed; it was harvested in October, under snow.

Yet out of adversity comes triumph. Rainfall in September refreshed the vines. And those plots on the Clos's slopes with richer water-retaining clay soils fared well in the cooler autumnal conditions. Picked much later than usual, the Riesling grapes were rich in both natural sugar and phenolic maturity; they were fermented to a rich, full dryness and an alcohol level of 13.5 percent ABV.

The color is a lustrous straw gold, and with plenty of air—a case for decanting the wine—the complex nose has hints of oily *goût de pétrole*, a character of maturing Riesling. The palate reveals a powerful, fat wine, for medium-term cellarage. **ME**

🍸🍸🍸🍸 Drink: to 2018

Château Nairac

2001

Origin France, Bordeaux, Sauternes, Barsac
Style Sweet white wine, 13.5% ABV
Grapes Sémillon 90%, S. Blanc 6%, Muscadelle 4%

Nairac is the first property you see on entering the village of Barsac from the north. After phylloxera, the vineyard was planted with red vines, with white vines only replanted just before World War I. By the 1960s the wine was being sold only in bulk. Tom Heeter and Nicole Tari (the daughter of the owner of Château Giscours) bought the property in 1971, and Tom, a wine enthusiast from Ohio, swiftly restored the vineyards and *chais*. He improved quality with a severe selection at harvest. He also kept separately dozens of lots, all barrel-fermented, so that he could monitor them before deciding on the final blend.

In 1993 their son Nicolas took over, and he was even more of a perfectionist than his father, seeking fully botrytized fruit and essentially hand-crafting the wine. Only barrels with which he was fully satisfied were blended and bottled. Consequently the production of this 40-acre (16 ha) estate is very limited. The wine is aged in about 65 percent new oak, and is usually far richer than most other Barsac wines. The 2001 has powerful stone fruit aromas; it is sumptuous, unctuous, and full-bodied, and has finesse, too, and a long, orangey finish. **SBr**

⊖⊖⊖ **Drink: to 2030**

Daniele Nardello
Recioto di Soave Suavissimus 2003

Origin Italy, Veneto, Soave
Style Sweet white wine, 14% ABV
Grape Garganega

Daniele and Federica Nardello are two brothers whose 34 acres (14 ha) of vineyards occupy the most southerly part of the Soave Classico area. The older vineyards are trained in the traditional Pergola Veronese way, whereas the recent ones are on the Guyot system, allowing for higher planting densities and better exposure of the vines to the sunlight.

The Recioto di Soave Suavissimus comes from the older vines of the estate, usually harvested over six weeks to ensure different levels of ripeness. The grapes are then left to dry indoors until the following March, when they are pressed. Each batch is then vinified separately in barriques, before being blended and left to harmonize over several months in stainless-steel vats. The wine is then bottled, and matures for a further year before being released.

The wine is deep gold in color, with a bouquet ranging from fresh yellow flowers to dried apricots, almonds, and honey. Some hints of citrus fruit (tangerine) refresh the whole picture. On the palate, it is intense, and the acidity balances the high sugar content, helping the wine retain its vibrancy through the long, well-focused finish. **AS**

⊖⊖⊖ **Drink: to 2020**

Navazos Niepoort
Vino Blanco 2012

Origin Spain, Jerez de la Frontera
Style Dry white wine, 12.5% ABV
Grape Palomino Fino

Beyond its initial aim of selecting and bottling some of the hidden and uncommercialized resources of established bodegas, Equipo Navazos has also taken part in collaborations to explore the identity of traditional Andalusian wines. This wine, made with Portuguese winemaker Dirk Niepoort, is a perfect exemplar of this curiosity in practice.

In the eighteenth century, fortification was rare in the wines of Sanlúcar de Barrameda. Jesús Barquín, one of the leading partners in Equipo Navazos, makes the point that in 1801 while the best grapes in Sanlúcar were the *listanes* (Palomino Fino) and the best vineyards those of *tierras blancas* (albariza soils), "if the grapes are of top quality, the whites need nothing more; it is true that some add a quarter of refined spirit to stabilize them, but they risk the wines becoming coarse as a result of this." The 2012 Vino Blanco employs the same approach. Grapes are fermented in butt using indigenous yeasts and then aged for eight months under a layer of naturally occurring *flor*. No alcohol was added and the wine finished at 12.5% ABV. This is a delicate low-acid wine with hints of sea spray and flowers. **FP**

⊖⊖ **Drink: on release and up to five to ten years**

Neudorf
Moutere Chardonnay 2010

Origin New Zealand, Nelson
Style Dry white wine, 14% ABV
Grape Chardonnay

Founded by Tim Finn and his wife Judy in 1978, Neudorf is the leader in the Nelson wine region. The estate's Chardonnay plantings spill down a gentle north-facing slope overlooking a side branch of the Moutere Valley on New Zealand's South Island. It is in one of the country's sunniest regions, where clear skies allow for rapid cooling at night, nurturing the slow development of flavors that comes with significant diurnal temperature variation. Grapes are hand-harvested from the old vine plantings, with a smaller portion from the neighboring Beuke vineyard also making the final blend.

Moutere tends to produce white wines of concentration and texture. The Chardonnay has strong minerality and a pronounced lime blossom opulence, according to Finn. Few people consider aging New Zealand Chardonnay in their cellar, but over five years this becomes a fine example of bottle-aged wine: rounded, supple, and elegant. The oak of its youth turns into a pronounced honeysuckle flavor. There is still plenty of lively acidity and fleshy fruit, confirming that this can be aged for several more years for further complexity. **SG**

⊖⊖⊖ **Drink: recent vintages for up to 10 years**

Newton Vineyards
Unfiltered Chardonnay 2005

Origin USA, California, Napa Valley
Style Dry white wine, 15.5% ABV
Grape Chardonnay

Dr. Su Hua Newton almost faced a mutiny from her assistant winemakers and many of her distributors when she decided to produce an unfiltered Chardonnay. But she and her husband Peter have often ventured into places where others have not dared to tread, being among the first to establish a winery on Spring Mountain in 1977. Dr. Newton has been the winemaker since the late 1990s.

The grapes from the thirty-five-year-old Wente clone Chardonnay vines are picked from dawn to 11 A.M. so they arrive cool at the winery. The juice is quickly put into barrels to ferment on native Carneros yeasts. As the cellar is built into Spring Mountain, the cool temperatures encourage long, slow fermentations of roughly eight months. *Bâtonnage* is eschewed so as not to obscure the expression of terroir and natural fruit purity. The wine is then blended and left in barrels for up to another year. It is never fined or filtered to preserve every nuance of aroma and flavor. It reveals tremendous mid-palate texture and density, and the persistence and layers of flavor of top white Burgundy—with which it shares the capacity to age for a decade or more. **LGr**

🍷🍷 Drink: to 2017+

Niepoort
Redoma Branco Reserva 2003

Origin Portugal, Douro Valley
Style Dry white wine, 14% ABV
Grapes Rabigato, Codega, Donzelinho, Viosinho, Arinto

Niepoort is a rare beast indeed these days—a small, family-run, independent Port shipper that, under Dirk Niepoort, has become one of the most innovative producers of unfortified wines in the Douro. The firm was established in 1842, with Dirk being the fifth generation to head the company.

Niepoort seeks out small, often unusual, plots of old vines for his best wines. He often finds little parcels of vines belonging to other growers and buys the grapes at a premium if they are what he wants. Redoma Branco is sourced from vineyards at 1,300 to 2,300 feet (400–700 m), where the cooler climate is more suited to white varieties.

Although cooler, these are still hot vineyards for white grapes, so hand selection before pressing is essential, to remove rotten berries and bunches where the excess sugar and lower acid levels would result in unbalanced wine. Fermentation and aging in French oak gives the wine a lovely toasty spiciness; but malolactic fermentation is avoided here, to preserve as much of the natural acidity as possible. The result is a wine with a remarkable resemblance to a fine white from the Côte de Beaune. **GS**

🍷🍷🍷 Drink: recent vintages for up to 10 years

Nigl
Riesling Privat 2005

Origin Austria, Kremstal
Style Dry white wine, 13% ABV
Grape Riesling

Kremstal refers to quite diverse locations around the legendary Nibelungen city of Krems. The massive granite hill and castle of Senftenberg is the most striking landmark on the Krems River, and also home to its most striking wine. From the Piri vineyard—the steepest and best spot on the Senftenberg—Martin Nigl crafts two batches each of Riesling and Grüner Veltliner; those from his oldest vines and sweetest spots are labeled Privat. Nigl was the first Krems-area vintner from outside the Wachau to achieve fervid international acclaim, firstly for his 1990 Riesling.

In the exceedingly ripe and botrytis-marked 2005 vintage, high elevation, ventilation, and rock nearly impervious to water all benefited the Piri. Even so, Nigl had to select stringently, shunting the botrytis Riesling bunches to a separate and less site- or estate-typical bottling. The Riesling Privat illustrates the minerality and intricacy one expects at this address, more so than any of Nigl's other 2005s.

Buddleia and verbena, cool mintiness, and an utterly fascinating mineral mélange reminiscent of scallops, shrimp shells, and ocean spray inform this rich yet refined and long-lived beauty. **DS**
🝫🝫🝫 **Drink: to 2017+**

Nikolaihof
Vom Stein Riesling Smaragd 2004

Origin Austria, Wachau
Style Dry white wine, 12.5% ABV
Grape Riesling

Nikolaihof, a family domain owned by Nikolaus and Christine Saahs, has the distinction of being the first biodynamic wine estate in Europe. The Saahs work with old vines (forty to fifty years old), and although they grow six different varieties, it is Riesling and Grüner Veltliner that star, with the former achieving a remarkable elegance. The combination of biodynamic viticulture, which encourages deep rooting, and old vines means that their vineyards do well even in difficult years. "2002 was a great year for us. Our neighbors had problems with rot but we had none," recalls Christine. "In 2003 when it was very hot we had no problems with alcohol and acidity. The root system means our vines never show stress."

In their youth, Nikolaihof wines are tight and reticent, with bright, mineralic flavors and good acidity. The Vom Stein Riesling Smaragd is typical 2004; it shows focused fruit with a touch of herbs. The palate shows high acid, minerals, lemony fruit, and great length. Nikolaihof's practice of releasing small volumes of mature wines under the Vinothek label shows that these wines repay cellaring; the Vom Stein 2004 is certainly one to keep. **JG**
🝫🝫🝫 **Drink: to 2025**

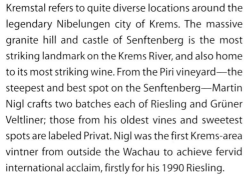

Oak Valley *Mountain Reserve Sauvignon Blanc* 2005

Origin South Africa, Elgin
Style Dry white wine, 13.4% ABV
Grape Sauvignon Blanc

The huge Oak Valley estate—which also farms deciduous fruit, flowers, and beef—was founded at the end of the nineteenth century by Antonie Viljoen, a Cape Colony senator. Vineyards were planted, and the area's first winery was established in 1908, although it fell into disuse a generation later. The estate's own wine production did not resume until the early twenty-first century.

The single-vineyard block that provides grapes for this wine (in the best vintages only) stands at an altitude of some 1,700 feet (518 m), on south-facing, unirrigated slopes above the Elgin Valley. The maiden Mountain Reserve 2005 emerged in recognition of the distinctive quality of this one vineyard, in a fine year for Sauvignon. Next would be the youthfully promising 2007. The Reserve's subtle power, elegant richness, and steely, flinty minerality combine to support the claim that Sauvignon can indeed offer complexity. If the Cape's Sauvignons are showing a convincing middle road between Loire classicism and the brilliant pungency of New Zealand, Oak Valley steers more toward the classic, reveling in the extremity of its own high origins. **TJ**

🍷🍷 **Drink: recent vintages within 5 years**

Jorge Ordoñez & Co *No. 3 Old Vines* 2005

Origin Spain, Malaga
Style Sweet white wine, 13% ABV
Grape Moscatel de Alejandría

In his book, *Wine: A Life Uncorked*, Hugh Johnson wrote about old bottles of "Mountain Wine" that he bought at auction from the Duke of Wellington's cellar. Winemaker Telmo Rodriguez and his U.S. importer, Jorge Ordóñez, decided to resurrect this special style of Malagan wine. Aided by Pepe Ávila of Bodegas Almijara, they explored the inaccessible schist and slate hills around Malaga, and purchased deep-rooted, drought-resistant Moscatel vines. Ordóñez appointed the late Austrian Alois Kracher (he died in 2007) as winemaker.

In the first vintage, 2004, they produced five wines, all numbered, as was Kracher's habit. No. 1 Selección Especial is made from overripe grapes left on the vines; No. 2 Victoria is based on grapes dried in a climate-controlled chamber; No. 3 Old Vines macerates the best of these dried grapes with the pulp and a one-year-old *crianza*; No. 4 is Essencia.

No. 3 is a full-bodied and intensely rich wine that possesses great acidity, incredible sweetness, and wonderful hazelnut, marmalade, coffee, and dried peach flavors. Drink it out of pure hedonism, after lunch, as if it were a dessert. **JMB**

🍷🍷🍷 **Drink: to 2020+**

◀ Vineyards variously oriented to catch the sun in Elgin.

Oremus

Tokaji Aszú 6 Puttonyos 1999

Origin Hungary, Tokaj
Style Sweet white wine, 11% ABV
Grapes Furmint, Hárslevelű, Muskalkoly

When the old communist wine company, or Borkombinát, split up in 1993, David Alvarez of Vega Sicilia in the Ribera del Duero (for many, Spain's greatest wine) was ready to buy up a decent portion of the domaine. The current director of Oremus provides an element of historical continuity, however: András Bacsó used to run the Borkombinát, and Oremus has the advantages of old stocks (including the fabulous 1972) and old vines.

The headquarters of Oremus are in the wine village of Tolcsva, where Aszú wine was first made in 1631. 1999 was the first vintage after 1989 when almost all the estates were making Aszú from fruit harvested on their own land, rather than buying it in. For that reason 1999 is really the earliest Aszú year when terroir character can be determined. At Oremus the wines are kept in cask for three years and a further two in bottle prior to release.

The 1999 6 Puttonyos wine is paler than most and redolent of peaches and crème caramel; the palate is dominated by peaches and apricots with a dash of honey. It has a powerful acidity. Best drunk with foie gras, blue cheese, or fruit-based desserts. **GM**
🅂🅂🅂🅂 **Drink: to 2019+**

Ossian

2011

Origin Spain, Rueda
Style Dry white wine, 14.5% ABV
Grape Verdejo

Ossian was born in 2005 as a joint venture between Javier Zaccagnini from Bodegas Aalto in Ribera del Duero and grower Samuel Gozalo. Rueda is the white wine appellation in central Spain whose only grape is Verdejo. But what is really unique here is that their 23 acres (9 ha) of organically farmed vineyards are still on their own roots, and predate phylloxera. Some vines are up to 180 years old. This is possible because Nieva, the village where the vines and winery are located, is a special area within the Rueda DO. It is far from the River Duero, and very high, at 2,800 feet (854 m), with an extreme continental climate characterized by much frost and snow.

Ossian's first vintage was only in 2005. It is normally a bright, green-gold color. The complex but well-focused nose shows a mix of oak and lactic notes (vanilla, smoke, *café au lait*, and toffee), lees, and flowers, together with white and yellow fruit, with citrus and medicinal touches. It is creamy in the mouth, showing plenty of oak, which will need time in bottle to integrate. Full of flavor, with pear, peach, and orange rind tones, the alcohol is well balanced by the acidity and the finish is very persistent. **LG**
🅂🅂 **Drink: recent vintages within 5 years**

André Ostertag *Muenchberg Grand Cru Riesling* 2005

Origin France, Alsace
Style Dry white wine, 12.5% ABV
Grape Riesling

Palacio de Bornos *Verdejo Fermentado en Barrica Rueda* 2012

Origin Spain, Rueda
Style Dry white wine, 13.5% ABV
Grape Verdejo

André Ostertag is one of Alsace's more outspoken practitioners. He cares about the quality of what the region as a whole produces as paternally as though he owned every last square foot of it.

The family estate, founded at Epfig in 1966, has gradually become entirely biodynamic. The Riesling produced from the grand cru vineyard of Muenchberg, of which Domaine Ostertag owns 3.25 acres (1.3 ha), is grown on gravelly, sandy soil, which results in wines that display the classic taut acidity of Alsace Riesling and levels of concentration that take several years to unravel.

In 2005, a hot, early summer was followed by cooler conditions in the latter half of August, resulting in a fine balance of ripeness and fresh acidity. This is evident from the very first aromatic impression of the Muenchberg Riesling, where the almost violent floral scents of the wine mingle with the steely, minerally streak typical of the grape. Over its first few years, its diamond-hard palatal texture has begun to yield up intense apple and lime fruit, without relinquishing so much as a petal of the gorgeous florality. **SW**
⊖⊖⊖ **Drink: to 2025**

Rueda is a white wine appellation centered around the village of Rueda, mainly in the province of Valladolid in Central Spain. Antonio Sanz is the fifth-generation descendant of Roque Sanz, who started a family winery more than 135 years ago. He is the most influential winemaker from the region.

The local Verdejo grape—which has only the name in common with the Portuguese versions—shares the honors here with the imported Sauvignon Blanc. Palacio de Bornos is the main brand, spanning Verdejo, Sauvignon, and blends of both, barrel- or tank-fermented. Palacio de Bornos Verdejo Fermentado en Barrica is most representative of their style, using vines at least forty-five years old.

The wine is straw yellow in color, and quite pale for a barrel-fermented white. On the nose, the barrel notes are well integrated with the green apple and pear fruit, showing laurel notes. The herbaceous character of the grape, the freshly cut grass notes, and the bitter touch to the finish combine well with the barrel notes. Depth, elegance, and complexity at an incredible price. This is one of the most reliable value white wines. **LG**
⊖ **Drink: recent vintages within 5 years**

Bodega del Palacio de Fefiñanes

Rías Baixas Albariño 2011

Origin Spain, Galicia, Rías Baixas
Style Dry white wine, 12.5% ABV
Grape Albariño

The Bodega del Palacio de Fefiñanes is the oldest winery in the region of Rías Baixas in Galicia. Founded in 1904, it is located in the cellars of the Palacio de Fefiñanes. The original owners were the first to bottle and label an Albariño wine, and their brand was registered as early as 1928. The winery owns 5 acres (2 ha) of vineyards and buys the rest of its grapes from growers in the region of Cambados, province of Pontevedra, where the winery is located.

The regular cuvée, also available in beautiful magnums, is fermented in stainless-steel tanks and bottled in its first year. In good vintages for this Atlantic appellation, the estate produces balanced and intense wines. The Albariño de Fefiñanes from such years is medium golden in color, with good intensity on the elegant nose, showing apple, floral, citric, and balsamic notes reminiscent of laurel. Medium-bodied in the mouth, with ripe acidity, the wine shows good weight of fruit, making it supple and long, with a typical bitter touch to the finish.

Contrary to popular belief, the best examples of Albariño drink better in their second or third year than when first released. **LG**

Drink: recent vintages within 5 years

Rafa Palacios

As Sortes 2012

Origin Spain, Valdeorras
Style Dry white wine, 13.5% ABV
Grape Godello

The Palacios are one of the major Spanish wine families. The second generation, represented by Álvaro Palacios, led the Priorat revolution at the end of the 1980s, and they later played a big part in the revival of Bierzo. In the meantime, young Rafael (Rafa) Palacios created Plácet, the iconic white Rioja.

At the start of the new century, Rafa left Rioja for Galicia to settle in Valdeorras—to many observers, the region with the greatest potential for quality whites in Spain. Here the native Godello grape had been producing some of the best and longest-lived whites in the country. Rafa, like his brother Álvaro, is passionate about poor hillside terroirs in forgotten or poorly developed viticultural regions of Spain. His vines are between twenty and forty-five years old, in small, scattered parcels. The climate is continental, with Atlantic influences, and the soil is granite.

As Sortes is generally golden in color, with good aromatic intensity and fine toasty notes that give way to ripe fruit (green apple, pineapple), aniseed, and a powerful mineral core of flint. Medium-bodied in the mouth, with good acidity, fresh and unctuous, leading to a remarkable finish. **LG**

Drink: recent vintages within 5 years

Pazo de Señorans
Albariño Selección de Añada 2006

Origin Spain, Galicia, Rías Baixas
Style Dry white wine, 12.5% ABV
Grape Albariño

Dom. Henry Pellé *Menetou-*
Salon Les Blanchais 2010

Origin France, Loire, Sancerre
Style Dry white wine, 12.5% ABV
Grape Sauvignon Blanc

The best things are often created or discovered accidentally, as is the case with Pazo de Señorans Selección de Añada. 1996 was one of the best modern vintages for Albariño, but a particular lot at Pazo de Señorans did not quite convince its owner—and president of the Rías Baixas DO—Marisol Bueno. So the wine was put to one side until they decided what to do with it. A couple of years later they tasted it and could hardly believe how the ugly duckling had turned into a beautiful swan. After years of experimenting, trying barrel fermentation or barrel aging, the tank-aging method was eventually identified. The 1996 was finally aged for twenty-seven months in stainless-steel tanks with its lees, bottled, and sold with great commercial success.

The wine clearly puts on weight with prolonged lees contact, as can be seen by the density and sensation in the mouth of a more mature vintage. Golden-yellow with greenish reflections, it has an aroma of good intensity; complex, with notes of black olive, flowers, and quince. Medium-bodied in the mouth, balanced by a very flavorful acidity, with lively fruit and a very persistent finish. **LG**

🛇🛇🛇 **Drink: recent vintages within 5 years**

Anne Pellé's father-in-law, Henry, was one of the pioneers of the AOC Menetou-Salon in the 1960s, her late husband continued the work, and her son, Paul-Henry, is gradually taking over from winemaker Julien Zernott. At their 100-acre (40 ha) domaine, commercial success has enabled experimentation. The zenith of this willingness to try new ideas is Clos des Blanchais, made from a single, southeast-facing, 6.4-acre (2.6 ha) vineyard, planted in the 1960s and vinified separately from the early 1980s.

The soil is Kimmeridgian limestone-clay and flint, embedded with thousands of tiny Jurassic oyster shells. Perhaps it is the power of suggestion, but after seeing these marine fossils scattered among the vines, it seems on tasting that a sea salt and iodine note has permeated into the wine. The 2005 nose was a delightful play of seaweed and honey. The palate had a spicy note, which came entirely from the terroir and the aging on lees, not from wood, and finished on a long, clean, saline note. The 2006 was crisp, light, and fresh as blossom on the nose, whereas the palate was intense and rich but with lots of acidity and a strong white sultana note. **KA**

🛇🛇🛇 **Drink: recent vintages within 5 years**

Peregrine
Rastasburn Riesling 2006

Origin New Zealand, Central Otago
Style Dry white wine, 12% ABV
Grape Riesling

André Perret
Condrieu Chéry 2004

Origin France, Northern Rhône, Condrieu
Style Dry white wine, 13% ABV
Grape Viognier

Central Otago is best known for its bold, fruity Pinot Noir, not least because Pinot Noir vines occupy around three-quarters of the region's vineyards. Riesling accounts for a more modest 4 percent of vineyard area, yet Central Otago is New Zealand's undisputed Riesling capital in terms of quality.

Cool, alpine Central Otago is New Zealand's only region with a continental climate. It also boasts schist slopes that suggest a rugged version of Germany's Mosel Valley. Central Otago Riesling is finer, tighter, and steelier than wine from other regions. A fine acid backbone and pronounced mineral flavors are what make Central Otago Riesling distinctive and special.

Peregrine is a progressive, experimental winery with access to vineyards in many parts of Central Otago, particularly the Cromwell Basin, source of some of the region's most exciting wines. Rastasburn Riesling was created from grapes grown in six Cromwell Basin vineyards. The 2006 has a more floral, perfumed character than usual, though the wine retains its strong citrus and mineral flavors. Ripe apricot, jasmine, grapefruit, and wet-slate characters amply testify to place and vintage. **BC**
🜚🜚 Drink: to 2018

Sepia photographs of the Condrieu hillsides taken at the time of World War I show slopes densely covered in vines. In the 1970s the hillsides were overgrown with brush, scrub, and tenacious acacia trees—and not a vine in sight. The Condrieu vineyard had dwindled to just under 30 acres (74 ha).

André Perret's grandfather came to Condrieu in 1925, and the first regular bottling of the wine from the Côteau de Chéry, the family's then only vineyard, started in those downtrodden early 1970s, when his father Pierre was at the helm. With Vernon, Chéry is one of the two most noble vineyards at Condrieu. For André, ownership of Viognier planted in 1948 and 1988 allows him to mix the fruit of very mature vines with that of more spritely plants.

Since the early 2000s, André has avoided extreme ripeness in his crop to achieve greater freshness, and to encourage what he terms, "the peach/apricot side of the aromas." Raised in new and young oak, with a small portion in steel vats, the Condrieu Chéry is bottled about one year after the harvest. 2004 was a vintage of generosity and abundance, tempered by a winsome elegance. **JL-L**
🜚🜚🜚 Drink: to 2017+

🄴 A Peregrine Wines vineyard hugs the valley floor at Gibbston.

R & A Pfaffl

Grüner Veltliner Hundsleiten 2005

Origin Austria, Weinviertel
Style Dry white wine, 13.5% ABV
Grape Grüner Veltliner

A vast arc of viticulture from the Danube to the Czech and Slovak frontiers, the Weinviertel earned its name through two centuries of quenching Austrian thirsts. The dominant grape in recent decades has been Grüner Veltliner. Roman and Adelheid Pfaffl were among the first Weinviertel vintners truly to distinguish themselves with the grape variety.

The Hundsleiten benefits from loess, the ocher glacial dust that so ably supports Grüner Veltliner in numerous growing regions. But there are also seams of water-retentive clay and heat-retaining stones that help to form an ideal medium for a wine of analogously layered complexity and structure. That these are the Pfaffls' oldest vines does not hurt quality, either. Enhance these features through late picking, spontaneous fermentation in wooden *fuder*, and a long nurturing sojourn on the lees, and the resulting wine combines exceptional succulent richness with vigor and precision. Blood orange, grapefruit zest, snap peas, cress, and green beans are all in evidence in the Hundsleiten 2005, a mix that will seem incongruous only to those not yet familiar with the wiles of Grüner Veltliner. **DS**

⊖⊖ Drink: to 2017+

F. X. Pichler

Grüner Veltliner Smaragd M 2001

Origin Austria, Wachau
Style Dry white wine, 14% ABV
Grape Grüner Veltliner

Grüner Veltliner dominates Austria's white vineyards as a workhorse grape, producing large volumes of fresh, lively, easy-drinking wines. However, it is also capable—in the right hands—of producing wines of real personality and power.

Franz Xaver Pichler—known to all as F. X.—is widely regarded as the Wachau's, and probably Austria's, greatest producer. M, standing for Monumental, was first produced in 1991. Its origin was an outstanding barrel of Grüner Veltliner in the winery, with an extra dimension of taste, which they subsequently aimed for deliberately. The grapes are harvested two to three weeks later than Pichler's single-vineyard wines.

M's calling card, especially in a great year like 2001, is the counterpoint of dryness and acidity on the one hand, with extract and complexity on the other. Several grams of residual sugar (up to 9 g/l are permitted) together with a high alcohol level contribute to an off-dry impression. This, allied to its density of flavor, suggests that the wine should be paired with either fairly rich, or at least decisively flavored, food such as dim sum or chili prawns. **SG**

⊖⊖⊖ Drink: to 2020+

A carving of St. Urban I, patron saint of winegrowers. ➜

PIEROPAN

VITICOLTORI IN SOAVE

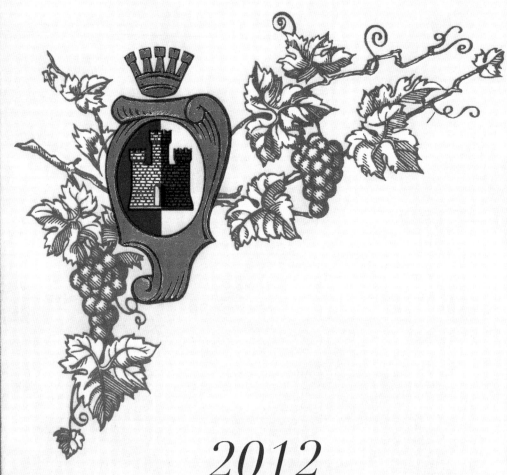

2012

La Rocca

Pieropan
Vigneto La Rocca 2012

Origin Italy, Veneto, Soave
Style Dry white wine, 13% ABV
Grape Garganega

Founded by Dr. Leonildo Pieropan in 1890, this distinguished Soave producer makes arguably the finest example of that dry white wine, which in other hands can be little better than insipid. Nino Pieropan and his wife Teresita fly the traditionalist flag in their winemaking, but have also long set the vinous standard in this part of northern Italy.

Pieropan's "basic" Soave Classico is a blend of the grapes of various vineyards scattered across the Soave Classico zone, lying just to the east of Verona. But the estate also produces two single-vineyard wines—Calvarino and La Rocca. The Calvarino vineyard, first bottled as such in 1971, is part of the original Pieropan estate and contains the traditional Soave varieties, Garganega and Trebbiano di Soave, grown on volcanic soil rich in basalt and tufa.

First made as a single-vineyard wine in 1978, La Rocca takes its name from the adjacent medieval castle that dominates the little town of Soave. The soil has more clay than Calvarino, and the vineyard is planted only with Garganega. The grapes are harvested relatively late to ensure maximum extract and ripeness. After aging for one year in oak barrels, the finished wine has more color, structure, and flavor than just about any other dry Soave. Also unusually for Soave, the wine ages well in the bottle (a tall flute rather than a Bordeaux-type bottle) for five or more years. When young, it is lively, crisp, and fruity, but with age it becomes more complex and rounded. La Rocca is ideal with fish like salmon and crab, and also excellent with white meat. **SG**

🍷🍷🍷 **Drink: recent vintages within 5 years**

Château Pierre-Bise
Quarts-de-Chaume 2002

Origin France, Loire, Anjou
Style Sweet white wine, 11.5% ABV
Grape Chenin Blanc

Claude Papin is as passionate about terroir as they come. Since taking over his father-in-law's estate in Beaulieu-sur-Layon in 1990, he has painstakingly used the concept of Unité Terroir de Base (Basic Terroir Unit) to identify twenty-five different mini-parcels across his 136 acres (55 ha) of vineyards. He believes that soil depth and the interception of solar radiation are the most important units, whereas wind speed has a huge impact on intensity.

Understanding these factors, and also his carboniferous, schist, and spilite soils, has helped Papin to differentiate precocious and later-ripening parcels that are vinified separately, according to their precise qualities. His focus on single-vineyard bottlings reflects his belief that a wine that emanates from different terroirs has no harmony or breeding. The proof is in the pudding, and the wines of Château Pierre-Bise are benchmark examples of their appellation, with a purity of expression and minerality that reflects Papin's meticulous vineyard practices and low yields.

The Quarts-de-Chaume appellation, 99 acres (40 ha), is renowned for powerful yet subtle sweet wines that are eminently age-worthy. High up on the appellation's steep, south-facing slope, with good exposure to the sun and wind, Château Pierre-Bise's precocious 6.6-acre (2.7 ha) parcel produces wines of great finesse and elegance. In 2002, a cool summer was followed by a fine autumn with good conditions for botrytis, which resulted in particularly well-balanced wines. **SA**

🍷🍷 **Drink: to 2050**

Pieropan's label features the fortress after which La Rocca is named.

Pierro
Chardonnay 2009

Origin Australia, Western Australia, Margaret River
Style Dry white wine, 13.5% ABV
Grape Chardonnay

After graduating in medicine from the University of Western Australia in 1973, Mike Peterkin gained a diploma in enology. From 1978 to 1981, he made wines at Enterprise in Clare, Cullen in Margaret River, and Alkoomi in Western Australia's Great Southern region—he was Margaret River's first professionally qualified winemaker. In the early 1980s, while still working as a locum doctor in Perth, he became increasingly intent on establishing his own winery. When a Busselton estate agent told him of a farm for sale, Peterkin left the city to check it out. He was not impressed but, hearing of another property on the agent's books at nearby Willyabrup, Peterkin insisted on seeing it—and promptly bought it.

Dissatisfied with the first three vintages after the inaugural 1983, Peterkin decided to make some radical changes, and the modern Pierro Chardonnay style was born with the 1986 vintage. Barrel-fermented, like white Burgundy, Pierro is perhaps the most powerful Chardonnay of the Margaret River region, though it has become finer in recent years. Pierro continues to earn its place among the most acclaimed small wineries in Australia. **SG**

☻☻☻ **Drink: recent vintages for up to 7 years**

Vincent Pinard
Harmonie 2010

Origin France, Loire, Sancerre
Style Dry white wine, 14% ABV
Grape Sauvignon Blanc

The grapes destined for Harmonie come from two plots, both in the Chêne Marchand *lieu-dit* of Sancerre. The plots are high up on the rolling hills above the village of Bué, where scattered white pebbles are evidence of the soil's high chalk content.

The Harmonie 2005 is still a very young, very closed wine. It has been aged in 100 percent new oak, and the wood flavors are obvious, as are crisp Cox apple flavors and fresh acidity. Yet it is still a little unknit. In 2006, Clement Pinard and his brother Florent, who had just taken over the winery, decided on a change. They aged one-third of the wine in oak barrels and the remaining two-thirds in older barrels. The flavor of wood is still there, but just as a backdrop, and the overall effect is much less robust.

The 2006 is an elegant and fine Sauvignon Blanc, with plenty of fruit and acidity, which suggests excellent aging potential. As an indication of its future, the 1996 is a beautiful wine, with a distinctive nose of white truffles, seaweed, oysters, and honey. The palate is very soft and subtle, with chalky flavors and notes of soft, floral fruit. The wood is obviously there—so it was correct to reduce it in 2006. **KA**

☻☻☻ **Drink: recent vintages for up to 10 years**

The town of Sancerre overlooks Loire vineyards from its hilltop site. ➜

Dom. Jo Pithon *Coteaux du Layon Les Bonnes Blanches* 2003

Robert & Bernard Plageoles *Gaillac Vin d'Autan* 2005

Origin France, Loire, Anjou
Style Sweet white wine, 12% ABV
Grape Chenin Blanc

Origin France, Southwest, Gaillac
Style Sweet white wine, 10.5% ABV
Grape Ondenc

Until the advent of dynamic, quality-focused producers like Jo Pithon, the sweet wines of Coteaux du Layon were often characterized by generous doses of sugar beet and sulfur. At the vanguard of the so-called "sugar hunters," who led a renaissance of naturally sweet Coteaux du Layon in the 1990s, Pithon enthralled critics with hyper-rich, exuberant cuvées of intoxicating sweetness.

Pithon produces a range of terroir-driven wines from a broad palette of tiny parcels of organically farmed Chenin Blanc in the Layon's best communes. Les Bonnes Blanches, in the commune of St.-Lambert-du-Lattay, is the village's foremost terroir. In 2003, a great vintage, Pithon's 2.5-acre (1 ha) vineyard produced two superb cuvées: Coteaux du Layon Les Bonnes Blanches 2003 and the flamboyant Coteaux du Layon Ambroisie.

Coteaux du Layon Les Bonnes Blanches 2003 was made from 100 percent botrytized grapes. Bottled in October 2005, the 2003 vintage is a corpulent wine that reflects Les Bonnes Blanches' signature elegance and underlying acidity. Its finish shows honeyed citrus and orchard fruits. **SA**

🍷🍷 **Drink: to 2018+**

Robert Plageoles is a man with a mission: to reclaim the almost lost heritage of the Gaillac region, not only in terms of local grape varieties, which were in danger of disappearing under the onslaught of more familiar "international" ones, but also in the method used to turn those grapes into a range of distinctive wine styles. Andrew Jefford describes him as a "viticultural archeologist."

The Vin d'Autan is made from the local Ondenc grape (from which Plageoles also makes a *sec* version). The wine is made by allowing the grapes to shrivel on the vine in the warm autumnal wind—a process accelerated by pinching off the bunches to suppress the flow of sap. This leads to miniscule yields, typically of 0.5 tons per acre. The grapes are further dried on straw mats and then fermented and aged in concrete tanks for twelve months.

In style, the 2005 resembles Tokay, with oxidative notes counterbalanced by bright acidity, and with an intense but not overpowering sweetness. On the palate, there are notes of bruised apple skins, quince, and walnuts. The finish is honeyed, but the vivid acidity keeps everything fresh. **JW**

🍷🍷🍷 **Drink: to 2030**

E. & W. Polz *Hochgrassnitzberg*
Sauvignon Blanc 2010

Origin Austria, South Styria
Style Dry white wine, 12.5% ABV
Grape Sauvignon Blanc

In the Austrian region of Südsteiermark (South Styria), Sauvignon Blanc excels, and instead of the usual assertive, grassy up-frontness that we have come to expect, Sauvignon here delivers a richer, more complex style of wine. Erich and Walter Polz have led the way in terms of Styrian fine wine production. Their family-run firm dates back to 1912, and in the mid-1980s ushered in the transition that has seen producers target the high-end market with their wines, rather than focus on quantity.

Altogether the brothers have access to 126 acres (51 ha) of vines. The source for this exceptional Sauvignon is the Hochgrassnitzberg vineyard, which abuts the Slovenian border. Its warm sand and limestone soils suit Sauvignon Blanc, producing ripe, flavorful grapes. These are fermented and matured in large oak barrels, with some vintages even seeing a bit of new oak, which marries surprisingly well with the bold, complex, herby flavors of Sauvignon from this site. The result is a serious white wine with a real sense of place, and some capacity to age, though this food-friendly white is perhaps best consumed early on in its life. **JG**

🔆🔆 **Drink: recent vintages for up to 8 years**

Domaine Ponsot
Morey St.-Denis Premier Cru 1990

Origin France, Burgundy, Côte de Nuits
Style Dry white wine, 13% ABV
Grapes Aligoté 50%, Chardonnay 50%

Although this is not the only great white wine in Burgundy's Côte de Nuits, none is so distinctive. Its austerity and uncompromising personality derive not only from its terroir but from its unusual varietal makeup. When, in 1911, William Ponsot came to plant a small limestone parcel in this Morey St.-Denis premier cru, he used a higher proportion of Aligoté than Chardonnay. According to Laurent Ponsot, now in charge of the domaine, Aligoté best expresses the character of the site, and most of the very old vines are still of this variety.

The wine is made with minimal intervention in natural processes, the better to translate the terroir, with no malolactic fermentation, no new oak, no *bâtonnage*, no fining, and no filtration. The aromas and flavors range from blossom and citrus, through apple, pear, and quince, to chalk, flint, smoke, honey, nuts, and nougat. The wine ages remarkably well. At the largest ever tasting of the wine, Master Sommelier Frank Kämmer gave his highest equal score to the 1990, which "combines the purity of a Manzanilla, the silkiness of a fine Burgundy, and the elegance of a Dom Pérignon." **NB**

🔆🔆🔆 **Drink: to 2020+**

Prager
Achleiten Riesling Smaragd 2001

Origin Austria, Wachau
Style Dry white wine, 14% ABV
Grape Riesling

Franz Prager of Weissenkirchen was one of the first Wachauer to recognize the quality of the region's dry white wines back in the 1950s. Along with other eminent winemakers, he created Vinea Wachau in 1983, which classifies the local wines according to three sorts: Steinfeder, a light, unchaptalized summer wine; Federspiel, a Kabinett with medium weight; and Smaragd, a powerful Kabinett or Spätlese that is akin to a dry Auslese in Germany.

Since 1992, the wines on this 31-acre (13 ha) estate have been made by Prager's son-in-law Anton ("Toni") Bodenstein. There was a high proportion of Riesling here from the start. Whereas the Wachau as a whole contains only 10 percent Riesling, the Prager lands are 63 percent and rising. The wine is grown in the large Achleiten vineyard, where the vines are now more than fifty-five years old, and the wines, including the 2001, are often marked by aromas of exotic fruits, mandarin blossom, ripe peaches, and tea leaves. The dominant note is of apricot and peach. These powerful, dry white wines—which benefit from bottle age—are excellent with Austria's rich veal dishes, and with pork and chicken. **GM**
⊖⊖⊖ **Drink: to 2017+**

J. J. Prüm *Wehlener Sonnenuhr*
Riesling Auslese Goldkapsel 1976

Origin Germany, Mosel-Saar-Ruwer
Style Sweet white wine, 7.5% ABV
Grape Riesling

In German wine history, 1976 has gone down as one of the "vintages of the century." High temperatures in May and June made for a "storybook flowering". The long hot spell was broken several times by short but heavy rains, meaning that ripening was never suspended by the high temperatures. The very early ripening process had already brought extraordinarily high must weights by the beginning of October. Some 80 percent of all Rieslings harvested this year in the Mosel-Saar-Ruwer were Spätleses or Ausleses.

Due to the low acidity levels, many of these wines were ready to drink very early, which today leads some tasters to worry about their further development. There need be no anxiety, however, about the exemplary Auslese Goldkapsel that Dr. Manfred Prüm created in this year. It very reluctantly revealed its full glory, but today shines brightly and has many more years of brilliance ahead.

Typically for this estate, Prüm's Auslese Goldkapsel 1976 is marked with the subtle inner tension of the finest acids and distinctive mineral richness, while at the same time exhibiting highly complex fruit flavors. **FK**
⊖⊖⊖⊖⊖ **Drink: to 2025**

J. J. Prüm *Wehlener Sonnenuhr*
Riesling Spätlese No. 16 2001

Origin Germany, Mosel-Saar-Ruwer
Style Sweet white wine, 7.5% ABV
Grape Riesling

Wehlener Sonnenuhr is without doubt regarded as one of the best white wine vineyards in the world. And although many other well-known producers own land here as well, this site is intrinsically linked to the name Joh. Jos. Prüm. This wine-grower dynasty can be traced back to the twelfth century.

Few wine growers have such an innate feeling for the Prädikat Spätlese as Dr. Manfred Prüm who, assisted by his daughter Katharina, is responsible for this wine's worldwide reputation. His wines in this weight class, with their finely tuned balance of beguiling sweetness, delicate fruit, intoxicating acidity, and feather-light alcohol, are textbook examples for superb German Spätleses. No one has won the *Gault Millau Weinguide*'s distinction for the best Riesling Spätlese in Germany as often as Prüm. With the 1999, 2000, and 2001 vintages, he achieved this for three consecutive years.

After about five years of bottle aging, the excellent 2001 Spätlese single-vat bottling No. 16 reached its plateau of maturity, on which it should remain for two decades. In its precision, elegance, and grace, it resembles a prima ballerina. **FK**

🍷🍷 **Drink: to 2030**

Jacques Puffeney
Arbois Vin Jaune 1998

Origin France, Jura, Arbois
Style Dry white wine, 14% ABV
Grape Savagnin

In Montigny-les-Arsures in AOC Arbois, Jura's largest wine-growing village, Jacques Puffeney has managed to bridge the gap between tradition and modern thinking in Jura winemaking. Puffeney's 5.5 acres (2.2 ha) of Savagnin are grown on classic blue/gray marl soils, most facing west or southwest.

Puffeney believes that constant selection during the six-year maturation period in barrel is the key to making fine Vin Jaune. The local wine laboratory tests each barrel twice a year. Puffeney relegates any not up to scratch, and in most years retains only one-third of the original barrels for Vin Jaune. After this aging period, he blends and holds the wine for a further year in large oak *foudres* in his cool cellars.

The 1998 vintage was bottled in the autumn of 2006 after the harvest. This burnished gold wine already shows complex flavors of curry spices, walnut, and crystallized fruit. A streak of lemon on the palate blends with a fullness that could cope—in Puffeney's opinion—with grilled lobster, as well as the more classic match of a young Comté cheese. It should be decanted a couple of hours before drinking and served at around 15°C (59°F). **WL**

🍷🍷🍷 **Drink: to 2040+**

André et Michel Quenard
Chignin-Bergeron Les Terrasses 2005

Origin France, Savoy, Chignin
Style Dry white wine, 13% ABV
Grape Bergeron (Roussanne)

Qupé
Marsanne Santa Ynez Valley 2011

Origin USA, California, Santa Ynez Valley
Style Dry white wine, 12% ABV
Grapes Marsanne 79%, Roussanne 21%

At an altitude of 1,050 feet (320 m), Michel Quenard's steep-terraced 7.5-acre (3 ha) vineyard, at the eastern end of the Chignin commune in the *lieu-dit* of Tormery, is planted almost entirely with Roussanne, locally named Bergeron, and in Savoy allowed to be grown only in Chignin. Surprisingly rare in the area, the terraces were created in the early 1980s using machines "borrowed" from workers constructing a motorway for the Albertville winter Olympics. The soil is extremely stony, but with gravel underneath, making it both well draining and better able to resist drought conditions than other nearby vineyards. Facing southeast, the vines inevitably capture the power of the sun, which is particularly strong in this valley, known as the Combe de Savoie.

The 2005 vintage could not have been more perfect and has a brilliant freshness. The grapes were exceptionally golden, with about 5 percent noble rot. The honeyed nose has aromas of apricot kernels and exotic flowers, with some light spice, too. Stony notes come through with the apricots on the palate. An alpine streak of lemony acidity will ensure several years of aging. Drink with pan-fried foie gras. **WL**

⊖ Drink: to 2017+

One of the first of California's so-called Rhône Rangers, Bob Lindquist is California through and through: A die-hard fan of the Los Angeles Dodgers and 1960s rock and roll, he is also a true pioneer in California winemaking. He released his inaugural vintage under the Qupé label in 1982, with this Marsanne as one of his offerings. Lindquist has since become best known for his Syrah, but his Marsanne testifies to the variety of California terroir.

Starting with Marsanne from a small Los Olivos vineyard and Roussanne from the Stoltman vineyard, Lindquist eventually had to buy additional fruit from other vineyards in his area. He picks his grapes relatively early, aiming for freshness and crisp acidity; the fruit is then pressed in whole clusters and left in tank, on lees, for forty-eight hours to pull in what he describes as a "canned corn" aroma. Barrel fermentation, in three-year-old French oak, lasts through the winter after harvest and into the early spring, allowing for malolactic fermentation. Lindquist says he can always pick his wines in a blind tasting by "the smell of the way a stone smells by a creek, or the way a street smells after rain." **DD**

⊖⊖ Drink: recent vintages for up to 10 years

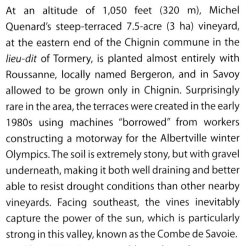

One of the vineyards used for Qupé wines bakes in the California sun. ➜

Château Rabaud-Promis 2003

Origin France, Bordeaux, Sauternes, Bommes
Style Sweet white wine, 13.5% ABV
Grapes Sémillon 80%, S. Blanc 18%, Muscadelle 2%

For more than a century, the history of Rabaud-Promis has been confusingly entangled with that of its neighbor Sigalas-Rabaud. The two formed a single estate until 1903, when part of the property was sold to Adrien Promis. However, the property was reunited in 1930, until 1952 when the estate was separated once again. Quality at Rabaud-Promis remained mediocre for many years, the wine stored in underground tanks and never seeing an oak barrel. After one of the owner's descendants married Philippe Dejean in 1972, he became the manager, and in 1981 he and his wife bought out the other family members. He was now free to make some badly needed investments.

With 80 acres (32 ha) under vine, this is quite a large property, with a modest eighteenth-century house and cellars at the top of the slope, surrounded by vines. Most of the vineyards are on gravelly soil with a good deal of clay beneath. The property also benefits from many old vines. As well as keeping yields at reasonable levels, Dejean introduced barrel fermentation in the late 1980s, though the wine was already showing signs of improvement from the 1983 vintage onward. By the time the great trio of vintages from 1988 to 1990 came around, Rabaud-Promis was very much back on form.

The 2003 vintage has plump apricot aromas, and the lushness one would expect from this super-ripe vintage. The texture is opulent and the finish spicy and fiery. **SBr**

☻☻☻ **Drink: to 2020**

FURTHER RECOMMENDATIONS		
Other great vintages		
1983 • 1988 • 1989 • 1990 • 1998 • 1999 • 2001 • 2005		
More Bommes wines		
Château Lafaurie-Peyraguey • Château Rayne-Vigneau		
Château Sigalas-Rabaud • Château La Tour Blanche		

Rabaud-Promis, returned to good form after a slide in quality. ➲

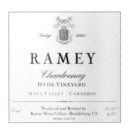

Ramey Hyde Vineyard
Carneros Chardonnay 2002

Origin USA, California, Napa Valley
Style Dry white wine, 14.5% ABV
Grape Chardonnay

David Ramey, one of California's most respected winemakers, set up his own winery in Healdsburg in 2003. He owns no vineyards, but long experience has taught him where to look for the best fruit. He remains a Chardonnay specialist, though he also makes red wines from Calistoga and Diamond Mountain, both in Napa Valley.

There are two primary sources for his Chardonnays—the Hyde vineyard and the Hudson vineyard, both in Carneros. Both are excellent wines, the Hudson being more muscular and more in tune with U.S. tastes than the more refined Hyde. Both wines are made from the so-called Old Wente clone, favored by Ramey for its lack of tropical fruit flavors.

The 2002 Hyde is a very rich wine, with broad, buttery aromas strongly marked by new oak. It is a wine of considerable ripeness and weight, but refreshed by good acidity and a mineral finish. David Ramey is well aware that the Californian climate delivers raw materials very different to those of, for example, a Meursault winery. Consequently, if the Hyde Chardonnay is refined by Californian standards, it remains unmistakably American. **SBr**
😊😊😊 Drink: 2017+

Domaine Ramonet
Bâtard-Montrachet GC 1995

Origin France, Burgundy, Côte de Beaune
Style Dry white wine, 13% ABV
Grape Chardonnay

At the top of Chassagne's hierarchy of addresses to seek out fine wine, you will find the Domaine Ramonet, the first to start selling in bottle, back in the 1930s. The Ramonet then was the legendary *père*, derived from his Christian name, Pierre. Today, his grandchildren Noël and Jean-Claude are in charge. They can offer you a wide range of top whites from Le Montrachet downward. The Bâtard-Montrachet comes from a 1.1-acre (0.45 ha) parcel adjoining their slightly larger holding in Bienvenues, in the Puligny section of the *climat*.

The winemaking approach is refreshingly pragmatic. The white wines are fermented on their gross lees with minimal stirring up of the sediment, so they can evolve at their own pace. In the case of the grands crus they are bottled after eighteen months. This results in some of the longest-lasting white wines in Burgundy. The 1995 comes from a short, but very fine vintage. It is a brilliant example, full, rich, concentrated, and still very vigorous, with just the faintest nuttiness underneath as a result of the new wood. It is multidimensional and, even after thirteen years, was only just ready to drink. **CC**
😊😊😊😊😊 Drink: to 2018

Domaine Raveneau *Chablis*
PC Montée de Tonnerre 2002

Origin France, Burgundy, Chablis
Style Dry white wine, 13% ABV
Grape Chardonnay

Although much of Chablis is ephemeral and devoid of character—for the most part, the vineyard is young, the yields are far too high, and the vines are largely machine-harvested—one domaine stands out ahead of the rest. This is Raveneau. It has mature vines; the crop is 45 hectoliters per hectare rather than 60 or so, and the fruit is gathered by hand. The juice is vinified and matured largely in tank, with around 20 percent in old oak barrels, so there is never an undue and unwelcome taste of new oak. The wines are pure, flinty, and terroir-distinctive.

Montée de Tonnerre, arguably Chablis' best premier cru, lies just to the east of the grands crus of Les Clos, Valmur, and Blanchots, on an extension of the same, more or less south-facing slope. Here the Raveneaus have their largest vineyard holding, at 6.6 acres (2.7 ha). This is Chablis' best example of a premier cru wine, and the 2002 comes from Chablis' best recent vintage. It is a very delicious, admirably steely wine, with splendidly impressive, ripe but austere fruit, and a great deal of depth. Chablis does not get much better than this; one only wishes there were more at this level of quality. **CC**

🝔🝔🝔🝔 **Drink: to 2018+**

Château Rayne-Vigneau
2003

Origin France, Bordeaux, Sauternes, Bommes
Style Sweet white wine, 14% ABV
Grapes Sémillon 80%, Sauvignon Blanc 20%

The vineyards of Rayne-Vigneau occupy various parts of one of the hills of Sauternes, a remarkable location thanks to the proliferation of semiprecious gems scattered in the soil. With 200 acres (80 ha) under vine, it is a large property, but the long-term director, Patrick Eymery, concedes that given the different soil types and expositions and elevations, only about 125 acres (50 ha) produce the first-rate wine that forms the basis of the grand vin.

The property, known previously as Vigneau, dates back to the end of the seventeenth century, and took its current name in 1892. However, the winery is ultramodern and there is nothing artisanal about the wine production. Nonetheless, quality is very high. Since 1986 Eymery has aged the wine in 50 percent new oak, though only since 2001 has the whole crop been barrel-fermented.

Rayne-Vigneau is a bright, fresh, beautifully balanced Sauternes with real elegance. In a vintage when many Sauternes are heavy, this 2003 has an appealing juiciness, and aromas of oranges and tropical fruit; it has excellent length and is one of the best sweet wines of this challenging year. **SBr**

🝔🝔🝔 **Drink: to 2030**

Rebholz *Birkweiler Kastanienbusch Riesling Spätlese Trocken GG* 2001

Origin Germany, Pfalz
Style Dry white wine, 12.5% ABV
Grape Riesling

Although the Rebholz estate in Siebeldingen near the Alsace border had been a quality pioneer in the southern Pfalz for three generations, few people in Germany even knew it existed when Hansjörg Rebholz took over after the premature death of his father some twenty-five years ago. Like his grandfather, Hansjörg continued to produce very individualistic dry wines, which often appear a little rough in their youth but develop marvelously. Since the late 1990s the quality has skyrocketed.

Long seen as the poor cousin of the Mittelhaardt, the reputation of the southern Pfalz has grown with that of Rebholz. The Kastanienbusch vineyard, in the neighboring village of Birkweiler, has played a significant role in that renaissance. The site sprawls across some 188 acres (76 ha) in an amphitheater west of the village, but only a part merits the classification Grosses Gewächs (great growth), and of that only a sliver has the weathered red slate soils on which Riesling thrives. This parcel is the highest and one of the steepest vineyards in the Pfalz.

Wild herbs and honey are the hallmarks of this vineyard that, despite the density of fruit, dances across the palate. The rigid acidic structure of the outstanding 2001 vintage will soften with age. Harvested on November 12—very late for a dry Riesling—it is only 12.5 percent ABV, but punches well above its weight. Fewer than 5,000 bottles were produced, so few will drink it at maturity. **JP**
🍸🍸🍸 **Drink: to 2020**

The Pfalz produces more wine than any other region in Germany. ➡

Remelluri
Blanco 2010

Origin Spain, Rioja
Style Dry white wine, 13% ABV
Grapes Viognier, Roussanne, Marsanne, Others

Remelluri is probably one of Spain's best white wines. It is also one of its more unusual. This original blend of eight white varieties (Viognier, Roussanne, Marsanne, Grenache Blanc, Sauvignon Blanc, Chardonnay, Muscat, and Petit Courbu) may suggest an expressive Burgundy or Condrieu, and no one would guess, in a blind tasting, that it came from the Rioja Alavesa, famed for its Tempranillo reds.

Remelluri's *tinto reserva* became a standard during the 1980s, and is now a modern classic. As for its white, it was first produced during the mid-1990s, almost as an experiment. Under the direction of the owner's son, Telmo Rodríguez, who also now runs his own winemaking business, various white grape varieties were planted in microplots at different altitudes, totaling 7.5 acres (3 ha). At the beginning, production was so scarce that they blended two years at a time. This is how they bottled the 94/95, 96/97, and 98/99 vintages for the U.S. market.

"The 1996 Remelluri white is the finest white wine I have ever tasted from Spain," wrote Robert Parker. "A spectacular, complex nose of honeysuckle, melons, smoke, and floral/tropical fruit aromas is followed by a medium to full-bodied, superbly concentrated, dry white that will turn heads. The bad news is that only 200 cases were made." The good news is that, under the technical management of enologist Ana Barrón, production of this fascinating white has risen to 12,000 bottles. **JMB**

Ⓢ Ⓢ **Drink: recent vintages within 5 years**

Remelluri is located in what used to be the monastery of Toloño. ➡

Max Ferd. Richter *Mülheimer*
Helenenkloster Riesling Eiswein 2001

Origin Germany, Mosel-Saar-Ruwer
Style Sweet white wine, 8% ABV
Grape Riesling

The tiny single vineyard Helenenkloster, only about 2.5 acres (1 ha) in size, has had the reputation of being one of the best terroirs for the production of fine Icewines on the Mosel for almost five decades. But what was harvested in the early morning hours of December 24, 2001, outdid everything that the Max Ferd. Richter estate had ever seen.

The production of Icewine is often a game of luck in which, with a lot of courage, a lot can be won. On December 23, 2001, temperatures on the Mosel sank to 16ºF (-9°C) in the afternoon. The coming holiday notwithstanding, Dr. Dirk Richter's team prepared for a very cold night and an Icewine grape harvest at five o'clock the next morning. With 223° Oechsle, a must weight record was set. Never in the estate's forty-year Icewine tradition had there been such a high level of sugar in the grapes.

The berries, frozen into rock-hard marbles at 8.5ºF (-13°C), were immediately pressed and fermented into an amazingly concentrated Icewine in which the 13.6 percent acidity creates the tangy backbone for 336 g/l residual sugar. It was rated in Germany with the maximum score of 100 points. **FK**
🜚🜚🜚🜚🜚 **Drink: to 2040+**

Château Rieussec
2004

Origin France, Bordeaux, Sauternes, Fargues
Style Sweet white wine, 14% ABV
Grapes Sémillon 95%, S. Blanc 3%, Muscadelle 2%

Château Rieussec, the only first growth in the commune of Fargues, is said to be the loftiest vineyard in the region other than Yquem, and with 198 acres (80 ha) under vine, it is also one of the largest. A former ecclesiastical property, it has had numerous owners. In 1984 the property was sold to the Lafite-Rothschild group. Charles Chevalier, now director of Lafite, ran Rieussec for many years and made continuous improvements in both the vineyards and cellar.

Chevalier and his successors returned Rieussec to a more classic style, in part by picking Sauvignon and Muscadelle earlier for greater freshness. From 1997 the entire crop has been barrel-fermented, and the winemakers compose their blend from around forty-five lots. The wine is aged for about two years; just over half the barrels are new.

Both botrytis and oak are evident on the nose of the 2004, which is suave and concentrated, with an unusually exotic fruit profile of pineapple as well as orange, which derives in part from the wine's excellent acidity. This was not an easy vintage, but Rieussec succeeded admirably. **SBr**
🜚🜚🜚 **Drink: to 2030**

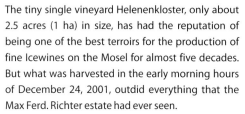

◄ Wine matures in the spacious Max Ferd. Richter cellars in Mulheim.

Telmo Rodríguez
Molino Real Mountain Wine 1998

Origin Spain, Andalusia, Málaga
Style Sweet white wine, 12% ABV
Grape Muscat

Emilio Rojo
Ribeiro 2011

Origin Spain, Galicia, Ribeiro
Style Dry white wine, 13% ABV
Grapes Lado, Treixadura, Albariño, Loureiro, Torrontés

Born into the family that owns Remelluri in Rioja, Telmo Rodríguez is the most famous winemaker in Spain. He left, then in 2010 returned to the family winery, in the interim founding his own Compañía de Vinos Telmo Rodríguez in 1994.

Relentlessly searching for forgotten areas and wines, he is interested in preserving traditions and saving old regions and styles. He once heard Hugh Johnson talk about a magical sweet wine from Málaga, and he could not get it out of his head. He went to Málaga and talked to everyone. He walked the few remaining vineyards, selected the best, and experimented. Finally, with the 1998 vintage, the first Molino Real Mountain Wine was born.

The Muscat grapes, grown on steep slate slopes in Cómpeta, Málaga, are sun-dried to concentrate the sugar. After twenty months in new French oak, the wine is full of floral notes, fruit, and exotic spices. A gorgeous golden color, and very fine and elegant in aroma, it has lactic and balsamic notes. Dense but medium-bodied in the mouth, it is balsamic and spicy, rich and long, with a sweetness well compensated by a fine acidity. **LG**

🔊🔊🔊 **Drink: to 2018**

The top Albariños produced in the coastal zone of Rías Baixas combine youthful aromatic complexity with moderate aging potential—all without the intervention of oak. These are precisely the virtues that characterize the best whites from inland Galicia, too. Among the latter shines Emilio Rojo's Ribeiro—already an almost mythical wine—produced every year from his tiny 5-acre (2 ha) estate.

Emilio abandoned his engineering studies in the 1980s to become a micro-vintner. As he puts it, his aim is not to grow but to shrink; his ultimate goal is a vineyard the size of a boxing ring—small amounts of product expressed with great power.

Unless you are quick enough to snatch one of the few bottles released to an enthusiastic and expectant public each year, it is hard to separate the wine from the winemaker in this case, and equally difficult to believe how authentic both can be. The young wine is angular as well as generous and unctuous, with excellent structure and a finely judged balance between acidity, oiliness, alcohol, and aromatic power. Better still, it gives every impression of needing a few more years to give of its best. **JB**

🔊🔊 **Drink: recent vintages for up to 7 years**

◀ The mountains of Málaga, which fascinated Telmo Rodriguez.

Rolly Gassmann
Muscat Moenchreben 2007

Origin France, Alsace
Style Dry white wine, 12.5% ABV
Grape Muscat

Rolly Gassmann *Riesling*
de Rorschwihr Cuvée Yves 2002

Origin France, Alsace
Style Dry white wine, 14% ABV
Grape Riesling

Louis Gassmann and his wife Marie-Thérèse (née Rolly) are highly respected in Europe for their consistent range of Alsace wines of full, voluptuous style. To be a little controversial, however, one does not always find in a Gassmann wine that supreme class shown by a Faller, Humbrecht, or Trimbach, and for a good reason: He does not have particularly good vineyards—no grands crus—and some of his holdings in Rorschwihr have a marked clay content, giving his Rieslings a strong *goût de pétrole* character that you either love or hate. What is clear, though, is that Louis (now aided by his son Pierre) is one of the best winemakers in Alsace, well aware of the marked character of his terroirs. From challenging material, he fashions some gorgeously pleasurable wines, often picked late to ensure full phenolic maturity in his grapes, eliminating any green, harsh edges.

The Muscat Moenchreben is a charmer, its grapey, sensuously sweet nose capturing the drama of late-season sunshine in the glass. The mouthfeel is very fat, the middle palate full of rich, succulent peachy flavors—a summer wine to be drunk on its own or with a slice of Alsace fruit tart. **ME**

☻☻☻ **Drink: recent vintages for up to 10 years**

In the past, by far the best wines made by Rolly-Gassmann were from Gewürztraminer, the grape best suited to the clay-rich soils of Rorschwihr and Louis Gassmann's penchant for a rich style touched by residual sugar. With Riesling, though, making a balanced, graceful wine from such soils and methods proved more difficult. In converting to biodynamic viticulture in recent years, Louis and his son Pierre have achieved real advances in the quality and character of their grapes, resulting in wines of greater purity, harmony, and class. The greatest improvements can be seen in this Riesling de Rorschwihr. (This vintage was named in honor of Louis's other son, Yves, who adopted the religious life the same year.)

The gentle variations in the 2002 growing season helped, of course. This was a year characterized by rains and mild temperatures. The result is a Riesling with a splendid frame of indestructible acidity in textbook balance with optimal maturity. This is a great bottle of endless complexity and class, which cautions the wise never to generalize about a wine, terroir, vintage—or particularly the producer. **ME**

☻☻☻ **Drink: to 2020+**

Rorschwihr's church with Château de Haut-Koenigsbourg on the hill. ➨

Dom. de la Romanée-Conti
Le Montrachet GC 2000

Origin France, Burgundy, Côte de Beaune
Style Dry white wine, 14% ABV
Grape Chardonnay

It would be hard to find a greater reference for outstanding white Burgundy than this. Domaine de La Romanée Conti owns only one of the 20 acres (0.7 of the 8 ha) of Le Montrachet, having bought parcels 31, 129, and 130 in 1963, 1965, and 1980 respectively. All the vines are in the Chassagne-Montrachet sector of the vineyard. The grapes are then vinified at the domaine's *cuvérie* in Vosne-Romanée by Bernard Noblet, and are bottled after around fifteen months of barrel aging.

The domaine makes a point of picking its Montrachet as late as possible, often well after all the other producers have completed their harvest. Co-owner Aubert de Villaine has noticed across the years that grapes in Le Montrachet retain their acidity even if left late on the vine. This late picking results in extraordinary opulence and an almost monolithic intensity that speak more of the producer than the vineyard. But after time in the glass, the incredible character of the vineyard starts to show. It is hard to define this in sensible words—the Abbé Arnoux, writing in 1727, could find "no words in either French or Latin to describe the *douceur* of this wine."

The 2000 vintage, recently tasted by this author as part of an extraordinary series of Montrachets in Nashville, Tennessee, was one of the stars of the show, a near-perfect wine. With time in the glass, the truly fabulous nose showed refinement as well as energy and power. So many layers of flavor came washing over the palate in gentle waves, persisting for an extraordinary length of time. **JM**
ӨӨӨӨӨ Drink: to 2030

Dom. Guy Roulot *Meursault*
Tessons Le Clos de Mon Plaisir 2005

Origin France, Burgundy, Côte de Beaune
Style Dry white wine, 13% ABV
Grape Chardonnay

One of the joys of Meursault as a wine village is the wealth of high-class bottles produced from a whole host of vineyards that have not been classified even as premier cru, let alone grand cru. They are therefore affordable and can offer some of the best value for white Burgundy. Among these *lieu-dit* vineyards one of the most exciting is Le Tesson (or Les Tessons), which lies on the mid to upper slope above the village, on a light and well-draining soil.

Le Tesson is divided into individual plots, several of which, curiously, have little summerhouses built on them. Domaine Roulot's plot is known as Le Clos de Mon Plaisir, an evocative name merited by the stylish quality of the wine. Jean-Marc Roulot, who returned to the family domaine after a spell in the movie industry, is one of Burgundy's more thoughtful winemakers, who has understood the importance of texture as well as fruit and structure in white wines. His Tesson has an attractive floral quality and a lively acidity to keep the palate fresh.

2005 is an outstanding vintage for white Burgundy. Its reputation has been slightly hidden behind the glory of the red wines of this exceptional year, and by the preference for the white wines of 2004 and 2006 over their red counterparts, but nonetheless the greatest white wines of this trio of vintages will certainly come from 2005. In their youth their lack of immediate aromatic qualities and the muscular nature of their concentration has won them fewer accolades than they deserve. It is the most complete vintage for a generation. **JM**
ӨӨӨ Drink: to 2017+

The entrance to Domaine de la Romanée-Conti.

Royal Tokaji Wine Co. *Mézes Mály Tokaji Aszú 6 Puttonyos* 1999

Origin Hungary, Tokaj
Style Sweet white wine, 10.5% ABV
Grape Furmint

The Royal Tokaji Wine Company was founded in September 1990 by a group of wine fanatics headed by Danish nobleman and Bordeaux winemaker Peter-Vinding-Diers and wine writer Hugh Johnson. At first they had the expertise of István Szepsy at their disposal, but Szepsy was to leave in 1993, at the time when the company was in difficulty and required recapitalization. In all, the owners mustered an impressive collection of vineyards totaling 264 acres (110 ha) in some of the areas that were classified in the first half of the eighteenth century.

The company is different to many in that it makes only Aszú wines and chiefly from top vineyards such as Szent Tamás, Nyulászó, and Betsek. Royal Tokaji was the first major company to put vineyard sites on its labels. Mézes Mály, with its loess soils, is a grand cru site, though not everyone is in agreement that the precise location of the cru has been found. Some people believe that the location is not at the back of the site, but in a frontal position, to the side of the other grand cru, Szarvas, but a little farther up the slope. Royal Tokaji has 50 acres (19 ha) in Mézes Mály.

This 6 Puttonyos wine is aged in cask for four years. Long maceration of the grapes means that the Royal Tokaji wines are normally darker than most, though this is an intense light gold with fresh, juicy, peachy fruit. Winemaker Károly Áts also detects peppermint, quince, and honey on the nose, as well as "great balance on the palate, wonderful structure, and a very long, lovely, quince aftertaste." **GM**
❸❸❸❸ **Drink: to 2020+**

Royal Tokaji Wine Co. *Szent Tamás Tokaji Aszú Esszencia* 1993

Origin Hungary, Tokaj
Style Sweet white wine, 7.5% ABV
Grapes Furmint 50%, Hárslevelű 50%

Esszencia (essence) is the *summum bonum* of quality in Tokaj wine. A lesser quality of Aszú Esszencia is also made, the equivalent of a 7 Puttonyos wine, but true *esszencia* is a fabulous beast, so rich in sugar that its fermentation is slow and partial. If you are lucky it might achieve 6 percent ABV. On the other hand, this essence of free-run must from nobly rotten fruit ages so slowly that it can survive for a century if kept in a good cellar, and its very longevity was formerly seen as a life-giving force. Kings and princes used to be the recipients of *esszencia*, and made presents of it to their friends and relations, at least those they wanted to survive into old age.

The Szent Tamás (or St. Thomas) vineyard is large and geologically amorphous. The soil is volcanic and contains tufa and quartz. With its 25 acres (11 ha), Royal Tokaji owns about one-fifth of the cru.

This *esszencia* is made from equal measures of Furmint and Hárslevelű and contains 304 g/l residual sugar, making it relatively vinous. The acidity is 11.5 g/l. Even at five years old the sweet wine was amber in color, the result of the policy at Royal Tokaji of using very small amounts of sulfur. The nose was a gorgeous whiff of Seville orange. The attack was very soft at the beginning, but it finished with the searing acidity of a Granny Smith apple.

Hungarians say that *esszencia* is best drunk by the thimble, full and simple of itself. Theoretically, anyone who takes the wine in this way will live for ever, but so far no long-lived individual has been found as evidence in support of the theory. **GM**
❸❸❸❸❸ **Drink: to 2050+**

Dark red-golden Tokajis age in the Royal Tokaji Wine Co. cellars. ➡

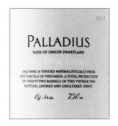

Rudera
Robusto Chenin Blanc 2002

Origin South Africa, Stellenbosch
Style Off-dry white wine, 14% ABV
Grape Chenin Blanc

South Africa's plantings of Chenin greatly exceed those of the grape's Loire homeland. Long used and abused in the Cape for everything from brandy to the occasional fine dessert wine, its star began to rise in the 1990s, when ambitious winemakers turned to the old, low-yielding Chenin vineyards and found, in some of the best sited of them, remarkable quality.

Winemaker Teddy Hall has been one of the grape's champions—first at Kanu, then at his own small Stellenbosch winery, Rudera. He makes Chenin wines in a variety of styles at Rudera, but the Robusto—well oaked, usually with just perceptible residual sugar, always showy and, yes, elegantly robust—is perhaps the best known of them all.

Grapes for the 2002 Robusto came from mature vineyards of bush-vine Chenin at the foot of the Helderberg near the town of Somerset West. Critic Michael Fridjhon noted the vineyards' potential to produce "intense, sumptuous fruit that transforms into an opulent, almost tropical, style of wine." He added, "The Rudera Robusto 2002 is amply textured, but with adequate acidity to rein in the fruit and to deliver length and persistence on the palate." **TJ**
🌓🌓 **Drink: to 2017**

Sadie Family
Palladius 2011

Origin South Africa, Swartland
Style Dry white wine, 13.5% ABV
Grapes Chenin, Grenache, Chardonnay, and others

A new genre of Cape white blends has emerged in recent years, drawing inspiration and grapes from the treasury of unirrigated, low-yielding old Chenin Blanc vines on the slopes of the granitic Perdeberg—"Horse Mountain"—named after the zebralike animal long since hunted to extinction. Augmented by various varieties, these blends are revealing great quality and expressive character.

Palladius, named like its Columella stablemate after a Roman viticulturist, was the first of them. There are now a dozen or two wines of this genre, but Palladius remains in the fore. Winemaker Eben Sadie has said, "You can blend for comfort or for complexity, which is what I'm trying for."

Still working on the composition and character of Palladius, Sadie directs most effort to his (leased) Perdeberg vineyards, which he farms largely organically. There is work in the cellar, too, as he continues to refine the blend, adding a little old-vine Clairette in the 2006. This is a big, powerful wine, rich and succulent, with good natural acidity and a graceful vein of tannic minerality, as well as earthy bass notes under the floral and fruity flourishes. **TJ**
🌓🌓🌓 **Drink: to 2021+**

Salomon-Undhof
Riesling Kögl 2005

Origin Austria, Weinviertel
Style Dry white wine, 13% ABV
Grape Grüner Veltiner

Sauer *Escherndorfer Lump*
Silvaner Trockenbeerenauslese 2003

Origin Germany, Franken
Style Sweet white wine, 8% ABV
Grape Sylvaner

Fritz Salomon was a pioneer of Austrian viticulture and among the country's earliest champions of Riesling and estate bottling. His sons, Erich and Berthold, now manage the Undhof. The Salomons' holdings in the steep, schistic, and loess-dusted terraces above Krems were owned for centuries by the distant bishopric of Passau in Bavaria, and still today a portion of each harvest is owed to the church in that cathedral city.

In the early 1990s economic considerations forced Erich Salomon to abandon wood for stainless steel, and quicken the pace at which Undhof wines evolved and were released. A decade later, with his younger brother at his side, it was time to loosen control of the nascent wines, and their Riesling Kögl 2005 fermented through January—long by recent standards—with subsequent time spent on its lees, rendering a creaminess of texture to complement its clarity of citrus and pit fruit, and wealth of nuances.

Quality depended in this particular vintage on a willingness to laboriously pick botrytis fruit. A later harvested Reserve Riesling Kögl displays additional richness but less clarity. **DS**

🍷🍷 **Drink: to 2017+**

Escherndorfer Lump is a parabola-shaped bluff facing south on the banks of the River Main. It has always been famous, not only for its individual microclimate but also for its difficulty of cultivation. In Germany this vineyard is considered one of the best sites for concentrated, juicy, and distinctively dry Sylvaner, but Horst Sauer has proved with remarkable regularity that world-class sweet wines can also be grown here. Almost no other winemaker is able to extract such overwhelming Trockenbeerenausleses from Sylvaner.

In 2003, the conditions here were perfect. On November 3, Sauer was able to harvest a highly elegant Trockenbeerenauslese, which may well be the very best wine from Franken in this great year. The wine's overwhelmingly exotic aromas of pineapple, mango, honey, and apricot are on the palate wrapped in a silky dress of delicate sweetness, and supported by a tightly woven acidity. The wine was sold at the winery for approximately $70 per half-liter bottle. By comparison with prices for Rieslings of similar quality and style from the Rhine and the Mosel, it represents spectacular value. **FK**

🍷🍷🍷 **Drink: to 2025**

Domaine Etienne Sauzet
Bâtard-Montrachet GC 1990

Origin France, Burgundy, Côte de Beaune
Style Dry white wine, 13.5% ABV
Grape Chardonnay

Based in Puligny-Montrachet, the Sauzet estate's operations have fluctuated over the years, with plantings peaking in the late 1940s. After the death of the founder in 1975, direction of Sauzet passed to Gérard Boudot, who had married into the family the year before. His conscientious stewardship has led to the estate being numbered among the top division of Chardonnay producers in the region.

Just 0.3 acres (0.13 ha) of Bâtard (a grand cru split between Puligny- and Chassagne-Montrachet) is held by Sauzet, and its annual production of this wine is supplemented by bought-in grapes. After a light pressing, the juice is transferred to barrel for an alcoholic fermentation of around three weeks. Tronçais and Allier oak are used to age the wine.

The 1990 vintage produced wines of immense fatness and richness, almost too much so for some purists. Sauzet's Bâtard is a massive, oily Chardonnay of stunning impact, speaking eloquently of forty-year-old vines and low yields. It sings out with baked apple and nutmeg on the nose, following up with a big-hitting palate that combines butterfat opulence and amazing, savory length. **SW**
Θ Θ Θ Θ Θ **Drink: to 2020+**

Willi Schaefer *Graacher*
Domprobst Riesling BA 2003

Origin Germany, Mosel-Saar-Ruwer
Style Sweet white wine, 7.5% ABV
Grape Riesling

If Willi and Christof Schaefer's estate were just being established, we would call them *garagistes*. This 8.5-acre (3.5 ha) property produces Mosel wine, exclusively from steep-slope Riesling vineyards in and near Graach. Willi Schaefer has never produced a Trockenbeerenauslese, nor does he seek to produce Eiswein. "Sure, we could have made TBA many times over the years," he says, "but the wines are maybe too concentrated. I enjoy them from other producers, but we want our wines to be light and elegant."

In "cool" vintages, Schaefer's wines can seem almost aloof, but in "warm" ones they shimmer with brilliance at every degree of ripeness. The greatness of these wines, indeed of this genre of wine, can be glimpsed in their most modest incarnations, but the gossamer lightness they attain even with fervid concentration and massive ripeness is both singular and miraculous. And never more so than in the vintage of 2003, when one might expect sprawling, mawkishly soft fruit. Instead, what one gets is a wine almost limpid, spring-loaded, and tightly wound. A tremendous volume of complex flavor is delivered on a frame so slight as to be almost evanescent. **TT**
Θ Θ Θ Θ Θ **Drink: 2030–2040**

The entrance to the Willi Schaefer winery. ➡

Mario Schiopetto
Pinot Grigio 2012

Origin Italy, Friuli, Collio
Style Dry white wine, 13% ABV
Grape Pinot Grigio

Schloss Gobelsburg *Lamm*
Grüner Veltliner Reserve 2011

Origin Austria, Kamptal
Style Dry white wine, 13.5% ABV
Grape Grüner Veltliner

Azienda Agricola Mario Schiopetto is one of the finest wine estates in the Collio area of northeast Italy. The Schiopetto family's 75 acres (30 ha) of vineyards are spread across Capriva del Friuli at Podere dei Blumeri and on the estate surrounding the former residence of the Bishop of Gorizia.

The late Mario Schiopetto began making wine in 1965. He traveled throughout Europe's wine regions, and was a pioneer of ultra-clean modern winemaking in Friuli. Camouflaged in the hills of Capriva, the splendid winery, designed by Tobia Scarpa, was completed in 1992.

Schiopetto first made Pinot Grigio in 1968, long before it became fashionable. Golden yellow in color, rather than the limpid green of so much wishy-washy wine made from this variety, the Schiopetto Pinot Grigio shows what can be done with this grape in the right hands. Rich, tasty, and characteristically low in acid, it is long, elegant, and pure, with not a trace of oak to mar the cleanly defined fruit. Although quite concentrated, this is best drunk young, because it loses its freshness and acidity after three or four years in bottle. **SG**

☻☻☻ Drink: recent vintages for up to 4 years

Tasting this icon of full-throttle Grüner Veltliner it is hard to believe Michael Moosbrugger assumed control of this property only in 1996. Gobelsburg is a centuries-old monastic property that gradually amassed many of the greatest vineyard sites in the Kamptal. In the early 1990s the order looked for someone to whom the property could be leased. Fortuitously, Moosbrugger was eager to become a vintner. The deal was brokered by Willi Bründlmayer, who signed on as a partner and consultant with a five-year plan, but by the third year he realized his consultation was not needed: "Why does he need me any more? He's sleeping on his casks."

The Lamm vineyard lies in a combe between the Gaisberg and Heiligenstein hills. It is protected from wind, and in truth it is very hot. Everyone with Veltliner vines there makes good wine, but none has been more impressive than Schloss Gobelsburg. The Lamm indicates a contrast between strength and delicacy, between intensity and precision, showing a brilliance, symmetrical and proportioned, with signature flavors of rosemary, rye-bread husks, and spit-roasted meat. **TT**

☻☻☻☻ Drink: recent vintages for up to 5 years

◧ Mario Schiopetto's vineyards at Capriva del Friuli in Gorizia.

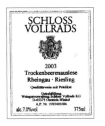

Schloss Lieser *Lieser Niederberg Helden Riesling AG* 2004

Origin Germany, Mosel-Saar-Ruwer
Style Sweet white wine, 7% ABV
Grape Riesling

Schloss Vollrads *Riesling Trockenbeerenauslese* 2003

Origin Germany, Rheingau
Style Sweet white wine, 7% ABV
Grape Riesling

For his region and profession, winemaker Wilhelm Haag is a revered father figure. In 1992, older son Thomas stepped in as cellar master for the once-renowned but since run-down Schloss Lieser, and from the first harvest it seemed that he had found his mission. Five years later he purchased the estate.

Thomas Haag demonstrated that the Niederberg Helden need not fear comparison with any of the Mosel's best slate sites. With the 2004 vintage, a new level of excellence was achieved. For a still-young man, Haag's approach is remarkably dominated by patience. Few of his neighbors harvest later or allow their Riesling to ferment cooler and longer, and his wines are correspondingly slow to emerge from a halo of yeasty, fermentative aromas, baby fat, and sheer sweetness.

The 2004 is a superb example of Riesling in synergy with noble rot. Pit fruits, citrus, melon, and honey saturate the palate and linger with memorable intensity. But only on the Mosel's slate slopes has it proven possible to render an ennobled wine with such delicacy and lift, one that for all of its creamy opulence offers such ravishing clarity. **DS**
🍷🍷🍷🍷 **Drink: to 2025**

The wines from the Schloss Vollrads, and the nearby Schloss Johannisberg, have been among the very finest German wines for centuries. For many years the castle was owned by the earls of Greiffenclau, one of the world's oldest wine dynasties.

Since a crisis in the 1990s, Dr. Rowald Hepp has restored the estate to its former grandeur. On September 23, 2003, the first batch of grapes for the Riesling Trockenbeerenauslese was harvested, and several more TBAs were to follow. Never before in the long history of the site had there been such highly concentrated TBAs; only the 1947 came close.

This wine was separately vinified—the fermentation lasted more than fifteen months, so high was the sugar level—and separately bottled. It had still to be released four years after the harvest, being permitted to rest in the castle cellar. But even the "normal" TBA of this almost alarmingly unusual vintage makes it clear how the natural gifts granted to the Schlossberg of Vollrads have made it a paradise for lovers of noble sweet jewels. With 306 g/l residual sugar, this is a concentrated elixir with immense scale and aristocratic distinction. **FK**
🍷🍷🍷🍷🍷 **Drink: to 2050+**

Schloss Vollrads, surrounded by the Schlossberg vineyard. ➔

Schlumberger *Gewurztraminer* SGN *Cuvée Anne* 2000

Heidi Schröck *Ruster Ausbruch* *Auf den Flügeln der Morgenröte* 2004

Origin France, Alsace
Style Sweet white wine, 14.7% ABV
Grape Gewürztraminer

Origin Austria, Burgenland, Neusiedlersee-Hügelland
Style Sweet white wine, 9.5% ABV
Grapes P. Blanc, Welschriesling, Sauvignon, Others

Schlumberger's 346 acres (140 ha) of vineyards constitute the largest viticultural estate in Alsace, and the quality of its production has blossomed under Serine Schlumberger, the seventh generation. All the wines Schlumberger makes are from its own vineyards, which extend 3.5 miles (5.6 km) from Guebwiller to Rouffach, and are so steep that they are terraced and still worked by horse. In fact, they have four horses, and employ four full-time masons to maintain over 30 miles (48 km) of terraces. Exactly half of this estate consists of four grands crus— Kessler, Kitterlé, Saering, and Spiegel. Cuvée Anne comes from the east- and southeast-facing grand cru Kessler, which has a sandy-clay soil over sandstone.

Schlumberger's Cuvée Anne was named after the daughter of Ernest Schlumberger, the great-great-grandson of the founder. It is an extremely rare wine, not only because it is a Sélection de Grains Nobles (SGN), but also due to its infrequent production, which averages just one vintage every seven years or so. It has an extraordinary elegance and finesse for such a big wine, with a long, lingering lusciousness of startling freshness on the finish. **TS**
🍷🍷🍷 **Drink: to 2040**

The Cercle Ruster Ausbruch was called to life in 1992 to restore the wine that made the reputation and the former wealth of tiny Freistadt Rust. Unexpectedly, the growers called on a young woman to chair their group. Since then, the name of Heidi Schröck has been associated with this nobly rotten genre, and no Burgenland grower can boast a greater quality or diversity of dry white wines than she.

Schröck began in vintage 2003 to bottle from diverse parcels, and her entire range of grape varieties includes an Ausbruch that would call to mind the multifarious field blends from which, until the past half century, wines here had always been made. The Psalmist's "on the wings of dawn" (*Auf den Flügeln der Morgenröte*) was suggested to her, she says, by early morning sunlight—a critical catalyst to true noble rot—glinting off, and then dissipating, fog on the lake known in German as Neusiedlersee.

This Ausbruch is almost trance-inducing as it rolls on to the palate, creamy yet ethereal and weightless like a bank of fog, then soaring into a finish of extraordinary intricacy, not in the least weighed down by its 200 g/l of residual sugar. **DS**
🍷🍷🍷 **Drink: to 2022+**

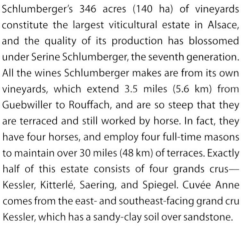

◪ Schlumberger vineyards at Guebwiller.

Selbach-Oster *Zeltinger Schlossberg Riesling Auslese Schmitt* 2003

Origin Germany, Mosel-Saar-Ruwer
Style Off-dry white wine, 8% ABV
Grape Riesling

In 2003, Johannes Selbach produced at least four separate Ausleses from the Schlossberg, a steep and rather unheralded site rising directly behind Zeltingen's pretty St. Stephanus church. Three of them were made in the usual way, with successive passes through the vineyard, and the riper among them (as well as those with more botrytis) were designated with stars—no star, one star, two stars.

Yet 2003 introduced a quiet revolution, in the form of an *en bloc* picking from the oldest and best-situated parcel, which carries the old site name of Schmitt. "We did no selections prior to harvesting," said Johannes. "This brings the usual diverse mix of greenish-yellow, golden, slightly overripe, and botrytis berries together, which creates a true expression of the site's terroir without the influence of human selection." The family have continued the program in each subsequent vintage, adding a second cuvée from a micro-parcel in the neighboring Sonnenuhr known as Rotlay.

Zeltinger Schlossberg provides a remarkably expressive, almost angular form of Mosel. The vineyards' Devonian slate soils create a taut and bracing minerality that seems to occupy the palate—one of the few places one can perhaps literally "taste the soil"—underscored with a singular forest-herb and lime zest mid-palate. The effect may be less genially charming than the Sonnenuhrs and Himmelreichs of the world, but it is delightfully, emphatically distinctive. **TT**
☻☻☻☻ **Drink: 2015–2025+**

FURTHER RECOMMENDATIONS
Other wines from the same producer
Bernkasteler Badstube • Graacher Domprobst
More Mosel-Saar-Ruwer producers
Fritz Haag • Karthäuserhof • Dr. Loosen • Maximin Grünhaus • Egon Müller • J. J. Prüm • Willi Schaefer

Harvesting Riesling in Selbach-Oster's Bratenhöfchen vineyard. ➡

Seresin
Marama Sauvignon Blanc 2009

Origin New Zealand, Marlborough
Style Dry white wine, 13% ABV
Grape Sauvignon Blanc

Seresin estate was founded in 1992 on the Wairau River terraces in Marlborough by Michael Seresin, a cinematographer of distinction whose film credits include *Bugsy Malone, Midnight Express, Fame,* and *Harry Potter and the Prisoner of Azkaban.*

Like Cloudy Bay, Seresin produces a "basic" Sauvignon Blanc, but also a more sophisticated version. The selection of the parcels for Marama is based on fruit flavors prior to harvesting, with three blocks in particular always giving extra depth and weight to the finished wine. Rather than adding yeast, the fermentation is induced by indigenous yeasts that occur naturally in the vineyard and winery. These different yeasts eventually add extra layers of flavor to the wine.

Marama is often more deeply colored than many other Sauvignon wines. At first, it smells of a typical Marlborough white wine, with capsicum and asparagus aromas leaping out of the glass, but toffee and yeast flavors are also apparent, derived from the barrel aging and wild yeast fermentation respectively. It is very atypical but so rich and long that you would forgive it almost anything. **SG**

⊖⊖ Drink: to 2017+

Shaw + Smith
M3 Chardonnay 2010

Origin Australia, South Australia, Adelaide Hills
Style Dry white wine, 13% ABV
Grape Chardonnay

Shaw + Smith began over a long lunch in 1989, when Martin Shaw and Michael Hill-Smith decided to realize a long-held dream to make wine together. Previously, in 1988, Michael had become the first Australian to pass the Master of Wine examination.

Although grapes were planted in the Adelaide Hills as early as 1839, it was not until 1979 that viticulture there was revived. Due to their altitude, the Adelaide Hills are significantly cooler than the nearby McLaren Vale and Barossa Valley wine regions. Sauvignon Blanc and Chardonnay are particularly well suited to these cooler conditions.

In 1994 the M3 vineyard at Woodside was planted at an average altitude of 1,378 feet (420 m). The grapes for M3 are hand-picked and whole-fruit pressed prior to 100 percent barrel fermentation and maturation in 35 to 40 percent new and 60 to 65 percent one- or two-year-old French oak. Since its first release with the 2000 vintage, Shaw + Smith's M3 Chardonnay has been distinguished by its balance of fruit, natural acidity, and oak. Hill-Smith described earlier vintages as "a work in progress," but now M3 is hitting its stride. **SG**

⊖⊖⊖ Drink: to 2020+

Edi Simčič
Sauvignon Blanc 1999

Origin Slovenia, Kozana, Goriška Brda
Style Dry white wine, 14.5% ABV
Grape Sauvignon Blanc

Château Smith-Haut-Lafitte
Pessac-Léognan 2004

Origin France, Bordeaux, Pessac-Léognan
Style Dry white wine, 13% ABV
Grapes S. Blanc 90%, S. Gris 5%, Sémillon 5%

In our golden age of wine, the white wines of Western Slovenia, touching the Italian border and the famed Friulian district of Collio, stand out—especially the Goriška Brda Sauvignons. The Simčičs have farmed these wine hills for more than 100 years, with their own label since 1990. Winemaking is now in the hands of Edi Simčič's son Aleks.

The Simčičs' Sauvignons really extend the taste spectrum of this grape variety. Both in their Kozana vineyard and in the winery, the approach is simple, natural, and rigorous. Yields are tiny (one bottle per plant). The grapes are hand-picked and harvested late. Barrel fermentation in French oak of mixed ages is employed, the wine staying in wood for twelve months. Aleks is essentially looking for richness and complexity rather than primary fruit, his Sauvignon Riserva rising well above the level of green fruits and leafiness endemic to the Loire.

When fully mature, the wine has opulent secondary characters on the nose. The palate is a perfect medley of full body, mineral core, and evolved stone-fruit and hedgerow flavors. The finish is long and multi-layered. *Bravissimo!* **ME**

☻☻☻ **Drink: recent vintages for up to 10 years**

Planted on a gravel shelf similar to the soil composition of Margaux, in a vineyard area known as Lafitte, this property came under the aegis in 1720 of a Scottish merchant, one George Smith, who added his sobriquet—not quite melodiously—to the château name. In 1990, it was acquired by the Cathiards, Daniel and Florence, who were Olympic downhill skiing champions in the 1960s.

The white wine is cool-fermented in stainless steel, then transferred to oak (50 percent of which is new) for a year's aging. Barriques are supplied from an on-site cooperage, another handy asset.

In 2004, the estate produced, by dint of late picking, the kind of dry white that would make a fine exemplar of the potential longevity of the best Graves whites. Its structure is austerely firm, even tannic, but without at all concealing the rapturous aromas of ripe greengage and nectarine, overlaid with a wisp of coffee steam from the barrel. A honey-rich palate offers up layers of complex fruit and intense minerality. This is a big, sturdy wine that means business, and one that will age gracefully to a fully satisfying maturity. **SW**

☻☻☻☻ **Drink: to 2019**

Soalheiro
Alvarinho Primeiras Vinhas 2010

Origin Portugal, Vinho Verde
Style Dry white wine, 12.5% ABV
Grape Alvarinho

Johann Stadlmann
Mandel-Höh Zierfandler 2011

Origin Austria, Thermenregion
Style Dry white wine, 13.5% ABV
Grape Zierfandler

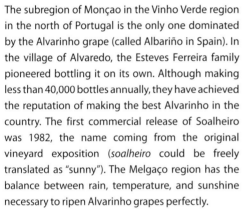

The subregion of Monçao in the Vinho Verde region in the north of Portugal is the only one dominated by the Alvarinho grape (called Albariño in Spain). In the village of Alvaredo, the Esteves Ferreira family pioneered bottling it on its own. Although making less than 40,000 bottles annually, they have achieved the reputation of making the best Alvarinho in the country. The first commercial release of Soalheiro was 1982, the name coming from the original vineyard exposition (*soalheiro* could be freely translated as "sunny"). The Melgaço region has the balance between rain, temperature, and sunshine necessary to ripen Alvarinho grapes perfectly.

In 2006, the Esteves Ferreira family joined forces with Dirk van der Niepoort of Port fame to produce a limited cuvée of some 3,000 bottles called Soalheiro Primeiras Vinhas (first vines), from vines they planted thirty years ago. The result is the essence of Soalheiro taken one step further in intensity, concentration, and minerality. Very light in color, and closed at first, it slowly reveals lemon oil and zest, hints of peaches, oyster shell, rainwater, and intense minerality with a great acidity. **LG**

🕘🕒 **Drink: 2017+**

Austria's so-called Thermal Region commences at the southern edge of Vienna and its famous woods. Traditionally Austria's largest wine supplier, although eclipsed in recent decades, this region and its center Gumpoldskirchen were home in the late Hapsburg era to some of the earliest research in the typing and propagation of individual grape varieties. As its alternate local name Spätrot suggests, Zierfandler needs Austria's long and usually balmy autumn to ripen properly, and then delivers fruit and spice in profusion, while retaining cut and freshness. However, the name suggests a red wine, while the wine pressed from these violet clusters is golden.

The stony, chalky Mandel-Höh was well known by 1840, when its terroir was spared by routing the Südbahn through Austria's first tunnel. Three generations of the Stadlmann family had made wine by the time the railroad came to Traiskirchen.

Mouth-wateringly redolent of quince, almond, apple, and mango, and satisfyingly rich in texture, Johann Stadlmann's Mandel-Höh generally retains subtle acidity, saline minerality, and pungent spice that help it finish long, lively, and invigorating. **DS**

🕘🕒 **Drink: 2020+**

Red-skinned Zierfandler grapes growing near Gumpoldskirchen. ➡

Steenberg
Magna Carta 2011

Origin South Africa, Constantia
Style Dry white wine, 13.5% ABV
Grapes Sauvignon Blanc 60%, Sémillon 40%

The lovely Constantia Valley has a winemaking history nearly as old as that of the Cape colony itself. Although the vineyards of Steenberg are much more recently planted, the farm was the first land grant made in the valley—remarkably enough, to a woman, Catharina Ras, in 1682. The modern estate's name means "Stone Mountain."

With a fine reputation for varietal expressions of both Sauvignon and Sémillon, it was inevitable that Steenberg would offer a blend of the two, given the great success achieved by such Bordeaux-inspired blends in the Cape since around 2000. Crucial to the quality of both varieties are the cool Atlantic breezes that allow (by South African standards) fairly slow and optimal ripening. Some vineyards show leaves burned by salt blown in from the ocean just 3 miles (5 km) away—this is Constantia's most exposed farm. A consequence is a herbaceous element in the Sauvignon, and there's a green aroma in the wine, which is made more complex by Sémillon's wax and lemon. The rich, broad palate has a vibrant acidity, with the oaking (40 percent new) unobtrusively supportive, and a succulently elegant, long finish. **TJ**
☻☻☻ **Drink: to 2021**

Stonier Estate
Reserve Chardonnay 2003

Origin Australia, Victoria, Mornington Peninsula
Style Dry white wine, 14% ABV
Grape Chardonnay

The Mornington Peninsula is one of Australia's cool climate wine-growing regions. The weather usually breaks during the fall here, so the region tends to specialize in Pinot Noir, Chardonnay, and Pinot Gris.

Now part of the Lion Nathan portfolio, Stonier was begun in 1978 when Brian Stonier and his wife Noel planted the first Chardonnay vines in the coastal town of Merricks. These vineyards are now almost twenty years old, and the vine age is bringing a natural balance and depth to the wines. Stonier now sources grapes from five different subregions.

Stonier's Chardonnays are not only in the top tier of Mornington wines, but among the best in Australia. The regular Chardonnay is of a very high quality, but the Reserve is even better. The 2003 has an intense, toasty, complex, herby nose. As you would expect from an Australian interpretation of this grape, it is boldly flavored, but with some minerally richness. There is a lot of weight and richness on the palate, which has a lovely texture and herby, toasty notes. It is a well integrated, powerful wine, made in a forward style, but there is also a lovely, lemony, minerally freshness. **JG**
☻☻ **Drink: to 2018**

◀ Steenberg vines ripen under the Cape sun.

Stony Hill
Chardonnay 1991

Château Suduiraut
S de Suduiraut 2011

Origin USA, California, Napa Valley
Style Dry white wine, 13% ABV
Grape Chardonnay

Origin France, Bordeaux, Sauternes
Style Dry white wine, 13% ABV
Grapes Sauvignon Blanc 60%, Sémillon 40%

Fred and Eleanor McCrea relocated to the Napa Valley in the 1940s after finding a goat ranch on the northeast slope of Spring Mountain. Initially they had no intention of growing grapes or making wine, but, encouraged by their neighbors, they planted Chardonnay and a little Pinot Blanc and Riesling. As it turned out, moderating climatic influences—such as northeast-facing slopes and an elevation between 400 and 800 feet (122–244 m) above the valley floor—turned out to suit Chardonnay.

Little has changed at Stony Hill since the 1940s. Apart from switching to a bladder press from the old basket press, vinification has remained constant. Stony Hill's philosophy is that the purest expression of fruit and vineyard comes through use of neutral wood. This also mandates suppression of the malolactic fermentation, which alters the acidity of the wine and introduces "extraneous" flavors.

The 1991 vintage had an unusual toasty, yeasty character from the start. In youth, Stony Hill Chardonnays are tightly wound, with firm citrus and floral flavors and a mineral core; it is only after five or ten years that their full complexity blossoms. **LGr**

🚫🚫🚫 **Drink: to 2021**

This is the dry wine of Château Suduiraut, one of the greatest of all Sauternes. Giving the dry wine just a casual initial for a name is a habit in these parts. But unlike many, this has a very short history indeed: 2004 was the first vintage to be released.

Suduiraut had long made a dry wine for domestic consumption. It is a natural thing to do: On a large estate like this one, with 220 acres (89 ha) under vine, there are inevitably some parts of the vineyard that are less susceptible to botrytis than others. But making a less-than-excellent Sauternes is not what Suduiraut is about; the obvious alternative was always to make a dry white.

This is a modern wine. It is often floral when young; then nuts and smoke will take over, still wrapped around a tight, concentrated core. The château had no particular model in mind when work began on the wine. Many of the other great Sauternes châteaux that make a dry wine have been wrestling with the question of how to update wines that are of extreme minority interest without losing the signature of the château. S de Suduiraut, arriving without any such baggage, can simply be itself. **MR**

🚫🚫 **Drink: recent vintages for up to 8 years**

Hand-harvesting of grapes at Château Suduiraut. ➡

Château Suduiraut 1989

Origin France, Bordeaux, Sauternes, Preignac
Style Sweet white wine, 14% ABV
Grapes Sémillon 90%, Sauvignon Blanc 10%

The Sauternes region is packed with fine châteaux in a wide range of architectural styles, suggesting how prosperous the Graves must have been in times past. Suduiraut is one of the grandest, dating from 1670 and surrounded by gardens designed by André Le Nôtre, whose most celebrated work was at Versailles. Long owned by the Suduiraut family, the château was acquired in 1992 by AXA Millésimes, which converted the property into a private hotel and conference center, while taking care to maintain the high quality of the wine.

This is an enormous property, with 220 acres (89 ha) under vine. Its rather flat, sandy clay soils are precocious and the grapes tend to ripen early. Yields are kept low, and different parcels and varieties are vinified separately—in barrels only, since 1992—giving winemaker Pierre Montegut more than fifty lots to work with. The creation of a second wine in 1992 also allowed the winemaking team to be more selective with the harvest.

1989 was a great vintage here. The last picking, on November 9, was rejected because it was tainted by rain, but the rest of the wine was aged for almost two years in 30 percent new oak. The nose is powerful, with aromas of oranges, barley sugar, and *crème brûlée*; although the wine is unquestionably rich, it is not heavy-handed and retains good acidity and length. In this vintage Suduiraut also produced 6,000 bottles of a magnificent Crème de Tête, but this regular bottling comes very close in quality. **SBr** ⊖⊖⊖ **Drink: to 2020+**

FURTHER RECOMMENDATIONS

Other great vintages

1959 • 1962 • 1967 • 1975 • 1982 • 1988 • 1990 • 1996 • 1997 • 1999 • 2001 • 2002 • 2005 • 2009 • 2010

More Preignac producers

Bastor-Lamontagne • de Malle • Gilette • Les Justices

The late-seventeenth-century Château Suduiraut. ⊞

Szepsy
Tokaji Esszencia 1999

Origin Hungary, Tokaj
Style Sweet white wine, 2% ABV
Grapes Furmint, Hárslevelű, Muscat Blanc à Petits Grains

Perhaps the rarest and most overwhelming of all sweet wines, Tokaji Esszencia is a lightly alcoholic syrup made from the small quantity of juice that drips from the Aszú (botrytis-affected) grapes before they are mashed to a paste. This juice is so high in sugar that it ferments extremely slowly, taking decades to achieve even as little as 5 to 6 percent alcohol. It is usually intended for blending with other wines, but occasionally, in the very best years, producers will bottle some Esszencia by itself.

The acknowledged master of contemporary Tokaji is István Szepsy, and he excelled himself in the great 1999 vintage. When tasted in 2004, Szepsy's Esszencia 1999 was creamy and grapey, though painfully sweet—it contains an incredible 500 g/l of residual sugar. Even more astonishingly, 1.8 ounces (50 g) of sugar were lost during fining and filtration—raw Esszencia is so thick and unctuous that it blocks the pores of the filtration sheets. Despite the awesome sweetness, it is not at all cloying, with very penetrating acidity and a mere 2 percent alcohol, so strictly speaking this is not wine at all but a lightly alcoholic beverage.

This is a wine—or rather grape juice—of simply astonishing sweetness, concentration, and length, and one that supports the legend of Tokaji as an elixir capable of raising the ill from their bed. Few who taste this wine will disagree that István Szepsy is able to work miracles. **SG**
❸❸❸❸❸ Drink: to 2050+

The town of Tokaj, at the confluence of the Tisza and Bodrog Rivers.. ➔

Tahbilk *Marsanne* 2006

Origin Australia, Victoria, Goulburn Valley
Style Dry white wine, 12.5% ABV
Grape Marsanne

Tahbilk is Victoria's oldest wine-producing estate, established in 1860, and has been owned by the Purbrick family since 1925. The estate's name is derived from the Aboriginal *tabilk-tabilk*, meaning "place of many waterholes." It produces two wines of particular distinction: the 1860 Shiraz, produced from ungrafted, pre-phylloxera vines planted on the property in 1860, and Marsanne, a remarkably inexpensive wine that develops superb complexity with bottle age.

Marsanne is a rare grape variety, with Tahbilk having the largest single holding in the world. Its spiritual home is the Hermitage region of the northern Rhône, where it makes a magnificently concentrated dry white wine. It is also grown in minute quantities in the United States and Switzerland. Tahbilk's Marsanne has been traced back to the 1860s, when cuttings from the St. Huberts vineyard in the Yarra Valley found their way to Goulburn. The estate now produces Marsanne from plantings dating back to 1927.

When young, the nose and palate exhibit completely unoaked, simple, and fresh aromas of lemon, honey, and peach. With about five years of bottle age, though, these develop into the very distinctive honeysuckle fragrance traditionally associated with mature Marsanne. Even in its second decade, the wine remains remarkably fresh and crisp. Tahbilk's Marsanne is a regional, and probably national, benchmark white wine. **SG**

🌕🌖 **Drink: to 2018+**

FURTHER RECOMMENDATIONS
Other great vintages
1996 • 1997 • 1999 • 2000 • 2001 • 2002 • 2003 • 2004
More wines from the same producer
1927 Vines Marsanne • 1860 Vines Shiraz • Eric Stevens Purbrick Cabernet Sauvignon • Eric Stevens Purbrick Shiraz

The Tahbilk sign hanging at the entrance to the winery. ➔

Domaine de la Taille aux Loups *Romulus Plus* 2003

Origin France, Loire, Touraine
Style Sweet white wine, 9% ABV
Grape Chenin Blanc

Former wine broker Jacky Blot created Domaine de la Taille aux Loups in 1989 out of a determination to restore the Loire appellation of Montlouis-sur-Loire. The domaine's old vines are situated on a south-facing stony limestone and clay plateau overlooking the river. The success of Blot's mission owes much to his fierce pruning and selection regime. Only the ripest, healthiest Chenin Blanc grapes survive the *trie de vendange*, followed by a final rigorous selection on the sorting table. This produces a tremendous concentration and purity of fruit, which is subtly enhanced by Blot's contemporary, barrel-fermented and matured style (10 percent new oak each year).

Most new oak is reserved for Cuvée Remus, an ambitious, dry Montlouis, whereas the sweet Cuvée Romulus owes its power and majesty to botrytis. Produced only in great years, Cuvée Romulus is made from the cream of the crop of botrytized grapes. Well endowed with 350 g/l of residual sugar, the wine's unusually opulent, tropical fruit with spice and honey finds structure and balance in a pithy acidity. It is an extraordinary digestif to enjoy in a mood of quiet contemplation. **SA**

🕒🕒🕒 **Drink: to 2025**

Tamellini *Soave Classico* *Le Bine de Costiola* 2004

Origin Italy, Veneto
Style Dry white wine, 13% ABV
Grape Garganega

The Soave DOC is enjoying a return to higher quality. Having been through a phase of "reorganization" that lasted for several years, the area now produces wines of a consistently high quality, vintage after vintage. One of the estates that emerged from this reorganization was Tamellini. The Tamellini family has been involved in wine production for many years, but the firm was created only in 1998.

Brothers Gaetano and Pio Francesco have appointed Federico Curtaz as the viticulturalist and Paolo Caciorgna as the winemaker. Many of their vineyards were planted in the first half of the 1970s, and are trained on the Guyot system or the traditional Pergola Veronese. The only grape variety is Garganega, the best grape of the Soave blend.

Their Soave Le Bine 2004 is a wine that does not make any concession to the "international palate." There is no oak whatsoever, and there are not the familiar, soft, almost tropical fruit aromas found in many Soaves made with Chardonnay or other international varieties in the blend. The wine is intense in both color and aroma, with the typical, refreshing, bitter almond appeal of this DOC. **AS**

🕒 **Drink: to 2019**

Cantina di Terlano
Chardonnay Rarità 1994

Origin Italy, Trentino Alto Adige
Style Dry white wine, 13% ABV
Grape Chardonnay

The Cantina di Terlano is a cooperative winery created in 1893 by twenty-four member growers. Today it has about 100 members, for a total vineyard area of 370 acres (150 ha). But do not let big numbers fool you; the Cantina di Terlano ranks among the best producers in Italy. The cellar houses 12,000 bottles of every vintage from 1955 to the present.

Every so often, the company releases a small amount of a mature wine that has been specially treated. The Chardonnay Rarità 1994 was partially fermented in barrique; after the blending, it was aged on its lees in stainless-steel vats for almost nine years. The wine was left to age in the bottle for a further eighteen months before release.

This wine somewhat resembles a great, mature Champagne. The color is unexpectedly youthful for such an old wine—bright gold-yellow, but no darker than many three-year-old, barrique-aged wines. The nose is enchanting, with intense notes of patisserie and dried herbs. On the palate, it is balanced, tightly textured, and complex. It is mouth-filling without ever being heavy, and has a lively, flinty acidity that helps it linger on the palate for minutes. **AS**

🌢🌢🌢🌢 **Drink: to 2018+**

Cantina di Terlano
Sauvignon Blanc Quarz 2011

Origin Italy, Trentino Alto Adige
Style Dry white wine, 13.5% ABV
Grape Sauvignon Blanc

The Cantina di Terlano officially produces three different ranges of wine—classics, crus, and selections. There is also a fourth range that comes in beautiful one-liter screwcap bottles, but that is only drunk locally: a good excuse to pay a visit.

Many of the cooperative's members have their vineyards around the village of Terlano itself. The soil there is mainly sandstone, but characterized by the presence of porphyry rocks, able to accumulate and redistribute the heat, thereby helping the ripening of the fruit. The sandstone is quite porous and is also able to absorb water and drain away any excess.

The Sauvignon Quarz is obtained from grapes grown in this type of soil, at an altitude of 980 to 1,150 feet (299–350 m). The fermentation takes place half in stainless-steel vats and half in oak casks. Once the fermentation is finished, the wine is blended and left to age on its fine lees for eight months. The wine is elegant and complex, with aromas of ripe apricot and white flowers, lightly accompanied by discreet toasty notes. On the palate, it is broad and mouth-filling, showing remarkable complexity, bracing minerality, and a long finish. **AS**

🌢🌢🌢 **Drink: recent vintages for up to 10 years**

Testalonga
El Bandito Chenin Blanc 2010

Origin South Africa, Swartland
Style Dry white wine, 13% ABV
Grape Chenin Blanc

This is one of the own-label wines of Craig Hawkins, the radical young viticulturist and winemaker at Lammershoek Winery in the Swartland, under which label he has also been doing fine work. Hawkins is experimental with this label, and the length of the maceration of the juice on the grape skins has varied from five weeks in 2008 to a remarkable two years in 2010: after carbonic maceration, the whole bunches—stems and all—remain solidly in their fermented juice in old wooden barrels.

This remarkable wine may not prove "easy" for those with fixed ideas. Made from organically farmed, fifty-five-year-old Chenin bushvines at Lammershoek, picked early by typical modern standards, its naked, "natural" winemaking involves no yeast inoculation, no acidification; nothing apart from a tiny amount of sulfur. It is transferred unfiltered to bottle. The wine's rich gold derives from the skins; it's bone-dry, and there's a great intensity of fruit flavors, held together by a formidable structure of grape tannin and acidity. It is possible, its maker surmises, that this wine could keep, well stored, for decades. **TJ**
🍷🍷 **Drink: to 2020+**

Jean Thévenet *Domaine de la*
BonGran Cuvée EJ Thévenet 2002

Origin France, Burgundy, Mâconnais
Style Dry white wine, 14% ABV
Grape Chardonnay

Jean Thévenet has first claim to be the father of fine winemaking in the Mâcon-Villages of southern Burgundy. Not that there is anything avant-garde about his approach. In truth, Jean follows a sensitively adapted form of classic white Burgundy making, in particular giving his wines the hand-crafted attention one associates more with the Côte de Beaune. He uses a combination of his father's old oak *foudres* and modern vats, always insistent that a moderate temperature during the first days is very important. He also strongly believes that fermentation should take place in its own time, which may be as long as six to eight months.

This unhurried approach depends on excellent grapes. Jean's best known domaine is La BonGran, located on the mid-slopes of Quintaine, the hamlet closest to the Saône. Harvesting takes place when the grapes are fully ripe, often as late as mid-October. Although the 2005, from a much-hyped vintage, is a strongly constituted, ripe wine, it will be interesting to see if it can ever match the grace of the BonGran Cuvée EJ Thévenet 2002—a great, focused wine, fresh yet golden, all lemon and honey. **ME**
🍷🍷🍷 **Drink: to 2017+**

Château Tirecul La Gravière
Cuvée Madame 2001

Origin France, Southwest, Monbazillac
Style Sweet white wine, 12% ABV
Grapes Muscadelle 50%, Sémillon 45%, S. Blanc 5%

If Monbazillac, with its vineyards just south of Bergerac, has lagged behind Sauternes not just in reputation but in quality, the reasons are primarily economic. Bruno Bilancini decided to buck the trend. He leased this property in 1992 and bought it outright five years later. A peculiarity of Tirecul La Gravière is that half the vines are Muscadelle, a variety that normally plays a mere supporting role to Sémillon and Sauvignon.

As well as the basic wine, Bilancini produces Cuvée Madame, a selection of the best and richest barrels, which is given extended oak-aging. It is not a limited-production wine, and the quantities produced vary considerably from vintage to vintage. Thus, in 1995, 80 percent of the crop qualified for Cuvée Madame. In 2001, Cuvée Madame had 210 g/l of residual sugar, at least 50 percent more than a fine Sauternes (but even the regular wine had 175 g/l). The nose oozes botrytis, with aromas of honey and peaches; it is very sweet, of course, but concentrated and enlivened with terrific acidity. By any criteria it is a superb wine, but then the regular wine, at about one-third of the price, is outstanding, too. **SBr**
🟢🟢🟢 **Drink: to 2030**

André & Mireille Tissot
La Mailloche 2005

Origin France, Jura, Arbois
Style Dry white wine, 13.5% ABV
Grape Chardonnay

Stéphane Tissot, the winemaker for the domaine since 1990, launched his first single-vineyard Chardonnays with the 1997 vintage, a radical step in the traditional Jura region. Among these, the 500-case La Mailloche has been the most successful, fully expressing the Jura terroir. East-facing, with vines of varied ages up to fifty years old, the vineyard has a compact clay soil from lias marl. There is never a ripeness problem, and the cool clay gives good acidity levels to the grapes, suiting Stéphane's reductive form of winemaking—fermentation in barrels (one-third new), with malolactic fermentation and regular lees stirring.

From August 20 for three weeks, the weather was perfect in 2005, a north wind drying out the grapes after earlier wet weather. Pale greeny lemon in color, La Mailloche has a powerful minerality on the nose (the lees aging combined with the soil) with some lemon rind, quince, and smoke. Lemony fruit emerges on the palate and spicy, toasty notes fill the mouth, yet neither oak nor alcohol dominates. The length is tremendous, giving an overall impression of a fresh, stony wine that will soften given time. **WL**
🟢🟢 **Drink: to 2020**

Marimar Torres Estate
Dobles Lias Chardonnay 2004

Origin USA, California, Sonoma County
Style Dry white wine, 14.1% ABV
Grape Chardonnay

Having made California her home, Marimar Torres persuaded her family in 1983 to expand their vineyard interests with the purchase of a 56-acre (23 ha) property in the rolling hills of western Sonoma County. Planting of Chardonnay and Pinot Noir began in 1986 on what is now the Don Miguel Vineyard, in a style she characterizes as European viticulture adapted to California conditions.

High-density planting limits vigor and encourages the vines to produce ripe, healthy, concentrated fruit. The vineyard, fully organic since 2003, is 10 miles (16 km) from the Pacific, in the heart of the Green Valley, where lighter soils ensure wines of elegance, not thrust. Torres opted to plant three distinctive Chardonnay clones.

The 2004 is composed of three barrels of the See clone, seven barrels of the Rued clone, and three of the Spring Mountain clone. The Dobles Lias was whole cluster pressed and barrel-fermented, with lees stirring throughout the malolactic fermentation. The following June, Torres selected the barrels for the blend, and added lees from other barrels being bottled. After eighteen months in French oak, the wine and lees were transferred to stainless-steel tanks, where they remained until bottling, unfiltered, in June 2006. With a lively, complex nose, the 2004 opens brilliantly on the palate, broad and textured but not fat, with a thin scrim of minerality carried through to a persistent finish. **LGr**
🝔🝔 **Drink: to 2017+**

Torres Marimar vines bask in the California sun. ➡

Château La Tour Blanche 2003

Origin France, Bordeaux, Sauternes, Bommes
Style Sweet white wine, 14% ABV
Grapes Sémillon 80%, Sauvignon Blanc 20%

In the 1855 classification, La Tour Blanche was placed immediately at the head of the first growths, with Yquem occupying a unique category as *capo di tutti capi*. Today the property leads a double existence as a functioning wine estate and a college for budding agronomists and winemakers. Owner and umbrella manufacturer Daniel Iffla, when he died in 1907, left the property to the state on condition that it was run as a free wine college. The college was duly constructed and the vines were leased to the merchant house of Cordier until 1955. The wine was unexciting until the arrival of a new director of the college, Jean-Piere Jausserand, in 1983.

Under Jausserand, different sectors of the 89-acre (36 ha) vineyard and different varieties were vinified and aged separately to give the estate about eighteen components for the final blend. Yields were slashed, and Jausserand insisted on using only bunches with high must weights for the grand vin. Pneumatic presses were installed in 1987, and chaptalization was abandoned. By 1989 the wine was being fermented and aged entirely in new oak.

The style is rich for Bommes—certainly compared with neighbor Clos Haut-Peyraguey—without being heavy, although initial density means that the wine can be slightly surly when young and thus benefits from bottle age. The 2003, typical of the vintage, is richer than usual, with peach syrup aromas, and a lushness on the palate moderated by some fresh acidity that gives good length. **SBr**
❸❸❸ **Drink: to 2025**

FURTHER RECOMMENDATIONS
Other great vintages
1990 · 1995 · 1996 · 1997 · 1998 · 1999 · 2001 · 2005
More Bommes producers
Lafaurie-Peyraguey · Rabaud-Promis *Rayne-Vigneau · Sigalas-Rabaud*

A white tower on the Château La Tour Blanche estate. ➡

David Traeger *Verdelho* 2002

Origin Australia, Victoria, Nagambie Lakes
Style Dry white wine, 12.5% ABV
Grape Verdelho

David Traeger established his winery in central Victoria in 1978, having learned his trade as assistant winemaker at Michelton. His vineyards are located at Hughes Creek, south of Nagambie, and contain Cabernet Sauvignon, Shiraz, Merlot, Petit Verdot, Tempranillo, Viognier, and Verdelho. There is another Shiraz and Grenache vineyard at Graytown (Heathcote), planted in 1891, that Traeger uses for his blockbuster red, The Baptista.

It is with his Verdelho, however, that Traeger really shines. Best known as one of the classic varieties of Madeira, where it makes a rich, medium-sweet wine with very high acidity, very little is made into dry wine anywhere, though it has been increasingly fashionable in Australia in recent years. Traeger planted Verdelho in the Nagambie Lakes region in 1994 principally because he wanted to avoid the ubiquitous Chardonnay.

The weather is very consistent in Nagambie, enabling Traeger to aim for a delicate and fragrant style of white wine rather than the usual Aussie powerhouse. In September 2005, David presented a fifteen-vintage vertical tasting of Verdelho from 1990 to 2004. The consistency of style and quality was highly impressive, as was the longevity, with older vintages from the inaugural 1990 onward still drinking well. When young, the wine is aromatic, with a distinctive honeysuckle and tropical fruit flavor, but with age it becomes biscuity and more fragrant. It is tremendous value for money, too. **SG**
☻☻☻ **Drink: to 2018+**

FURTHER RECOMMENDATIONS		
Other great vintages		
1991 · 1993 · 1994 · 1996 · 1998 · 1999 · 2001 · 2003		
More wines from the same producer		
David Traeger Cabernet / Merlot		
David Traeger Shiraz · David Traeger Baptista Shiraz		

Grapes are crushed mechanically after picking at Nagambie Lakes. ➡

Trimbach
Clos Ste.-Hune Riesling 1990

Origin France, Alsace
Style Dry white wine, 13% ABV
Grape Riesling

Angerhof Tschida
Trockenbeerenauslese Sämling 2007

Origin Austria, Burgenland, Illmitz
Style Sweet white wine, 9% ABV
Grape Scheurebe

Although the Trimbach family of Ribeauvillé has owned the tiny 3.2-acre (1.3 ha) vineyard of Clos Ste.-Hune for more than 200 years, wine was not named for it until 1919. In November 2005, wine auctioneer John Kapon tasted thirteen vintages of Clos Ste.-Hune. Afterward, he declared, "The 1990 quickly laid claim to wine of the night. It had a fabulous nose, full of musk, rainwater, citrus, nut, and a sweet Asian spice. The richness, length, and breed of the wine were all superlative. Flavors of tender, juicy white meat, rain, citrus dust, and oil were all delicious. It was rich, exotic, and incredible."

Bureaucracy dictates that the name of any solely owned vineyard in Alsace cannot be used as a grand cru, therefore the Trimbachs would have to put the name Rosacker—the grand cru in which Clos Ste.-Hune sits—on the label of the wine, rather than that of Clos Ste.-Hune itself. The Trimbachs have long rejected this reasoning, and continue to bottle the wine as a plain AOC Alsace. Despite its "official" lowly status, this is one of the world's greatest dry white wines, and fetches a higher price than any other dry Alsace wine. **SG**

🍷🍷🍷🍷 Drink: to 2020+

With the small town of Illmitz home to more than sixty Tschidas, it is not surprising that Hans Tschida named his property Angerhof to distinguish it from other Tschida estates. He has been making wines since 1982, but first bottled them in 1988. With 99 acres (40 ha) under vine here, he also produces some red wines. But his real passion has always been sweet botrytis wines and straw wines from unbotrytized fruit in years when noble rot is clearly lacking.

Sämling, the Austrian name for Scheurebe, usually makes the finest TBAs here, though in some years Chardonnay and Welschriesling can come close in quality. The year 2007 was an exceptional vintage for botrytis wines. Gold in color, the Sämling has voluptuous aromas of peaches and tropical fruit, with a touch of honey. The attack is splendid, with a sweet and sour tone on the palate thanks to the high acidity (11.5 grams per liter) required to balance the residual sugar of 271 grams. The wine is racy, clean, and intense, with an excellent and persistent tangy finish. It is not remotely heavy but its balance should ensure a very long life, though it is not a wine that demands further cellaring. **SBr**

🍷🍷🍷 Drink: to 2040

◧ Harvested Riesling grapes arriving at the Trimbach winery.

Tyrrell's
Vat 1 Semillon 1999

Origin Australia, New South Wales, Hunter Valley
Style Dry white wine, 10.5% ABV
Grape Sémillon

Valentini
Trebbiano d'Abruzzo 1992

Origin Italy, Abruzzo
Style Dry white wine, 12.5% ABV
Grape Trebbiano d'Abruzzo

Tyrrell's could claim to be the masters of Hunter Valley Sémillon, producing seven different labels of fine Sémillon every year, including three individual vineyard bottlings. The flagship wine is not a single-vineyard one, though: Vat 1 comes from three vineyards, all in the same locality, on the dry creek bed at the bottom of the hill in front of the winery, a total of nearly 15 acres (6 ha). The soils are all similar: light, sandy, and alluvial, some with a calcite base.

Vat 1 was first bottled in 1962 as Vat 1 Hunter River Riesling, its traditional name. This changed in 1990 to Vat 1 Semillon. A major difference between Tyrrell's and Mount Pleasant styles is that Tyrrell's ferments less highly clarified juice, giving a slightly richer, more fleshy style. The 1999 vintage was one of the biggest, with what Bruce Tyrrell describes as a high juice yield. "But it's very good quality, with very good chemistry, and it will age well," he says.

No oak is used. The 1999 still has a green tinge to its bright light yellow color, whereas the nose is delicately lemony and faintly herbal, with a hint of toast creeping in. In the mouth, it is fresh and clean, fine and lingering, with great balance. **HH**
🍷🍷 Drink: to 2020+

Trebbiano d'Abruzzo can be considered an exception among Trebbiano-based wines. The Trebbiano d'Abruzzo name identifies both the legal name of the wine but also one of the two grape varieties admitted by the DOC law for its production. These are Trebbiano d'Abruzzo itself, otherwise known as Bombino Bianco, and the (sadly) more famous Trebbiano Toscano, responsible in the recent past for the dilution of many traditional DOCs and DOCGs, including Chianti. The Bombino Bianco is quite different. Bombino is the modern distortion of the name Bonvino or Buon Vino (good wine).

The Valentini family has been an interpreter of Trebbiano d'Abruzzo for many generations. Edoardo Valentini passed away in April 2006, passing the family firm to his son, Francesco Paolo, but what mattered to him was a wine able to "speak the dialect," rather than the science of the winemaking.

The 1992 is an incredible wine, with notes of dried leaves, biscuits, spices, coffee, and chamomile flowers. On the palate, it is superb, with a freshness and vibrancy one would never expect from a 1992, and enviable body and length. **AS**
🍷🍷🍷🍷 Drink: to 2017+

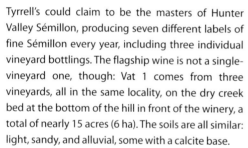

◧ An iconic Southern Cross windpump in the Hunter Valley.

Van Volxem *Scharzhofberger Pergentsknopp Riesling* 2005

Origin Germany, Mosel-Saar-Ruwer
Style Off-dry white wine, 12% ABV
Grape Riesling

Roman Niewodniczanski's ambitions are as tall and unorthodox as the man himself. He has taken the van Volxem estate in Wiltingen to unprecedented heights since his family purchased it in 1999. At the same time he has aroused the ire of some of his colleagues in the valley by making little or no use of classical terms like Kabinett, which he considers too light to be taken seriously, or Spätlese, preferring instead to favor a hedonistic, some would say off-dry, style that is at once rich and dense with a spicy character. He is also unusual in using subplots with historical precedence, such as the Pergentsknopp in the heart of the world-renowned Scharzhofberg vineyard, or *Alte Reben*, which means "old vines," to designate his finest wines. Those in the Pergentsknopp are more than 100 years old.

Although some object that his ostensibly dry wines are not dry at all, Niewo is quick to retort that the Spätlese and Auslese produced today are too sweet. "If you look at the Spätlese produced in the 1950s, they often had little more residual sugar than my dry wines do today."

The grapes in 2005 were exceptionally ripe, with a fine acidic structure. The wine is a pale golden yellow, with yeasty aromas of wild peach, sweet herbs, and nut oils. On the palate it is pungent, with smoky apricot pit fruit, riveting nerve, and uplifting mineral salts. It is nonetheless subtle, with toasted almonds on a seductively long finish. Niewo drinks his wines three to eight years after harvest. **JP**

🍷🍷🍷 **Drink: to 2035**

FURTHER RECOMMENDATIONS
Other great vintages
2001 • 2004
More wines from the same producer
Kanzemer Altenberg Alte Reben Riesling • Scharzhofberger Riesling • Wiltinger Gottesfuß Alte Reben Riesling

Pruning vines into the heart shape typical of the Mosel. ➡

Vergelegen
White 2005

Origin South Africa, Stellenbosch
Style Dry white wine, 14% ABV
Grapes Sémillon 67%, Sauvignon Blanc 33%

Many critics believe that the Cape's white wines are its chief glory, and an inevitably cited example is this flagship of one of the Cape's finest producers.

The confident poise of this wine belies the fact that it encompasses only a half decade of development. The first, 2001, vintage was not only much more heavily wooded, but had reverse proportions of the grape varieties, with nearly 80 percent Sauvignon to give the "up-front fruit" that initially reassured an uncharacteristically insecure André van Rensburg. Now the winemaker is seeking a wine that will mature over—he believes—at least a decade. Van Rensburg's confidence lies in the proven quality of his vineyards high on the Helderberg.

In the cellar a fairly oxidative regime is followed. The two varieties are separately bunch-pressed then fermented in oak (mostly new for the Sémillon, mostly older for the Sauvignon) for some ten months before being blended. The wood is assertive on the youthful wine, but within a few years it is absorbed into supporting the growing complexity of its discreet richness, serene intensity of flavor, and subtle power, informed by a fine vein of acidity. **TJ**
🍷🍷 **Drink: to 2017+**

Verget
St.-Véran Les Terres Noires 2005

Origin France, Burgundy, Mâconnais
Style Dry white wine, 13% ABV
Grape Chardonnay

Since the mid-1980s, a role reversal in Burgundy has seen growers become more like *négociants*, buying in grapes, must, or wine, and *négociants* become more like growers, with a higher proportion of their production coming from their own vineyards. Among the former, one of the most ambitious of a new breed of small *négociant* firms is Verget, established in 1990 by Belgian Jean-Marie Guffens, who had founded his own Domaine Guffens-Heynen in Pouilly-Fuissé a decade earlier.

Guffens prefers to buy grapes rather than must or wine, the better to control quality, and offers representative wines from Chablis and the Côte d'Or as well as from the Mâconnais. While some of the most prestigious bottlings fully justify their grand or premier cru status, it is those from less exalted appellations further south that really over-deliver.

A classic case in point is this relatively humble St.-Véran Terres Noires. From the black earth comes white gold, glimmering with the promise of the richness within. Compact, dense, and focused, the wine has crisp, almost crunchy stone fruit with an exciting mineral charge. **NB**
🍷🍷 **Drink: 2017+**

Georges Vernay
Condrieu Coteau de Vernon 2010

Origin France, Northern Rhône, Condrieu
Style Dry white wine, 14% ABV
Grape Viognier

Vie di Romans
Chardonnay 2004

Origin Italy, Friuli Venezia Giulia
Style Dry white wine, 14% ABV
Grape Chardonnay

Few wine-growing areas owe as much to one emblematic vineyard as Condrieu does to Georges Vernay's Coteau de Vernon. Perched above the eponymous town, these 5 acres (2 ha) of lonely vines winked like a lighthouse throughout the dark days of the 1950s, '60s, and '70s, when Condrieu (and with it Viognier) nearly slipped beneath the waves.

The average age of the vines is sixty years, implying a root structure of great penetration. Sometimes the grapes are briefly skin-macerated, sometimes not; the juice is then barrel-fermented (20 percent new wood) and left on its fine lees for twelve to eighteen months before bottling.

Whether it is due to those deep roots or to the fundamental aptitude of the site itself is an open question, but this is a Condrieu that always repays storage before being broached. After eight to ten years the wine will have taken a little summer gold in its color, and the diagnostic floral aromas will be deepening into something creamier, fruitier, sometimes even smokier. The palate will be filled out with honeyed pear and apricot fruits that taper away gracefully in a sprinkling of powdered stone. **AJ**

🖐🖐🖐 **Drink: recent vintages for up to 10 years**

The name Vie di Romans comes from the local dialect and means "the ancient Roman road." The Gallo family (no relation to the Californian one) has owned and worked this land for more than a century. Gianfranco Gallo took over the family business in 1978, and implemented revolutionary vineyard and cellar practices (at least for this region at this time) that led some of his neighbors to label him as "mad." If wines such as his Sauvignon Blancs or his Chardonnays are the fruit of madness, then let there be more of the madness.

The Vie di Romans Chardonnay 2004 is a flamboyant wine. A bright yet deep golden-yellow color in the glass prepares you for what might come next. You already know that wines of such color might be heaven or hell, but certainly will not leave you indifferent. This is heaven. It exhibits a virtually seamless harmony, with notes of golden apples, cedar, and ripe pears, but also yellow flowers and bay leaves, leaving you wishing you had come across this jewel when it was more readily available. The big structure and the mercifully high acidity will guarantee medium- to long-term cellaring. **AS**

🖐🖐 **Drink: to 2017+**

Vigneti Massa
Timorasso Costa del Vento 2012

Origin Italy, Piedmont, Langhe
Style Dry white wine, 13% ABV
Grape Timorasso

Walter Massa has been the first producer to believe in, to grow, and to make into wine an ancient grape variety that was, at the end of the 1980s, on the brink of extinction. The Timorasso grape is the traditional variety of the Tortona hills in southern Piedmont. Today it is grown by nearly twenty different producers, but in 1987 Walter was on his own.

With no literature to rely on and no one's example to follow, Walter had to progress by trial and error until his turning point, the 1996 vintage, when the lack of space in his cellar forced him to leave a batch of wine in the vats and on its lees. This experimental 1996 was the wine that convinced Walter that Timorasso needed more time on its lees in order to develop its full potential.

Walter's Costa del Vento 2002 is a bit like the man himself: Restrained, understated elegance and complexity are the main traits. Subtle citrus and green apple notes are the foreword to a more complex nose, with mineral and petrollike notes. On the palate, it shows an unsuspected array of spices, especially white pepper, then closes with more honeyed, waxy flavors. Still a long life ahead. **AS**

🟢🟢🟢 **Drink: to 2017+**

Domaine A. et P. de Villaine
Bouzeron 2012

Origin France, Burgundy, Côte Chalonnaise
Style Dry white wine, 12.5% ABV
Grape Aligoté

In the public eye, Aubert de Villaine's name is inextricably linked with the great Domaine de la Romanée-Conti (DRC). But Aubert de Villaine is also interested in seeking out more affordable wines and terroirs of quality in the quieter corners of Burgundy.

In 1973, he and his U.S. wife Pamela bought a run-down wine estate at Bouzeron near Chagny. Bouzeron had always been known for Aligoté, and here on the village's limestone hillsides it is capable of producing wines of depth and structure. The de Villaines replanted the vineyards and, in the case of Aligoté, chose the best strain of it, called *doré*. The wine is given bespoke care from the vine to the glass—controlled grape yields, manual harvesting, fermentation in both used oak *foudres* from the DRC (80 percent) and modern vats, then six to eight months of aging before bottling.

The wine is simply labeled Bouzeron, in line with its promoted village AOC status. It has a seamlessly integrated green-gold color, hinting at the richness and density to come. It also has a crisp freshness and fine notes of walnut and chestnut. An invigorating wine, perfect with Epoisses cheese. **ME**

🟢🟢🟢 **Drink: to 2017+**

Aubert de Villaine, one of Burgundy's best-known winemakers. ➡

Domaine Comte Georges de Vogüé *Bourgogne Blanc* 1996

Vollenweider *Wolfer Goldgrube Riesling ALG* 2005

Origin France, Burgundy, Côte de Nuits
Style Dry white wine, 12.5% ABV
Grape Chardonnay

Origin Germany, Mosel-Saar-Ruwer
Style Sweet white wine, 7% ABV
Grape Riesling

This historic domaine went through a difficult patch toward the end of Georges de Vogüé's life (he died in 1987), but his daughter Elisabeth de Ladoucette, who ran things from the late 1980s until 2002, reversed the trend by hiring François Millet as winemaker and Gérard Gaudeau as *chef de vignes*.

De Vogüé is the only domaine on the Côte de Nuits to have been making grand cru white wine. In the 1970s and early 1980s there was no replanting, so when Millet and Gaudeau joined in 1986 they uprooted most of the old vines. It was decided that the Musigny Blanc would be released as Bourgogne Blanc until the vines reach the required age, and the wine the required quality for grand cru status. It comes from 1 acre (0.4 ha) of young vines at the top of Musigny, planted in 1986, 1987, and 1991. Another half acre (0.2 ha) was replanted in 1997.

The de Vogüé Bourgogne Blanc 1996 is a brilliant white Burgundy, with a lovely, minerally, slightly stinky, cabbagy nose that is complex and full. The palate is savory but fresh, still with lovely acidity. It is full-flavored, with a lemony freshness to the nutty fruit, showing great definition and precision. **JG**

🍷🍷 Drink: to 2017+

Daniel Vollenweider came to wine out of infatuation. After studies in his native Switzerland, he planned a brief apprenticeship with Ernst Loosen on the Mosel, and then with Meursault's Dominique Lafon. He never made it to Lafon. Learning how many distinguished Mosel vineyards were dying from neglect, Vollenweider one day pedaled out to the Wolfer Goldgrube. It was love at first site.

Steep parcels with ancient terraces and vines—many ungrafted, since the Goldgrube had resisted phylloxera—were to be had for modest prices. Vollenweider started buying land, located a moribund cellar, then threw himself passionately into the pursuit of spontaneous, slow-fermentation wines of elegant sweetness.

Vollenweider's "long gold capsule" Goldgrube Auslese from 2005—there is also a "regular" Goldkapsel bottling—testifies to this vineyard's fabulous potential and the vintner's fanaticism. Honey, grilled grapefruit, caramelized pear, candied pineapple, white raisin, and brown spices abundantly inform an opulent, oozingly viscous, yet bell-clear, subtly saline, refreshing little miracle. **DS**

🍷🍷🍷🍷 Drink: to 2025

◀ The courtyard of Domaine Comte Georges de Vogüé.

Robert Weil *Kiedricher Gräfenberg Riesling TBA G 316* 2003

Origin Germany, Rheingau
Style Sweet white wine, 6% ABV
Grape Riesling

Since the early 1990s, the 173-acre (70 ha) Robert Weil estate has caused a paradigm shift in the production of noble sweet dessert wines in Germany. Although its dry Rieslings are also beginning to match the depth of those from Leitz, its Spätlese and Auslese have long set the benchmark for the style. The estate was founded in 1875 by Dr. Robert Weil, a professor of German at the Sorbonne in Paris who left to escape the Franco-Prussian war. He settled in Kiedrich, and his choice of vineyards was impeccable. The site, first mentioned in the twelfth century as the *mons Rhingravii*, is a steep southwesterly slope exposed to the setting sun.

Although a Trockenbeerenauslese has been produced from this site each year since 1989, there have been only three gold-capsule bottlings—in 1995, 1999, and 2003. In fact, in the 2003 vintage, which brought forth a cornucopia of noble sweet Rieslings, two were produced—one with a must weight of 282° Oechsle, and this one with 316° Oechsle, the highest on record at the estate.

A dazzling golden yellow, the wine has an explosive aroma of caramelized apricot, guava, and lemon oil embedded in layer upon layer of honeyed botrytis. It is incredibly dense, richly creamy in texture, with a juicy, almost salty, tanginess. Extremely elegant, despite the enormous weight and depth, its brilliant spiciness rises at the back of the palate, and there is stunning length. **JP**
ⓢⓢⓢⓢⓢ **Drink: to 2100**

The historic Robert Weil manor house. ➨

Domaine Weinbach
Cuvée Théo Gewurztraminer 2002

Origin France, Alsace
Style Dry white wine, 13.5% ABV
Grape Gewürztraminer

Domaine Weinbach
Schlossberg GC Riesling 2002

Origin France, Alsace
Style Dry white wine, 13.5% ABV
Grape Riesling

The Domaine Weinbach is one of the oldest and most distinguished wine estates in Alsace. Records relate that wine was made at Kayserberg during the Carolingian era in the ninth century. Later, in the early 1600s, a religious and winemaking community was established here by the Capucins, who gave their name to the surrounding 5-acre (2 ha) *clos*.

In 1894, the property was bought by the Faller brothers, and it was their son and nephew Théo who brought the wines to the first rank of Alsace by realizing the full potential of his magnificent holdings in the grands crus Kayserberg, Furstentum, and Altenbourg. Théo Faller pioneered the use of indigenous yeasts, low yields, and long, slow fermentation in neutral large old casks.

Weinbach wines are often named after a member of the family rather than the *cru* from which they come. This 2002 Gewurztraminer comes from grapes grown in the Clos des Capucins, where Théo rests. The eponymous Cuvée Théo has exquisite aromas of rose, jasmine, spices, and crystallized citrus fruit. The mouthfeel is velvety, fine, and elegant, in line with the style of the vintage. **ME**
🍷🍷🍷🍷 **Drink: to 2017+**

The 57-acre (23 ha) Domaine Weinbach at Kayserberg and Kienzheim is one of the three best natural sources of great wine in Alsace, and the slopes of the grand cru Schlossberg in particular are the prize location of the domaine's finest Rieslings.

The mother rock of Schlossberg is granite, the soils sandy and full of minerals. At the top of the slope, at an altitude of 1,300 feet (400 m), these soils are not very deep, so the vines penetrate to the mother rock, making for wines of racy minerality and pure fruitiness—ideal for this dry, grand cru cuvée, where all the sugar is fully fermented out.

This brisk yet generous style fully suits the classy, subtle character of the 2002 vintage, a warm but not overly hot year that needed the intuitive "feeling" for which winemaker Laurence Faller is renowned. The fragrant, tense, and pure nature of this Schlossberg 2002 is entirely compatible with the marine flavor of oysters, or simply grilled seabass. The Cuvée Ste. Catherine (which was great in 2000) is another Weinbach Riesling from the lower, richer part of the Schlossberg. This wine is perfect for sauced lobster or the splendid Alsace dish, Coq au Riesling. **ME**
🍷🍷🍷🍷 **Drink: to 2017+**

The Faller family own Weinbach, hence the name on their winery wall. ➡

Weingut Wittmann *Westhofener Morstein Riesling Trocken* 2001

Origin Germany, Rheinhessen
Style Dry white wine, 13% ABV
Grape Riesling

Together with his colleague Klaus Keller, whose winery is located a few miles away, Philipp Wittmann has managed to bring the southern Rheinhessen hinterland back into the consciousness of connoisseurs worldwide. Certainly by 2001, with the help of his phenomenal Morstein wine from that vintage, he proved that even here, in the rather flat region about 5 miles (8 km) away from the Rhein, Rieslings can be grown that rank among the best representatives of their kind.

This wine, granted ninety-four points as the best dry German Riesling of this vintage by Gault Millau, is distinguished by its "inimitable combination of elegance and potency . . . a fruit explosion." The Morstein site was first documented in 1282, when important monasteries in the Rhine Valley, in the Palatinate, and in Alsace owned property here. The vineyard is dominated by limestone rock. The topsoil, barely 1 foot (30 cm) deep, is of heavy, clayish marl, whereas the equally heavy subsoil is characterized by water-bearing layers of limestone.

Philipp Wittmann and his family have been cultivating this terroir according to ecological guidelines for many years. The grapes of the Morstein Riesling 2001 were harvested in the last week of October after repeated preselection. This is a true grand cru, with a distinct personality that combines the mineral richness of the wines of the northern Rheinfront with the juicy, overwhelming fruit flavors of the wines from the Palatinate. **FK**
⊖⊖⊖ **Drink: to 2019+**

FURTHER RECOMMENDATIONS
Other great vintages
2002 • 2004 • 2005 • 2012
More wines from the same producer
Westhofener Aulerde Chardonnay and Riesling
Westhofener Steingrube Riesling

This tower provides a vantage point across the Morstein vineyard. ▶

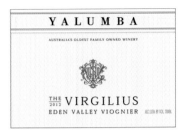

Yalumba

The Virgilius Viognier 2012

Origin Australia, South Australia, Barossa Valley
Style Dry white wine, 13.5% ABV
Grape Viognier

Yalumba's chief winemaker, Louisa Rose, has surely done more to promote the once near-extinct white Rhône variety, Viognier, as a grape capable of great things than anyone else, leading the clonal selection program in Australia and, in 2002, organizing the first International Viognier Symposium.

The Virgilius is the flagship Viognier of Australia's oldest family producer Yalumba, and is universally acknowledged as Australia's best Viognier. Yalumba's empire includes vine nurseries, allowing access to new varieties and better clones. In 1980, they planted 3 acres (1.2 ha) in the Eden Valley, though they weren't the first (Elgee Park in the Mornington Peninsula and Heathcote Winery in Heathcote beat them by a year or two). The first Virgilius was released in 1998, from the 1980 plantings.

The barrels used are around four or five years old, previously used for Chardonnay. The wine is bottled after twelve months, after severe barrel selection. The 2012 is the best yet. The nose has a delightful, opulent, apricot-kernel flavor, but it is not overblown. It has spice, floral, and peach notes, with an underlying hint of nettles and ginger, and a long finish. **KG**

ⓈⓈⓈ Drink: to 2020

Château d'Yquem

2001

Origin France, Bordeaux, Sauternes
Style Sweet white wine, 13.5% ABV
Grapes Sémillon 80%, Sauvignon Blanc 20%

Château d'Yquem looks down upon its Sauternais neighbors in every sense. Perched atop a hill that overlooks Lafaurie-Peyraguey, Guiraud, and Rieussec, Yquem was the only wine to be classified as Premier Cru Supérieur in the 1855 classification.

On average, only 110,000 bottles are produced each year. In a poor vintage, the entire crop is deemed unworthy of bearing the château's name. At least half a dozen *tries* are undertaken in each vintage to ensure that only the botrytized grapes are selected. The legend is that just one glass of wine is produced from each vine.

After the "bargain" 1999, which was probably the least expensive Yquem ever released—at about $140 (£70; €95) a bottle—2001 marked a return to the high prices that only top wines in top vintages can command. Released on September 29, 2005, to great acclaim, by mid-2007 it was selling for $1,000 (£500; €670) a bottle. With its perfect balance of fruit, botrytis, sugar, and acidity, and gorgeous flavors of crème brûlée, peaches, and apricots, it could be drunk young with immense pleasure, but will probably last for a century. **SG**

ⓈⓈⓈⓈⓈ Drink: to 2050+

Dusk falls over Château d'Yquem and its vineyards. ➋

Zilliken *Saarburger Rausch*
Riesling TBA A.P. #2 2005

Origin Germany, Mosel-Saar-Ruwer
Style Sweet white wine, 7% ABV
Grape Riesling

Domaine Zind-Humbrecht
Clos Jebsal Pinot Gris 2002

Origin France, Alsace
Style Dry white wine, 13.5% ABV
Grape Pinot Gris

As its name (meaning "intoxication") suggests, Saarburg's Rausch vineyard is among Germany's most vertiginous. Hanno Zilliken's wines are known for their complexity and for the balance they can achieve at stratospheric levels of sugar. In 2005, between October 10 and 22, warm, steady breezes desiccated nearly all of Zilliken's Riesling, yielding a concentration of acidity as well as sugar, extract, and flavor not unlike that achieved in Eiswein. Picking began with Beerenauslese and Trockenbeerenauslese, and continued with a sheer volume of Auslesen never before recorded.

Two different TBAs were harvested—one for sale at auction, and the other (with a tiny numeral two on the label as the second-from-last digit in its registration number) was sold directly to the trade and private customers. Musk, smoked meats, brown spices, caramel, lemon oil, and distilled plum are just a few of the aromas on display here. Layers of fresh, jamlike, and caramelized pit fruits follow on the palate, along with alluring mocha and butter cream. Compulsively, one returns to take up the glass with a reverence that few wines can command. **DS**

🍷🍷🍷🍷🍷 Drink: to 2055

The story of Zind-Humbrecht is one of a family of Alsace vignerons who over the course of fifty years have become icons of white winemaking. Léonard Humbrecht's family had been growers in Gueberswihr since the mid-seventeenth century, but it was his marriage to Geneviève Zind of Wintzenheim in 1959, and the uniting of the two families' vineyards, that created an important domaine of 45 acres (18 ha). It now offers a range of single-vineyard wines from some of the finest sites in Alsace—none more so than the Clos Jebsal.

Located in the uplands of Turckheim, the Clos is blessed with ideal exposure to light and sunshine. High levels of natural sugar are reached in the grape, so it is an ideal spot for Pinot Gris. Yet the soils are very complex, marl and gypsum in particular giving the wine fine minerality to balance any tendency to overripeness. The 2002 was a stylish, not too hot, vintage requiring real "feeling" to make. Of medium yellow color, the magical nose is honeyed yet smoky; the palate has plenty of concentration, yet the harmony of fruit, racy acidity, and residual sugar makes for a near-perfect wine. **ME**

🍷🍷🍷🍷 Drink: to 2017+

Pinot Gris vines in the Brand vineyard of the Domaine Zind-Humbrecht. ➡

Dom. Zind-Humbrecht *GC*
Rangen Clos St.-Urbain Riesling 2002

Origin France, Alsace
Style Dry white wine, 12.5% ABV
Grape Riesling

Olivier Humbrecht is a winemaker's winemaker, a man steeped in the technical arcana of the profession, the first Frenchman to pass the Institute of Masters of Wine examinations. Under the wise tutelage of his father Léonard, he has helped to propel the Zind-Humbrecht estate, founded only in 1959, into pole position among Alsace producers.

Operating on yields that are barely half the permitted maximum, Zind-Humbrecht disposes holdings in four of the grands crus. As well as Hengst, Brand, and Goldert, there is Rangen, a steeply shelving, south-facing vineyard planted on a mixture of light sandstone, volcanic rubble, and ash, overlooking the River Thur. Clos St.-Urbain is an enclave within the Rangen cru.

The vines are tended along biodynamic principles, and consequently Humbrecht regards the phases of the moon as quite as important to the vineyard as the weather outlook. Minerality is a treasured taste reference, particularly in the Rieslings. That quality appears in the Clos St.-Urbain Riesling as a gentle acerbity. In the Alsace vintage of 2002, the wine has deep, intense color, and powerful grapefruit and lime aromas. On the palate it has low-yield viscosity, allied to commanding fruit concentration, and an acid profile as highly polished as a guardsman's boots. As it leaves the mouth, it casts a tenacious vapor trail of gorgeous floral and citrus notes behind it. **SW**
☻☻☻☻ **Drink: to 2020+**

Zind-Humbrecht's Clos St.-Urbain above the town of Thann. ➨

Château Gi

Grand Cru Cl

CLASSEMENT OFFICIEL DE

MARGAU

1970

APPELLATION MARGAUX

NICOLAS TARI, PROPRIÉTAIRE A LABARDE

MIS EN BOUTEILLES AU

cours

é

TROLÉE

ARGAUX - 33

HATEAU

BERTHON - LIBOURNE

Bodegas Aalto *PS* 2001

Origin Spain, Ribera del Duero
Style Dry red wine, 14% ABV
Grape Tinto Fino (Tempranillo)

Bodegas Aalto was founded in 1999 by Javier Zaccagnini, formerly director of the Consejo Regulador de Ribera del Duero from 1992 to 1998, and Mariano García, who was head winemaker at Vega Sicilia from 1968 to 1998. Aalto wines are the product of 247 acres (100 ha) of vines, comprising more than 250 parcels spread out over the various terroirs of the Denominación de Origen Ribera del Duero. No parcel is more than 7.5 acres (3 ha), and no vine is less than forty years old. The standard cuvée is named simply Aalto, with the bodega's top wine called Aalto PS—Pagos Seleccionados (selected parcels). Tinto Fino (also called Tempranillo) is the only grape used for the wines, but Aalto PS is made from vineyards planted in the 1920s or earlier.

For the 1999 and 2000 vintages, grapes were purchased from local growers. From the 2001 vintage, Aalto has used its own 79 acres (32 ha) of old vines, in the provinces of Valladolid, Burgos, and La Horra. Until 2005, wines were made at a rented winery facility in Roa, but Aalto is now based in a bespoke winery at Quintanilla de Arriba. The basic wine undergoes malolactic fermentation in steel vats, but for the PS barrels are used.

From a highly regarded Ribera del Duero vintage, the Aalto PS 2001 has much greater extraction than the basic wine and probably needs up to ten years in bottle to show its best. It is a wine of power and extract rather than of elegance, but is very drinkable with suitably robust food. **SG**
☺☺☺☺ **Drink: to 2020**

FURTHER RECOMMENDATIONS
Other great vintages
2000 • 2003 • 2004
More producers from Ribera del Duero
Alión • Dominio de Atauta • Hacienda Monasterio *Hermanos Sastre • Pesquera • Pingus • Vega Sicilia*

Iron traces give Ribera del Duero soil a reddish tint. ➔

Accornero *Barbera del Monferrato Superiore Bricco Battista* 2004

Origin Italy, Piedmont, Langhe
Style Dry red wine, 14.5% ABV
Grape Barbera

Situated in the rolling Monferrato hills between the provinces of Asti and Alessandria, the Monferrato DOC largely overlaps that of Asti, and many producers can choose between making Barbera d'Asti, from a slightly more restrictive zone, or Barbera del Monferrato, the name of the larger growing area. The Accornero family have opted for Barbera del Monferrato, since they feel more tied to the surrounding hills than to the Asti denomination.

Their 49-acre (20 ha) property, bought in 1897 by Bartolomeo Accornero and his son Giuseppe, is today owned by Giulio Accornero, who runs it with his sons Ermanno and Massimo. Their well-structured Barbera Superiore Bricco Battista comes from three parcels of land covering about 7 acres (3 ha) on the Battista hill, about 1,000 feet (308 m) above sea level, where the vines are more than forty years old. "These old vines make all the difference, and give our Barbera natural fruit concentration and complexity," says Ermanno. Since Barbera inherently lacks tannin, malolactic fermentation and aging occurs in wooden barrels, 80 percent of which are massive *tonneaux* made of French oak, whereas the remainder are smaller barriques.

2004 was a classic vintage in Piedmont, unlike the disastrous 2002 and scorching 2003 vintages. With ripe black fruit and hints of spice balanced by fresh acidity and compact tannins, this wine should still give pleasure at fifteen years of age. **KO**
🍷🍷🍷 **Drink: to 2019+**

The Monferrato hills, stretching toward Altavilla from Grazzano. ➜

Achával Ferrer
Finca Altamira Malbec 2001

Origin Argentina, Mendoza
Style Dry red wine, 13.8% ABV
Grape Malbec

Alaverdi Monastery
Saperavi 2010

Origin Georgia, Kakheti
Style Dry red wine, 13.5% ABV
Grape Saperavi

Achával Ferrer is a boutique Mendoza producer making a critically acclaimed range of Malbecs. "These are single-vineyard Malbec varietals, all three of them from very old, low-producing vines in very special places in Mendoza," says Santiago Achával.

Finca Altamira is one of these select wines. This 13.5-acre (5.5 ha) Malbec vineyard lies alongside the Tunuyan River, in the southwestern part of the Uco Valley, at 3,400 feet (1,050 m) above sea level. Soils are sandy, with gravel and boulders mixed in. The eighty-year-old plants produce a miserly 12 ounces (350 g) of grapes per plant, which works out as one bottle of wine for every three plants. "This allows a minerality in the wine not found in wines of high-yield vineyards," says Achával. The Altamira vines are ungrafted and the soil is poor and sandy, with lots of alluvial sediment. Daytime temperatures approach 100ºF (38ºC), with a low of 54ºF (12ºC) at night.

The Altamira 2001 is an arresting, compelling wine. As well as the concentrated, almost lush fruit, there is some serious structure, minerality, and good acidity. This is a wine that speaks of its origins just as surely as a leading Malbec from Cahors. **JG**
🝰🝰🝰 **Drink: 2017+**

With the discovery of fossilized wine grape pips in Georgia dating back to 6000 BCE, the country had proof of a winemaking tradition extending back 8,000 vintages. Few, if any, have been more critical in the recent renaissance of this tradition than Bishop Davit (Makharadze) of the Alaverdi Monastery, and consulting winemaker Teimuraz Glonti.

The grapes for this wine come from the monastery's own vines, planted in the dark, alluvial soils of the Akhasheni appellation of Kakheti, eastern Georgia. The wine is produced in the traditional manner: after crushing, the grapes and stems are run into the cone-shaped qvevri vessels for the first five-to-six days of fermentation. Once both the alcoholic and malolactic fermentation are completed, the wine is racked into new qvevris, which are sealed until the springtime. Elevage is strictly in qvevri, then barrel.

The wine vibrates with intense color and has a nose of blackberries, minerals, and violet flowers; there are black cherry and berry flavors, firm but ripe chalky tannins, and a sapid, crisp finish. Over years of aging, the mineral character will become more evident, adding additional complexity and nuance. **LG**
🝰🝰 **Drink: to 2020+**

Allegrini
La Poja 1997

Origin Italy, Veneto
Style Dry red wine, 14% ABV
Grape Corvina Veronese

Allende
Aurus 2001

Origin Spain, Rioja
Style Dry red wine, 14.5% ABV
Grapes Tempranillo, Graciano

The Allegrini family has been a proud and very reliable interpreter of the grapes of the Valpolicella since the sixteenth century. Giovanni Allegrini was widely regarded as one of the first in the Valpolicella area to concentrate on quality production. The aim of his children is clearly the same. La Poja is a wine produced exclusively from Corvina Veronese grapes, the most highly regarded variety of the Valpolicella DOC. This was an innovation because monovarietal wines were previously unheard of in the area.

The color of the 1997 is a very deep ruby red, with some light garnet hues at the edges. On the nose it is dense and spicy, with fruity tones redolent of dark summer berries. Given the warmth that characterized the vintage, one might expect to find some jamlike fruit aromas, though happily there is no whiff of these. Instead of maturing into stewed fruit, the nose has minty, balsamic hints, which give the impression of being the natural continuation of the still rich, primary aromas. On the palate it is classy, round, and velvety, gradually revealing a moving range of flavors, very good depth, and a long, spicy, but still sharply focused finish. **AS**

🍷🍷🍷 **Drink: to 2017+**

Having finished his university studies in agriculture, Miguel Angel de Gregorio took the post of technical director at Bodegas Bretón in Rioja as his day job. But his curiosity and determination to go one step further led him to create Finca Allende, and to make his own wine, Allende (an old word meaning "further"), in 1995. By 1997 he had given up his job and was dedicated to his own project, which was enlarged with Aurus (from the Latin for "gold"), a wine that strives for the golden mean through perfectly balanced Tempranillo and Graciano.

In 2001, Finca Allende built a new winery in the village of Briones in Rioja Alavesa, next to a stone house that became the company headquarters. 2001 was also one of Rioja's best modern vintages. The Aurus 2001 characteristically goes one step further in balance and elegance, thanks to the old vines grown on a slope with a high clay content, and rigorous selection in both vineyard and winery. Dark in color and very aromatic, in its youth it combines ripe berry fruit with floral notes (violets), black olives, and oak. Full-bodied, with lively acidity, plenty of fruit and tannin, it is balanced and elegant. **LG**

🍷🍷🍷🍷 **Drink: to 2020**

Alta Vista
Alto 2002

Origin Argentina, Mendoza
Style Dry red wine, 14.5% ABV
Grapes Malbec 80%, Cabernet Sauvignon 20%

The Casa del Rey winery in Chacras de Coria, Mendoza, was bought in 1997 by Jean-Michel Arcaute of Pomerol's Château Clinet and Patrick d'Aulan, owner of St.-Emilion's Château Sansonnet; they renamed it Alta Vista. Rare for Argentina, the winery had an underground cellar that would provide ideal, slightly cool aging conditions for top-of-the-range, barrel-aged red wines such as Alto, which spends around eighteen months in oak. Of particular interest was the potential of Argentina's Malbec.

In 2002, Mendoza in general, and Alta Vista in particular, enjoyed its best ever vintage. Alta Vista's wines were made by José Spisso, one of the brightest of all the Argentine winemakers.

The oldest Malbec vines date from the 1920s, grown along the upper part of the Mendoza river valley at Las Compuertas, some 3,445 feet (1,050 m) above sea level. This area of acid soils is renowned for its gloriously dense Malbecs, with distinctive chestnut flavors. Allowing the young wine to experience its secondary, acid-softening (malolactic) fermentation in French barrels has given its bulging red fruit flavors a nonintrusive oak sheen. **MW**
🥂🥂🥂 **Drink: 2017+**

Elio Altare
Barolo 1989

Origin Italy, Piedmont, Langhe
Style Dry red wine, 14% ABV
Grape Nebbiolo

The son of a grape grower, Elio Altare was disheartened by the stagnant scene in Barolo in the 1970s. Following a visit to Burgundy, he began to thin out grape bunches in the vineyards in order to reduce yields and increase concentration, and he shunned chemical fertilizers that pushed quantity over quality—all to the horror of his father, since growers were rewarded on the basis of quantity rather than quality. When he then sawed his father's large oak casks in half with a chainsaw, Elio was disinherited. But after his father passed away in 1985, Elio bought the winery back from his sisters and began to make his revolutionary Barolos.

Using small barrels made of French oak, and drastically reducing maceration time, Elio's elegant and softer Barolos caused a commotion. Graceful and polished rather than muscular, Elio's Barolos are rich in fruit with hints of spice and round tannins. Enjoyable sooner than the Barolos of yore, they are also capable of lengthy cellaring. The 1989, an excellent year in Piedmont, is smooth and supple, with complex layers of black fruit and spice balanced by moderate tannins and fresh acidity. **KO**
🥂🥂🥂🥂 **Drink: to 2020+**

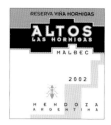

Altos Las Hormigas *Malbec*
Reserva Viña Hormigas 2002

Château Angélus
2000

Origin Argentina, Mendoza
Style Dry red wine, 14.3% ABV
Grape Malbec

Origin France, Bordeaux, St.-Emilion
Style Dry red wine, 13% ABV
Grapes Merlot 50%, Cabernet Franc 50%

Altos Las Hormigas was founded in 1995 by a group of Italians led by winemaker Alberto Antonini and entrepreneur Antonio Morescalchi. A vineyard was planted on the loamy soils of Luján de Cuyo, adjacent to where the winery now stands, but the vines came under almost immediate attack from ants—*hormigas*—hence the name of the winery.

The founders decided that their reserve Malbec would, in the first few years at least, benefit from being partly sourced from vines dating to the 1920s in another Mendoza subregion called La Consulta, lying at nearly 3,300 feet (1,000 m) above sea level. Malbec from La Consulta stands out thanks to its inherent freshness. The extra few hundred feet of altitude over Luján and a greater proximity to the Andean snowline result in grapes that are crunchier to chew and crisper to taste.

Freshness begets the aromatic and textural depth needed for red wines like Viña Hormigas to withstand eighteen months in mainly new barrels. 2002 is the greatest vintage in Mendoza since 1997, and this wine has the dense, viscous, black fruit characteristics of Malbec in this vintage. **MW**

🍷🍷🍷 Drink: to 2017+

Until the mid-1980s, L'Angélus (it became plain Angélus in 1990) was a well-regarded St.-Emilion estate that produced good wine but seldom made anything special. However, since his first vintage in 1985, Hubert de Boüard de Laforest, aided by his cousin by marriage Jean-Bernard Grenié, has achieved a much deserved promotion from Grand Cru Classé to Premier Grand Cru Classé in 1996.

Angélus had a fine run of vintages in the 1990s, culminating in the excellent 2000. This is a wine of great structure, depth, and tannin. At early barrel tastings, it seemed almost over the top, smelling and tasting like Amarone, but since then the wine has settled down to evoke the savory Angélus terroir. Like Cheval Blanc, Angélus is blended from Merlot and Cabernet Franc grapes, with recent vintages slightly biased toward Merlot, though the 2000 is an even blend. After an extensive tasting, Serena Sutcliffe MW wrote, "I can never escape (nor would I wish to) the image of the Millet *Angélus* bell tolling over the fields when I broach a bottle of its namesake wine. There is something eternal about the picture it presents—like wine itself." **SG**

🍷🍷🍷🍷 Drink: to 2030+

Domaine Marquis d'Angerville
Volnay PC Clos des Ducs 2002

Origin France, Burgundy, Côte de Beaune
Style Dry red wine, 13% ABV
Grape Pinot Noir

Although completely surrounded by a retaining wall, the southeasterly-sloping Clos des Ducs site was first mentioned in the sixteenth century as a part of the surrounding vineyards of Caillerets, Taillepieds, and Champans. It was acquired in 1804 by the Baron du Mesnil, and in 1906 noble cuttings were planted after the ravages of phylloxera. The work was done by the grandfather of the present-day owner, Guillaume d'Angerville; a fervent defender of authentic wines, he was one of the first growers to bottle and sell his own wine.

Guillaume's father Jacques continued in his father's footsteps for the fifty-two vintages that he managed the estate. The 2002 was his last, and the 2005 the first stunning vintage of Guillaume, who appears to be maturing in his role as the senior member of the clan. The 2002 is a wine of subtle balance and silky elegance, from the original 5.4 acres (2.1 ha) planted with a noble, low-yielding clone of Pinot Noir known in professional circles as the Pinot d'Angerville. When tasted from barrel shortly before bottling, there was every reason to believe that the 2005 will one day be even better. **JP**
🍷🍷🍷🍷 **Drink: to 2027**

Château d'Angludet
2001

Origin France, Bordeaux, Margaux
Style Dry red wine, 13% ABV
Grapes Cabernet Sauvignon, Merlot, Petit Verdot

In appearance, Angludet, inland from the major Margaux vineyards near the estuary, is a modest farmhouse, and it was acquired in 1961 by Bordeaux merchant Peter Sichel, part-owner of Château Palmer. In 1989 he entrusted its management to one of his sons, Benjamin, who had always been fascinated by viticulture. The terroir of Angludet will never produce a wine with the refinement and intensity of Palmer or Château Margaux itself. The Sichels prefer to maintain Angludet as a sturdy, well-structured wine offered at a reasonable price but capable of giving pleasure over many years.

The 2001 has a touch more opulence than is customary at Angludet, but it also has a good deal of spice, vigor, and grip. Older vintages such as 1983 aged enjoyably for many years, and the well-balanced 2001 may well do the same. Angludet is the very model of what used to be called a Cru Bourgeois, and many insiders were surprised when it failed to be classified as a Cru Bourgeois Exceptionnel in 2003. That classification is now history, but the wine lives on as an exemplary classic Bordeaux that one can actually afford to drink. **SBr**
🍷🍷🍷 **Drink: to 2020**

Angludet stands on the gravel plateau known as Le Grand Poujeau. ➡

Ànima Negra
Vinyes de Son Negre 2010

Origin Spain, Majorca
Style Dry red wine, 14% ABV
Grapes Callet, Manto Negro, Fogoneu

This winery started as no more than a hobby, even a joke, for a group of friends from Majorca in 1994. They started blending Cabernet Sauvignon with other autochthonous grapes from the island, fermenting the grapes in a milk tank and carrying out everything in the traditional manner, with improvised and secondhand equipment. But the wine had a marked personality, and it soon grabbed the attention of aficionados, distributors, and the press, and the winery was born.

The wine, called Ànima Negra—later changed to simply AN because of conflicts with the name—was the first serious attempt to use some largely unknown varieties—Callet with a little Fogoneu and Manto Negro. To produce serious wine from these varieties, it is necessary to have very low yields, so Ànima Negra searched for very old, dry-farmed vines, pruned in the traditional gobelet way.

The wine is intense and wild, very spicy, unmistakably Mediterranean, with plenty of balsamic notes and wild herbs. It is concentrated, but in the style of Burgundy rather than Bordeaux, harmonious, exotic, and highly individual. **LG**

☻☻☻ **Drink: recent vintages for up to 12 years**

Antinori
Guado al Tasso 2003

Origin Italy, Tuscany, Bolgheri
Style Dry red wine, 13.5% ABV
Grapes Cabernet Sauvignon, Merlot, Syrah, Others

Tuscan winemaking scion Piero Antinori, one of the pioneers in revamping the wilting Chianti Classico DOC in the 1970s, and creator of Tignanello, one of the original Super-Tuscans, first released Guado al Tasso in 1990. After the success of his uncle's illustrious Sassicaia, and his brother Lodovico's Ornellaia, Piero upgraded his nearby rosato-producing Belvedere holdings in Bolgheri, which he renamed Guado al Tasso. The 2,224-acre (900 ha) estate stretches from the gentle hills to the Tyrrhenian Sea, on the sliver of Tuscan shore known as the Maremma—often referred to as the Gold Coast because some of the most sought-after and expensive wines in Italy are made here.

The 2003 vintage in Italy was one of the hottest and driest on record. Near Bolgheri, grapes ripened early, and by mid-August the earliest ripening varieties already showed very high sugar levels, though yields were slightly lower than usual due to the lack of water. Boasting an intense ruby color, with ripe cherry aromas and hints of oak, coffee, and chocolate, the Guado al Tasso 2003 is surprisingly fresh for the vintage, with soft, sweet tannins. **KO**

☻☻☻ **Drink: 2017+**

Antinori
Solaia 1985

Origin Italy, Tuscany
Style Dry red wine, 12.5% ABV
Grapes C. Sauvignon, Sangiovese, C. Franc

Solaia, which means "the sunny one" in Italian, is a 25-acre (10 ha) southwest-facing vineyard planted 1,150 to 1,300 feet (351–396 m) above sea level on stony calcareous soil of marl and friable albarese rock. It is located at Santa Cristina, cheek by jowl with the renowned Tignanello vineyard, in the Mercatale Val di Pesa zone of Chianti Classico.

Antinori first produced a single-vineyard wine from this site in the 1978 vintage, but this was a limited release in Italy only. Because of the "non-Chianti" grapes used (the Cabernets), Solaia was classified as a lowly Vino da Tavola di Toscana rather than DOCG Chianti Classico.

On November 8, 2006, Christie's held an Antinori master class in London, hosted by Albiera Antinori. The wines included Solaia 1985, from the best Tuscan vintage of the decade. With 10 percent Cabernet Franc rather than the usual 5 percent, the wine was still not fully mature, although it hinted at more to come. Albiera suggested that the optimum age for Solaia is fifteen to twenty-five years, which seems reasonable considering the acidity and tannin levels of the wine. **SG**
Ⓢ Ⓢ Ⓢ Ⓢ **Drink: to 2020**

Antinori
Tignanello 2010

Origin Italy, Tuscany
Style Dry red wine, 12.5% ABV
Grapes Sangiovese, C. Sauvignon, C. Franc

One of the original "Super-Tuscan" wines, Tignanello is produced exclusively from the eponymous vineyard, a 116-acre (47 ha) southwest-facing, calcareous rocky marl and limestone plot, planted between 1,150 and 1,312 feet (350–400 m) above sea level at Antinori's Santa Cristina estate.

Tignanello was originally a Chianti Classico Riserva called Vigneto Tignanello, but was first vinified as a single-vineyard wine in 1970, when it still contained the traditional Tuscan white grapes Canaiolo, Trebbiano, and Malvasia. From the 1975 vintage, white grapes were totally eliminated.

Tasted in November 2006, the 1985—probably the best vintage to that date for Tignanello—had a beautiful, herbaceous nose. It was perfectly mature, and a really lovely wine, made with a much lighter touch than its Antinori sibling Solaia. Although Tim Atkin MW felt that the Cabernet character had become more conspicuous with age, "Tignanello is very Tuscan," commented Albiera Antinori; "the '85's aromas are so typical of Sangiovese of a certain age." Albiera suggested that the optimum age for Tignanello is ten to fifteen years. **SG**
Ⓢ Ⓢ Ⓢ **Drink: recent vintages for up to 15 years**

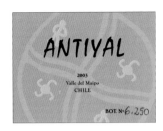

Antiyal

2003

Origin Chile, Maipo Valley
Style Dry red wine, 14.5% ABV
Grapes Carmenère, Merlot, C. Sauvignon, Syrah

Chile's first garage wine, Antiyal, was first produced in 1998 by Alvaro Espinoza, who had already made a name for himself at Santa Rita's offshoot, Carmen. Espinoza and his wife, Marina, converted a small barn in their front garden into a winery. The grapes for Antiyal come from Espinoza's front garden and other Maipo Valley vines belong to Alvaro's mother. Both Chilean Cabernet Sauvignon and Carmenère benefit from a dose of Syrah to give the wine the breadth its otherwise linear profile demands—a profile accentuated by Espinoza's then thoroughly unorthodox, non-interventionist approach.

Apart from aging in French barrels (some of which come secondhand from Santa Rita), Antiyal, which in the local Mapuche dialect means "sons of the sun," bears no winemaking airs and graces—as evinced by the 2003, a vintage of perfect balance and ripeness. Antiyal's new home from 2007 is Chile's first green winery, which makes use of solar and wind power, and even has a lunar window that can be opened to allow the barrels access to beneficial lunar forces during propitious periods. **MW**
🟢🟢 **Drink: to 2018**

The stunning Maipo Valley, Chile, with the Andes in the distance. ➡

Anwilka Estate/ Klein Constantia *Anwilka* 2009

Araujo Estate Wines *Eisele Vineyard* 2001

Origin South Africa, Stellenbosch
Style Dry red wine, 14% ABV
Grapes Syrah 56%, Cabernet Sauvignon 44%,

Origin USA, California, Napa Valley
Style Dry red wine, 14.4% ABV
Grapes C. Sauvignon 75%, C. Franc 25%

Anwilka started as a joint venture between Lowell Jooste of Klein Constantia, Bruno Prats (formerly of Cos d'Estournel), and Hubert de Boüard de Laforest of Angélus, but is now owned by Klein Constantia.

Anwilka's vineyards, purchased in 1997, are in Helderberg, southwest of Stellenbosch. Extensive replanting took place in 1998 to ensure that the vineyards were virus free (vineyard virus is endemic in the Cape). The philosophy of the partners is "to spare no cost when it comes to wine quality." The wine was released in South Africa on March 3, 2006, a month before the remainder was released into the Bordeaux trade for international distribution at a surprisingly high price for a South African red. Nonetheless, a prompt sellout ensued when critic Robert Parker described Anwilka as, "the finest red wine I have ever had from South Africa."

And the wine itself? Deep, inky, and viscous. The nose is slightly volatile and dusty, with very rich fruit and creamy oak aromas. The wine is warm and spicy, very concentrated but velvety in texture. A couple of years to smooth out the rough edges will result in a very drinkable wine in the "international" style. **SG**
⊖⊖⊖ **Drink: to 2020+**

The 35-acre (14 ha) rocky Eisele Vineyard, named for its original owners, is one of the first Napa Valley vineyards to be identified on a wine label. Originally planted in the nineteenth century, with Cabernet Sauvignon introduced in 1964, the vineyard garnered renown in the 1970s when Ridge and then Joseph Phelps purchased the grapes to craft brilliantly complex, rich wines. In 1990 Bart and Daphne Araujo purchased the vineyard, located southeast of Calistoga at the foot of the Palisades Mountains, which protect the vines from the north.

The splendid 2001 growing season began with a mild winter with relatively low rainfall, followed by a warm, dry spring. Cooler weather in July and August brought fruit and tannin maturity into equipoise, with firm natural acidities and intense flavors, which were also retained via night harvesting throughout the month of September. After cold soaks and extended maceration in stainless-steel tanks, the wine aged in 100 percent new French oak barrels for twenty-two months. Minty on the nose, with a palate at once lush and mineral, the wine is firm, with tight yet supple tannins. **LGr**
⊖⊖⊖⊖⊖ **Drink: to 2025**

◀ The Anwilka vineyards nestle close to Helderberg Mountain.

Argiano
Brunello di Montalcino 1995

Origin Italy, Tuscany, Montalcino
Style Dry red wine, 13.5% ABV
Grape Sangiovese

Located at the top of a hill in Sant'Angelo in Colle, southwest of Montalcino, Argiano derives its name from Ara Jani, the altar of the Roman god Janus. During the Renaissance, a noble family from Siena built a magnificent villa on the hilltop, and eventually the holdings were bequeathed to the counts of Lovatelli. In 1992, the current owner, Noemi Marone Cinzano, acquired the property and set about revamping its cellars and Brunello production. That same year she engaged the services of legendary enologist Giacomo Tachis, who retired in 2003.

The 247-acre (100 ha) estate is protected from storms and hail by Mount Amiata, and the warm winds from the Maremma create a warm, dry microclimate that allows grapes to reach a healthy maturity. In 1995, a five-star vintage for Montalcino, Tachis decided to put all the best grapes into a single Brunello and renounced making a Riserva version. The Brunello 1995, which aged for two years in wood, half in barriques and half in large Slavonian oak casks, is rich with ripe fruit and floral aromas that carry over to the palate. It is impeccably balanced, with firm tannins that will soften over time. **KO**

🆂🆂🆂 **Drink: to 2020**

Argiolas
Turriga 2001

Origin Italy, Sardinia
Style Dry red wine, 14% ABV
Grapes Cannonau 85%, Others 15%

When, in the late 1970s, many of Sardinia's farmers gratefully pulled up their vines in exchange for European subsidies, Antonio Argiolas made the brave decision to invest extensively in Sardinia's native grapes. The family transformed their vineyards, updated the cellars to maximize quality, and engaged the services of legendary enologist Giacomo Tachis, whose love of Sardinia's native varieties was to become a passion, to guide resident winemaker Mariano Murru.

Their flagship wine, Turriga, is based on Cannonau and other local red varieties, along with Malvasia Nera. This powerful red was made with a flair that soon set the standard for the rest of the region. First released in 1988, it is from the estate's best vineyard, Turriga, located 1,755 feet (230 m) above sea level with chalky, slightly stony soil and perfect exposure. The wine's hallmark sensations include ripe fruit, spice, and myrtle. The excellent 2001 vintage was characterized by a dry start, so the winery resorted to emergency irrigation in June. Full-bodied and powerful, the 2001 will age wonderfully thanks to its impressive structure. **KO**

🆂🆂🆂 **Drink: to 2020**

🄴 The Castello di Argiano overlooks Argiano winery's vineyards.

Domaine du Comte Armand
Pommard PC Clos des Epeneaux 2003

Origin France, Burgundy, Côte de Beaune
Style Dry red wine, 13.5% ABV
Grape Pinot Noir

Pommard has no grands crus, but it is widely agreed that its two outstanding sites are Rugiens and Les Epenots. The latter occupies about 74 acres (30 ha) between the village and the boundary with Beaune, and is divided into three sectors. The smallest, and arguably the best, of these is the walled 12-acre (5 ha) Clos des Epeneaux, a monopoly of the biodynamic Comte Armand estate.

Benjamin Leroux, who has been Comte Armand's winemaker since 1999, routinely produces four wines from the *clos*, based on the age of the vines as well as on location; these are subsequently blended. The youngest vines are used to produce the estate's Pommard Premier Cru; the rest goes into the Clos des Epeneaux. The oldest vines in the *clos* are about sixty years old.

Les Epenots gives very tannic wines that usually need many years to shed their aggression. Wine from the Clos des Epeneaux can be impenetrable when young, and the 2003 is no exception. Yet there is tremendous aromatic richness here, with complex aromas of raspberries and oak; the fruit is sweet and spicy, but the alcohol gives a peppery finish. **SBr**
🝖🝖🝖 Drink: to 2020

Artadi
Viña El Pisón 2004

Origin Spain, Rioja
Style Dry red wine, 14% ABV
Grape Tempranillo

Artadi started as a cooperative producing approachable, simple red wines in 1985, but in less than a decade was among Rioja's best. This astonishing achievement is due to the determination of Juan Carlos López de Lacalle, Artadi's guiding light, to produce world-class wines.

Viña El Pisón is one of the first single-vineyard wines from Rioja, a region where blending grapes or wines, not only from different vineyards but from different subregions, was the tradition. It is planted with very old vines of Tempranillo, probably with a small proportion of other varieties (even white varieties) mixed in, as usually happens in old vineyards. Its 6 acres (2.5 ha) were planted in 1945 by Juan Carlos's grandfather.

Artadi is a wine that maintains its quality vintage after vintage, but maybe the 2004, from a superb vintage, shows an extra degree of elegance. With a deep and intense color in its youth, it has balsamic notes mixed with ripe red and black forest fruits, graphite, and beautifully integrated oak. In the mouth it shows medium body and great intensity, with bright acidity and plenty of ripe tannins. **LG**
🝖🝖🝖🝖 Drink: to 2025

A taster checks the color and the "legs" of the wine. ➜

Ata Rangi *Pinot Noir* 2011

Origin New Zealand, Martinborough
Style Dry red wine, 13.5% ABV
Grape Pinot Noir

Ata Rangi—Maori for "new beginning" or "dawn sky"—was a barren 12-acre (5 ha) paddock when Clive Paton bought it in 1980. He was one of a handful of winemaking pioneers attracted to the Martinborough area by the localized, free-draining shingle terrace some 66 feet (20 m) deep, the lowest rainfall records of anywhere in the North Island, and the proximity to the capital city of Wellington, a mere 50 miles (80 km) away.

Paton chose mainly red varieties—Pinot Noir, Cabernet Sauvignon, Merlot, and Syrah. Pinot Noir's potential shone from the start, and today Ata Rangi is judged by many to be New Zealand's finest example of this tricky grape variety. Among the main Pinot clones favored and planted is Abel (also known as the Ata Rangi "gumboot" clone), which was allegedly brought in illegally from France in the late 1970s. In the small winery, the tanks are named after sporting people, such as "Blowers," named in honor of English cricket commentator Henry Blofeld.

The estate is owned and managed by Paton, his wife Phyll (formerly a winemaker at Montana), and his sister Alison. The affability of the Ata Rangi team is reflected in its wines. The benchmark Pinot Noir has a typically aromatic Kiwi Pinot nose, but further probing reveals far greater depths than most other New Zealand reds. The palate is quite savory, though still luscious, with great length and concentration of flavor. Ata Rangi also makes a Syrah, Cabernet, and Merlot blend called Célèbre. **SG**

⊖⊖⊖ Drink: recent vintages for up to 10 years

FURTHER RECOMMENDATIONS
Other great vintages
1999 • 2000 • 2001 • 2003
More producers from Martinborough
Craggy Range • Dry River
Martinborough Vineyard • Palliser

Signatures of delegates at a winemakers' conference at Ata Rangi.

Dominio de Atauta
Ribera del Duero 2001

Origin Spain, Ribera del Duero
Style Dry red wine, 13.5% ABV
Grape Tinto Fino (Tempranillo)

Au Bon Climat
Pinot Noir 2005

Origin USA, California, Santa Barbara County
Style Dry red wine, 13.5% ABV
Grapes Pinot Noir 82%, Mondeuse 18%

Miguel Sánchez is a native of the easternmost part of Ribera del Duero, in the cold province of Soria. He had known for a long time of the ungrafted and, in many cases, centenarian vines surrounding the tiny village of Atauta, and had a dream to make world-class wines from them. The opportunity arose when he met French winemaker Bertrand Sourdais.

Dominio de Atauta is their flagship wine, but they also produce very limited quantities of special cuvées or single-vineyard wines under the names Valdegatiles, Llanos del Almendro, El Panderón, La Mala, San Juan (for sale only in Puerto Rico), or La Roza. The pair search for balance and elegance, freshness and good acidity rather than raw power. 2000 was the first, almost experimental vintage, but 2001 was the first "serious" wine, as well as a leap in quality, from an exceptional vintage. This Atauta is very dark garnet in color. With good complexity, elegance, and intensity on the nose, it shows plenty of ripe, red fruit, spice, and orange rind. Medium-bodied, it has lively acidity, lovely balance, great fruit, and great persistence—all the components required to evolve rewardingly in bottle. **LG**
🍷🍷🍷 **Drink: to 2017+**

Nowhere in the world outside Burgundy's Côte d'Or has the pursuit of exceptional Pinot Noir been so utterly single-minded as it has in California. The collective efforts have been reaping rich rewards since the 1980s, and among the first rank has been Jim Clendenen's Au Bon Climat (ABC) winery, established in 1982.

The sustained warm, dry conditions of the 2005 California vintage delivered fruit of unimaginable ripeness and concentration. Coupled with the growing maturity of the vineyards, it is not hard to see why Clendenen feels that this is probably the best entry-level Pinot ABC has yet produced.

An opulent deep ruby in color, the bouquet opens up with purest Pinot raspberry, but quickly adds smoky oak tones, a fugitive note of violet, a suggestion of ground cilantro. The palate is a pile driver, big and burly, and yet somehow soft and yielding in the center, too. It is exactly the sort of Pinot that is approachable young, for the ripeness and pliancy of its acidity and its glorious fruit, but that will perform graciously in the bottle over several years too, if that is what you want it to do. **SW**
🍷🍷🍷 **Drink: to 2020**

Bien Nacido is the primary source of grapes for Au Bon Climat. ➡

Château Ausone 2003

Origin France, Bordeaux, St.-Emilion
Style Dry red wine, 14% ABV
Grapes Cabernet Franc 55%, Merlot 45%

Ausone is the smallest of the first growths of Bordeaux, but few wines of the region enjoy such a glittering reputation. Perched on a limestone spur overlooking the town of St.-Emilion, Ausone took its name from the Roman poet Ausonius. Bottles survive from the 1840s, and those fortunate enough to have tasted nineteenth-century vintages testify to their quality and staying power.

In more recent times, ownership was divided between two feuding families. This state of affairs, which lasted twenty years, was hardly designed to guarantee fine quality, though nature assured that excellent wines were often made during the period. In 1995 the battling came to an end and Alain Vauthier took full control of the property. Under his intelligent and open-minded direction, Ausone has scaled new heights. Even in such a notoriously tricky vintage as the torrid 2003, Ausone made superb wine. Its limestone soils prevented the vines from suffering drought stress, and the high proportion of Cabernet Franc gave a perfume and complexity that are unusual in 2003 but very typical of Ausone.

Vauthier is a meticulous vineyard manager, aiming to bring the grapes to full ripeness before harvest. This means that the wines are at the powerful end of the spectrum, and consistently concentrated flavors are generated by vines that are an average of fifty years old. Yet the wines, even in 2003, have freshness too, and a structure that guarantees a very long life ahead. **SBr**
🍷🍷🍷🍷🍷 **Drink: to 2030**

FURTHER RECOMMENDATIONS
Other great vintages
1982 · 1995 · 1998 · 2000 · 2001 · 2005 · 2009 · 2010
More producers from Côtes St.-Emilion
Belair · La Gaffelière · Magdelaine · La Mondotte · Pavie Pavie-Macquin · Tertre Roteboeuf · Troplong Mondot

This fine doorway at Ausone proclaims the château's success. ➲

Azelia
Barolo San Rocco 1999

Origin Italy, Piedmont, Langhe
Style Dry red wine, 14% ABV
Grape Nebbiolo

Domaine Denis Bachelet
Charmes-Chambertin GC 1999

Origin France, Burgundy, Côte de Nuits
Style Dry red wine, 12.5% ABV
Grape Pinot Noir

Founded by his grandfather in 1920, Luigi Scavino's small Azelia estate in Castiglione Falletto has been making Barolo for decades. Their flagship Barolo San Rocco comes from grapes grown in a 4.5-acre (1.8 ha) vineyard of the same name located in the celebrated commune of Serralunga, famed for more deeply colored Barolos of great structure and longevity, thanks to its iron-rich calcareous soil dating back to the Helvetian period. Following Modernist principles that allow Barolo to be enjoyed upon release, rather than after ten years or so when the tannins have softened, Luigi has reduced maceration and fermentation to between ten and twelve days. New and used barriques tame the aggressive tannins and add a touch of vanilla and spice.

The 1999 vintage, awarded five stars by the Barolo and Barbaresco Consorzio, was indeed excellent in Piedmont, producing well-structured and complex wines capable of long cellaring. Azelia's Barolo San Rocco 1999 is densely colored and has a rich floral nose with balsamic notes. Succulent black fruit and well-integrated oak on the palate are balanced by smooth and supple tannins. **KO**

⊖⊖⊖ **Drink: to 2019**

Denis Bachelet does not consort much with the other vignerons of Gevrey-Chambertin and his wines do not conform to a school or style. Born in Belgium in 1963, he returned to Gevrey in the early 1980s to take over from his grandfather. This is a tiny domaine of just over 5 acres (2 ha), with vineyards centered on the village of Gevrey, including premier cru Les Corbeaux and grand cru Charmes-Chambertin. The Bachelet 1-acre (0.4 ha) holding of Charmes-Chambertin is in the upper, and better, part of the vineyard. Some vines may date from immediate post-phylloxera replanting, but most were planted by his great aunt in the 1920s, occasionally assisted by her younger sister, Denis's grandmother.

His Charmes-Chambertin 1999 still displays an intense deep purple color. There is a haunting, enchantingly perfumed quality to the fruit, which blossoms on the nose. The 50 percent new wood is not in evidence at all, subdued by the opulence of the fruit. The palate is broad and luxurious, poised and exciting, with a marvelous and complex basket of rich, red fruit and a perfect, long finish. Just one sniff or sip will bring a smile to your face. **JM**

⊖⊖⊖⊖ **Drink: to 2020+**

Balnaves *The Tally*
Cabernet Sauvignon 2005

Origin Australia, South Australia, Coonawarra
Style Dry red wine, 14.5% ABV
Grape Cabernet Sauvignon

Banfi *Brunello di Montalcino*
Poggio all'Oro 1988

Origin Italy, Tuscany, Montalcino
Style Dry red wine, 13% ABV
Grape Sangiovese

Balnaves is a small, family-owned company in the heart of the famous Terra Rossa strip of Coonawarra. Since the planting of the first 13 acres (5 ha) of vines in 1976, the estate has grown steadily, and now covers a total of 140 acres (57 ha) of prime Terra Rossa soil. In 1995 Peter Bissell joined as the company winemaker.

Among his many previous pursuits, the affable family patriarch Doug Balnaves was a shearer of Merino sheep. A shearer is paid by the number of sheep he shears, and the "tally" is recorded. The higher the tally, the greater the recognition for skill and hard work, and the higher the remuneration. As a nod toward this noble Australian tradition, the Balnaves family named its finest wine "The Tally."

Made from grapes from the best vineyards in the best years—though rather perversely, Doug Balnaves insists the best grapes are not from the Terra Rossa vineyards—The Tally is a tightly structured but rounded and age-worthy red. With its strong acidity and taut backbone, it is a classic example of Coonawarra, becoming ever more minty and leafy with bottle age. **SG**

🍷🍷🍷 Drink: to 2020

Although 1988 was not a great year in many parts of Italy, it was a stellar year with a small crop of outstanding quality in Tuscany. According to Michael Broadbent, "The best wines were from Montalcino." Banfi's Poggio all'Oro (Golden Hill) single-vineyard Brunello Riserva is a good example of the vintage, still with ripe fruit and depth. Banfi's select Poggio all'Oro Riserva is produced only in excellent years.

The Poggio all'Oro vineyard, situated at 820 feet (250 m) above sea level, was the first to be replanted by Banfi in 1980, with ten different clones chosen from the best Sangiovese plants selected throughout the territory. The 1985 debut vintage was made in a more traditional style, having been aged for forty-two months in large Slavonian oak casks, and was immediately hailed by critics for its dense complexity. In later years, the winemaking has taken on a more international profile, and today Poggio all'Oro is aged for two and a half years in small French oak and is a favorite in export markets, particularly the United States. Banfi is credited with bringing Brunello, once considered a rarity, to consumers around the world. **KO**

🍷🍷🍷🍷 Drink: to 2018

Barca Velha
1999

Jim Barry
The Armagh Shiraz 2001

Origin Portugal, Douro Valley
Style Dry red wine, 13.5% ABV
Grapes Tinta Roriz, Touriga Franca, T. Nacional

Origin Australia, South Australia, Clare Valley
Style Dry red wine, 14.5% ABV
Grape Shiraz

The rugged Douro Valley in northern Portugal is one of the most dramatic vineyard regions on earth. But for decades, until the turn of the twenty-first century, only one unfortified wine came to any international prominence—Barca Velha. This was the brainchild of Fernando Nicolau de Almeida, then winemaker at Ferreira in the 1950s. Having visited Bordeaux in the 1940s, he returned to Portugal fired with an ambition to make a Portuguese "first growth."

Small parcels of higher-altitude vineyard are used to give freshness and complexity to the blend. Only the very best grapes from selected vineyards are chosen. Aging is in small, new oak barrels for between twelve and eighteen months, plus further time in bottle before release—typically six years after the harvest. Releases are remarkably rare, with only fifteen vintages ever having been sold.

The 1999 exhibits gloriously fresh, concentrated fruit flavors of black fruit, the aroma overlaid with cedar and vanilla from the maturation in wood, with chocolate and floral hints. Great concentration and depth on the palate is balanced by a fine elegance rarely seen in wines of this power. **GS**

🍷🍷🍷🍷 Drink: to 2020+

Jim Barry bought land near Clare in 1959 and planted much of it with vines. The winery was built in 1973 and the first Jim Barry wines were available in 1974. The estate now comprises almost 618 acres (250 ha) of old vines in the upper Clare district.

In 1985, Barry released the first Armagh Shiraz, made from low-yielding vines that he had planted in 1968—in an unusual curving formation—and used previously in his Sentimental Bloke Port blend, named after a poem by local author C. J. Dennis. Unusually, the Shiraz clone came from Israel.

Named after nearby Armagh, which was settled by the Irish in 1859, this is perhaps the apotheosis of South Australian Shiraz—a massively concentrated and proportioned wine. This is as big as Aussie Shiraz gets —and that is very big indeed.

When tasted in 2004, the 2001 was quite closed on the nose, and a bit minty. The palate was very tightly structured, the juicy acidity making it more approachable, though the finish was still immensely tannic and powerful. There was more than enough here to suggest great aging potential. The Armagh is a serious wine from a serious winery. **SG**

🍷🍷🍷 Drink: to 2019

Domaine Ghislaine Barthod
Chambolle-Musigny PC Les Cras 2002

Origin France, Burgundy, Côte de Nuits
Style Dry red wine, 13% ABV
Grape Pinot Noir

Bass Phillip
Premium Pinot Noir 2004

Origin Australia, Victoria, Gippsland
Style Dry red wine, 13.5% ABV
Grape Pinot Noir

Chambolle-Musigny has the reputation of being one of Burgundy's more "feminine" wines, with the accent on charm and finesse rather than power. By and large the reputation is deserved, but it would be a mistake to think of Chambolle as a short-term wine. It ages extremely well, especially from its best sites. Les Cras, not far from the village, has white soils similar to those found in parts of the grand cru Bonnes Mares, and it also benefits from a southerly as well as easterly exposition.

It was Ghislaine Barthod's father, Gaston, who assembled the 17-acre (7 ha) domaine that now bears her name, and her first vintage was 1986. Les Cras is the largest of her premiers crus, with 2.12 acres (0.86 ha) under vine. When young, Les Cras can be distinctly dense, yet it is always marked by a fine perfume, sometimes cherries, at other times raspberries; with age the nose becomes more leafy and sensuous. If austere when young, it becomes sweeter and more supple after about five years in bottle. The 2002 is especially elegant. Though compact and robust, the rich fruit and fine length guarantee a promising future. **SBr**

☻☻☻ **Drink: to 2020**

Phillip Jones is one of the gurus of Australian wine, at the extreme end of the extreme sport of Pinot Noir making, and with a cluster of four vineyards almost entirely dedicated to the grape. He first planted in 1979, in a cool, lush part of southern Victoria—natural dairy country—which is one of the few regions to be spared the ongoing drought. The pinnacles of the many Pinot Noirs he crafts each year are the Reserve and Premium labels, the former just a single barrel or two, made only in the best years.

Both wines are sourced from the same sections of the same vineyard each year. At Leongatha, the rainfall is high and the humidity may well be the highest of any Australian wine-growing area. The very deep, well-drained soil is the saving grace. It is a silty loam, very old and rich in minerals (especially iron) and volcanic-based. Time in oak has been shortened somewhat, from between sixteen and eighteen months to between thirteen and fifteen. The favored oak is lightly toasted Allier. The Premium 2004 has a palish color but a fine, heady fragrance. Haunting, spicy cherry aromas and great silky finesse on the palate make this a memorable drink. **HH**

☻☻☻☻ **Drink: to 2018**

Battle of Bosworth
White Boar 2004

Origin Australia, South Australia, McLaren Vale
Style Dry red wine, 15% ABV
Grape Shiraz

Located to the south of the McLaren Vale township, Edgehill Vineyard was established in the early 1970s by Peter and Anthea Bosworth. Willunga itself was settled in the late 1830s, and Bosworths have been growing grapes in the district since the late 1840s. Their son, Joch Bosworth, took over the management and day-to-day running of the vineyards in 1995. He named his brand "Battle of Bosworth" to suggest the challenges presented by his organic viticultural practices.

Though inspired by the Amarone wines of north Italy, Joch Bosworth's White Boar is quite different. Rather than harvesting his grapes and drying them on racks (as with Amarone), the vines' canes are cut once the desired flavor spectrum has developed, and the grapes are allowed to dry and then raisin on the vine itself. After two weeks of this process, the grapes are hand-picked before being gently guided through a slow fermentation. With more fruit and color than a typical Amarone, the nose and palate of White Boar show flavors of tar, mace, nutmeg, earth, pudding fruits, soy, roses, cedary oak, Turkish Delight, rum, raisin, and chocolate. **SG**

❺❺❺ Drink: to 2019+

Château de Beaucastel
Hommage à Jacques Perrin 1998

Origin France, Southern Rhône, Châteauneuf-du-Pape
Style Dry red wine, 13.5% ABV
Grapes Mourvèdre, Others

The Beaucastel family was living in Courthezon by the middle of the sixteenth century. According to records, in 1549 "Noble Pierre de Beaucastel" bought "a barn with its plot of land extending to 52 *saumées* at Coudoulet." In 1909, Pierre Tramier bought the property. Beaucastel then passed to his son-in-law Pierre Perrin, and afterward to Jacques Perrin. Today, Château de Beaucastel is run by Jean-Pierre and François, Jacques's sons.

In 1989, conditions were so favorable that the Perrins decided to make a special cuvée in honor of their father. The Hommage à Jacques Perrin is made mostly from very old Mourvèdre vines that yield tiny quantities of intensely ripe, concentrated fruit.

The wine stole the show in a 2006 *World of Fine Wine* blind tasting of Châteauneuf-du-Pape, with four vintages of Château de Beaucastel Hommage à Jacques Perrin taking the top four spots, confirming its status as arguably the southern Rhône's greatest wine. Stephen Browett described the 1998 as "a gorgeous wine, full of sweet, ripe fruit, and more than a hint of milk chocolate." The Perrins call it "a wine to be kept for your retirement." **SG**

❺❺❺❺ Drink: to 2020+

Beaulieu Vineyard *Georges de Latour Cabernet Sauvignon* 1976

Origin USA, California, Napa Valley
Style Dry red wine, 14.5% ABV
Grape Cabernet Sauvignon

Looking back, one might wonder if the 1976 vintage presaged the evolution of a style that now, at the beginning of the twenty-first century, defines Napa Valley Cabernet Sauvignon. Notwithstanding some rain during harvest, it was the first of two major drought vintages in Napa Valley, resulting in yields half the norm and wines that were more intense, tannic, powerful, and jammy than previously seen.

Beaulieu was founded in 1900 by Georges de Latour, but the first vintage of the Private Reserve was not produced until 1936, by which time Latour had lured Andre Tchelistcheff to be his winemaker. Considered by many to be the most influential winemaker in U.S. history, Tchelistcheff set the style for this limited edition wine and directed its winemaking until his retirement in 1973.

The 1976 Private Reserve, which Robert Parker, writing in 1995, deemed "spectacular from its release . . . the quintessential example of the BV Private Reserve style," is a powerfully spicy wine, a bit alcoholic, with the particularly strong dusty flavors of the Rutherford Bench, even more intense than usual given the dryness of the vintage. **LGr**
🍷🍷🍷🍷 **Drink: to 2021**

Château Beauséjour Duffau-Lagarrosse 1990

Origin France, Bordeaux, St.-Emilion
Style Dry red wine, 13% ABV
Grapes Merlot 60%, C. Franc 25%, C. Sauvignon 15%

Before 1990, the 17-acre (7 ha) St.-Emilion Premier Grand Cru Classé estate of Château Beauséjour Duffau-Lagarrosse was largely unknown. That was before the château overshadowed the exceptional wines of Ausone, Angélus, and Cheval Blanc in the hot St.-Emilion vintage of 1990.

There is one reason why this wine is so sought-after: Robert Parker. In the February 1997 edition of his bimonthly newsletter, *The Wine Advocate*, Parker gave the Beauséjour 1990 a perfect score of 100, describing it as "fabulously concentrated, with outstanding purity, and a nearly unprecedented combination of richness, complexity, and overall balance and harmony." Only three other Bordeaux wines attained a 100-point score in 1990: Margaux, Pétrus, and Montrose.

Released at about $45 (£22; €33) a bottle, by 2006 Château Beauséjour Duffau-Lagarrosse 1990 was fetching up to $10,000 (£4,995; €7,360) a case at U.S. auctions. Owner Jean Duffau and winemaker Jean-Michel Dubos seem indifferent to the huge cult surrounding their 1990 vintage, but have yet to create anything remotely similar in quality. **SG**
🍷🍷🍷🍷🍷 **Drink: to 2020+**

Château Beau-Séjour Bécot 2002

Origin France, Bordeaux, St.-Emilion
Style Dry red wine, 13.5% ABV
Grapes Merlot 70%, C. Franc 24%, C. Sauvignon 6%

Michel Bécot was born into a wine-growing family that has lived in St.-Emilion since 1760 and owned Château La Carte since 1929. He purchased the Beau-Séjour estate in 1969. In 1979, the Bécot family further enlarged the estate with the purchase of 11 acres (4.5 ha) on the Trois Moulins plateau. The estate, which then became known as Château Beau-Séjour Bécot, is today a substantial 41-acre (16 ha) holding on a perfectly uniform terroir.

When Michel retired in 1985, his sons Gérard and Dominique took on the management of the property. In that year, Beau-Séjour Bécot was controversially stripped of its Premier Grand Cru Classé status and relegated to the lower category of St.-Emilion Grand Cru because of Michel Bécot's incorporation of a couple of non-Premier Grand Cru vineyards. The decision was reversed in 1996, and Beau-Séjour Bécot is now one of the leading Premiers Grands Crus Classés B.

The château's 49 acres (20 ha) of vineyards are sited on a limestone plateau in the northwest part of the appellation. The wine is matured in oak barriques (50 to 70 percent of them new) for eighteen to twenty months. The ubiquitous Michel Rolland is a consultant, and the wine is made in his image. The 2002 is full-bodied, concentrated, and rich, with layers of cassis-scented fruits and hints of new oak. In a blind Grand Jury Européen tasting of more than 200 wines from this underrated vintage, this wine came top. **SG**

🍷🍷🍷🍷 **Drink: to 2022**

FURTHER RECOMMENDATIONS
Other great vintages
1982 • 1988 • 1990 • 1998 • 2000 • 2001 • 2003
More St.-Emilion Premiers GCs Classés (B)
Angélus • Beauséjour Duffau-Lagarrosse
Canon • Clos Fourtet

A *cave* hints at Beau-Séjour Bécot's medieval religious connections. ➡

Beaux Frères

Pinot Noir 2002

Origin USA, Oregon, Willamette Valley
Style Dry red wine, 14.2% ABV
Grape Pinot Noir

The wines of Beaux Frères would be distinctive on their own terms even if they did not have Robert Parker as one of the owners. Winemaker and brother-in-law Michael Etzel is dedicated to producing Pinot Noir only in a manner that, in his view, will reflect the essence of that grape as grown in their pocket of Ribbon Ridge.

The Ribbon Ridge is a small sub-appellation of the Willamette Valley where the moderate climate is warmer and slightly drier than the valley floor. The ridge has sloping hillsides containing primarily sedimentary, silty-clay loam soils of the Willakenzie soil series. The moderately deep soils are of low fertility and are finer and more uniform than the alluvial and volcanic soils of neighboring regions.

Willakenzie soils tend to produce black fruit wines (as distinct from the red fruits produced by Jory loam soils elsewhere in the Willamette), and Etzel's Beaux Frères Pinot Noirs are true to type, with an intensely extracted palate of black cherries, blackberries, mineral, and smoke. 2002 produced profoundly ripe fruit and a sophisticated, spicy wine with firm structure, fine acidity, and complexity. **LGr**
☻☻☻ **Drink: to 2017+**

Château Bélair-Monange

2012

Origin France, Bordeaux, St.-Emilion
Style Dry red wine, 13.5% ABV
Grapes 85% Merlot, 15% Cabernet Franc

This ancient property, a Premier Cru Classé, belonged in the fourteenth century to Sir Robert de Knolles. The first vintage to be bottled by his descendants was in 1802. In 1916, Bélair was bought by the Dubois-Challon family, who were also the owners of Château Ausone. After the death of Mme. Jean Dubois-Challon in 2003, she left the estate to her long-time winemaker, Pascal Delbeck. Delbeck sadly found the taxes on the property too crippling, and from 2006 the firm of J. P. Moueix began acquiring shares, and finally bought the property in 2008, changing its name to Bélair-Monange.

The Moueix family ploughed the vineyards and replaced Delbeck's punchdowns with more conventional pumpovers. In 2012, they decided to merge the vineyards with those of nearby Château Magdelaine, another Premier Cru Classé, which had long been owned by the Moueix family. This brought the surface under vine to 57 acres (23 ha).

The 2012 has delicate red-fruit aromas, and the palate shows finesse, lift, and great polish, adding up to a wine of tension and persistence rather than great weight and power. **SBr**
☻☻☻☻ **Drink: to 2030**

Beringer *Private Reserve*
Cabernet Sauvignon 2001

Origin USA, California, Napa Valley
Style Dry red wine, 14.9% ABV
Grapes C. Sauvignon 94%, C. Franc 6%

Château Berliquet
2001

Origin France, Bordeaux, St.-Emilion
Style Dry red wine, 13% ABV
Grapes Merlot 75%, C. Franc 20%, C. Sauvignon 5%

Beringer is the oldest continuously operating winery in Napa Valley. When chief winemaker Ed Sbragia and his predecessor, Myron Nightingale, happened on a lot of grapes in 1977 that promised a distinctive Cabernet in a big, rich style, he kept that portion apart two years in French oak barrels to be bottled as the first vintage of Beringer Private Reserve.

That original bottling came from what is now called Chabot Vineyard; over time, as Beringer acquired access to prime vineyard properties, the Private Reserve became a blend of prime lots designed to express vintage character in a bold, rich style. Fruit from the St.-Helena Home Vineyard, like nearby Chabot, provides rich fruit, supple tannins, and a fleshy texture; Bancroft Ranch Vineyard, Rancho del Oso, and Steinhauer Ranch on Howell Mountain, and Marsden on Spring Mountain add concentrated Cabernet backbone and structure.

At a blind tasting of Napa Valley 2001 vintage wines in September 2004, the Beringer Private Reserve stood out among its companions: concentrated, but harmonious; ripe, but elegant and structured; complex, virile, and vibrant. **LGr**
🍷🍷🍷🍷 **Drink: to 2025+**

This property is very well located on the plateau and slopes near Magdelaine, Canon, and other fine properties. In the 1950s, the vineyards were allowed to decline and the wines were produced by the cooperative. After the death of Vicomte de Lesquen and his wife in the late 1960s, the present owner, Vicomte Patrick, gave up his banking career in Paris to run the property. He persuaded the cooperative to build a cellar at Berliquet, which qualified the estate to be promoted to Grand Cru Classé in 1986.

Lesquen knows he has a fine terroir here, so in 1996 he left the cooperative and in 1997 hired Patrick Valette as his consultant enologist. Although Berliquet has only 22 acres (9 ha) of vines, the soils are complex, and Valette's skills are employed to make the best possible blend. Lesquen is adamant that he wants elegance rather than power, and since 1997 that is exactly what the wine delivers. Even in tricky vintages such as 1997 and 1999, Berliquet made sound and refined wine. The excellent 2000 is outclassed by the even better 2001, in which the richness and body are countered by lively acidity that gives the wine length and balance. **SBr**
🍷🍷🍷 **Drink: to 2020**

Biondi-Santi
Tenuta Greppo Brunello di Montalcino Riserva 1975

Origin Italy, Tuscany, Montalcino
Style Dry red wine, 12.5% ABV
Grape Sangiovese

Biondi-Santi is the name behind the mythic Brunello that has become one of Italy's three top generics. It was Ferruccio, grandfather of Franco Biondi-Santi (who died in 2013), who "invented" the name Brunello for that clone of Sangiovese grown principally (then, if not now) in the vineyards of Montalcino. His son, Tancredi, initiated the idea of Brunello di Montalcino being capable of lasting 100 years.

Franco Biondi-Santi described himself as a "continuer, not an initiator," though no one can deny that he was a gritty fighter, having had to endure ridicule and opposition for sticking to his highly traditional style. Well into his eighties, he still used his own homegrown clones of what he called Sangiovese Grosso; he still insisted on grapes for Riserva coming from vines at least twenty-five years old; he still eschewed mechanical temperature control in the fermentation; and he aged in large old Slavonian oak casks. In their youth his wines had little charm and so much structure in terms of tannin and acidity that you somehow doubted whether the fruit would ever burst through the austerity. But burst through it does, along with all kinds of subtle and fleeting tertiary aromas.

The 1975, topped up in 2000, is probably at its peak more than thirty years on—as extraordinary and impressive as any wine Franco's father made in his lifetime. **NBel**

ΘΘΘΘ **Drink: to 2020+**

FURTHER RECOMMENDATIONS
Other great vintages
1925 • 1945 • 1955 • 1964 • 1982 • 1995 • 2001
More producers from Montalcino
Argiano • Case Basse • Costanti
Lisini • Pieve di Santa Restituta

The Biondi-Santi estate is the spiritual home of Brunello di Montalcino. ➜

Boekenhoutskloof
Syrah 2009

Origin South Africa, Coastal Region
Style Dry red wine, 14.5% ABV
Grape Syrah

Internationally, Boekenhoutskloof Syrah is perhaps the most consistently celebrated Cape red, from the maiden 1997 onward, and in its homeland a panel of judges in 2006 voted it "best red wine"—and the winery as a whole among the country's top five.

In what some regard as a national scandal, the Somerset West vineyard that produced the famous first vintage of the Syrah disappeared under an industrial park. Thwarted by such progress, cellar master Marc Kent (also one of the seven owner-partners represented by the chairs on the label) turned elsewhere. A mature, low-yielding hillside vineyard in the Wellington area has been the source of grapes since 1998, though vinification and *élevage* is done in the Franschhoek cellar of the Boekenhoutskloof winery.

As for the names, the winery's is Dutch in origin and means "Cape beech ravine," whereas the French name for the grape commonly called Shiraz in South Africa tends to be used there for wines of European inspiration (or aspiration)—and this one is, as Jancis Robinson says, "deliciously 'French' Syrah." Although demand and reputation bring it as close to "cult" status as any South African wine, it is also the only contender to use indigenous yeast and no new oak. Big but not bold (with the substantial alcohol beautifully balanced and reclusive), ripe but restrained and fresh, it has both grace and power, packed with focused, savory fruit. **TJ**

🍷🍷🍷 **Drink: recent vintages for up to 10 years**

The winery is located in a corner of the stunning Franschhoek Valley. ➡

Château Le Bon Pasteur 2005

Origin France, Bordeaux, Pomerol
Style Dry red wine, 13% ABV
Grapes Merlot 80%, Cabernet Sauvignon 20%

Michel Rolland is so well known as a wine consultant that it is easy to forget that he and his family own properties on the right bank of Bordeaux. The best known is Le Bon Pasteur in Pomerol, which has been in his family for three generations. As is common in Pomerol, the property consists of numerous parcels, though the château itself is located in the hamlet of Maillet on the very edge of the appellation. Some of the best parcels of vines are well located near Gazin and L'Evangile. Other sectors are sandier. The vines are old and the style of the wine quite powerful.

Not surprisingly, Rolland applies his standard techniques to his own wine, with green-harvesting and leaf-pulling in the vineyard, late harvesting even at the risk of picking some overripe fruit, careful sorting at the winery, and no crushing of the grapes. The Burgundian technique of punching down the cap is used for the Merlot, and the winery is equipped with a modern vertical press. At least 80 percent new oak is used to age the wine, which also undergoes malolactic fermentation in new oak.

The result is a rich, fleshy wine that is accessible and enjoyable when drunk young, though it will age well in the medium term. The 2005 is particularly successful, with aromas of cherries and mint leaf and oak, while the palate is both voluptuous and very concentrated. But it is worth noting that the 2005 comes, for Le Bon Pasteur, at a high price, and that better value, even if slightly less spectacular quality, can be found in preceding vintages. **SBr**

ⓈⓈⓈⓈ **Drink: to 2020**

FURTHER RECOMMENDATIONS
Other great vintages
1989 • 1990 • 1995 • 1998 • 2000 • 2001 • 2009 • 2010
More producers from Pomerol
La Conseillante • L'Eglise-Clinet • Lafleur
Pétrus • Le Pin • Trotanoy • Vieux Château Certan

Le Bon Pasteur lies at the edge of the Pomerol appellation. ➡

Henri Bonneau *Châteauneuf-du-Pape Réserve des Célestins* 1998

Origin France, Southern Rhône, Châteauneuf-du-Pape
Style Dry red wine, 14.5% ABV
Grape Grenache

Described by Andrew Jefford as "one of the Rhône's great right-wing eccentrics," Henri Bonneau has been making wine since 1956 from his tiny holdings—just 15 acres (6 ha)—in the famed La Crau area of the Châteauneuf-du-Pape winemaking zone. Bonneau makes several different cuvées, selected according to his judgment of their quality. There is the basic Châteauneuf-du-Pape; the Cuvée Marie Beurrier; and finally the Réserve des Célestins, which Bonneau calls his "grand vin."

The Réserve des Célestins 1998 was assessed in a *World of Fine Wine* tasting in 2006. Stephen Browett of Farr Vintners said, "This smells just like Banyuls. Very, very ripe and sweet Grenache that has a suggestion of spirit on the nose. Tastes just like it smells and if this is less than 15 percent alcohol I'm a Dutchman." For Franco Ziliani, it was, "A wine already arrived at the end of the road." And Simon Field MW concluded, "A *folie de grandeur* that is starting to show a few cracks. . . ."

As these tasters' comments suggest, Bonneau's wines are highly idiosyncratic and do not necessarily represent everybody's idea of what fine Châteauneuf-du-Pape should taste like. But the Réserve des Célestins, more than any other of Bonneau's wines, represents the archetype of wine production carried out on a small scale—artisanal wine that is, for many people, the ideal of what winemaking should be. **SG**

🍷🍷🍷🍷 Drink: to 2018+

Harvesting Grenache grapes at Châteauneuf-du-Pape. ➡

Bonny Doon
Le Cigare Volant 2005

Origin USA, California, Santa Cruz
Style Dry red wine, 13.5% ABV
Grapes Grenache, Syrah, Mourvèdre

Bonny Doon
Vin Gris de Cigare 2012

Origin USA, California, Santa Cruz
Style Dry rosé wine, 13% ABV
Grapes Grenache, Mourvèdre, Pinot Noir, G. Blanc

In the mid-1980s, Randall Grahm, presiding genius of Bonny Doon Vineyard, elected to shun the pseudo-Burgundian obsession with Pinot Noir and Chardonnay and strike out into relatively undiscovered French-inspired territory. If Grahm did not invent the California taste for Rhône blends alone, he was certainly one of its leading lights.

His principal Rhône-style red is named for an obscure bit of Gallic lunacy whereby, in 1954, at the height of UFO hysteria, the growers of Châteauneuf-du-Pape secured the passing of a by-law that forbade flying saucers (*cigares volants*) from landing in their vineyards.

The composition of the wine changes from year to year, with Syrah and Mourvèdre sometimes edging out Grenache. The result is usually a wine of astonishing levels of extract and spice intensity, as is the case with the wondrous 2005 vintage. It throws a fistful of black pepper in your nose, before following up with violet-tinged blackberry and black plum fruits. The tannins are elegant but fairly severe, ensuring that the wine will unwind in its own good time, perhaps over fifteen years or so. **SW**

🍷🍷🍷 **Drink: to 2020**

Bonny Doon's dry rosé wine is modeled on those of Provence, where *petits rosés d'été* are known as *vins gris*, or gray wines. But there is nothing gray about the personality of Bonny Doon's Vin Gris. The grape blend has altered with the years, sometimes foregrounding Mourvèdre, sometimes Grenache, but now bringing in some Grenache Blanc. The last ingredient adds aromatic vigor to the wine, conferring an infectious peachiness on the wine's aromas, from which a young pink richly benefits.

The wine is impeccably dry, avoiding the overly evident note of residual sugar that is often thought to help a rosé along. It has whistle-clean aromas of rosehip and watermelon, opening to more substantial peach and raspberry tones on the palate. There is more than a touch of savory spice to it as well, reflecting the peppery, clovelike aromatics of those southern Rhône grape varieties, together with a generous pinch of *herbes de Provence*. Though intended for drinking relatively young, it holds up well for a couple of years after the vintage. Always fairly priced, this is one of the great value rosés in all of California. **SW**

🍷🍷 **Drink: recent vintages within 2 years**

Borie de Maurel
Cuvée Sylla 2010

Origin France, Minervois, La Lavinière
Style Dry red wine, 14.5% ABV
Grape Syrah

Rugged, extrovert, and lyrical, Michel Escande is one of those French winemakers so inebriated by words and ideas that he seems sometimes to be following in the wake of Arthur Rimbaud and his *bateau ivre* as much as in the footsteps of his avowed master, Jacques Reynaud of Château Rayas.

The Borie de Maurel range includes two blends of Syrah, Grenache, and Carignan: Esprit d'Automne and Féline; the pure Grenache Belle de Nuit and the pure Mourvèdre Maxime; the white Aude (90 percent Marsanne balanced by Muscat) and a Mourvèdre-Syrah Rosé.

The pure Syrah Cuvée Sylla comes from a number of parcels sited at around 980 feet (299 m). The height and what Escande calls the *aérologie* are perfect for Syrah, bringing it slowly to the full yet poised ripeness that represents Escande's ideal. The fruit is hand-picked and carefully sorted, then fermented uncrushed. It sees no wood. Escande intends this to be one of the most pure yet aerial of southern France's great Syrahs, and it is: smooth yet soaring, rich-fruited yet aromatically enchanting, its tannins like cumulus on the tongue. **AJ**

🔊🔊 **Drink: to 2025**

Borsao
Tres Picos 2012

Origin Spain, Aragón, Campo de Borja
Style Dry red wine, 14.5% ABV
Grape Garnacha (Grenache)

Aragón in Spain is the mother country of Garnacha, even if France is the country producing the most prestigious and fashionable Grenache wines.

For any Spanish wine aficionado whose eyes opened to wine in the 1980s, Borsao must be a favorite name, even though the winery was then called Cooperativa del Campo de Borja. There is no little merit in maintaining good to very good quality levels for more than twenty years, with respectable production volumes and ludicrously low prices. The best Borsao wines are those where the fruit is allowed to express itself fully: The plain and simple Borsao label and the recently introduced Borsao Garnacha Mítica are champions of silky fruit, with the structure of wines three to six times the price.

But the extraordinary Tres Picos cuvée, from old vines, is a dramatic qualitative jump into the territory of complexity and concentration, without renouncing subtlety or fruit character. It is a delicious wine, savory and with suggestive underbrush notes, long and fresh thanks to its sound acidity and perfectly integrated alcohol, and with aromas and flavors that grow with aeration. **JB**

🔊 **Drink: recent vintages for up to 7 years**

Boscarelli *Vino Nobile*
Nocio dei Boscarelli 2003

Origin Italy, Tuscany, Montepulciano
Style Dry red wine, 14.5% ABV
Grapes Sangiovese 80%, Merlot 15%, Mammolo 5%

The Boscarelli estate was founded in 1962 and the first Vino Nobile released in 1968. The DOC law for Vino Nobile di Montepulciano states that the minimum proportion of Sangiovese must be 70 percent, but is quite permissive regarding the rest. With such latitude, it is difficult to know what real Vino Nobile di Montepulciano should taste like: Our suggestion is to use the Nocio dei Boscarelli as a benchmark example.

Despite the presence of Merlot, in the Nocio it seems that the terroir manages to override the varietal expression. The 2003 vintage was excessively hot and dry, but the drawbacks of this extreme weather are not detectable in the wine. The not-too-deep color (a trademark of real Sangiovese) tends to sober garnet tinges, and introduces a nose of sour cherries and menthol, possibly because of the oak aging. Take a sip and let it conquer your palate; the perfectly measured velvety richness is not disturbed by the dry tannins that spoil all too many 2003s, and supports a nicely complex mid-palate. The finish is soft and warm—the only concession made to this famously hot vintage. **AS**
☻☻☻ **Drink: to 2018+**

Bouchard Père & Fils
Clos de Vougeot Grand Cru 1999

Origin France, Burgundy, Côte de Nuits
Style Dry red wine, 13.5% ABV
Grape Pinot Noir

The Bouchard family, and the reputation of their house, stumbled in the early 1990s, and when Champagne producer Joseph Henriot, a former president of Veuve Clicquot, heard that it was for sale, he jumped at the chance. In 1995, he became the new owner. He immediately set about restoring the house's reputation by declassifying or simply pouring away bottles he considered substandard. He also invested in the vineyards and commissioned a new gravity-operated winery in Savigny.

Bouchard owns about 1 acre (0.4 ha) within Clos de Vougeot, mostly in the upper part, which Henriot bought from Ropiteau-Mignon, as well as a plot lower down near the Route Nationale; the winemaker Philippe Prost insists that the blend of the two is better than either on its own. Some 2,000 bottles are produced. Like all the top Bouchard wines, the Clos de Vougeot is aged in no more than 40 percent new oak. The 1999 is exemplary, with its somber aromas of cherries and wax, and a sumptuous palate that is spicy and vigorous but shows no rough edges. The finish is long and tangy, and this wine is likely to be very long-lived. **SBr**
☻☻☻☻ **Drink: to 2019+**

Bouchard Père & Fils is based at the magnificent Château de Beaune. ➲

Bouchard-Finlayson *Galpin Peak Tête de Cuvée Pinot Noir* 2005

Braida *Bricco dell'Uccellone Barbera d'Asti* 1997

Origin South Africa, Walker Bay
Style Dry red wine, 14.2% ABV
Grape Pinot Noir

Origin Italy, Piedmont, Monferrato
Style Dry red wine, 14% ABV
Grape Barbera

Not far from the southernmost tip of Africa, just a few miles from the sea, is the Hemel-en-Aarde valley, one of the Cape's coolest wine-growing areas.

The valley has been closely associated with the Burgundian varieties for the comparatively short time of its modern winemaking existence—and so too has Peter Finlayson, a pioneering winemaker who struck out in 1990 with Paul Bouchard from the famous Burgundian family of Bouchard Aîné et Fils. Finlayson had Burgundian experience himself, but the early Bouchard touch was important.

The wines aim at classicism rather than fruity exuberance. The regular Galpin Peak Pinot Noir is named for the mountain overlooking the vineyards; Tête de Cuvée is a barrel selection made in the best years only and matured with a higher proportion of new wood, requiring greater patience on the part of drinkers. 2005 provided excellent ripening conditions, giving concentrated fruit in the wine—the youthful oakiness not too obscuring of the raspberry and cherry notes, within a well-structured tannic and acid framework, leading to a lengthy, sensual finish. **TJ**

🜂🜂🜂 **Drink: to 2017+**

Until the late Giacomo Bologna stunned critics and connoisseurs alike with his barrique-aged, single-vineyard Bricco dell'Uccellone, Barbera d'Asti was considered as merely the coarse, everyday dinner companion for many northwestern Italians.

While studying the techniques of the best French winemakers in the late 1970s, Bologna learned how malolactic fermentation in wood could soften Barbera's strident acidity and add tannins that the grape inherently lacks. He realized that, if used wisely, barriques would not only add subtle flavors to Barbera, but polish its rustic edges. At the 1985 edition of Vinitaly, the country's largest annual wine show, Bologna launched his Bricco dell'Uccellone 1982, and within five days all 9,800 bottles were pre-sold. Other producers noted the wine's success, and soon an enological revolution was underway.

Although most Barbera d'Asti is consumed within the first three to five years, Bricco dell'Uccellone has great aging potential. The 1997 vintage, one of the greatest of the last century, is still remarkably fresh, with silky smooth tannins and excellent fruit with licorice notes. **KO**

🜂🜂🜂 **Drink: to 2017+**

Bricco dell'Uccellone is arguably the finest Barbera d'Asti. ◢

Château Branaire-Ducru
2005

Origin France, Bordeaux, St.-Julien
Style Dry red wine, 13% ABV
Grapes C. Sauvignon 70%, Merlot 22%, Others 8%

Driving through St.-Julien, it is easy to miss Branaire-Ducru, which stands opposite the grander, more showy Château Beychevelle. Branaire's mansion is more modest, yet is still engagingly stately. In the seventeenth century, Branaire's vineyards formed part of the Beychevelle estate. Since its separation, Branaire has passed through numerous hands, including the two families that gave the estate its present name. In 1988 the property was bought by Patrick Maroteaux, who invested heavily, renovating the buildings and the 120 acres (48 ha) of vineyards. With the skilled Philippe Dhalluin as winemaker and manager, he reduced yields and introduced a stricter selection by creating a second wine.

Under Dhalluin and his successor, Jean-Dominique Videau, Branaire's wine has gone from strength to strength. Although it has gained in richness and weight since the 1980s, it has always retained its typicity as a refined and balanced St.-Julien. Branaire preserves a high proportion of Cabernet Sauvignon at a time when many Médoc estates are increasing their plantings of Merlot. Yet the wine is never austere, even if it has a firm tannic structure. This is particularly apparent in a vintage such as 2005, when richness and succulence are beautifully balanced by tannin and acidity.

Although Branaire-Ducru is not perceived as a top-notch estate, it has not produced a mediocre wine since the mid-1990s. Its profile is as modest as the early nineteenth-century château, but the quality of its wines is beyond reproach. **SBr**
🄢🄢🄢🄢 **Drink: to 2030**

Château Brane-Cantenac
2000

Origin France, Bordeaux, Margaux
Style Dry red wine, 13% ABV
Grapes Merlot 55%, C. Sauvignon 42%, C. Franc 3%

This distinguished Margaux property takes its name from Baron Hector de Brane, nicknamed Napoleon des Vignes, who bought it in 1833, having sold Brane-Mouton (later Mouton Rothschild) in 1830. The property, at 222 acres (90 ha), is now the largest of the five second growths in Margaux, but it is almost certainly the original parcels of vines to the front of the château, on the magnificent Cantenac *croupe* (terrace), that contribute most to the wine's breed, charm, delicacy, and finesse. Here 75 acres (30 ha) of vines benefit from good air circulation, drainage, and reflected warmth from soils rich in gravel and quartz, and up to 40 feet (12 m) deep.

The property has been in the Lurton family, one of Bordeaux's most important land-owning dynasties, since 1925. Henri Lurton was born at the château, and since taking over from his father in the 1990s has been determined to prove that it is fully worthy of its second-growth status.

The largest tasting of Brane-Cantenac ever held (almost fifty vintages, some more than 100 years old) showed that there is a distinct identity and quality to the wines, which are often pleasantly surprising in lesser years. They are also, however, fully worthy of the property and the vintage in great years—such as this 2000, though even then only 27 percent of production went into the grand vin. Aristocratic, brilliantly clear, and fresh on the nose, the wine is dense but elegant and nimble on the palate, with fine-grained, ripe, and refined tannins, excellent transparency of flavor, and elegant length. **NB**
🄢🄢🄢 **Drink: to 2030+**

Since the 1964 vintage, Henri Lurton has increased the Merlot in the wine. ➜

GRAND CR...

CHÂTEAU

BRANE CANTEN...

MARGAUX

1964

APPELLATION MARGAUX CONT...

L. LURTON, PROPRIÉTAIRE A CANTENAC...

MIS EN BOUTEILLES AU CH...

Brokenwood
Graveyard Shiraz 1991

Origin Australia, New South Wales, Hunter Valley
Style Dry red wine, 13.5% ABV
Grape Shiraz

Brokenwood was established in 1970 when three lawyers, James Halliday, Tony Albert, and John Beeston, bought a 10-acre (4 ha) block in Pokolbin. Over the next few years they got their hands dirty, before making their first wine in 1973.

In 1978 Brokenwood purchased the neighboring Graveyard vineyard—a 35-acre (14 ha) plot facing east, with heavy red clay loam soils, originally planted in 1969. Most of the plantings are Shiraz, and the first release under the Graveyard vineyard designation was in 1983. This was also the year that Halliday severed his association with the winery.

Graveyard Shiraz is not a wine that impresses with power or concentration; what is special about it is the way it communicates its origins, consistently displaying the Hunter characteristics of leather and spice, combined with genuine longevity. The 1991 was a drought vintage, and the wines suffered some water stress, which perhaps accounts for the relatively low alcohol level of this wine. It is a structured, muscular interpretation of Graveyard that will continue to evolve for a few years yet, and will last for many more. **JG**

🍷🍷🍷 **Drink: to 2019+**

Château Brown
2004

Origin France, Bordeaux, Pessac-Léognan
Style Dry red wine, 13% ABV
Grape C. Sauvignon 55%, Merlot 43%, P. Verdot 2%

This attractive Bordeaux estate takes its name from John Lewis Brown, an eighteenth-century Scottish-born wine merchant. In 1939, AndréBonnel acquired Brown, but winemaking was abandoned in the 1950s and the estate was ineligible for the Graves Classifications of 1953 and 1959, so it has remained a plain Pessac-Léognan, without Cru Classé status.

The 2004 vintage was the first wine at Brown produced under the auspices of the Mau family of Bordeaux negociants, who (in partnership with Dutch wine and spirit group Dirkzwager) took over the estate in December of that year. Stéphane Derenoncourt, who also works at Châteaux Pavie-Macquin, Canon-la-Gaffelière, and La Mondotte, supervises the vinification of the red wines.

The influence of the new regime was apparent with the 2004 wine, which was better balanced and with more depth than in the past. It is medium rather than heavy weight, in a lightly earthy, lean style, with some elegance.

Tasted in January 2009, it was still firmly tannic, suggesting that further aging was required for the wine to show its best. **SG**

🍷🍷🍷 **Drink: to 2019+**

▣ The pumping-over process being carried out at Brokenwood.

David Bruce *Santa Cruz Mountains Pinot Noir* 2004

Origin USA, California, Santa Cruz Mountains
Style Dry red wine, 14.2% ABV
Grape Pinot Noir

Bussaco Palace Hotel *Buçaco Tinto Reservado* 2005

Origin Portugal, Luso
Style Dry red wine, 13% ABV
Grapes Baga, Touriga Nacional

One of California's least appreciated but highest quality wine-growing regions, the Santa Cruz Mountains lie between the city of San Jose, at the southern end of San Francisco Bay, and the Pacific Ocean beach town of Santa Cruz. Foggy mornings and warm afternoons are standard fare among these heavily wooded and surprisingly remote ridges and valleys, making for a long, gentle growing season.

Dr. David Bruce's first career was in dermatology; this supported his winemaking until 1985, when he committed to it full time. The core property of the David Bruce winery is a 15-acre (6 ha) estate located at 2,100 feet (640 m) above sea level, where fog reaches only rarely. Bruce is locally famous for being among the first to understand the potential of Santa Cruz Mountain terroir—especially for Chardonnay and Pinot Noir. As a result, his Pinot Noir is widely considered the definitive one from this region.

A blend made from estate grapes and those from nearby vineyards, this is a big, full-flavored Pinot Noir, with a core of concentrated red fruit flavors and subtle toast, nutmeg, and vanilla notes from fifteen months spent in new French oak. **DD**

☻☻☻ Drink: 2019+

Wineries with guest houses are ten a penny but hotels that make wine are a rare breed. Conceived as "a cathedral of wine" by its founder Alexandre de Almeida, the vineyards and cellars of the Bussaco Palace Hotel have produced some of Portugal's most highly regarded wines for close to a century.

Other than a label change and, in 2000, the introduction of 79-gallon (300-liter) French oak barrels to replace the aged *toneis* (wooden vats), Buçaco Tinto Reservado remains true to tradition. The grapes (Touriga Nacional from Dão and Baga from Bairrada) are foot-trodden and fermented in granite *lagares* (with around 50 percent stems) before being aged for up to twelve months in 50 percent new and 50 percent second-use French oak. The wine is usually released four years after bottling, and will age for very many more (the hotel still lists wines from the 1940s).

Although the wines are generally very austere in their youth, this 2005 is more expressive and fleshy, with hedonistic, soaring incense spice and rock rose to its red-fruited nose and palate. A very long, precise finish bodes well for aging. Surely one of the best Tinto Reservados the hotel has produced. **SA**

☻☻☻ Drink: to 2030+

Tommaso Bussola *Recioto della Valpolicella Classico* 2003

Ca' Marcanda
IGT Toscana 2004

Origin Italy, Veneto, Valpolicella
Style Sweet red wine, 12% ABV
Grapes Corvina/Corvinone 70%, Others 30%

Origin Italy, Tuscany, Bolgheri
Style Dry red wine, 14% ABV
Grapes Merlot 50%, C. Sauvignon 25%, C. Franc 25%

This is a wine whose origins reach far back in time. *Recioto* is made with grapes laid out in bunches to dry under the eaves of the winery for up to six months, after which time the berries have shriveled to up to half their original weight, and have become so concentrated that the resulting wine, slowly vinified over a period of years, may consist of solid matter, in the form of sugars, phenols, and flavonoids, at up to 30 percent of total weight.

Tommaso Bussola is one of the great individualist producers of *Recioto*. It is to his *viticoltore* uncle Giuseppe Bussola that Tommaso owes his passion for, and expertise in, the ways of the grapes that grow on Valpolicella Classico's beautiful hills and terraces. He also sat at the feet of Valpolicella's doyen and maestro, Giuseppe Quintarelli, whose property is visible from Tommaso's recently enlarged and expanded winery at San Peretto in Negrar. Tommaso's style is less oxidative, and less ethereal than that of Quintarelli, a powerhouse of rich, bittersweet cherry and cranberry fruit. But he also achieves some remarkable undertones of herb, flower, and cedar, and, with age, leather, meat, spice, and tar. **NBel**
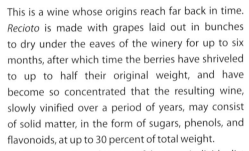 **Drink: to 2030+**

Angelo Gaja is one of Italy's most dynamic and discussed winemakers. In 1961, when he first took over the family's Barbaresco firm and began cutting back yields, and later, when he began using barriques as part of the aging process for his red wines, local growers and producers watched in shocked amusement. But thanks to the international success of Gaja's wines, other winemakers were soon adopting many of the same quality techniques.

In 1996 Gaja bought 250 acres (101 ha) in Castagneto di Carducci, near Bolgheri. International red varieties excel in this area, thanks to the favorable conditions near the coast and also to land that has not been depleted by centuries of farming.

Ca' Marcanda's flagship wine, Magari (the name means "if only"), was named to reflect the Piedmontese custom of downplaying one's accomplishments. Made from Merlot, Cabernet Sauvignon, and Cabernet Franc, Magari is a Bordeaux blend that reflects the warmth of the Tuscan sun. The 2004, an exemplary vintage in Bolgheri that led to perfect ripening, is earthy, with ripe yet restrained fruit, fresh acidity, and sweet tannins. **KO**
☻☻☻ **Drink: to 2019+**

Ca'Viola
Bric du Luv 2001

Château Calon-Ségur
2003

Origin Italy, Piedmont, Langhe
Style Dry red wine, 14.5% ABV
Grapes 85% Barbera, 15% Pinot Noir

Origin France, Bordeaux, St.-Estèphe
Style Dry red wine, 13% ABV
Grapes Cabernet Sauvignon 60%, Merlot 40%

Giuseppe Caviola is a young, talented Piedmontese winemaker who, besides producing his own wines, lends his expertise to producers all around Italy.

His Bric du Luv 2001 is a stunner of a wine, in a style that will be quite difficult to repeat because of a change in the blend. The vast majority of the 2001 blend was Barbera, the rest Pinot Noir. In 2002, Bric du Luv was not produced because of the unfavorable climatic conditions; and from 2003 onward, the Pinot Noir was replaced by an even smaller proportion of Nebbiolo (the Pinot Noir destined for Luv was hijacked for a charity project sponsored by nine Langhe producers).

The Bric du Luv 2001 is a very deep ruby red, still with some faint purple tinges. Its nose is well articulated and complex, uniting with the nicely primary aromas of cherries, raspberries, and strawberries, and some more evolved, pleasantly medicinal, almost iodinelike notes. After such an alluring nose you might wonder whether the palate could ever live up to your expectations: Well, it does. The wine is full, powerful, and nicely juicy at every sip, without ever becoming cloying. **AS**

🍷🍷🍷 Drink: to 2017+

Calon-Ségur lies just to the north of St.-Estèphe and comprises 183 acres (74 ha) of vineyards, as well as a beautiful château and gardens. The heart on the label owes its place to the eighteenth-century owner, Nicolas-Alexandre de Ségur, whose heart was at Calon even though he also owned Latour and Lafite at the time. More recently, after a quiet period, the 1995 and 1996 vintages were much acclaimed as a change in style, after Madame Gasqueton took over the estate in succession to her late husband.

The year 2003 will be remembered for a generation at least for its summer of record-breaking temperatures. Hot, sunny weather may normally suit the vine, but not to this degree as far as most of Bordeaux was concerned. The cool, deep, gravel-on-clay soils of St.-Estèphe, however, were able to survive the torrid heat much better than elsewhere, and yielded the star wines of the vintage. The Calon-Ségur 2003 is immensely concentrated in color and full of an unusually lush version of the typical St.-Estèphe black-currant fruit. The tannins are overlaid by a wealth of fruit that should all come together over the next ten to fifteen years. **JM**

🍷🍷🍷🍷 Drink: to 2025

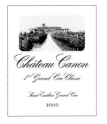

Candido

Cappello di Prete 2011

Origin Italy, Puglia, Salento
Style Dry red wine, 13.5% ABV
Grape Negroamaro

The Francesco Candido estate is one of the biggest family-owned wine cellars in southern Italy, run today by the third generation of Candidos.

The property stretches between the provinces of Lecce and Brindisi, in the Salento plain, where the soil is calcareous but rich in clay. The growing season climate is characterized by hot days and quite cool nights, which help the grapes preserve their primary aromas and good acidity levels. The main red grape variety of the Salento is Negroamaro, a grape that takes its name from the dark color of the berries and the bitterish finish of the wine produced from it.

Cappello di Prete is one of the wines that makes you understand why southern Italy has become such a popular region among wine aficionados. The color is a bright, moderately intense ruby red, with a touch of garnet. The nose is classy—broad, soft, rich yet elegant and complex, with hints of spices, tobacco, and spirit-steeped soft fruits. On the palate it is round and deep, its tannins plentiful but quite fine. The wine lingers pleasantly on the palate, moving slowly toward its announced and expected bitterish finish. **AS**

🍷🍷🍷 **Drink: recent vintages for up to 12 years**

Château Canon

2000

Origin France, Bordeaux, St.-Emilion
Style Dry red wine, 13% ABV
Grapes Merlot 75%, C. Franc 25%

This large estate was purchased in the mid-1990s by the Wertheimers of New York, who brought in John Kolasa—the manager of Rauzan-Ségla in Margaux—to deal with its serious problems.

Many vines were virused, so Kolasa embarked on a major program of replanting. Even though he bought some acres of old vines that he was allowed to incorporate into the Canon holdings, the average age of the vines remains young and it will be many years before the wines return to the splendor of the past. Nevertheless, the change in ownership brought immediate improvements and the 1995 is a very good wine. Canon is aged in up to 65 percent new oak and only half the crop ends up in the grand vin, so selection is severe.

Today's vintages are medium-bodied yet, in their youth, firm and even austere, but with sufficient plummy fruit and underlying suppleness to suggest a fine future. The 2000, a mighty wine that may not be entirely typical of Canon, has great power and richness of black cherry and chocolate flavors; it should age effortlessly, though lesser vintages such as 2004 may show more charm and finesse. **SBr**

🍷🍷🍷 **Drink: to 2025**

Château Canon-La-Gaffelière

2005

Canopy

Malpaso 2010

Origin France, Bordeaux, St.-Emilion
Style Dry red wine, 13% ABV
Grapes Merlot 55%, C. Franc 40%, C. Sauvignon 5%

Origin Spain, Castilla-La Mancha, Méntrida
Style Dry red wine, 14.5% ABV
Grape Syrah

Graf Stephan von Neipperg knew precisely what he wanted to do when he took over this property, owned by his father, in 1985. He renovated the winery and hired a little known (but now celebrated) winemaker called Stéphane Derenoncourt.

It has taken some time to restore vineyards that were abused by the regular deployment of herbicides in the 1970s, but essentially organic treatments have restored them to health. There was much venerable Cabernet Franc that contributed an elegant character to the wine, and this has been scrupulously preserved. Neipperg is also well aware that some lower sectors of the vineyard, on sandier soil, are of lesser quality and these rarely enter the grand vin.

In style Canon-La-Gaffelière is a fleshy but charming wine, often marked by the freshness imparted by Cabernet Franc. At the same time it has a seductive quality not unrelated to the generous use of new oak. It is a wine that usually shows well when young but is certainly capable of aging. The 2005 has precisely that combination of succulence and freshness that marks the wine at its best. **SBr**

🍷🍷🍷 **Drink: to 2025**

Canopy is one of the most spontaneous and unusual success stories in recent Spanish wine history. It enjoyed instant success right from the start, when, as recently as 2004, Belarmino Fernández teamed up with associates to develop his own project under the impulse of his multitalented brother, Alberto F. Bombín, popular restaurateur, wine taster, writer, distributor, actor, and TV showman.

Prioritizing the selection of the most propitious terroirs and varieties, the first thing they did was to choose forty-year-old Grenache and younger Syrah vines in Méntrida, one of the oldest wine-producing regions in central Spain, in Toledo, near Madrid. The appellation Méntrida is not at all prestigious, and until recent times has traditionally concentrated on the production of bulk wines. The area does, however, possess what it takes to produce great wines: an individual terroir, and old vineyards.

Belarmino and his associates always manage to obtain good fruit definition from their Syrah, even in more challenging vintages like 2006. Year in, year out, the oak is handled judiciously, resulting in a savory and powerful red wine. **JB**

🍷 **Drink: to 2017**

◄ Château Canon-La-Gaffelière is one of St.-Emilion's top labels.

Celler de Capçanes
Montsant Cabrida 2004

Origin Spain, Catalonia, Montsant
Style Dry red wine, 14.5% ABV
Grape Garnacha

Celler de Capçanes is a modern cooperative in the province of Tarragona. Like most cooperative wineries, it was founded a long time ago—1933 in this case—but did not start bottling its own wines until 1979. Nowadays it has 125 members, who own a total of 550 acres (222 ha) of vines, and produce 528,350 gallons (2 million liters) of wine every year.

Its portfolio is very wide with plenty of labels—Mas Colet, Lasendal, Vall de Calàs, and Costers del Gravet—covering different price brackets. Cabrida is at the top of its range. The name derives from when the vineyards were abandoned and taken over by goats (*cabra* means goat). The wine is 100 percent Garnacha, from fifteen small plots of very old vines (ranging from sixty to a hundred years old), on slopes and old terraces rich in clay, granite, and slate.

2004 was a superb vintage in the region, and one of the best for Cabrida. This is not a shy wine, but dark and powerful, with plenty of oak influence, which needs some bottle age to dissipate. Notes of black fruit, chocolate, and espresso coffee on the nose are followed by a full-bodied palate, with good acidity and a very long finish. It needs time. **LG**
🍷🍷🍷 Drink: to 2020

Villa di Capezzana
Carmignano 1997

Origin Italy, Tuscany, Carmignano
Style Dry red wine, 13% ABV
Grapes Sangiovese 80%, Cabernet Sauvignon 20%

Unknown to many wine consumers, north-central Italy has for centuries been home to a number of traditional *denominazioni* besides Chianti.

One such is Carmignano, a small redoubt to the west of Florence, where Cabernet Sauvignon was first admitted to the hallowed company of the indigenous Sangiovese. Commitment to quality winemaking among its growers saw the DOC elevated to DOCG status in 1990. Chief among those growers is the Contini Bonacossi family, whose Capezzana estate has long been the principal name in the export markets.

The estate's low-altitude vineyards mean hotter ripening days, with the result that Capezzana harvests about a fortnight earlier than greater Tuscany manages. The 1997 vintage in these parts has passed into legend already. It produced wines of rich color, astonishing intensity, and great longevity. Villa di Capezzana made a wine that gushes forth plums and black currants, with the kind of muscular concentration for which much Chianti would (or should) surrender its Trebbiano, and a perfect, tripartite balance of acidity, tannin, and alcohol. **SW**
🍷🍷🍷 Drink: to 2017+

Arnaldo Caprai *Sagrantino di Montefalco 25 Anni* 1998

Origin Italy, Umbria, Montefalco
Style Dry red wine, 14% ABV
Grape Sagrantino

Podere Il Carnasciale

Il Caberlot 2009

Origin Italy, Tuscany, Valdarno
Style Dry red wine, 13.5% ABV
Grape Caberlot

Until about thirty years ago Sagrantino was grown, not so much in vineyards, but in gardens, a few plants at a time, to make a sweet *recioto*-style blockbuster of a dried-grape wine today known as Sagrantino Passito. The dry style, which now prevails, was not made until the 1970s.

Very little research had been done on Sagrantino before the early 1990s, when Marco, son of Arnaldo Caprai, began his experiments in vineyard and *cantina*. Working with his illustrious enologist Attilio Pagli, it was, and still is, Marco's intention to prove that Sagrantino is one of the great grapes of Italy.

The top cru, 25 Anni, was introduced in 1996, twenty-five years after Arnaldo purchased the estate, to fulfill just this function. The problem with Sagrantino is its heroic tannin levels, but Caprai's work on clones and Pagli's management of wood-aging has brought forth a cru that, without losing the essential power and concentration of the original, can be considered for drinking not just at Christmas but any time: a rich, structured red, displaying a broad spectrum of fresh and dried fruit, tar, coffee, and dark chocolate aromas. **NBel**

🍷🍷🍷 **Drink: to 2020+**

"Unique" is a much overused word in the world of wine, but this wine certainly merits the term: the only wine in the world made from Caberlot, a biotype presumed to be a natural cross between Cabernet Franc and Merlot, cultivated by only one producer.

Passionate wine lovers Wolf and Bettina Rogosky began developing their small estate, Il Carnasciale, in the mid-1980s. After they were introduced to agronomist Dr. Remigio Bordini, they agreed to plant Caberlot, to which Bordini held the reproduction rights. He rewarded their trust by agreeing not to supply the variety to any other producer.

Wolf died in 1996, but his dream has been brilliantly realized by Bettina and their son Moritz. The arrival of Peter Schilling as winemaker (first vintage 2003) has led to less extraction and less new wood, and, as a spectacular vertical of the first twenty vintages in Florence in 2014 showed, these wines are now even finer. More Cabernet Franc than Merlot in character, they are black-fruited, peppery, and roseate on the nose, effortlessly expansive and richly silken but still elegant, fine, and pure on the palate, with a flourishing, harmonious finish. **NB**

🍷🍷🍷🍷🍷 **Drink: to 2025+**

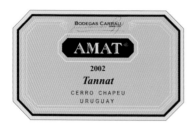

Bodegas Carrau
Amat 2002

Origin Uruguay, Rivera
Style Dry red wine, 14.5% ABV
Grape Tannat

In comparison with the Carrau family's traditionally designed Las Violetas winery at the southern end of Uruguay, Cerro Chapeu—established in 1976 in the hills of the same name (otherwise known as "bowler hat peak") on Uruguay's verdant northeastern border with Brazil—is positively space age.

The grapes come from a 4-acre (1.6 ha) plot planted in 1976 and arrive, hand-picked, at ground level, dropping into a circular set of small stainless-steel tanks, which allow gentle hand-punching of the skins down to extract color and flavor without the excess tannin that mechanical pumping would risk. The wine is then run by gravity into new barrels of French and American oak for around twenty months before being bottled, unfiltered.

Amat is a notably rich, heady version of Uruguay's flagship red grape, the Tannat, with tannins tenderized by being grown on sandy soils in a consistently warm climate. The grapes' inherently smooth tannins are aided by sensitive winemaking and a refusal to blast the wine with oak, allowing an appealingly wide range of dark fruit flavors to the fore in a medium- to full-bodied wine. **MW**

🍷🍷 **Drink: to 2017+**

Casa Castillo
Pie Franco 1999

Origin Spain, Murcia, Jumilla
Style Red wine, 14.5% ABV
Grape Monastrell

Wines like Casa Castillo Pie Franco take us back centuries, to the days when Monastrell had not yet abandoned eastern Spain to become, in a foreign land, one of the great red wine varieties under the names Mourvèdre and Mataró.

Allowing the grape to express itself, by nurturing it and keeping human intervention to a minimum, is what characterizes the recent boom in Spanish winemaking. Among the outstanding producers working in this way, we must count the Vicente family, whose most authentic and exclusive product is this Casa Castillo Pie Franco. The 1999 vintage of this wine reaches an admirable balance and harmony, and will likely be at its peak around 2015.

The 430 acres (174 ha) owned by Julia Roch e Hijos (the company name behind Casa Castillo wines) are divided into four plots. The oldest of these is La Solana, planted in 1941 to ungrafted (pre-phylloxera) Monastrell vines. It is a very low-yielding plot, and one sadly doomed to disappear sooner or later, because every year a small percentage of the vines die as a consequence of phylloxera—though the process is slow due to the sandy soils. **JB**

🍷🍷 **Drink: to 2020**

Casa Gualda
Selección C&J 2009

Origin Spain, La Mancha
Style Dry red wine, 12.5% ABV
Grape Cencibel (Tempranillo)

La Mancha in central Spain is the biggest vineyard in the world, with some 500,000 acres (202,350 ha) planted. The white Airén grape is also the most planted grape variety in the world, with close to 1 million acres (404,700 ha), all of them in Spain, and most of them in the center of the peninsula.

The Cooperativa Nuestra Señora de la Cabeza, located in Pozoamargo, was founded in 1958, with some 135 members controlling roughly 2,100 acres (850 ha) under vine. It is a dynamic and modern winery, thanks to the work of manager José Miguel Jávega. Having so many raw materials to choose from, he decided to select the best grapes, then to ferment, raise, and bottle the wines separately as Casa Gualda Selección C&J.

This is honest Tempranillo, more concentrated than the norm for the region, but still very well suited to food, and terrific value. The wine shows aromas of good intensity—fine, elegant, and floral, with red fruit, cinnamon, and light-toasted oak, easily recognizable as Tempranillo. Supple in the mouth, where red fruit again emerges, it is at once ample and slightly astringent, with fine tannins. **LG**

⑤ Drink: recent vintages for up to 12 years

Casa Lapostolle
Clos Apalta 2000

Origin Chile, Colchagua Valley, Apalta
Style Dry red wine, 14.5% ABV
Grapes Merlot, Carmenère, Cabernet Sauvignon

When Alexandra Marnier-Lapostolle landed in Chile in the mid-1990s, she signed a deal with a family of Chilean grape growers with vineyards dating back to the 1920s. These furnish the Clos Apalta fruit.

The oldest ungrafted Cabernet Sauvignon plots enjoy their own amphitheater, which captures the heat needed for the late-ripening Carmenère and Cabernet. The grapes are prevented from ripening too quickly by cooling evening thermal winds, raised by the presence of the nearby Tinguirririca (Colchagua) River, and by the south-facing aspect of the vines. Below ground, the roots have to work hard because the water table is constantly rising and falling. This minimizes the need for irrigation, while providing the stress in hot periods needed for naturally complex and concentrated grapes.

Slightly lower fermentation temperatures than is customary in Bordeaux are employed, to prevent the grapes' inherent richness becoming overbearing. In 2000, the maturation of the grape tannins was relatively slow, so the dominant fruit flavors (black cherry, blackberry) are nice and restrained, despite the wine's impressive concentration. **MW**

⑤ Drink: to 2017+

Viña Casablanca
Neblus 2000

Origin Chile, Aconcagua , Casablanca Valley
Style Dry red wine, 13.2% ABV
Grapes C. Sauvignon, Merlot, Carmenère

If any wine in this book could be forgiven for having an identity crisis, it is Neblus. In its first vintage, 1996, Neblus was a white wine, a noble rot-affected sweet Chardonnay, aiming to cement the Casablanca Valley's reputation as Chile's primary region for white wines of all styles. As Viña Casablanca's key UK export market wanted only dry white wines, or the Bordeaux-style reds Chile produced so effortlessly, Neblus was rebranded to become a premium red.

Neblus shows the edgy tannins, crisp fruit, but full body associated with wines grown in cool parts of otherwise hot countries. The twelve months that the 2000 vintage spent in Allier oak have tempered the riper-tasting fruit flavors imparted by grapes from warmer regions such as Colchagua Valley. These grapes, plus those from Casablanca itself, were picked several weeks later than usual, the harvest being delayed by cool, humid weather just as the grapes were changing color. An event like this would be frowned on in Bordeaux, but should be welcomed in Chile if, as it did in 2000, it aids the healthiest vineyards to enjoy extended, and thus potentially more complex, ripening. **MW**

🜨🜨 Drink: to 2017+

Cascina Corte *Dolcetto di*
Dogliani Vigna Pirochetta 2011

Origin Italy, Piedmont, Langhe
Style Dry red wine, 13.5% ABV
Grape Dolcetto

Cascina Corte was built as a farmhouse around the year 1700. Three hundred years later it lay abandoned until Amalia Battaglia and Sandro Barosi bought the ruins along with the old vineyards surrounding it. They knew that on their own they could not take on the technical aspects of a new career as wine producers, so they hired Beppe Caviola to support them on the winemaking side and Giampiero Romana as a viticulturalist.

Amalia and Sandro produce a few bottles of Barbera and Nebbiolo from a vineyard they planted in 2002, but Dogliani is a village famous for its Dolcetto and that is what they are concentrating on. They produce two wines from it—an entry level one from a southerly exposed vineyard, and a cru, Pirochetta, from sixty-year-old vines facing east.

In good years, Pirochetta is as juicy a wine as you could ever imagine. It is a nicely deep ruby red color with assertive purple tinges. On the nose it is dark and fruity, with a hint of spice, and on the palate its big, round mouthfeel is balanced by a pleasantly vibrant acidity that manages to sustain it through a fairly long finish. **AS**

🜨🜨🜨 Drink: recent vintages for up to 8 years

Castaño
Hécula Monastrell 2012

Origin Spain, Catalonia, Yecla
Style Dry red wine, 14.5% ABV
Grape Monastrell

Castello dei Rampolla
Vigna d'Alceo 1996

Origin Italy, Tuscany
Style Dry red wine, 14% ABV
Grapes Cabernet Sauvignon 85%, Petit Verdot 15%

Castaño and Yecla are almost synonymous, because for years the Castaño family was the only winery bottling wines at this Mediterranean *Denominación de Origen* in the province of Murcia in Spain. They have cultivated their vineyards since the 1950s, and it was not until the 1970s that they built their winery and started making their wines.

Their identity is the Monastrell grape, which in France is called Mourvèdre, and makes reputed wines such as Bandol. In Spain it has little prestige, and is mainly used to make bulk wines, full of color and alcohol. Monastrell represents 80 percent of the family's nearly 900 acres (364 ha).

Hécula, their "modern" wine, first produced in 1995, can be drunk on release to enjoy the exuberance of young Monastrell, or can be kept for six or seven years to let it develop in the bottle. In its frequent very good vintages, Hécula is a dense wine, of a dark purple, opaque color. The nose combines red and black fruit, balsamic notes, Mediterranean *sousbois* aromas, tree bark, and a well-integrated background of oak. It is supple, rich, dense, long, easy to drink—and very good value. **LG**

Ⓢ **Drink: recent vintages for up to 8 years**

This small estate produces its wines from grapes grown in the heart of the Chianti Classico area. The largest part of the vineyards is located in the village of Panzano (Greve in Chianti). The soil is light, calcareous, stony, and with little clay.

The man who founded the estate was the Principe Alceo di Napoli Rampolla who, in 1964, decided to turn the old family properties (which date back to 1739) into a commercial operation. Principe Alceo was one of the first to advocate Cabernet Sauvignon in the area. Many narrow-minded locals did not like his ideas at the time, but were eventually proved wrong. His Sammarco (95 percent Cabernet Sauvignon, 5 percent Sangiovese) won the praise of both consumers and the press with its very first release (1980). Principe Alceo passed away in 1991, and in 1996 his sons Luca and Maurizia honored his memory by producing the first vintage of what is today one of Tuscany's most prized wines.

The 1996 is a classic, showing black currant, mint, and lead pencil aromas on the nose. In the mouth it is velvety yet possesses good grip, amazing depth, and impressive concentration. **AS**

ⓈⓈⓈⓈⓈ **Drink: to 2030**

Castello del Terriccio
Lupicaia 1997

Origin Italy, Tuscany, Bolgheri
Style Dry red wine, 14.5% ABV
Grapes C. Sauvignon 90%, Merlot 10%

Castello del Terriccio is a 106-acre (43 ha) estate on the Tuscan coast in the extreme south of the province of Pisa, owned by the family of Gian Annibale Rossi di Medelana e Serafini Ferri since 1922. He himself took over in 1975, and for a while tried farming various crops, but in the 1980s decided to concentrate all his efforts on grapes and olives.

Taking his cue from the neighbors in nearby Bolgheri, and hiring perhaps the most "international" of Tuscany's enological consultants, Carlo Ferrini, Dr. Rossi early on took the decision to plant a preponderance of French grapes. His first mission was to make a Cabernet Sauvignon that might challenge Sassicaia and the *crus classés* of Bordeaux, and it was to the Lupicaia vineyard that he looked first to produce the grapes. He switched to another vineyard half a mile (800 m) away, but the name Lupicaia (meaning "place of wolves") was retained.

Lupicaia is a wine of top quality, barrique-aged, and made from imported varieties. The mythic Tuscan year of 1997 was hot, but, as Dr. Rossi puts it: "The good lord gave us the key to the faucet"—meaning that the rains fell just at the right times, and not during vintage. The color is somewhat evolved but the nose is very expressive—loganberries, cherries, eucalyptus, and truffles. There is excellent balance on the palate, with fruit, tannins, acidity, and alcohol coming together in a harmonious whole. It will last for at least one more decade. **NBel**
ⓈⓈⓈⓈⓈ **Drink: to 2017+**

◧ Cabernet Sauvignon vines in Castello del Terriccio's Lupicaia vineyard.

Castello di Ama *Chianti Classico Vigneto Bellavista* 2001

Origin Italy, Tuscany, Chianti Classico
Style Dry red wine, 14% ABV
Grapes Sangiovese 80%, Malvasia Nera 20%

Long noted for its wines, the medieval hamlet of Ama was acquired by four Roman families in the 1970s. They converted the property into a modern winemaking estate and quickly succeeded, with the help of Marco Pallanti, one of Italy's most dynamic winemakers, in producing world-class wines.

Pallanti chose the best vineyard sites for Chianti Classico to allow maximum ripening and the highest quality. He also began experimenting with training systems that would improve ripening further. Ama now make their flagship Castello di Ama Chianti Classico from a combination of top vineyards, but in exceptional vintages they also produce a cult single-vineyard bottling from the Bellavista vineyard.

Few other Chianti Classicos enjoy the sterling reputation of Vigneto Bellavista. First released in 1978, it is a selection from the estate's oldest vineyard. Perfect ripening and the high vine age generate rich flavor concentration, whereas the altitude means sharp differences between day and night temperatures, enhancing the wine's exquisite aromas and complexity. The 2001, a stellar vintage in Chianti Classico, is one of its finest expressions. **KO**
🍷🍷🍷🍷 **Drink: to 2021**

Castelluccio *Ronco dei Ciliegi* 2003

Origin Italy, Emilia Romagna
Style Dry red wine, 13.5% ABV
Grape Sangiovese

The Castelluccio estate is located in Modigliara, in the region of Emilia Romagna, an area where the soils are a thick layer of calcareous marls, so dense and heavy, in fact, that they are not normally suitable for the cultivation of the vine.

In 1975, however, a few micro areas were identified that were suitable for the production of high-quality grapes. The then owner hired the agronomist Vittorio Fiore, who planted and managed the vineyards of Castelluccio, using methods that were quite revolutionary at the time.

Castelluccio produces wines from only two grape varieties: Sangiovese and Sauvignon Blanc. The Ronco dei Ciliegi is thus a 100 percent Sangiovese, but this wine has a much more fruity appeal than its Tuscan relatives. The rough edges that sometimes characterize Chiantis and Brunellos are nowhere to be seen, but the grape's renowned rustic elegance is all there. The tannins are definitely present, yet as smooth as silk. Long aging potential is guaranteed by its remarkable concentration and by a perfect balance between acidity and fine, subtle astringency. **AS**
🍷🍷🍷 **Drink: to 2018+**

Castillo de Perelada
Gran Claustro 2009

Origin Spain, Catalonia, Costa Brava
Style Dry red wine, 14% ABV
Grapes C. Sauvignon, Merlot, Cariñena, Grenache

Catena Alta
Malbec 2010

Origin Argentina, Mendoza
Style Dry red wine, 14.1% ABV
Grape Malbec

The castle of Perelada hosts a popular summer festival, a casino, a wine therapy spa, and a well-known bodega. The castle was purchased in 1923 by industrialist Miguel Mateu Plá, and in its Carmelite cellar his nephew Arturo Suqué has established a successful winemaking business that has led the DO Empordá-Costa Brava since its foundation in 1975.

A less ambitious family might well have been content with the profits from its Cavas, its best-selling Blanc Pescador (5 million bottles a year), and other inexpensive high-volume wines. But in the 1990s they purchased several privileged plots, taking the total vineyard to 370 acres (150 ha), renovated the original bodega, and started a new experimental winery, producing there a selection of cult wines called Ex Ex (Exceptional Experiences).

Gran Claustro showed its true colors from its first vintage in 1993. With a name referring to the castle's Grand Cloister, it shies away from other more recent wines of this bodega. Almost opaque, it offers an intense nose of blackberries, balsamic, cocoa, and forest floor. In the mouth it is very powerful, with ripe fruit, rich tannins, and an extended finish. **JMB**

🍷🍷🍷 **Drink: recent vintages for up to 15 years**

The Catena vineyards on the slopes of the Andes range in altitude from 2,560 feet (780 m) in Este Mendocino to 4,920 feet (1,500 m) in Valle de Uco. Altitude is important: With it, Malbec ripens more slowly, preserving acidity and greater levels of anthocyanins and phenolics because of the enhanced UV light exposure. The result is wine with more intensity and color, and with fresher acidity.

Nicolás Catena has led the way in raising the international profile of Malbec, Argentina's most widely planted red variety. He has instituted a research program to understand the factors influencing quality in Malbec wines. The first Catena Alta Malbec was made in 1996. Originally a single-vineyard wine from the Angélica vineyard in the Lunlunta district, the Alta Malbec is now a blend from five vineyard blocks. It is this blending of different sites with distinctive characteristics that helps make the Alta Malbec the wine that it is.

Even the fairly frequent warm vintages still represent what is good about this wine: The hallmark of the Catena style is refinement and balance, but with a big personality. **JG**

🍷🍷 **Drink: recent vintages for up to 10 years**

Dom. Sylvain Cathiard *Vosne-Romanée PC Les Malconsorts* 2000

Origin France, Burgundy, Côte de Nuits
Style Dry red wine, 13% ABV
Grape Pinot Noir

Les Malconsorts is an outstanding premier cru, one of the half dozen most distinguished of its rank. In any village other than Vosne-Romanée it would surely have been classified as grand cru. It lies immediately to the south of La Tâche on the same mid-slope elevation. The wines have a consistent quality across the vintages, with an exceptional density of fruit in a harmonious register. The Cathiards own 1.85 acres (0.75 ha) of the total 14.5 acres (6 ha). Sylvain's grandfather, a foundling from Savoy, came to Burgundy and found work with Domaines de la Romanée-Conti and Lamarche, before buying a few parcels of vineyards for himself.

Sylvain Cathiard succeeded like no other vigneron in 2000. At a tasting of over 200 wines from this vintage two years after bottling, Cathiard's Malconsorts far outshone all other premiers crus and all but two grands crus. The wine is glorious to drink in its youth, a scintillating mouthful of ripe red fruit that floods to all parts of the palate. It will be several years before secondary aromas bring a further level of complexity to the party, though for those with the patience it will be well worth the wait. **JM**

ϴϴϴϴ **Drink: to 2017+**

Cavallotto *Barolo Riserva Bricco Boschis Vigna San Giuseppe* 1999

Origin Italy, Piedmont, Langhe
Style Dry red wine, 14.5% ABV
Grape Nebbiolo

The village of Castiglione Falletto is one of only three towns whose entire area qualifies for Barolo production. It is also the hottest of all the growing zones. The village's complex soils yield wines of ample bouquet and complexity.

Barolos from leading estate Cavallotto are noted for their power, grace, and balance. Both their cellars and the vineyards are located on the Bricco Boschis hill. Their 8.5-acre (3.5 ha) vineyard in the middle of the hill, Vigna San Giuseppe, which produces the best grapes, is bottled separately as Riserva Vigna San Giuseppe. Fifty-year-old vines generate concentrated flavors and the soil mix of sand with calcareous marls lends the wine its finesse, and clay its longevity. The near Mediterranean microclimate of the famed cru is evident in the estate's exotic plants, including banana trees, which thrive in the heat and sheltered slopes of Bricco Boschis.

Cavallotto makes Barolo in a classical style, and the 1999, an exceptional vintage for Barolo, has an ample bouquet, impeccable balance, and concentrated flavors. It will continue to age beautifully for years. **KO**

ϴϴϴ **Drink: to 2029+**

Domaine du Cayron
Gigondas 1998

Origin France, Southern Rhône, Gigondas
Style Dry red wine, 14.5% ABV
Grapes Grenache Noir, Syrah, Cinsaut, Mourvèdre

Château de Chamirey *Mercurey*
Premier Cru Les Cinq 2010

Origin France, Burgundy, Côte Chalonnaise
Style Dry red wine, 13.5% ABV
Grape Pinot Noir

Michel Faraud is the fourth generation of his family to run the 40-acre (16 ha) Gigondas estate since 1840. He works with his three daughters. Just one cuvée is produced, from 70 percent Grenache, with the rest Syrah and Cinsaut, and a touch of Mourvèdre. The average age of the vines is forty-five years and the yields are kept decidedly low. The wine is aged in old tuns for six months to a year. It is bottled without recourse to either fining or filtration. They make somewhat more than 60,000 bottles a year.

The soils are clay-based, and Gigondas is often seen as the more masculine, less subtle face of Châteauneuf-du-Pape. The identifying characteristic of a good Gigondas is the aroma of brown sugar, to which Domaine du Cayron also adds something earthy. This is coupled with the smells of meat and Provencal herbs. Robert Parker, in particular, admires this "sexy Provencal fruit bomb," in which he finds licorice, kirsch, smoke, and incense.

This is above all a food wine, to drink with a highly flavored southern daube (beef braised in olive oil and wine), with lots of garlic, rosemary, and thyme. **GM**

🍷🍷🍷 **Drink: to 2018**

Château de Chamirey is one of the most dynamic and historic producers in the Côte Chalonnaise, and is helping to raise the reputation of a region that has been steadily improving over recent years.

Mercurey is the largest appellation in the Côte Chalonnaise and produces its most profound and powerful reds. Château de Chamirey owns 91½ acres (37 ha) here, of which 37 acres (15 ha) are premier cru. The Marquis de Jouennes was bottling red Mercurey under the name of the Château in 1934, and the property is now managed by his son-in-law, Bertrand Devillard, and his children Amaury and Aurore.

In 2009, a great vintage, they decided to bottle a special cuvée called Les Cinq, because it was a blend of the best barrels of their five premiers crus. In 2010, another very successful year, they blended only eight barrels from these fives sites, for a total of 1,904 bottles. Although all the barrels are new, the oak is beautifully integrated in a wine that is effortlessly grand: fine and focused but with exceptional depth, harmony, and silken suavity of tannin, and a fantastic, flourishing finish, it is a sumptuous wine that is as highly rated as any in the region. **NB**

🍷🍷🍷🍷 **Drink: to 2025+**

Château du Cèdre
Le Cèdre 2002

Origin France, Southwest, Cahors
Style Dry red wine, 14.1% ABV
Grape Malbec

In 1987 Pascal Verghaeghe and his brother Jean-Marc took over the Château du Cèdre domaine, which was founded by their father in 1956.

Cahors has three main terroirs: river gravels, clay-limestone terraces, and the pure limestone upland. All the Cèdre wines are blends of the first two. "I had to forget my initial Burgundian idea of one wine, one terroir; here the Bordeaux notion of blending works better, with power from the gravels and finesse and fat from the clay-limestone." Le Cèdre is pure Malbec, made from low-yielding, forty-year-old vines. After sorting and destemming, the grapes are lightly pressed. Extraction is long and slow, using hand-punching and a forty-day maceration period. The wine goes into new oak for malolactic, and stays there for twenty months.

Opaque black in color, this wine is chiefly remarkable for the density and explosive definition of its taut, almost bitter-edged sloe fruits. The oak shapes that fruit, though near invisibly; smoke and iron provide forest whispers. This is the dense, ambitious Cahors of historical legend rendered intelligibly sumptuous for a new century. **AJ**

🅖🅖🅖 Drink: to 2017+

M. Chapoutier *Châteauneuf-du-Pape, Barbe Rac* 2001

Origin France, Southern Rhône, Châteauneuf-du-Pape
Style Dry red wine, 15.2% ABV
Grape Grenache Noir

Michel Chapoutier was an enormous fan of the late Jacques Reynaud of Château Rayas, whose wines were reputedly 100 percent Grenache Noir. The Chapoutiers have a 79-acre (32 ha) plot in Châteauneuf from which they produce an enduring Grenache-based wine called La Bernadine. Although the Chapoutiers are *négociants* based in the Northern Rhône, their wines have none of the jaded character of the branded wines of the region. Once the brothers Michel and Marc Chapoutier inherited the family business from their father in the early 1990s, Michel set out to make an all-Grenache cuvée with Barbe Rac from a 10-acre (4 ha) hilltop site west of the village of Châteauneuf, using some of his oldest Grenache vines.

The first vintage of Barbe Rac was made in 1991. Since then the Chapoutiers have embraced biodynamism and have been championed by Robert Parker. The 2001 vintage is now a mature take on Barbe Rac. Parker describes it as smelling of "garrigue, licorice, kirsch liqueur, cassis, and new saddle leather," and gives it a life of fifteen to twenty years. It is at its best with Provençal lamb. **GM**

🅖🅖🅖🅖🅖 Drink: to 2021

Châteauneuf-du-Pape's ruined castle was built by Pope John XXII. ➡

M. Chapoutier
Ermitage Le Pavillon 1999

Origin France, Northern Rhône, Hermitage
Style Dry red wine, 13% ABV
Grape Syrah

Michel Chapoutier is small, dynamic, and obsessive; and his obsession is terroir. "I want to make a perfect photograph of the terroir," he says.

The terroir of Ermitage Le Pavillon is about 10 acres (4 ha) of Les Bessards, composed of granite subsoil under sedimentary deposits. This is the soil known as gore, decomposed and ferruginous. The Syrah vines, averaging sixty-five years of age, are cultivated biodynamically; this, along with barriques to replace the old chestnut casks that had filled the winery in his father's day, was one of the great innovations that Michel made when he took over in the late 1980s.

One of the reasons winemakers go biodynamic is to enable their wines to express the terroir more clearly, and Michel has taken this to its logical conclusion by releasing various individual cuvées, of which this is one. In youth it can have an almost floral nose, with savory, deep, coffee, and coal-smoke fruit, black cherries, and a silky texture. This 1999 is dense and sleek, vigorous and muscular, with flavors of tar, herbs, and black olives, lovely balance and grace, and a long finish. **MR**

ᕫᕫᕫᕫ **Drink: to 2030**

Chappellet *Signature*
Cabernet Sauvignon 2004

Origin USA, California, Napa Valley
Style Dry red wine, 15% ABV
Grapes C. Sauvignon 80%, Merlot 13%, Others 7%

Vines were planted at Chappellet in 1963 and the estate—one of the oldest in the region—bought by Donn Chappellet in 1967. The robust Cabernets produced here in the 1970s soon won acclaim.

It is a superb site. The stony soil gives the wines a lot of extract, and an elevation of 1,200 feet (366 m) helps retain acidity. Donn's son Cyril has revitalized the estate, replanting underperforming vineyards, altering the varietal mix, improving farming techniques, and installing drip irrigation. By the early 2000s the vineyards were all organic. Today the focus is very much on Cabernet Sauvignon, which does exceptionally well in this area. The regular bottling is the Signature Selection, and there is also a considerably more expensive Pritchard Hill cuvée made in far smaller quantities, though it is usually only a notch superior to the Signature Selection.

The 2004 is exceptional, with black fruits and a discreet smokiness on the nose. It is very ripe, displaying ample blackberry fruit, without being too jammy, and there is a juiciness and vigor that fires up the palate; again, there is that smoky oakiness on the long finish. **SBr**

ᕫᕫᕫ **Drink: to 2025**

Domaine Chave
Ermitage Cuvée Cathelin 1990

Origin France, Northern Rhône, Hermitage
Style Dry red wine, 14% ABV
Grape Syrah

Château Cheval Blanc
1998

Origin France, Bordeaux, St.-Emilion
Style Dry red wine, 13% ABV
Grapes Merlot 55%, Cabernet Franc 45%

Gérard Chave—known as the winemaker's favorite winemaker—is retired now and has handed on the reins to his son and successor, Jean-Louis. The clue to his magnificence was great land, ripe grapes, and meticulous construction. His vines in the *lieux-dits* of Diognères, Péléat, Beaumes, Bessards, and Hermite all played their roles in constructing the greatest of all Hermitages.

Chave wanted to make the best from what was a small but manageable domaine operated from an unpretentious house on the left bank of the Rhône. The cellars behind were covered in venerable candyfloss mold, which would have had many New World winemakers running for cover. After he acquired the estate of the Irish archaeologist Terence Gray, he had nearly 40 acres (16 ha) on the hill of Hermitage plus another 2.5 acres (1 ha) in St.-Joseph. His production was around 40,000 bottles a year.

The Cuvée Cathelin 1990 was considered perfection by Robert Parker. It is decidedly meaty: roast beef with cubes of smoked bacon and a good twist of pepper. It would be wonderful with braised beef and black olives. **GM**

🍷🍷🍷🍷🍷 Drink: to 2025

Clive Coates MW describes Cheval Blanc as "the only great wine in the world made predominantly from Cabernet Franc." The *encépagement* of the 1998, however, uses more Merlot than Cabernet Franc.

Early picking meant that the Merlot was harvested before heavy rains on September 27, avoiding any risk of dilution. Overall yields were remarkably low, resulting in a wine of huge concentration and richness. As one might expect of such a formidable wine, it is still relatively closed, though it already suggests spicy, cedarwood complexity with the characteristic Cheval Blanc berry fruit character.

Although only two years older than the 2000, the 1998 is already far more advanced and complex. The deliciously luscious palate also shows restraint and elegance. This lacks the sheer concentration of the 2000 but has finer tannins to match its velvety fruit texture, with simply wonderful length. Cheval Blanc 1998, as with the 2001 and 2000, has an alcohol level in excess of 13 percent. An outstanding Cheval Blanc that will assume legendary status alongside the 1947 and 1921 as it develops. **SG**

🍷🍷🍷🍷🍷 Drink: to 2030+

Domaine de Chevalier

1995

Origin France, Bordeaux, Pessac-Léognan
Style Dry red wine, 13% ABV
Grapes C. Sauvignon, Merlot, C. Franc, Petit Verdot

As you approach Chevalier from the town of Léognan, you can see how the vineyard is fringed by the pine forests of the Landes. Indeed, this is one of most westerly, and thus coolest, vineyards in Bordeaux. Such conditions clearly benefit the estate's white wine, but the red vines, which make up by far the largest proportion of the vineyard, can struggle to ripen. But ripen they usually do, urged on by owner Olivier Bernard's attention to yields.

The relative coolness of Chevalier means that the domaine never delivers a hefty red wine. No Latour or Pavie will ever emerge from here. The finest examples of red Chevalier are miracles of finesse rather than power. Their delicacy can lead them to be underestimated in their youth, yet with bottle age, mysteriously, they often take on more density and weight. Bernard admits to using a concentrator in most vintages, just to raise the alcohol level by half a degree or so, which, in his view, gives the wine greater vinosity. Unusually, the vinification includes the Burgundian method of *pigeage* (punching down the cap) rather than the more Bordelais pumpovers.

The elegant 1995 is particularly voluptuous here, with wonderfully complex aromas of woodsmoke, truffles, and tobacco, as well as red fruits. The delicious fruit is balanced by fine acidity, and although not a fleshy wine, it is tight and complex and beautifully structured. Hitting its prime after twelve years, it will cruise on for many more. **SBr**
🚫🚫🚫 **Drink: to 2025+**

Bottles laid out for a vertical tasting of Domaine de Chevalier. ➜

VICARD
TONNELLERIE

DISTINCTION

Thin / Medium plus toast / Toasted heads

CHIMNEY ROCK

Chimney Rock *Stags Leap*
Cabernet Sauvignon Reserve 2003

Origin USA, California, Napa Valley
Style Dry red wine, 14.2% ABV
Grapes Cabernet Sauvignon, Merlot, Petit Verdot

Chryseia
2005

Origin Portugal, Douro Valley
Style Dry red wine, 13% ABV
Grapes Touriga Nacional, Touriga Franca, Tinta Roriz

In 1980 Sheldon "Hack" Wilson and his wife, Stella, purchased the Chimney Rock golf course on the Silverado Trail in Napa Valley's Stags Leap District and converted nine holes into 75 acres (30 ha), mostly planted to Cabernet Sauvignon. The Terlato family, who first joined as partners and have had sole ownership since 2004, recently converted the last nine holes to grapevines.

Replanting after Napa's phylloxera epidemic in the 1990s led Chimney Rock to focus on red wines crafted to reveal soft, elegant fruit. The grapes are destemmed, but not crushed, and no press wine is used in the blend. This, along with *élevage* in French oak (50 percent new) to highlight the fruit, has caused the wines' texture to become legendary, with language such as "plush," "supple," and "rich" consistently being used to characterize the wines.

Chimney Rock's 2003 Cabernet Sauvignon, with its genesis in a cooler year, shows silky, elegant fruit and tannin structure, dark cassis flavors, subtle mineral notes, and firmer acidity, suggesting greater longevity than the more voluptuous, perhaps more obvious, 2002. **LGr**

🍷🍷🍷 **Drink: to 2025+**

Chryseia is one of the new wave of unfortified Douro wines and the first to be a joint venture with a winemaker closely associated with the finest of Bordeaux—in this case, Bruno Prats, the former owner of Château Cos d'Estournel.

Only the best years will be released; in lesser years, only the second label Post-Scriptum will be made. Grapes are sourced from the steep vineyards of Quintas Vila Velha, Bomfim, and Perdiz, along with Vesuvio in some years. Rigorous *triage* limits the production. The wine is vinified at the ultra-modern Quinta do Sol winery, downstream from Pinhão. It was released through the Bordeaux *négociants*, ensuring wide availability despite limited volumes.

The 2005 is a lighter and more elegant wine than the 2003 or 2004. In flavor, it is clearly Portuguese, having the classic aromas of Touriga Nacional. In style, it is more New World, yet the Bordeaux influence is still clear in the finesse and elegance of touch. Black-currant fruit is overlaid with cedar and vanilla, with a perfumed floral character from the Touriga Nacional. Firm yet velvety, with an integrated tannic structure—all very harmonious. **GS**

🍷🍷🍷 **Drink: to 2017+**

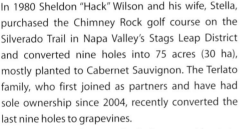

Chimney Rock ages its wines in French oak barrels.

Domaine Auguste Clape
Cornas 1990

Origin France, Northern Rhône, Cornas
Style Dry red wine, 13% ABV
Grape Syrah

Domenico Clerico
Barolo Percristina 2000

Origin Italy, Piedmont, Langhe
Style Dry red wine, 14.5% ABV
Grape Nebbiolo

Of the great red appellations of the northern Rhône, Cornas is perhaps the least easily understood. Its wines often appear more tightly clenched in their youth than other young Syrahs, and they can eerily resemble Syrah-based blends from further south when grown in the less propitious sites. Not so Clape.

The vineyards of this estate are set back on south-facing terraces, protected from the desiccating effect of the Mistral. Soils are the typical granitic clay. All these factors contribute to grapes that habitually ripen to formidable levels of potential alcohol and possess unearthly concentration.

Vinification in open wooden fermenters is followed by a combination of pumping and treading to maximize color and phenolic extraction; the wine is then given as much as two years' barrel maturation in a mixture of large *foudres* and smaller barriques. In its second decade, the glorious 1990 vintage began to acquire aromas of dried fruits—figs and raisins—allied to the strongly gamey notes that mature Rhônes take on. Tannins and fruit are in perfect balance; there are wafts of coffee and herbs, and the wine ends with a beautifully integrated finish. **SW**
😊😊😊😊😊 Drink: to 2020+

Domenico Clerico, who bottled his first Barolo in 1979, is one of the founding members of Barolo's Modernist school. He and his colleagues have been accused by more traditionally minded neighbors of betraying Barolo's traditionally austere and aristocratic nature, but Clerico remains unruffled by the criticism of his fruit-driven wines, believing that prudent use of new oak can round out Barolo's harsh edges and enhance the flavor profile.

Clerico's Percristina is made from the Cristina vineyard, situated at 1,214 feet (370 m) above sea level. He acquired his vines here in 1995, some of them up to fifty-six years old.

The hot 2000 vintage was highly acclaimed in Piedmont, though the wines have slightly lower acidity than normal, balanced by velvety tannins. Barolos from this vintage are enjoyable earlier than normal but will still improve over the medium term. Clerico's Percristina, layered with ripe cherry and hints of spice, was aged for twenty-five months in new barriques, and although it will continue to age gracefully for several more years, it was also enjoyable in its youth. **KO**
😊😊😊😊 Drink: to 2020+

Clonakilla
Shiraz/Viognier 2006

Origin Australia, New South Wales, Canberra
Style Dry red wine, 14.5% ABV
Grapes Shiraz 94%, Viognier 6%

In 1971, Irish-born John Kirk bought a 44-acre (18 ha) farm near the village of Murrumbateman, 25 miles (40 km) north of Canberra, and planted 1.2 acres (0.5 ha) each of Cabernet Sauvignon and Riesling.

Throughout the 1970s and 1980s, the Cabernet and Shiraz were blended together in the then traditional Australian style. Wines from the 1990 vintage were bottled separately and the Shiraz won several awards, alerting Kirk to the potential of Murrumbateman Shiraz. Inspired by Marcel Guigal's single-vineyard blends of Shiraz and Viognier, Clonakilla began including a small amount of Viognier in its own Shiraz from 1992.

Bottled alone, New South Wales Shiraz tends to be peppery, with burly tannins, but Clonakilla's blend captures the best of both worlds and reflects its relatively cool-climate origins. Ranked "Outstanding" in Langton's "Classification of Australian Wine," the 2006 vintage marks the fifteenth release of this wine. Its only rival as an Australasian Shiraz/Viognier blend is Torbreck's RunRig. In 1998 the Kirks began bottling some Viognier by itself, and this, too, is now seen as an Australian benchmark for the style. **SG**

⊖⊖⊖ **Drink: to 2018+**

Clos de l'Oratoire
1998

Origin France, Bordeaux, St.-Emilion
Style Dry red wine, 13% ABV
Grapes Merlot 90%, C. Sauvignon 5%, C. Franc 5%

Once Graf Stephan von Neipperg had restored the fortunes of Canon La Gaffelière, he turned his attention to Clos de l'Oratoire, which his father had bought in 1971. The vines here are planted on a clay-limestone slope, with sandier soils lower down.

The viticulture is essentially organic, with green cover planted between the rows. Vinification is similar to that at Canon La Gaffelière, with fermentation in wooden vats and punching-down of the cap. Neipperg and his consultant, Stéphane Derenoncourt, increase the hedonistic appeal of the wine by aging it in a high proportion of new barrels.

Neipperg keeps the price of the wine at reasonable levels because he knows well that this is a location that gives exceptional results only in warm years when the grapes ripen fully. In cooler years, which have become something of a rarity, Clos de l'Oratoire can be less successful. 1998 was a splendid year, and the wine has admirable lushness and plumpness, without succumbing to flabbiness. It retains some tannic structure and an admirable balance. It was a pleasure to drink in its youth, but has kept its opulent fruit and stylishness. **SBr**

⊖⊖ **Drink: to 2018**

Clos de los Siete

2004

Origin Argentina, Mendoza, Uco Valley
Style Dry red wine, 15% ABV
Grapes Malbec 45%, Merlot 35%, Others 20%

You would expect a blockbuster project (hatched by winemaker Michel Rolland and the late Jean-Michel Arcaute in the late 1990s) to produce a blockbuster wine. Yet although Clos de los Siete is a big, ripe, concentrated wine, it is not so dense, extracted, or over-oaked as to be fairly described as such.

Part of the reason is Rolland's switch from his Old World technique to soaking the juice on the chilled skins before fermentation starts; this extracts flavor without too much tannin. Leaving the red in oak barrels after fermentation can flesh out the tannins, and add a touch of flavor complexity. The grapes come from vineyards (planted by some of France's leading wine families) at Vistaflores, in the Tunuyán department of Mendoza's high Uco Valley region.

Rolland's task is to select the best vats from which to make the Clos de los Siete (Club of Seven) blend. Anything left over is used by each investor for their own brands. The combination of Michel Rolland's enological restraint and the Uco Valley's terroir, which favors wines with a higher natural acidity than those from the rest of Mendoza, is a mouthwatering combination. **MW**

🍷🍷 **Drink: to 2020**

Clos de Tart

2005

Origin France, Burgundy, Côte de Nuits
Style Dry red wine, 13.5% ABV
Grape Pinot Noir

The 17-acre (7 ha) Clos de Tart was created in the twelfth century by the abbey of Tart, and remained in ecclesiastical hands until secularization was imposed during the French Revolution. Like so many Burgundian estates, the Clos underperformed in the 1960s and 1970s, but renaissance came after the appointment in 1995 of Sylvain Pitiot as manager.

The Clos de Tart forms a square of vineyards, planted on rather poor clay-limestone soils that enjoy exceptional drainage. Pitiot has divided the vineyards into various sectors, giving him a wide palate of wines from which to form his final blend.

Pitiot destems but does not crush the bunches, favors a cold soak for about one week, ferments with natural yeasts, and keeps the barrels in a very cool cellar so as to delay the malolactic fermentation for as long as possible. The whole crop is aged in new oak. The magnificent 2005 is typical of Clos de Tart at its best. There are cherries on the nose, but also an aroma of violets frequently found in this wine. The texture is velvety, the fruit pure, ripe, and concentrated but still reticent, and fine, almost racy acidity sustains the very long finish. **SBr**

🍷🍷🍷🍷 **Drink: to 2030**

Clos des Papes

2001

Origin France, Southern Rhône, Châteauneuf-du-Pape
Style Dry red wine, 13.5% ABV
Grapes Grenache 65%, Mourvèdre 20%, Others 15%

As early as 1896, the great-grandfather of current owner Vincent Avril started bottling wine under the Clos des Papes name. Today, Burgundy-trained Vincent runs the property with his family. Despite its name, the estate actually draws fruit from eighteen separate parcels scattered across 79 acres (32 ha) of prime Châteauneuf territory.

Clos des Papes' red Châteauneuf is made from up to thirteen different grape varieties, though the emphasis is on Grenache and Mourvèdre. The wine is aged in only 20 percent new oak, so as not to overpower its fruit. Avril has installed a "fogging machine" to keep the maturing wines in an atmosphere of high humidity, even when the warm Mistral wind is blowing through the Rhône Valley.

Because of its rich fruit, Clos des Papes can be consumed at or near release, though the finest examples will age gracefully for up to twenty years or more. It starts to show its best after five or so years of cellaring, and can be drunk pleasurably with lamb, duck, or game. The Avrils also make a non-vintage wine called Le Petit d'Avril, which is usually a blend of their three most recent vintages. **SG**

🍷🍷🍷 **Drink: to 2020+**

Clos Erasmus

1998

Origin Spain, Catalonia, Priorat
Style Dry red wine, 14.5% ABV
Grapes Grenache, Syrah, Cabernet Sauvignon

During the 1980s, Daphne Glorian was working in the wine trade in Europe. When René Barbier and Alvaro Palacios decided to settle in Priorat to resurrect this forgotten region, they invited some friends to join them. One of those was Glorian.

Glorian's wine, Clos Erasmus, is now one of the few cult wines from Spain. She sought out dry-farmed, old-vine Grenache, grown on steep slopes where the soil is mainly slate, planting some supplementary Syrah and Cabernet Sauvignon. Her barrels rested in Barbier's cellars until 2000 when she moved to her own space, the old theater in Gratallops that had previously hosted Palacios.

In 1989, the first vintage, all the grapes were fermented together, then bottled separately, giving birth to the new Priorat. Nearly ten years later, 1998 provided the ideal circumstances for producing a most impressive Erasmus. The color is very deep, close to black in its youth, and the aroma complex, with plenty of ripe berries, violets, dried herbs, and smoky notes from the barrel aging. Full-bodied in the mouth, it is dense, powerfully mineral (wet slate), persistent, long, and complex. **LG**

🍷🍷🍷🍷 **Drink: to 2025**

Clos Mogador 2001

Origin Spain, Catalonia, Priorat
Style Dry red wine, 14.5% ABV
Grapes Grenache, C. Sauvignon, Syrah, Others

René Barbier is, without doubt, the father of modern Priorat, the catalyst for the rebirth of the region's wines from 1989. He was the first really to believe in the potential of the region and his enthusiasm was very contagious, therefore he was able to convince others to move there with the aim of producing world-class wines. His belief and determination made it a reality.

Barbier is a descendant of French wine growers who established themselves in Penedès; the René Barbier label used to belong to them but was sold a long time ago. His vineyard is an immense slate amphitheater above the Siurana River, where he grows a variety of grapes—the typical ones from Priorat, but also some unusual ones like Pinot Noir and Monastrell, which may give his wine the little added dimension not found in others.

Sometimes tannic, backward, and reduced in its youth, Clos Mogador often does not show well in early blind tastings, but given time it is the most consistent, year in, year out, of all the Priorats. In more difficult years, it is not only a very good wine for the vintage, but a very good wine, period. And in great years, like 2001, it shines even brighter.

René Barbier junior is now working with his father and, so convivial is Priorat, he has married the girl from Clos Martinet (another one of the five original *clos* in the appellation), where they are currently making wine together with the help of other friends. The tradition continues. **LG**

🕉🕉🕉 **Drink: to 2018+**

FURTHER RECOMMENDATIONS
Other great vintages
1994 • 1998 • 1999 • 2004 • 2010
More producers from Priorat
Clos Erasmus • Costers del Siurana
Mas Martinet • Alvaro Palacios

Clos Mogador started the Priorat wine revolution. ➡

Coldstream Hills *Reserve Pinot Noir* 2005

Origin Australia, Victoria, Yarra Valley
Style Dry red wine, 13.5% ABV
Grape Pinot Noir

James Halliday and his wife Suzanne established Coldstream Hills in 1985 and it has grown to become one of Australia's leading small wineries. Although sold to Southcorp in 1996, Halliday continues to consult for Coldstream Hills and still lives in a house on the property. Coldstream Hills is located in the Yarra Valley, which, in vinous/climatic terms, is cooler than Bordeaux but a little warmer than Burgundy. It is recognized for producing some of the finest Pinot Noir and Chardonnay in Australia.

Based largely on grapes from the low-yielding Amphitheatre A Block—a steep, north-facing slope below the winery, planted in 1985, and bottled separately from the 2006 vintage—the estate's top wine has been its Reserve Pinot Noir, made from these superior parcels of grapes, which are then earmarked for special attention during vinification. "A higher percentage of new French oak, longer time in barrel, and selecting the best grapes places the emphasis on the wine's structure," says Coldstream Hills winemaker Andrew Fleming.

Reserve Pinot Noir is not made every year, and never exceeds 10 percent of the total Pinot Noir made, claims the estate. This highly regarded Australian cool-climate Pinot Noir displays strong varietal character, and is suitable for medium-term cellaring. Some have criticized it for almost caricaturing Burgundy, but in its best years it is an authentic portrait of cool-climate Australian Pinot Noir at its most compelling. **SG**
ⓈⓈⓈ **Drink: to 2017+**

FURTHER RECOMMENDATIONS
Other great vintages
1995 • 1996 • 1997 • 1998 • 2002 • 2004 • 2005
More Yarra Valley Pinot Noirs
De Bortoli • Mount Mary
Yarra Yering • Yering Station

Coldstream Hills is one of the loveliest wine estates in Australia. ➜

Colgin Cellars *Herb Lamb Vineyard Cabernet Sauvignon* 2001

Origin USA, California, Napa Valley
Style Dry red wine, 15% ABV
Grape Cabernet Sauvignon

Concha y Toro *Almaviva* 2000

Origin Chile, Maipo Valley
Style Dry red wine, 13.5% ABV
Grapes Cabernet Sauvignon 86%, Carmenère 14%

Through a fine art career, Ann Colgin learned a bit about what constitutes "cachet" and "fine," so when it came time to design her eponymous wine, she corralled the best and the brightest.

Colgin's first bottling in 1992 came exclusively from the Herb Lamb Vineyard, a 7.4-acre (3 ha) plot owned by Herb and Jennifer Lamb. The following year they planted 5 acres (2 ha) of Cabernet Sauvignon on a steep, rocky hillside. The Lambs have replanted more than half the vineyard to Clone 7 grafted on to 110R rootstock. Colgin's fruit comes from selected rows at the top of the vineyard.

The winemaking is state of the art: early morning picking, double sorting, cold soaking, fermentation in stainless-steel tanks, twice-daily pump-overs, two to three week fermentations, and an additional thirty to forty days of post-fermentation maceration. Malolactic is in barrel, and the 2001 was aged for nineteen months in 100 percent new Taransaud barrels. The wine is neither fined nor filtered. Colgin Cellars now has two other estate vineyards, but it is the Herb Lamb bottling that sets the standard: It is seamless and exquisitely elegant. **LGr**

◒◒◒◒ **Drink: to 2025+**

Philippine, daughter of the late Baron Philippe de Rothschild, decided to follow her father's template of combining the natural resources of an emerging wine country with the experience of a more established one—and thus Almaviva was born, with Chile's Concha y Toro winery the other parent.

Before the deal was finalized, Concha y Toro's winemakers had been going through its best vineyards in the favored Puente Alto area that formed the backbone of their premium Don Melchor. Microvinification of small lots allowed the winemakers enough grapes for Almaviva, while making sure that they could make the most of those left for Don Melchor.

The 2000 wine was blended by Mouton's technical director, Patrick Léon, and Concha y Toro's French-trained winemaker, Enrique Tirado. It was the first vintage to be fermented and aged in Almaviva's futuristically curved winery, and is a clear step up in quality from previous vintages. The vineyard work done in previous years is most clearly felt on the wine's mid-palate, which combines juicy fruit flavors with fine fruit and oak tannins. **MW**

◒◒◒ **Drink: to 2018+**

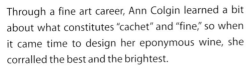

◪ Uninterrupted vines stride across the Napa Valley.

Concha y Toro
Don Melchor 2008

Origin Chile, Maipo Valley
Style Dry red wine, 14% ABV
Grapes Cabernet Sauvignon, Cabernet Franc

Château La Conseillante
2004

Origin France, Bordeaux, Pomerol
Style Dry red wine, 13% ABV
Grapes Merlot 80%, Cabernet Franc 20%

The influence of the Bordelais has always been apparent at Chile's largest wine producer, Concha y Toro. Company founder, businessman, and politician Don Melchor Concha y Toro started out with vines from the French region in the 1880s, with the help of a French winemaker. So when, a century later, the company decided to introduce a wine named after the Don that they intended to compete with the world's best red wines, it was only natural they should seek the advice of the leading Bordelais winemakers of the time, Emile Peynaud and his colleague, Eric Boissenot.

Chilean Enrique Tirado has, since 1997, overseen the development of the 282-acre (114-ha) Puente Alto vineyard in the Alto Maipo. In Tirado's hands, the wine has a distinctive Chilean—or Puente Alto—character, an expression of Cabernet Sauvignon from seven distinct gravel plots with varying (but always small) proportions of Cabernet Franc that has a core of the region's generous, ripe black currant fruit, shaded with mint and French oak, and a texture of fine-grained tannins and balancing natural acidity that gives the wine long-term cellaring potential. **DW**
🍷🍷🍷 **Drink: to 2025**

Château La Conseillante is unusual, at least in Pomerol, in having been under the same ownership—the Nicolas family of Libourne—since 1871. Since 2004 the director and winemaker has been the energetic Jean-Michel Laporte, who has maintained the estate's extremely high standards.

The soils, as so often in Pomerol, are varied. Just more than half the vines are planted on clay soils, the rest on sandy gravel, with some stonier sectors close to Pétrus. No doubt, all this contributes to the complexity and subtlety of the wine.

Although La Conseillante is impressive in its youth, it needs ten years to show its immense sensuous appeal, its aromas of truffles and licorice, its velvety texture, its succulent fruitiness, its impeccable balance and length. The 2004 in its youth had explosive black-cherry aromas, a firm tannic grip behind its svelte texture, but the wine will evolve superbly over decades. For some reason, La Conseillante has been underrated by some wine critics, which means that, although prices are far from cheap, they remain reasonable given the quality and staying power of the wine. **SBr**
🍷🍷🍷 **Drink: to 2030**

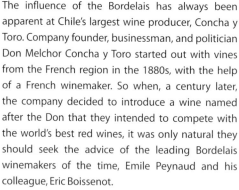

Conseillante wines are renowned for their staying power. ➡

CRU POMET O...

CONSEILLAN

1912

N

Contador

2004

Origin Spain, Rioja
Style Dry red wine, 14% ABV
Grape Tempranillo

Benjamín Romeo's personal project Contador took off in the late 1990s as a small bodega—just 38 acres (15 ha), with a self-imposed future production limit of 20,000 bottles. Romeo's first few years there coincided with his last ones at Artadi, where he worked as enologist for fifteen years.

Although there is no venerable track record to support the reputation of Contador's reds (named Contador, Cueva del Contador, and La Viña de Andrés), they speak for themselves every time a cork is pulled. If one believes that some young wines really can be worth several hundred dollars a bottle, then Contador 2004 (and do not overlook the excellent 2005) must be among that group. It is a great wine, of firm but silky tannins, brilliant acidity, excellent fruit expression, and voluptuous mouthfeel, all wrapped in superlative elegance.

Every aficionado has felt at some point a certain perverse satisfaction when tasting a wine of high price and prestige that fails to match the high expectations it has created. Assuredly, this is far from being the case with Benjamín Romeo's wines, least of all his magnificent Contador 2004. **JB**
🍇🍇🍇🍇🍇 Drink: to 2020+

Giacomo Conterno

Barolo Monfortino Riserva 1990

Origin Italy, Piedmont, Langhe
Style Dry red wine, 14% ABV
Grape Nebbiolo

The 1990 vintage was nearly perfect in Piedmont thanks to a hot, dry summer with just enough rain and naturally occurring low yields. Giacomo Conterno's Barolo Monfortino from this vintage is undoubtedly one of Italy's greatest wines, known for its heroic structure and marathon aging potential.

The 1990s were bellicose years for winemakers in Italy, and Barolo in particular, because traditionalists were criticized for adhering to what many regarded as old-fashioned cellar techniques, particularly in regard to wood-aging. Giovanni Conterno carried on regardless, aging the Monfortino 1990 for seven years in large oak casks. Adhering loyally to his late father's philosophy, Roberto Conterno has not reduced Monfortino's length of wood-aging, blatantly eschewing the smaller French barriques that tend to soften the complex character of Barolo.

The Monfortino 1990 has proudly triumphed as a quintessential Barolo of power and class, and is still very youthful with firm but silky tannins and crisp acidity. The wine's hallmark sensations of licorice, mint, and floral nuances evolve slowly in the glass, and the wine still needs years to reach its peak. **KO**
🍇🍇🍇🍇🍇 Drink: to 2040+

Conterno Fantino
Barolo Parussi 2001

Origin Italy, Piedmont, Langhe
Style Dry red wine, 14% ABV
Grape Nebbiolo

Cousins by marriage, Guido Fantino and Claudio Conterno founded Conterno Fantino in 1982, at first working their fathers' holdings in Monforte and later acquiring more vineyards.

Conterno advocates sustainable viticulture, using only organic nutrition and sowing field beans and other legumes in every other row to keep a natural balance. Fantino is in charge of the cellar where, after some years of experimentation, he switched to new barriques for malolactic fermentation and aging.

The Parussi vineyard is one of the top sites in Castiglione Falletto, and Conterno Fantino leased land here from 1997 to 2001, during which time it produced its single-vineyard Barolo of the same name. Thanks to the lighter calcareous soil, Parussi yields elegant Barolos with softer tannins by comparison with the more muscular Barolos from Monforte. The Parussi 2001, the last to be bottled by Conterno Fantino before the vineyard owners decided to take back the vineyard and make the wine themselves, is well structured but refined, with ripe fruit and sweet tannins. Although enjoyable young, it should age well for several years yet. **KO**

🍷🍷🍷 **Drink: to 2021+**

Contino
Viña del Olivo 1996

Origin Spain, Rioja
Style Dry red wine, 13.5% ABV
Grapes Tempranillo 95%, Graciano 5%

Founded in 1973, Contino produces wines only from its own grapes. It was a pioneer in single-vineyard wines in this region, where blending was the norm.

The style was revolutionary for the mid-1970s: darker in color, with more fruit, French rather than American oak, the Tempranillo being complemented by a little Graciano—almost extinct by then, but happily recovered now, partly thanks to Contino.

Viña del Olivo was first produced in 1995 as the top-of-the-range bottling. Contino wanted to experiment with some techniques, such as malolactic in new barrels, and started with a stricter selection of grapes so that they could withstand the new processes. It selected a vineyard on a chalky slope, planted about twenty years previously, that was producing very small berries. After twenty-four months in barrel, a legendary new Rioja was born.

In 2000, this 1996 was voted the best red wine in Spain by some top Spanish enologists. Dark in color, complex, and elegant on the nose, with plenty of ripe red fruit, fine leather, and spicy, toasty, balsamic notes, it is flavorsome and rich in the mouth. It should age magnificently. **LG**

🍷🍷🍷🍷 **Drink: to 2020+**

Coppo
Barbera d'Asti Pomorosso 2004

Origin Italy, Piedmont, Monferrato
Style Dry red wine, 14% ABV
Grape Barbera

The Coppo family has been in the wine trade since the early 1900s, but it is the founder's four grandsons who have changed the emphasis toward high-quality production, focusing on Barbera.

The astuteness of the four young brothers allowed them to predict what would become the winning trends, and 1984 saw the birth of their Barbera Pomorosso, which they aged in small French oak barrels. Barbera, which was once scorned, became the pride of the entire region and today receives its due recognition.

Pomorosso, Coppo's flagship Barbera, is aged for fifteen months in barrique and offers a complex and fragrant bouquet of ripe cherries and blackberry, integrated with subtle notes of cherry liqueur, chocolate, espresso, and vanilla. A welcome change after the bizarre extremes of 2002 and 2003, 2004 was a classic vintage in Piedmont, yielding outstanding Barberas of freshness and structure. The Pomorosso 2004 is a hallmark Barbera d'Asti, sumptuous yet elegant, with crisp acidity and velvety tannins, which are still sufficiently structured to sustain the wine for several years. **KO**

🍷🍷🍷 **Drink: to 2019**

Coriole
Lloyd Reserve Shiraz 1994

Origin Australia, South Australia, McLaren Vale
Style Dry red wine, 14% ABV
Grape Shiraz

Coriole was established in 1967 by Hugh Lloyd and his wife Molly, and it is still very much a family affair, with their son, Mark, now in charge.

Lloyd Reserve is Coriole's flagship. Full-blooded and super-ripe, the wine avoids Portiness, excessive alcohol, or dead-fruit character because the grapes are never picked too late nor allowed to stress. It is a single-vineyard wine, from a block of old vines near the winery, planted in 1919 on poor, shaley soils. The site is slightly east-facing and relatively cool, which explains the elegance of the wine.

Fermentation is floating cap, with plunging and pump-over, and the decision to press is made by tasting, not by Baumé levels. Pressings are also added back according to taste. The wine finishes fermenting in tank before being transferred to oak—these days, 100 percent French. The 1994, an excellent red wine vintage, was made during the transition from American to French oak and was 50/50. Winemaker Simon White says Lloyd Reserve's peak drinking time is at ten to fifteen years, by which time the typical seaweed/iodine character of the Seaview subregion has asserted itself. **HH**

🍷🍷🍷 **Drink: to 2017+**

Corison *Cabernet Sauvignon*
Kronos Vineyard 2001

Matteo Correggia
Roero Ròche d'Ampsèj 1996

Origin USA, California, Napa Valley
Style Dry red wine, 13.8% ABV
Grape Cabernet Sauvignon

Origin Italy, Piedmont, Langhe
Style Dry red wine, 14.5% ABV
Grape Nebbiolo

Cathy Corison, like many who have worked for others, felt the persistent tug to make wine on her own terms, longing for the chance to make wines that are "both elegant and powerful."

It is the benchland alluvial soil on which all her vines grow that distinguishes the character of her Cabernet Sauvignon. Known as Bale gravelly loam, the soil has a small percentage of clay, which stores water to nourish the vines as they grow. Corison manages the vine to produce "purple, red, blue, and black fruits," with lush, fully resolved tannins right out of the vineyard. Elegant and sensual, Corison Cabernets offer a subtle sinew and no dearth of fresh fruit, while communicating a clear provenance with subtle "Rutherford dust" texture on the back palate.

Corison has owned the Kronos Vineyard since 1996. Planted in soils stonier than her other sources, the grapes retain their natural acidity, which Corison wants for both backbone and longevity. The Kronos 2001, aged in 50 percent new French barrels, is more understated than those from bigger vintages or styles; but with its firm structure, it exudes elegance, energy, and dynamic complexity. **LGr**

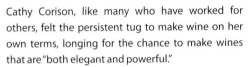 **Drink: to 2025**

Perhaps more than any other wine, Matteo Correggia's iconic Ròche d'Ampsèj accurately encapsulates the dreams and the passion of one man. The steep, sandy hills of his native Roero had long been considered viticulturally inferior to Barolo and Barbaresco, and its wines, produced from Nebbiolo and Arneis, were unfashionable. Matteo recognized that the area lacked nothing except investment. Stainless-steel tanks and new oak were both in short supply and yields were far too high.

Determined to raise the region's profile, and armed with a 7-acre (3 ha) parcel of twenty-five-year-old, high-density Nebbiolo, Matteo reduced yields, trimmed the maceration time to less than a week, and introduced 100 percent new oak. The improvement was as rapid as it was spectacular, and his uncompromising regime soon caught the eye of the press; by 1996 his Ròche d'Ampsèj had already scooped Italy's most desirable wine medal, the *Tre Bicchiere*. Largely through the efforts of this one man, who was tragically killed by a freak accident in 2001, the Roero ceased to be a viticultural backwater and was promoted to DOCG status in 2005. **MP**

⊖⊖⊖⊖ **Drink: to 2025+**

Cortes de Cima
Incógnito 2003

Origin Portugal, Alentejo
Style Dry red wine, 14.5% ABV
Grape Syrah

Cortes de Cima, one of the leading estates in Portugal's sunny Alentejo region, was established by Hans and Carrie Jorgensen in the late 1980s.

At the time the vineyard was planted, one of the key varieties here, Syrah, was illegal. As a result, the Jorgensens labeled the wine it yielded as Incognito. Since the first vintage, in 1998, this has gone on to become a standard-bearer for the Alentejo, reaching cult status within Portugal.

The Incógnito 2003 comes from a hot vintage, when the excessive heat actually delayed phenolic maturity in the grapes, but this has not had a negative effect on the wine. A staggered harvest occurred under cloudless skies, resulting in a dense, ripe wine that is extremely seductive, but that also has a more serious side. Although its warm climate origins are reflected in the ripeness of the fruit, it is a wine that sits somewhere between, say, the Barossa and the northern Rhône, though it is closer to the former than to the latter. Aged in a mix of half-French and half-American new oak barrels for eight months, this is a wine that should settle down with a year or two in bottle and drink well for many more. **JG**

🔇🔇 **Drink: to 2018**

COS
Cerasuolo di Vittoria 2010

Origin Italy, Sicily, Vittoria
Style Dry red wine, 13% ABV
Grapes Nero d'Avola, Frappato

In 1980, three school friends from Vittoria—Gianbattista Cilia, Giusto Occhipinti, and Giuseppina Strano—decided to make wine from their parents' vineyards to kill time before they went to university. On a shoestring budget, they crushed grapes by foot in an ancient cellar and fermented in an old concrete vat. In doing so, they resurrected the languishing Cerasuolo di Vittoria DOC and, unknowingly, became among the first pioneers in Sicily's wine renaissance.

In the late 1980s and early 1990s Cilia and Occhipinti visited California and were for a while influenced by its winemaking. But then they took a step back and began recycling barriques and using differently sized barrels. At a time when most firms were investing heavily in international varieties, COS continued to focus on native grapes Nero d'Avola and Frappato, blended together in Cerasuola.

COS insists on keeping the winemaking as natural as possible, shunning chemical treatments in the vineyards and cultured yeasts in the winery, where the red wines are bottled unfiltered. The Cerasuola di Vittoria is earthy and rich, with sweet fruit and a long mineral close. **KO**

🔇🔇 **Drink: to 2020+**

Château Cos d'Estournel
2002

Andrea Costanti
Brunello di Montalcino 2001

Origin France, Bordeaux, St.-Estèphe
Style Dry red wine, 13% ABV
Grapes C. Sauvignon 58%, Merlot 38%, Others 4%

Origin Italy, Tuscany, Montalcino
Style Dry red wine, 14% ABV
Grape Sangiovese

Château Cos d'Estournel was established in the early nineteenth century. In 1917 it was acquired by the Ginestet family and passed through marriage to the Prats family. In 1998 Bruno Prats sold the estate, but his son Jean-Guillaume remains as administrator, so that a measure of continuity is maintained.

In general, the vineyards of St.-Estèphe have considerably more clay than those of its neighbor Pauillac, but Cos d'Estournel is something of an exception, sharing a gravelly soil that is quite similar to that found at the great growths of Pauillac. However, Cos d'Estournel has considerably more Merlot planted than would be customary in Pauillac. Without it, the wine would be much more rugged and tannic, because the Merlot moderates the very structured Cabernet that the soils produce. In style the wine is sumptuous and concentrated, deep in color and flavor, yet it has more elegance than many wines from St.-Estèphe. It ages well.

The 2002 vintage, not universally successful in the Médoc, is excellent here, with toasty, chocolaty aromas from the substantial proportion of new oak, ample succulence, and a long, luxurious finish. **SBr**

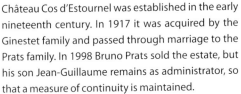 **Drink: to 2025**

A four-star vintage for Brunello, 2001 was exceptional in the higher reaches of the denomination. Here, in the original growing area, Sangiovese can reach unprecedented elegance and refinement, as at the Conti Costanti estate located at Colle al Matrichese. The vintage was so exceptional that Costanti even made a tiny amount of Riserva, the first since the great 1997 vintage.

The Costanti family relocated to Montalcino from Siena in the mid-1500s. They came into possession of vast holdings and built a large villa in which the family still resides. Tito Costanti was among the early pioneers who first vinified Sangiovese *in purezza* in the late nineteenth century, calling the wine Brunello. Conte Emilio built on his ancestor's achievements and began bottling Brunello in the 1960s.

Andrea Costanti took over in 1983 and continues the tradition of making stellar-quality Brunellos. He has enlisted the services of enologist Vittorio Fiore and, by skillfully blending tradition with innovation, using barrels of various sizes and ages, they produce highly fragrant and graceful wines. **KO**

🍷🍷🍷 **Drink: to 2020**

Costers del Siurana
Clos de l'Obac 1995

Origin Spain, Priorat
Style Dry red wine, 13.5% ABV
Grapes Garnacha, Cariñena, Syrah, Others

Couly-Dutheil
Chinon Clos de l'Echo 2005

Origin France, Loire, Touraine
Style Dry red wine, 13.5% ABV
Grape Cabernet Franc

This is the property of Carlos Pastrana and his wife Mariona Jarque, local folk among the group of five pioneers responsible for the comeback of wines from Priorat. Their winery name, Costers del Siurana ("banks of the Siurana"), refers to Siurana River.

Costers del Siurana was founded in 1987—the first vintage was 1989—but the Pastranas began work at the end of the 1970s, recovering old vineyards, planting new grape varieties, and restoring historical properties like Mas d'en Bruno. They use only grapes grown on their own properties, from dry-farmed vineyards, never use any pesticides or chemical products, and always vinify the same grape varieties for their different wines—the white Kyrie, red Miserere, sweet Dolç de l'Obac, and the top-of-the-range red Clos de l'Obac.

Clos de l'Obac is somehow different from other Priorats, leaning more toward finesse, with less color and concentration—a more elegant Priorat. The 1995 is still the best example. Offering an abundance of balsamic, mineral, and *garrigue* notes, it is full-bodied but well balanced and elegant, with cedar and eucalyptus on the long, satisfying finish. **LG**
❺❺❺❺ Drink: to 2020

In a region where most vignerons own small parcels, Couly-Dutheil has 225 acres (91 ha), and the *négociant* branch of the company a further 75 acres (30 ha). The bulk of Couly-Dutheil's product is good, though not exceptional. But then there is Clos de l'Echo, a beautiful, south-facing, 40-acre (16 ha) *lieu-dit*, on a mixture of clay and limestone, located next to the Château de Chinon. The world-class wines from this *clos* are aged in stainless-steel tanks in the cellars that extend into the cliff behind the winery.

In their youth, Clos de l'Echo wines like the 2005 are meaty, packed with black fruit flavors, high in tannins, and matched with a fair slug of acidity, so need five or more years before they really come into their own. The meaty flavors become soft and gamey, the black fruit becomes more aromatic, the tannins become finer, and the acidity keeps everything fresh. To illustrate, a Clos de l'Echo 1952 had an elegant nose with undernotes of hay, mushroom, and woodland undergrowth. The palate was soft, with a touch of leather and some raspberry fruit. Although it had a shortish finish, this was still a very sprightly fifty-year-old wine. **KA**
❺❺❺ Drink: to 2020+

Viña Cousiño Macul *Antiguas Reservas Cabernet Sauvignon* 2003

Craggy Range *Syrah Block 14 Gimblett Gravels Vineyard* 2005

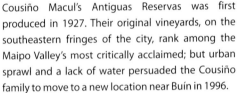

Origin Chile, Maipo Valley
Style Dry red wine, 13.5% ABV
Grape Cabernet Sauvignon

Origin New Zealand, Hawke's Bay
Style Dry red wine, 13% ABV
Grape Syrah

Cousiño Macul's Antiguas Reservas was first produced in 1927. Their original vineyards, on the southeastern fringes of the city, rank among the Maipo Valley's most critically acclaimed; but urban sprawl and a lack of water persuaded the Cousiño family to move to a new location near Buín in 1996.

Far from being a death knell, the move, with the addition of extra vineyards, plus a new winery in which fermenting tanks can be left in sealed chambers for temperature control, produced cleaner, riper, more balanced wines—the cramped surroundings of the old winery in the Santiago suburbs were conducive neither to picking at the right time, nor to the most hygienic storage.

Since 2002, Antiguas Reservas has reclaimed its position as a benchmark Chilean Cabernet, thanks to its expressive black fruit, fine-grained but generous tannin, and reasonable alcohol levels. Perhaps the fact that the winery remains family owned explains why the Cousiños refined their winemaking rather than renouncing it, as have so many of their peers, in favor of the modern French tendency for overextraction, overoaking, and overpricing. **MW**
🔊🔊 Drink: to 2018+

In the late 1980s, Australia-based businessman Terry Peabody decided to enter the wine business. Steve Smith MW advised him to buy the last available parcel of high-quality wine-growing land in the Gimblett Road subregion of Hawke's Bay. The Gimblett Gravels appellation is strictly determined by the gravelly soils laid down by the old Ngaruroro River and exposed after a huge flood in the 1860s.

Craggy Range (the costliest ever start-up for a New Zealand winery) produced its first wines in the 1999 vintage from its vineyards in Marlborough and Hawke's Bay. Two facilities, both located in Hawke's Bay, serve all production—the Giant's Winery, overlooked by Te Mata Peak, and the larger SH50.

Although it also makes high-quality Merlot and Pinot Noir (and white wines, too), Craggy Range does Syrah best of all. The 2005 is a deep, viscous purple, raising expectations of a blockbuster. However, Craggy makes its wines with a light touch, and this is remarkably restrained. The dark, brooding nose hints at Syrah spiciness and savory flavors. There are chalky tannins on the finish, and no hint of the alcohol burn that often mars Kiwi Syrah. **SG**
🔊🔊🔊 Drink: to 2017+

Cullen *Diana Madeline Cabernet Sauvignon Merlot* 2001

Origin Australia, Western Australia, Margaret River
Style Dry red wine, 14% ABV
Grapes Cabernet Sauvignon 75%, Merlot 25%

Dr. Kevin Cullen and his wife, Di, planted Margaret River's first experimental vines in 1966. In 1981, a decade after establishing the vineyards in Wilyabrup, Di became the full-time winemaker and planted Western Australia's first Merlot and Cabernet Franc, sowing the seeds of their flagship Bordeaux blend.

Di was succeeded as chief winemaker in 1989 by her daughter Vanya, under whose stewardship the vineyards were certified organic in 2003 and biodynamic in 2004. In 2000, Vanya won the Qantas Winemaker of the Year award. The judges described the flagship Cabernet Sauvignon Merlot as "simply the greatest wine of its style made in Australia."

This wine owes its imposing structure and intense concentration of dark fruits, mulberry, and plum to shy-yielding, dry-farmed vines planted on poor, well-drained ironstone gravel soils. Scott Henry trellising and minimal handling in the winery account for its signature fine-grained tannins. Its unworked style shows an excellent integration of wood with fruit. With age, it unravels complex notes of warm earth, tobacco, and bitumen.

The 2001 vintage, the driest for 126 years, produced superb wines, especially the Cabernet Sauvignon; there was no addition of Cabernet Franc, Malbec, or Petit Verdot this year. When Di Cullen passed away in 2003, the flagship wine, starting with the 2001 vintage, was renamed Diana Madeline Cabernet Sauvignon Merlot in her honor. **SA**

🕙🕙 **Drink: to 2025**

Biodynamic viticulture is practiced at the Cullen vineyards. ➡

CVNE *Real de Asúa Rioja Reserva* 1994

Origin Spain, Rioja
Style Dry red wine, 13% ABV
Grapes Tempranillo 95%, Graciano 5%

Established in 1879, the Compañía Vinicola del Norte de España (known as CVNE or Cuné) comprises the Imperial, Viña Real, and Contino labels, among others. Real de Asúa is a concept borne out of the then highly regarded 1994 harvest, although the idea had been with the Cuné directors for some years. The Real de Asúa brothers were two of the founding partners of Cuné. One of the first vineyards they acquired was at Villalba, 3 miles (5 km) to the northwest of Haro, in the heart of Rioja Alavesa. The new wine was produced using grapes mainly from that old vineyard—sited 1,772 feet (540 m) above sea level—which usually contributes to the Imperial Rioja blend.

The Cuné winery is made up of a group of mostly nineteenth-century buildings, arranged around a courtyard surrounded by pavilions for wine production, maturation, and bottling. Real de Asúa is vinified in its own little cellar here. The hand-picked grapes are placed in a refrigeration room prior to manual sorting. The final crushed grape juice is then fermented in small oak vats. Post-fermentation, this wine is gravity fed into new French oak casks.

Real de Asúa is at the forefront of modern-style Rioja. It is a big, full-bodied wine, deeply colored, and very firm, with tannins that can take ten years or more to settle down. More recent vintages have moved toward even greater ripeness and roundness, with more use of new French oak, and the wine has found great favor in the U.S. market. **SG**

🍷🍷🍷 **Drink: to 2019+**

FURTHER RECOMMENDATIONS
Other great vintages
1995 · 1996 · 1999 · 2000 · 2001 · 2004
More CVNE red wines
CVNE Crianza · CVNE Reserva · Contino Reserva
Viña del Olivo · Viña Real Gran Reserva

CVNE'S nineteenth-century winery still holds many ancient vintages. ➡

Romano Dal Forno
Amarone della Valpolicella 1985

Origin Italy, Veneto, Illasi
Style Dry red wine, 15% ABV
Grapes Corvina, Rondinella, Oseleta

The Illasi Valley lies approximately 15 miles (25 km) east of Verona and forms the eastern border of the Valpolicella and Soave DOCs. It has never been considered part of the Classico zone, which includes the more famous communes of Negrar and Fumane.

Romano Dal Forno was born in 1957 to a family with more than three generations of cooperative viticultural experience. Romano's destiny would have been identical to that of thousands of other grape growers but for a chance meeting, in 1979, with Giuseppe Quintarelli, the master of Valpolicella. Leading a crusade to uphold the region, Quintarelli was one of the few who worked only with their own grapes and who vinified and bottled their entire production themselves. For Romano, the encounter proved that quality Valpolicella was within reach.

Romano's combination of high density vineyards, tiny yields, and lengthy *appassimento* resulted in a wine of Herculean proportions, with remarkable natural acidity providing both proportion and balance. The Dal Forno winery's epic 1985 Amarone remains a benchmark for complexity, structure, and longevity. **MP**

❸❸❸❸❸ Drink: to 2020+

Dalla Valle
Maya 2000

Origin USA, California, Napa Valley
Style Dry red wine, 14% ABV
Grapes C. Sauvignon 65%, C. Franc 35%

When Gustav Dalla Valle retired, he and his wife Naoko moved to the Napa Valley. In 1982, they found a small property on hillsides just east of Oakville: They had found a fine spot, with rocky, volcanic soils; the vines were just above the fog line, giving a warm microclimate. Since Gustav died in 1995, the property has been run by his widow.

Two wines are produced: a Cabernet Sauvignon, with around 10 percent Cabernet Franc blended in, and Maya, which has far more Cabernet Franc. The Maya has cemented Dalla Valle's reputation with a superb depth of flavor and striking harmony. Young Maya can be a bit austere, but this sets it apart from the big, jammy, alcoholic wines that now dominate Napa Valley. Unfortunately, the vineyards were hit by leafroll virus in the 1990s, but replanting was completed in 2007, and levels are gradually rising.

The 2000 has dense chocolaty aromas, but the 75 percent new French oak is perfectly integrated into the wine. It is very rich and succulent, with a firm tannic backbone, and a fresh aftertaste to which the 35 percent Cabernet Franc surely contributes. Well balanced and stylish, it will age effortlessly. **SBr**

❸❸❸❸❸ Drink: to 2022

Dard et Ribo
C'est le Printemps 2012

Origin France, Northern Rhône Valley
Style Dry red wine, 12.5% ABV
Grape Syrah

The story of René-Jean Dard's and François Ribo's collaboration has a novelistic neatness. The duo were born, a year apart, into wine-growing families, both of whom supplied the local cooperative, but on opposite sides of the Rhône river: Dard in Tain, Ribo in Tournon. But it was only once both had left the region to study at the Beaune Wine School in Burgundy that they would meet, become friends, and then pool their meager resources in 1984 to set up a winemaking shop in a small cellar in Tain.

That they met in Burgundy is significant, since their Syrah has a kinship with that region's Pinot Noir: the Dard et Ribo house style is about lightness of touch, drinkability, and silkiness rather than power. To achieve that, they have been pioneers in adopting the philosophy that has come to be described as "natural": a hands-off approach with minimal chemical additions in both their 17¼-acre (7-ha) collection of vineyard plots in Crozes-Hermitage and in their cellar. C'est le Printemps is the style at its most joyful, a wine released in the spring after vintage (hence the name) that is supple, succulent, and full of Syrah's natural peppery spice. **DW**

🌓 **Drink: to 2017**

D'Arenberg
Dead Arm Shiraz 2003

Origin Australia, South Australia, McLaren Vale
Style Dry red wine, 14.5% ABV
Grape Shiraz

In 1912 Joseph Osborn purchased the well-established Milton Vineyards in what is now McLaren Vale. Joseph's grandson Francis d'Arenberg (d'Arry), returned from school in 1943 to help his ailing father run what was then a relatively conservative and traditional business. He eventually assumed full management in 1957. Frequent successes in the Australian wine show system, including a Jimmy Watson Trophy at the 1969 Royal Melbourne Wine Show, helped d'Arenberg along the road to being an important producer.

The Dead Arm Shiraz is d'Arenberg's flagship wine, named after the disease (Eutypa Lata) that afflicts some of the oldest vines at d'Arenberg: It slowly reduces one of the "arms" of the vines to dead wood, so the other arm of the vine produces small volumes of concentrated and highly flavored grapes—ideal for making a blockbuster red wine.

The Dead Arm Shiraz shows ripe, plummy, cassis fruit aromas, and is very concentrated, with toasty American oak flavors. It is best drunk with bold, rich, robust meals, especially roasted meats and vegetables, stews and casseroles. **SG**

🌓🌓🌓🌓 **Drink: to 2018+**

De Trafford
Elevation 393 2003

Origin South Africa, Stellenbosch
Style Dry red wine, 14.8% ABV
Grapes C. Sauvignon 42%, Merlot 33%, Others 25%

The name refers to the altitude in meters of the home vineyard of the Mont Fleur farm, where this small family winery is located. Elevation 393 also plays on architectural vocabulary: Close inspection of the label reveals that it depicts the winery's north and west elevations.

David Trafford is an architect by training but a wine grower by conviction—perhaps the most prominent of any recent generation Cape winemaker with no formal qualifications. This has not prevented a growing international reputation, notably for this wine and a splendid varietal Shiraz.

The inclusion of Shiraz in a Bordeaux-style blend marks this wine as one of an ambitious handful, mostly from the Helderberg area of Stellenbosch, responding in this way to local traditions and conditions. The wine, from one of the best vintages of recent years, has fine fruit and dense supple tannins, together suggesting a good developmental future. In its ripe, forthright power, heavy-textured richness, and lavish French-oaking it reveals its modernity, though the complementary naturalness of the winemaking completes the story. **TJ**

☻☻☻ **Drink: to 2018+**

DeLille Cellars
Chaleur Estate 2005

Origin USA, Washington State, Yakima Valley
Style Dry red wine, 15.2% ABV
Grapes C. Sauvignon, Merlot, C. Franc, Petit Verdot

From its inception in 1992, the partnership behind DeLille Cellars has desired nothing more than to produce exceptional wines—the powerful ones founder Chris Upchurch loves. When others focused on varietal wines, DeLille staked its claim on the synergy of blended grapes. Upchurch believes in blending not just varieties, but different vineyard sites. Although Chaleur Estate is essentially a warm-climate, Red Mountain wine, Upchurch finds balance by blending cooler-climate Merlot from Boushey Vineyard to soften the ripe, but tannic, Cabernet Sauvignon. Cabernet Franc adds aromatic complexity. Petit Verdot, Upchurch says, elevates all. This is a wine that coheres harmoniously.

Chaleur Estate usually ages in 100 percent French oak barriques for eighteen months, primarily for natural clarification and fresh spice notes. The wine is fined but never filtered. The 2005 vintage is regarded as the best in Washington State for at least ten years. Even young, the seamlessly structured, complex, and rich Chaleur exhibits glorious, high-toned fruits above a concentrated core of herbs, dark fruits, and minerality. **LGr**

☻☻☻ **Drink: to 2017+**

Faux-medieval ironmongery defends the wines at DeLille Cellars. ➡

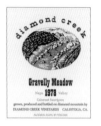

Azienda Agricola Dettori

Cannonau Dettori Romangia 2009

Origin Italy, Sardinia
Style Dry red wine, 17.5% ABV
Grape Cannonau (Grenache)

Diamond Creek Vineyards

Gravelly Meadow 1978

Origin USA, California, Napa Valley
Style Dry red wine, 13.5 % ABV
Grapes C. Sauvignon 88%, C. Franc 6%, Merlot 6%

Sardinia's sparse, arid interior is deeply agrarian, its inhabitants still fiercely proud of tradition. At first meeting Alessandro Dettori appears to break this mold, but it soon becomes apparent that he is an ardent supporter of the old-fashioned ways. Alessandro decided to call his greatest wine Dettori, to reflect his family's dedication to viticulture.

For this wine, ancient, bush-vine Cannonau with an average age of more than a century is grown, unirrigated, on chalky soils in Sardinia's northwestern extremity, just 2.5 miles (4 km) from the sea. The scorching sun and low yields ensure an exceptional degree of ripeness, which even the indigenous yeasts struggle to ferment to dryness. Hand-harvested, the grapes are fermented in cement tanks. Dettori does not encounter wood; and wood could scarcely begin to tame this colossus.

How do the grapes develop such levels of sugar without losing their acidity? How do the yeasts produce so much alcohol without a whiff of volatile acidity? Dettori is a pre-historic conundrum, a reminder that Mother Nature, despite our best attempts to tame her, remains firmly in charge. **MP**
ΘΘΘΘ **Drink: recent vintages for up to 5 years**

When the late Al Brounstein began clearing his Diamond Mountain vineyard properties in 1968, he could see how Diamond Creek comprised distinct areas, all with different soil types and exposures, and decided to vinify them separately. The relatively flat land that constitutes Gravelly Meadow originated as a riverbed. It is Diamond Creek's second coolest vineyard, with a thin scrim of gravel over bedrock.

The Diamond Creek wines have always been powerfully structured wines with tremendous tannic intensity; those from the 1990s forward show a smidgen more accessibility. Nevertheless, these are firm, pure mountain fruit wines that need ten to twelve years of bottle age to sing.

After the uneven 1976 and 1977 vintages, heavy winter rains and a frost-free spring led to a warm summer with several hot spells. It was the first year that fruit from the Lake Vineyard was not blended into Gravelly Meadow, and its absence may have contributed to the more opulent, fleshier nature of the bottling that year. Outside fermentation in open wooden vats, followed by French barrique aging, produced a singular wine. **LGr**
ΘΘΘΘ **Drink: to 2018+**

Gravelly Meadow vineyard is planted on a prehistoric riverbed. ➋

Domaine A
Cabernet Sauvignon 2000

Origin Australia, Tasmania, Coal River
Style Dry red wine, 13.5% ABV
Grapes C. Sauvignon, Merlot, Petit Verdot, C. Franc

Domaine A, a 50-acre (20 ha) property in the lovely Coal River Valley of southern Tasmania, was originally planted in 1973. It is now owned by Peter and Ruth Althaus. Despite the cool climate, Althaus believes that proper grape ripeness is possible because of the prevailing dry northern winds that funnel up the valley during the growing season.

Cabernet Sauvignon is the flagship wine of Domaine A and is arguably Tasmania's top Cabernet. The second label—Stoney Vineyard—is made year in, year out, but Domaine A wines are produced only in high-quality vintages.

The Cabernet Sauvignon 2000 was made using the classic Bordeaux blend of varieties and was matured in 100 percent new French oak for twenty-four months. During this period in oak, the wine was racked eight times and then bottled unfiltered. After a further twelve months in the cellar, the wine was released in September 2004. Deep crimson with a dark cherry rim, the wine has pronounced Cabernet Sauvignon aromas of cassis and red berry fruits, with underlying hints of something more leafy and savory, à la Coonawarra. **SG**
 Drink: to 2018+

Domaine de l'A
2001

Origin France, Bordeaux, Côtes de Castillon
Style Dry red wine, 13% ABV
Grapes Merlot, Cabernet Franc, C. Sauvignon

With his wife, Christine, Stéphane Derenoncourt acquired the Domaine de l'A in 1999 and quickly increased the average planting density to 6,000 roots per hectare in order to balance better the low yields over a larger number of vines, thus reducing the individual charge per plant. The average age of the vineyard today is about thirty-five years.

The property is located on the slopes above the Dordogne in the village of Ste.-Colombe, contiguous to those of St.-Emilion. Although most of the soils are chalky clay, some suggest those of Fronsac. Everything here, from pruning to harvest, is done by hand. In the cellar, Stéphane is a minimalist. The wine is racked only once, never fined.

Stéphane Derenoncourt has never admired wines that appear constructed or overblown, preferring the discreet reserve that is a sign of his own character. Not surprisingly, he has also long enjoyed overlooked, more classical vintages such as 2001, which he prefers to the New World pomp of 2000, 2003, or even 2005. The Domaine de l'A 2001 is a perfect example of his preference, a lesson in subtlety, balance, and drinkability. **JP**
 Drink: to 2018+

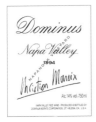

Dominus

1994

Domaine Drouhin *Oregon*
Pinot Noir Cuvée Laurène 2002

Origin USA, California, Napa Valley
Style Dry red wine, 14% ABV
Grape C. Sauvignon, Merlot, C. Franc, Petit Verdot

Origin USA, Oregon, Willamette Valley
Style Dry red wine, 13.5% ABV
Grape Pinot Noir

Christian Moueix—the owner of Pétrus and other prestigious properties in Bordeaux—began his love affair with the Napa Valley and its wines while studying at U.C. Davis in 1968 and 1969. After many years of searching for the ideal vineyard location, in 1982 he entered into a joint venture with Robin Lail and Marcia Smith, the daughters of John Daniel, who made Inglenook Cask Selection from the famed Napanook vineyard in Yountville, California.

The first vintage of Dominus was in 1983, four years after the pioneering Bordeaux/Napa collaboration at Opus One. Dominus 1994 was the first vintage produced solely by Christian Moueix. Robert Parker awarded the 1994 a score of 99 points.

In the early years of Dominus, a series of artists' portraits of Christian Moueix was commissioned for the labels, the most distinguished of which was probably by Peter Blake, who did the 1988 version. From 1991, though, a *faux* Bordeaux label has replaced the artist series. The Dominus winery—designed by Swiss architects Herzog and De Meuron, well known for the Tate Modern in London—is notable in its own right. **SG**

🍷🍷🍷🍷 **Drink: to 2019+**

From inception, Cuvée Laurène has been a winery blend. It had to be, because it takes vintages, perhaps generations, to understand the character of specific plots and the wines they produce.

Véronique Drouhin had generations of family experience to guide her in the vineyard. Both when the estate was founded and as it has added vineyards, farming practices differed from those normal in Oregon before their arrival. Although the first plantings were with own-rooted Pommard (UCD 5) and Wadenswil (UCD 2A) clones of Pinot, they planted them far more densely than usual. They later switched to clones such as 115 and 777, and grafted these on to phylloxera-resistant rootstocks.

This, and severe fruit selection, partly accounts for the concentration and complexity of Cuvée Laurène. The wine is left on the skins for four to five days before pressing with a maximum 2 percent press wine in the final blend. Warm days and cool nights characterized the relatively stable 2002 vintage, producing an elegantly textured, firmly structured, dynamic Cuvée Laurène, filled with forest fruit and licorice flavors. **LGr**

🍷🍷🍷 **Drink: to 2017+**

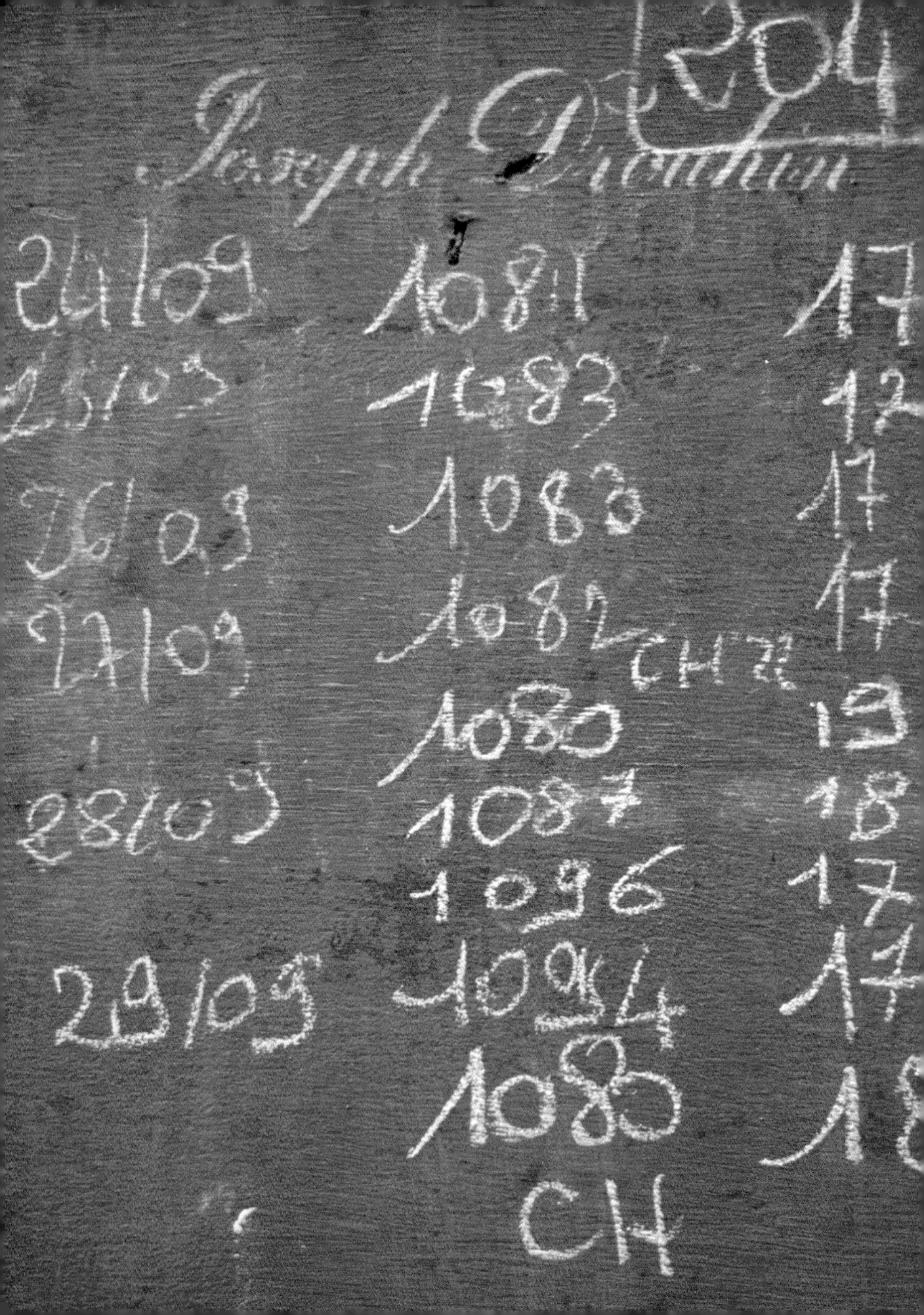

204

Joseph Drouhin

24/09	1081	17
25/09	1083	17
26/09	1083	17
27/09	1082	17
	1080 CH2	19
28/09	1087	18
	1096	17
29/09	1094	17
	1080	18
	CH	

Domaine Joseph Drouhin
Musigny Grand Cru 1978

Origin France, Burgundy, Côte de Nuits
Style Dry red wine, 12.5% ABV
Grape Pinot Noir

Although Joseph Drouhin traces its history back to its eponymous founder and the year 1880, it was Robert Drouhin who took the helm in 1957 at the age of twenty-four, who set the company on its present course. His desire to improve quality had many facets. Not only did he limit fertilizers, curb chemical treatments, and reduce yields, but more importantly he purchased vineyards in Chambertin-Clos de Bèze, Bonnes Mares, and Musigny.

In 1973 he hired the first woman enologist in Burgundy—Laurence Jobard—and it was she who made this wine, in the magnificent vaulted Gothic cellar under the former Palace of the Dukes of Burgundy, built originally for the kings of France.

To the north of Beaune, after Grands-Echézeaux and Clos Vougeot, and shortly before the village of Chambolle, there is a small promontory with a splendid view over the plain below. The soil feels light and is strewn with small pebbles. This is Musigny, which produces a wine of exceptional purity. In its youth, aromas of cherry and violet predominate, but it is only with age that the true flavors appear. Refined and complex, they take on nuances of fallen leaves, exotic woods, and even hints of leather. On the palate it is a wine of incomparable finesse, harmony, and elegance. At its best, it is the purest expression of Pinot Noir in the world, a fist of steel in a velvet glove. 1978 was a memorable year in all of Burgundy. As total production of the 1999 Musigny was only 220 cases, those who call a bottle their own are very lucky. **JP**

🍷🍷🍷🍷 **Drink: to 2020**

Pierre-Jacques Druet
Bourgueil Vaumoreau 1989

Origin France, Loire, Touraine
Style Dry red wine, 13% ABV
Grape Cabernet Franc

Pierre-Jacques Druet, a first-generation winemaker, makes wine from grapes grown in both Chinon and Bourgueil, though it is his wines from Bourgueil that carry his reputation most forcefully. Many believe that these are the finest made in the whole appellation. The son of a *négociant* from Montrichard, a small town between Blois and Tours, Druet studied in Beaune as well as at Montpelier and Bordeaux. After managing an exporter in Bordeaux he eventually started to produce wine, setting up in Benais, on the north bank of the Loire between Saumur and Tours, in time for the 1980 vintage.

As well as his Chinons, he makes four different cuvées of Bourgueil from his 32-acre (13 ha) holdings. The grandest cuvées here are the Grand Mont and Vaumoreau, but the others, Les Cent Boiselees and Beauvais, are both excellent wines, albeit in a lighter (though by no means light) style. The flagship cuvée, Vaumoreau, is produced from low-yielding Cabernet Franc vines planted in the 1910s. The Vaumoreau is matured for two to three years in wood before bottling.

Make no mistake, these are serious wines requiring patience, but they offer complexity, intensity, and finesse, particularly in the better years. The 1989 growing season in the Loire was hot and dry, giving sufficient ripe fruit and tannins to balance the acidity. Druet's Vaumoreau 1989 is a powerful wine, with aromas and flavors of blackberries, violets, and an underlying earthiness. The finish is fresh, with hints of herbs and chocolate. **JW**

🍷🍷🍷🍷 **Drink: to 2019**

Dry River *Pinot Noir* 2009

Origin New Zealand, Martinborough
Style Dry red wine, 13% ABV
Grape Pinot Noir

The Martinborough region makes perhaps the most Burgundian of New Zealand's Pinot Noirs. The most renowned producer here is Dry River, whose Pinot is often New Zealand's most concentrated and long-lived. The original owner Neil McCallum sold his estate to U.S. owners but stayed on as a consultant until 2011.

The Dry River winemaking process is meticulous. Selection of the appropriate clone of Pinot Noir is important for quality. Clone 5, the "Pommard" clone, is used (among others), which produces wines with a great deal of upfront fruit. Reflective tape is placed under the vines to ensure greater ripening, and in the winery, whole-bunch fermentation is employed. This is an ultra-traditional Burgundy method of red wine fermentation that can create a more generous style.

With its deep color, Dry River's Pinot Noir looks atypical when young. It has a tight and restrained nose, with a crisp, very rich, and supple palate that develops earthy and eucalyptus flavors with age. The high acid/low tannin structure means that the wine drinks well when young, but can also be cellared for up to ten years. This rich style of Pinot is not for everyone—indeed, McCallum warned drinkers of his 1996 vintage, "It is not a wine for wimps, but neither has it sacrificed the elegance essential to fine Pinot Noir." At the Pinot Noir conference held in Wellington in 2004, after tasting the 2001 vintage, Aussie wine guru James Halliday declared, "Dry River is the Pommard of New Zealand Pinot Noir." **SG**

🜏🜏🜏 **Drink: recent vintages for up to 10 years**

FURTHER RECOMMENDATIONS
Other great vintages
2002 · 2003 · 2005 · 2006 · 2008
More producers from Martinborough
Ata Rangi · Craggy Range
Martinborough Vineyard · Palliser

The entrance gateway to the Dry River winery in Martinborough. ➡

DRY RIVER

Duas Quintas *Reserva Especial* 2003

Origin Portugal, Douro Valley
Style Dry red wine, 14.5% ABV
Grapes Touriga Nacional, Tinta Barroca

The Duas Quintas label is owned by Ramos Pinto, a company established by Adriano Ramos Pinto in 1880. At that time Ramos Pinto was a Port company that, like all others, bottled unfortified wine only in small quantities for personal consumption.

In the twentieth century it was Ramos Pinto, then directed by José Ramos Pinto Rosas and his nephew João Nicolau de Almeida, that led the research into vine varieties in the Douro, resulting in the list of recommended types used today. Previously, most vineyards were mixed plantings of myriad different, often unidentified, varieties.

The family-owned company was sold to Champagne Louis Roederer in 1990, but is still headed by the ebullient João Nicolau de Almeida. His was one of the first houses to consider the possibilities of making fine table wine here, largely a result of the influence of Fernando Nicolau de Almeida, João Nicolau de Almeida's father. The Duas Quintas label refers to wine from two estates, these usually being Quintas Ervamoira and Bons Ares.

The Reserva Especial, however, is a return to traditionalism. The grapes come from old plantings of mixed varieties at Quintas Bom Retiro and Urtiga, both in the Rio Torto Valley. Foot-treading, with minimal stalk removal, employs the winemaking technology of biblical days. The use of new wood for this vintage was limited. The result is a rich, voluminous wine with great, ripe, tannic structure; it has a great future ahead of it. **GS**

🝐🝐🝐 **Drink: to 2024**

FURTHER RECOMMENDATIONS
Other great vintages
2000 • 2004 • 2007 • 2009
More Douro Valley table wines
Chryseia • Niepoort Batuta • Niepoort Charme
Quinta do Crasto • Quinta do Noval • Romaneira

The Douro Valley vineyards produce fine table wines as well as Port. ➡

Georges Duboeuf *Fleurie La Madone* 2009

Origin France, Beaujolais, Fleurie
Style Dry red wine, 13.5% ABV
Grape Gamay

Of the ten cru wines of Beaujolais, Fleurie retains the most ardent affection in aficionados' hearts. Its name evokes the flowers with which the house of Duboeuf garlands many of its Beaujolais labels, and it is often one of the most attractive wines in its youth.

The La Madone vineyard, established at the outset of the twentieth century, is planted on the granite soils that are typical throughout the region. Duboeuf's wine comes from an estate that covers 15 acres (6 ha) of vineyard land, with vines that are on average fifty years old. The proprietor is Roger Darroze, still a hands-on vineyard director in his nineties. Duboeuf has been buying and bottling the entirety of the production for more than thirty years.

What they (and we) get is a fine, structured Fleurie cuvée, one-eighth of which is aged in new oak. The wine displays the classic Gamay wild strawberries and rose petals on the nose, just subtly sharpened with the cedary influence of the wood. In the mouth, it opens up with ripe, pulpy red fruits held in place by a gently assertive tannic structure. Much cru Beaujolais is drunk too young and, although it does not have the longevity of its Pinot neighbors to the north, a wine such as this will handsomely repay some keeping. What you are waiting for is the nervy acidity of the young wine to settle down, though in a good vintage like 2009, it has to be said, the ripeness and sleekness is so succulent that the temptation to embark on it early will need to be met by iron-willed resistance. **SW**

🍷🍷 **Drink: recent vintages for up to 8 years**

FURTHER RECOMMENDATIONS
Other great vintages
1999 • 2000 • 2001 • 2003 • 2004 • 2009 • 2010
More producers from Fleurie
Pierre Chermette • Michel Chignard • Clos de la Roilette
Andre Colonge • Guy Depardon • Domaine de la Presle

The chapel of La Madone overlooks Fleurie. ➡

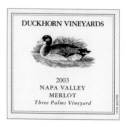

Duckhorn Vineyards
Three Palms Merlot 2003

Origin USA, California, Napa Valley
Style Dry red wine, 14.5% ABV
Grapes Merlot 75% , C. Sauvignon 10%, Others 15%

Château Ducru-Beaucaillou
2000

Origin France, Bordeaux, St.-Julien
Style Dry red wine, 13% ABV
Grapes C. Sauvignon 65%, Merlot, 25%, C. Franc 10%

Napa Valley Merlot's reputation for intense, ripe-fruit character and concentration belied by seductively soft texture was set by Dan and Margaret Duckhorn, who focused on producing top-quality Merlot from their first vintage in 1979. Their 83-acre (33 ha) Three Palms Vineyard is named for all that was left on the property of a San Francisco socialite once her house had fallen into disrepair. Located on an alluvial fan on the northeast side of the valley, the site is covered with volcanic stones washed down over the centuries from Dutch Henry Canyon. Originally planted in 1967 by the Upton brothers (now partners with the Duckhorns), the vineyard was replanted after phylloxera between 1990 and 1999.

The Three Palms flagship wine differs from the Estate Merlot largely in intensity and concentration; more tightly wound, it is less accessible upon release, and benefits from three or four years' bottle maturation, opening on to a developmental plateau lasting fifteen years from the vintage date. Although 2003 was a fairly difficult year, it resulted in a wine with subtle complexity, a clearly delineated structure, and well-integrated toasty oak. **LGr**

❺❺❺❺ **Drink: to 2018+**

Planted on deep gravel soils with high clay content, the vineyards of this deuxième cru St.-Julien (long considered to be in the top rank of the second growths) produce what is often felt to be the textbook style of a St.-Julien claret—soft and yielding, with luscious blackberry fruit, but lacking nothing in aging potential. The wines are given an eighteen-month maturation in cask, with more than half of the oak renewed each year.

One of the fascinating aspects of the wines is that they always show very deeply extracted color in their youth, leading one to anticipate a heavy, tannin-dominated experience, and yet it is for their subtlety, elegance, even relative delicacy that the wines of this property are celebrated.

The legendary 2000 vintage produced wines of extraordinary finesse and concentration. Ducru-Beaucaillou opens with sweetly ripe blackberries and raspberries on the nose, with deep aromas of singed red meats, toast, and thyme. The palate is both intense and immense, its tannins majestic but perfectly balanced with ripe fruit, soft acidity, and long, vanilla extract oak tones. **SW**

❺❺❺❺ **Drink: to 2030+**

The château is nineteenth-century, but the estate is much older. ◆

Domaine Claude Dugat
Griotte-Chambertin GC 1996

Origin France, Burgundy, Côte de Nuits
Style Dry red wine, 13% ABV
Grape Pinot Noir

On the northwestern side of Gevrey-Chambertin village is a building described as the Cellier des Dîmes. This is where, today, Claude Dugat keeps the wine from his very fine estate. There have been Dugats in Gevrey since at least as far back as the French Revolution. In the previous generation there were Maurice, Pierre, and Thérèse. Claude, born in 1956, is the son of Maurice. Bernard Dugat-Py is the son of Pierre, and makes very good wine just around the corner. Thérèse married into the Humbert family, again nearby, again highly respected for their wine.

The inexorable consequences of the French laws of succession led, inevitably, to the fragmentation of a family's vineyard. The result is that Claude Dugat, now with his two children, looks after a mere 9 acres (4 ha) of vines. The wines include old vine village Gevrey-Chambertin; a premier cru that is a mixture of Craipillot and Perrières; and Lavaux-Saint-Jacques. At grand cru level we have three wines, but in miniscule quantities: Chapelle-Chambertin, Charmes-Chambertin, and Griotte-Chambertin. There are not quite four barrels of the latter.

Wine commentators often find a flavor of cherries in the wines of Griotte. There is nothing wrong with this, but it has nothing to do with the fact that a *griotte* is a variety of bitter cherry, best for making into jam. Here Griotte refers to the soil, to its limestone origin. Claude Dugat's Griotte is the most austere, the latest to evolve, of his wines, but the most profound. This 1996 is only now coming into its own, the fruit now becoming really succulent. **CC**
ӨӨӨӨӨ **Drink: to 2026**

Domaine Dugat-Py *Mazis-Chambertin Grand Cru* 1999

Origin France, Burgundy, Côte de Nuits
Style Dry red wine, 13% ABV
Grape Pinot Noir

Bernard Dugat may not own the finest vineyards, but no other vintner does more perfect work with the material at his disposal. His key to coaxing the finest out of each vineyard is old vines, low yields, and long fermentations with whole clusters. With no filtration, no fining, and little intervention during vinification, his Burgundies are clean, racy, and seductive.

Tasting Dugat's wines in his vaulted cellar, a former monastery above the village of Gevrey, is often a spiritual experience—and his 1999s were breathtaking, electrifying the palate with uncompromising purity. In 1999 he picked early and quickly, finishing on September 22, a day before the weather turned irreversibly wet. This same year Dugat began experimenting with organic farming, a practice he now follows in all his vineyards. With success catching up to his micro-winery, he has also expanded his holdings and now cultivates 25 acres (10 ha) with his wife Jocelyne and son Loïc.

All of his wines are dark, brooding, and better structured than almost anything else you will find in Burgundy. Although surprisingly dense, they are in no way artificial or constructed. Yes, they are made from exceptionally ripe grapes, but without the heaviness of over-maturity. Dugat's 1999 Mazis-Chambertin, made from seventy-year-old vines that were plowed by horse, shows incredible depth and expression of blackberry and hazelnut flavors. One of the outstanding wines of the vintage, it is concentrated and structured, with velvety, mouth-coating tannins and an extremely long finish. **JP**
ӨӨӨӨӨ **Drink: to 2050**

Domaine Dujac *Gevrey-Chambertin PC Aux Combottes* 1999

Origin France, Burgundy, Côte de Nuits
Style Dry red wine, 13% ABV
Grape Pinot Noir

When Jacques Seysses began his apprenticeship with Gérard Potel in Volnay in the 1960s, being a winemaker did not have the allure that is does today. Nor did buying an estate, which he did in 1967, appear to be a great investment. As fortune would have it, his first vintage was the worst of his career. Since then, many memorable years have followed, and the estate has grown from 12 acres (5 ha) to almost 32 acres (13 ha). Today he is assisted by his son Jeremy, whose wife Diana manages the cellar.

Although the domaine also has five grands crus, its premiers crus are of the first order, with Combottes, literally surrounded by grands crus, certainly one of the finest such sites in Gevrey-Chambertin. Combottes derives its character from being a synthesis of the three surrounding vineyards—Clos de la Roche, Latricières-Chambertin, and Charmes-Chambertin. Of the total 7.4-acre (3 ha) area of Combottes, Dujac owns slightly more than a third.

Whether 1999 is the finest vintage of Combottes is a matter of speculation. In any case, it is one of the most unusual vintages ever harvested here. Rich, dense, and with enormous structure, it is still extremely closed. The only way to make it look tame today would be to pair it with wild meats. Jacques Seysses thinks that 2005 may be his best ever vintage, but it will be another fifteen or twenty years before it reaches its apogee. Instead, 1997 is the vintage that he prefers drinking today, "because it is so delicate, while still showing youthful fruit." **JP**

😊😊😊😊 Drink: to 2030

Dunn Vineyards *Howell Mountain C. Sauvignon* 1994

Origin USA, California, Napa Valley
Style Dry red wine, 13.5% ABV
Grape Cabernet Sauvignon

Randy Dunn was the winemaker at Caymus as it rose to prominence in the 1980s, but his own wine is in many ways the polar opposite of theirs. Pure mountain fruit, his wines are densely concentrated and tightly wound. Dunn's wines are not for those seeking immediate gratification; most vintages require at least twelve years before the layers of complexity unfold.

The growing conditions on his Howell Mountain property differ from those elsewhere in Napa. At 2,000 feet (610 m) above sea level, the vineyards are above the fog line, so they warm up more quickly, even if daytime temperatures are 10 to 15°F (6–8°C) cooler than the valley floor. Nighttime temperatures are warmer than down in the valley, so that while the cooler spring means a later budbreak, the vines catch up by the autumn to have a harvest time similar to elsewhere in Napa.

Dunn's wines are designed to be inaccessible when young; after hand-picking, destemming, and crushing the crop, he inoculates and allows fermentation, but shuns the extended maceration that might add softness. Malolactic fermentation is induced in tank before the transfer to barrels. Most vintages age thirty months in up to 50 percent new French barriques. The wine is filtered but never fined. The Howell Mountain 1994 is quintessential Dunn—"a behemoth," Parker called it. Full-bodied, with tremendous extract and intensity, it is dynamic and long on the palate, with multiple layers of black fruits, floral aromatics, and a mineral core. **LGr**

😊😊😊😊 Drink: to 2030+

Château Durfort-Vivens
2004

Origin France, Bordeaux, Margaux
Style Dry red wine, 13% ABV
Grapes C. Sauvignon 65%, Merlot 23%, C. Franc 12%

Classified as a second growth, Durfort-Vivens clearly had considerable potential, but in 1937 the property was sold to Château Margaux, which raided its vineyards, so that the Durfort label almost disappeared. In 1962 Lucien Lurton bought the property and began to claw back its vineyards. The château itself, opposite the cellars, was retained by Bernard Ginestet, the former owner of Margaux.

Lucien Lurton handed over Durfort-Vivens to his son Gonzague in 1992. Rather than green-harvest, Gonzague prunes short to achieve low yields, and never uses more than 40 percent new oak. He seeks finesse rather than excessive richness, and some critics dismiss his wines as too light for a second growth. In some vintages the wine is indeed rather light, but it needs time for its perfume and poise to emerge. It is the spice and succulence, both unusually pronounced for Durfort, that mark out the 2004 as an exceptional wine from this estate. Gonzague Lurton's wines are sometimes underrated, but prices are reasonable, and their restraint and finesse are welcome at a time when many estates are moving in the opposite stylistic direction. **SBr**
❸❸❸ **Drink: to 2020**

Château L'Eglise-Clinet
2002

Origin France, Bordeaux, Pomerol
Style Dry red wine, 13.5% ABV
Grapes Merlot 75%, C. Franc 20%, Malbec 5%

Although this 15-acre (6 ha) property has been owned by the family of Denis Durantou since 1882, Durantou does not let tradition dictate how he produces wine. He has many old vines, but has replanted about one-third of them because he found the rootstock unsatisfactory and incapable of giving the quality he was looking for. He is particularly keen on his Cabernet Franc because of the floral quality it gives to his wine. The vineyards are on different soils, which contribute to the wine's complexity: Clay gives it power, gravel its finesse.

Rather than sort at the winery, Durantou prefers to prepare his vineyards carefully before the harvest, eliminating any unripe or otherwise satisfactory bunches. He argues that the small amount of leaves and stalks that may enter the vats makes no significant difference to the quality of the wine.

Durantou says that appreciative wine drinkers should accept good levels of tannin and acidity in an age-worthy wine. He makes excellent wine in lesser vintages, too, as the 2002 amply demonstrates. It is very concentrated, but not at the expense of sweet ripe fruit, and the tannins are fine-grained. **SBr**
❸❸❸❸ **Drink: to 2020**

Under Durantou, L'Eglise-Clinet has become a great Pomerol estate. ➡

PICHONNEAU SA
CONSTRUCTEUR

16102 COGNAC · FRANCE · B.P 79

TYPE   N°

MADE IN FRANCE

CHATEAU
L'EGLISE CLINET
1989
POMEROL

El Nido
Clio Jumilla 2008

Origin Spain, Murcia, Jumilla
Style Dry red wine, 14% ABV
Grapes Monastrell, Cabernet Sauvignon

This wine is produced by Bodegas El Nido, a firm co-owned by the Gil Vera family and the powerful U.S. importer Jorge Ordóñez. In some respects it is a parallel project to Bodega Hijos de Juan Gil, where the key figure is Miguel Gil. At Finca Luzón he had been one of the main protagonists in the extraordinary takeoff of Jumilla reds in the 1990s, while other outstanding wines include Casa Castillo Las Gravas and Valtosca, and Casa de la Ermita Petit Verdot. Both this Clio and the awesome and (for many) excessive El Nido—its bigger brother in terms of concentration and price—are produced under the technical supervision of Australian enologist Chris Ringland, who established his formidable reputation with his own Three Rivers Barossa Shiraz. Ringland is also a participant in another of Ordóñez's Spanish winemaking ventures.

The El Nido winery is located in the Paraje de la Aragona, about 6 miles (10 km) from Jumilla, the town that lends its name to the appellation. The facilities are modest in size, as befits the ambitious quality-oriented purpose of this winery. Such elite wines can be made only under strict control of the grapes and of each step in the production process.

Clío is a wine in which power and finesse coexist, a rare combination that demands privileged raw materials as well as a special sensibility to orchestrate them into something exceptional. Robert Parker praised the 2004 as "a totally hedonistic effort with exceptional length and balance. It is remarkably light on its feet for such a powerful wine." **JB**

🄢🄢 **Drink: recent vintages for up to 8 years**

Viña El Principal *El Principal*
Cabernet Sauvignon 2001

Origin Chile, Maipo Valley
Style Dry red wine, 14% ABV
Grapes C. Sauvignon, Merlot/Carmenère, C. Franc

After Patrick Valette's father sold Château Pavie in 1998, he returned to the land of his birth, Chile, and launched El Principal. This was a partnership with the Fontaine family, former owners of Viña Santa Rita, and now vineyard owners in Pirque, a Maipo Valley subregion 19 miles (30 km) southeast of Santiago. Pirque's warm spring winds allow Merlot to flower early (mid-September) and safely enough not to lose too many of its fragile flowers.

Pirque's main attribute, however, is the deep bed of pebble-rich soil, washed down from the Andes by the Maipo River to the north, underpinning the vineyards. This allows young vines to put down deep main roots and a complex web of finer roots relatively quickly, and provides quick drainage to minimize the effect of wet weather, should this come in off the Pacific when the later ripening grapes like Carmenère and Cabernet Sauvignon are still hanging on the vine.

With his father's health in decline (he died in 2002), Patrick Valette made the El Principal 2001, plus a second-tier red wine called Memorias. At his own Bordeaux estate in St.-Emilion, Château Franc Grace Dieu, Patrick Valette produced wines with a lightness of touch. But with El Principal's bolder and more alcoholic grapes, he could produce something intrinsically more forceful, despite the relative youth of the vines (most have been planted since 1994). Its defining characteristics are ripeness and leanness, with menthol, pepper, and blackcurrant flavors topped off by a generous touch of French oak. **MW**

🄢 **Drink: to 2018**

Ernie Els
2004

Domaine René Engel
Clos de Vougeot Grand Cru 1992

Origin South Africa, Stellenbosch
Style Dry red wine, 14.5% ABV
Grapes C. Sauvignon 62%, Merlot 24%, Others 14%

Origin France, Burgundy, Côte de Nuits
Style Dry red wine, 13% ABV
Grape Pinot Noir

The involvement of professional golfers with making wine is a big issue—think Greg Norman, David Frost, Arnold Palmer, Mike Weir, and Nick Faldo, for example, quite apart from Ernie Els. Judging a range of these wines in 2005, *Golf Connoisseur* unkindly suggested that South Africa "has been turning out world-class golfers far longer than world-class wines." But the magazine still gave the Ernie Els 2002 its "Best Red Wine by a Pro" award, joining a chorus of U.S. praise for the label since the inaugural 2000.

The golfer's venture into wine is in partnership with an old friend, Jean Engelbrecht of Rust en Vrede estate, where the first vintages were produced (and where Els had met his wife). As Els said at the announcement of the project, "It's the way I play my golf—getting professionals involved." In 2004, an independent home for Ernie Els Wines was acquired when some prime Helderberg land (already supplying some of the grapes for the blend) was acquired, and a new cellar was built to take in grapes from the 2005 harvest, with winemaker Louis Strydom there to receive them.

The aim with the wine, as suggested by Els's public relations, "is to capture everything that Ernie stands for: big in stature and gentle in character." It is also starting to acquire the golfer's substantial reputation for excellence. Oriented to Napa more than to Bordeaux, which ultimately inspired the varietal mix, the 2004 is deep-colored, full-bodied, and full-flavored, with a sweet touch to the fruit, a ripe tannic structure, and a tense, mineral grip. **TJ**
🍷🍷🍷🍷 Drink: to 2017

The grand cru Clos de Vougeot is one of Burgundy's many enigmas. Though theoretically a single vineyard, enclosed since the fourteenth century by drystone walls, the 124 acres (50 ha) are subdivided among as many as eighty different producers, and there are notable variations in potential quality due both to the location of particular vines within the *clos* and to the competence of the grower. The Engel holding of 3.4 acres (1.4 ha) is favorably situated on the upper-mid slope just south of the Château de Clos de Vougeot itself.

The domaine was created by René Engel (1896–1991). It used to own Echézeaux and Grands Echézeaux, Vosne-Romanée Les Brulées, and village Vosne-Romanée, but after the sudden and unexpected death of grandson Philippe Engel in 2005 it was sold to François Pinault (owner of Château Latour) and renamed Domaine d'Eugénie.

1992 is not a celebrated vintage for red Burgundy. The wines showed the effect of summer rainfall and, though pleasing to drink early in life, rarely showed much concentration. This Clos de Vougeot is the exception—a wine that won for Philippe the coveted trophy of Jeune Vigneron de l'Année (Young Winemaker of the Year). Even at fifteen years old this remained an intense, youthful wine with little flashes of vibrant black fruit among the more classical, softer red notes of Burgundian Pinot Noir. The oak component (70 percent new barrels) is perfectly integrated into this wine, which fills the palate in a most satisfying manner. **JM**
🍷🍷🍷🍷🍷 Drink: to 2017

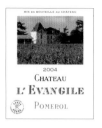

Domaine Sylvie Esmonin
Gevrey-Chambertin VV 2012

Origin France, Burgundy, Côte de Nuits
Style Dry red wine, 13.5% ABV
Grape Pinot Noir

Château L'Evangile
2004

Origin France, Bordeaux, Pomerol
Style Dry red wine, 13% ABV
Grapes Merlot 70%, Cabernet Franc 30%

This beautiful wine hails from one of the most diminutive and shy vigneronnes not just of Gevrey-Chambertin, but of the whole of Burgundy: Sylvie Esmonin. If the lady is shy, her wines are most certainly not. Vieilles Vignes is an "old-school" wine that has been tailored, if only modestly, for the modern world. It is often the best "village" wine of Gevrey-Chambertin.

This wine has been produced from some of the oldest vines of the estate, and using whole clusters of Pinot Noir fruit rather than stripping the grapes from their stems. This whole-cluster character is present in the wine, providing a herbal, smoky aroma when the wine is young. As the wine ages, these aromas slowly transform into a more floral perfume and the herbal aspect becomes fainter.

Age brings additional character to the flavors, too, bringing more focus and freshness. The 2012 is a concentrated vintage, so for that reason this wine should not be drunk in its first flush of youth, but rather when it is at least ten years old, and it will be delicious for at least another ten years after that. Your patience will be amply rewarded. **BN**

🍷🍷🍷 Drink: to 2025+

L'Evangile in full sail is one of Pomerol's most glorious wines. Although the 34-acre (13.7 ha) estate is quite close to Cheval Blanc, the terroir is quite different. Many of the parcels near the château are on heavy clay, and elsewhere there are plots of gravel over clay. There are also some vines planted on sandier soils, but these are never used for the grand vin.

Until 1990 L'Evangile was owned by a Madame Ducasse. In that year Eric de Rothschild took a 70 percent share in the property, only to discover that the redoubtable Mme. Ducasse would not relinquish her control of the estate. No significant changes were permitted, and the only evolution she allowed was the introduction of a second wine. At a great age, she died in 2000 and at last the Rothschild team could take complete control. They introduced harvesting in the small containers called *cagettes*, constructed a new winery with a circular cellar, and increased the proportion of new oak to 100 percent.

The 2004 wears its cloak of new oak gracefully, and there are attractive aromas of red fruits and plums. The palate has a lot of flesh for 2004, despite an underlying severity that will go with time. **SBr**

🍷🍷🍷🍷 Drink: to 2030

Château L'Evangile, behind rows of newly planted vines. ➡

Eyrie Vineyards *South Block Reserve Pinot Noir* 1975

Origin USA, Oregon, Willamette Valley
Style Dry red wine, 12.5% ABV
Grape Pinot Noir

Fable Mountain Vineyards *Syrah* 2011

Origin South Africa, Tulbagh, Western Cape
Style Dry red wine, 14.7% ABV
Grape Syrah

In 1979 the publishers Gault Millau sponsored a wine olympiad that matched some of the best wines of France against a selection of the international competition. The success of David Lett's Eyrie Vineyards South Block Reserve Pinot Noir 1975 raised eyebrows, most notably those of Robert Drouhin who, reluctant to believe the results, decided to stage a replay in Beaune in 1980. With the same wines but a different panel of competent judges, the Eyrie Pinot came in second, beaten by two-tenths of a point by Drouhin's Chambolle-Musigny 1959, but still managing to push the Chambertin-Clos de Bèze 1961 into third place. Suddenly, anyone interested in the Côte d'Or had also heard of the Dundee Hills in Oregon's northern Willamette Valley.

The 1975 Eyrie wine, like all of David Lett's wines, is a model of delicacy and restraint, of perfumed finesse rather than overextraction and power. The style of wine that Lett set out to make, and of which the 1975 is a perfect example, is the style he still makes today. In the past, it had often been said that good Pinot could not be made outside Burgundy. The Eyrie Vineyards 1975 wine changed all that. **SG**
🜨🜨🜨🜨🜨 Drink: to 2020

This beautiful farm in the inland Tulbagh district was acquired in 2010 by Terroir Selections, the company of American wine and hospitality man Charles Banks. He changed the name from Tulbagh Mountain Vineyards, as the estate was known when vines were first planted in the early 1990s.

Rebecca Tanner in the winery and Paul Nicholls in the vineyard have formed a harmonious partnership since 2009 and overseen the continuing improvement (assisted by consultation with Banks' American team). While the property has always been farmed organically, a biodynamic approach now "gives us the best results," says Rebecca, "since it is a great way to enhance the health of the farm organism as well as being best for wine quality."

Grapes for the Syrah are picked notably ripe, and there is a plush intensity to it, but it is dry, and its new-oak influence is modest. The element of red- and black-fruited elegance is augmented by the use of a proportion of whole bunches, stems and all, in the fermenting juice. If quality continues to improve at Fable, future vintages will be even more marvelous, but already there are hints of profundity. **TJ**
🜨🜨 Drink: to 2021

Fable Mountain's vineyards nestle in the shadow of the Witzenberg Mountains. ➡

Domaine Faiveley *Chambertin-Clos de Bèze Les Ouvrées Rodin* 2010

Origin France, Burgundy, Côte de Nuits
Style Dry red wine, 13.5% ABV
Grape Pinot Noir

Maison J. Faiveley, founded in 1825, has long been one of Burgundy's most respected négociants, but as Domaine Faiveley it also owns many top vineyards, including four grands crus in the Côte de Beaune and six in the Côte de Nuits, of which Chambertin-Clos de Bèze may be the brightest jewel in the crown.

The firm has been enjoying a renaissance since 2007 under Erwan Faiveley, the current generation of the owning family; Bernard Hervet, the managing director; and Jérôme Flous, the talented technical director. The wines, which were often austere, dry, and tannic, now have greater elegance, purity, and succulence, due in part to the adoption of five high-quality coopers and more sensitive vinification.

In the great 2010 vintage, the firm decided to release for the first time a special cuvée of Clos de Bèze called Les Ouvrées Rodin, from the oldest of its three plots. The other Clos de Bèze cuvée has hardly suffered as a result and is also superb. But separate vinification for a few years prior to the first release showed that the oldest plot produced an even more magical wine, of astonishing depth and intensity, but also harmony and sublime silken refinement. **NB**
😊😊😊😊😊 **Drink: to 2030+**

Château Falfas *Le Chevalier* 2000

Origin France, Bordeaux, Côtes de Bourg
Style Dry red wine, 13.5% ABV
Grapes Merlot 55%, C. Sauvignon 30%, Others 15%

Tucked away on a slope in the undulating Côtes de Bourg, Falfas is a substantial and charming Renaissance château dating from 1612. In 1988 the property was bought by John Cochran, a U.S. lawyer then based in Paris. His wife, Véronique, is the daughter of one of France's leading biodynamic consultants, and one of Cochran's first decisions was to convert the vineyards to biodynamism.

With 54 acres (22 ha) of vines, this is quite a large property, and the vines are planted on varying soils. The Cochrans are not fans of green-harvesting, but nonetheless yields are kept low. The wines are fermented with indigenous yeasts and aged in one-third new oak. In 1990 the Cochrans introduced a special bottling called Le Chevalier, which is produced from the oldest vines, some of which are seventy years old and give a very low crop.

The oak is evident on the Le Chevalier 2000, as one would expect, but it is not too dominant. It is an assertive and robust wine with plenty of grip; it is built to last and has good length and a chewy finish. The regular Falfas can be drunk young, but the Le Chevalier benefits from aging. **SBr**
😊😊 **Drink: to 2018+**

The Château Falfas *chais*, behind the estate's autumnal vines. ➡

Far Niente
Cabernet Sauvignon 2001

Origin USA, California, Napa Valley
Style Dry red wine, 13.5% ABV
Grapes C. Sauvignon 93%, Merlot 4%, Petit Verdot 3%

From the first harvest at the Far Niente winery in 1982, Dirk Hampson has been involved in the winemaking, whether as winemaker or director of winemaking. This rare consistency is one of the factors distinguishing Far Niente from properties that employ itinerant winemakers.

Gil Nickel, an Oklahoma nurseryman, purchased the winery that was to become Far Niente in 1979, restoring an 1885 gravity flow winery (abandoned since Prohibition) to produce a wine with the perfume and elegance of a Margaux. Nickel remained involved until his early death in 2003.

2001 was the first year that Far Niente Cabernet Sauvignon was produced from 100 percent Oakville estate fruit, blended from the select lots of the 100-acre (40 ha) Stelling Vineyard and the 42-acre (17 ha) Sullenger Vineyard. Stelling fruit, the core of the wine (90 percent of the 2001) is grown in the gravelly loam behind the winery, leading up to the western hills of Oakville. The soils of the Oakville alluvial fans here contribute to the berrylike fruit, rounded tannins, and sensual character of the Far Niente Cabernets. The 2001 vintage, harvested over the last week of September into the first week of October, was aged for twenty months in French oak (95 percent new barrels). The relatively moderate season produced a classically elegant and stylish wine in the Far Niente fashion, promising a graceful evolution and harmonious character as it ages. **LGr**
🜚🜚🜚🜚 **Drink: to 2020**

Fog from San Pablo Bay blankets Oakville vineyards. ➡

Fattoria La Massa *Chianti Classico Giorgio Primo* 1997

Fèlsina Berardenga *Chianti Classico Riserva Rancia* 1988

Origin Italy, Tuscany, Chianti Classico
Style Dry red wine, 14% ABV
Grapes Sangiovese 91%, Merlot 9%

Origin Italy, Tuscany, Chianti Classico
Style Dry red wine, 13% ABV
Grape Sangiovese

Fattoria La Massa, located in the area of Panzano in Chianti, has been producing wine since the thirteenth century. Owner Giampaolo Motta undertook an apprenticeship with highly regarded Tuscan producers (Fontodi, Castello dei Rampolla) before he purchased Fattoria La Massa in 1992.

Motta hired Carlo Ferrini as a consultant winemaker, but continued to take some important technical decisions himself. Keeping the wine on its fine lees, with frequent *bâtonnage*, was something quite new in Chianti, particularly for the Sangiovese grape. With this rather untraditional approach, wines such as the Giorgio Primo 1997 managed to capture the attention of wine journalists.

Motta insists that if he had possessed in 1997 the knowledge that he has today, he would have produced a far better wine, because the grapes that year were of sensational quality. As it is, the wine still shows a certain primary character, both in its color and on the nose. On the palate, it is quite sound, showing continuity with the character on the nose—very fruity, slightly roasted, with earthy nuances of leather and licorice. **AS**

☺☺☺☺ Drink: to 2017+

The Grancia of Fèlsina, from which the Rancia vineyard takes its name, was a complex of buildings and properties controlled by Benedictine monks. It formed part of Santa Maria della Scala, which was one of the great hospital complexes of medieval Europe. The vineyard is at an altitude of more than 1,345 feet (410 m), covering about 15 acres (6 ha), with south-facing exposure. Vines were first planted in 1958. Situated in the commune of Castelnuovo Berardenga, in the extreme southeast corner of the Chianti Classico zone, Fèlsina was acquired by Domenico Poggiali in 1961. After his daughter Gloria married the Veneto schoolteacher Giuseppe Mazzocolin, the latter abandoned the classroom for winemaking. He now runs the estate with consultant Franco Bernabei.

Mazzocolin and Bernabei had found their feet by 1988, creating one of their best ever wines in that vintage. The wine is unusual for Chianti Classico in being made from 100 percent Sangiovese. Tightly structured when young, Rancia blossoms after five or so years in bottle into a gorgeous mouthful of herbs, tea leaves, and rich, plummy fruit. **SG**

☺☺☺☺ Drink: to 2018+

Felton Road
Block 3 Pinot Noir 2002

Origin New Zealand, Central Otago
Style Dry red wine, 14% ABV
Grape Pinot Noir

Fiddlehead
Lollapalooza Pinot Noir 2002

Origin USA, California, Santa Barbara County
Style Dry red wine, 14% ABV
Grape Pinot Noir

Nigel Greening was a U.K.-based movie producer who enjoyed the wines of New Zealand's Felton Road estate so much that he once drove around all his local wine merchants to buy every bottle available. Like Victor Kiam and his electric shavers, Greening liked the company so much that he bought it. Greening already owned his own vineyard in nearby Cornish Point.

Bannockburn in Central Otago is the most southerly wine-growing region in the world, and the only one in New Zealand with a continental rather than a maritime climate. This brings the risk of frost, but has the benefits of low rainfall and high sunshine hours. Such a marginal climate is ideally suited to the production of high-quality Pinot Noir.

Felton Road's Block 3 vineyard is perfectly north-facing with a deep topsoil layer of windblown loess. The outstanding 2002 vintage is richly flavored, with high acidity but low tannin, and a soft, lingering finish. The aromas suggest red fruits with a hint of spice. The wine is best enjoyed young, but can be aged for up to fifteen years. Nigel Greening believes it to be one of the best they have yet produced. **SG**

🍷🍷🍷 **Drink: to 2017+**

Kathy Joseph, originally a microbiologist, became fascinated by winemaking and worked until 1989 for Pecota in Napa Valley. In 1989, she founded her own company based in Santa Barbara. Her two principal varieties were Sauvignon Blanc and Pinot Noir, and the latter came not only from local Santa Barbara vineyards but from Oregon, too. There is a playful, almost whimsical side to her approach, with Sauvignon cuvées named Goosebury [*sic*] and Honeysuckle, and a Pinot called Lollapalooza.

In 1997 she bought land opposite the famous Sanford & Benedict Vineyard, and planted 100 acres (40 ha) of Pinot Noir at high density. The site is cool and well drained. This she named the Fiddlestix Vineyard, and her first vintage was in 2000.

As well as the regular Pinot Noir from Fiddlestix, labeled "728," Joseph makes Lollapalooza, a selection from the finest barrels. Like the 728, this is aged in almost 50 percent new oak. The 2002 is particularly successful, with elegant cherry aromas, integrated oak, a plump texture, ample sweet fruit, and ripe tannins. It is well structured, given that the vines are still young, and it has fine length of flavor. **SBr**

🍷🍷🍷 **Drink: to 2017+**

Château Figeac
2001

Finca Luzón
Altos de Luzón 2002

Origin France, Bordeaux, St.-Emilion
Style Dry red wine, 13% ABV
Grapes C. Franc 35%, C. Sauvignon 35%, Merlot 30%

Origin Spain, Murcia, Jumilla
Style Dry red wine, 14.5% ABV
Grapes Monastrell, C. Sauvignon, Tempranillo

The numerous other St.-Emilion properties with Figeac in their name testify to the fact that in the past the property was far larger than it is today; even so, with 100 acres (40 ha) under vine, Figeac remains substantial. Unlike many St.-Emilion estates, its vineyards have a low clay content; indeed the terroir has much in common with the Médoc, with vines planted on three gravelly slopes. The terrain also influences the grape varieties cultivated, with a high proportion of Cabernet Franc and, remarkably, a good deal of Cabernet Sauvignon, too.

In contrast to richer, fleshier St.-Emilions, including most of the other first growths, Figeac is more restrained and austere in its youth. This sometimes means the wine is underestimated when young, but Figeac, when mature, is a model of elegance and harmony. Although the wine is refined, it is by no means fragile, and has enough body to withstand aging in 100 percent new barrels.

2001 was an exceptional vintage in St.-Emilion. The new oak is very apparent, both on the nose and the palate, but the wine is dominated by exquisite flavors of cherries and red fruits. **SBr**
🗲🗲🗲 **Drink: to 2025**

After a change of ownership in 2005, Finca Luzón became simply Bodegas Luzón. Its vineyard area of 1,730 acres (700 ha) is planted mostly to the traditional Monastrell, but also to Tempranillo, Cabernet, Merlot, Syrah, and other varieties.

As a consequence of the change of ownership, there were also a few significant management changes. Miguel Gil, aided by the work of enologist Joaquín Gálvez, was responsible for promoting Finca Luzón from the status of bulk wine producer to the enviable position it would later occupy in southeast Spain. Since 2005 both men have followed their own paths to some of the most exciting projects in their area: Gil at his own Jumillan brainchild, Hijos de Juan Gil, and Gálvez at Beryna in Alicante, next to Rafael Bernabé. Neither move, however, seems to have deflected Luzón from its orientation toward quality.

Altos de Luzón shows, year in and year out but perhaps particularly in 2002, the great potential of Spanish Monastrell-based wines. This local grape, first grown in southeast Spain in the Middle Ages, now provides harmonious wines of power under control, thanks to a judicious use of oak. **JB**
🗲 **Drink: to 2017+**

Finca Sandoval
2005

Origin Spain, Castilla-La Mancha, Manchuela
Style Dry red wine, 14.5% ABV
Grapes Syrah, Monastrell, Bobal

Flowers *Camp Meeting Ridge*
Sonoma Coast Pinot Noir 2001

Origin USA, California, Sonoma Coast
Style Dry red wine, 14% ABV
Grape Pinot Noir

Some wine lovers take their passion to the extreme and start their own winemaking project. If the protagonist also happens to be a first-class wine writer, as is the case with Víctor de la Serna, founder and owner of Finca Sandoval, he also brings an important perspective—that of one who knows all about vineyards. Víctor de la Serna also enjoys the help of a fine local enologist—Rafael Orozco.

Finca Sandoval is a property of 25 acres (10 ha) planted with Syrah on clay-chalky soils, at a height of 2,526 feet (770 m) above sea level. Syrah was chosen because of its potential in this particular climate and soil. The company also owns, or has rights over, several acres of Mourvèdre, Bobal, Garnacha Tintorera, and Touriga Nacional.

The 2002 vintage was excellent in the warmer areas of Spain, Manchuela included, and the Finca Sandoval of this year is, undoubtedly, a great wine, with an unusual balance between Atlantic and Mediterranean nuances. But one vintage that indicates the future quality and style of this wine is the 2005, which is already magnificent and will only gain in stature over the years. **JB**

🍷🍷🍷 **Drink: to 2020**

The two Flowers vineyards are perched high in the Sonoma coastal range, only 2 miles (3.2 km) from the shore. Walt Flowers was a nurseryman in Pennsylvania, who first planted vines here on the Sonoma Coast in 1991. Camp Meeting Ridge, his first vineyard, is at an elevation ranging from 1,100 to 1,400 feet (335–427 m). In 1998 Flowers planted an even higher ridgetop vineyard. Through the tangled scrub and woodland, he discerned the soil was red and volcanic with clay particles. Soil analyses and aerial surveys persuaded Flowers that his hunch was sound, and the first vintage from the cleared and planted Flowers Ranch vineyard was in 2004. Yields are very low at both sites.

Finesse is the hallmark of the Flowers Pinot Noir, but that does not mean there is any lack of fruit or that its tone is attenuated. The basic Pinot Noir cuvée, combining grapes from the Flowers vineyards with those from other sites controlled though not owned by the Flowers team, sets a high standard. The 2001 blends aromatically fine raspberry fruit and a discreet toastiness, and the flavors are bright, juicy, and concentrated, with a long, pure finish. **SBr**

🍷🍷🍷 **Drink: to 2017+**

Fontodi
Flaccianello della Pieve 1997

Origin Italy, Tuscany
Style Dry red wine, 13.5% ABV
Grape Sangiovese

Foradori
Granato 2004

Origin Italy, Trentino, Mezzolombardo
Style Dry red wine, 14% ABV
Grape Teroldego

One of the most acclaimed IGT Sangiovese wines, Flaccianello takes its name from a southwest-facing 25-acre (10 ha) vineyard, situated 1,312 feet (400 m) above sea level at Panzano in Chianti, in the valley of the Conca d'Oro (Golden Basin). The name Fontodi is of Roman origin, from the Latin *Fons-odi*.

The Manetti family has been producing traditional terra cotta in the Chianti region for more than three centuries. In 1968 the family bought Fontodi, and ever since has quietly been acquiring new sites and improving the quality of its wines.

Flaccianello 1997 shows all the richness associated with that great Tuscan vintage. When young, it had magnificently pure Sangiovese characteristics, smelling of tea leaves and herbs, with underlying cherry and plum fruit. With such an ideal balance of fruit, acidity, and tannins, it was tempting to drink the wine young. At ten years of age, well-cellared examples were still very youthful, though starting to become more complex and meaty in flavor. The wine has won several accolades, including a Tre Bicchieri rating from the influential Italian wine guide *Gambero Rosso*. **SG**

🍷🍷🍷🍷 **Drink: to 2020+**

Granato means "pomegranate" in Italian. Grapevines and pomegranates have the same origins in the Mediterranean, and so the name was given to the concentrated and dense Teroldego, unquestionably Trentino's best red grape variety. The building blocks of this world-class wine have been a careful selection of the variety's best phenotypes, the biodiversity of the vineyard, and a lowering of the yields.

The Granato 2004 won the "Three Glasses" award in the 2007 *Gambero Rosso* guide. The wine comes from Teroldego vineyards around Foradori's hometown of Mezzolombardo, and specifically from single sites in Morei, Sgarzon, and Cesura, where the alluvial soils are stony with lots of pebbles.

Fermented in large open oak casks, then aged for eighteen months in small barriques, the wine has a dramatic, very deep ruby color that hints at the intensity of the aromas and flavors. The nose is fabulous—opulent, herbal, almost viscous in its intensity yet also magically elegant. The wine is built on a powerful base of interweaving tannins relieved by a soft medley of hedgerow fruits and even, as one taster has remarked, ripe pomegranate seeds. **ME**

🍷🍷🍷🍷 **Drink: to 2020**

Château Fourcas-Hosten
2005

Origin France, Bordeaux, Listrac
Style Dry red wine, 13% ABV
Grapes Merlot 45%, C. Sauvignon 45%, C. Franc 10%

Domaine Fourrier
Griotte-Chambertin GC 2005

Origin France, Burgundy, Côte de Nuits
Style Dry red wine, 13% ABV
Grape Pinot Noir

Listrac, which lies a good distance west of the most prestigious vineyards of the Médoc, has a reputation for rather tough, rustic wines. Indeed, this reputation is often justified. On the other hand, the wines can age very well. A number of properties bear the Fourcas name, and this is the most charming of the Fourcas châteaux, a well-proportioned and modest country house located near the village church.

In 1983 the then owner, New York wine merchant Peter M. F. Sichel, asked Patrick Pagès, the owner of the neighboring Château Fourcas-Dupré, to manage the property and oversee its winemaking. Some of the vineyards are picked by machine and the wine is aged for twelve months in one-third-new barriques.

Pagès, although very familiar with the vineyards, is puzzled that the wine is so different from his own at Fourcas-Dupré. When young, there can be some rusticity, but after ten or more years in bottle more complex aromas and flavors begin to emerge. For example, the 1971, although not an outstanding wine, was still full of life and character at more than thirty years old. The 2005 has plenty of fruit on the nose, and the palate has more flesh than usual. **SBr**

🍷🍷 **Drink: to 2025**

Griotte-Chambertin, down the slope from Clos de Bèze, is, at 6.75 acres (2.73 ha), the smallest grand cru in the commune, and there are only some half a dozen owners. Among the most highly-regarded, for quality if not for volume, for only some four casks are annually produced, is that of Domaine Fourrier.

At the time Jean-Marie Fourrier joined his father Jean-Claude in the late 1980s, the reputation of the estate was at a low ebb: fine wines in the 1950s and '60s, but disappointing thereafter. Jean-Marie had been an intern *chez* the late, great Henri Jayer, and had also worked with Domaine Drouhin in Oregon. He fine-tuned the production, reduced the crop, and separately vinified the four Gevrey-Chambertin premiers crus (the fifth, Clos St.-Jacques, had always been individually treated). The wines, since 1993, have once again been excellent.

2005 is a great Burgundy vintage. Griotte (from a corruption of *crai*, chalky limestone, and nothing to do with cherries, for all that the wine is, indeed, black cherry flavored) makes one of the commune's most refined wines; a Gevrey with a hint of Musigny, perhaps. This is a very lovely example. **CC**

🍷🍷🍷🍷🍷 **Drink: 2019–2035+**

Freemark Abbey
Sycamore Cabernet Sauvignon 2003

Origin USA, California, Napa Valley
Style Dry red wine, 14% ABV
Grapes C. Sauvignon 85%, Merlot 8%, C. Franc 7%

Frog's Leap
Rutherford 2002

Origin USA, California, Napa Valley
Style Dry red wine, 13.6% ABV
Grapes C. Sauvignon 89%, C. Franc 11%

A winery stood on this spot, just north of St. Helena, in 1886. It closed its doors in 1955, but was reactivated in 1967. Over the years there were numerous changes in ownership. In 2001, the winery and brand, though not the vineyards, were sold to the Legacy Estates Group, to be bought in 2006 by Jess Jackson, though the Freemark label lives on.

From the 1970s onward, Freemark Abbey became renowned for a single-vintage Cabernet from the dry-farmed Bosché vineyard. In 1984, a second Cabernet was added to the portfolio from the Sycamore vineyard. Sycamore is superbly located in Rutherford, and produces a denser, more structured wine than Bosché. A small proportion of Cabernet Franc and Merlot from the same vineyard are blended in to give additional complexity.

The Sycamore Cabernet 2003 has immense aromatic richness, with black cherry fruit and a streak of mint, and an overt ripeness that comes close to jamminess. The palate is immensely concentrated, and although the tannins are formidable there is no excessive extraction, and the finish is vigorous and long. In short, classic Napa Cabernet. **SBr**

◐◐◐ **Drink: to 2025**

Frog's Leap Rutherford cuvée is the antidote to stuffy Californian wines, often too precious in their claim to "unparalleled quality." Developed by Larry Turley and John Williams in 1981, Frog's Leap set a standard for supple, delicious wines drawn from valley fruit, accessible and of a place rather than a price point.

Although intended to be enjoyed with good humor and zest for life, the flagship cuvée lacks no gravitas. It is crafted to exemplify what legendary winemaker André Tchelistcheff believed to be the essence of Napa Valley: intense aromatics, dark-berried fruits lifted by subtle green-olive scents, and a harmonious palate texture he termed "Rutherford Dust," likened to velvet over pebbles.

To make a soft, supple wine with just enough grip, Williams eschews concentration devices and favors extended maceration for up to thirty days; he shuns new oak treatment that would obscure the natural texture of the terroir. The warm 2002 summer offered optimal conditions for a quintessential Frog's Leap Rutherford cuvée: vibrant ripe fruits jumping out of the glass, and a succulent palate with firm, dusty tannins subtly tugging on the back palate. **LGr**

◐◐◐ **Drink: to 2017+**

Harvesting Merlot grapes at Frog's Leap. ➡

Fromm Winery
Clayvin Vineyard Pinot Noir 2001

Origin New Zealand, Marlborough
Style Dry red wine, 14% ABV
Grape Pinot Noir

Elena Fucci
Aglianico del Vulture Titolo 2004

Origin Italy, Basilicata, Vulture
Style Dry red wine, 13.5% ABV
Grape Aglianico

Although Fromm Winery offers several good varietal wines, more than half of production is now Pinot Noir, as owner Georg Fromm believes that this "will achieve the highest international standard of any grape variety grown in New Zealand."

In addition to La Strada Pinot Noir, blended from two Brancott Valley sites, Fromm bottles two single-vineyard versions—Fromm Vineyard and Clayvin Vineyard. The latter is a beautiful, well-exposed, hillside site, also in Brancott Valley, in one of the highest parts of Marlborough, and takes its name from its complex clay soils. The 37 acres (15 ha) were first planted in 1991 by two local viticulturalists, who supplied fruit to Fromm before selling them and UK shipper Lay and Wheeler the vineyard in 1998.

Georg describes the 2001 vintage as the best since 1996. It represented Marlborough at New Zealand's Pinot Noir Celebration in 2004, receiving praise from French wine writer, Michel Bettane. On the nose, it is composed, darkly fruited, gently smoky, and vivid, while on the palate it is harmonious and luxuriously textured, with the minerality and personality of its privileged site. **NB**
🔴🔴🔴 **Drink: to 2017**

Elena Fucci is a young estate, born only in 2000. The owner, Elena herself, is also young, and a recently qualified professional winemaker. She was still completing her studies in Pisa when the first wine of the estate (2001) was created under the supervision of her father, Salvatore, and consultant winemaker Sergio Paternoster. The Aglianico del Vulture Titolo is made from grapes grown in the vineyard of the same name—a vineyard so aptly positioned and so small that it could easily be mistaken for the backyard of the Fuccis' house, in the village of Barile.

The Titolo 2001 was an amazing preview of the potential of the estate. 2002 and 2003 were two very different and difficult vintages, which highlighted how well this producer could cope with extreme situations. Maturity came with the 2004 vintage.

The Titolo 2004 has a deep, vibrant color and an amazingly complex nose, showing a character of ripe, juicy dark berries and light, more earthy/leathery notes. The bouquet is completed by a hint of balsamic and mint. Elena Fucci dreams of one day seeing Barile become the Montalcino of Basilicata, and that recognition should not be too far off. **AS**
🔴🔴🔴 **Drink: to 2025+**

Gago Pago La Jara
2004

Origin Spain, Toro
Style Dry red wine, 14.5% ABV
Grape Tinta de Toro (Tempranillo)

After ten years at the family winery, Remelluri in Rioja, Telmo Rodríguez created his own company in 1994 with other Spanish winemakers also educated in Bordeaux. Together they are rediscovering many appellations in Spain and creating wines there.

Telmo's *modus operandi* is to begin in collaboration with a local grower, make a simple and inexpensive wine, come to understand the character of the grapes and the soil and climate of the region, then look for exceptional vineyards from which to create a top bottling. This was the case in Toro, where he made Dehesa Gago and Gago before he made this Pago La Jara. The fruit for this cuvée is sourced from three small plots of ungrafted old vines, planted in the 1940s at 2,250 feet (686 m), on slopes of clay-limestone soil covered by pebbles.

2004 is a classic vintage in Toro. Initially, it may be seen as hard and tannic, in comparison to lusher vintages like 2003 and 2005. The wine has mineral notes of peat and graphite, spices, smoke, black fruit (blackberry and blueberry), and hints of violet. In the mouth, it is big and powerful, but balanced, with fresh fruit. It is long and persistent. **LG**

❸❸❸ **Drink: to 2019**

Gaia Estate
Agiorghitiko 1998

Origin Greece, Peloponnese, Nemea
Style Dry red wine, 13.5% ABV
Grape Agiorghitiko

The Peloponnese is the southernmost part of the Greek mainland. Here, on limestone soils, is the village of Koutis, home to Gaia, named after the ancient Greek goddess of the earth. Gaia was created in 1997 in the appellation of Nemea by the young Greek winemaking duo of Leon Karatsalous and Yannis Parakevopoulos. They started their wine careers on the island of Santorini, where they still produce one of Greece's signature white wines.

A lot of Nemea is pleasant, easy-drinking wine made from vineyards planted on the flatter plateaus among the hills, from vines where the yields are the highest allowed under the appellation rules. That is not the case at Gaia Estate. Leon and Yannis bought vineyards on hill slopes and pruned the vines to give low yields of outstanding quality fruit from the little-known but fine grape Agiorghitiko (St. George).

The 1998 is deep, almost opaque, with aromas and flavors of ripe, dark fruits (black cherries and damsons), with sweet spice and toast. On the palate, the ripeness of fruit is perfectly balanced by the acidity and soft, velvety tannins. Gaia Estate is clearly at the forefront of world-class Greek wine. **GL**

❸❸❸❸ **Drink: to 2018**

Gaja *Barbaresco* 2001

Origin Italy, Piedmont, Langhe
Style Dry red wine, 13.5% ABV
Grape Nebbiolo

BARBARESCO
DENOMINAZIONE DI ORIGINE CONTROLLATA E GARANTITA
2001

The Gaja family settled in Piedmont in the mid-seventeenth century, and Giovanni Gaja founded the eponymous winery in 1859. Angelo joined the business in 1961, and today the family owns 250 acres (101 ha) of prime vineyards in Barbaresco and Barolo, as well as two further estates in Tuscany. Although Angelo is the front man and marketer extraordinaire, Guido Rivella is the winemaker.

Gaja's Langhe portfolio includes a number of Barbaresco single-vineyard wines: Sorí Tildin, Sorí San Lorenzo, and Costa Russi. There are also two Barolo crus: Sperss and Conteisa Cerequio, produced at the rented Gromis estate. But the Barbaresco *tout court* remains the Gaja estate's flagship wine, blended from fourteen different parcels of vines.

The 2000 and 2001 vintages were the last two of an extraordinary run of fine vintages that the wines of Alba enjoyed from 1995 onward, and came to be dubbed the "seven fat years." Now that the wines have been bottled for some time, 2001 has emerged as the finer vintage, having more grace and elegance, and more staying power in the long term. Tasted in March 2006, Gaja's Barbaresco 2001 was a classic of its kind, with a superbly pure and ripe Nebbiolo nose. The palate was unsurprisingly still closed and undeveloped, but the magnificent concentration and length were already apparent. In a fine year like 2001, top Barbaresco can age for thirty years or more, though this will perhaps start to be approachable after ten years or so. **SG**
😊😊😊😊 **Drink: to 2031+**

FURTHER RECOMMENDATIONS
Other great vintages
1964 · 1971 · 1985 · 1989 · 1990 · 1996 · 1997 · 2004
More Gaja wines
Barolo Sperss · Costa Russi · Gaja and Rey Chardonnay · Sorí San Lorenzo · Sorí Tildin

Domaine Gauby *Côtes du Roussillon-Villages Rouge Muntada* 2003

Origin France, Roussillon
Style Dry red wine, 13.5% ABV
Grapes Syrah 45%, Grenache 30%, Carignan 25%

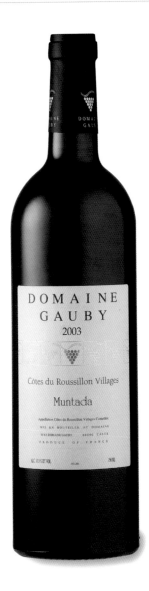

The son of a former French international rugby player, Gérard Gauby is often described as the "uncrowned king of the Roussillon." When he inherited his maternal grandfather's vines in 1985, he had under his control just 12 acres (5 ha) of vines, the crop of which was taken to the local cooperative. He has since systematically expanded the estate, so that today he cultivates a total of 111 acres (45 ha) of vines in the remote Agly valley, west of Perpignan.

Most of the vineyards are in the village of Calce, though Gauby has also purchased vineyards further inland, in the fashionable Fenouillèdes region. The soils are mainly chalky—hence the name Calce, from *calcaire*. Grenache predominates; some vines were planted in 1947, and yields are extremely low.

The flagship wine is Muntada, a red Côtes du Roussillon-Villages. Muntada used to average 15 percent alcohol, but in the late 1990s Gauby became convinced that there was something wrong with Roussillon's vineyards, which needed constant spraying with chemicals. He weaned his vineyards off chemicals and since 2000 has been completely biodynamic. As the physiognomy of his vines changed, so too did the style of the wine. He is using less new oak and fewer extractive techniques in the winery, too. The objective is to produce wines of greater finesse, an aim explained by his love of great Burgundy. What was once a high-alcohol blockbuster is now a much fresher and more restrained wine that demands aging. **SG**

❾❾❾❾ **Drink: to 2018+**

FURTHER RECOMMENDATIONS
Other great vintages
1998 • 1999 • 2000 • 2001 • 2002 • 2007
More Gauby wines
Les Calcinaires • La Coume Ginestre
Vieilles Vignes

Château Gazin
2004

Origin France, Bordeaux, Pomerol
Style Dry red wine, 13% ABV
Grapes Merlot 90%, C. Sauvignon 7%, C. Franc 3%

Jean-René Germanier
Cayas Syrah du Valais Réserve 2005

Origin Switzerland, Valais, Vétroz
Style Dry red wine, 13% ABV
Grape Syrah

Unlike its mighty neighbor, Château Pétrus, Gazin has a proper château, an elegant country mansion that has been inhabited for ninety years by the Bailliencourt family. In the 1970s Gazin went through a bad patch. The family also owned Château La Dominique in St.-Emilion, but to keep hold of Gazin, they were forced to sell their other property, as well as almost 12 acres (4.8 ha) of Gazin's own vineyards. The purchaser was none other than Pétrus, and this sale robbed Gazin of some of its best parcels.

Not all of Gazin's vines are ideally located, but about two-thirds of its 60 acres (24 ha) are on the celebrated Pomerol plateau, shared with Pétrus and a handful of other properties. Gazin does not have the same power and weight as Pétrus, though when young it can be dense and tannic. Since 1988 the wine has been very good indeed, though often underrated, perhaps because it is made in good quantities for a Pomerol and thus lacks the cachet of its low-production rivals. The 2004 shows how fine the wine can be in a less-than-stellar vintage. It is perfumed and intense on the nose, yet the palate shows great richness, spice, and elegance. **SBr**

🥂🥂🥂 **Drink: to 2025**

The Swiss canton of Valais is not only the biggest wine canton in the country but also the source of the River Rhône. Wine grower Jean-René Germanier always dreamed of producing a great Syrah wine. His winery's history goes back to 1896, when Urban Germanier founded the vineyard at Balavaud Vétroz. Today, Gilles Besse, the nephew of Jean-René Germanier, is in charge of the winemaking.

The first vintage of the 100 percent Syrah Cayas was 1995—released then as Syrah du Valais. The name Cayas refers to *caillou* (French for "pebble") and to the slate soil in the region of Vétroz. Since that first vintage, Cayas has been regarded as the best Syrah of Switzerland, marked by elegance, concentration, power, and length. In 2004, the winery launched a second wine, called simply Syrah 2004, with the aim of raising higher still the quality of the Cayas.

The Cayas 2005 has a dark, almost violet color. On the nose, there are aromatics of black currant, forest floor, and coffee. The palate is very elegant and fresh, with a good balance between ripe red fruits and earthy, mineral, spicy notes. The tannins are dense and firm, and the finish long. **CK**

🥂🥂🥂 **Drink: to 2017+**

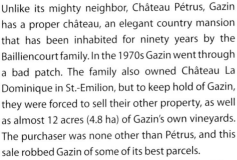

◧ The newly arrived grapes are destemmed in the Gazin winery.

Gerovassiliou *Avaton* 2002

Origin Greece, Macedonia, Epanomi
Style Dry red wine, 14% ABV
Grapes Limnio, Mavroudi, Mavrotragano

Evangelos Gerovassiliou's eponymous domaine, perhaps the best in Greece, is located in Epanomi, some 15 miles (24 km) southwest of Thessaloniki. The current estate has its genesis in a family vineyard of 6 acres (2.5 ha), in which Vangelos began planting Greek and foreign varieties in 1981. Vangelos has the right background to make fine wine: He trained in Bordeaux, counting among his influences the great Emile Peynaud, and from 1976 to 1999 he was employed as chief enologist at Château Carras.

The original vineyard has since expanded to a sizable 111 acres (45 ha), planted still with a mix of Greek and foreign varieties. International stars Chardonnay, Sauvignon Blanc, Viognier, Grenache, Syrah, and Merlot rub shoulders with Greek varieties Assyrtiko, Malagousia, Limnio, Mavroudi, and Mavrotragano. Malagousia is Gerovassiliou's pride and joy because this variety was rescued from near extinction by Vangelos himself, and he was the first to demonstrate its undoubted potential by vinifying it for the first time using modern techniques.

Gerovassiliou's whites are impressive, but it is the reds that particularly stand out. The Gerovassiliou Syrah is a striking effort, but Avaton is possibly his best red wine, all the more interesting for the fact that it is a blend of three Greek varieties—Limnio, Mavroudi, and Mavrotragano. This is a substantial wine showing modern, earthy black fruits coupled with a lovely, spicy structure. A true vin de garde, this will develop over twenty years in the cellar. **JG**

🚫🟢 **Drink: to 2020+**

FURTHER RECOMMENDATIONS
Other great vintages
2001 • 2003 • 2004
More Gerovassiliou wines
Ktima Gerovassiliou (Red and White) • Ktima Gerovassiliou Fumé, Chardonnay, Viognier, Syrah

Harvested Limnio grapes arrive at the Gerovassiliou winery. ➡

Giaconda
Warner Vineyard Shiraz 2002

Origin Australia, Victoria, Beechworth
Style Dry red wine, 13.5% ABV
Grape Shiraz

The unassuming, quietly spoken Rick Kinzbrunner, a guru among Australian wine producers, is a true vigneron who puts as much effort into growing the right grapes as he does into making superb wine. Giaconda produced its first wine in 1985, quickly becoming celebrated for Chardonnay and, to a slightly lesser degree, Cabernet Sauvignon and Pinot Noir. It was not until 1999 that Shiraz appeared, to instant acclaim. Within four vintages, critics were ranking it among the best Shirazes in Australia, a country not short on competitive Shiraz wines.

The Shiraz grapes were first grown by a neighbor named Warner a short distance away from Giaconda's vineyard. These were joined by fruit from the younger, 2-acre (0.8 ha) estate vineyard—an estate Shiraz is a possibility in the future. The soil of both vineyards is granitic.

The 2002 is a big, concentrated wine with superbly brooding color and loads of opulent fruit: Plum, blackberry, and pepper and clove aromas predominate. The palate is dense and rich, almost chewy, yet also elegant. This is wine with a twenty-year life expectancy, at least. **HH**

🍷🍷🍷 **Drink: to 2022**

Bruno Giacosa
Asili di Barbaresco 2001

Origin Italy, Piedmont, Langhe
Style Dry red wine, 14% ABV
Grape Nebbiolo

Italy can boast many excellent wine producers and a few outstanding ones. But when it comes to genius, there may be only one: Bruno Giacosa. Bruno began as a *commerciante*, what the French call a *négociant*, buying grapes, as his father had before him, from growers with whom they had long relations, and crafting them into very special crus. Bruno always knew which ones were going to merit his highest accolade, the red label of the Riserva.

Bruno went on to purchase major vineyards in Asili in Barbaresco and Falletto in Serralunga, Barolo. Asili is famous not so much for its power as its elegance and grace; Falletto for its austerity and firmness, its tendency to take a long time to mature and its ability to age extremely well.

Giacosa's top wines, such as the Asili 2001 or 2000 Falleto Riserva, can be positively symphonic in their range and variety of aroma and flavor, sweet mixing with bitter, fruit with acidity and tannin, herb with flower, leather and tar with oak (though he uses only large *botti* for Barolo and Barbaresco), not forgetting the elements of mushroom, sometimes truffle, meat, and game. **NBel**

🍷🍷🍷🍷🍷 **Drink: to 2030+**

The Barbaresco village of Neive, the home of Bruno Giacosa. ➡

Château Giscours

1970

Origin France, Bordeaux, Margaux
Style Dry red wine, 12.5% ABV
Grapes C. Sauvignon 53%, Merlot 42%, Others 5%

This property was known, grimly enough, as a fortified dungeon in the fourteenth century. It had become a vineyard, however, by the time of its sale in 1552, making it one of the more venerable *crus classés*. During the Second Empire (1852–70), it was rebuilt using the banking fortune of its then proprietor, the Comte de Pescatore, in a style suitable for receiving Empress Eugénie. Nicolas Tari and his son Pierre ushered the vineyard into an era of glory after World War II, this to be consolidated in recent years under the control of the Francophile Jelgersma family of Dutch financiers.

The estate extends over four separate plots, planted on the Médoc's gravelly, sandy soil, with a rough, pebbly top layer allowing for all-important permeability. In 1970 it shared in the climatic renaissance enjoyed by Bordeaux as a whole, as the region put the ghastly vintages of the late 1960s behind it. The Médoc in particular turned out concentrated wines of extraordinary longevity, partly as a result of an unusually late harvest, which did not really get under way until October.

Giscours 1970 is dense and dark, still offering up licorice hints as well as fistfuls of pulpy blackberries as it embarked on its maturity in the early 1990s. Secondary development added dried figs and an herbal note (possibly oregano), but the ample muscle of the wine, supported by elegant tannins that have aged gracefully, continues to sustain it. **SW**
🍷🍷🍷🍷 **Drink: to 2020+**

The grand château was built by owner Count de Pescatore in 1847. ➡

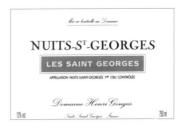

Goldwater
Goldie 2004

Domaine Henri Gouges *Nuits-St.-Georges PC Les St.-Georges* 2005

Origin New Zealand, Waiheke Island
Style Dry red wine, 13.5% ABV
Grapes Cabernet Sauvignon, Merlot

Origin France, Burgundy, Côte de Nuits
Style Dry red wine, 13% ABV
Grape Pinot Noir

Kim and Jeanette Goldwater pioneered grape growing on Waiheke Island when they planted their first vines in 1978. They quickly proved that the island was ideally suited for the production of high-quality Cabernet Sauvignon and Merlot.

The success of this Cabernet Sauvignon/Merlot blend, christened Goldie from the 2002 vintage, encouraged other aspiring winemakers to plant vines on Waiheke Island. Most discovered that wine made from low-yielding vines grown on expensive real estate was at best marginally profitable. Goldwater was the exception, boosting revenue by also making wine from Marlborough-grown grapes.

A move toward new vineyard sites and improved clones of Cabernet Sauvignon and Merlot has led to rising quality. The wine has become denser, with riper flavors, and now shows a stronger influence of classier oak. In 2004, the wine was made in many small parcels, allowing the individual characteristics of each clone and vineyard block to be retained prior to blending. It is an intense yet elegant red wine with primary fruit flavors of dark berry, anise, licorice, and a suggestion of Asian spices. **BC**

🍷🍷🍷 **Drink: to 2019**

The Gouges estate is sequestered behind a nondescript wall in Nuits-St.-Georges. In 1929, when most farmers were selling their grapes to shippers, Henri Gouges bottled his first wines. His sons took over in 1967 and expanded the estate to its current 37 acres (15 ha) of vineyard. Since 1985, two cousins have run the estate. Pierre manages the vineyards, taking a natural, organic approach to farming. Christian is in charge of the highly modern cellars.

In the late nineteenth century, the village of Nuits began calling itself Nuits-St.-Georges, adding the name of its most illustrious vineyard to its moniker. That site, which has been planted for more than a thousand years, faces the sunrise just south of the village. Its 17 acres (7 ha) are divided among fifteen growers. Gouges, with 2.5 acres (1 ha) of fifty-year-old vines, is one of the largest.

The 2005 was a very dry vintage. Bottled in early 2007, it is a dense, uncompromising wine. Austere in its youth, such a wine is generally an acquired taste. It has more flesh and suppleness than its predecessors, with blackberry and mineral notes. It could be the finest St.-Georges the estate has ever produced. **JP**

🍷🍷🍷🍷 **Drink: to 2030**

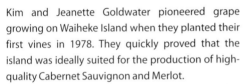

◀ Waiheke Island lies just off the coast of Auckland and is covered in vines.

Grace Family Vineyards
Cabernet Sauvignon 1995

Origin USA, California, Napa Valley
Style Dry red wine, 13.5% ABV
Grapes Cabernet Sauvignon

Grace Family Vineyards emerged in 1976, when a 1-acre (0.4 ha) plot was planted by Dick Grace with Cabernet Sauvignon budwood from the Bouché Vineyard in Rutherford. The fruit caught the attention of Charlie Wagner of Caymus, who made its wine as a special bottling until a dispute between the two men led Dick to set out on his own.

With its micro-production and mailing-list-only sales policy, Grace Family Vineyards produced arguably the first cult Cabernet in California. Annual production was often below 200 cases and more than 4,000 people were on the waiting list. If cult wines are defined by the star power behind the label, Grace Family Cabernet can boast a fine pedigree, with Gary Galleron, Heidi Peterson Barrett, Gary Brookman, and David Abreu all present at its creation. Dick Grace's son Kirk now manages the vineyard, which required considerable replanting in the early 1990s following a phylloxera infestation.

Few wines can compete with Grace Family Cabernet in terms of performance at auction. At the 1985 Napa Valley Wine Auction, a specially packaged five-bottle collection won the highest bid, selling for $10,000. Demand for Grace wines has continued unabated, with a 12-liter, engraved bottle of the 2003 vintage selling at the 2006 Naples Wine Auction for $90,000. The 1995, the first bottling by Heidi Peterson Barrett, is regarded as the quintessence of Napa Valley Cabernet. **LGr**
🍷🍷🍷🍷🍷 **Drink: to 2020+**

The Grace family home is located on the estate. ➡

Alain Graillot
Crozes-Hermitage 2001

Origin France, Northern Rhône, Crozes-Hermitage
Style Dry red wine, 13% ABV
Grape Syrah

Autodidacts are relatively rare in the wine world and so Alain Graillot is something of a phenomenon. An agricultural machinery salesman turned *récolteur-vigneron*, Graillot's first vintage under his own domaine name appeared in 1985. The Crozes-Hermitage is grown on a plot near the Rhône's confluence with the River Isère, where the land is an alluvial mix of gravel, sand, and small rocks.

The grapes are given a preferment maceration on their stems of between two and five days. After clarifying, the wine is given a mixed maturation treatment. 20 percent of it remains in vat, while the rest is divided among a mixture of one- and three-year-old oak barriques, where it spends up to a year.

A broiling August in 2001 was followed by a relatively cool, but mercifully dry, September. The conditions produced smallish grapes with thick skins, good acidity, and full physiological maturity. Picking began in the final week of September. As with other northern Rhône appellations, the 2001 vintage turned out better balanced wines than the excessively vaunted 2000.

Graillot's Crozes 2001 is a characteristically dark, dense wine, ink-black in its infancy, solid with ripe fruit tannin, and possessed of the smoky, meaty intensity of fine Rhône Syrah. On the palate, its raspberry-blackberry fruit emerges slowly from this initial shell, and had begun to assert itself in the balance after around three years. **SW**
ⓢ ⓢ ⓢ **Drink: to 2017**

◧ A Rhône winemaker samples wine that has been aging in barrel.

Château Grand-Puy-Lacoste 2000

Origin France, Bordeaux, Pauillac
Style Dry red wine, 13% ABV
Grapes C. Sauvignon 70%, Merlot 25%, C. Franc 5%

Although less well known than other wines from this commune, Grand-Puy-Lacoste has a track record as an excellent and sensibly priced Pauillac. It forms part of the stable of properties owned by the Borie family of *négociants*. Francois-Xavier Borie runs the estate, as well as another classified growth, Château Haut-Batailley, while his brother Bruno looks after the St.-Julien super-second of Ducru-Beaucaillou. The château itself dates from the 1850s and behind it is a rambling English-style garden and pool quite unexpected in a region where gardens tend to be formal and manicured.

The vineyards are located on two gravelly mounds and have scarcely altered in their dimensions in 150 years. The average age of the vines is about forty years, which helps to give the wine its concentration and focus. Grand-Puy-Lacoste is virile, but never rustic or clumsy.

The grapes are well sorted before vinification, and Borie is careful not to overextract; if a vintage lacks stuffing, he will add more press wine. The balance of Grand-Puy-Lacoste is usually exemplary, exhibiting the natural force of a typical Pauillac, while at the same time conserving a high degree of finesse and up-front fruitiness. The 2000 vintage is unusually sumptuous and possesses an incredible hedonistic quality that is hard to resist, being lush, velvety, chocolaty, and amazingly long. It will undoubtedly age well, just as the delicious and irresistibly fruity 1982 has done. **SBr**

🍷🍷🍷 **Drink: to 2030**

FURTHER RECOMMENDATIONS
Other great vintages
1961 · 1982 · 1988 · 1990 · 1995 · 1996 · 2005 · 2010
More fifth growths from Pauillac
d'Armailhac · Batailley · Clerc-Milon *Lynch-Bages · Pontet-Canet*

Grand-Puy-Lacoste has a history stretching back to the fifteenth century. ➡

Grange des Pères
2010

Elio Grasso
Barolo Runcot 2001

Origin France, Languedoc
Style Dry red wine, 13.5% ABV
Grapes Syrah, Mourvèdre, C. Sauvignon, Counoise

Origin Italy, Piedmont, Langhe
Style Dry red wine, 14% ABV
Grape Nebbiolo

Back in the 1970s, it was Aniane-based Mas de Daumas Gassac that first showed the world that the Languedoc could produce fine wine, with a fragrant, long-lived Cabernet Sauvignon made under the tutelage of the great Emile Peynaud. So it is perhaps no coincidence that Aniane is also home to the estate that some critics reckon has succeeded Daumas Gassac as the Languedoc's leading wine domaine—Laurent Vaillé's Grange des Pères. Vaillé, a physiotherapist by training, established his 27-acre domaine (11 ha) in the early 1990s, with the first vintage being 1992.

Yields are low, and the wine is a blend of Syrah, Mourvèdre, and Cabernet Sauvignon, with a tiny amount of Counoise. It is the presence of this last grape in the blend that results in this wine being labeled as a Vin de Pays, as opposed to AOC Coteaux du Languedoc. But who cares about appellations when the wine is this good? The wine completes an extended twenty-month *élevage* in oak barrels.

The key to the success of Grange des Pères, as with many fine wines, is balance, and this is shown in the 2010. It is not a heavy, dark wine, but instead shows an expressive nose that is slightly animally, with delicate ripe fruit character. The palate is profound, with an open, slightly sweet, herbal, animally edge to the intense, savory fruit. This is a Languedoc star with a hint of the northern Rhône about it. The balance and extended *élevage* also mean that this is a wine that will cellar well for at least a decade, and perhaps even longer. **JG**
🝳🝳🝳 **Drink: recent vintages for up to 12 years**

The winemaker Elio Grasso has undoubtedly become one the household names in Barolo and is part of the local echelon reverently known as *Barolisti*. A former banker who took on the family business in the late 1970s, Grasso replanted the vineyards and began bottling Barolo in 1978. He describes himself as being neither traditionalist nor modernist, and eschews being labeled as one or the other. What is important to him is to bottle the ultimate expression of the grapes in his vineyards, and he insists that it is better to be applauded as a grape grower than as a wine producer.

Grasso's 35 acres (14 ha) of vineyards in a hamlet of Monforte d'Alba are on the magnificent Gavarini hillside. He makes three different Barolos—Gavarini Vigna Chiniera, Ginestra Vigna Casa Maté, and single-vineyard Runcot. Elio's son Gianluca wanted to create a more modern expression for Runcot, and ages this wine in new French barriques to tame the powerful tannins. The south-facing 4.5-acre (1.8 ha) vineyard is slightly lower in altitude than his others, with limestone and clay soil that naturally gives the wine structure. Runcot is only bottled in the best years, starting with the 1995 vintage.

Although the 2001 vintage as a whole was given only four stars by the Barolo and Barbaresco Consorzio, it really deserved to be rated as a five-star vintage according to most producers, and is certainly capable of lengthy cellaring. The Runcot 2001 is sleek and polished, with complex layers of ripe fruit, oak, and spice, and great length. **KO**
🝳🝳🝳🝳 **Drink: to 2021+**

Silvio Grasso
Barolo Bricco Luciani 1997

Origin Italy, Piedmont, Langhe
Style Dry red wine, 14% ABV
Grape Nebbiolo

The Silvio Grasso estate was founded in 1927 and is now run by Federico Grasso, who is also the agronomist and the winemaker of the firm. The estate covers 34 acres (14 ha), half of which are planted with Nebbiolo. It surrounds the village of La Morra, where the soils, lighter and more sandy than those of Monforte and Serralunga d'Alba, allow for more elegant and forward wines.

Federico Grasso can be considered as a member of the "modernist" contingent among Barolo producers, though he also makes a very traditionally styled wine—André—that, far from being dedicated to someone of that name, is so-called after the Piedmontese word for "backward." This Barolo has very long maceration (up to forty days) and is aged in traditional large oak casks.

The Bricco Luciani comes from one of the finest *crus* of the village of La Morra, and is produced with a much more modern approach to that of André. Short maceration and aging in small barriques ensure that this wine is enjoyable from the date of release. The 1997 is a bold example. The color is intense, even though there is no sign of youthful, purple vibrancy. The nose is quite open, intense, penetrating, and very elegant, with notes of dried flowers and undergrowth over little red berries. The palate is dense, full-bodied, and warm, crammed with very fine and sweet tannins. Although already very enjoyable at around ten years of age, this wine will reward those with the patience to wait a few more years before opening. **AS**

🍷🍷🍷🍷 **Drink: to 2025**

Grattamacco
2003

Origin Italy, Tuscany, Bolgheri
Style Dry red wine, 13.5% ABV
Grapes C. Sauvignon 65%, Merlot 20%, Sangiovese 15%

The Grattamacco estate is one of the historic wine producers of Bolgheri in the province of Livorno. The first wine sold under the Grattamacco label was the 1978 vintage, and it was an instant success among wine enthusiasts. Grattamacco was sold in 2002, and now belongs to Dottor Tipa, a Swiss Italian who also owns the Colle Massari estate, a beautiful property in the up-and-coming Montecucco DOC area.

The Grattamacco property is situated on a hill at 300 feet (91 m) above sea level, between the villages of Bolgheri and Castagneto Carducci. The climate here is very mild and dry, with appreciable differences in day and nighttime temperatures toward the end of the summer, when the ripening grapes need them the most. The estate extends over 74 acres (30 ha), of which 27 acres (11 ha) are vineyards and 7.5 acres (3 ha) are olive groves. The remainder of the estate is woodland.

The 2003 vintage was exceptionally hot and dry in most of Europe, and Tuscany was no exception, but the Grattamacco shows none of the unpleasant traits of this Saharan vintage. The nose is fresh and vibrant, with notes of soft, ripe fruits (blackberry, blueberry). The oak is perfectly integrated and never overwhelms the fruit. It enters the mouth in a very sensual, smooth, and fleshy manner, and then opens to show its full scale, though it is never overdone. Its depth is outstanding, and so is its length, kept interesting by a welcome (and maybe unexpected) acidity. The tannins are not dry or tough, and they promise much for the wine's aging potential. **AS**

🍷🍷🍷🍷 **Drink: to 2020+**

Greenock Creek
Roennfeldt Road Shiraz 1998

Origin Australia, South Australia, Barossa Valley
Style Dry red wine, 15% ABV
Grape Shiraz

The rise of Greenock Creek to Barossa superstardom was meteoric, particularly in the United States, and was based on grapes from low-yielding, dry-farmed Shiraz, Cabernet Sauvignon, and Grenache vines, all estate grown, from ten to seventy years in age.

Many of the Greenock Creek cuvées come from the Marananga and Seppeltsfield vineyards, on soils ranging from alluvial deposits to heavy loams and loams overlying limestones and granites. The wines were originally made by Chris Ringland of Rockford, who now makes his own much sought-after prestige wines. Michael Waugh is now in sole charge of winemaking at Greenock Creek.

At least five cuvées of Shiraz are made here, from the Seven Acre, Creek Block, Alice's, Apricot Block, and Roennfeldt vineyards. The fruit for the Roennfeldt wine comes from a Marananga vineyard. 1998 was an excellent vintage in the Barossa Valley. This wine shows a dense purple color, with massive concentration on both nose and palate. The palate has a rich mouthfeel, and is dominated by blackcurrant and blackberry together with notes of smoke and tar on the long finish. **JW**

🝖🝖🝖🝖 **Drink: to 2025**

Miljenko Grgić
Plavac Mali 2004

Origin Croatia, Pelješac, Dingač
Style Dry red wine, 13.5% ABV
Grape Plavac Mali

The Pelješac peninsula lies about an hour's drive northwest of Dubrovnik. The native grape is Plavac Mali, like California's Zinfandel a descendant of the ancient Croat variety Crljenac, and a variety perfectly adapted to its environment. The appellation of Dingač is the pride of this region. Here, slopes plunging steeply into the Adriatic Sea tilt an unbelievably narrow strip of vines toward the sun.

Miljenko Grgić is a native Croat who left for Germany, then Canada, and eventually the United States, where he worked for a number of wineries, including Robert Mondavi, before co-founding Grgich Hills Cellars and developing a reputation for superlative Chardonnays. He never lost his love for his homeland, however, and in 1995 founded his own modern and well-equipped winery in Pelješac.

Grgić's Plavac Mali from Dingač is a fusion of ancient vineyard and modern technology. Everything about the wine is big. The color is deep and the nose pronounced, with ripe black fruits and an almost raisinlike richness that follows through onto the palate. The alcohol and tannins are high yet perfectly integrated. A truly outstanding wine. **GL**

🝖🝖🝖 **Drink: to 2019**

Domaine Jean Grivot
Richebourg Grand Cru 2002

Origin France, Burgundy, Côte de Nuits
Style Dry red wine, 13.5% ABV
Grape Pinot Noir

Domaine Anne Gros
Richebourg Grand Cru 2000

Origin France, Burgundy, Côte de Nuits
Style Dry red wine, 13.5% ABV
Grape Pinot Noir

The Grivot family has been in the Burgundy region since the late eighteenth century. Initially they were mixed farmers and coopers, but were already bottling their own wines by the mid-1930s. Jean Grivot acquired his parcel in Richebourg in 1984, bringing the domaine to its present total of 39.5 acres (16 ha). Meanwhile, Jean's son Etienne, a student of viticulture, became involved in the winemaking and transformed the vineyard.

Richebourg is one of the greatest grands crus within that marvelous swathe of them behind the village of Vosne-Romanée. The Grivots own 0.8 acres (0.3 ha) of sixty-year-old vines in a single parcel. Although the cru is often associated with Burgundies of unusual power, Grivot has no wish to make a wine he describes as "brutal"; instead he hopes to fashion a wine of great energy with a distinctly airy quality. 2002 was a great vintage at Grivot, and Etienne prefers it to the acclaimed 1999. The nose is exquisite, with intense cherry fruit. Blessed with fine acidity and splendid balance, it is nonetheless a monumental wine of richness and power, sustained by weighty, ripe tannins. **SBr**
😊😊😊😊 **Drink: to 2025+**

This property used to be part of Domaine Louis Gros, until, in 1963, it branched off on its own under François Gros. He retired in 1988, and since that time his daughter Anne has had complete control of the domaine. Until 1994 it continued to be known as Domaine Anne et François Gros.

Quality here used to be middling but has risen sharply under Anne's care. Although not certified as such, since 2000 the domaine has been organic. Vinification is straightforward, with fermentation in open wooden vats with natural yeasts, and a generous portion of new oak, around 80 percent, for the grands crus. Anne insists that she detests dry tannins in a wine, and aims to provide a sensation of unctuosity and, above all, fruit.

Although Richebourg sometimes has the reputation of being a massive wine by Burgundian standards, this is not the case here. Instead there is intensity, extremely fine tannins, discreet power, an oakiness more present on the nose than the palate, and exceptional length. Anne Gros's Richebourg is stylistically consistent while remaining true to the vintage. **SBr**
😊😊😊😊 **Drink: to 2025**

Château Gruaud-Larose

2005

GS

Cabernet 1966

Origin France, Bordeaux, St.-Julien
Style Dry red wine, 13% ABV
Grapes C. Sauvignon 57%, Merlot 31%, Others 12%

Origin South Africa, Durbanville
Style Dry red wine, 12% ABV
Grape Cabernet Sauvignon

This property shows the Médoc at its grandest, with a château, completed in 1875, and a tower overlooking the 200-acre (80 ha) vineyard. The wine was highly regarded in the mid-eighteenth century but the property was under joint ownership a century later with two separate labels, even though the wine was identical. The merchant Désiré Cordier bought one sector in 1917 and the other in 1935, thus reuniting the property. Today the estate is owned by another great *négociant* family, the Merlauts. They retained the services of Cordier's veteran winemaker, Georges Pauli, who oversees the property with great energy.

Stylistically, there is nothing dogged or heavy-handed about Gruaud-Larose, and its muscularity is balanced by freshness and vigor. The 2005 shows the property at the top of its form. The aromas are seductively ripe, floral, and spicy, whereas the palate has a vibrant dramatic quality; it is a wine with energy, vigor, and excellent length. Perhaps because it is promoted with less flamboyance than many other top St.-Juliens, Gruaud-Larose is sometimes underrated, but in great years it is a truly outstanding and harmonious wine. **SBr**
🍷🍷🍷 **Drink: to 2035**

Embarrassingly little is known of a wine regarded as among the finest from South Africa's wine prehistory. Only more recently have foreigners taken an interest in a wine that rarely surfaces for resale; it was never commercially released, mysteriously finding its way into the cellars of the well connected.

The wine was bottled by Stellenbosch Farmers' Winery, bearing the initials of the then production director, George Spies, indicating his belief in what was clearly some sort of experiment. Part of the experiment, indicated by the tiny "100%" on the minimalist label, was to show doubters that the Cape could make serious wine solely from Cabernet Sauvignon. Labeling regulations were then scarcely demanding, and the term "Cabernet" frequently concealed a much larger proportion of Cinsaut.

Two facts are clear: Maturation was in only large old vats, and primary vinification was done on the Durbanville farm where the grapes were sourced. The vineyard was, unfortunately, built over soon after. Only one other—also impressive—wine was made from its grapes under this label, in 1968. No one knows what happened to the 1967. **TJ**
🍷🍷🍷 **Drink: to 2021+**

◩ Gruaud-Larose is a leading Médoc second growth.

Guelbenzu
Lautus 2004

Origin Spain, Navarra, Cascante
Style Dry red wine, 13.5% ABV
Grapes Tempranillo, C. Sauvignon, Merlot, Grenache

Guigal
Côte-Rôtie La Mouline 2003

Origin France, Northern Rhône, Côte-Rôtie
Style Dry red wine, 13% ABV
Grapes Syrah 90%, Viognier 10%

In 1989 Ricardo Guelbenzu, a former lawyer, was entrusted by his seven brothers with the task of resuscitating their old family firm Bodega del Jardín. No one could have imagined that as Bodegas Guelbenzu it would become one of the undisputed leaders of the region, still less that Ricardo would also become a winemaker in Aragón and in Chile.

Lautus, the family's pride and joy, comes from the best 6 acres (2.5 ha) of their 91 acres (37 ha) in the valley of Queiles, close to the village of Cascante. The sand, chalk, clay, and limestone soils, together with the fresh continental climate, favor the four varieties in the blend. *Lautus* means "magnificent" in Latin, and the wine was first produced in 1996.

Since then only the 1999, 2001, 2004, and 2005 vintages have been released, because the wine spends twelve months in new French barrels then three years in bottle before going on the market. Despite its intensity, it strikes a magnificent balance between fruit and wood. It has a cherry color, with an aroma of fine berries, spice, toast, and balsamic notes. Full, polished, and round in the mouth, it has ripe tannins and an elegant, lingering finish. **JMB**

🍷🍷🍷 Drink: recent vintages for up to 15 years

In the past thirty years, Marcel Guigal has gone from strength to strength with his Côte-Rôtie crus: La Landonne, La Mouline, and La Turque. They found admirers in John Livingstone-Learmonth and Melvyn Masters; ten years later, Robert Parker stepped in and the prices went ballistic.

Syrah is in its element here, on these slopes of sandy gneiss south of Lyon. La Mouline is a Côte Blonde from seventy-five-year-old vines, and is more Burgundian than the Côte Brune, although that could be because most growers add up to 30 percent of the aromatic Viognier. At Guigal it is more like 11 percent. Guigal also destems La Mouline, but leaves all that saucy roughness in his La Landonne.

The wine is soft and seductive, with a distinct aroma of black currants and a whiff of leather that marks it out as predominantly Syrah. The 2003 wines were aged in 100 percent new oak for forty-two months, and should last fully thirty years. Steve Tanzer finds flavors of "black raspberry, smoked meat, and roasted nut" in the wines, with chocolate tastes on the finish. They are at their best with roast woodcock or, failing that, partridge. **GM**

🍷🍷🍷🍷🍷 Drink: to 2030+

Hacienda Monasterio
Ribera del Duero Reserva 2003

Origin Spain, Ribera del Duero
Style Dry red wine, 14% ABV
Grapes Tempranillo, Cabernet Sauvignon, Merlot

Viña Haras de Pirque
Haras Character Syrah 2010

Origin Chile, Maipo Valley
Style Dry red wine, 14.8% ABV
Grapes Syrah 85%, Cabernet Sauvignon 15%

At the beginning of the 1990s, Ribera del Duero was exploding. A group of investors decided to establish a new winery between two of the most famous villages—Valbuena de Duero and Pesquera de Duero. The young Dane Peter Sisseck arrived in Spain to take care of the technical direction of Bodegas Monasterio, quickly establishing a formidable reputation both for himself and for his wines.

The Reserva is a selection that complies with the longer *élevage* time required—a minimum of thirty-six months, with no less than twelve months in oak barrels—but the Crianza also ranks among the best in the category. The year 2003 was very warm in Europe, but Sisseck managed to make a very balanced wine. The Cabernet and Merlot add freshness to the Tempranillo, and sometimes also a minty note. The color is deep, with good intensity on the nose, where the oak will integrate over time. On the palate it is dominated by ripe black fruit and spice, medium-bodied, elegant, and long. It is ideal with roast lamb, the specialty of the region. Decant in advance to give it time to open up if consumed young. **LG**

🌢🌢🌢 Drink: to 2020

In 1991, Chilean businessman Eduardo Matte Rosas and his son bought a thoroughbred farm at Pirque in the Maipo Valley. As the track, paddocks, and stabling area for the horses took up less than half the estate, the Mattes immediately set about planting a vineyard. The hills offered a tantalizing range of mesoclimates, elevations, and expositions for Alejandro Hernández, who oversaw the planting.

Haras de Pirque's own winery was built from 1997, with Hernández bringing in Alvaro Espinoza to oversee the winemaking. Hernández and Espinoza had both trained in Bordeaux, but were convinced that Syrah could thrive in the Maipo Valley, despite the received Chilean wisdom of planting Syrah only in the country's hotter subregions like the Aconcagua Valley, Colchagua Valley, and the coastal foothills, rather than the Maipo Valley and the Andean foothills. Their belief in Maipo Syrah appears vindicated in the Haras Character Syrah, whose tannic structure is linear rather than expansive, and whose flavors of red fruit and underbrush reveal themselves gently, rather than loudly, in a reassuringly mouth-filling but cleansing wine. **MW**

🌢 Drink: recent vintages for up to 9 years

Hardys *Eileen Hardy Shiraz* 2001

Origin Australia, South Australia
Style Dry red wine, 14.5% ABV
Grape Shiraz

In 1850, at the age of twenty, Thomas Hardy came to the new colony of South Australia from Devon, England. He established a winery on the banks of Adelaide's River Torrens in 1853. By the mid-1970s, five generations of the Hardy family had guided and shaped Thomas Hardy & Sons. Named after the family matriarch Eileen Hardy, 500 cases of the eponymous wine, made from the very best selected cuvées, were bottled as her annual birthday gift from the company. First released commercially in 1973 to honor "Auntie Eileen's" eightieth birthday, the wine was originally made from Shiraz and then Cabernet Sauvignon. Now it is made exclusively from Shiraz sourced in Clare, Padthaway, and McLaren Vale.

For the 2001 vintage, fruit was sourced from the Schobers vineyard in the Clare Valley; Upper Tintara in McLaren Vale; Yeenunga and Frankland River; and Padthaway. The grapes were fermented in concrete open-top fermenters before being pressed in a traditional basket press. After malolactic fermentation, all of the wine was aged for eighteen months in new and one-year-old French barriques, rather than the more typical American oak used for big South Australian red wines. Although usually a burly, alcoholic red wine, the Eileen Hardy 2001 is relatively elegant and restrained. Renowned Australian wine writer James Halliday described it as, "One of the most elegant to date under this label; medium-bodied, silky texture, and very long in the mouth; perfect aftertaste." **SG**

ⓢⓢⓢ **Drink: to 2017+**

FURTHER RECOMMENDATIONS
Other great vintages
1987 · 1988 · 1993 · 1995 · 1997 · 1998 · 2000 · 2004
More Hardys wines
Eileen Hardy Chardonnay
Thomas Hardy Cabernet Sauvignon

Eileen Hardy with friends at a cricket match in Singapore in the 1920s. ▶

Harlan Estate *Proprietary Red Wine* 1994

Origin USA, California, Napa Valley
Style Dry red wine, 14.5% ABV
Grapes C. Sauvignon 70%, Merlot 20%, Others 10%

After an earlier venture involving a property too cold, with ground too fertile, to grow fine wine, Bill Harlan set out to discover the properties that produced great wines with extraordinary intrinsic quality, personality, and a legacy.

Recognizing that many of the top French sites were hillside vineyards, Harlan scouted for property in Napa near well-regarded sites, but on hillsides. The property he found in 1983 lies on the western side of Oakville, on the western edge of Heitz's Martha's Vineyard, not far from the To-Kalon Vineyard. Whereas these vineyards lie on the valley floor, Harlan's vines are planted at an altitude of 300 to 600 feet (92–184 m), with good drainage and sun exposure. Harlan was one of the first to recognize the talents of David Abreu, who oversaw the initial planting. Meticulous care at every stage is designed to capture greatness: severe grape-by-grape selection; small-batch fermentation, some in stainless, the rest in wood; and aging in French oak.

It is no wonder Harlan's Proprietary Red, characterized by multiple layers of aroma and flavor, a luxurious texture befitting a luxury wine, and dense palate concentration, frequently receives 100-point scores from Robert Parker, who characterized the 1994 as embodying "immortality in a glass." The 1994, the first vintage that seized critical acclaim, remains a brilliant performer at auction. In 2007, a single bottle of Harlan Estate 1994 was hammered down at $1,600 (£800; €1,150). **LGr**

Ϭ Ϭ Ϭ Ϭ Ϭ **Drink: to 2019+**

FURTHER RECOMMENDATIONS
Other great vintages
1995 · 1996 · 1997 · 1999 · 2001 · 2002 · 2003
More producers from Napa
Caymus · Colgin · Corison · Diamond Creek · Duckhorn Grace Family · Heitz · Quintessa · Rubicon Estate

Harlan Estate vines sprawl across Oakville's hills. ➡

Château Haut-Bailly 2005

Origin France, Bordeaux, Pessac-Léognan
Style Dry red wine, 13% ABV
Grapes C. Sauvignon 65%, Merlot 25%, C. Franc 10%

Most of the estates of the Graves produce both red and white wine, often of equal quality, especially in the northern Graves. Haut-Bailly is unusual in that its terroir only permits the cultivation of red varieties. It has regained the high reputation it enjoyed in the late nineteenth century, after changes in ownership led to a dull patch from the 1920s to 1950s. In 1955 it was bought by a Belgian wine merchant, Daniel Sanders, and he was succeeded in 1979 by his son Jean, who restored and expanded the property. By the 1980s Haut-Bailly was established as one of the best red wines of the Graves.

Sadly, Jean Sanders's sisters opted to sell their share of the property. Haut-Bailly was sold in 1998 and the new owner was a New York banker called Robert Wilmers. Wilmers appointed Jean's daughter Véronique as manager, and an advisory team was appointed. They are aided by a plethora of old plants, including some ancient ungrafted vines and some Carmenère. The Haut-Bailly team also commissioned a detailed soil analysis to gain an even more profound understanding of the terroir.

Haut-Bailly's hallmark is elegance, but it is not a thin or attenuated wine. There is flesh and well-judged oak, but also no lack of density. The tannins are never too overt, and there is a seamless character to its texture in the best vintages. The sleek, stylish 2005 shows Haut-Bailly at its best. Like previous vintages it will quickly show its character and charm, yet retain its distinction for many decades. **SBr**
🍷🍷🍷 **Drink: to 2030**

FURTHER RECOMMENDATIONS
Other great vintages
1945 · 1947 · 1959 · 1961 · 1970 · 1978 · 1983 · 1985 1986 · 1990 · 1995 · 2000 · 2001 · 2004 · 2009 · 2010
More producers from Pessac-Léognan
Dom. de Chevalier · Fieuzal · Haut-Brion · La Louvière

Until the 1940s, Haut-Bailly's price was at a similar level to that of the first growths. ➡

Les Grands Vins de la Gironde (Illustrés)
par Henry Guillièr

Libourne
Bordeaux

Vincit Omnia Veritas

Reproduction Interdite
Droits Réservés

LÉOGNAN (GRAVES)
CHATEAU HAUT-BAILLY
CRÛ EXCEPTIONNEL

PAUILLAC (MÉDOC)
CHATEAU LAFITE
1er GRAND CRÛ CLASSÉ

PAUILLAC (MÉDOC)
CHATEAU LATOUR
1er GRAND CRÛ CLASSÉ

PAUILLAC (MÉDOC)
CHATEAU MOUTON ROTHSCHILD
GRAND CRÛ CLASSÉ

SAUTERNES
CHATEAU YQUEM
1er GRAND CRÛ CLASSÉ

SAINT-EMILION
CHATEAU AUSONE
1er GRAND CRÛ CLASSÉ

MARGAUX (MÉDOC)
CHATEAU MARGAUX
1er GRAND CRÛ CLASSÉ

PESSAC (GRAVES)
CHATEAU HAUT-BRION
1er GRAND CRÛ CLASSÉ

Château Haut-Brion

1989

Origin France, Bordeaux, Pessac-Léognan
Style Dry red wine, 13% ABV
Grapes C. Sauvignon 45%, Merlot 37%, C. Franc 18%

It is one of the remarkable features of the 1855 classification that the sole Graves property to be accorded supreme status as a first growth was Haut-Brion. History has confirmed that judgment. It was already renowned in the seventeeth century, when the commercially astute owners, the Pontac family, successfully marketed the wine in London.

Now entirely surrounded by the Bordeaux suburbs, this wonderful vineyard has been impeccably maintained. Haut-Brion has benefited from a tranquil continuity since 1935, when the U.S. banker Clarence Dillon bought the estate. His granddaughter, the Duchesse de Mouchy, and her son Prince Robert of Luxembourg oversee the property today. The estate has been managed by three generations of the Delmas family since 1921. Jean-Bernard Delmas created here in 1961 the first stainless-steel fermentation hall in Bordeaux, and he also conducted extremely detailed research into the clones and rootstocks planted here. The vineyards are higher than they look, and although fundamentally on deep gravel soils, there are also some parcels with a high clay content.

The 1989 is a classic year at Haut-Brion: voluptuously aromatic, with aromas of cedar, black currant, and chocolate; even at close to twenty years of age it retains a burly yet velvety power that is never coarse, and an extraordinary length of flavor. This legendary wine will live for decades. **SBr**
Drink: to 2025

Haut-Brion's turreted château dates from the sixteenth century.

Château Haut-Marbuzet
1999

Heitz Wine Cellars *Martha's Vineyard Cabernet Sauvignon* 1974

Origin France, Bordeaux, St.-Estèphe
Style Dry red wine, 13% ABV
Grapes Merlot 50%, C. Sauvignon 40%, C. Franc 10%

Origin USA, California, Napa Valley
Style Dry red wine, 13.5% ABV
Grape Cabernet Sauvignon

Henri Dubosq owns a cluster of properties in the southeast corner of the appellation and Haut-Marbuzet is the best of them. Since 1952, when Henri's father began buying vines in the area, the Dubosqs have applied themselves to reconstituting the ancient Domaine du Marbuzet, fragmented in 1948, and the process was completed only in 1996.

There is plenty of clay in the soil at Haut-Marbuzet, which accounts for the generous proportion of Merlot, giving the wine its sensuous appeal. Another factor behind its popularity is that Dubosq ages the wine entirely in new oak. Curiously, the wine does not taste that oaky, but the new oak probably contributes to its sweetness, accessibility, and svelte texture. St.-Estèphe has a reputation for rather tough wines, but Haut-Marbuzet is always attractive from the moment of release, though it keeps well, peaking at about fifteen years of age.

The 1999, which Dubosq prefers to the 2000, is a perfect example of Haut-Marbuzet: aromatic, concentrated, and spicy, yet with integrated tannins and fine length of flavor. Haut-Marbuzet rarely lets you down. **SBr**

♦♦♦ **Drink: to 2020**

From the initial release of the acclaimed 1974 Napa Valley Cabernet Sauvignons, Heitz's Martha's Vineyard bottling was declared the wine of the vintage. Along with the 1968 and 1970, the 1974 is considered the finest wine Joe Heitz ever made—except he didn't make it. In fact, Joe Heitz lay in bed with a sore back when harvesting began; it was his son David who harvested and vinified the wine, marking his first vintage as winemaker. What a beginning for a young winemaker: The wine remains one of the earliest and most sought-after California cult wines of all.

Planted entirely to Cabernet Sauvignon, the vineyard's alluvial fan and bale loam soils back up against the western foothills of Napa Valley. The uniqueness of the terroir manifests itself in a distinctive eucalyptus aroma in the wine.

The 1974, described by Robert Parker twice in one review as "monumental," was extolled for its "staggering" concentration. Thirty years from vintage, the flavor remained deep and saturated, with fully integrated tannins and sweet, rich fruit. A truly legendary wine. **LGr**

♦♦♦♦♦ **Drink: to 2027**

Henschke
Hill of Grace 1998

Origin Australia, South Australia, Eden Valley
Style Dry red wine, 14% ABV
Grape Shiraz

Second only to Penfolds Grange in the Australian red wine hierarchy, Henschke's Hill of Grace is very different to Grange—a single-vineyard wine rather than a multiregion blend, and a wine that aims to achieve elegance rather than power.

"The Grandfathers," as the oldest part of the vineyard is called, was probably planted in the 1860s. These vines are planted on their own roots from pre-phylloxera material brought from Europe by the early settlers. The vineyard is planted predominantly to Shiraz, but it also includes other varieties such as Riesling, Sémillon, and Mataro (also called Mourvèdre).

The wine itself typically has plum, blackberry, and chocolate flavors, with supple and chalky tannins, and huge length. It can be aged with confidence for at least ten years. Current owners Stephen and Prue Henschke assert that dry growing, the age of the vines, and day/night temperature fluctuations at the vineyard are the secrets behind Hill of Grace's stunning quality. For some, however, Henschke's other single-vineyard Shiraz, Mount Edelstone, is sometimes at least its equal. **SG**
⊖⊖⊖⊖⊖ **Drink: to 2018+**

Herdade de Cartuxa
Pera Manca 1995

Origin Portugal, Alentejo
Style Dry red wine, 14.6% ABV
Grapes Trincadeira, Aragonez, Cabernet Sauvignon

The Convento de Cartuxa is a former Carthusian monastery, which was founded in 1587, becoming a private estate in 1834. It was occupied by farm workers following Portugal's "Carnation Revolution" in 1974, and when the property was returned to its owners, it was in an appallingly neglected state, and the vineyards had to be thoroughly overhauled.

The estate's finest wine is Pera Manca. It was a well-known wine prior to the outbreak of phylloxera but after the epidemic had run its course, the land was forested and it was only in 1987 that Pera Manca was revived.

The wines are only released in the best years, and the 1995 is one of the most successful vintages, exuding power and richness, with a bitter-sweet, chocolate-like intensity of flavor akin to Vintage Port. The Cabernet just penetrates the aroma, and black currant punctuates the dense morello cherry and raisin-like fruit. A somewhat burned, feral character develops in the wine with age. Pera Manca commands stupendous prices, and has rapidly become the cult wine of southern Portugal, comparable with Barca Velha in the north. **RM**
⊖⊖⊖⊖⊖ **Drink: to 2020+**

Herdade de Mouchão

2001

Origin Portugal, Alentejo
Style Dry red wine, 13% ABV
Grapes Alicante Bouschet 70%, Trincadeira 30%

Herdade do Esporão

Esporão Reserva 2004

Origin Portugal, Alentejo
Style Dry red wine, 14.5% ABV
Grapes Tempranillo, C. Sauvignon, Trincadeira

Mouchão has been owned by the Reynolds family since the mid-nineteenth century, when Thomas Reynolds set out south from Porto in search of a cork estate. Even today the estate is mostly cork grove, though it is best known for its wine.

In the 1974 revolution the Alentejo region was the setting for a rural uprising and the Mouchão estate was taken over by locals, who trashed the vineyards and drank a lot of the wine that was stored here. The property was restored to the family, who returned in 1985 and started a rebuilding program. The vineyards have been completely replanted, but the winery has been left more or less alone.

The 2001 is the hundredth vintage at the estate. A blend of 70 percent Alicante with 30 percent Trincadeira, it has a dark, savory, intensely spicy nose, with a strong, savory meaty streak. The palate is dark, savory, and spicy with firm tannic structure and a distinctive meaty, spicy edge. Stylistically, this wine is partly modern and fruit-driven, but under the surface there is savory, Old World complexity. Drinking well early in its life, this will reward cellaring if the 1990 is anything to go by. **JG**

❸❸❸ **Drink: to 2017+**

In many ways, the Esporão estate was the first to put the Alentejo on the wine map. This was partly due to the sheer size of the property, the largest in the country, and partly to the influence of the Australian winemaker, David Baverstock, whose skills as both winemaker and chief communicator have captured the attention of the world's wine drinkers.

Esporão is 120 miles (193 km) south and inland from Portugal's capital, Lisbon, in Reguengos de Monsaraz. The terrain is a total contrast to that of the north: Vast, open, gently rolling plains are the norm, baking hot in the summer, with very low rainfall and the constant threat of drought. There has not been a long history of fine wine production, although now a vast dam has been constructed for irrigation.

Only a small percentage of the 9,000 tons of grapes crushed here each vintage end up under the Esporão label. Esporão Reserva is the flagship wine, made from a careful selection of the best grapes each vintage. The result has a dark berry and cassis nose, obvious vanilla, and a palate that is more New World than most Portuguese reds, softer and less structured than many, yet rich and full flavored. **GS**

❸❸ **Drink: to 2020**

Herzog
Montepulciano 2005

Origin New Zealand, Marlborough
Style Dry red wine, 14.6% ABV
Grape Montepulciano

Hans and Therese Herzog owned a winery and Michelin-starred restaurant in their native Switzerland before moving to Marlborough. Why leave their life of security and success? "Because I wanted to make great red wine of a type that I couldn't make at home," explained Hans.

On the face of it, Marlborough's climate appears to be too cool to ripen Montepulciano—an unlikely bedfellow to Sauvignon Blanc, Riesling, and Pinot Noir, the region's star performers. Herzog deliberately chose one of the warmest vineyard sites in Marlborough, and harvests a tiny yield of grapes from his vines in order to guarantee full physiological ripeness. Low yields also give impressive flavor concentration. A long, slow fermentation using wild yeasts promotes intensity of flavor and color.

Montepulciano does not have a successful track record in New Zealand, or indeed outside Italy. Herzog is making wine dangerously close to the edge and succeeding brilliantly. 2005 is the best vintage since the first in 1998. Intense and brooding, it has layers of flavors suggesting plum, dark berry, violet, chocolate, anise, and mixed spice. **BC**

🝔🝔🝔 **Drink: to 2017**

Hirsch Vineyards
Pinot Noir 2004

Origin USA, California, Sonoma Coast
Style Dry red wine, 14.3% ABV
Grape Pinot Noir

David Hirsch's vineyards occupy a rocky ridge 3 miles (5 km) from the Pacific and about 1,000 feet (305 m) above sea level—high enough to raise them above coastal fog. This is the Sonoma Coast—a thin strip of land lying north of the Russian River, including the first three or four ridges that run along the edge of the continent. Hirsch bought land here in 1978 to use as an isolated retreat, until a friend mentioned that if he planted Pinot Noir it would be world class.

The vineyards lie on a mixture of ocean floor sediments and chunks of ocean crust known as the Franciscan Melange. The land is full of geologic faults: Rocks of drastically different character abut one another, and soil variation is random and abrupt. The topography is complex, the mesoclimates varied, the rootstocks and clones diverse. Grapes from each block are distinctive in their character. Having established his own label in 2002, Hirsch now makes use of this complexity by keeping wine from each of some thirty-five blocks and sub-blocks separate until blending. The 2004 has the intense aromatics, acid balance, integrated tannins, and earthy undertones that characterize Hirsch Pinot Noir. **JS**

🝔🝔🝔 **Drink: to 2020**

Château Hosanna

2000

Origin France, Bordeaux, Pomerol
Style Dry red wine, 13.5% ABV
Grapes Merlot 70%, C. Franc 30%

This is a newcomer to Pomerol, but one with a history. Until 1998, when Etablissements Moueix purchased the estate, this property was known as Certan-Giraud. It consisted of 11 acres (4.5 ha) in a single block, with gravel soils over a clay subsoil. The vineyards lie between Pétrus and the village of Pomerol, and the neighbors include Lafleur, Lafleur-Pétrus, and Certan de May. After the purchase, Christian Moueix selected the best and highest sectors of the vineyard and renamed them Hosanna, a counterpart of his Napa Valley estate Dominus.

Despite the fine location of the vineyards, Certan-Giraud did not enjoy much of a reputation before Moueix acquired it. Christian Moueix judged that the property was poorly drained, and he soon installed a pumping system to assist with drainage.

The 2000 vintage shows how swift the progress has been here since the purchase just two years earlier. Its aromas of black currants are reticent, but on the palate the wine is rich, full-bodied, and concentrated, with opulence of fruit, fine balance, an overall elegance, and splendid persistence. Quality is consistently high, but so are the prices. **SBr**

☻☻☻☻☻ Drink: to 2020

Isole e Olena

Cepparello Toscana IGT 1997

Origin Italy, Tuscany
Style Dry red wine, 13.5% ABV
Grape Sangiovese

Paolo de Marchi's wine, Cepparello, would have been a Chianti Classico had varietal Sangiovese been allowed in Chianti Classico under Italian wine laws in the early 1980s when the wine was first initiated. It was one of the first of its Super-Tuscan type and remains among the best.

De Marchi, whose Piedmontese family bought the estate in the 1960s, took charge in the 1970s, and he soon began to conceive the style of Cepparello—a barrel-aged 100 percent Sangiovese, made from the best sites on the Isole e Olena estate. He is one of the very few proprietors in the Chianti Classico zone, and certainly among those not native to Tuscany, who commands operations in both the vineyards and winery (with a little help from his friends Donato Lanati and Giampaolo Chiatini).

Like many other Tuscan producers, Isole e Olena excelled in the 1997 vintage, although only a relatively modest 3,900 cases were made. Lauded by *Wine Spectator* as "the best wine ever from Paolo di Marchi," the 1997 was Cepparello's first appearance in the magazine's annual Top 100 feature. Cepparello is a wine from heaven. **SG**

☻☻☻☻ Drink: to 2017+

Viña Izadi
Rioja Expresión 2001

Origin Spain, Rioja
Style Dry red wine, 14.5% ABV
Grape Tempranillo

In recent years Rioja has faced an identity crisis. On one side are the traditional wines, venerable Gran Reservas of great depth and complexity. On the other are the so-called *Alta Expresión* ("high expression") wines that, for many, epitomize the big, powerful, lavishly oaked, "international" style.

After many years of owning vineyards in Villabuena de Alaba, the Anton family founded Viña Izadi in 1987. The winery's philosophy was transformed in 1997, when Don Gonzalo Anton hired Mariano García, the former winemaker for thirty years at Vega Sicilia. Together with Izadi's incumbent winemaker Angel Ortega, Anton and García took the wines into the *Alta Expresión* style.

In the excellent 2001 Rioja vintage, Izadi produced perhaps their best Expresión yet. However, it only just scraped into the top twenty of a *World of Fine Wine* tasting of Rioja held in 2005. Despite praise for its richness, the tasters were ambivalent about the wine's *Alta Expresión* clothing. Spanish wine expert John Radford wrote: "This is a heavyweight with tremendous extraction, but is this what people expect when they buy Rioja?" **SG**

🍷🍷🍷🍷 **Drink: to 2021+**

Paul Jaboulet Aîné
Hermitage La Chapelle 1978

Origin France, Northern Rhône, Hermitage
Style Dry red wine, 13.4% ABV
Grapes Syrah, Others

One of the great red wines of the world, Paul Jaboulet Aîné's Hermitage La Chapelle is blended from several vineyards spread across the great Hill of Hermitage that overlooks the River Rhône and the little town of Tain l'Hermitage.

In what was a great year throughout the northern Rhône, Jaboulet's wine is still the benchmark of excellence. By mid-2007, La Chapelle 1978 was fetching $1,000 (£500; €735) a bottle, though even this is a relative bargain compared to the $6,000 (£3,000; €4,420) commanded by the 1961, which is probably the greatest and rarest La Chapelle vintage.

Production of La Chapelle has increased considerably in recent years, with a detrimental effect on quality. After a vertical tasting of thirty-three vintages from the 1950s to 1999, Jancis Robinson wrote: "Something happened to this legendary wine in the 1990s. The 1990 continues to be a truly great wine. . . . But the most recent Hermitage La Chapelle with any real excitement was made in 1991." The 1978, though, continues to shine and now under new ownership, future vintages should as well. **SG**

🍷🍷🍷🍷🍷 **Drink: to 2018+**

Jade Mountain
Paras Vineyard Syrah 2000

Origin USA, California, Napa Valley, Mount Veeder
Style Dry red wine, 15% ABV
Grapes Syrah 94%, Viognier 3%, Grenache 3%

Jade Mountain was established in 1984 by the San Francisco psychiatrist Douglass Cartwright, and by the end of the decade it had already gained a fine reputation for its Rhône-varietal wines. Today, Syrah and Viognier are produced in most parts of California, but twenty years ago they were rare, with just a handful of properties focusing on Rhône-style wines. Not all the wines were made from estate-grown grapes, but many of the best came from the Paras vineyard, a 20-acre (8 ha) site 1,200 feet (366 m) up on Mount Veeder. Terraced on steep shale slopes, the site was replanted by Cartwright.

Jade Mountain produces numerous wines, many of them blends. Paras Vineyard Syrah usually includes some Viognier and Grenache. The wine is aged for around eighteen months in at least 50 percent new French oak. In certain good vintages, a block called P10 is vinified and released separately. The Paras Syrah normally has a dense nose of blackberries and black pepper; it has formidable concentration and massive fruit on the palate, but the alcohol is not too evident and there is sufficient vigor to assure it of good length. **SBr**
ΘΘΘ **Drink: to 2017+**

Jasper Hill
Emily's Paddock Shiraz 1997

Origin Australia, Victoria, Heathcote
Style Dry red wine, 14% ABV
Grapes Shiraz 90–95%, C. Franc 5–10%

Ron Laughton planted the Jasper Hill vineyard in 1975, naming two vine plots after his daughters, Emily and Georgia. The vines are ungrafted, unirrigated, and farmed with organic and biodynamic techniques.

In the case of Emily's Paddock, both Shiraz (90 to 95 percent) and Cabernet Franc (5 to 10 percent) vines were interplanted. They are hand-picked and cofermented, with Emily's aging in French oak and Georgia's in both French and sweeter-tasting American oak. Heathcote Shiraz is renowned for its fruit flavors, ripe rather than minty or peppery.

Wines from both Emily's and Georgia's Paddocks are known for producing Shiraz tasting of the soil, rather than merely of the grape. Emily's Paddock is more exposed, higher and sunnier than Georgia's, and has shallower topsoil. "Emily's Paddock gives lighter colored wines and of greater minerality and elegance compared to Georgia's," says Ron, "because all the vine roots, bar the superficial ones, are embedded in primary rock." Emily's naturally lower yields mean less overt fruit sweetness and increased minerality, perfume, and tannic structure. **MW**
ΘΘΘ **Drink: to 2030**

Domaine Henri Jayer *Vosne-Romanée PC Cros Parantoux* 1988

K Vintners
Milbrandt Syrah 2005

Origin France, Burgundy, Côte de Nuits
Style Dry red wine, 13% ABV
Grape Pinot Noir

Origin USA, Washington State, Columbia Valley
Style Dry red wine, 13.9% ABV
Grape Syrah

Henri Jayer, who died in 2006, occupies a special place in the annals of Burgundy. In World War II he was entrusted with the vines of the Domaine Méo-Camuzet on a sharecropping basis. Henri was not so much interested in the vines as with what went on in the cellar. He insisted on absolute cleanliness, regular topping-up of the barrels, and minimal manipulation. His opposition to fermenting with the stems is now shared by most Burgundian estates.

The 2.47-acre (1 ha) Parantoux vineyard, sandwiched between Richebourg and Vosne-Romanée Les Brulées, was derelict, but the land was owned by the Méo-Camuzet family. Henri planted it after the war. His nephew and successor Emmanuel Rouget owns one-third, the Méos the rest. Since the vines have been of age, the wine has invariably been one of the very best of the premiers crus.

The 1988 was the last wine where the whole vineyard was made as one wine. As with all Jayer wines, the new oak is definitely apparent, but underneath are ripe tannins, weight, and a mellow richness uncommon in this vintage, in which some wines are on the lean side of austere. **CC**

🍷🍷🍷🍷🍷 Drink: to 2038

The Wahluke Slope is one of the warmest regions in the state of Washington, producing consistently ripe fruit year after year. Growers have learned a lot since the string of hot vintages in the 1990s, tweaking their canopy management, irrigation regimes, and crop loads to better accommodate a mid-season heat spell.

Butch and Jerry Milbrandt's 550-acre (222 ha) vineyard, planted in 1997, is the source for Charles Smith's Milbrandt Syrah. The 2005 vintage here was terrific: Droughtlike, mild winter conditions ended with spring rains and snowfall. Dry conditions helpfully returned for flowering and fruit set, with healthy development through July. Heat finally hit in late July and August, with a string of days when temperatures exceeded 100°F (38°C). But the real beauty of 2005 was a perfect September and October—moderate, warm, and sunny—allowing an extended harvest. Harmony is the operative word for the top wines, and this Syrah expresses it beautifully, unfolding a savory complexity of smoked meats that complements a sweet, berry-fruit core, and a broad but balanced structure. **LGr**

🍷🍷 Drink: to 2017+

Kanonkop
Paul Sauer 2003

Origin South Africa, Simonsberg-Stellenbosch
Style Dry red wine, 13.5% ABV
Grapes C. Sauvignon 64%, C. Franc 30%, Merlot 6%

The maiden vintage of this wine in 1981 was one of South Africa's earliest red blends made in the image of Bordeaux, and was named after the eminent politician who farmed the property in the 1930s. Kanonkop, incidentally, means Cannon Hill, and refers to the seventeenth-century practice of firing a cannon from a nearby peak, to signal to farmers in outlying areas that a ship sailing between Europe and the Far East had entered Table Bay.

There have been substantial changes in the Kanonkop winemaking approach since 1981, when the idea of an alcohol level around 14% ABV, which the Paul Sauer can occasionally reach, would have been disconcerting, and the use of all-new oak barrels for maturation a crazy dream. But the wine is still fermented in the old open cement tanks, and the reputation of Paul Sauer as one of the Cape's finest red wines has been steadily maintained. In its youth, the 2003 is dominated by oak's tobacco and cedar notes, but rich dark fruit lurks purposefully on the firmly structured palate, signaling its presence with characteristic violets, tea leaf, and black berries. **TJ**

🟢🟢🟢 **Drink: to 2018**

Kanonkop
Pinotage 2009

Origin South Africa, Simonsberg-Stellenbosch
Style Dry red wine, 14% ABV
Grape Pinotage

For some, Pinotage is South Africa's contribution to the list of noble varieties; for others, it is a grape with inherent problems of structure and flavor—though few would deny that Kanonkop has produced some fine varietal Pinotages.

Although the first wine from Pinotage was the Lanzerac 1959, the grape was developed as early as 1925. In that year Abraham Perold's experiments produced what took decades to be accepted as a useful and undeniably distinctive new variety, through a cross of Pinot Noir and Cinsaut. Kanonkop was one of the first properties to plant Pinotage, and its commitment to the variety was strengthened by the passionate conviction of Beyers Truter, winemaker there from 1980 until 2002. It was the Pinotage 1989 that won Truter the Robert Mondavi International Winemaker of the Year award at the 1991 International Wine and Spirit Competition.

Good vintages show how well Pinotage can develop, with sweet plum flavors gaining complexity from notes of tomato cocktail, mushroom, and earth, the spice of mostly new oak well absorbed, and a firm, savory, tannic structure. **TJ**

🟢🟢 **Drink: to 2024**

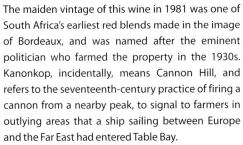

◀ The wine museum at the Kanonkop estate.

Katnook Estate *Odyssey Cabernet Sauvignon* 2002

Origin Australia, South Australia, Coonawarra
Style Dry red wine, 14.5% ABV
Grape Cabernet Sauvignon

Wayne Stehbens has been winemaker ever since the Katnook brand was released in 1980. Odyssey, only produced in the best vintages, came much later; the first vintage was the 1991. Stehbens says Odyssey is his attempt to make a great Cabernet, not necessarily a great Coonawarra. Indeed, the regular Katnook Estate Cabernet Sauvignon could be said to be more typical of the region. The three vineyards that supply the wine's backbone are low-yielding, mature vines on some of the highest land on the limestone ridge, where the topsoil is thinnest. Katnook's best vineyard sites are on the original cigar-shaped strip of central Coonawarra, where the soil is the classic terra rossa red soil over limestone.

Odyssey is a barrel selection of the most powerful, concentrated, and age-worthy batches of Cabernet. Fermentation is in stainless-steel tanks, at 64 to 77ºF (18 to 25ºC). The wine is matured in new barriques for thirty-six months—a long time for a Coonawarra wine, but its extreme concentration permits this. Uncommon for Coonawarra Cabernet, there is about one-third American oak, the rest being French. The result is a complex bouquet and fleshy, velvet-smooth palate texture, the wine unusually high in extract for a Coonawarra Cabernet. The 2002 vintage was a cool, extremely low-yielding one, and the wine is a typical Odyssey. It is loaded with cedar/cigarbox and chocolate/mocha aromas interwoven with black currant; the palate is quite profound, rich and silky in its tannins. **HH**
🝖🝖🝖 **Drink: to 2025**

FURTHER RECOMMENDATIONS
Other great vintages
1991 · 1992 · 1994 · 1996 · 1999 · 2001 · 2004 · 2005
More producers from Coonawarra
Balnaves · Bowen Estate · Majella · Parker Estate Penley Estate · Petaluma · Rymill · Wynns

Signs to a host of wineries at Penola in Coonawarra. ➔

Hungerford Hill

Katnook Estate

Leconfield WINES

BOWEN ESTATE

PENOWARRA WINES

Château Kefraya *Comte de M* 1996

Origin Lebanon, Bekaa Valley
Style Dry red wine, 14% ABV
Grapes C. Sauvignon 60%, Syrah 20%, Mourvèdre 20%

Nobody knows when wine was first made in Lebanon, although the Phoenician ancestors of today's Lebanese were certainly among the very earliest winemakers. Later, in the Greco-Roman era, a wine cult flourished, as the ruins of the Temple of Bacchus in Lebanon's Bekaa Valley prove.

In 1947, Michel de Bustros took over the family estate at Kefraya. He cleared the clay limestone ground and planted about 750 acres (303 ha) with grape varieties imported from France, including Cinsault, Carignan, Grenache, Mourvèdre, and Cabernet Sauvignon. Kefraya's vineyards grow at 3,280 feet (1,000 m) above sea level—appropriately, the company's motto is *Semper Ultra* (always higher).

With the help of a French company, De Bustros built a winery in 1978—in the middle of a war. In 1984, Kefraya's French winemaker, Yves Morard, was caught in the middle of an artillery battle between the Syrian and Israeli armies, and briefly ended up in a Tel Aviv jail. Morard was from the Rhône, and because the Bekaa has a similar climate to his homeland, he suggested planting the same vines. Impressed by the quality of these new vineyards, De Bustros and his new winemaker, Jean-Michel Fernandez, made a wine in 1996, aged in oak barrels for one year and released after a further three years. The full-bodied, concentrated, and rich Comte de M 1996 received a similar reception to that of Serge Hochar and his Bekaa red wine Château Musar at Bristol in 1977. **SG**

☻☻☻ **Drink: to 2018+**

FURTHER RECOMMENDATIONS		
Other great vintages		
1997 · 1998 · 1999 · 2000 · 2001		
More producers from Lebanon		
Clos St.-Thomas · Kouroum · Château Ksara		
Massaya · Château Musar · Wardy		

Harvesters take a well-earned break at Château Kefraya. ➡

Staatsweingüter Kloster Eberbach Assmannshäuser
Höllenberg Spätburgunder Cabinet 1947

Origin Germany, Rheingau
Style Dry red wine, ABV not available
Grape Pinot Noir

Comparing Spätburgunder (Pinot Noir) with Burgundy's reds may seem unfair; but when the Spätburgunder is a matured Assmannshäuser Höllenberg from a good vintage, the contest becomes a lot closer. Indeed, Jancis Robinson places the German wine in a class of its own: "The out and out star...was the 1947 Assmannshäuser Höllenberg Spätburgunder trocken Cabinet, as stunning a variant on red Burgundy as I have enjoyed in many a year. It was followed by three 1947 grand cru Burgundies...., but every one of them was knocked into a cocked hat by the majestic Spätburgunder."

This wine was grown in Germany's most famous red wine site—a very steep, south-by-southwest-facing slope on the western end of the Rheingau. Pinot Noir has been grown here on the Höllenberg (Hell Mountain) since at least 1470, and even Riesling-loving Goethe appreciated this red wine during his trip through the Rhine valley in 1814.

The slate soil lends the wine a very subtle berry taste and a typical striking bitter almond note in the finish. Even after six decades, this wine displays an intoxicatingly complex fruit flavor and remarkable freshness. "The 1947 Spätburgunder was still dark purplish crimson and amazingly rich, lively, and dramatic. Powerfully reminiscent of violets, woodsmoke, licorice, and truffles, it still has an exciting life ahead," concluded Jancis Robinson. **FK**
😊😊😊😊😊 Drink: to 2017+

FURTHER RECOMMENDATIONS
Other great vintages
1893 • 1921 • 1953 • 2003 • 2005
More German Pinot Noir producers
Dautel • Deutzerhof • Dr. Heger • Fürst • Huber
Johner • Kesseler • Knipser • Meyer-Näkel

The sun setting over the walls of the steep Höllenberg vineyards. ➡

Château Ksara
Cuvée du Troisième Millénaire 2009

Origin Lebanon, Bekaa Valley
Style Dry red wine, 13.5% ABV
Grapes Petit Verdot, C. Franc, C. Sauvignon, Syrah

The Ksara estate is the senior and biggest wine producer in Lebanon, and lies in the heart of the Bekaa, near Baalbeck. It is so named because it was the site of a *ksar*, or fortress, at the time of the Crusades. Jesuit fathers acquired the property in 1857. A resident priest, Father Kirn, pioneered the introduction of better vines in Lebanon (imported from Algeria), and new varietals were cultivated. At 3,609 feet (1,100 m) altitude in the Bekaa, Ksara has some of the highest vineyards in the world.

Ksara's wine cellar is a grotto discovered by the Romans, who consolidated part of the vault and dug several narrow tunnels from the cave into the surrounding chalk. In 1972, Ksara came into the hands of a business consortium when the Jesuits were told to sell the estate to conform to the directives of the Vatican II synod. At the time, Ksara represented 85 percent of all Lebanese wine production and was a hugely successful business—too successful, said the Vatican. Today, it represents 38 percent of Lebanese wine production.

Château Ksara's flagship and most individual wine is its Cuvée du Troisième Millénaire. Made principally from the relatively obscure Bordeaux variety Petit Verdot, it is less extracted and more elegant than some other Ksara wines, and can be enjoyed immediately, but develops well with an additional two or three years of aging. **SG**

🕲🕲🕲 **Drink: to 2017+**

FURTHER RECOMMENDATIONS
Other great vintages
2001 • 2002 • 2003
More wines from Château Ksara
Blanc de l'Observatoire
Cuvée de Printemps • Réserve du Convent

The vines have adapted to the high altitude of Lebanon's Bekaa Valley. ➡

Château La Dominique

2001

Origin France, Bordeaux, St.-Emilion
Style Dry red wine, 13% ABV
Grapes Merlot 86%, C. Franc 12%, C. Sauvignon 2%

Château La Fleur-Pétrus

1998

Origin France, Bordeaux, Pomerol
Style Dry red wine, 13% ABV
Grapes Merlot 90%, Cabernet Franc 10%

The eighteenth-century founder of this estate made his fortune in the Caribbean, and named his property after one of the French islands in the region. Between 1933 and 1969 it was owned by the De Bailliencourts of Château Gazin in Pomerol, and was then sold to construction tycoon Clément Fayat, who acquired other properties in the Médoc and Pomerol. With advice from Michel Rolland, the property was renovated, but, in 2006, Fayat changed his strategy by hiring Jean-Luc Thunevin, *négociant* and owner of Château Valandraud, to manage all his properties.

At seven years of age, the 2001, with its plummy, oaky aromas and its sweet, stylish palate, showed better than the 2000. Although there have been some excellent vintages of La Dominique over recent years, it must be said that the wine has yet to deliver a consistent style or, for that matter, quality. There is usually ample opulence and ripeness, but there is something hit and miss about La Dominique. The location of the vineyards suggests that it ought to be capable of delivering wine that is truly distinguished. Perhaps the radical changes initiated by Clément Fayat will do the trick. **SB**

🍷🍷🍷 Drink: to 2020

Jean Pierre Moueix has owned Château La Fleur-Pétrus since 1952. Four years after it was purchased, the vineyards were destroyed by the terrible frost that ravaged Bordeaux, and most of the vines had to be replanted. La Fleur-Pétrus has 22 acres (9 ha) of gravel-rich soil on a plateau east of Pomerol, sandwiched between the great estates of Lafleur and Pétrus, the latter also owned by Moueix.

Like so many Pomerol producers, La Fleur-Pétrus excelled in the 1998 vintage. Tasted in 2005, the wine was just starting to mature. At first the nose was perfumed and pronounced, but after half an hour or so it completely closed up. The palate was more forthcoming but still very tight, with dense layers of savory, earthy, spicy flavors underscored by vanilla oak. The structure was just about perfect; the acidity was mouth-puckering, suggesting that this is built for the long haul. The mid-palate was extraordinarily rich and elegant, but still tight on the finish. It is surprisingly drinkable at the moment, yet shy rather than surly. With its marvelous balance of ripeness and savoriness, this is the apotheosis of modern fine red Bordeaux. **SG**

🍷🍷🍷🍷🍷 Drink: to 2020+

◀ Nutrients are plowed into the soil of a La Dominique vineyard.

Château La Gomerie
2003

Origin France, Bordeaux, St.-Emilion
Style Dry red wine, 13% ABV
Grape Merlot

This new St.-Emilion superstar came into being almost by accident. The modest house with its 6 acres (2.5 ha) of vineyards lies about half a mile (1 km) outside St.-Emilion along the road to Libourne. For the Bécot family, who own Beau-Séjour-Bécot and bought La Gomerie in 1995, its attraction was that part of it lay adjacent to their Premier Grand Cru Classé. Possibly, part of its vineyards could become part of the first growth.

The Bécots were probably not aware how fine the terroir was when they bought the property. The soil is sandy on the surface but there was clay and iron clinker below. Moreover, the soil and microclimate are precocious, so the vines can be harvested before those of the first growth.

La Gomerie, which sells for higher prices than Beau-Séjour-Bécot, has been derided as yet another vin de garage. This is to do it an injustice, for the grapes are grown on a distinguished terroir fringing the St.-Emilion plateau. The wine's quality was confirmed in 2005 when, based on a blind tasting of three vintages, La Gomerie won the St.-Emilion Coupe, which is awarded every two years. **SB**
$)$ $)$ $)$ $)$ **Drink: to 2018**

La Jota Vineyard Company
20th Anniversary 2001

Origin USA, California, Napa Valley
Style Dry red wine, 14.9% ABV
Grape Cabernet Sauvignon

La Jota Vineyard Company has come a long way from its founding in 1898 by Frederick Hess, who planted vines, built a stone winery out of the volcanic rock that distinguishes the wines, and named it after the Spanish land grant on which it was built. Acclaimed at the beginning of the twentieth century, it closed during Prohibition and remained deserted until purchased in 1974 by Bill and Joan Smith, who reestablished the estate and its reputation and then sold it on to Jess Jackson and Barbara Banke in 2004.

Howell Mountain was the first subappellation in the Napa Valley, distinguished by its 1,400-foot (427 m) elevation, taking the vineyards above the fog line. La Jota's vineyards, on the south side, have well-draining, poor, volcanic ash soils that naturally devigor the vines and produce concentrated fruit.

The 20th Anniversary 2001 is a brooding and intense wine, with a sweet fruit and dried herb character and a mid-palate minerality true to its mountain origin. The extensive investment and attention the new owners are dedicating to the property suggest that La Jota will be a wine to watch in subsequent vintages as well. **LGr**
$)$ $)$ $)$ $)$ **Drink: to 2020+**

◄ Small vineyards flourish amid the buildings of St.-Emilion.

Château La Mission Haut-Brion 1982

La Mondotte 2000

Origin France, Bordeaux, Pessac-Léognan
Style Dry red wine, 13% ABV
Grapes C. Sauvignon 48%, Merlot 45%, C. Franc 7%

Origin France, Bordeaux, St.-Emilion
Style Dry red wine, 13.5% ABV
Grapes Merlot, Cabernet Franc

Beginning life as part of neighboring Château Haut-Brion, the estate was sold in 1630 to the Lazarites, a priestly community founded by St. Vincent de Paul. The wine they produced established a formidable reputation and provided financial support for the Mission's pastoral work among society's poor.

The French Revolution destroyed the ecclesiastical connection, but the property was lucky in its subsequent owners, who combined viticultural savvy with commercial bullishness. After World War I, the estate was acquired by the Woltner family, whose scion Henri established the château's latter-day reputation. In 1984, it was reacquired by its neighbor, Haut-Brion, and is now under the direction of Jean-Philippe Delmas.

In 1982 conditions conspired to produce a wine of midnight-black concentration and intensity. Black currants abound in the bouquet, twenty-five years after its release, but are now joined by the truffley notes of bottle age. Like all the best wines of the vintage, there is a haunting combination of tannic backbone and velvet softness to the structure, while the finish is a triumphant *sostenuto*. **SW**

🍷🍷🍷🍷🍷 Drink: to 2040

La Mondotte was purchased in 1971 by present proprietor Stefan von Neipperg's father and initially used as an informal second wine for Canon-la-Gaffelière. When Stefan von Neipperg sought to regularize this arrangement with the St.-Emilion authorities at the time of the 1996 classification, he was told he had to build a separate cellar for the wine. In order to make the investment worthwhile, he decided to "do something special." The result was La Mondotte. It exploded on to the Bordeaux market with the 1996 vintage, winning an instant 95–98 rating from Robert Parker. Consultant Stéphane Derenoncourt has worked on La Mondotte with Von Neipperg throughout, and together the pair have made it an "experimentation center."

The result, in the case of the 2000, is a wine of intoxicating aromatic power, hinting at incense, resin, chocolate, and kirsch. The wine's backbone becomes increasingly apparent in its arc through the mouth. Derenoncourt and Von Neipperg are looking for precision and finesse without abandoning the powerful sensuality that lies close to the heart of St.-Emilion's appeal. **AJ**

🍷🍷🍷🍷🍷 Drink: to 2025

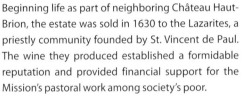

◧ A Gothic gateway proclaims La Mission's ecclesiastical origins.

La Rioja Alta
Rioja Gran Reserva 890 1985

Origin Spain, Rioja
Style Dry red wine, 12.5% ABV
Grapes Tempranillo, Mazuelo

La Rioja Alta was founded by five wine growers from Rioja and the Basque country in 1890, and is still in the hands of those five families today. It is situated in the Barrio de la Estación in Haro, next door to other well-known names like Muga, López Heredia, Bodegas Bilbaínas, and CVNE. After initial fermentation in stainless steel, the wine was put into century-old oak vats for malolactic fermentation and clarification. It then spent eight years in American oak casks, and was hand-racked by candlelight fifteen times. The wire netting on this wine originally acted as a protective seal to stop unscrupulous people changing the contents of the bottle for wine of inferior quality and then reselling it. These days it is used for aesthetic reasons and to maintain a link with the past.

The wine's color is translucent orange rather than red, the coloring matter having precipitated during the long upbringing in barrel and the subsequent years in bottle. The nose has mostly tertiary aromas, with leather, mushrooms, a whiff of truffle, and spices. On the palate it is polished, with suave tannins and a persistent finish. **LG**

🍷🍷🍷🍷 Drink: to 2020

La Spinetta
Barbaresco Vigneto Starderi 1999

Origin Italy, Piedmont, Langhe
Style Dry red wine, 14.5% ABV
Grape Nebbiolo

Giuseppe Rivetti bought the estate of La Spinetta, in the village of Castagnole Lanze, in 1977. The area is famous for the production of Moscato, which is how Giuseppe started in 1978, making the first single cru Moscato in Italy. The first red wine, a Barbera, followed in 1985, and in 1989 Giuseppe's sons released Pin, a revolutionary blend of Nebbiolo and Barbera dedicated to their father. The first Barbaresco, Gallina, emerged in 1995.

The Barbaresco Vigneto Starderi has been produced since 1996 from the Starderi vineyard in the area of Neive. Technically, this wine would fall under the category of "modern" Barbaresco, but older vintages show that, in the long run, the variety wins over the vinification and maturation techniques.

The 1999 was an amazing vintage for Nebbiolo. The Vigneto Starderi 1999 shows a beautifully intense ruby-red color, with some light garnet hues at the rim. The nose is ample and expressive, with the initial balsamic notes complemented by soft, sweet fruits, spices, and dark chocolate. On the palate, another more aniseedlike note completes the warm, pleasantly tannic and very long aftertaste. **AS**

🍷🍷🍷🍷 Drink: to 2025

Domaine Michel Lafarge
Volnay PC Clos des Chênes 1990

Château Lafite Rothschild
1996

Origin France, Burgundy, Côte de Beaune
Style Dry red wine, 13% ABV
Grape Pinot Noir

Origin France, Bordeaux, Pauillac
Style Dry red wine, 13% ABV
Grapes C. Sauvignon 83%, Merlot 7%, Others 10%

The first mention of this vineyard, as Cloux des Chaignes, is not until 1476—relatively late by Volnay standards. Despite being ranked only as a *troisième cuvée* by Dr. Lavalle in 1855, today Clos des Chênes is considered by many to be among the finest expressions of Volnay. This may be in part thanks to the exceptional quality of Michel Lafarge's wine. His 2.5 acres (1 ha) of vines are located in the lower part of the vineyard, the prime sector being well exposed to the south and east on a well-drained slope with brown soil on the classic Jurassic limestone base.

Since 1990, the making of classical red Burgundy has passed more into the hands of Michel's son Frédéric, who continues in the same mold, though with a quiet transition to biodynamic farming methods. Little new oak is used in the eighteen-month maturation process in the Lafarge's rabbit warren of a cellar in the middle of Volnay.

The 1990 is still a powerful, brooding wine that has not yet had the opportunity to reveal all its complexities, nor the graceful opulence that is the hallmark of a great Lafarge wine. The fruit and the structure will undoubtedly emerge with time. **JM**

🥂🥂🥂🥂 **Drink: to 2020**

Systematic winemaking began at Lafite in the seventeenth century, with the establishment of the property's ancestral vineyards by its then owner, Jacques de Ségur. Sixty years later, its reputation had spread widely enough that it found favor with the first British prime minister, Robert Walpole, who put in a quarterly repeat order for the wine during his term in office.

Lafite endured some difficult times in the twentieth century. It suffered the indignity of being transformed into a Nazi garrison, and many felt that it underperformed against the other first growths during the 1960s and early 1970s. Jean Crété set it back on the road to recovery in 1976 and, in 1983, was ably succeeded by Gilbert Rokvam. The Lafite 1996 is a towering wine, equipped with the muscle, perfume, and finesse one looks for in wines of this caliber. Sweet spice and complex notes of preserved berry fruits open up on the bouquet, while the palate shows a rounded, sinuous, high-powered wine with awe-inspiring tannic heft, but nimbleness and agility too. It will continue to sail serenely on through the coming decades. **SW**

🥂🥂🥂🥂🥂 **Drink: to 2050+**

Château Lafleur
2004

Origin France, Bordeaux, Pomerol
Style Dry red wine, 13.5% ABV
Grapes Merlot 50%, Cabernet Franc 50%

Domaine des Comtes Lafon
Volnay PC Santenots-du-Milieu 2002

Origin France, Burgundy, Côte de Beaune
Style Dry red wine, 13% ABV
Grape Pinot Noir

Not far from Pétrus and La Fleur-Pétrus stands a rather shabby farmhouse, which produces one of Bordeaux's greatest and costliest wines. Like Château Le Gay, it used to be owned by the frugal Robin sisters. On the death of Thérèse Robin in 1984, her sister Marie leased Lafleur to their cousin Jacques Guinaudeau, who made the wine from 1985 onward. When Marie died in 2001, Guinaudeau managed to fight off his rivals and secure the property.

Despite Lafleur's small size, the property has four distinct terroirs. These give the wines their complexity, but other factors contribute to their grandeur: the venerable vines, the very low yields, and the practice of selective harvesting to ensure that only the ripest grapes enter the winery. Guinaudeau's perfectionism means there is no such thing as a mediocre Lafleur. The 2004 is magnificent: Scented with elegant oak, mint, and a distinctive floral character, it is a voluptuous mouthful, complex but balanced, with a long life ahead of it. Small quantities and voracious demand mean that only a lucky few ever have the opportunity to taste a mature example of this stellar Pomerol. **SBr**
🔱🔱🔱🔱🔱 Drink: 2015–2035

Dominique Lafon, who became the winemaker at Comtes Lafon in 1984 at the age of only twenty-six, is best known for his Chardonnays, which are seductively fruity and powerfully spiced. However, he makes far better Pinot Noirs than most people imagine, an exercise in discerning subtle differences in soil and climate. Some, like the Santenots-du-Milieu, are actually grown in the village of Meursault, but are allowed by law to be labeled as Volnay.

After Dominique took over from his father René, he gradually terminated the sharecropping agreements his ancestors had signed, in order to exploit the family's excellent vineyards himself. Since then he has established a reputation for wines of richness, precision, and balance.

"Improving the reds, which lacked both concentration and acidity, was a challenge, but once you get healthier grapes, with better natural balance, you become less aggressive in the cellar," he says. "Now we do less extraction and the wines are more elegant." Dominique says that the 2002 is still very closed. For those of us lacking time or patience, the 1997 and 1992 are now drinking beautifully. **JP**
🔱🔱🔱🔱 Drink: to 2027

The Lafon château's roof tiles are typical of Burgundian architecture. ➡

Château Lagrange

2000

Origin	France, Bordeaux, St.-Julien
Style	Dry red wine, 13% ABV
Grapes	C. Sauvignon 65%, Merlot 28%, Petit Verdot 7%

Château Lagrézette

Cuvée Pigeonnier 2001

Origin	France, Southwest, Cahors
Style	Dry red wine, 14% ABV
Grape	Malbec

In 1983 the Japanese company Suntory bought Lagrange and began restoring neglected buildings, and buying back the vineyard parcels sold off by previous owners. They made an astute choice of director and winemaker in Marcel Ducasse, who nurtured the estate from 1983 until retiring in 2007.

The estate's soils never produce a massive, powerful wine. Lagrange is lighter and more elegant than, for example, Léoville-LasCases, though Ducasse greatly admires the finesse of Léoville-Barton. The Lagrange winemakers work hard to avoid excessive tannins in the wine. They look instead for balance. Although Lagrange is a wine that ages well, it is not structured for exceptionally long cellaring.

The 2000 is an excellent example of Lagrange's quality. The nose hints at sweet black currants, with a smokiness that comes from the 60 percent new oak in which the wine is aged. Its sumptuousness is a hallmark, but there is sufficient freshness to keep the wine lively and long. Ducasse's retirement brings a golden age for Lagrange to an end, but his successor, Bruno Eynard, has been his technical director for many years, so continuity is assured. **SBr**

☻☻☻ **Drink: to 2020**

This 160-acre (65 ha) showcase property belongs to Alain Dominique Perrin of the luxury goods company Richemont, which owns Cartier and other brands. He bought it in 1980, and spent ten years restoring it to its present magnificence.

Named after the pigeon house standing in the midst of its vines, Pigeonnier was first made serendipitously in 1997, when a late frost resulted in a miserly yield that was fermented in a single oak vat. The wine impressed Perrin and his team so much that a decision was made to produce a wine like this each year by pruning hard to induce low yields. An average of 7,000 bottles per year is made, and it is easily the most expensive wine from Cahors.

The opaque color of the Pigeonnier 2001 is in keeping with Cahors's reputation as the "black wine" of medieval renown. Ultra-modern in style, with ripe fruit and a lick of new oak, this is concentrated, thickly textured, and tannic, finishing powerfully and built to last. Pigeonnier lacks the charm and suppleness of Lagrézette's Cuvée Dame Honneur, but for those who like expensive blockbusters, it is one of the best of its type. **SG**

☻☻☻☻☻ **Drink: to 2017+**

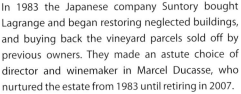

◄ Lagrange's Italianate tower was added to the château in 1820.

La Grande Rue

Domaine
François Lamarche

Domaine Lamarche
La Grande Rue PC 1962

Origin France, Burgundy, Côte de Nuits
Style Dry red wine, 13% ABV
Grape Pinot Noir

Leaving the hill of Corton aside, Burgundy's red wine grands crus begin with La Tâche, at the southern end of the commune of Vosne-Romanée, and continue almost uninterrupted up to the gates of the village of Gevrey-Chambertin. However, between La Tache and the swathe that begins with La Romanée at the top, then continues through La Romanée-Conti and ends in Romanée-St.-Vivant, there is a gap. This is the 4-acre (1.65 ha) vineyard of La Grande Rue, monopoly of the Lamarche family.

Legend has it that Henri Lamarche did not apply for grand cru status back in 1936, when the laws of today were first enacted—he feared he would have to pay more taxes. La Grande Rue was not made a grand cru until 1992, so this particular wine, the 1962, is only a premier cru, but it was made at a time when quality here was high. Subsequently standards slumped, but they have revived in the last fifteen years.

This 1962 shows the seductive magic that is old Pinot Noir. Mellow and soft to the point of a chiffon of silk; earthy, mushroomy, and sensual. And yet, despite being more than forty-five years old, the wine still has a freshness that gives it dimension and length on the palate. Do not drink this wine with food. Open the bottle after the meal is over, when you are comfortably replete. Close the curtains, turn off the music, and most of the lights. Drink it slowly and gently, as you would a Vintage Port. **CC**
🍷🍷🍷🍷 **Drink: to 2017+**

◀ The La Grande Rue Grand Cru vineyard of Domaine Lamarche.

Domaine des Lambrays
Clos des Lambrays GC 2005

Origin France, Burgundy, Côte de Nuits
Style Dry red wine, 13.5% ABV
Grape Pinot Noir

Just north of the Clos de Tart is another grand cru, Clos des Lambrays. Almost all of Clos des Lambrays is owned by the Domaine des Lambrays, which has been a grand cru only since 1981. Ironically, at that time the vineyard, neglected for many years, needed widespread replanting, which was bound to diminish the quality of the wine. However, Clos des Lambrays was considered superb in the 1940s.

In 1996 the property was sold to a German tycoon called Gunter Freund; since 1980 it has been managed by Thierry Brouin. The vineyards are on a fairly high slope, on impoverished limestone soils. It is quite a virile wine but in no way coarse. There is perfume and refinement, as well as structure and backbone. The wine has been sound for many years, but it is only since the mid-1990s that Clos des Lambrays has attained absolute grand cru quality.

The 2005 is an exquisite wine, highly perfumed with red-fruit aromas and a pronounced floral tone; there is rich fruit, of course, but also a fluidity, a sleekness, a balance of concentration and freshness, and great persistence. It adds up to a wine of extraordinary equilibrium and complexity. **SBr**
ⓢⓢⓢⓢ **Drink: to 2030**

Landmark *Kastania Vineyard*
Sonoma Pinot Noir 2002

Origin USA, California, Sonoma Valley
Style Dry red wine, 14.5% ABV
Grape Pinot Noir

The Landmark winery is located in the hamlet of Kenwood along the highway that runs the length of Sonoma Valley. The Mabry family created the Landmark brand, but in 1989 Damaris Deere Ethridge, a partner in the company, bought out the other shareholders and brought in her son Michael and her daughter-in-law Mary to help run the winery. As a descendant of John Deere, whose name is stamped on almost every tractor in the United States, she did not lack means. The winery has long specialized in Chardonnay and Pinot Noir, although a few other wines, such as Syrah, are also produced.

Landmark produces a reliable Pinot Noir called Grand Detour, which is a blend from five sites, including one in Santa Barbara. Kastania is a single-vineyard wine from a site planted with Pinot Noir in 1994 with a blend of Dijon clones, as well as long-established Californian clones such as Pommard.

The 2002 has alluring aromas of cherries, tobacco, tea, and toast, almost heady in its fragrance. It is a lush wine, full-bodied and silky, with discernible new oak behind the opulent black-cherry fruit, and some acidity on the finish. **SBr**
ⓢⓢⓢ **Drink: to 2017+**

Landmark at the base of Sugarloaf Mountain in the Sonoma Valley. ▶

Château Latour 2003

Origin France, Bordeaux, Pauillac
Style Dry red wine, 13.3% ABV
Grapes C. Sauvignon 81%, Merlot 18%, Petit Verdot 1%

The tower after which the estate is named was built in the late fourteenth century as a fortress during the Hundred Years' War (1337–1453). The tower is long gone, but was replaced in the early part of the seventeenth century by the tower that stands today, a circular, domed affair that was actually intended as a pigeon roost.

Included among the Firsts in the 1855 classification (some argue that it appeared behind Lafite on the list only on alphabetical grounds), Latour has maintained a degree of consistency that befits a world-renowned wine. Deep-rooted vines on highly gravelly soils produce wines that are perhaps the most long-lived of all the first growths, and the high Cabernet content (more than 80 percent in some vintages) means that the wines should in no event be approached much before the onset of their third decade. That said, the 2003 is an uncommonly forward wine, as a result of the intense ripeness of the vintage. Produced in a furious heat wave that caused widespread calamity throughout Europe, the wine is black as sin and will prove at least twice as tempting. It displays a gorgeously floral nose of black currants, black plums, and smoky oak, and, despite its firm tannins, it has such gentle acidity and sweet fruit on the palate that it's likely to be drunk too early by primary fruit fans. At 13.3 percent alcohol, it is also quite a blockbuster, and yet the horsepower behind it is perfectly integrated with its fruit concentration. **SW**

🜚🜚🜚🜚 **Drink: 2020–2075+**

FURTHER RECOMMENDATIONS
Other great vintages
1982 · 1986 · 1989 · 1990 · 1995 · 1998 · 2000 · 2009
More producers from Pauillac
Lafite Rothschild · Mouton Rothschild · Pichon-Longueville (Baron) · Pichon-Longueville (Comtesse)

An elaborate dovecote on the Latour estate, dating from c. 1630. ▸

Château Latour-à-Pomerol

1961

Origin France, Bordeaux, Pomerol
Style Dry red wine, 13% ABV
Grapes Merlot, Cabernet Franc

Le Dôme

1998

Origin France, Bordeaux, St.-Emilion
Style Dry red wine, 13% ABV
Grapes Cabernet Franc 75%, Merlot 25%

This Château Latour is usually suffixed by "à Pomerol" to distinguish it from the many other La Tours in Bordeaux. The first owners were called Chambeaud. In 1875 their only daughter married Louis Garitey. Garitey's eldest daughter and heiress at Latour was the redoubtable Mme. Edouard Loubat, who as well as enlarging Latour was consolidating Pétrus.

Château Latour, managed by Ets. J. P. Moueix since 1962, but owned by Mme. Lily Lacoste, daughter of Mme. Loubat, is indisputably one of Pomerol's top estates. The 20-acre (8 ha) vineyard lies in two main parcels and is planted in the ratio of 90 percent Merlot and 10 percent Cabernet Franc. It normally produces a bigger wine than its stablemate in the Moueix lineup, Château La Fleur-Pétrus—they sell for the same price—although not as refined.

Back in 1961 the vineyard was of a venerable average age, for this was before the young vines planted after the 1956 frosts were incorporated into the grand vin. This, together with the concentration of this very short but perfectly balanced vintage, has produced a memorable wine. Rich, creamy, opulent, balanced, and succulent. **CC**
🍷🍷🍷🍷🍷 **Drink: to 2017+**

When Englishman Jonathan Maltus first made Le Dôme in 1996, it was labeled *garagiste*. Yet in style Le Dôme is surprisingly classic: surprising because Maltus, in Bordeaux at least, is a professional outsider, a habitual breaker of conventions. It is almost as if those early vintages have turned out classic in spite of him.

Maltus's principle has always been that as a single-vineyard wine, everything from the vineyard should go into the blend. The early vintages received 150 percent new oak—100 percent new oak to begin with, then racking into 50 percent new oak. (He has since dispensed with the extra 50 percent.) This made for some distinctly chewy tasting experiences, and yet the wines were never overextracted, always balanced, and always had that indefinable something that makes even a sullen barrel sample sing. The high proportion of Cabernet Franc gives marvelous aromatic freshness—on this 1998, now approaching maturity, there are notes of raspberries and black fruits, a firm but discreet structure, and an immensely long, aromatic finish. It is fascinating and utterly addictive. **MR**
🍷🍷🍷🍷🍷 **Drink: to 2030**

Le Due Terre
Sacrisassi 1998

Origin Italy, Friuli
Style Dry red wine, 13% ABV
Grapes 50% Refosco, 50% Schioppettino

Le Due Terre is a small estate set up in 1984 by Silvana and Flavio Basilicata. The cellar is in the Colli Orientali del Friuli, which stretches along the border with Slovenia in the hilly part of the Udine province. This is traditionally a white wine area, but recent red wines have also been promising. The most important local red grape varieties are the Refosco dal Peduncolo Rosso, better known in the rest of the world as Mondeuse, and the Schioppettino, a grape variety capable of yielding lightly colored, interesting wines, with black pepper as their trademark. Le Due Terre's Sacrisassi Rosso unites the characters of the two grapes: The delicate yet baroque elegance of the Schioppettino smoothes the somewhat rough edges of the Refosco, which in return adds color and flesh to the blend.

The 1998 shows a refreshing and typical northeastern Italian greenness, supported by a warm, deep, and dark fruit. The tannins are lightly present, but it is the acidity that defines and supports the fruit during the pleasantly focused finish. This is a wine to fall in love with for its unique personality and for its strong sense of origin. **AS**

🍷🍷🍷 **Drink: to 2018**

Le Macchiole
Paleo Rosso 2001

Origin Italy, Tuscany, Bolgheri
Style Dry red wine, 14% ABV
Grape Cabernet Franc

Le Macchiole is the brainchild of the late Eugenio Campolmi who, at the beginning of the 1980s, decided to pursue his strong passion for wine and invested large amounts of money in the reconversion of his family's vineyards. He also planted international grape varieties such as Cabernet Franc, Cabernet Sauvignon, and Merlot, and in 1991 he hired young Luca D'Attoma to consult on the winemaking. When Eugenio died prematurely in 2002 the running of the estate passed into the capable hands of his wife Cinzia. She quickly proved to be just as capable and meticulous as Eugenio in the uncompromising search for quality. In particular, she insisted that a great wine is made in the vineyard.

Paleo Rosso is one wine into which Eugenio invested a lot of energy. This wine assumed its definitive shape in the 2001 vintage when, instead of being a blend of Cabernet Sauvignon and Cabernet Franc, it was made exclusively from the latter variety. The wine shows a bright ruby color. The nose combines elegantly vegetal (never green) notes and red fruits, with a light underlying butteriness. **AS**

🍷🍷🍷 **Drink: to 2018+**

Le Pin

2001

Origin France, Bordeaux, Pomerol
Style Dry red wine, 13% ABV
Grapes Merlot 92%, Cabernet Franc 8%

One of the most sought-after wines in the world, Le Pin is the original garage wine, so-called because it is made in the basement of a very plain farmhouse in Pomerol. Indeed, the property is so modest that it stops short of calling itself a château and is simply named after a nearby pine tree.

The Thienpont family are long-established Belgian wine merchants who also own Château Labégorce-Zédé in Margaux and other properties in the Côtes de Francs. They acquired Le Pin in 1979 from the widow Madame Laubie, who had always cultivated the 2.5-acre (1 ha) vineyard organically but sold the grapes as anonymous generic Pomerol. With such a miniscule vineyard, Le Pin produces just 600 to 700 cases each year; by comparison, Château Lafite-Rothschild produces approximately 29,000 cases of wine a year, and even Pétrus manages about 4,000. The combination of extreme rarity and high international demand has created exalted prices.

A wine that is both iconoclastic and hedonistic, Le Pin is often dismissed by those brought up on "classic" Bordeaux because it undermines—both stylistically and financially—the long-established wine hierarchy of Bordeaux. The affable Jacques Thienpont is bemused by the prices fetched by his wine, but remains philosophical. "I am not a banker," he says, "but if you buy a wine and the value goes down, you can always drink it. If you buy a piece of paper, and the value goes down, you can't eat it." **SG**
🍷🍷🍷🍷 **Drink: to 2020**

◀ The Le Pin farmhouse, in front of the eponymous pine tree.

Le Riche *Cabernet Sauvignon Reserve* 2003

Origin South Africa, Stellenbosch
Style Dry red wine, 14% ABV
Grape Cabernet Sauvignon

Etienne le Riche is one of many winemakers at established domaines who have felt the urge to do their own thing, but one of the few who actually did. In the mid-1990s, after twenty years at the established grandeur of Rustenberg estate, he left for a considerably more modest enterprise, renting a small farm in Stellenbosch's Jonkershoek Valley.

In 2013, the successful concern moved into its own newly built cellar on a smallholding in Stellenbosch, alongside one of the vineyards that supply their Cabernet Sauvignon grapes (on the basis of "long-term friendship agreements"). By then, son Christo had assumed prime responsibility for the wines. The new winery retains the old-fashioned open-top concrete fermenters Etienne always favored, alongside more modern features.

It is fairly unusual in the Cape for the flagship wine to be a varietal Cabernet; most opt for the blended model of Bordeaux. Yet this fresh and harmonious Reserve has a classic completeness that sometimes eludes the straight varietal. While the more recent vintages of Le Riche perhaps signal a turn to riper, oakier opulence, the 2003 is typical of the cellar's earlier approach. There is a fruit-intense gentleness, a refinement, vitally informed by a firm structure of tannin and acidity, while the oaking is restrained. Etienne le Riche (now an advisor to his son, in the new winery, with a repackaging exercise just undertaken) sees essential continuity: "There are lots of changes, but really no change . . . ." **TJ**

🍷🍷 **Drink: to 2018**

FURTHER RECOMMENDATIONS		
Other great vintages		
1997 • 2000 • 2001 • 2007 • 2009		
More producers from Stellenbosch		
Kanonkop • Meerlust • Morgenster		
Rustenberg • Rust en Vrede • Thelema		

Le Riche draws its grapes from vineyards in mountainous Stellenbosch. ➔

L'Ecole No. 41 *Walla Walla Seven Hills Vineyard Syrah* 2005

Origin USA, Washington State, Columbia Valley
Style Dry red wine, 14.5% ABV
Grape Syrah

Wine production in Washington State is a relatively recent development, but expansion has been rapid. Although the state's coastal strip around Seattle is too wet for viticulture, the inland valleys are semi-arid, making irrigation mandatory if grapes are to ripen fully. These valleys have hot days, cool nights, and, because of their northerly latitude, more daylight hours and sunshine than California. This gives Washington's wines a long growing season and considerable freshness and elegance.

L'Ecole No. 41 was founded in 1983, and has been run for many years by Marty Clubb. In its early years, the winery developed a strong reputation for Chenin Blanc and for rather oaky Sémillon, but recently the red wines have proved the stronger suit. The best of them are varietals or Bordeaux blends sourced mostly from the esteemed Pepper Bridge and Seven Hills vineyards in nearby Walla Walla.

Early vintages in new wine regions can seem clumsy as winemakers explore the potential of the fruit being grown. This was certainly true at L'Ecole No. 41, but by the late 1990s winemaker Michael Sharon had come to grips with Walla Walla fruit and the wines were far more consistent. The Seven Hills Syrah 2005, aged in one-third new barriques, has a dense color, sweet blueberry fruit on the nose, with considerable charm, and fine intensity on the palate. It may be less lush than some Syrahs from warmer areas such as Napa, but its piquancy, vigor, and mint-leaf freshness more than make up for it. **SBr**

🟢🟢🟢 **Drink: to 2018**

FURTHER RECOMMENDATIONS
Other great vintages
2001 • 2002 • 2003 • 2004
More producers in Washington State
Canoe Ridge • Château Ste. Michelle
Leonetti Cellars • Quilceda Creek

Built in 1915, this former schoolhouse became L'Ecole No. 41's winery. ➜

Peter Lehmann
Stonewell Shiraz 1998

Origin Australia, South Australia, Barossa Valley
Style Dry red wine, 14.5% ABV
Grape Shiraz

Barossan Peter Lehmann, who died in 2013, was winemaker and manager at Saltram Wines until 1980. It was here that he developed strong relationships with local grape growers, completing deals with a handshake rather than a contract.

By 1979, there was a serious glut of grapes and wine. Saltram ordered Lehmann to go back on his word to the growers that he would buy their crop. He refused, and set about establishing a new winery. The first vintage was processed in 1980, and in 1982 the winery was named Peter Lehmann Wines.

The grapes for Stonewell Shiraz come from old, low-yielding vineyards in the drier western areas of the Barossa. After a lean period in the mid-1990s, 1998 was a return to form in the area, and many excellent reds were produced. Like the man himself, this wine is big, with lots of fruit, alcohol, and acidity. The flavors are quintessentially Barossan—leather, spice, cassis, and sweet oak. But despite its larger-than-life structure, the 1998 is surprisingly drinkable and elegant. It has won many prizes, including gold medal at the Adelaide, Brisbane, and Hobart National Wine Shows in 2000. **SG**

🍷🍷 **Drink: to 2018+**

Leonetti Cellars
Merlot 2005

Origin USA, Washington State, Columbia Valley
Style Dry red wine, 14.3% ABV
Grapes Merlot 85%, C. Sauvignon 8%, Petit Verdot 7%

Gary Figgins's early wines were big, rich, and chewy—relatively easy to make in Washington State's desert-hot climate. As he and son Chris have matured as wine growers, the style has become more elegant and harmonious. Accessible upon release, the wines also benefit from cellaring.

Figgins blends his Merlot from as many as six different vineyards throughout the Columbia Valley. The wine is kept in new French and American barrels for fourteen months, but Figgins never stacks more than two barrels high, to maintain the air circulation that contributes to the wine's development.

This 2005 is an exciting vintage as new plantings were introduced to the blend. After the frost of 2004 cut production by one-third, growers enjoyed a brilliant growing season in 2005. A cooler summer than 2003, stable autumn weather, and frost-free harvest allowed slow accumulation of flavors and retention of acidities to produce balanced, elegant, harmonious wines bursting with ripe fruit. The 2005 is an elegant, silky, middle-weight wine, even across the palate, accessible and harmonious, with pure fruit flavors leading into a minerally finish. **LGr**

🍷🍷🍷 **Drink: to 2020+**

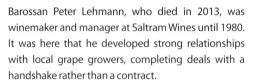

Bird netting protects young vines at a Peter Lehmann vineyard.

Château Léoville-Barton 2000

Origin France, Bordeaux, St.-Julien
Style Dry red wine, 12.5% ABV
Grapes C. Sauvignon 72%, Merlot 20%, C. Franc 8%

There has been a major Irish presence in Bordeaux ever since the 1690 victory of the Protestant William of Orange at the Battle of the Boyne forced many Roman Catholic Irish to emigrate. They may not have had the proprietorial rights the English once enjoyed in the region, but the number of Irish hearts with "Bordeaux" engraved on them is legion. The Bartons are one such dynasty. Arriving in 1821, they liked the wines and the ambience of Château Langoa so much that they bought the place. In time, they acquired a minority parcel of the Léoville estate to go with it and the two wines have evolved symbiotically ever since. At close to two centuries, this is the longest tenure of any winemaking family in Bordeaux.

Lying at the heart of the St.-Julien appellation and planted on gravel-clay soils, the Léoville estate comprises 120 acres (49 ha). The wines have a traditional vinification, being held in barriques (around half are new each year) for eighteen to twenty months before blending and bottling.

The miracle vintage of 2000 produced prodigies almost wherever one looked, so it is all the more extraordinary for a particular property to stand out so prominently. The Léoville 2000 is a career-defining wine, intensely weighty, rich, and opulent, with a fine layer of smoky oak supporting layers of lush, decadent cassis fruit, held together with tannin struts as elegant as Doric columns. It is a sublime wine that will produce surprises at every stage of its development. **SW**

◔◔◔◔ **Drink: to 2040+**

FURTHER RECOMMENDATIONS
Other great vintages
1989 · 1990 · 1995 · 1996 · 1998 · 2001 · 2003 · 2005
More producers from St.-Julien
Ducru-Beaucaillou · Gruaud-Larose · Lagrange Langoa-Barton · Léoville-Las Cases · Talbot

Anthony Barton, proprietor of Château Léoville-Barton. ➡

Château Léoville-Las Cases

1996

Origin France, Bordeaux, St.-Julien
Style Dry red wine, 13% ABV
Grapes C. Sauvignon 65%, Merlot 20%, Others 15%

For decades the Delon family have considered their property of first-growth quality, and in great vintages their wine is of comparable quality with the first growths. Selection is scrupulous and often no more than 40 percent of the crop ends up in the grand vin, with the rest being used for the Clos du Marquis.

Léoville-Las Cases is masculine and muscular, a dense, dark, brooding wine with imposing tannins and a structure that seems rugged in the wine's youth, but which promises a very long life in bottle. The wine has its detractors, however, who argue that it has become too extracted and too reliant on techniques such as reverse osmosis to concentrate the wine artificially, and excessively.

The 1996 demonstrates very well that Léoville-Las Cases is a wine that demands patience. In its youth it was decidedly aggressive and the fruit was masked by the tannins. By now the sheer class of the wine is evident, with lean, cedary, black currant aromas of great elegance, though on the palate the wine is still rather dense and tight. It will take a few more years for the tannins to become more supple and for the richness of the fruit to emerge. **SBr**
☻☻☻☻☻ **Drink: to 2030**

Château Léoville-Poyferré

2004

Origin France, Bordeaux, St.-Julien
Style Dry red wine, 13% ABV
Grapes C. Sauvignon 65%, Merlot 25%, Others 10%

The mighty Léoville estate was carved up after the French Revolution and this sector consists primarily of vineyards planted on gravelly soil along the road to Pauillac. It has been owned by the Cuvelier family, originally wine merchants in northern France, since 1920, and is currently managed by Didier Cuvelier.

The style of Léoville-Poyferré is very different to the more classic, even austere Léoville-Barton, and the super-concentrated, powerful, and dramatic Léoville-Las Cases. It is more lush, more hedonistic, more appealing in its youth. Its sheer sensuality is hard to resist, even if in this respect it is less typically St.-Julien than the other two wines. But Cuvelier aims to produce an ageworthy wine and has reduced the proportion of Merlot in the vineyard when many other Médoc estates have been increasing it.

The 2004 shows the property at its best. The black currany aromas do not lack succulence and charm, yet the wine has considerable power, vigor, and balance, with an abundance of black fruit flavors and fine length. Dependable and consistent, Léoville-Poyferré also offers, for a second growth, good value for money. **SBr**
☻☻☻ **Drink: to 2022**

A courtyard separates Léoville-Las Cases (left) and Léoville-Poyferré (right). ▶

Domaine Leroy *Romanée-St.-Vivant Grand Cru* 2002

Origin France, Burgundy, Côte de Nuits
Style Dry red wine, 13% ABV
Grape Pinot Noir

In 1988 Mme. Lalou Bize-Leroy, at the time co-manager of Domaine de la Romanée-Conti (DRC), as well as director of her family's Maison Leroy, was invited to inspect the Charles Nöellat domaine, based in Vosne-Romanée, which was looking for a purchaser. Half of the vines were missing; the remainder were suffering from years of neglect. Nevertheless they were old and they were the old-fashioned, high-quality Pinot hardly found any more. Potentially they could produce magnificent wine. The Nöellats had a deal.

The Leroy parcel of Romanée-St.-Vivant covers 2.45 acres (0.99 ha). Mme. Bize makes her wine much as it is made at the DRC, yet you would not confuse these two Romanée-St.-Vivants. The Leroy wines never hint that they come from whole grape vinification. They are fatter, richer, and more voluptuous, generous rather than restrained. This 2002, bottled after less than a year—here the approaches do differ—is full-bodied and very densely concentrated, absolutely crammed with ripe fruit, and has the splendid acidity of the vintage. It will last and last. A magnificent wine. **CC**

🆂🆂🆂🆂🆂 Drink: 2015–2050

L'Enclos de Château Lezongars 2001

Origin France, Bordeaux, Premières Côtes de Bordeaux
Style Dry red wine, 13% ABV
Grapes Merlot 70%, C. Franc 15%, C. Sauvignon 15%

This attractive property, set within the village of Villenave-de-Rions in the hills above the Garonne, was bought by a British couple, Russell and Sarah Iles, in 1998. They still run the property, aided by their son Philip and their winemaker Marielle Cazeau.

The basic Lezongars is aged for nine months in one-third new barriques. The best barrels are given longer barrel aging and released under the L'Enclos de Château Lezongars label. Since 2000, there has also been the Special Cuvée, sourced from the most gravelly slopes on the property, made almost entirely from Merlot, and aged in a much higher proportion of new oak.

Given the short time that the family has been running the property, its progress has been swift and impressive. Admittedly, the Special Cuvée seems something of a marketing exercise, but the premium L'Enclos has been a very consistent wine in quality and style. It exhibits sweet, elegant, cherry aromas, a rounded fleshy texture, good but not excessive fruit concentration, and a long, spicy finish. Moreover, the price makes it eminently affordable: a fine, modern-style claret to enjoy relatively young. **SBr**

🆂🆂 Drink: to 2017+

Elegant Château Lezongars, home of the Iles family. ➡

Domaine du Comte Liger-Belair *La Romanée GC* 2005

Origin France, Burgundy, Côte de Nuits
Style Dry red wine, 13% ABV
Grape Pinot Noir

Of all the grands crus in Burgundy, La Romanée, with an area of 2 acres (0.83 ha), is the tiniest. As each *cru* possesses its own, individual *appellation contrôlée*, La Romanée is the smallest AOC in all France. The vineyard, unusually planted in a north-to-south orientation and not from east to west, up and down the prevailing slope, lies immediately above La Romanée-Conti, and, like that estate, is a monopoly, in this case of the Liger-Belair family since 1827.

Prior to 2001, the vineyard was tended and the wine made by Régis Forey, a local Vosne-Romanée *vigneron* who also operated his own independent estate, but the wine was matured, bottled, and marketed by Bouchard Père et Fils of Beaune, albeit under its own special label. This system ceased when young winemaker Louis-Michel Liger-Belair arrived on the scene, the lease with Forey having come to its end. For the next three vintages, half of the La Romanée was reared by Bouchard, half by Louis-Michel (it is interesting to compare the 2002s, because there is just a little more delicacy and finesse in Louis-Michel's example), but from 2005 all the wine is Liger-Belair's own work.

Like Romanée-Conti itself, La Romanée is a lighter and more feminine wine that La Tâche or Richebourg. Hitherto it was always a bit leaner than Romanée-Conti, and it did not have the breed. This is no longer the case. This 2005 is simply exquisite: complex, profound, pure, harmonious, and very lovely indeed. Perhaps it is the best wine of all in this excellent harvest. We must wait and see. **CC**

🙂🙂🙂🙂 Drink: 2020–2040+

Lisini *Brunello di Montalcino Ugolaia* 1990

Origin Italy, Tuscany, Sant'Angelo in Colle
Style Dry red wine, 14% ABV
Grape Sangiovese

Located in the hamlet of Sant'Angelo in Colle, the Lisini estate has played a leading role in Montalcino since the late 1960s. Elina Lisini, still active in the family estate, was one of the founding members of the Consorzio in 1967, well before Brunello became known around the world. The family began a thorough restructuring of the property and the cellars in the 1970s, and their 1975 Riserva is a hallmark Brunello from this great vintage.

In 1983 the firm engaged consulting enologist and Sangiovese specialist Franco Bernabei, whose terroir-driven philosophy induced Elina's nephew Lorenzo Lisini and his family to highlight their most exceptional vineyard. Lisini labeled the single-vineyard bottling Ugolaia, after this vineyard. Situated between Sant'Angelo in Colle, one of the hotter Montalcino growing areas, and Castelnuovo d'Abate at 1,050 feet (320 m) above sea level, this 3.7-acre (1.5 ha) parcel, with its perfect southwestern exposure, generates the best grapes, yielding long-lived, concentrated Brunellos of great complexity.

Ugolaia, which is produced only in exceptional vintages, is made in the classic style, and aged for thirty-six months in large Slavonian oak barrels. Replanted in the late 1970s with the best vines from the estate, Ugolaia is at the powerful end of the spectrum. The Ugolaia 1990, from one of the most lauded vintages in the last century, is a superb wine of breeding and class that, according to wine writer Franco Ziliani, "deserves a standing ovation" for its complexity and powerful structure. **KO**

🙂🙂🙂 Drink: to 2020+

This cellar device indicates that the barrel is full and can admit no air. ➡

Littorai Wines
The Haven Pinot Noir 2005

Origin USA, California, Sonoma Coast
Style Dry red wine, 13.8% ABV
Grape Pinot Noir

López de Heredia
Viña Tondonia Rioja GR 1964

Origin Spain, Rioja
Style Dry red wine, 12.5% ABV
Grapes Tempranillo 75%, Garnacho 15%, Others 10%

Ted Lemon was the first American to serve as manager and winemaker at a Burgundian estate: Domaine Guy Rulot in Meursault. He returned to the United States in the 1990s and established Littorai with the goal of producing terroir-based wines, choosing Pinot Noir and Chardonnay as the varieties most likely to express the subtle qualities of the site.

The Haven is Lemon's premier vineyard. It lies at 1,200 feet (366 m), a few miles from the coast in an exceptionally cool location. The substrate is diverse, with each soil type planted, picked, and vinified separately. Lemon prefers dry farming where possible, but irrigates to establish the vines.

Spring rains shattered the 2005 bloom, leaving a drastically reduced crop. The berries were tiny, but held none of the harsh tannins and aggressive character that so often result from low yields. Intense in color, this 2005 wine has wonderful black fruit, fine acid balance, and tannins that do not intrude. Unfortunately, only a tiny quantity was made. Along with the 2006, it is a fine example of Lemon's determination to focus his primary energy on place, in order to let the wine best reflect its origins. **JS**

⊝⊝⊝⊝ **Drink: to 2017+**

López de Heredia was founded in 1877 by Don Rafael López de Heredia y Landeta. Between 1913 and 1914 he planted the Tondonia vineyard on the left bank of the Ebro River, which was to become one of the most famous vineyards and brands in Rioja. Successive generations have done their best to preserve the traditions of the estate. The grapes are hand-harvested and fermented in seventy-two vats of different sizes and oak origin. Malolactic is carried out in these vats or in barriques; only wood, and never new, is used for the production of the wines.

"In Rioja they call it the vintage of the century," explains María José López de Heredia of 1964, "but we call it the miracle vintage, as it does not seem to age." This vintage stayed in barrel for nine years, and was hand-racked eighteen times. It was fined with egg white and bottled, unfiltered, in 1973. It now has a nice, light red color, with some brick on the rim. The bouquet is fully mature but still vibrant, with autumn leaves, porcini mushrooms, leather, sweet cherry fruit, tea, maraschino, and tobacco. The palate is polished, with fully resolved tannins and a good acid spine. So, still a long life ahead. **LG**

⊝⊝⊝⊝⊝ **Drink: to 2025**

Château Lynch-Bages
1989

Origin France, Bordeaux, Pauillac
Style Dry red wine, 12.5% ABV
Grapes C. Sauvignon 73%, Merlot 15%, Others 12%

John Lynch emigrated to Bordeaux from Ireland in 1691, and though he dealt in textiles, wool, and leather, his son Thomas developed a nose for wine. In the eighteenth century the family acquired a pair of properties in Pauillac, and christened them Lynch-Moussas and Lynch-Bages. The estates went their separate ways over the next couple of centuries, though both were included among the fifth growths when the 1855 classification was formulated.

The Cazes family bought Lynch-Bages on the eve of World War II, and, since then, the estate has come a long way from its 1855 classification. Its deuxième-quality wines are masterpieces of intensity; hugely long-lived wines, but possessed of the kind of grace and approachability for which there really is no better word than *charmant*. The 1989 vintage generally produced seductive, supple, deliciously curvaceous wines, and none more so than Lynch-Bages. There is a hefty tannic structure to the wine, but also a load of purple fruits, overlaid with the characteristic mintiness of Pauillac Cabernet, shading to haunting eucalyptus, and concluding with a massive, though elegant, finish. **SW**
🜲🜲🜲🜲🜲 Drink: to 2030+

Macari Vineyard
Merlot Reserve 2001

Origin USA, New York, Long Island, North Fork
Style Dry red wine, 13% ABV
Grape Merlot

"This whole area is an experiment," says Joe Macari, who fell into managing a vineyard and winery almost by accident. His father had owned land on the North Fork of Long Island since 1963, and suggested that he and Joe experiment with wine growing. They planted their first vines in 1995 and have been experimenting ever since. The Mattituck property reaches northwest to the bluffs rising 100 to 275 feet (30–84 m) above the Long Island Sound, which moderates the area's temperature. The vineyard's sandy loam soils contribute to middle-weight wines with lively acidities and a purity of flavor that Macari has learned to respect.

Macari began experimenting in the 1990s with organic, and especially biodynamic, viticulture. A biodynamic consultant told him that Long Island is simply too humid to farm biodynamically but Macari begins each season biodynamically and stops only when threatened with the loss of his crop.

A product only of warmer vintages, the Reserve wine is quintessential Long Island Merlot—bursting with raspberries, with undertones of tobacco and minerals, and propelled by vibrant acidity. **LGr**
🜲🜲 Drink: to 2017+

Château Magdelaine

1990

Origin France, Bordeaux, St.-Emilion
Style Dry red wine, 13% ABV
Grapes Merlot 95%, Cabernet Franc 5%

In 1952 the Moueix family took over the property, and soon replanted most of the vineyard, which they found in poor shape. The density is unusually high for St.-Emilion, at around 3,600 vines per acre (9,000 vines per hectare). The location is exceptional, too, with Bélair to the east, and Canon just to the north.

Magdelaine is distinctive in that it has a higher proportion of Merlot in its vineyard than any other first growth of St.-Emilion. The soils are composed of limestone mixed with clay. Some of the parcels are plowed by horse, a rarity in St.-Emilion. The vinification is in the classic Moueix mold, with every effort made to avoid overextraction.

Despite the high proportion of Merlot, Magdelaine is not especially voluptuous initially. Compared with the denser, oakier St.-Emilion premiers, it can seem almost too restrained when young, but it is a wine that effortlessly takes on weight and complexity as it ages. Today the 1990 has pure, refined aromas, a silkiness on the palate, and exquisite harmony, while maintaining a firm tannic structure and striking length. Immensely drinkable now, it will develop over many years. **SBr**

♥♥♥♥ **Drink: to 2020**

Majella
The Malleea Cabernet/Shiraz 1998

Origin Australia, South Australia, Coonawarra
Style Dry red wine, 13.5% ABV
Grapes Cabernet Sauvignon, Shiraz

The Majella winery occupies land first used for the Lynn family's lamb-rearing business. In 1968 Brian Lynn, known as "Prof," began to plant grapes. These were contracted to Eric Brand for Hardys, and later for Wynn's Coonawarra Estate. In 1991 Majella began making its own wine, a Shiraz, which was produced at Brand's Laira winery by winemaker Bruce Gregory. This arrangement continues, although Majella have since established their own winemaking facilities.

The Shiraz was joined in 1996 by a premium red blend of Cabernet Sauvignon and Shiraz called The Malleea, an aboriginal word for "green paddock." Production at Majella is increasing as commitments to supply grapes to others expire. There are 150 acres (60 ha) under vine, mostly Cabernet Sauvignon but also including Merlot and Riesling.

The Malleea 1998 is a big, traditionally styled Australian wine, with aromas of mint, cinnamon, and oak spices. The palate is dominated by big black fruit flavors and a major dose of ripe tannins. The finish is long and complex, and with age the tannins on the finish have begun to soften and integrate seamlessly with the intense fruit and acidity. **JW**

♥♥♥ **Drink: to 2020**

Malvirà

Roero Superiore Mombeltramo 2001

Origin Italy, Piedmont, Langhe
Style Dry red wine, 14% ABV
Grape Nebbiolo

Marcarini

Barolo Brunate 1978

Origin Italy, Piedmont, Langhe
Style Dry red wine, 13.5% ABV
Grape Nebbiolo

Malvirà, wryly meaning "wrongly situated," refers to the former location in Canale of this leading Roero winery, which faced north instead of south. Malvirà makes a dazzling range of whites and reds, expressing just how good Arneis and Nebbiolo can be when grown on the left bank of the Tanaro River near Alba. The estate was founded in the 1950s by Giuseppe Damonte, and is now run by his sons Massimo and Roberto. The brothers are custodians of their father's commitment to classic winemaking, while embracing the best of modern methods.

This Roero Mombeltramo 2001 is made from pure Nebbiolo grown around the family's new Canova winery. The wine was fermented in oak barriques for up to twenty months and bottled two years after the vintage. The 2001 is a great classic year throughout Piedmont, as reflected in the wine's full ruby color, which is also bright and clear, almost Burgundian, a trait that resurfaces in a lovely bouquet of raspberries tinged with spice. The mouthfeel is deceptively soft and velvety at first, but after a few seconds dry but elegantly ripe tannins underpin the end flavor. A complete wine. **ME**
☻☻☻ **Drink: to 2017+**

Famed for producing the most perfumed and graceful Barolos, the hilltop village of La Morra offers breathtaking views of the vine-covered, rolling hills below. The reason for this more gentle expression of Barolo apparently resides in the hamlet's magnesium-rich soil. One of La Morra's most esteemed producers, Marcarini has been producing Barolos of extreme elegance since the 1950s.

Managed by Anna Marcarini Bava, her daughter Luisa, and son-in-law Manuel Marchetti, the firm produces classically styled Barolos. Marcarini has been a pioneer in lowering yields and raising the profile of individual vineyards. Back in 1958, Marcarini released its first single-vineyard Barolo from the Brunate vineyard, of which it owns a large share. The Marcarinis proudly point out that Brunate has been one of the Langhe's most important zones since it was first documented as such in 1477.

Marcarini's Brunates have an enticing bouquet with hints of tobacco, and a great complexity and finesse. They are also very long lived, as is persuasively shown by the 1978 vintage, which has aged splendidly. **KO**
☻☻☻ **Drink: to 2018**

Château Margaux

2004

Origin France, Bordeaux, Margaux
Style Dry red wine, 13% ABV
Grapes C. Sauvignon 78%, Merlot 18%, Petit Verdot 4%

The only eponymous *cru classé* among the districts brought under the 1855 umbrella, Margaux was once known as La Mothe de Margaux, a *mothe* being a mound, and mounds being highly prized for their exposure on the flattish terrain of the Médoc.

In 1977 André Mentzelopoulos, a Greek hotelier's son, purchased Margaux. Incomers have always played prominent roles among the classed growths, but none perhaps at quite such a high-profile estate as this. Mentzelopoulos died cruelly early in his tenure, but the improvements he had overseen—including a vast new underground *chai*—had set Margaux back on the road to recovering its reputation. The 1978 was a turning-point vintage, and since then the wine has soared magisterially from one pinnacle to another.

An important aspect of the performance of any wine estate is what it makes of the lesser vintages. Sandwiched between the towering twins, 2003 and 2005, the 2004 has inevitably found itself in the shade. By no means a poor year, it would amply have passed muster as a solid, reliable vintage in normal climatic times. The 2004, partly harvested in showery conditions, is a leaner Margaux than normal in terms of body and tannin, but lacks nothing in richly flowing aromatic splendor, or dazzling complexity on the palate. It has floral notes dancing around the spicy-cored black-currant fruit, and a finish rounded out with judiciously applied oak. **SW**
ⓢⓢⓢⓢⓢ **Drink: to 2030+**

◧ The Marquis de la Colonilla commissioned the château in 1810.

Marqués de Griñón
Dominio de Valdepusa Syrah 1999

Origin Spain, Montes de Toledo
Style Dry red wine, 13.5% ABV
Grape Syrah

Marqués de Murrieta *Castillo*
Ygay Rioja GR Especial 1959

Origin Spain, Rioja
Style Dry red wine, 13% ABV
Grapes Tempranillo, Mazuelo, Garnacha, Graciano

Carlos Falcó y Fernández de Córdova, Marqués de Griñón, besides being part of the Spanish aristocracy and a public personality, is one of the pioneers of modern viticulture and winemaking in Spain. In 1974 he planted a vineyard surrounding his family home, Dominio de Valdepusa in Malpica de Tajo, in the Montes de Toledo.

Syrah is a very fashionable grape in Spain today, but Falcó was probably the first to plant it and to make and sell a varietal wine from it, in 1991. The 104 acres (42 ha) of vineyards are mainly Cabernet Sauvignon, but he also planted Syrah, Merlot, Chardonnay, and Petit Verdot. Since 2002, his estate has held the first appellation in Spain for a single vineyard: Dominio de Valdepusa is a Denominación de Origen in its own right.

In 1999 the Syrah performed especially well. A deep cherry color, it is almost opaque. There is good intensity on the nose, with strawberry jam, black olives, spices, and toasty oak in the background. Very concentrated and full-bodied in the mouth, tasty, with notable acidity and a long finish. A wine of great personality. **LG**
🍷🍷 Drink: to 2019

The foundations for Rioja's oldest winery were laid in 1825, when the first grapes were planted at the estate of Ygay. The winery was started in 1852 by Luciano Francisco Ramón de Murrieta, later Marqués de Murrieta. In 1878 he acquired the Ygay estate and vineyards that have been home ever since to one of the great bodegas in Spain.

The winery has 445 acres (180 ha) of vineyards, 14,000 American oak barrels, and a stock of 3 million bottles aging in its cellars. The wine was originally called Château Ygay but the name was finally changed to Castillo Ygay. It was produced as a Gran Reserva Especial only in the best vintages.

The characteristics of the wines are good color and structure, with enough alcohol and acidity to age for a long time. The 1959 was bottled in May 1986, after six months in vat and twenty-six years in American oak. It then spent six and a half years resting in bottle before it was put on the market in 1991. Its orange hue reveals its age. The nose is clean and fresh, oaky with vanilla, hinting at the use of properly dried wood, and a core of cherry fruit. It has good structure and penetrating flavors. **LG**
🍷🍷🍷🍷 Drink: to 2019+

Marqués de Riscal
Rioja RM (Reserva Médoc) 1945

Origin Spain, Rioja
Style Dry red wine, 11.9% ABV
Grapes Cabernet Sauvignon 70%, Tempranillo 30%

Martínez-Bujanda
Finca Valpiedra Rioja Reserva 1994

Origin Spain, Rioja
Style Dry red wine, 13.2% ABV
Grapes Tempranillo, Cabernet Sauvignon

In 1858, Camilo Hurtado de Amézaga, Marqués de Riscal, founded a winery in Rioja. He had been living in Bordeaux since 1836, so decided to experiment with French varieties at his estate at Elciego. His wines soon started winning prizes, and became so popular that to prevent against fakes he had to invent the wire netting that would make it impossible to extract the cork without breaking it. Today, Marqués de Riscal has one of the most impressive wineries in the world. Designed by Frank Gehry, it contains every vintage produced since 1862, as well as a hotel and a wine spa.

By the 1940s Marqués de Riscal was producing two million bottles. In some very special years, such as 1945, it kept thirty or forty barrels of what it called Reserva Médoc, with a high percentage of Cabernet Sauvignon. On rare occasions, Francisco Hurtado de Amézaga, winery director, presents this for tasting. The wine still appears dark and youthful. As tasted in March 2000, the nose still shows berry fruit with some minty notes. Full-bodied, with some tannins in the mouth, it is dense and long with plenty of flavor. Surely one of the world's best wines. **LG**

☻☻☻☻☻ **Drink: to 2025**

Finca Valpiedra is one of the more modern traditional Riojas—or one of the more traditional modern ones. The idea was to produce a wine with more fruit and color, fresher, with less time in oak than the old norm, but still unmistakably Rioja. It was the brainchild of the Martinez-Bujanda family, producers of the popular Conde de Valdemar wines, with a business going back to 1889. The Martínez-Bujandas wanted to make a château-style wine from fruit grown at the finca, and they eventually built a completely separate winery, first used for the 1997 vintage, to make this single-vineyard wine.

1994 was a very good year for the region, and also the starting point for Finca Valpiedra. The 1994 has an intense garnet color and a complex aroma, with black berry fruit, lactic and balsamic notes, ink, chocolate, leather, *sousbois*, and star anise. Earthy and spicy in the mouth, it is medium-bodied, with good fruit weight, acidity, finesse, and a remarkable finish. The baroque-looking label of the early vintages was soon replaced by a minimalist, modern one consisting of a black-and-white image of a rolling stone—Valpiedra means stone valley. **LG**

☻☻☻ **Drink: to 2019**

Mas de Daumas Gassac
1990

Origin France, Languedoc , Pays de l'Hérault
Style Dry red wine, 14% ABV
Grapes Cabernet Sauvignon 70%, Others 30%

Italy has its Super-Tuscans; Ribera del Duero has Vega Sicilia; and the Languedoc has Mas de Daumas Gassac. Labeled as a mere Vin de Pays de l'Hérault, its red wine has already ascended into the halls of the anointed. The estate was purchased by a Parisian glove maker, Aimé Guibert, initially without the intention of making wine until a professor of enology pointed out the potential of its local *garrigue* soils with a red glacial layer below, and the cool air currents of the high-altitude vineyard.

Predominantly planted with cuttings of old Médoc Cabernet, the remainder of the blend changes from year to year. There are now 75 acres (30 ha) planted. The potential of the debut vintage, 1978, was immediately apparent. Mas de Daumas Gassac is an unfiltered wine of immense textural and tannic density, and corresponding longevity.

On the nose, the 1990 was, at ten years old, full of secondary aromas, with tar and seasoned leather backing up the blackberry-raspberry fruit. The tannic shell was still quite intact, but the spices—licorice, ginger, pepper—deepened and burnished the already formidable, savory complexity of the wine. **SW**

☻☻☻ **Drink: to 2020**

Mas Doix
Costers de Vinyes Velles 2004

Origin Spain, Priorat
Style Dry red wine, 15% ABV
Grapes Cariñena, Garnacha, Merlot

It is not uncommon for a grape-growing family to start making and bottling their own wine. In the case of Mas Doix, however, the wine produced went straight to the top of its region and was wildly acclaimed all over the world. The winery is the project of the Doix and Llagostera families, grape growers for five generations, and began in 1998 when Ramón Llagostera took over the business. The company now owns 50 acres (20 ha) of vines in Poboleda, Priorat, planted to the traditional grapes, Cariñena and Garnacha, complemented by some Syrah, Cabernet Sauvignon, and Merlot.

Costers de Vinyes Velles comes from the company's oldest vines, between seventy and 100 years old, more or less half Cariñena and half Garnacha, with a small amount of Merlot. The 2004 is very dark in color. The aroma, of good intensity, shows plenty of very ripe black fruit, with some well-integrated toasty oak in the background. In the mouth it shows plenty of structure, good acidity, and fruit intensity. It is quite tannic when young, but the 15 percent alcohol does not show at all, and it is well wrapped by dense fruit, glycerine, and acidity. **LG**

☻☻☻ **Drink: to 2019**

Mas Martinet
Clos Martinet Priorat 2000

Origin Spain, Catalonia, Priorat
Style Dry red wine, 14.7% ABV
Grapes Garnacha, Syrah, C. Sauvignon, Cariñena

Driving from Falset to Gratallops you come to a big palm tree, the icon of the Mas Martinet winery of the Martinet i Ovejero family. They have 17 acres (7 ha) of vineyards in production, and new plantings are slowly coming on stream.

Their first wine is called Clos Martinet, its first vintage being 1989, and 2000 represents one of the finest they have made. It was a very good year for Priorat, albeit not an easy one. In June a dry wind blocked the development of the vines, at the start of a hot, dry summer. At Martinet they had to help their vines, eliminating bunches to help the remainder reach maturity. Harvested between September 12 (Syrah) and October 21 (Cariñena), the varieties were vinified separately in stainless steel with one month of maceration. They were bottled unfined in April 2002 after eighteen months in new French fine-grained oak barrels. The wine has an intense garnet color. The nose is powerful but elegant, with plenty of well-ripened red fruit and mineral notes. Rich and savory in the mouth, it has abundant fruit and an interesting finish. Decant well in advance or, even better, let it mature in bottle for a few more years. **LG**

☻☻☻ **Drink: to 2020**

Más Que Vinos
La Plazuela 2004

Origin Spain, Castilla
Style Dry red wine, 14% ABV
Grapes Cencibel (Tempranillo) 85%, Garnacha 15%

Más Que Vinos (meaning "more than wines") is the name of a young company created by three prestigious enologists—Gonzalo Rodríguez, his wife Mai Madrigal, and German-born Alexandra Schmedes—who met in Rioja in 1998 while consulting for different wineries. They decided to produce their own wines in Dosbarrios, Toledo.

La Plazuela—"the small square," referring to the center of the village where it is produced—is their top wine. It is a *vino de la tierra de Castilla*, the Spanish equivalent of the French vin du pays. Considered by some Spanish critics to be the top wine from central Spain, it is even referred to as a Castillian Pomerol. It certainly has the lushness of some of the prestigious Bordeaux wines but with a clear local accent, including the unmistakably sweet coconut from the small percentage of American oak used. Very deep in color, it is almost black. It is very expressive on the nose, with some graphite and peat notes, licorice, and a core of ripe, black fruit. It has very good structure in the mouth, very well-balanced acidity, and intense flavors, with tannins that still need some polishing in the bottle. **LG**

☻☻☻ **Drink: to 2019**

Bartolo Mascarello
Barolo 1989

Origin Italy, Piedmont, Langhe
Style Dry red wine, 13.5% ABV
Grape Nebbiolo

Bartolo Mascarello, who died in 2005, was the embodiment of traditional Barolo—not the bad old Barolo, orange with a brownish edge and reeking of Marmite and Bovril, but Barolo made with attention and passion. Certainly, a Modernist wine will be much deeper, much redder of color, less volatile, more sumptuous, and less austere, with a tannin-acid structure that will not frighten away the squeamish when it is young. But it will also be less magical, and less long-lasting. A Bartolo Mascarello Barolo has soul. Those who are tuned in to soul will detect it. Those who are not will deny it.

A Bartolo Barolo is traditional also in the sense of being a blend of crus rather than from a single vineyard. Normally four vineyards contribute—Canubbi, San Lorenzo, and Ruè in the commune of Barolo, and Rocche di Torriglione in La Morra. The 1989, the middle and perhaps greatest of a run of three top vintages, does not contain Ruè, as the vineyard had been taken out prior to replanting. But the concept is the same, and remains so under the aegis of Bartolo's daughter Maria Teresa. Even in these heathen times, soul is not dead. **NBel**
🍷🍷🍷🍷🍷 Drink: to 2030+

Giuseppe Mascarello
Barolo Monprivato 1998

Origin Italy, Piedmont, Langhe
Style Dry red wine, 14% ABV
Grape Nebbiolo

Of all the great Barolo crus, few have the prestige of Monprivato in Castiglione Falletto, right at the heart of the Barolo growing zone. Mauro Mascarello, who runs the winery started by his grandfather in 1881, likes to point out that Monprivato is a historic vineyard, already registered in the land archives of Castiglione Falletto in 1666, thus preceding the birth of Barolo as a dry red wine by nearly 200 years.

Although the Mascarellos have owned part of the vineyard since 1904, it was not until 1970 that Mauro decided to vinify the grapes from Monprivato separately, and their single-vineyard bottling is only produced in excellent years. Mauro maintains a traditional approach to winemaking.

The 1998 vintage, awarded five stars by the Barolo Consorzio, is less popular than the more flamboyant and publicized 1997 and 1999 vintages, thanks to an initial austerity. But Monprivato 1998 is exquisite and extremely elegant, with the wine's hallmark, delicate ruby-garnet hue and a complex bouquet of roses, cherry, and smoke. Fruit flavors with a hint of licorice and tobacco are impeccably balanced by abundant but silky smooth tannins. **KO**
🍷🍷🍷 Drink: to 2018+

Vines fan out from the village of Castiglione Falletto. ➡

Mastroberardino
Taurasi Riserva Radici 1997

Origin Italy, Campania, Altripalda
Style Dry red wine, 14% ABV
Grape Aglianico

Matetic
EQ Pinot Noir 2005

Origin Chile, Aconcagua, San Antonio
Style Dry red wine, 14.5% ABV
Grape Pinot Noir

Despite the recent wine renaissance in southern Italy, the famous house of Mastroberardino remains the region's most admired producer, and can trace its winemaking roots back to the seventeenth century. Their family firm was founded in 1878 and for years was the only ray of light in a region that was in the vinous Dark Ages until the late twentieth century.

The firm's perennial commitment to local varieties—in particular to the ancient Aglianico grape, from which the celebrated Taurasi is made—was crucial in catapulting this wine to worldwide fame. Antonio Mastroberardino's Taurasi Radici, a selection made with the best grapes from different parcels, was first produced in 1986 to celebrate the rebirth of the family winery after the devastating earthquake of 1980. The Radici Riserva 1997 is one of the best-ever releases, with a floral bouquet layered with hints of leather and truffle, wild cherry flavors, and a long, licorice finish. Impeccably balanced, the 1997 is a wonderful expression of Aglianico from one of the most celebrated of all Italian vintages— a vintage "to gladden Italian hearts," as Michael Broadbent has rightly remarked. **KO**

🔆🔆🔆 **Drink: to 2030**

The Matetic family left their native Croatia in 1900 to settle in Chile, building businesses from galvanized barbed wire to luxury hotels. Their decision to convert part of their 25,000-acre (10,000 ha) farm from beef cows to vineyards appears seminal in any debate linking the falling demand for beef and the growing demand for fine wine.

Its Pacific coast location in an ultra-cool south-western spur of Chile's already famed Casablanca Valley seems to be the perfect fit. Matetic planted three ungrafted Pinot Noir clones for EQ (meaning "equilibrium"): the early ripening 777 (50 percent), for its crisp red cherry aromas; the mid-season ripening 115 (30 percent), for velvet texture; and the late ripening and genetically mixed "Valdivieso" selection (20 percent), for tannic breadth and color.

The Matetic vines were certified organic and biodynamically managed, tight pruned and minimally drip irrigated, giving yields low enough to express a sense of place. The 2005 was a notably cool year, necessitating the gentle winemaking that has produced aromatic Pinot Noir of agreeably taut ripeness and immediacy. **MW**

🔆🔆 **Drink: to 2017**

◱ Frescoes in the Mastroberardino cellars by De Rosa, Micozzi, and Botez.

Red wines | 659

Domaine Maume
Mazis-Chambertin GC 2002

Origin France, Burgundy, Côte de Nuits
Style Dry red wine, 13% ABV
Grape Pinot Noir

The Maume winery is in Gevrey-Chambertin, on the main road from Nuits to Dijon. Winemaker Bernard Maume led a dual life: when not in his cellar he was a professor, researching in yeasts at Dijon University. He has now mostly retired from winemaking and his place has been taken by his son Bertrand.

Domaine Maume covers about 11 acres (4.5 ha), all of it in Gevrey. Heading its list of wines are two grands crus, Mazis- and Charmes-Chambertin; rather more is produced of the former than the latter. As you might expect from a glance round the somewhat artisanal cellar, there is something old-fashioned, even rustic about the wines, but in the best sense. They are full-bodied, tannic, somewhat sinewy, a bit muscular, assertive rather than elegant. But they have plenty of depth and last well. The two grands crus contrast with each other: the Charmes is softer, more civilized; the Mazis a gypsy, almost feral.

The 2002 Mazis-Chambertin benefits from the finesse of the vintage. Currently it is a bit rugged; the tannins are very evident. But underneath there is plenty of well-balanced fruit, and the promise of wild abandon. Drink it with a gamey stew. **CC**

🍷🍷🍷🍷 **Drink: to 2027**

Mauro
Terreus Pago de Cueva Baja 1996

Origin Spain, Castilla
Style Dry red wine, 14% ABV
Grape Tempranillo

Mariano García is the most famous winemaker from Spain. He worked for Vega Sicilia for thirty years, between 1968 and 1998, where he created some monumental wines. In 1984, he started a small family winery in the town of Tudela de Duero, just outside the limits of the Ribera del Duero appellation, and named it Mauro after his father. The regular Mauro and, later, Mauro Vendimia Seleccionada, put them at the top of the hierarchy of the Duero region. Today his two sons have joined him at the winery.

Terreus, meaning "made from the soil," was born with the 1996 vintage. It comes from a single, 7.5-acre (3 ha) vineyard, Pago de la Cueva Baja, planted before 1950 with Tempranillo and a little Grenache, that gives very small yields. It is only made in the best vintages and destined for long aging in bottle.

The wine is aged for thirty months in new French oak barrels and shows plenty of wood and toasty notes in its youth. The wine is dark, with a complex nose of ripe, red fruit. Huge structure in the mouth, velvety tannins, sweet fruit, but with balancing acidity that gives a fresh sensation. The 1996 is the most elegant of all the Terreus wines so far. **LG**

🍷🍷🍷🍷 **Drink: to 2018+**

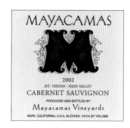

Maurodos

San Román Toro 2001

Origin Spain, Toro
Style Dry red wine, 14% ABV
Grape Tinta de Toro (Tempranillo)

Maurodos is the name of the Mauro winery in Toro, owned by the García family—father Mariano, and sons Alberto and Eduardo. San Román is one of the "new generation" wines from Toro. It is named after the tiny village where the modern-looking winery and the bulk of their vineyards are located.

In Toro the climate is extreme—very hot in summer and cold in winter. The soil has a high clay content and the vineyards, traditionally pruned and trained *en gobelet*, are covered with rolling stones. The wines from the region are certainly powerful. So the key here is to find some balance and finesse.

The first vintage of San Román included some Garnacha, but it is a grape that does not develop easily in Toro, so in 2001 the wine was 100 percent Tinta de Toro, the local clone of Tempranillo. It stayed for twenty-two months in French and American oak before being bottled. It has a very deep color. There is good intensity on the nose, with plums and other black fruit, some violet notes, a lactic touch, and a toasty background. Medium- to full-bodied, and with fresh acidity, it is dense and long, but the tannins still require the final polish of several years in bottle. **LG**
🍷🍷🍷 **Drink: to 2020**

Mayacamas

Cabernet Sauvignon 1979

Origin USA, California, Napa Valley
Style Dry red wine, 12.5% ABV
Grapes C. Sauvignon 90%, Merlot 5%, C. Franc 5%

Perched at more than 2,000 feet (610 m), high up in the Mayacamas Mountains, stands this old stone winery. The German Fischer family, who founded the estate in the 1890s, soon spotted the virtues of this well-ventilated, well-drained mountain site. In 1968 a San Francisco stockbroker called Bob Travers bought the 52-acre (21 ha) property.

Numerous wines were made here in the 1970s, but the best was always the superb Cabernet Sauvignon, modeled on Bordeaux. The winemaking is old-fashioned, the Cabernet being aged initially in large casks for about two years and then for a year in French oak barrels of which about 20 percent are new. Travers does not pick at very high ripeness levels, so the Cabernet is tannic when young.

Travers likes to drink his own wines at twenty-five years, and a recently tasted 1979 shows why. The color is dark, with only a hint of evolution. The nose is dense, though there are some leathery tones to suggest age. There is considerable sweetness of fruit, as well as some bracing tannins and a slight earthiness; it has exceptional length. Not for everyone, but it is undoubtedly a Napa classic. **SBr**
🍷🍷🍷🍷 **Drink: to 2019+**

Josephus Mayr
Maso Unterganzner Lamarein 2004

Origin Italy, Alto Adige
Style Dry red wine, 13% ABV
Grape Lagrein

Taste this wine from Maso Unterganzner and you are sure to surrender to it. The Mayr family has owned and run a *maso* (alpine farm) here since 1629. Josephus and Barbara, the present owners, represent the tenth generation. The farm produces not only grapes and wine, but also chestnuts, apples, walnuts, kiwi fruit, and olives, all evidence of the climate benefiting this part of the Alto Adige.

Maso Unterganzner is located in the far eastern point of the wide Bolzano Basin, where the River Ega flows into the Isarco, at an altitude of about 950 feet (290 m) above sea level. The Mayr family's attachment to their traditional heritage is reflected in the training system of the vines, although this is slightly modified to limit yields and allow for a higher planting density. The soil here is warm and rich in porphyry rocks—just about perfect growing conditions for the Lagrein grape.

The Lamarein 2004 is the apotheosis of fruit: An unbelievable concentration of dark yet very fragrant cherry and blackberry fruit opens on to sweeter and more subtle notes of soft spices, vanilla, and peppermint. The wine on the tongue is pure, thick velvet, but manages to remain vibrant through fine-grained tannins. The clean-cut acidity is so natural as to be reminiscent of the refreshing sourness of fresh summer berries, and helps the flavor linger, still well defined, for what seems like the better part of a minute. Simply awesome. **AS**
🅢🅢🅢 **Drink: to 2019**

The label for Josephus Mayr's Maso Unterganzner Lamarein 2004. ➜

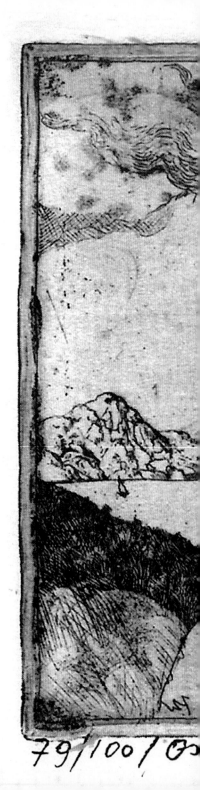

d von Wolkenstein Oskar Kokoschka

Meerlust *Rubicon* 1996

Origin South Africa, Stellenbosch
Style Dry red wine, 13.5% ABV
Grapes C. Sauvignon 70%, Merlot 20%, C. Franc 10%

This distinguished South African estate was founded in 1693, when the governor of the Cape, Simon van der Stel, granted the land to Henning Hüsing, who named the farm Meerlust (love of the sea) after the sea breezes that blew inland from False Bay. Johannes Albertus Myburgh bought Meerlust in January 1757; today, Hannes Myburgh is the eighth-generation owner of the estate.

Meerlust's flagship red wine is Rubicon, a Bordeaux blend with the emphasis firmly on Cabernet Sauvignon. It was first made in 1980, but the 1990s produced an excellent series of vintages for Rubicon, with 1996 perhaps the highlight. Although this is a much-maligned and rain-sodden Cape vintage, Meerlust's Italian winemaker Giorgio dalla Cia, now retired, waited longer than most of his colleagues to harvest. Meerlust's cellar records reveal a prolonged, quite opportunistic picking schedule, where care and rigor repaid the investment.

At ten years of age, Rubicon 1996 had a brownish hue, with a pleasingly mature nose that is a ringer for a mature Pauillac: cedarwood and cigar-box aromas to the fore, but underscored by spicy berry fruits. There is still some sweetly juicy fruit in the mouth, though the flavors were more gamey than the nose. Good depth and concentration is balanced by the chalky tannins, which for many years were heavy and sullen, but have now settled down. Once this Rubicon has been broached, there is no turning back. **SG**
🆂🆂🆂 **Drink: to 2017+**

FURTHER RECOMMENDATIONS
Other great vintages
1992 · 1995 · 1998 · 2000 · 2001 · 2003 · 2005 · 2009
More producers from Stellenbosch
Kanonkop · Le Riche · Morgenster *Rustenberg · Rust en Vrede · Thelema*

Meerlust's Cape Dutch complex was made a National Monument in 1989. ➡

Charles Melton *Nine Popes* 2004

Origin Australia, South Australia, Barossa Valley
Style Dry red wine, 14.5% ABV
Grapes Grenache 54%, Shiraz 44%, Mourvèdre 2%

In 1973, a Sydney boy named Graeme Melton arrived in South Australia's Barossa Valley. Graeme and a mate needed jobs to fix their broken-down Holden to continue their road trip across Australia. There were two jobs on offer—one as a cellar hand at a local winery called Krondorf, and another pruning at a vineyard down the road. They flipped a coin, and Melton got the job as cellar hand.

At Krondorf, Melton met the Barossa winemaker Peter Lehmann, moving with him when he set up his eponymous winery six years later. For some still unexplained reason, Lehmann named his protégé "Charlie." The name stuck. Over the next ten years, Melton honed his winemaking skills under Lehmann and traveled to France, where he gained a passion for the wines of the Rhône Valley, in particular the Southern Rhône where Grenache, Shiraz, and Mourvèdre are blended with up to eleven other varieties in red Châteauneuf-du-Pape.

At the same time as Melton was building his own winery and cellar in 1984, the Australian government was paying growers to pull out their Barossa Shiraz and Grenache vines as they had become unfashionable. But Melton had seen the possibilities for these varieties in France, and created his "Nine Popes" blend, a pun on Châteauneuf's name. Aged twenty months in barriques, the 2004 has raspberry, cherry, and plum aromas, with a touch of spicy oak. Peppery, rich, and long, this is Australia's premier southern Rhône-style red. **SG**

ΘΘΘ **Drink: to 2019**

FURTHER RECOMMENDATIONS
Other great vintages
1993 · 1996 · 1997 · 1998 · 2002 · 2006
More Charles Melton wines
Barossa Valley Shiraz
Rose of Virginia · Sotto di Ferro

Bush-trained Charles Melton vines at Tanunda in the Barossa. ➦

Abel Mendoza
Selección Personal 2004

Origin Spain, Rioja
Style Dry red wine, 13.5% ABV
Grape Tempranillo

Abel Mendoza Monge is the owner of a small property in San Vicente de la Sonsierra. He is the viticulturalist, and his wife Maite Fernández is the chief enologist, and they strive for balanced, elegant, naturally expressive wines. The bodega was established in 1988, with 44 acres (18 ha) of family vineyards on the Ebro River's left bank, where the soils are a mix of clay, marl, and sand. The old vines are mostly Tempranillo, with a little Graciano, Garnacha, and white varieties such as Garnacha Blanca, Malvasía Riojana, Turruntés, and Viura.

The flagship wine from the 1998 vintage onward has been the Selección Personal. From a 5-acre (2 ha) vineyard with forty-year-old vines in El Sacramento, the wine ferments in large vats and after malolactic spends twelve months in new one- or two-year-old French barrels. Abel also likes to add a small amount of white wine, as in the Côte Rôtie, for finesse, acidity, and freshness. The result is an intense dark cherry red, with an aroma of blackberries, chocolate, spice, laurel, and light toast. In the mouth it is medium-bodied, with good acidity and structure, smooth tannins, and excellent fruity persistence. **JMB**

🅢🅢 **Drink: to 2019**

E. Mendoza
Estrecho 2004

Origin Spain, Alicante
Style Dry red wine, 14% ABV
Grape Monastrell (Mourvèdre)

You cannot get much more Mediterranean than Alicante. This appellation covers fifty-one villages in the province of the same name, and a small part of Murcia. The coastal areas, where the climate is truly Mediterranean, with high humidity, are better known for sweet Muscats, and the more continental interior, next to Almansa, Yecla, and Jumilla, for reds.

In the 1960s, Enrique Mendoza, a salesman in love with wine, started planting vineyards in the village of l'Alfàs del Pi, very close to Benidorm, where the winery is located. In 1990, he started producing and bottling wines from his own vineyards, and soon became the undisputed leader of quality in Alicante.

Today, the business is driven by Enrique's sons—Pepe, who makes the wine, and Julián, who sells it. They made Estrecho for the first time in 2003. Sourced from a single plot of Monastrell vines more than fifty years old, it has an intense color, and a fine nose with balsamic and red fruit notes. Medium-bodied with a velvety texture in the mouth, it is elegant and somehow Burgundian in style. It has none of the rusticity often found in Monastrell, nor Alicante's failings of overripeness and oxidation. **LG**

🅢🅢 **Drink: to 2017+**

Domaine Méo-Camuzet
Richebourg Grand Cru 2005

Origin France, Burgundy, Côte de Nuits
Style Dry red wine, 13% ABV
Grape Pinot Noir

Denis Mercier
Cornalin 2005

Origin Switzerland, Valais, Sierre
Style Dry red wine, 13% ABV
Grape Cornalin

Take a drive out of Vosne-Romanée with Jean-Nicolas Méo, stop a short distance up the road to Concoeur, and you will be able to walk uphill with him through his vines in the premiers crus of Brulées and Cros Parantoux to those he owns in Richebourg. Here he possesses 0.86 acres (0.35 ha)—enough, say, for five barrels or 125 cases of twelve bottles.

The Méos and the Camuzets were upper-class, absentee landlords, civil servants and politicians, and for forty-five years their considerable 37-acre (15 ha) estate was share-cropped by Henri Jayer. In the early days both the Méo and the Jayer shares were sold in bulk to local merchants. From the 1970s onward Jayer began to bottle his entitlement, as he did the produce of his own, small, family domaine. With these wines he cemented his reputation. He retired in 1988. Jean-Nicolas Méo, then twenty-four, decided to take over, employing Jayer as an avuncular consultant for a number of vintages.

Richebourg is an ample wine. This Méo 2005 is a yardstick example: full-bodied, quite tannic, definitely oaky, though not in a dominating way, and above all very, very rich and concentrated. **CC**
🝙🝙🝙🝙🝙 Drink: 2020–2040

The grape variety Cornalin has been enjoying a boom in the Valais. In the 1950s, Cornalin (also called Rouge du Valais and Rouge du Pays) was found only in the villages of Granges and Lens; now it is spread all over the Valais. In 1972, Jean Nicollier gave Rouge du Valais the name Cornalin du Valais because he was inspired by a similar grape planted in the Vallée d'Aoste. Recent research on the DNA of the grape, conducted by José Vouillamoz, has shown that the two Cornalins are unrelated. On the other hand, Cornalin d'Aoste is also cultivated in the Valais under the name Humagne Rouge. Cornalin is very sensitive to rot and generally very difficult to grow.

The wine-grower couple Anne-Catherine and Denis Mercier have cultivated 15 acres (6 ha) of grapes in the Valais since 1982. Some 10 percent is planted with Cornalin, on terroirs called Goubing, Pradec, and Corin, and ever since its first vintage in 1991 it has been the best wine in their portfolio.

The 2005 is a shining red color, with notes of ripe red berries and dark chocolate. On the palate, it is intense, with fresh acidity, lots of lively black currant and cherry flavor, fine tannins, and a long finish. **CK**
🝙🝙🝙 Drink: to 2017

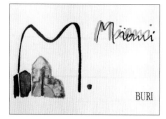

Meyer-Näkel *Dernau Pfarrwingert Spätburgunder ATG* 2003

Origin Germany, Ahr
Style Dry red wine, 14.5% ABV
Grape Pinot Noir

Miani *Merlot* 1998

Origin Italy, Friuli
Style Dry red wine, 14.5% ABV
Grape Merlot

It never fails to amaze that the Ahr valley, one of the northernmost German wine-growing areas, is mainly a red wine-producing region. This very small Anbaugebiet, with only 1,344 acres (544 ha) of vineyards, produces the highest proportion of red wine (88 percent) of all German regions, and yields some of the finest Spätburgunders.

South of Bonn and opening into the Rhine, this tightly carved valley, with its often extremely steep slate slopes and perfect south-facing vineyards, produces Pinot Noir wines that often reach up to 14 percent ABV without any chaptalization. The high alcohol content notwithstanding, the Ahr Spätburgunders display extraordinary finesse.

This is particularly noticeable in the wine from the Dernauer Pfarrwingert, with which Werner Näkel gained the reputation of being one of Germany's best red wine producers. The vineyard yields intensely fragrant wines, with complex fruit flavors, finely zesty tones, and a silky texture. The marked mineral richness of the soil provides for a bouquet that brings red currants, cherries, and huckleberries to mind, and exhibits chocolate and violet notes. **FK**
😊😊😊😊 **Drink: to 2018**

The area of Colli Orientali del Friuli in northeast Italy is home to some of the country's best white wines, but performs very well with reds, too. The soil is rich in calcareous marls and sandstone, and the area boasts an incredible array of microclimates. The Miani estate accounts for just less than 30 acres (12 ha) of land and produces a total of only 1,000 cases per year. Miani's wine does not come cheap, but it is worth every penny.

The Merlot 1998 is simply one of the best Merlots ever produced. The juice coming from these forty-year-old vineyards, which give only around 1 pound (0.45 kg) per plant, is so rich in body, elegance, and personality that it will leave you wondering what the antipathy to this variety in the *Sideways* movie was really all about. The color is impenetrable and the nose amazingly rich, ranging from fruits to cinnamon and tobacco, chocolate to iodine, mint to vanilla, then closing on a more earthy note. The silky, warm, caressing, but powerful palate is even better: The alcohol is balanced by the very fine tannin, whereas the full, harmonious mouthfeel is refreshed by a perfect acidity and nicely savory minerality. **AS**
😊😊😊😊😊 **Drink: to 2020+**

Peter Michael Winery
Les Pavots 2004

Origin USA, California, Sonoma County
Style Dry red wine, 15.1% ABV
Grapes Cabernet Sauvignon, Cabernet Franc, Merlot

The Cabernet Sauvignon, Cabernet Franc, and Merlot used for this wine are grown above Knights Valley in eastern Sonoma County, at 1,500 feet (457m) in elevation. Lady Michael named the Les Pavots vineyard after the poppies growing on the mountain hillsides, and it is easy to be intoxicated by this wine's heady mix of elegance, firm, concentrated structure, and dynamic aromatic complexity.

The vineyard was planted in 1989 on rocky, well-drained, Rhyolite soil with a high potassium level that encourages photosynthesis, imparting deeper color and flavor development to the grapes. Southerly exposure facilitates full maturity, but Pacific breezes waft through the vines, encouraging the slow ripening process that enables the grapes to capture their distinctive mineral characteristics. The vines are classical, small-cluster clones prized for producing wines of concentration and structure.

The blend in Les Pavots varies, but always has Cabernet Sauvignon at its core. The glory of this wine is not its immediate accessibility, but rather how it will bloom over time, revealing increased depth, complexity, and harmony. **LGr**

⊖⊖⊖⊖ **Drink: to 2019+**

Moccagatta
Barbaresco Basarin 1998

Origin Italy, Piedmont, Barbaresco
Style Dry red wine, 14% ABV
Grape Nebbiolo

Sergio Minuto founded this estate in 1912. He had two sons, Mario and Lorenzo, who worked together in the running of the family business until 1952, when they decided to separate their careers. Mario's two sons, Sergio and Franco, are the present owners.

The name Moccagatta was adopted in 1979 from the area on which the cellar is built. Together with the Cru Cole, the Cru Basarin is the best and oldest single-vineyard wine of the estate. The less well-known Bric Balin represented a critical step in the estate's evolution, because it was the first wine on which the Minutos felt free to experiment with new winemaking and aging techniques.

It was through the trials with Nebbiolo grapes for Bric Balin that they eventually decided to age all their Barbarescos in barriques rather than in traditional, large oak casks. The Basarin 1998 shows a beautiful color of medium intensity, with elegant garnet hues. The nose is enthralling, with softly floral notes accompanied by earthy, leathery, balsamic (eucalyptus) aromas. On the palate, the tannins are present but fine, helping the wine's flavor to expand and to linger pleasantly on the long finish. **AS**

⊖⊖⊖⊖ **Drink: to 2025**

Salvatore Molettieri *Taurasi*
Riserva Vigna Cinque Querce 2001

Origin Italy, Campania, Irpinia
Style Dry red wine, 15% ABV
Grape Aglianico

The DOCG Taurasi, spiritual home of Aglianico, is in the mountains that ring Naples. It is from its meager volcanic subsoils that Salvatore Molettieri fashions an Aglianico of such intensity that *Gambero Rosso*, Italy's leading wine guide, awarded him Cellar of the Year in 2005—an award previously bestowed upon such luminaries as Angelo Gaja and Roberto Voerzio.

Aglianico's lineage traces directly to the Greek invasion of Puglia in the seventh century BCE. The Romans christened the grape Vitis Hellenica, whence its current name derives. Known as the "Barolo of the South," Taurasi shares with Nebbiolo a Burgundian synthesis of power and elegance. Given its diminutive size—just 556 acres (225 ha) of vineyards—Taurasi is held in very high regard.

Sourced from a parcel of old-vine Aglianico planted on uncharacteristically clay-rich soil, the tiny yields produce this wine, rich in alcohol and saturated with the raspberry, tobacco, and violet notes typical of the grape. The 20 percent new French barriques add a fine distinction, the perfume and the weight together offering a sensual rusticity never before seen so far south of Beaune. **MP**

🍷🍷🍷 **Drink: to 2021+**

Robert Mondavi
Cabernet Sauvignon Reserve 1978

Origin USA, California, Napa Valley
Style Dry red wine, 13% ABV
Grapes Cabernet Sauvignon, Cabernet Franc

Fashion and taste may change, but legends live on. Robert Mondavi's most ambitious wine, aspiring to compete with the greatest wines of the world, often seems overshadowed by the "new, new thing," an artisanal creation or cult wine. But over the decades, regardless of changes in fashion, ownership, and family drama, this wine has stayed a course, reflecting a consistency of style and quality. The Mondavi Reserve has never been a blockbuster wine; rather, the elegant style reflects vintage variation in the Napa Valley. Cooler (later) vintages are more aromatic, with an elegant structure; warmer (early) vintages have a more assertive structure and brawnier fruit.

In 1978 a growing and harvest season that was mostly dry and warm saw several heat spikes, which produced a bountiful crop of extremely ripe fruit. While other (cooler) vintages might reveal more finesse, the 1978 Mondavi Cabernet Sauvignon Reserve was always intended to live at least thirty years from vintage. It remains quite alive, of a piece with the other great vintages that built the legend of the wine and its visionary creator. **LGr**

🍷🍷🍷🍷🍷 **Drink: to 2018+**

Evening light plays on Robert Mondavi vineyards at Carneros. ➡

Château Montaiguillon
2010

Chateau Montelena
Cabernet Sauvignon 2003

Origin France, Bordeaux, Montagne St.-Emilion
Style Dry red wine, 13% ABV
Grapes Merlot 60%, C. Franc 20%, C. Sauvignon 20%

Origin USA, California, Napa Valley
Style Dry red wine, 13.5% ABV
Grapes C. Sauvignon 90%, Merlot 5%, C. Franc 5%

The appellation of Montagne St.-Emilion lies just north of St.-Emilion beyond the Barbanne River. The soils are essentially clay-limestone, though they are quite varied. Montaiguillon is one of the best established properties; the grandfather of the present owner, Chantal Amart Ternault, bought the estate in 1949. It is quite a substantial vineyard, with almost 75 acres (30 ha) in a single parcel facing south and southwest toward the Barbanne valley.

Madame Ternault insists that her viticultural practices—deleafing, green-harvesting, minimal treatments—are the same as they would be were the vineyards in St.-Emilion. She finds that in most years the Cabernets ripen well here, and add backbone to the wine. The vineyards are picked both by hand and by machine. The wine is aged in one-third new oak for twelve months and bottled without filtration.

These are not wines intended for very extensive aging, and Madame Ternault considers that they are at their best at between seven and ten years old. The wine shows a fair amount of oak on the nose; it has ample concentration and a robust but not hard character, with ample fruit on the finish. **SBr**

🍷🍷 **Drink: recent vintages for up to 10 years**

Montelena is located in Calistoga, at the northern end of the Napa Valley. It is one of the hotter areas within the valley, giving firm, robust, long-lived Cabernets. The property was founded in 1882.

By 1981, Bo Barrett, the son of the principal owner, was in charge of the restored winery, and he is still making the wines today. Some 80 acres (32 ha) are planted with Cabernet, and since the rootstock was St. George, they survived the scourge of phylloxera that afflicted the valley twenty years ago. The soils vary; some are alluvial gravel, but some are volcanic, allowing Barrett to compose the blend each year depending on the success of the various sectors. A little Cabernet Franc is blended in to give the wine a more immediate attack. Barrel aging is prolonged at up to two years, but only 25 percent new oak is used.

The 2003 is a resplendent Cabernet, with intense black currant and bramble tones on the nose. In the mouth, the wine is voluptuous, even luxurious, highly concentrated, but with plenty of punch and grip. Impressive now, it will certainly benefit from bottle aging. **SBr**

🍷🍷🍷🍷 **Drink: to 2030**

◀ Montaiguillon's vineyards and château in Montagne St.-Emilion.

Montes *Folly* 2005

Origin Chile, Santa Cruz, Colchagua
Style Dry red wine, 15% ABV
Grape Syrah

Montes can trace its origins back to 1987, when Aurelio Montes and Douglas Murray, both of whom had long-standing experience in the wine industry, joined forces. A year later, Alfredo Vidaurre and Pedro Grand came aboard, and Viña Montes was formally born. Montes Folly, billed as "Chile's first ultra-premium Syrah," was first made in 2000. The back label testified, "From Chile with pride." A $6.5 million (£3.3 million; €4.4 million) Feng Shui-inspired winery was completed in February 2005.

The grapes for Folly are grown on the very highest and steepest slopes of Montes's Finca de Apalta vineyard in Apalta Valley. The wine was so named because other winemakers considered it insane to plant Syrah, which was then a relatively untested variety in Chile. Some would still consider it madness to harvest grapes by hand on a 45-degree slope at 984 feet (300 m) altitude—and at night, too.

Yields are kept low, with grapes and clusters that are much smaller and even more concentrated than in the vineyard's lower slopes—"pure, ripe fruit," as Aurelio puts it. They consequently deliver more color and tannins, making Montes Folly richly colored, deep, and powerful, and typically with more than 14 percent alcohol. Only 9,000 bottles are produced in any given vintage. After the blockbuster 2004, the 2005 was a return to the softer and more approachable style of the wine previously seen in 2003. Warm, spicy, lusciously ripe, and immensely drinkable, it will age for up to twelve years. **SG**
❂❂❂❂ **Drink: to 2017**

FURTHER RECOMMENDATIONS
Other great vintages
2000 · 2001 · 2002 · 2003 · 2004
More Montes wines
Alpha M
Angel · Cherub

The Folly label, with artwork by British cartoonist Ralph Steadman. ➲

MONTES Folly ®

'Apalta Valley was where my dreams and instincts led, searching for the best terroir for red wines in Chile. My partners agreed and "La Finca de Apalta", a mountain Estate, was cleared as high as we could and Syrah —untested in this region— planted in the steeper slopes. Both were considered folly by the conventional wine trade. This wild wine, harvested by acrobats, is the result. Only the genius of Ralph Steadman could translate this emotional wine into a label, to him our gratitude'.

2005

Aurelio Montes

Montevertine

Le Pergole Torte Vino da Tavola 1990

Origin Italy, Tuscany, Radda in Chianti
Style Dry red wine, 13% ABV
Grape Sangiovese

Sergio Manetti, who died in 2000, was viewed by some as one of the iconoclasts of the Italian wine *rinascimento*. That he was a rebel is undeniable. But his legacy is entirely positive, the wines he created the noblest expression of Tuscan enology. An industrialist, Sergio purchased this small property in 1967 and, first as a hobby, later as a passion, set about making it a center for what in those days was a scarce commodity in Tuscany—top-quality wine. To his aid he recruited the great Giulio Gambelli, the "master taster" and guru of Tuscan quality wine.

Like Gambelli, Sergio believed in making wine in as natural a way as possible: no additives, minimum handling, no filtration, eschewing even the then trendy and generally considered essential control of temperature during vinification. But his main fetish was Sangiovese, Sergio resisting to the end of his days the movement toward blending with French grapes. As one would expect, therefore, the wines, today under the unswerving care of son Martino, have their rustic side, while simultaneously demonstrating all the complexity and personality of which Sangiovese is capable in the right hands. **NBel**
🍷🍷🍷🍷🍷 Drink: to 2020

Montevetrano

2004

Origin Italy, Campania
Style Dry red wine, 13% ABV
Grapes C. Sauvignon 60%, Merlot 30%, Aglianico 10%

The history of the Montevetrano estate really started in 1985, the year in which the owner, Silvia Imparato, began working with the then-unknown Riccardo Cotarella, now one of Italy's most prominent winemakers. New practices in both vineyard and winery preceded their first release in 1991. After this experiment, in which Aglianico played a more important role, it was decided that from 1993 there would be a higher proportion of Merlot.

Montevetrano is a unique wine loaded with personality and style. The 2004 vintage was the only wine (together with one from Tuscany) to be awarded the maximum score by the 2007 edition of all the main five Italian wine guides. On the nose, notes of freshly cut grass and minted black currants begin the memorable aromatic progression through Mediterranean bush aromas, musk, lead pencil, and black pepper. In the mouth it is the embodiment of harmony, with a perfect amount of well-integrated oak, and the acidity to keep it interesting and vibrant without ever making it seem tart. The present but nicely smooth tannins will ensure that the wine will age gracefully for many years to come. **AS**
🍷🍷🍷🍷 Drink: to 2022+

◀ The Montevertine hilltop property was originally a vacation villa.

Domaine Hubert de Montille *Volnay PC Les Taillepieds* 1985

Origin France, Burgundy, Côte de Beaune
Style Dry red wine, 12% ABV
Grape Pinot Noir

A door in a wall on Volnay's rue de Combe leads to an enclosed series of old buildings and a handsome period house, which is the summer residence of Maître Hubert de Montille, a distinguished Dijon advocate and one of the finest growers and winemakers in Burgundy. The domaine, now largely run by his son Etienne, continues to make benchmark examples of four premiers crus in Volnay and Pommard, joined by more recently acquired plots in Beaune and Corton.

It is in Maître Hubert's greatest wine, the Premier Cru Volnay Les Taillepieds, that one can taste the essence of his rigorously classical winemaking. De Montille believes that chaptalization should never raise the alcoholic strength of the wine beyond 12 to 12.5 percent. This approach began by accident in 1959, when Hubert made a mistake in the amount of sugar he added to his Taillepieds: The wine reached only 11.5 percent ABV but, to his delight, became his best wine of the year, showing more subtle nuances of flavor and fruit than the others.

The de Montille Taillepieds 1985 can still be bought at auction or on the secondary market. Despite the warmth of that golden autumn, the color is an alluringly clear ruby grading to garnet rim. With a little air, the aroma of intense Pinot fruit is in perfect balance with the racy tension of the *lieu-dit*. The mouthfeel again stresses lovely fruit, very 1985, merging with gently oxidative vinosity. The finish is long, fine, and very complex. **ME**
🍷🍷🍷 **Drink: to 2020+**

FURTHER RECOMMENDATIONS
Other great vintages
1966 • 1971 • 1978 • 1987 • 1999 • 2002 • 2005
More Domaine Hubert de Montille wines
Pommard PC Pézerolles • Pommard PC Rugiens
Puligny-Montrachet PC Les Caillerets • Volnay PC Rugiens

A vineyard worker drives in the prestigious wine village of Volnay. ➡

Château Montrose

2003

Origin France, Bordeaux, St.-Estèphe
Style Dry red wine, 13% ABV
Grapes C. Sauvignon 65%, Merlot 25%, C. Franc 10%

The history of Montrose only gets under way at the outset of the nineteenth century, when Etienne Théodore Dumoulin, having inherited it as a fallow part of the estate of Château Calon, decided to clear what was then a parcel of scrubby moorland and plant the vines to which it was eminently suited. Then known as La Lande de l'Escargeon, it was found to be a prime viticultural site, so much so that Dumoulin built a château to go with it and renamed the estate Montrose. Rapidly growing to 125 acres (50 ha), the property had, within a generation, begun producing wines of such renown that they effortlessly made it in among the Seconds in 1855.

Vintages do not come much bigger than 2003, when a searing heat wave of a summer produced Cabernet and Merlot grapes of colossal, almost fearsome concentration. The wine is densely colored, intensely perfumed, and immensely structured, with notes of cassis, toasty oak, vanilla, roses, and sage emerging from the girderlike tannic framework. It is powerful on the finish, almost hot in youth, but with so much succulent fruit that it will take thirty years' aging in its stride. **SW**

🍷🍷🍷🍷 **Drink: to 2040+**

Château Montus

Cuvée Prestige 2001

Origin France, Madiran
Style Dry red wine, 14% ABV
Grape Tannat

In a world full of taste-alike "international" wines, the red wines of southwest France are a breath of fresh air. Notably, the Montus and Boucasse wines of Alain Brumont have been gladly received into the fine wine pantheon. It was back in 1979 that Brumont decided to go it alone and plant the first vines at Montus, 1982 being the first released vintage.

One of the perennial difficulties with Madiran has been working with the Tannat grape which, left to its own devices, can make wines that are impossibly tannic in their youth, but that lose their fruit before the structure resolves. Brumont uses 100 percent destemming and small oak, of which some is new, to tame Tannat—but not too much.

The Cuvée Prestige 2001, a selection from the best blocks in the vineyard, is an impressive wine that manages to capture the wildness of reds from this corner of southwest France while avoiding rusticity. It is a big wine dominated by bold, dark fruits, with great density and structure, but with refinement and a touch of new oak. This is a wine that will continue to evolve for some years, but that is already beginning to drink well. **JG**

🍷🍷🍷 **Drink: to 2020+**

Domaine de la Mordorée
Cuvée de la Reine des Bois 2001

Origin France, Southern Rhône, Châteauneuf-du-Pape
Style Dry red wine, 15% ABV
Grape Grenache Noir

The year 2000 in Châteauneuf-du-Pape did not please everyone: It was just that bit too hot, and that meant power, and alcohol, and every now and then, coarseness. The following year, 2001, was the wine for the people in the know: Elegant and balanced, it gives every indication of being built to last.

The Domaine de la Mordorée is not old. It was created by Francis Delorme and his son Christophe as recently as 1986, and named after the woodcock—a bird they admire. They made their first wine in 1989. The Delormes have estates in neighboring Tavel and Lirac, and have recently bought land in Condrieu. All in all they have 132 acres (53 ha) in thirty-eight separate parcels.

The Cuvée de la Reine des Bois comes from an 8.5-acre plot (3.5 ha). The wine has won many accolades, including *coups de coeur* in the important French *Guide Hachette*. The 2001 received the best present a wine can ever receive in this world—a 100-point score from Robert Parker. It is inky, and its bouquet reminiscent of dark, sour cherries. The palate is spicy. It is best with woodcock, wild boar, or some other strongly flavored game. **GM**

😊😊😊😊😊 Drink: to 2025

Moric *Lutzmannsburg*
Blaufränkisch Alte Reben 2009

Origin Austria, Mittelburgenland
Style Dry red wine, 13.5% ABV
Grape Blaufränkisch

For many years Roland Velich worked for the family winery, known for its Chardonnay. But by 2001 he had developed a project specializing in old-vine Blaufränkisch. Velich was determined to show that native Austrian varieties such as Blaufränkisch could make great wine unaided by Cabernet or Merlot. He had little difficulty acquiring or leasing venerable Blaufränkisch sites, as they were then undervalued, especially since the yields were low. He now controls 62 acres (25 ha), and also produces Grüner Veltliner.

His finest red wine is usually the Alte Reben from Lutzmannsburg. Here the oldest vines were planted in 1902 and 1904, and the youngest in the 1920s. The wine is fermented with natural yeasts and aged in 396-gallon (1,500-liter) casks for twelve months, and is then aged further in *tonneaux*.

The 2009 comes from a very ripe year and there is a slight jamminess on the nose. The palate is sleek, concentrated, and beautifully textured. There is tannin present, but also freshness, lift, and length. It is an example of the heights to which Blaufränkisch can rise from an old, well-tended vineyard, especially in the hands of a skilled winemaker. **SBr**

😊😊😊😊 Drink: to 2025

Moris Farms *Avvoltore* 2004

Origin Italy, Tuscany, Massa Marittima
Style Dry red wine, 14% ABV
Grapes Sangiovese 75%, C. Sauvignon 20%, Syrah 5%

Two centuries ago, the Moris family left Spain and moved to Tuscan Maremma, but it was only in the past few decades that it converted entirely from agriculture to viticulture. The Moris estate divides into two different properties: One extends over 1,037 acres (420 ha) near Massa Marittima in northern Maremma; the other over 138 acres (56 ha) south of the River Ombrone. The total vineyard area is 173 acres (70 ha), divided into roughly equal parts between the northern property (in the Monteregio di Massa Marittima DOC) and the southern one (in the Morellino di Scansano DOC).

Avvoltore is the flagship wine of the estate, produced from grapes grown on the northern property. The vineyards are situated at an altitude that ranges from 260 to 330 feet (80 to 100 m) above sea level. The soil is rich in clay but very well drained—perfect conditions for the production of well-structured red wines.

The Avvoltore 2004 is dark ruby red with purple tinges. The grape blend seems to work perfectly, with the Sangiovese giving structure and nerve, and the Cabernet Sauvignon giving depth, juiciness, and flesh. On the nose the Cabernet seems to prevail, because the wine shows notes of blackberry and bell pepper. The aromatic picture is completed by the pleasant mintiness of the oak. On the palate, the wine is elegant and somewhat tense (distinctive traits of Sangiovese), but recalls the nose while adding a soft yet assertive mouthfeel. **AS**
☻☻☻ **Drink: to 2025**

FURTHER RECOMMENDATIONS

Other great vintages

1990 · 1997 · 2001 · 2003

More wines from Maremma

Ca'Marcanda · Grattamacco · Guado al Tasso · Lupicaia Ornellaia · Sassicaia · Michele Satta

The creeper-covered Moris Farms winery at Poggio la Mozza ➥

EMILIO MORO

Emilio Moro
Malleolus 2004

Origin Spain, Ribera del Duero
Style Dry red wine, 14% ABV
Grape Tempranillo

In the late 1980s a number of new bodegas emerged in the Ribera del Duero region, many of them founded by locals who had previously sold wines in bulk or supplied grapes, must, or wine to other producers. Bodegas Emilio Moro dates back three generations, and most of their production comes from their own vineyards, now mostly replanted with a clone selected from their oldest vines.

Bodegas Emilio Moro produce a range of wines characterized by aromas of ripe fruit and toasty notes, with a house style that in recent years has been polished to achieve greater balance and finesse. Within their portfolio, Malleolus 2004 represents a high-quality level wine at a moderate price, and still at a relatively high production volume, unlike the more exclusive and expensive micro-cuvées Malleolus de Sanchomartín and Malleolus de Valderramiro. *Malleolus* is the Latin source of the Spanish *majuelo*, one of the many names for "plot" in this area, and the one most commonly used in the neighborhood of Pesquera de Duero. The grapes for this wine are sourced from vines between twenty-five and seventy-five years of age. **JB**

☻☻☻ **Drink: to 2018**

Moss Wood
Cabernet Sauvignon 2001

Origin Australia, Western Australia, Margaret River
Style Dry red wine, 14.5% ABV
Grapes C. Sauvignon, C. Franc, Petit Verdot, Merlot

Moss Wood is rated in the top tier of Langton's classification of Australian wines, and its Cabernet Sauvignon is widely regarded as one of Australia's finest examples, offering elegance, restrained power, and cellaring potential. Before 2001, the benchmarks for the Moss Wood Cabernet Sauvignon style were the wines made between 1974 and 1977. Langton's sold a bottle of the 1973 (its first vintage) for a claimed post-1970 Australian vintage record price of $1,850 (£900; €1,285) at its Melbourne online auction in September 2007. A bottle of the 1974 fetched approximately $1,400 (£675; €960).

Perfumed and finely structured, the Moss Wood Cabernet Sauvignon 2001 is arguably the greatest wine yet released from this producer. It has cassis black-currant aromas and hints of cedar and violet. Since 1996, extended oak aging to twenty-four months and the introduction of Cabernet Franc, Petit Verdot, and Merlot into the blend has made the wine deeper in color, more aromatic, and more textured, with a better balance of oak and fruit. Only time will tell if the 2001 will age as well as the now-legendary 1973 and 1974. **SG**

☻☻☻ **Drink: to 2020+**

◄ A bold mural painting announces the Emilio Moro winery.

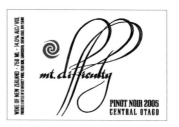

Château du Moulin-à-Vent
Croix des Vérillats 2011

Origin France, Beaujolais, Moulin-à-Vent
Style Dry red wine, 13% ABV
Grape Gamay

Mount Difficulty
Long Gully Pinot Noir 2005

Origin New Zealand, Central Otago
Style Dry red wine, 14% ABV
Grape Pinot Noir

Of the ten Beaujolais crus, Moulin-à-Vent is often the longest-lived and the richest, and since its acquisition in 2009 by Jean-Jacques Parinet, ably assisted by his son Edouard, Château du Moulin-à-Vent has again been producing some of the best wines not only of this famous village but of the region as a whole.

The property has 74 acres (30 ha) under vine, all at the heart of the appellation. From scattered parcels of old vines the Parinets produce their flagship wine, Château du Moulin-à-Vent, and from younger vines the delicious Couvent des Thorins. But they also bottle separately the wine from two outstanding lieux-dits—Champ de Cour and Croix des Vérillats.

Both of the latter wines are vinified in large oak vats, followed by at least ten months in barrels, only 10 to 20 percent new. But their characters are different: Champ de Cour faces southeast, on granite, while Croix des Vérillats faces east, on pink granite sand. The latter is more *airien*, elegant, and supple. An intense, luminous ruby red, it has an alluring nose of pure but ripe black fruit, gently plummy and spicy, and a palate that is racy, sapid, silky, and vital. Delicious in youth, it still has the structure to age gracefully. **NB**
🍷🍷🍷 Drink: to 2022+

Mount Difficulty owns or manages seven vineyards in the heart of Bannockburn, Central Otago's finest subregion. Each vineyard was mapped to record differing soil patterns, with up to six plots in a single vineyard. Different clones of Pinot Noir appropriate to each soil type were then planted in each plot.

Winemaker Matt Dicey has identified the section in each vineyard most likely to make a single-vineyard wine. That plot is then pruned, shoot-thinned, and fruit-thinned to limit grape yield to 1 ton per acre (around 20 hl/ha). If vintage conditions are good, then a single-vineyard wine may be made, though these are not produced every year.

2005 was a moderately cool vintage that favored Bannockburn, one of the region's warmest areas. Long Gully vineyard is, at sixteen years of age, one of Mount Difficulty's oldest sites and boasts moderately heavy soils by Central Otago standards, reducing the need for irrigation. The vineyard has now "come of age" and is likely to make single-vineyard wines regularly in the future. The wine has wonderful fruit purity, with a peacock's tail of cherry, plum, floral, and spice flavors emerging on the finish. **BC**
🍷🍷🍷 Drink: to 2017+

A Mount Difficulty vineyard, formerly a scene of gold prospecting. ➡

Mount Langi Ghiran
Shiraz 2003

Mount Mary
Quintet Cabernet 2003

Origin Australia, Victoria, Grampians
Style Dry red wine, 15% ABV
Grape Shiraz

Origin Australia, Victoria, Yarra Valley
Style Dry red wine, 13% ABV
Grapes C. Sauvignon 50%, C. Franc 30%, Others 20%

Trevor Mast has been making wine in the Grampians region of Victoria since the mid-1970s. Inspired by a tank of Shiraz from the Italian Fratin brothers' vineyard, Mast sought work with the Fratins as their winemaker, and in 1987 bought the Mount Langi Ghiran property. The vineyards are in a spectacular setting, lying 1,148 feet (350 m) above sea level at the base of Mount Langi Ghiran's cliff face.

The original vineyards, planted in the 1870s, were replaced by sheep at the turn of the century, but the site was re-established in 1963 by the Fratins. The Shiraz is made from fruit from this "Old Block," with topsoils of granitic sands and silt together with red clay loams. This varied soil profile gives some control of water supply, allowing the vines to stress naturally during critical growth periods, with resultant concentration of fruit flavors.

Mount Langi Ghiran is in a powerful but elegant Shiraz style. The warm 2003 season is reflected in the glass, showing ripe blueberries as well as the trademark pepper. A big, chewy wine when young, Mount Langi Ghiran softens with five or more years' bottle age into a fine cool-climate Shiraz. **SG**

🍷🍷🍷 **Drink: to 2018**

The Yarra Valley is a region reborn. For a number of reasons—including the Depression and the fact that Australia lost interest in table wines, turning to beer and fortifieds instead—wine growing in Australia's Yarra Valley had a fifty-year break, beginning in the 1920s. Then, in the 1970s, a small band of pioneers returned to the Yarra, including Dr. John Middleton. In 1971 Middleton planted 25 acres (10 ha) with several grapes, including Cabernet and Pinot Noir.

Over a while Mount Mary became one of Australia's cult wines. They are not universally appreciated, though. In particular, Robert Parker recently gave them a negative write-up. How did Middleton react? The offending Parker review was displayed on the end of a barrel for everyone to see.

Perhaps the most famous of Mount Mary's wines is the Quintet. Complex sweet black-currant fruit dominates the nose, with a spicy, savory, almost minty earthy/gravelly edge. The palate is concentrated, with nice gravelly complexity to the ripe black-currant and red-berry fruit. This, like many of the Mount Mary wines, is one to put in the cellar and forget about for a decade or more. **JG**

🍷🍷🍷 **Drink: to 2025**

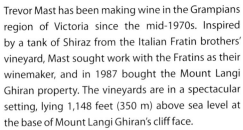

◀ Widely spaced Mount Langi Ghiran vines near Ararat in the Grampians.

Château Mouton Rothschild
1945

Origin France, Bordeaux, Pauillac
Style Dry red wine, 13% ABV
Grapes C. Sauvignon 85%, Merlot 8%, C. Franc 7%

Coming at the end of World War II, the "victory vintage" of 1945 was a wonderful symbol of peace. Throughout France, ungrafted, mature vines—none had been replaced during the war—gave the highest quality grapes. In Bordeaux, Mouton Rothschild, despite having an ill-equipped winery, was particularly brilliant, and is now acclaimed as one of the greatest wines of all time. Broadbent has famously described Mouton 1945 as "a Churchill of a wine," and not just in reference to the wine itself. To commemorate the end of the war, this was the first vintage of Mouton to feature a bespoke label, based on Churchill's "V for victory," by a young French artist called Philippe Jullian. Every vintage since, Mouton has enlisted an artist to design a new label.

In June 1993, the château's owner Baronne Philippine de Rothschild served the 1945 to more than 200 guests at a dinner. The idea was to pour magnums, of which only 1,475 were made. However, when a magnum was opened for inspection, the *maître de chai* decided that the wine was not yet ready and bottles were served instead. This is truly a wine built to last. **SG**

☻☻☻☻☻ **Drink: to 2050**

Muga *Prado Enea*
Gran Reserva Rioja 1994

Origin Spain, Rioja
Style Dry red wine, 13.5% ABV
Grapes Tempranillo, Mazuelo, Graciano

Bodegas Muga was created in 1932 by Isaac Muga Martínez in the town of Haro. His company is now in the hands of the third generation, brothers and cousins splitting the duties in the vineyard, the winery, and the local and export markets.

Muga's trademark is the use of oak, and only oak, in its winemaking. The grapes are fermented in 160 vats, and the wines raised in 14,000 barrels. The whole process is very traditional, from the use of wild yeast to the fining with egg whites. The methods are traditional, but the wines are quite modern without losing their identity, and they appeal to both traditionalists and modernists.

In 1994, modern Rioja exploded. The Prado Enea, always a ruby color with some orange reflections, showing the extended aging in vat, barrel, and bottle before being put on the market six or seven years after the harvest date, has an intoxicating nose of red berries and forest floor, hinting at porcini mushrooms and truffles. Spice, leather, and citrus are also common descriptors here. With medium body, a nice acidity, soft tannins, and a very long finish, this is a Rioja for Burgundy lovers. **LG**

☻☻☻ **Drink: to 2020**

⬛ Bottles of the Mouton 1945 flank the 1924, the first with a picture label.

Domaine Jacques-Frédéric Mugnier *Le Musigny GC* 1999

Mullineux Family Wines *Schist Syrah* 2011

Origin France, Burgundy, Côte de Nuits
Style Dry red wine, 13% ABV
Grape Pinot Noir

Origin South Africa, Swartland
Style Dry red wine, 13.7%
Grape Syrah

Frédéric Mugnier—Freddy to his friends—is a fortunate fellow. Now the custodian of both the handsome Château de Chambolle-Musigny and the wines from his superb vineyards in Chambolle and Nuits, he was formerly an off-shore oil engineer and commercial pilot before returning full time to manage the estate in 1998.

Of his vineyards in Chambolle, which include a parcel of the premier cru Les Fuées and another of the seductive Amoureuses, Freddy's finest plot is a generous 3.5-acre (1.4 ha) portion of grand cru Le Musigny. The vines were planted between 1947 and 1962— unequaled raw material for what is, for many collectors, the best wine in the appellation.

The 1999 vintage was a hot year by Burgundy's standards, a year when Freddy's approach paid off. "Great wine," he says, "is a creation of the soil, and our craft is to respect the living equilibrium in the soil and the grape. We are not dogmatic in our methods. But we monitor the environmental side effects and we avoid processes that would traumatize the wine." This wine has that scented ethereal quality of the greatest Côte de Nuits. **ME**

ϴϴϴϴϴ **Drink: to 2025+**

Following their maiden 2008 releases, Chris and Andrea Mullineux rapidly gained recognition as shining among the leading lights of the Swartland. Now included in their range are small bottlings of three expressively different single-origin Syrahs— from schist, granite, and iron soils respectively, and named accordingly. These wines are sourced from specific parcels that have been carefully nurtured to provide grapes whose wines can stand alone, with sufficient complexity and balance. The maiden release of Schist and Granite was 2010.

Schist comes from a fifteen-year-old dryland vineyard on a steep, east-facing slope near the town of Riebeek-Kasteel. The wine is vinified with minimal manipulation—no yeast inoculation, no additives, the bunches not destemmed, matured in 132-gallon (500-liter) oak barrels, half of them new. In its youth this is a rich, intense, and dense wine, yet with a genuine freshness and some elegance. The structure is paramount: tannins are firm, fine, and harmonious; together with the bright natural acidity, they should carry the ample fruit to a finer maturity a decade or more after the vintage. **TJ**

ϴϴϴ **Drink: to 2026+**

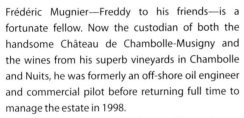

◀ The church of Chambolle-Musigny, at the heart of the Côte de Nuits.

René Muré
Pinot Noir Cuvée "V" 2004

Origin France, Alsace
Style Dry red wine, 13.5% ABV
Grape Pinot Noir

Château Musar
1999

Origin Lebanon, Bekaa Valley
Style Dry red wine, 14% ABV
Grapes Cabernet Sauvignon, Cinsault, Carignan

The "V" of this Cuvée represents the first letter of Vorbourg, the name of the Côte de Rouffach's grand cru in southern Alsace. Its excellent location and those of other fine hillsides in the Rouffach area have attracted vine growers and winemakers since Roman times. The vines for this Pinot Noir are indeed located in the grand cru Vorbourg, but because the only grapes permitted for the appellation grand cru are Riesling, Pinot Gris, Gewürztraminer, and Muscat, the wine cannot be called Vorbourg.

This 2004 is an exceptional Pinot Noir from a year that brought great color, vivid fruitiness, and phenolic maturity to what is a powerful but not overextracted wine. It was neither filtered nor fined. Of deep, dark ruby hue, the first aromas are an exotic medley of violets, pink pepper, and fresh, dark fruits combining with hot spices like cinnamon and clove. The wine has real volume in the mouth, the smooth tannins melding happily with a luxuriant flavor of black cherries and raspberries. The finish is focused and long, a touch of ripe acidity and minerality completing an impressive Pinot that is a natural partner to roast guinea fowl or game birds. **ME**
🍷🍷🍷 **Drink: to 2019**

After a long stay in France, Gaston Hochar returned to Lebanon and in 1930 created Château Musar in the cellars of the seventeenth-century Mzar castle in Ghazir, overlooking the Mediterranean. In 1959, after completing his enology diploma in Bordeaux, Gaston's eldest son, Serge, entered the business. Serge's younger brother Ronald took over Château Musar's marketing and finance departments in 1962. The brothers were given complete control in 1966.

Château Musar is notorious for smelling of *Brettanomyces* (a yeast genus that causes "mousy" and "old sock" smells) and volatile acidity (acetic acid, which makes the wine smell vinegary). These could be considered to be faults, but with Musar they form part of the wine's unique character.

The varietal composition varies from one vintage to the next, giving Château Musar a different character and identity each year. The 1999 is relatively pale in color, as many of Musar's best vintages are, with the characteristic "old sock" nose balanced by rich and ripe fruit flavors. The acidity is quite low, and it was drinking beautifully by 2007, but could be aged for another ten years. **SG**
🍷🍷🍷 **Drink: to 2017**

A Bedouin woman picks grapes in Château Musar's Aana vineyard. ➡

Fiorenzo Nada
Barbaresco Rombone 2001

Origin Italy, Piedmont, Langhe
Style Dry red wine, 14% ABV
Grape Nebbiolo

Château de la Négly
La Porte du Ciel 2001

Origin France, Coteaux du Languedoc, La Clape
Style Dry red wine, 14.5% ABV
Grape Syrah

Bruno Nada's story is a morality tale with a happy ending. Born in 1951 in Treiso, where his father Fiorenzo had a small Barbaresco estate, Bruno left the land for the city in search of a professional career and a more affluent lifestyle. After studying at technical college in Turin, he later became a lecturer at the hotel school in Barolo. There the pull of his beloved Langhe was so strong that he started courses in food and wine appreciation.

Finally, in the early 1980s, Bruno went to his father, who had previously sold his wine in bulk, and suggested they try something new and market the wine directly. Fiorenzo's laconic reply was *Pruvuma* (let's try). Since then, they have been content to make a small number of wines with infinite care and respect for local traditions.

The Rombone is a majestic wine of marked austerity when young, particularly in the first-rate, structured 2001 vintage. The ample aromas are very Barbaresco, akin to violets and blackberries, with an almost Burgundian luxuriance. In the mouth, this is a warm, strong wine—tannic yet ripe—of muscular texture and great length. It will live for decades. **ME**
🍷🍷🍷🍷 Drink: to 2030+

This 124-acre (50 ha) estate on the eastern slopes of the coastal limestone lump of La Clape produces a range of showy but stimulating and clearly differentiated wines. Owner Jean Paux-Rosset, his dreams for fine Languedoc wine frustrated by a family that persisted with the productivist viticulture of the past, took over the domain in 1992, and has steadily been renovating both vineyards and cellar ever since. Claude Gros now consults.

Of the reds, La Falaise and the preponderantly Mourvèdre-based l'Ancely are both serious, dense wines of satisfying complexity. The two finest wines, though, are both pure Syrah: Clos des Truffiers, made with Jeffrey Davies, comes from vineyards at St.-Pargeoire, whereas Clos du Ciel (of which there are at least three in the wine world) is part of the Négly estate itself. La Porte du Ciel is lush, sumptuous, and dense, the distinctive salty edge lent by the marine location easily subsumed within its glossy fruit architecture. (The salt is more evident, gratifyingly, on the white Brise Marine.) Perhaps Paux-Rosset's father, Max, was not so wrong in his thinking after all: It was he who first planted Syrah on La Clape. **AJ**
🍷🍷🍷 Drink: to 2017

Nino Negri
Sfursat 5 Stelle 2003

Origin Italy, Lombardy, Valtellina
Style Dry red wine, 14.5% ABV
Grape Chiavennasca (Nebbiolo)

Niebaum-Coppola Estate
Rubicon 2003

Origin USA, California, Napa Valley
Style Dry red wine, 14.5% ABV
Grapes C. Sauvignon, C. Franc, Merlot, Petit Verdot

In the last of Lombardy's Alpine valleys before Switzerland, Valtellina is one small Italian wine region outside Piedmont where the great Nebbiolo grape, known locally as Chiavennasca, regularly succeeds. Nino Negri is the leading producer. Indeed, the consistent excellence of Valtellino owes a lot to Casimiro Maule, Negri's enologist and winemaker, because since 1976 he has set the yardstick for the winemaking revival in the valley. His Sfursat 5 Stelle is his greatest wine, and this 2003 is among the best vintages, a great achievement in such a torrid year.

The 2003 has an intense garnet color with just a hint of brick at the glass's rim; the heat of the year gives initially rich and spicy aromas, prunes and raisins, almost balsamic in their unctuousness. With air, the bouquet develops classy Nebbiolo scents of old roses mingling with toasted, torrefied notes of nuts and coffee, and a touch of vanilla. Miraculously, the palate has an aristocratic, tightly knit character, a lot in reserve, elegance and poise winning by a short head over raw power. Casimiro Maule's masterly touch can also be savored in the Sfursat Normale 2003, suffused with the taste of black cherries. **ME**
🥂🥂🥂🥂 **Drink: to 2018**

In 1871 William C. Watson purchased 78 acres (32 ha) of farmland in Napa and planted it with grape vines, naming the estate Inglenook. The Finnish-born Captain Gustave Niebaum, who had amassed a fortune in the Alaskan fur trade, bought Inglenook in 1880. The estate's wines soon gained a high reputation: In 1901 travelers dining on the Southern Pacific Railroad were ordering Inglenook Claret.

The estate was divided in 1964 when Allied Grape Growers bought the Inglenook brand name, the château, and 94 acres (38 ha) of vineyards. The whole estate later became the property of renowned movie director Francis Ford Coppola, although he almost lost everything in the late 1970s when he used it as collateral to fund *Apocalypse Now*.

Coppola's first Rubicon vintage was 1978, but it was not released until 1985, after seven years in barrel. Early vintages were very dense and tannic, but since the 1990s the style has become much more accessible. The 2003 is surprisingly supple by Napa standards but will age gracefully. The Niebaum-Coppola name was retired in 2006, and the estate itself is now known as Rubicon. **SG**
🥂🥂🥂🥂🥂 **Drink: to 2018+**

Ignaz Niedrist
Lagrein Berger Gei 2010

Origin Italy, Alto Adige
Style Dry red wine, 13% ABV
Grape Lagrein

Niepoort
Batuta 2004

Origin Portugal, Douro
Style Dry red wine, 14% ABV
Grapes Field blend of many indigenous varieties

This wine estate has been the property of the Niedrist family since 1870. For decades the family sold their grapes to the local cooperative cellar of Cornaiano, but at the start of the 1990s they uprooted their Schiava (Trollinger) vines in order to make their own wine from the Lagrein grape.

The village of Cornaiano is situated just north of the Caldaro Lake. Here Lagrein thrives in the warm, well-draining soils formed millions of years ago by the withdrawal of the glaciers. Lagrein is a variety that is grown exclusively in the southern part of Alto Adige. Although it is also used for producing fruity rosé wines (Lagrein Kretzer), it is very rich in color and quite low in tannin. When fermented on its skins it gives deep, very robust, yet soft red wines that win favor through their fruit-driven appeal.

In the glass, the Lagrein Berger Gei appears to be almost pitch black, with vibrant purple hints. On the nose it offers aromas of blackberries, cranberries, and soft ripe fruits, with a spiced, cocoa/tobaccolike finish. On the palate it is thickly textured, with the concentration of a fruit jam but the vibrancy of freshly squeezed summer berries. **AS**

🍷🍷 **Drink: recent vintages for up to 10 years**

Dirk Niepoort is in the lucky position of being a serious wine nut who also has a winery and some of the world's greatest terroirs to play with. These terroirs—specifically, the terraced schistous slopes of the Cima Corgo region of Portugal's Douro—have been dedicated to Port production, but for his fine red table wines Niepoort prefers north-facing, cooler vineyards. He reckons that the best Port vineyards are not the best vineyards for table wines.

Batuta was first made in 1999, and stylistically it most resembles a classed growth Bordeaux. It spends thirty to forty-five days on skins—to achieve not bigger, but rather finer, tannins. The wine is wild and intense, but very refined at the same time, with great length and finesse.

Probably the best vintage to date is the 2004. It is not as wild as Redoma can be, but is powerful yet elegant, intense yet refined. The lovely full, fresh nose shows sweet, dark chocolaty and spicy notes along with the tight fruit; there is great definition. The palate is concentrated with rich, sweet fruit, but under this the structure is huge. A fresh, tight style offers lots of potential for aging. **JG**

🍷🍷🍷 **Drink: to 2030**

Winemaker Dirk Niepoort in one of his barrel rooms. ➡

Niepoort

Charme 2002

Origin Portugal, Douro
Style Dry red wine, 13% ABV
Grapes Field blend of many indigenous varieties

Possibly the leading figure in the Douro table wine revolution, Dirk Niepoort is obsessed with fine wine; and of all the world's wine regions, it is Burgundy he most admires. While he was achieving fame for his Redoma and Batuta reds, and strikingly Burgundian Redoma Branco Reserva, he was busy developing a rather different expression of the Douro: Charme.

"The difference between a good wine and a great wine is a hundred little details," says Niepoort. The grapes are foot-trodden in *lagares* with the stems, and the length of the maceration is a critical detail. A lot has to be extracted very early on in the *lagar*, then the rest has to be extracted very gently. Niepoort says that in 2001 they missed the timing by as little as a few hours and as a result no Charme was released from this year.

The first released vintage of Charme was the 2002. The wine has a smooth, ripe, elegant nose. There is richness and depth, with a bit of stemmy spiciness. On the palate it is smooth and ripe, with a spiciness and some structure to the tannins. This wine shows that the Douro is capable of elegance and finesse as well as power and wildness. **JG**

⊖⊖⊖ Drink: to 2025+

Bodega Noemía de Patagonia

Noemía 2004

Origin Argentina, Patagonia, Río Negro Valley
Style Dry red wine, 14.5% ABV
Grape Malbec

Noemía is the flagship wine of Noemi Marone Cinzano and winemaker Hans Vinding-Diers. In 2001 Hans was working in the Río Negro Valley in Patagonia, when he stumbled across a vineyard planted there in the 1930s with a genetically diverse selection of French Côt, the "real" Malbec (the later ripening one). It had been planted by Italian immigrants as a "mother" vineyard for southern Argentina. The debut 2001 vintage from this vineyard produced Argentina's first garage wine.

Noemía was fermented with no pumps (or other mechanical aids) in the cool rooms of a fruit-packing warehouse by Vinding-Diers before Cinzano, for whom Vinding-Diers was working as a consultant in Tuscany, came on board. Together they built a dedicated winery for Noemía, for the 2004 vintage.

The wine is bottled by gravity and unfiltered, so decant it over a day or more before drinking. The wine has immensely concentrated fruit and exotic tannins, but retains its elegance despite its mass. It also shows the best characteristics of the Malbec grape: an unrivaled breadth of tannin in a wine that does not taste "tannic" at all. **MW**

⊖⊖⊖⊖ Drink: to 2017

Andrea Oberto
Barbera Giada 2010

Origin Italy, Piedmont
Style Dry red wine, 14.5% ABV
Grape Barbera

Ojai Vineyard
Thompson Syrah 2003

Origin USA, California, Santa Barbara
Style Dry red wine, 13.5% ABV
Grape Syrah

This estate was created in 1978 by Andrea Oberto, who wanted to continue the family's grape-growing tradition. The time at which he began his business was hardly ideal, with many producers actually giving away one case of Barolo with every ten to fifteen cases of Barbera sold. Barolo might be Piedmont's flagship wine, but Barbera is the grape variety (and the wine) more dear to Piedmontese people. Back then there were not many non-Piedmontese palates that could have dealt with the typically fierce acidity of the Barbera grape.

Oberto's Barbera Giada, first produced in 1988, was among the first Barberas enjoyed by non-Piedmontese wine lovers. The vines used to produce Giada were planted in 1951, and ensure a high quality of fruit. The yields are kept quite low. The grapes are fermented at a controlled temperature, and the juice pumped over many times to obtain richness and extraction. This is a Barbera to make many people change their opinion of the grape. The 2010 is the liquid personification of elegant and succulent fruit tones. Try it with a leg of lamb roasted with copious amounts of rosemary and garlic. **AS**

🍷🍷🍷 **Drink: recent vintages for up to 7 years**

Neither the little resort town of Ojai nor U.S. Syrah were well known when Adam and Helen Tolmach planted their small Syrah vineyard in 1981. Pierce's disease ultimately ravaged the vineyard, but Tolmach decided not to replant, the better to work more intensively with the growers he has come to know. Tolmach, who has focused exclusively on his own wines since 1991, has always been inquisitive, trying to understand the causal relationships in every act of wine growing and winemaking. The course of his career has been a journey of producing a variety of distinctive single-vineyard wines in the Santa Barbara region of California.

Along the way, realizing that high sugar levels, and therefore high alcohol levels, were antithetical to complex flavor expression, his journey has been a search for ever-cooler sites suited to wines of elegance and longevity. 2003 was a relatively easy vintage, producing the low yields Tolmach seeks. The Thompson Syrah is a powerful, dense, and concentrated wine, with a latent complexity destined to become harmonious and integrated ten years and more from the vintage. **LGr**

🍷🍷🍷 **Drink: to 2018**

Willi Opitz
Opitz One 1999

Origin Austria, Neusiedlersee/Seewinkel, Illmitz
Style Sweet red wine, 11% ABV
Grapes Blauburger or other Austrian black varieties

Willi Opitz originally tended his minute vineyard only at the weekends. He has since given up the day job and acquired a bit more land, and he also receives regular parcels of nobly rotten fruit from local growers who, for one reason or another, do not wish to use it themselves. Everything is strictly graded and placed in different cuvées to make wines at various levels of sweetness, from Spätlese to Trockenbeerenauslese. In years without botrytis, the grapes are either left on the vine until the frosts (this is hazardous in Illmitz because it is close to a national park that is also a bird sanctuary) or they are laid on dry reeds to make Schilfwein, a style revived by Opitz in the 1980s and which he calls Schilfmandl (little man of straw).

An innovation is Opitz One, his excellent red reed wine. It is made from the Austrian Blauburger crossing (Blauer Portugieser X Blaufränkisch—one of Friedrich Zweigelt's creations) or a combination of red varieties. The 1999 is characterized by a pinky red color and an immense taste of nougat, Rumtopf, and chocolate mousse. The wine is best consumed with a slice of Sacher torte. **GM**

❸❸❸❸ **Drink: to 2019+**

Opus One
1987

Origin USA, California, Napa Valley
Style Dry red wine, 13.5% ABV
Grapes C. Sauvignon 95%, C. Franc 3%, Merlot 2%

In "Show Me What You Got," Jay–Z raps, "I'm just getting better with time/I'm like Opus One." Although not commanding as much attention as some other Napa wineries these days, Opus One was the first "designer" or "boutique" winery in Napa. Robert Mondavi and Baron Philippe de Rothschild first met in 1970 in Hawaii. Eight years later, they met again in Bordeaux. It took one hour for them to agree to a joint venture in California. The cachet of their names would bring buyers at high prices.

It took a few vintages for Opus One to find its feet, but it then settled into a distinctive style that married fruit grown in the California style with winemaking *à la bordelaise*. Opus One could never be mistaken for a Bordeaux wine—it is too ripe and alcoholic for that—but it is a good deal more savory and less alcoholic than the completely over-the-top California Cabernets that have emerged since.

Still deeply colored in 2006, the Opus One 1987 displays a not unattractive green note on the nose at first, and then, with aeration, tobacco. This wine is full and concentrated, with a big, tannic finish, and is capable of aging for several more years. **SG**

❺❺❺❺❺ **Drink: to 2017+**

The large, semicircular Grand Chai, or barrel room, at Opus One. ▶

Siro Pacenti
Brunello di Montalcino 2001

Origin Italy, Toscana, Montalcino
Style Dry red wine, 14% ABV
Grape Sangiovese

Pago de los Capellanes *Parcela*
El Picón Ribera del Duero 2003

Origin Spain, Ribera del Duero
Style Dry red wine, 14.5% ABV
Grapes Tinto Fino (Tempranillo), C. Sauvignon

Giancarlo Pacenti's father, Siro, bought 49 acres (20 ha) of prime Montalcino real estate in 1960; his grandfather had worked the land as a share cropper a generation earlier. The family's 17 acres (7 ha) of Sangiovese in the extreme north of the DOCG profit from the cool climate and the sandy soils, and give rise to wines of exceptional aromatic complexity. Their 32 acres (13 ha) in the south of the appellation are cultivated on rich, alluvial soils with a high proportion of limestone, and the grapes produced here give wines of substantial power and alcohol. It is the marriage of fruit from these two sub-zones that imbues the Pacenti wines with such extraordinary complexity and longevity.

In Giancarlo's opinion, the 2001 is the ultimate expression of Sangiovese. Vinified in a glorious underground cathedral of a cellar, the wine saw twenty days' maceration on the skins followed by twenty-four months in French oak barriques, and was neither fined nor filtered. The Pacentis have worked tirelessly to preserve as much of the Montalcino terroir as possible through the winemaking process. The 2001 is a fitting legacy. **MP**

🍷🍷🍷 **Drink: to 2025**

Pago de los Capellanes is a very young winery in Ribera del Duero. The name means "Vineyard of the Chaplains," because it used to belong to the church and was tended by chaplains from the village of Pedrosa. The Rodero-Villa family owns it and more than 250 acres (101 ha) of vineyards surrounding the winery, 80 percent of which are Tempranillo, the rest Cabernet Sauvignon and Merlot.

Parcela el Picón is a single-vineyard bottling from a 5-acre plot (2 ha) of a special clone of Tinto Fino (Tempranillo), with a mesoclimate that gives an exceptional quality to the tannins. It is one of the few single-vineyard bottlings from Ribera del Duero, and is produced only in years considered exceptional— the first three being 1998, 1999, and 2003.

The 2003 harvest was extremely small and the production of Picón was no more than a quarter of that in 1999. The color is very dark garnet, almost black at the core. The aroma is of good intensity, complex, with meat, spices, very mature red fruit, and well-integrated wood. On the palate the wine is medium-bodied with good acidity, flavorful, fresh, and with a very long finish. **LG**

🍷🍷🍷🍷 **Drink: to 2018**

Pahlmeyer
Proprietary Red 1997

Origin USA, California, Napa Valley
Style Dry red wine, 14.7% ABV
Grapes C. Sauvignon, Merlot, Malbec, Others

Jason Pahlmeyer is a well-known figure in Napa Valley society—a former banker and trial lawyer, he developed excellent vineyards in the Coombsville and Atlas Peak districts. He also showed the world how the Napa Valley can produce superb Bordeaux-style reds using strictly traditional, Old World grape-growing and winemaking techniques. More importantly, he has done this in a region where technology dominates, where single-varietal labeling was and remains the norm, and where blends labeled simply as "red wine" have in the past been so terrible as to alienate consumers.

The fruit for Pahlmeyer's Proprietary Red Wine—a traditional Bordeaux blend of Cabernet Sauvignon, Merlot, Malbec, Cabernet Franc, and Petit Verdot—comes largely from steep, low-yield, hillside plantings. He harvests at the extremes of ripeness, with very high sugar content. The wine gets two years of barrel aging in 80 percent new oak and 20 percent one-year-old oak before being bottled unfined and unfiltered. Year after year, the result is a red wine of smooth tannins, bottomless fruit, and overwhelming force. **DD**

ⓈⓈⓈⓈⓈ **Drink: to 2017**

Paitin
Barbaresco Sorì Paitin 1999

Origin Italy, Piedmont, Langhi
Style Dry red wine, 14% ABV
Grape Nebbiolo

The official birth date of the prestigious Barbaresco DOCG is 1894, but Nebbiolo di Barbaresco was produced long before that date. The Barbaresco of the Sorì Paitin (*sorì* in Piedmontese dialect meaning a southerly exposed vineyard) had been bottled since 1893. The original property was bought in 1796 by Benedetto Elia from the Pelissero family. Today the cellar is run by Secondo Pasquero Elia and his two sons, Giovanni and Silvano.

The grapes for Sorì Paitin have a short maceration of eight or nine days at a temperature of about 90°F (32°C). Some 60 percent of the wine is then left to age in Slavonian oak casks, the remainder in French oak barriques. About 20 percent of the barriques are new each year.

Many producers were astonished by how much color Nebbiolo gave in 1999. The wine shows a deep but bright ruby-red color with light garnet hues. The nose is very elegant and complex, with tones of violets and red fruits (pomegranate, cherry), along with darker, tarry notes. Rich, soft, warm, and caressing, the wine has good nerve from its fine tannins and nicely integrated acidity. **AS**

ⓈⓈⓈⓈ **Drink: to 2030**

Alvaro Palacios
L'Ermita 2000

Origin Spain, Priorat
Style Dry red wine, 14% ABV
Grapes Grenache, Cabernet Sauvignon, Carignan

Descendientes de J. Palacios
Corullón 2001

Origin Spain, Bierzo
Style Dry red wine, 13.5% ABV
Grape Mencía

In the 1980s, René Barbier was the sales director for the Palacios Remondo winery in Rioja. Young Alvaro Palacios was often his travel companion, selling the family wines throughout the world. But both had a vision to make world-class wine on their own, in a new region. They finally settled in Priorat, where they created respectively Clos Mogador and Clos Dofí—later Finca Dofí, as technically it is not a *clos*.

But Álvaro wanted to go a step further. He scouted out the vineyards until he found what he was looking for. The amphitheater that forms the vineyard of L'Ermita is mainly planted with bush-trained, old-vine Grenache, complemented by some Carignan and a little Cabernet Sauvignon. It is a terraced slope of decomposed slate, known locally as *llicorella*, which transmits minerality to the wines.

In 2000 Palacios achieved a great balance for L'Ermita. The wine has a very intense, dark garnet color, a complex, intense aroma, with floral and mineral (graphite) notes, and plenty of ripe, dark fruit. Rich and fleshy mouthfeel, clean and precise, supple and full, with a very long finish. L'Ermita is deservedly Spain's most expensive wine. **LG**

🍷🍷🍷🍷🍷 **Drink: to 2020**

Bierzo is the gate between Castilla and Galicia, with a humid, warm climate. Nobody paid much attention to the local grape, Mencía, until Ricardo Pérez Palacios and his uncle Álvaro Palacios got there. They looked for old vineyards high in the mountains, where the berries were small, the juice concentrated and well colored. Until then, Mencía was considered a grape to make rosé but not much more.

The tiny mountain village, Corullón, where this wine's grapes are sourced, has very small plots of old-vine Mencía growing on slate slopes so steep that they have to be worked with a horse. 2001 was a very balanced vintage for the Bierzo region, making for elegant and balanced wines that age very slowly and well, taking time to reveal themselves.

In the 2001, the dark robe is followed on the nose by plenty of balsamic notes intermixed with acid strawberry, red currant, blueberry, and flowers, while on the palate there is a nice spine of lively acidity and focused flavors. The Palacios were looking for balance and elegance from the beginning—a style well represented in this long and beautifully defined 2001. **LG**

🍷🍷🍷 **Drink: to 2017**

Palari Faro

2004

Origin Italy, Sicily
Style Dry red wine, 14% ABV
Grapes Nerello Mascalese, N. Cappuccio, Others

Château Palmer

1961

Origin France, Bordeaux, Margaux
Style Dry red wine, 13% ABV
Grapes C. Sauvignon 47%, Merlot 47%, C. Franc 6%

Faro wine has been produced on the Messina Strait's hills for centuries. Apart from the period of Arab domination, wine flourished on Sicily until the first half of the twentieth century, when phylloxera ravished the vineyards. From then wine production was in decline, reaching its lowest ebb in 1985.

It was then that Salvatore Geraci was talked into saving the Faro DOC by Luigi Veronelli, father of Italian food and wine journalism. Geraci asked Piedmontese winemaker Donato Lanati to take a look at his vineyards—17 acres (7 ha) of incredibly steep terraces facing the sea and planted with very old vines of local and obscure grape varieties. Lanati, of course, fell in love with them and took up the challenge. The result is the Faro we know today—the height of elegance and personality.

The color is a not too deep ruby red, tending to orangey tinges with age. The nose is ample, earthy, spicy, and floral, with tones of red fruits enriched by hints of raw meat and fragrant Eastern spices. The palate is nicely dry and well proportioned, the round, sweet tannins supporting the fruit and sustaining the long, clean finish. **AS**

🥂🥂🥂 **Drink: to 2017**

A legendary wine from a legendary vintage, Château Palmer 1961 is one of those perfect wines one never forgets. One of the greatest vintages of the postwar period, 1961 got off to a difficult start with two harsh frosts, but a small crop of healthy, ripe grapes was collected. Small volumes and high concentration combined to produce wines of exceptional quality.

The Finnish wine connoisseur Pekka Nuikki sampled a bottle in July 2006, his seventh tasting of the wine: "The nose was incredible: wide open, with an odd but seductive mix of chocolate, truffle, black-currant, and caramel aromas. A full, rich, and sweet wine, with a soft, well-balanced finish. Not as deep, fat, and concentrated as I was expecting, but one of the best Palmer '61s that I have tasted. This was very enjoyable, but again unfortunately not as good as its legendary reputation led me to hope. This Palmer is excellent to drink now, and . . . my earnest advice is don't wait, don't sell—just be kind to yourself and enjoy it now."

As Nuikki's experience shows, this wine is capricious nowadays; he afterward admitted, "I still haven't found the 'perfect bottle' of 1961 Palmer." **SG**

🥂🥂🥂🥂🥂 **Drink: to 2021+**

Château Palmer, bought in 1816 by Englishman John Palmer. ➡

Château Pape-Clément 2000

Origin France, Bordeaux, Pessac-Léognan
Style Dry red wine, 13% ABV
Grapes Cabernet Sauvignon 60%, Merlot 40%

The reference to Pope Clement is no idle proprietorial fancy. In 1305, Bertrand de Goth, a major landowner in Bordeaux as well as its archbishop, became Pope Clement V, and the city named this estate in his honor. From 1939 it was owned by the Montagne family, and passed by marriage into the ownership of one of Bordeaux's most powerful *négociants*, Bernard Magrez. Pape-Clément remains his flagship estate in Bordeaux and, under his stewardship, quality has risen significantly.

The vineyards are less precocious than those of Haut-Brion, but the soils are clearly outstanding. The vinification is in the modern style, with a cold soak, punching-down of the cap, and extensive aging in mostly new oak barrels. Low yields ensure a high level of concentration. Since 1994 there has been a small production of excellent white wine. There always was a patch of white vines here, but the crop was never sold commercially. Then Bernard Magrez planted a further 5 acres (2 ha) alongside the château, and the result is a refined, if very oaky and costly white wine.

Few would question that Pape-Clément has become one of the most sumptuous and luxurious wines of Pessac-Léognan. Despite the concentration and oakiness, it retains a good deal of finesse. The 2000 epitomizes this style, with smoky, licorice-tinged, black-fruit aromas; it is full-bodied, tannic, and has considerable power, elegance, spiciness, and length. **SBr**

🍷🍷🍷🍷 **Drink: to 2020+**

FURTHER RECOMMENDATIONS
Other great vintages
1986 • 1989 • 1990 • 1995 • 1996 • 1998 • 2002 • 2005
More producers from Pessac-Léognan
Haut-Bailly • Haut-Brion • La Louvière
La Mission-Haut-Brion • Smith-Haut-Lafitte

Château Pape-Clément, home to Pope Clément V in his early life. ➡

Parker *Coonawarra Estate Terra Rossa First Growth* 1996

Origin Australia, South Australia, Coonawarra
Style Dry red wine, 14.5% ABV
Grapes Cabernet Sauvignon, Merlot

Parker Estate was established by the late John Parker in 1985 and sold to the Rathbone family, owners of Yering Station, in 2004. Being located in the southern end of Coonawarra, a notably cooler mesoclimate than the north end, great attention is paid to shoot positioning, to optimize ripening, and bunch thinning to restrict crop level.

The cheekily named First Growth is a selection of the best batches of wine off the back section of the 1985-planted Parker vineyard, augmented by some parcels from the nearby Balnaves vineyard. The soils are all classic Coonawarra *terra rossa*, with more gravel under the Cabernet and a shallow claypan under the Merlot.

Pete Bissell has made all the wines at Balnaves starting with the 1996 vintage. The First Growth is the flagship of the three Parker Estate reds, and is not produced every year (missing 1992, 1995, 1997, 2002, and 2003). The Merlot content varies between 10 and 14 percent. The grapes are machine-harvested and fermentation takes place in stainless steel, with extraction by rack and return. About 80 percent of the wine has a long maceration—up to thirty days on skins—"to get the right structure," says Bissell. It spends twenty months in new French oak. The First Growth has always been a rich, liberally oaked wine, its aromas turning to mocha and smoked charcuterie with bottle age. It is concentrated, fleshy, and rich in the mouth, with extra weight and alcohol warmth. **HH**
🝖🝖🝖 **Drink: to 2018**

FURTHER RECOMMENDATIONS
Other great vintages
1998 · 1999 · 2001 · 2004 · 2005
More producers from Coonawarra
Balnaves · Bowen Estate · Katnook
Majella · Penley · Rymill · Wynns

The Parker winery was built among the Coonawarra vineyards. ➡

Parusso
Barolo Bussia 2001

Origin Italy, Piedmont, Langhe
Style Dry red wine, 14% ABV
Grape Nebbiolo

The Bussia 2001 comes from three glorious crus on the Bussia hill, where the age of the vines ranges from ten to fifty years. The Bussia hill is in Monforte d'Alba, famous for yielding some of the most powerful, structured, and long-lived Barolos.

Brothers Marco and Tiziana Parusso run the family estate—Tiziana looking after the administrative side, and Marco the winemaking. Marco is always keen to try new ways of improving his wines—first on an experimental scale, then with what actually reaches the shelves. Despite this constant striving, his wines manage to taste effortlessly elegant and remarkably spontaneous.

The Barolo Bussia 2001 is a wine of amazing concentration and depth, with aromas ranging from the intensely fruity (bing cherries, cranberries, citrus), to the delicately floral, the spicy (vanilla, nutmeg), and the earthy (tar, leather). On the palate, it is so intense that it gives the impression of viscosity, but the rich smoothness is balanced by copious, beautifully fine-grained tannins. The perfect balance between the acidity and the tannins promises a long life for this serious wine. **AS**

☻☻☻☻ Drink: to 2040

Domaine Sylvain Pataille
Marsannay Fleur du Pinot 2011

Origin France, Burgundy, Côte de Nuits
Style Dry rosé wine, 13% ABV
Grape Pinot Noir

Dry rosé wine in Burgundy was virtually invented as a concept in the early 1900s in Marsannay, just south of Dijon. Today, Marsannay remains the spiritual home of Burgundian Rosé and, as such, is endowed with its own appellation: Marsannay Rosé.

Rosé has been around in Burgundy for almost 100 years, but a short list of producers make "great" Marsannay Rosé, and Sylvain Pataille, owner of a 35-acre (14-ha) domaine, is a master of this art. Pataille's pale, strawberry-colored wine is made from low-yielding, almost sixty-year-old Pinot Noir vines. He then ages it for almost two years before releasing it—half that time in oak and half that time in stainless-steel tanks. The only marked difference in his production method for the reds is that the grape skins have only a short contact time with their juice, limiting the amount of color that can be extracted from those skins. So as you can imagine, this is priced just like a red Marsannay—and a good one at that.

Although this wine has been specifically made by Pataille to age, and ten-plus years should not be a problem, even as a "baby" it remains one delicious mouthful of wine. **BN**

☻☻ Drink: to 2020

Paternoster *Aglianico del Vulture Don Anselmo* 1999

Origin Italy, Basilicata
Style Dry red wine, 13.5% ABV
Grape Aglianico

Filipa Pato
Nossa Tinto Calcario 2010

Origin Portugal, Bairrada
Style Dry red wine, 13.6% ABV
Grape Baga

Today it is difficult to explain Aglianico del Vulture in a few words. With the DOC a work in progress, very good, established producers are competing with good newcomers and "wannabes" charging silly prices for wines with impressive figures but no history or pedigree whatsoever.

The Paternoster family is one of the longest established wine families here, with its headquarters in Barile, one of the villages included in the DOC close to Mount Vulture itself. Mount Vulture is an extinct volcano, and having vineyards close to it means that the vines can exploit its special type of soil. This soil is rich in tufa, and in particular silicates, which are able to retain water and sustain the vines through the long and often dry growing season.

The Don Anselmo 1999 is a great wine, and as such it needed time to come out. It has a garnet color and a complex nose that goes from sour cherries to black truffles, from spices to mint and balsamic tones. On the palate its tannins are grippy but very fine grained, supporting the wine without being cumbersome. The finish is long, complex, clearly defined and deeply satisfying. **AS**

🍷🍷🍷 Drink: to 2025

Filipa Pato's father, one of Bairrada's leading lights, has been a champion of the region's notoriously difficult high-acid, high-tannin Baga grape. Like him, she is a self-trained winemaker whose inquiring mind and gentle touch are taking this variety to elegant new heights.

Since Pato started making her own wines in 2001 she has created an enviable portfolio of old, densely planted Baga vineyards on well-drained chalky clay soils. These low-yielding, organically cultivated vineyards produce complex, balanced wines.

First made in 2009, this wine is sourced from Pato's best vineyards, which average eighty years old. Reviving a Roman tradition, Nossa is part-fermented in oak *lagares* (shallow open fermenters), which results in a very gentle extraction. The balance is fermented in small closed-oak fermenters (*balseiro*) in which all the wine undergoes a two-month maceration on skins to refine the tannins. With its ultrafine tannins and Atlantic freshness, Pato has cracked the modern conundrum. Nossa is an elegant, very precise Baga with delicate red fruits. It is broachable, yet can be cellared with confidence. **SA**

🍷🍷🍷 Drink: to 2030+

Luis Pato *Quinta do Ribeirinho*
Pé Franco Bairrada 1999

Origin Portugal, Bairrada
Style Dry red wine, 13% ABV
Grape Baga

Luis Pato is, in his own words, the "defender of Baga, the most original grape of Bairrada." Baga is the traditional variety for Bairrada, even though it needs the best vineyards and vintages to show its mettle. Without these, it can be harsh in the extreme, with massive tannic structure hiding what fruit there is.

Quinta do Ribeirinho Pé Franco is the conclusion of a lifetime's ambition for Pato—an attempt to make a pre-phylloxera wine in the modern age. Some of the Pato vineyards are sandy, and fortunately phylloxera does not like sand, so a small vineyard was planted in 1988 with ungrafted Baga vines.

The vineyard has been expanded to 8.5 acres (3.5 ha) since the first planting, but low yields from the ungrafted vines mean, in effect, only one glass of wine from each vine each vintage—the equivalent of just 1,800 bottles per year. Long maceration gives the wine a classic Bairrada structure, with very firm tannins, but supporting a more modern fruit-forward style than is often the case, with sweet cherry and plum aromas overlaid with spice and licorice from its one year in oak. A very modern wine, but firmly in the classic Bairrada tradition. **GS**

☙☙☙ Drink: to 2020

Château Pavie
2003

Origin France, Bordeaux, St.-Emilion
Style Dry red wine, 14% ABV
Grapes Merlot 70%, C. Franc 20%, C. Sauvignon 10%

There is no wine in Bordeaux more controversial than Gérard Perse's Château Pavie, and the 2003 vintage divided opinions like no claret before or since. After his first taste of the wine during the 2003 en primeur campaign, Robert Parker wrote: "An off-the-chart effort from perfectionist proprietors Chantal and Gérard Perse . . . a wine of sublime richness, minerality, delineation, and nobleness."

Jancis Robinson MW, however, was less impressed: "Completely unappetizing overripe aromas. . . . More reminiscent of a late-harvest Zinfandel than a red Bordeaux, with its unappetizing green notes." Clive Coates MW declared: "Anyone who thinks this is good wine needs a brain and palate transplant." And Michael Schuster, reporting on the 2003 Bordeaux campaign for *The World of Fine Wine*, wrote, ". . . very strange nose for claret; a ripe, raisiny, slightly medicinal combination of Port and the bitter almonds of Amarone di Valpolicella . . . . No score." And on it went, exploding into a British versus U.S. critics battle, with Parker labeling the British "classicists" as "reactionaries." Buy a bottle and decide for yourself. **SG**

☙☙☙☙ Drink: to 2020+

The Château Pavie winery lies just below Château Ausone. ➦

Château Pavie-Macquin 1999

Origin France, Bordeaux, St.-Emilion
Style Dry red wine, 13% ABV
Grapes Merlot 70%, C. Franc 25%, C. Sauvignon 5%

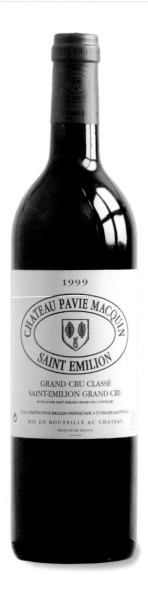

Albert Macquin, who died in 1911 and was an early owner of this property, was one of the heroes of European viticulture, grafting vines on to U.S. rootstocks after phylloxera decimated the vineyards of France. In 1990 this was one of the first Bordeaux properties to adopt biodynamism, but a catastrophic attack of mildew in 1993 persuaded Nicolas Thienpont, who took over the management in 1994, to abandon the system.

The soils are fairly uniform and in some places quite deep, giving wines with considerable power. When young, Pavie-Macquin can be somewhat overwhelmed by its tannins, though after a few years the fruit does re-emerge. Vinification is traditional, although, in a rare flight of whimsy, the vats carry names reminiscent of nineteenth-century bodice-ripper fiction: Cunégonde, Berthe, and Eliane.

In the new St.-Emilion classification of 2006, Pavie-Macquin was promoted to Premier Cru Classé, only to discover a short time later that a court, in response to lawsuits from disgruntled proprietors whose estates had been demoted, had suspended the classification. Nicolas Thienpont was not greatly perturbed by this. His peers, wine critics, and the marketplace in general had recognized the outstanding quality of Pavie-Macquin. The 1999 was not an acclaimed vintage in St.-Emilion, but at Pavie-Macquin the terroir spoke out: The wine is tannic, still formidable, and highly concentrated, yet the fruit shines through. **SBr**

🍷🍷🍷 **Drink: to 2020**

FURTHER RECOMMENDATIONS
Other great vintages
1998 • 2000 • 2001 • 2004 • 2005 • 2009 • 2010
More producers from St.-Emilion
l'Angélus • Beau-Séjour Bécot
Cheval Blanc • Magdelaine • Pavie

Gnarled old vines, the priceless legacy of this St.-Emilion château. ➡

Peay Vineyards
Pinot Noir 2004

Origin USA, California, Sonoma Coast
Style Dry red wine, 13.9% ABV
Grape Pinot Noir

Peay is one of a handful of small-production wine growers whose exceptional wines have brought increasing attention to this land of rugged hills, deep canyons, coastal fog, and cool climate.

In the 1990s, Nick and Andy Peay dreamed of finding a climate and terrain where Pinot Noir might develop the full character of the grape in the context of a distinctive location. After buying this former sheep ranch they planted mostly to Pinot Noir and Syrah, with some Chardonnay and tiny amounts of Viognier, Roussanne, and Marsanne.

The Peays seek to produce Pinot Noir that has "volume without weight." Meticulous care in the vineyard and a gentle touch in the winery have created wines of great integrity, balance, and structure. The 2004 has depth and concentration balanced by the fresh acidity and minerality that seem to characterize the site. In 2005, they produced two Pinot Noirs, recognizing that the vines have matured enough to reflect differences in the terroir. If the vineyard continues to evolve on its present trajectory, Peay Pinot Noir will surely become one of the most coveted wines in the United States. **JS**

🚫🚫🚫 **Drink: to 2019**

Giorgio Pelissero
Barbaresco Vanotu 1999

Origin Italy, Piedmont, Langhe
Style Dry red wine, 14% ABV
Grape Nebbiolo

The family-run Pelissero estate is located in the district of Treiso in the Barbaresco production zone. The family has transformed the Pelissero grape-growing business into one of the most respected winemaking firms in Barbaresco. The first bottles date back to 1960 and were produced by Luigi, now succeeded by his enologist son Giorgio.

Vanotu, the nickname for Giovanni in the local dialect, is the name of the vineyard that belonged to Giorgio's grandfather, Giovanni, and is also the name of the firm's flagship single-vineyard bottling. Thanks to its unique location, climate, and predominantly calcareous soil, the Vanotu vineyard yields very good wine even in lesser vintages.

Giorgio has given the wine an unmistakably modern ethos and ages it in barriques, 80 percent new, for eighteen months to create a wine with good fruit concentration and sweet tannins that can be enjoyed relatively young. Despite rains in mid-September, 1999 was an excellent vintage in Piedmont. The Vanotu 1999 has rich raspberry and cherry aromas and flavors, with well-integrated vanilla and spice, and velvety tannins. **KO**

🚫🚫🚫 **Drink: to 2019**

◀ Pinot Noir wine is swirled against a light to reveal its color.

Penfolds *Bin 95 Grange* 1971

Origin Australia, South Australia
Style Dry red wine, 12.3% ABV
Grapes Shiraz 87%, Cabernet Sauvignon 13%

Penfolds's flagship red wine, the brainchild of Max Schubert in the early 1950s, was conceived as an Australian take on the style of classed-growth Bordeaux. In an era when the country's output was focused on fortified wines, Schubert had the vision to produce something as complex and ageworthy as the best of classic France. Short of all but the scarcest plantings of the Bordeaux varieties, he had to fall back on Shiraz—then, as now, the most widely disseminated red grape in South Australia.

Astonishingly, Grange found no commercial takers in its earliest vintages. The moment of serendipity came in 1960 when, on a visit to the Magill facility where the wine was made, a Penfolds board member asked to retaste the first efforts. Returning to company HQ in Sydney, he spread the news: The wine was on its way to becoming a legend.

Speaking in 1993, Schubert said, "If you had to point to a wine that fulfilled all the ambitions of Grange, it would have to be 1971." At the Wine Olympiad in Paris in 1979, it won a gold medal and topped a class that included the northern Rhône's finest. It was an extravagantly great harvest, and the fruit quality is reflected in a wine that has stayed the distance effortlessly. Aged for eighteen months in new American oak, it is laden with aromas of preserved fruits, backed by the complex, earthy, truffly notes of bottle age. Its tannic structure was still intact, though beautifully supple, at thirty-five years old, and the finish is brilliantly sustained. **SW** ☉☉☉☉☉ **Drink: to 2021+**

FURTHER RECOMMENDATIONS

Other great vintages

1966 • 1986 • 1991 • 1994 • 1996 • 1998 • 2004 • 2005

More Australian Shiraz-based wines

Jim Barry The Armagh • Glaetzer Amon-Ra
Henschke's Hill of Grace • Wyndham Estate Black Cluster

Penfolds *Bin 707 Cabernet Sauvignon* 2004

Origin Australia, South Australia
Style Dry red wine, 13.5% ABV
Grape Cabernet Sauvignon

The Cabernet equivalent of Grange, Bin 707 was famously named after the Boeing jet by a former Qantas marketing man and first sold as such with the 1964 vintage—though Penfolds had made Cabernet wines from the renowned Kalimna Block 42 vineyard (the vines of which were planted in 1888) since 1948. Indeed, Max Schubert experimented with Cabernet from Kalimna in the early days of his Grange project, but conceded that the vineyard was ultimately too inconsistent and too small to produce commercially viable volumes of fine wine. Because of this inconsistency of fruit supply and wine style, no Bin 707 was made between 1970 and 1975. But in 1976, Coonawarra grapes were used for the first time and, since then, the wine has established itself as a benchmark Australian Cabernet Sauvignon.

Bin 707 is built like the jet plane after which it is named—an extremely powerful wine, with high alcohol, ripe tannins, and lots of sweet fruit. Grapes are sourced from across South Australia's premium red wine regions, including the Barossa Valley, Coonawarra, and McLaren Vale. The blended wine is then usually aged for up to eighteen months in new American oak hogsheads.

In the very best years, Block 42 is made as a separate wine (this occurred most recently in 1996 and 2004)—although Bin 707 was also made in these vintages. The 2004 used 4,500 liters of Block 42, and this helped to produce one of the best Bin 707s for several years. **SG**

☺☺☺☺ **Drink: to 2020**

FURTHER RECOMMENDATIONS
Other great vintages
1991 · 1995 · 1996 · 1997 · 1998 · 2002 · 2004 · 2007
More Penfolds red wines
Kalimna Bin 28 · Magill Estate
RWT · St. Henri · Special Bins (42, 60A)

Penfolds *Block 42 Kalimna Cabernet Sauvignon* 2004

Origin Australia, South Australia
Style Dry red wine, 13.5% ABV
Grape Cabernet Sauvignon

Tinto Pesquera *Janus Gran Reserva* 1995

Origin Spain, Ribera del Duero
Style Dry red wine, 13% ABV
Grape Tinto Fino (Tempranillo)

Even in the uniquely rich and varied Penfolds range, the Special Bins, of which this wine is one, have a particular cachet. A wine from Kalimna Block 42 was the second commercial release of Grange (the 1953) and another the first of Bin 707 (the 1964). The only other released vintages of Kalimna Block 42 have been 1961, 1963, 1996, and 2004.

Block 42 is on the edge of the 10-acre (4-ha) Kalimna Vineyard in Barossa Valley and was planted in the mid-1880s, making these the oldest Cabernet Sauvignon vines in the world. The naturally low yields of these ancient vines, which are on their own roots rather than grafted onto phylloxera-resistant rootstock as most vines are, must surely contribute to the extraordinary density and purity of the wines.

The 2004 was fermented in stainless-steel vats, before finishing its fermentation and maturation in oak barrels. It is awe-inspiring in its apparently contradictory qualities: astonishingly intense aromas of opulent but very vivid black fruit and incense, and an expressive palate that is at once dense and graceful, refined and saturated, with the floating quality achieved by only the greatest wines. **NB**
🍷🍷🍷🍷🍷 **Drink: to 2050+**

Alejandro Fernández created Pesquera, one of the first wines in the region, in 1972. There are three labels with the Pesquera name—all made exclusively from the Tempranillo grape.

In 1982, the birth year of the Ribera del Duero appellation, Alejandro experimented by starting with the same grapes, fermenting half of them in full bunches in medieval stone *lagares* and pressed in the traditional way, the other half, destemmed, in stainless-steel tanks. Both wines were blended and aged for three years in old American oak barrels. The wine was subsequently produced following the same labor-intensive recipe, but only in the very best years and in very limited quantities.

1995 was one of those special years in Ribera, so Fernández bottled a very serious Janus, even austere in its youth, representing the elegant rusticity that is the essence of Pesquera. Dark ruby color, intense aroma with red fruit, lactic notes, spicy oak, elegant tertiary sensations, leather and grilled meat, a hint of truffle. Medium to full-bodied in the mouth, with good acidity, balanced, with a strong core of fruit, supple and persistent. **LG**
🍷🍷🍷🍷 **Drink: to 2020**

Old, bush-trained Tinto Fino vines near Pesquera de Douro. ➜

Château Petit-Village
2000

Origin France, Bordeaux, Pomerol
Style Dry red wine, 13% ABV
Grapes Merlot 75%, C. Sauvignon 17%, C. Franc 8%

The vineyards of Petit-Village lie in a triangular plot on quite stony, gravelly soils. The property was owned by the Prats family, then sold by Bruno Prats to AXA Millésimes in 1989.

In the past, Petit-Village had a mixed reputation and Pomerol insiders suggest that Prats tolerated yields that were too high, because he was more used to the larger crops obtained in the Médoc. The AXA team introduced a second wine in 1995, which allowed them to select more carefully the wine released as the grand vin. They also restructured the winery to allow more parcel selections in the vineyard. The proportion of new oak has varied; in some vintages it was as high as 100 percent, but more recently it has been maintained at 70 percent.

Many vintages of the 1990s were unsatisfactory, but by 2000 Petit-Village had hit its stride. The new oak is certainly evident on the nose, but there is richness of fruit and elegance, too. Whereas the palate is marked by concentration and fleshiness, with big ripe tannins to give it structure, the finish is as sumptuous as one would hope for from a top-flight Pomerol. **SBr**

🚫🚫🚫 **Drink: to 2025**

Petrolo
Galatrona 2004

Origin Italy, Tuscany
Style Dry red wine, 14.5% ABV
Grape Merlot

Galatrona is the brainchild of Lucia Bazzocchi Sanjust and her son Luca. The Bazzocchi family has owned the estate since the 1940s, but it is only since the 1980s that the wine production has been devoted to uncompromising quality. This change was carried out thanks to the consultancy of two key figures in Tuscan winemaking—Carlo Ferrini and Giulio Gambelli.

The Galatrona 2004 is a wine bound to impress as soon as the first drop makes its way from bottle to glass. The color is deep, with a bluish, purplish vibrancy to it. This liveliness of color heightens the expectation of sweet and sour ripeness of dark summer fruit. But on sniffing and sipping, even these expectations will be exceeded.

On the tongue, it is like a thick caress of glycerin, with immense and perfectly shaped waves of black currant, morello cherry, and cranberry, then more earthy, black trufflelike tones, closing with a refreshing, uplifting, balsamic zing. The tannins are very fine and evenly distributed, and together with the superbly balanced acidity will ensure the graceful aging of this wine over many years. **AS**

🚫🚫🚫🚫🚫 **Drink: to 2030**

◀ The modest buildings of the Petit-Village estate in Pomerol.

Pétrus 1989

Origin France, Bordeaux, Pomerol
Style Dry red wine, 13.5% ABV
Grapes Merlot 95%, Cabernet Franc 5%

Pétrus has become a wine of legend. Its fame is far from recent, and the wine was fetching high prices a century ago. The Loubat family were the owners from 1925 onwards, but the Moueix family became the sole agents for Pétrus in 1943, thus beginning their long association with the property. In a deal that remained secret for decades, Moueix became majority shareholders as long ago as 1969.

If the château itself, as so often in Pomerol, is unremarkable, the same is hardly true of the vineyards. Within the complex soil structure of the Pomerol plateau, where the best vineyards are located, there is a 49-acre (20 ha) sector composed of deep blueish clay soils with a marked iron content, and Pétrus occupies over half of this. Only 2.47 acres (1 ha) of the Pétrus vineyard is on gravelly soil.

If Pétrus is a powerful and very long-lived wine, that has more to do with its vines and soil than with a heavy hand in the winery. The vineyard just happens to lie on a quite superb parcel of land, and the owners of neighboring Château Gazin, who sold 10 acres (4 ha) of vines to Pétrus in 1969, have been kicking themselves ever since. Pétrus is never a brutal or extracted wine, as the 1989 demonstrates. Even today, the color shows little evolution, and the might of the wine is evident on the nose, which is sumptuous and oaky, yet airily elegant. The palate is richly fruity and voluptuous, and although there are powerful tannins here, the finish is delicious and bright, elegant as well as majestic. **SBr**

❸❸❸❸❸ **Drink: to 2035**

FURTHER RECOMMENDATIONS
Other great vintages
1929 · 1945 · 1947 · 1961 · 1964 · 1970 · 1975 · 1982 1990 · 1995 · 1998 · 2000 · 2001 · 2003 · 2005 · 2006
More Mouiex properties
Hosannah · La Fleur-Pétrus · Trotanoy · Providence

Pétrus has long been one of the world's most sought-after wines. ➦

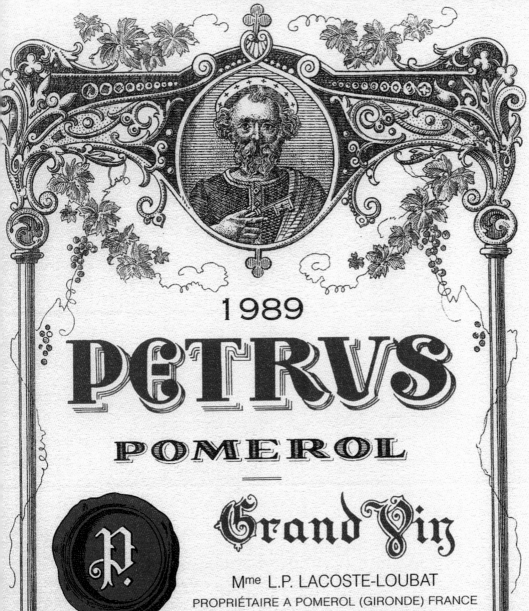

1989

PETRVS

POMEROL

Grand Vin

Mme L.P. LACOSTE-LOUBAT

PROPRIÉTAIRE A POMEROL (GIRONDE) FRANCE

MIS en BOUTEILLES au CHATEAU

LP98201

Alc. 13.5% vol.   APPELLATION POMEROL CONTRÔLEE   75 cl

Château de Pez 2001

Origin France, Bordeaux, St.-Estèphe
Style Dry red wine, 13% ABV
Grapes C. Sauvignon 45%, Merlot 44%, Others 11%

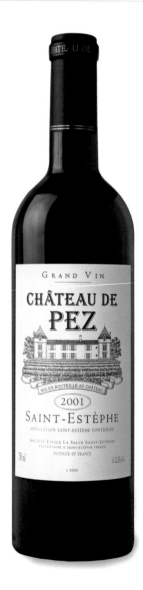

This property has existed for about 500 years, although vines were only planted in the late sixteenth century. Until the estate was acquired by the Rouzaud family of Champagne Roederer in 1995, it was owned by Robert Dousson. In 1970 Dousson decided to bottle separately one barrel of each of the five traditional Bordeaux varieties. Since monoculture is virtually unheard of in the Médoc, this gave tasters a fascinating opportunity to see how the grape varieties matured when unblended.

When the Dousson era came to an end in 1995, the new owners, the Rouzauds, made numerous changes in the vineyard, introducing a more severe selection at harvest and installing temperature control in the old wooden fermentation vats. Dousson's wines were medium-bodied yet had an austerity commonly encountered in St.-Estèphe, due to his high proportion of Cabernet Sauvignon. Under the Rouzauds, the proportion of Merlot has been increased and the extraction is probably gentler than it was during Dousson's time.

Whereas the old style of de Pez required about a decade in bottle to show it at its best, the new wine is far more supple and approachable, though it is just as likely to age well. The 2000 is robust and firm, though not harsh, and the 2002 is charming and stylish. The 2001 strikes the perfect note: with sufficient structure to gain in complexity, but with a supple texture and enough freshness to give the wine immediate appeal. **SBr**

Ө Ө Ө **Drink: to 2017**

FURTHER RECOMMENDATIONS
Other great vintages
1982 • 1995 • 1998 • 2000 • 2002 • 2005 • 2009 • 2010
More St.-Estèphe châteaux
Calon-Ségur • Cos d'Estournel • Haut-Marbuzét • Lafon-Rochet • Montrose • Les Ormes-de-Pez • Phélan-Ségur

An1899 advertisement for le Pez featuring a view of the Gironde. ➔

Joseph Phelps
Insignia 2002

Origin USA, California, Napa Valley
Style Dry red wine, 14% ABV
Grapes C. Sauvignon 78%, Merlot 14%, Others 8%

Piaggia
Carmignano Riserva 1999

Origin Italy, Tuscany
Style Dry red wine, 13% ABV
Grapes Sangiovese 70%, C. Sauvignon 20%, Merlot 10%

Insignia was born in 1974, but its first few vintages were either Cabernet or Merlot. Only in 1977 did it become established as a blend.

Stylistically, the wine changed during the 1990s. The proportion of new oak increased, and the winemakers chose high-ripeness lots, so alcohol levels rose to 14 percent or more. Barrel aging was prolonged, usually between twenty-four and twenty-eight months. By the end of the decade, Petit Verdot was finding its way into the blend, and in 2004 Insignia, for the first time, contained only estate-grown fruit. In line with Phelps's evolution in the 2000s, production became more limited.

Insignia has been consistently excellent over three decades, despite being produced in substantial volumes. With its opaque color and its sumptuous aromas of black fruits, toast, and coffee, the Insignia 2002 is typical of this magisterial wine. It is plump, highly concentrated, and its weight of fruit is sustained by powerful tannins rather than by forceful acidity. Although slightly austere in its youth, Insignia is designed to be aged, which it does with ease, gaining complexity with the years. **SBr**

🍷🍷🍷🍷 Drink: to 2030

One of the most neglected Italian DOCGs, Carmignano has an ancient history and boasts what can be considered to be the first appellation law in the world, dating back to 1716.

With such a long history, some ups and downs were inevitable. In 1932, when Italy was under fascist rule, the Carmignano area was incorporated into the Chianti DOC—a move that threatened to destroy centuries of tradition. In 1960 a few producers started reclaiming Carmignano's autonomy. The DOC was conceded in 1975, and the DOCG in 1990.

The Carmignano Riserva 1999 is a great wine, showing a bright ruby color with a brick-orange rim. The nose offers blueberry, cranberry, and cherry notes before exerting an earthier appeal and closing with a bitter chocolate aroma that balances the sweet ripe fruit. In the mouth it is quite bold and fleshy, pleasantly mineral, with perfectly balanced acidity and tannins that are very finely textured. The abiding impression is of a superlative wine, very enjoyable if drunk in its first decade but still with pleasant surprises dependably in store if allowed to age for a few more years. **AS**

🍷🍷 Drink: to 2020

Château Pichon-Longueville Baron 2004

Château Pichon-Longueville Comtesse de Lalande 1982

Origin France, Bordeaux, Pauillac
Style Dry red wine, 13.5% ABV
Grapes C. Sauvignon, Merlot, C. Franc, Petit Verdot

Origin France, Bordeaux, Pauillac
Style Dry red wine, 12.5% ABV
Grapes C. Sauvignon 45%, Merlot 35%, Others 20%

Until the mid-nineteenth century, the Pichon-Longueville and Pichon-Lalande estates were one. Family disputes led to the eventual division of the property, and in 1933 Pichon-Longueville was bought by the Bouteillier family. Under their stewardship, the estate and its dashing château became run down, until in 1987 it was acquired by the present owners, AXA Millésimes.

The quality of the wines had been fairly poor in the 1960s and 1970s, especially for a second growth, but Jean-Michel Cazes and his able team worked swiftly to restore the wines, as well as the château, to its former grandeur. Practices such as machine-harvesting were immediately halted, and increased attention was paid to viticulture and yields.

The results have been triumphant. The 2004, although less prized than 2000 or 2005, nonetheless shows Pichon in all its glory. The nose, with its notes of chocolate and licorice as well as black currant, has real power, while the wine is mouth-filling, highly concentrated, and shows no rough edges. Power and structure can be fatiguing, but Pichon is also remarkably fresh, with no excessive extraction. **SBr**
🍷🍷🍷🍷 Drink: to 2030+

Anomalies in both the history and location of this estate led, for a time, to the bureaucratic insistence that two separate appellation wines be produced from it. A process of untiring appeal eventually led to its being accepted that the estate has always been thought of as Pauillac, and not as St.-Julien.

The estate is planted on clay-based gravel beds. A mainstream modern vinification involves eighteen months' aging in barrique, with around half the wood renewed in each vintage. Traditionally seen as softer and more "feminine" than the majority of Pauillacs, the debate arises as to which exercises the greater influence over the style—the relatively high Merlot content or the St.-Julien factor.

The 1982 is one of the more singular wines of a generally heroic vintage. From the start, there was an overripe style to the fruit that one authority found reminiscent of prunes. It had a ravishing floral top note, too, in its youth, which has yielded to secondary and tertiary aromas of wild mushrooms and earth. The tannins have melded into the wine, but the full-blown cherry and blackberry fruit on it remain intact. **SW**
🍷🍷🍷🍷 Drink: to 2017+

Pieve di Santa Restituta *Brunello di Montalcino Sugarille* 2000

Origin Italy, Tuscany, Montalcino
Style Dry red wine, 13% ABV
Grape Sangiovese

Dominio del Pingus

2004

Origin Spain, Ribera del Duero
Style Dry red wine, 14% ABV
Grape Tempranillo

The church of Santa Restituta has very ancient origins, featuring on documents dating back to 650 CE. Records exist of wine being produced from the church's vineyard in the twelfth century.

The property was sold in 1972 to Roberto Bellini who, with his wife Franca, extended the vineyards, constructed the modern winemaking facilities, and restored the ancient cellar. They found an experienced partner in Angelo Gaja, who took over the estate's wine production in the 1990s.

Gaja produces three wines at Santa Restituta—an IGT (Promis) and two Brunellos, the Rennina and the Sugarille. Both are convincing Brunellos, but maybe the Sugarille is the more compelling of the two, thanks to its masculine, less tamed appeal. The Sugarille 2000, in particular, is a great example of a Brunello that manages to combine complexity with great purity of fruit. The engaging sour cherry and sweet leather notes are beautifully matched by a powerful but never intrusive tannin, which is somewhat smoothed by the toasty oak. Although drinking well eight years after the vintage, it will be improving for two or three times as long. **AS**

❸❸❸❸ **Drink: to 2030**

Danish-born Peter Sisseck established Pingus in 1995. His aim was to produce "an unmistakably Spanish, terroir-driven wine . . . a garage wine." Its fame soared after Robert Parker awarded the inaugural 1995 a score of 96 out of 100 points.

"Pingus" was the nickname given to Sisseck by his uncle Peter Vinding-Diers, who sent him to Ribera del Duero to embark on a new project at Hacienda Monasterio. Inspired by Jean-Luc Thunevin's efforts at Château Valandraud in St.-Emilion, Sisseck located three separate plots, each containing very old vines of Tinto Fino (Tempranillo), and set up the Pingus winery. Sisseck uses "natural" methods—severe cropping from old vines, fermenting the must in new oak barrels, and racking the wine into more new oak barrels—to produce a very big, rich, powerful wine, with up to 15 percent alcohol.

Sisseck called the 1995 and 1996 "big and brutal," but several subsequent vintages have shown more restraint and elegance. The 2004 vintage of Pingus, which received a perfect 100-point Parker score, was sold at more than $1,430 (£700; €1,045) a bottle by a London wine merchant in 2007. **SG**

❸❸❸❸❸ **Drink: to 2035+**

Pintia
Toro 2003

Origin Spain, Toro
Style Dry red wine, 15% ABV
Grape Tinta de Toro (Tempranillo)

Pintia is the name of the Toro wine from Vega Sicilia—its producers were among the first to focus on the appellation. Their project started with the purchase of old and ungrafted vines in the villages of Toro and San Román de Hornija, where the winery was later built. They also planted some new vines, also on their own roots and pruned *en gobelet*.

The winery is almost identical to Alión, and built by the same architect. What is different is the huge cold room, where the harvested grapes are stored overnight to cool down to about 41°F (5°C), allowing a four-day natural prefermentation maceration.

In the extremely warm 2003 vintage, the challenge was to avoid the heat showing in the wine. The Pintia is extremely dark in color, almost black and opaque. Intense, even if a bit closed on the nose at first, with black fruits, flowers, minerals (chalk), and well-integrated wood. Although the wine is full-bodied and generous in structure, the alcohol is perfectly integrated and balanced by the acidity, with fresh fruit and a long finish. There are still some tannins that will be more highly polished after a few more years in bottle. **LG**

🜂🜂 **Drink: to 2018**

Podere *Salicutti Brunello*
di Montalcino Piaggione 2003

Origin Italy, Tuscany, Montalcino
Style Dry red wine, 15% ABV
Grape Sangiovese

Francesco Leanza came to winemaking late in life, but lost no time in establishing a formidable reputation in Montalcino. Humble, hard-working, and with no false modesty, he confesses to being as surprised as anyone by his success. An analytical chemist by training, Francesco purchased the estate in 1990, and planted 9 acres (4 ha) of organically cultivated vineyards in 1994. Piaggione, the only vineyard from which he sources grapes for Brunello, enjoys a textbook, southern exposure and is rich in the limestone responsible for the exceptional power of the wines of Montalcino.

In the late twentieth century, Brunello di Montalcino enjoyed an unprecedented renaissance in popularity. Investment poured in, and the value of both land and grapes skyrocketed. With investors clamoring for returns, few wines now merit the prices they command. Francesco Leanza is swimming against that tide, however. Given the relative youth of the Piaggione vineyard, the 2003 is nothing short of a miracle. Fat and sleek in the mouth, it has deftly judged acidity and layers of black fruit, cherry, licorice, sweet spice, and tar. **MP**

🜂🜂🜂🜂 **Drink: to 2020**

Poliziano *Vino Nobile di Montepulciano Asinone* 2001

Origin Italy, Tuscany, Montepulciano
Style Dry red wine, 14% ABV
Grapes Prugnolo Gentile (Sangiovese) 90%, Others 10%

Federico Carletti has run the Poliziano estate since 1980, after completing a degree in agricultural science and doing a stint in a northern Italian wine cellar. He quickly understood that the success of the venture depended on knowledge of the most advanced techniques of international viticulture and winemaking. For this, his friendship with former fellow student Carlo Ferrini and with Maurizio Castelli was essential.

Today Carletti also owns a property in the Tuscan Maremma, in one of the best areas of the Morellino di Scansano DOC. His most important wine to date, however, is Asinone, a Vino Nobile di Montepulciano that combines the best local traditions with the most cutting-edge international winemaking.

The Prugnolo Gentile grapes used for its production are the result of a mass selection back in the 1960s. The bunches are much smaller and more compact than those of regular Sangiovese. The wine is dark and dense in appearance. On the palate it is powerful but smooth and complex, with the balsamic notes from the oak refreshing its ripe and soft fruit appeal. **AS**

🍷🍷🍷 **Drink: to 2020+**

Domaine Ponsot *Clos de la Roche Vieilles Vignes* 2001

Origin France, Burgundy, Côte de Nuits
Style Dry red wine, 13% ABV
Grape Pinot Noir

"The best Pinot Noir is made outside of Burgundy," quips Laurent Ponsot with a wry smile. "We make Burgundy here." One of his finest comes from the Clos de la Roche, an enclosed vineyard planted with grapes since the Middle Ages. The Clos is also a nursery, and it has long been a Ponsot tradition to select cuttings from their own vineyards. In the 1940s, Laurent's father, Jean Marie, planted the vines that now constitute the "Vieilles Vignes."

The estate has long been willing to take risks, often harvesting extremely late to avoid chaptalizing. Laurent has been more regular, developing a style that is rich, dense, and incredibly long on the palate. He hit the right balance in 2001, a vintage that benefited from a new, naturally cooled, gravity-flow winery dug into a hill.

Very outspoken, Laurent ages all of his wines in old barrels, because "new wood masks the true quality of a wine." Often showing poorly in blind tastings against sexier wines lavishly influenced by new oak, their subdued, alluring aromas, with hints of spiced black plums, raspberries, and cocoa seduce the educated palate, as does the vibrant acidity. **JP**

🍷🍷🍷🍷 **Drink: to 2030**

Château Pontet-Canet

2004

Origin France, Bordeaux, Pauillac
Style Dry red wine, 13% ABV
Grapes C. Sauvignon 62%, Merlot 32%, Others 6%

In 1975, a Cognac producer called Guy Tesseron bought this property, whose wines were marketed by former owners as a non-vintage wine supplied to French railways. When his son Alfred took over, he instituted changes that soon ameliorated quality. He is aided by a superb winemaker in Jean-Michel Comme, and consultant Michel Rolland.

Jean-Michel Comme is an instinctive winemaker: He has not been afraid, for instance, to dispense with temperature control—he would rather keep his vats under personal observation, cosseting the young wine into a long, slow fermentation. Although the team here favor a gentle extraction, Pontet-Canet, with its high proportion of Cabernet and aging in a substantial percentage of new oak, remains a powerful, tannic wine that requires years of bottle age to reveal its full glory.

Recent vintages have seen the ascent of Pontet-Canet into one of the great wines of Pauillac. Prices have been rising, but Pontet-Canet remains undervalued, because the trade and customers remain unaware of the extraordinary progress made by Alfred Tesseron and his team. **SBr**

🍷🍷🍷 **Drink: to 2035**

Château Poujeaux

2005

Origin France, Bordeaux, Moulis
Style Dry red wine, 13% ABV
Grapes C. Sauvignon 50%, Merlot 40%, Others 10%

Poujeaux has been owned by the Theil family since 1921. In those days, the property had been broken into three estates, but over time the Theils managed to reunite the property. The viticulture is attentive, with plowing of the soil and green-harvesting when necessary; the winemaking is scrupulous.

In its youthful appeal, its succulence and fine texture, and its ability to age, Poujeaux has long been the very model of a fine Cru Bourgeois. In 2003, it was one of nine properties to be promoted to Cru Bourgeois Exceptionnel. The category of Cru Bourgeois is now defunct, but Poujeaux retains the features that made it so admirable in the first place.

Château Poujeaux is a serious wine, generously tannic without being extracted or overwrought. It never seems to go through a phase at which it is less than highly drinkable, and vintages such as 1990 continue to age beautifully.

The superb 2005 is in the same mold. There is plenty of oak on the nose, but the wine is suave and elegant; impeccably balanced, it impresses without striving to impress. And over the years it has demonstrated remarkable consistency. **SBr**

🍷🍷 **Drink: to 2020**

The 1922 vintage, made soon after the Theils took over Poujeaux. ▶

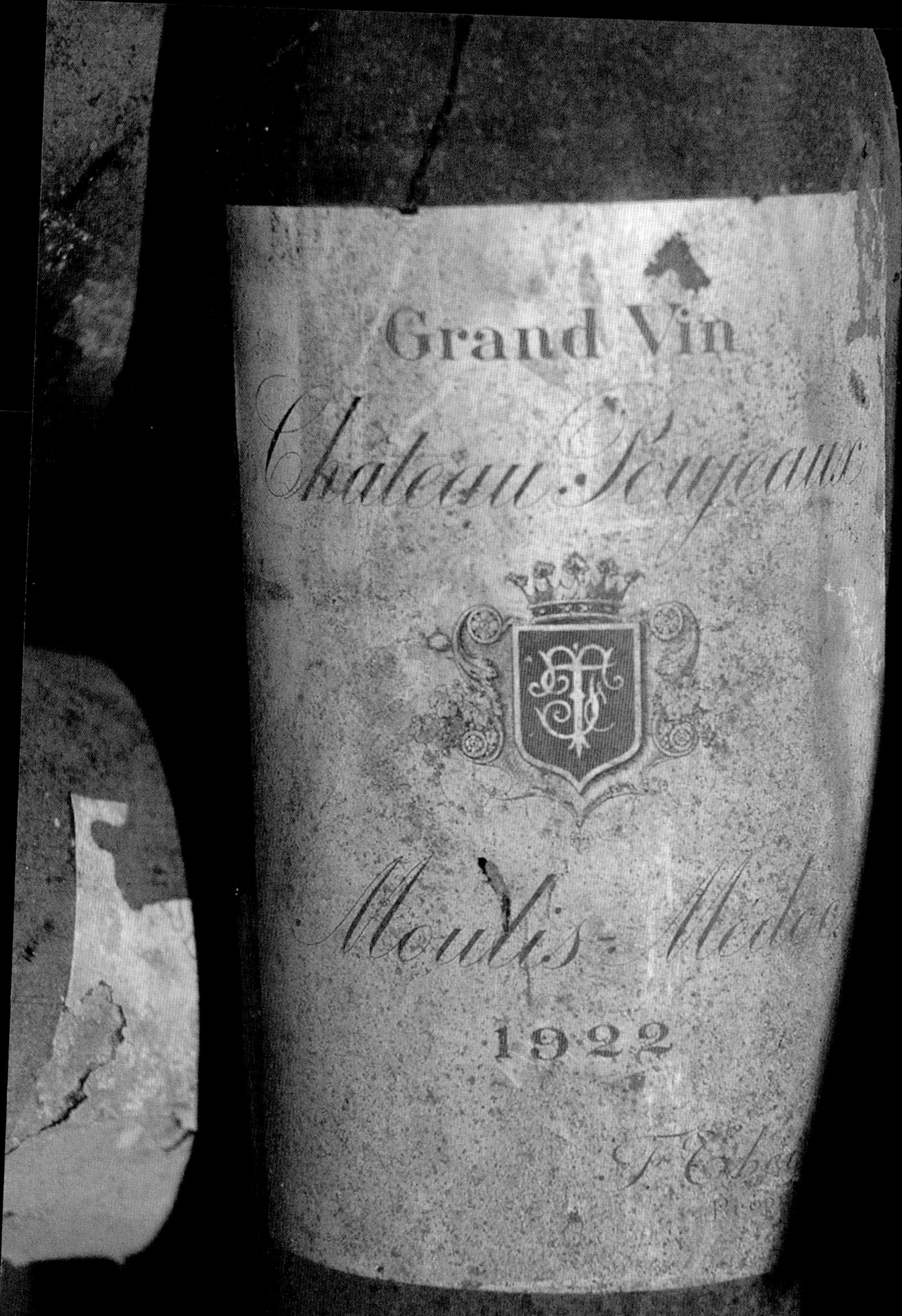

Grand Vin

Château Poujeaux

Moulis-Médoc

1922

Pride Mountain
Reserve Cabernet Sauvignon 1997

Origin USA, California, Napa/Sonoma Valleys
Style Dry red wine, 14.1% ABV
Grape Cabernet Sauvignon

Directly astride the Napa–Sonoma border, on the high ridgeline of the Mayacamas range, lies the Pride Mountain estate, also known as Summit Ranch. Trying the estate's Reserve Cabernet Sauvignon is the best way to understand the distinctiveness of Northern California's finest mountaintop terroir.

Perched 2,100 feet (640 m) above sea level, with rocky and well-drained volcanic soils, the vineyards of the Pride Mountain estate float high above the cold and wet fog banks that swing in from the Pacific Ocean and bring steep temperature swings to the Napa and Sonoma Valley floors. Pride Mountain does get some cooling effect from the air that accompanies those fog banks—and also from the simple fact of its high altitude—but it also gets considerably more sunshine over the course of a growing season than do the valley floors. That extra sun translates not into excess ripeness but into a longer and steadier growing season.

Although Napa Valley floor Cabernet Sauvignons tend to have smoother, more velvety tannins, this wine—perhaps the very finest of its kind—has a richer, rougher, black-fruit character. **DD**
🍷🍷🍷🍷 Drink: to 2017+

Prieler
Blaufränkisch Goldberg 2003

Origin Austria, Burgenland, Neusiedlersee-Hügelland
Style Dry red wine, 14% ABV
Grape Blaufränkisch

The iron- and quartzite-rich chalk and mica-schist outcroppings of Burgenland—peaking in the Goldberg—resisted eons of erosion, the remnants of which form a sandy residue at lower levels. The Prielers' range of vines also peaks in Goldberg, with a Blaufränkisch from its stonier sections.

In 1993, the Prielers elected to segregate the Goldberg Blaufränkisch. A Swiss agent was smitten, and rescued the Prielers after they had sold a mere twenty-four bottles domestically. With the 1994—today a pungently smoky and still freshly black-fruited wine of superb refinement—Austrian sales rose to sixty bottles.

Only with the 1997 came recognition, as Ernst Triebaumer in neighboring Rust helped beat the drum with his Blaufränkisch Mariental. A decade later, few Austrian wines command a higher price than these two reds. Bittersweet nut oils, cassis, violets, cardamom, and peat dominate the Goldberg 2003, its palate-coating fine tannins, and subtly salt-tinged and tartly fresh black fruits belying both the searing extremity of the vintage and the new barrels in which the wine was raised. **DS**
🍷🍷🍷🍷 Drink: to 2020+

Dom. Prieuré St.-Christophe
Mondeuse Prestige 2004

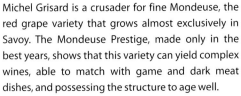

Origin France, Savoy
Style Dry red wine, 12% ABV
Grape Mondeuse

Michel Grisard is a crusader for fine Mondeuse, the red grape variety that grows almost exclusively in Savoy. The Mondeuse Prestige, made only in the best years, shows that this variety can yield complex wines, able to match with game and dark meat dishes, and possessing the structure to age well.

The domaine is in the village of Fréterive, known for its vine nurseries, including those of the Grisard family. The Mondeuse Prestige 2004 comes from vines in Fréterive and in Arbin. The vines withstood the 2003 heat well so, for this domaine, 2004 was not overproductive. Even in the best years, Mondeuse achieves only 11 per cent alcohol naturally, but still manages to give wonderful red fruit flavors.

The wine has a youthful purply/crimson color, and is quite plummy on the nose, with some spicy cinnamon oak notes and a touch of jam. The acid balance is excellent, with medium, rounded tannins. Plums and *griotte* cherries blend with a spicy, toasty character and a herbal edge on the finish. It is still tight and youthful, and may well close up for a year or more before aging gracefully. It would benefit from decanting. **WL**
🍷🍷🍷 **Drink: to 2030**

Prieuré de St.-Jean de Bébian
2001

Origin France, Coteaux du Languedoc
Style Dry red wine, 14% ABV
Grapes Grenache, Syrah, Mourvèdre

Having given up their careers as full-time wine writers, Chantal Lecouty and Jean-Claude Lebrun settled down in the Languedoc in 1994, and were particularly taken with this former monastic property dating back to the twelfth century. In recent years it had been owned by Alain Roux, who had started to plant Syrah and Mourvèdre.

The property boasts clay and pebble soils similar to Châteauneuf-du-Pape, which encouraged Chantal and Jean-Claude to plant all thirteen of the Châteauneuf-du-Pape varieties. They went shopping for suitable vines, and brought in Syrah from Chave in Hermitage, Châteauneuf varieties from Château Rayas, and Mourvèdre from Domaine Tempier in Bandol. These complemented the estate Grenache.

The Prieuré is the domaine's top red. Grenache makes up around half the cuvée, with the rest in Syrah and Mourvèdre. The wine is aged in barriques, around one-third of which are renewed annually. Michel Bettane and Thierry Desseauve have praised the Prieuré 2001 for its "size, breed, and richness." It would be at its best served with a plate of grilled squab pigeons. **GM**
🍷🍷🍷 **Drink: to 2017+**

Produttori del Barbaresco
Barbaresco Riserva Rabajà 2001

Origin Italy, Piedmont, Langhe
Style Dry red wine, 13.5% ABV
Grape Nebbiolo

It is universally agreed that this is one of the greatest vineyard sites in Barbaresco. One of its defining qualities is its particular mesoclimate, influenced by cooling breezes rising up from the River Tanaro. Rabajà's predominantly sandy and limestone soils produce elegant yet full-bodied Barbarescos that are charming while young but are also among the most age-worthy in the denomination.

Produttori del Barbaresco was founded in 1958 at the site of the original cellars used by Barbaresco's founding father, Domizio Cavazza. Under the direction of Aldo Vacca, Produttori continues to make outstanding Barbarescos. Traditionally crafted from grapes hailing from some of the most sought-after vineyards in Barbaresco, the cooperative's single-vineyard Riservas represent some of the greatest values in Italian wine.

One of the greatest recent bottlings to be released by Produttori del Barbaresco is its Rabajà Riserva 2001. A superb vintage, it is full-bodied yet elegant, with impeccable balance. Its tannic structure and freshness will allow it to age and evolve for decades. **KO**

🍷🍷🍷 **Drink: to 2025**

Château Providence
2005

Origin France, Bordeaux, Pomerol
Style Dry red wine, 13% ABV
Grapes Merlot 95%, Cabernet Franc 5%

Because Pomerol as a whole has been a latecomer to stardom, there are still patches of vines that have never been fully exploited. One of these was a plot called La Providence, located near Château Certan de May. Christian Moueix had his eye on these vines, and in 2002 agreed with the owner, a M. Dupuy, to a form of co-ownership. Three years later, in 2005, Moueix bought out M. Dupuy and purchased the remaining stocks. To mark his acquisition of the property, Christian Moueix changed its name from La Providence to the blunter Providence.

The vineyards, with a surface of nearly 7 acres (3 ha), are well drained, on soils of gravel and reddish clay. Cabernet Franc plays a minor role here, but the varieties are interplanted and the new owner does not yet know precisely how much there is.

Providence is, and will remain, quite a rare wine, since only 1,000 cases are produced. Although the 2000 is fleshy and delicious, it is surpassed by the 2005, which has a remarkable aromatic purity. The texture is sleek and silky, but it does not lack tannin or concentration. The Moueix imprint lies in the balance and stylishness of the wine. **SBr**

🍷🍷🍷 **Drink: to 2022**

◀ The leaves of Nebbiolo vines turn red during fall in Barbaresco.

Agricola Querciabella
Chianti Classico 1999

Origin Italy, Tuscany, Chianti
Style Dry red wine, 13% ABV
Grapes Sangiovese 95%, Cabernet Sauvignon 5%

The wealthy industrialist Giuseppe Castiglioni, an avid collector of French wines and owner of the largest collection of Louis Roederer Cristal in Italy, founded Agricola Querciabella in 1974. Situated in Greve-in-Chianti, the estate initially had only 2.5 acres (1 ha) of vines and a few old buildings. Since then, the area under vine has expanded to 64 acres (26 ha), with a further 30 acres (12 ha) dedicated to olive growing.

Agricola Querciabella produces four wines in all. Batàr is a blend of Chardonnay and Pinot Blanc; Camartina is a blend of Sangiovese and Cabernet Sauvignon; and Palafreno is a blend of Merlot and Sangiovese. These IGT bottles are superstars of Italian wine, but Querciabella's top wine—and its only wine to be classified as DOCG—is its Chianti Classico. The grapes for this wine come from the vineyards of Faule, Solatio, and Santa Lucia, which face south, southwest, and southeast respectively, and are at 1,148 to 1,640 feet (350–500 m) above sea level. The estate is run according to biodynamic principles; average production is 144,000 bottles.

Described by Hugh Johnson OBE as a "leader in Chianti Classico," Querciabella is one of the top examples of this famous Tuscan wine and achieved *Tre Bicchieri* (three glasses) status in the Italian wine guide *Gambero Rosso* in 1995. Good vintages such as the 1999, with its firm structure, can be drunk upon release, but will age well for up to twenty years. **SG**
$ $ $ **Drink: to 2019**

◄ Tuscan hills surround one of Querciabella's vineyards near Greve.

Quilceda Creek
Cabernet Sauvignon 2002

Origin USA, Washington State
Style Dry red wine, 15% ABV
Grapes C. Sauvignon 97%, Merlot 2%, C. Franc 1%

Andre Golitzin made his first barrel of Cabernet Sauvignon in 1974, in his garage, with Yakima Valley grapes. Experiments led to bonding of the winery in 1978; the first Quilceda Creek Cabernet was vintage 1979; son Paul took over the winemaking in 1995; and they finally built a winery in 2004.

There is general consensus that the wines took a qualitative leap upward once Paul took over; his father acknowledges that Paul simply has a brilliant palate. He also believes in blending.

The 2002 is blended from four different vineyard sources. Grapes are harvested only when they taste fully ripe; after destemming and light crushing, they fall by gravity into the fermenters. Specific commercial yeasts initiate the fermentation and continue until dryness, after which the wine is pumped into new French oak for the malolactic. The wines typically age in barrel for twenty-two months, with an additional nine months in bottle before release. The Quilceda Creek 2002 is a formidably impressive wine: intense yet elegant, with dynamic, complex aromas and flavors, a firm but supple tannic spine, and great length. **LGr**
🍷🍷🍷🍷 **Drink: to 2025+**

Quinta do Côtto
Grande Escolha 2001

Origin Portugal, Douro Valley
Style Dry red wine, 13% ABV
Grapes Touriga Nacional, Tinta Roriz

Quinta do Côtto is one of the oldest properties in the Douro Valley, dating back to the fourteenth century. There is some evidence that the estate was settled before the advent of Portugal itself.

Situated in the lower part of the Douro, Côtto was one of the estates to be included in the first demarcation of the region, in 1756. It was also one of the first quintas to take advantage of the 1986 relaxation of the law that finally allowed Port wine to be exported from the Douro, without having to be sold through the shippers in Vila Nova da Gaia.

Unfortified wine has been made on the estate since the 1970s, making it one of the first companies to take the style seriously. Most other Port houses at the time were making small volumes of table wine for personal consumption, but never for sale. Two unfortified wines are currently made here: one from younger vines, and the Grande Escolha, produced only in exceptional vintages. Old vines, more than twenty-five years old, are used for the latter, and three weeks of maceration ensure a deep, rich wine with plenty of tannic backbone, softened slightly by aging in Portuguese oak for up to two years. **GS**
🍷🍷 **Drink: to 2030**

Quinta do Mouro
Alentejo 2008

Origin Portugal, Alentejo
Style Dry red wine, 14.5% ABV
Grapes Tempranillo, Alicante Bouschet, Others

Quinta do Vale Meão
2000

Origin Portugal, Douro Valley
Style Dry red wine, 14.5% ABV
Grapes T. Nacional, T. Franca, Others

Among the pioneers of fine wine in the hot, dry Alentejo region, in southern Portugal, is Luis Louro, who first planted vines in 1989. The vineyard, of schistous soil, has now been extended to a total of 54 acres (22 ha), mostly planted with Portuguese varieties—Aragonês (also known as Tinta Roriz or Tempranillo), Alicante Bouschet, Touriga Nacional, and Trincadeira, but with some French imports too.

Quinta do Mouro, made entirely from quinta-grown fruit, uses a marvelous mixture of old and new. The grapes are crushed by foot-treading for two days, followed by fermentation in temperature-controlled stainless-steel tanks—essential if anyone is going to make fine wine in this hot climate. Maturation is in a combination of French and Portuguese oak.

Wines from very hot regions can be baked and jamlike, but Quinta do Mouro manages to maintain an elegance and finesse. Moderately deep in color, with a sweet, black fruit and smoky, cedarwood nose, the fine yet firm tannic grip balances the body and the alcohol, leaving a fruit-driven finish with some floral complexity to it. **GS**

🔇🔊 **Drink: to 2022**

Quinta do Vale Meão was made famous by one wine—Ferreira's Barca Velha, which was sourced here for many years. The estate was originally established by Dona Antónia Ferreira, the Port industry's answer to Veuve Clicquot, the legendary widow of the Douro. It was her last great achievement, since the Quinta was completed in the year she died, 1896.

Deep in the Douro Superior, Quinta do Vale Meão is now owned by a great-great-grandson of Dona Antónia Ferreira, Francisco Javier de Olazabal. Formerly president of A. A. Ferreira, he resigned in 1998 to concentrate on making his own single quinta wine. The first release was the 1999, but Francisco de Olazabal considers the 2000 to be the baptism vintage, one of the best they have made.

The estate vineyards vary from low-lying riverside plantings to sites of more than 656 feet (200 m) in altitude. They are planted with the usual combination of traditional grape varieties—Touriga Nacional, Tinta Roriz, Touriga Francesa, Tinta Amarela, Tinta Barroca, and Tinto Cão—but it is the sweet, black fruit character of Touriga Nacional that dominates the flavor of Quinta do Vale Meão. **GS**

🔇🔊 **Drink: to 2018+**

Quinta dos Roques *Dão Touriga Nacional* 2005

Origin Portugal, Dão
Style Dry red wine, 14% ABV
Grape Touriga Nacional

Quinta dos Roques is one of the finest wine estates in the Dão region of north-central Portugal. The Dão is therefore dominated by the cooperative movement, with farmers selling their production to the cooperative where it becomes an anonymous part of a large blend. In 1978, Luis Lourenço, the owner of Quinta dos Roques, took the decision to replant the vineyard with the most suitable grapes, and to start making and bottling estate wine.

The vineyards have been expanded and now make up about 100 acres (40 ha), divided into twelve vineyard plots. The soils here are predominantly granitic sand, and the vineyards are at relatively high altitudes, giving freshness and structure despite the high natural alcohol levels.

Wines under the Quinta label were first produced in 1990, initially in the form of blends. The varietal range was launched in 1996. These latter wines, and in particular the Touriga Nacional, soon found international critical acclaim. The pure Touriga Nacional wine is made in the new winery, which combines traditional granite *lagares* with state-of-the-art modern equipment. Aged for fifteen months in new French oak barriques, the wine has a classic Touriga nose of black cherry and bramble jam, overlaid with chocolaty herbal notes. The full, rich body, with a great acid–tannin balance, gives a firm grip to the palate. The structure here makes it a wine that, while delicious on release, will repay cellaring for a decade or more. **GS**
☉☉ **Drink: to 2020+**

FURTHER RECOMMENDATIONS
Other great vintages
1996 • 2000
More Dão wines
Duque de Viseu • Fonte do Ouro
Grão Vasco • Porta dos Cavalheiros

A woman carries maize past a vineyard at Mangualde in the Dão region. ➔

Quintarelli
Amarone della Valpolicella 1995

Origin Italy, Veneto
Style Dry red wine, 15.5% ABV
Grapes Corvina, Rondinella, Molinara

"I still remember those times when, if the Recioto kept on fermenting and consumed all its sugars to become dry, that brought shame on all the family," says Giuseppe Quintarelli of his roots in the Valpolicella tradition. A dry Recioto is of course nothing other than our beloved Amarone: *Amaro* literally means bitter, but here it really means "dry." Recioto Amaro was its original name, when it was considered a rather unwelcome accident. Apparently the name Amarone was created by a very talented cellarmaster of the Cantina Sociale di Valpolicella called Adelino Lucchese. When sampling a dry Recioto from vat in the spring of 1936, he enthused: "This is not a Recioto Amaro, this is an Amarone!"

The aromas of Quintarelli's Amarone 1995 literally fill the room. Notes of morello cherries, chocolate, dried figs, freshly ground spices, and even aromatic herbs seem to affect the drinker nearly as much as does the high alcohol itself. In the mouth, the wine delivers on its aromatic promise: A sip of the opulent, glycerin-rich nectar will keep the favors lingering for minutes—yet the wine never comes across as overextracted or muscular. **AS**

🍷🍷🍷🍷🍷 **Drink: to 2035+**

Quintessa
2000

Origin USA, California, Napa Valley
Style Dry red wine, 14.5% ABV
Grapes C. Sauvignon 70%, Merlot 20%, C. Franc 10%

The Quintessa vineyard and winery occupies a magnificent lakeside site in Rutherford beneath a knoll on the western side of the Silverado Trail. When acquired in 1990, it was valued as one of the last undeveloped sites in the Napa Valley. It was developed by the Franciscan wine estate as the source of a pricy, no-holds-barred Bordeaux blend. The first vintage was in 1993.

The contoured vineyards, about 160 acres (65 ha) in all, are divided into twenty-six different blocks, allowing the winemakers to structure their blends carefully. Any wines that seem unsatisfactory are sold off. The soils are mostly alluvial with many volcanic traces, and since 2004 the estate has been cultivated biodynamically. The wine is aged for eighteen months in 60 percent new French oak.

The 2000 is typical of Quintessa in that the new oak is prominent on the nose. The palate is luxurious and very oaky, but the sumptuous texture is nicely undercut by spice and sufficient acidity to give ample persistence. It is a beautifully made wine but one that, it could be argued, lacks some personality, offering voluptuousness but little minerality. **SBr**

🍷🍷🍷🍷 **Drink: to 2020**

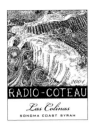

Qupé
20th Anniversary Syrah 2001

Origin USA, California, Santa Barbara
Style Dry red wine, 13.5% ABV
Grape Syrah

Radio-Coteau
Cherry Camp Syrah 2004

Origin USA, California, Sonoma Coast
Style Dry red wine, 15% ABV
Grape Syrah

Bob Lindquist established Qupé in 1982, and since 1989 he and Jim Clendenen have shared a winery on the Bien Nacido vineyard in the Santa Maria Valley. Over the years, Lindquist has preferred to produce a cool-climate Syrah, somewhat restrained in style and age-worthy.

The Anniversary Syrah commemorates Qupé's twentieth vintage and is intended to last another twenty years. All the fruit comes from the original 5-acre (2 ha) "X" Block at Bien Nacido, the vineyard's oldest Syrah block. One-third of the grapes in the fermentor were whole clusters, with stems, designed to add noticeable spice character and firmer tannin. A fourteen-day fermentation in a small, open-top fermentor, with twice-daily punch-downs, was followed by a five-day postfermentation maceration, pressing, and racking into French oak barrels for aging. Lindquist used neutral barrels to emphasize the Bien Nacido terroir, and the *élevage* in barrel continued for twenty months.

The Anniversary Syrah 2001 is a tight, restrained wine, with firm grip and taut aromas of tar, leather, smoked meats, blueberries, and spice. **LGr**
☻☻☻ **Drink: to 2021+**

With extensive experience in France, Washington State, and California, Eric Sussman set out on his own in 2002 to produce wines reflecting variety and site, honoring Old World approaches in a New World setting. His interest lies in cool-climate, near-coast settings that can be farmed with the minimum input of water and nutrients. He works closely with vineyard owners and carries his minimalist approach into the winery, where his goal is to leave, at most, a "gentle human fingerprint" on the wine.

Cherry Camp vineyard lies on a ridge above the town of Freestone, on the edge of the Russian River Valley area, but is, in character, a true coastal setting. After a century as a cherry orchard, the property was replanted to Syrah in 2002, with 2004 as the first vintage. The 2004 was closed on release, but one already sensed the inherent quality in a dense concentration of aromas and flavors, the layers of spice, earth, and fruit balanced by fine natural acids. The 2005 showed a similar character. It was an extraordinary beginning for a vineyard and wine destined to become classic points of reference for California cool-climate Syrah. **JS**
☻☻☻ **Drink: to 2017+**

Château Rauzan-Ségla

2000

Origin France, Bordeaux, Margaux
Style Dry red wine, 13% ABV
Grapes C. Sauvignon 54%, Merlot 41%, Others 5%

In 1855, this Margaux property was rated as one of the finest second growths. Those who tasted the wines from the 1960s to the 1980s would have been perplexed by this high ranking, as the wine was plainly mediocre. Rauzan was put on the market in the early 1990s. In 1994 it was bought by the Wertheimers of New York, whose primary business was the fashion house of Chanel. The family had been hoping to bag Latour but were unsuccessful and settled for Rauzan instead. It was a good choice; the price was far less, and there was clearly an enormous potential to be realized. Scotsman John Kolasa was appointed to manage the property.

Kolasa set to his task with energy, backed, fortunately, by the resources of the Chanel group. He replanted many of the vines, improving the varietal balance, increased the vineyard density, and installed new drainage. In the winery he acquired smaller fermentation tanks to allow for more parcel selections. The new team got off to a good start with a fine 1994 and the wines have steadily improved. Since many of the vines are still young, Kolasa takes care not to overextract, always aware that the hallmark of Margaux is elegance rather than power.

The 2000 is a formidable wine, with a distinct oakiness (Rauzan-Ségla is usually aged in 50 percent new oak); but persistence of flavor overrides any brawniness, and the fruit emerges clearly. Its fine balance should bring a long, rewarding future. **SBr**
ꙮꙮꙮꙮ **Drink: to 2025**

The château was built in the twentieth century by the Cruse family. ➡

Ravenswood *Sonoma County* *Old Hill Vineyard Zinfandel* 2002

Origin USA, California, Sonoma Valley
Style Dry red wine, 14.2% ABV
Grapes Zinfandel 75%, Others 25%

Ravenswood, founded in 1976, began life as a ramshackle roadside winery in a former garage. Its owner and winemaker, Joel Peterson, had a day job as an immunologist, which he retained until 1987. He found that making wine perfectly combined the scientific and artistic sides of his nature.

Peterson relied on indigenous yeasts, punched down the cap frequently, and aged the wine in varying proportions of new Nevers oak. It was rarely filtered. He developed a portfolio of single-vineyard wines, mostly from old Sonoma vines. At the same time he released a range called Vintner's Blend, which offered full-bodied Zinfandel in larger volumes and at a moderate price.

The winery's motto, "No Wimpy Wines," does Peterson's winemaking skills an injustice. Some of his Zinfandels are certainly big, powerful wines, but they usually have an elegance rarely encountered with this grape variety. In 2001, the vast Constellation group bought the winery. Volumes have expanded considerably, with inevitable compromises, but Peterson has maintained production of his splendid single-vineyard wines. Old Hill Ranch has very low-yielding nineteenth-century vines, some planted in 1880. It is organically farmed with at least fourteen varieties, though Zinfandel dominates. The 2002 is exemplary, with elegant cherry and vanilla aromas, a sleek texture, lively acidity, fine concentration and persistence, and a very long finish. **SBr**
ⱺⱺⱺ **Drink: to 2017**

Zinfandel grapes growing in Ravenswood's Old Hill Vineyard. ⇨

Château Rayas
1990

Remírez de Ganuza
Rioja Reserva 2003

Origin France, Southern Rhône, Châteauneuf-du-Pape
Style Dry red wine, 14% ABV
Grape Grenache

Origin Spain, Rioja
Style Dry red wine, 13% ABV
Grapes Tempranillo, Graciano

Very little has changed at Châteauneuf-du-Pape's most famous estate, Château Rayas, since the early 1970s. The feather touch of the Reynaud family's blending skills has been handed down by the founder Louis to son Jacques Reynaud and then to his nephew Emmanuel. Here is an estate defying much of local Châteauneuf convention: all or mostly Grenache, harvested at tiny yields; the use of creaking old barrels for *élevage*, their misshapen fronts coded in ancient Greek letters, the vintage numbers reversed; the bottle-by-bottle hand labeling; the tasting glass with a broken stem for undesirable, usually unannounced, visitors.

In these days of blockbusters, along trundles Château Rayas with its glimmering pale red that swiftly turns to a rather dull strawberry hue. Where are the massive aromas, the potent hit on the palate? This wine sits at peace in the glass, suggesting there are more spices to come given enough time. The 1990 has a round, sweet bouquet, with hints of cooked fruits. There is good palate depth, with controlled vigor, and a real finesse comes out in the delicious, chewy finish. **JL-L**

🍷🍷🍷🍷🍷 Drink: to 2030

Fernando Remírez de Ganuza acquired his knowledge of vineyards and his desire to become a winemaker from his time as an estate agent, when he also traded in vineyards. He established his own small bodega in the village of Samaniego in 1989, committed to the renewal of Riojan wines, through two fundamental principles: working only with his own grapes from the best plots in the Rioja Alavesa, and vinifying them in an intuitive, original way. His 140 acres (47 ha) of south-facing vineyards have clay and limestone soils and vines ranging from thirty-five to 100 years old: 90 percent is Tempranillo.

Remírez de Ganuza is one of the standard-bearers of the Riojan renaissance. The Remírez de Ganuza Reserva, his first red, launched with the 1992 vintage, with a twenty-four-month *crianza* in cask and a similar period in the bottle, remains his most emblematic and reliable wine. An intense cherry color, it has a leafy aroma backed by fine toast and ripe fruit. Beautifully balanced on the palate, it is delicious and velvety, while retaining great vivacity. An elegant *reserva* with real presence, which usually needs a few more years to develop in bottle. **JMB**

🍷🍷🍷 Drink: to 2018+

Domaine Louis Rémy
Latricières-Chambertin GC 2002

Origin France, Burgundy, Côte de Nuits
Style Dry red wine, 13% ABV
Grape Pinot Noir

Mme. Marie-Louise Rémy and her daughter Chantal Rémy-Rosier are the surviving Rémys in the wine business, the Gevrey-based domaine of Mme. Rémy's brother-in-law Philippe having been sold to Mme. Lalou Bize-Leroy in 1989. At the top of the village of Morey-St.-Denis, under Clos des Lambrays and facing on to the Place du Monument, Mme. Rémy lives opposite a splendid two-level, deep vaulted cellar, somewhat too extensive, it would appear, for their 6.42-acre (2.6 ha) domaine.

It was here that quality, splendid in the 1940s, '50s, and '60s, subsequently took a turn for the worse. Louis Rémy died during the vintage in 1982, but standards had long been declining. However, Chantal Rémy is a qualified enologist, and under her direction quality has risen. This was apparent in the 1999 vintage, and even more so in 2002.

Latricières-Chambertin lies above the Route des Grands Vins just south of Chambertin itself. There is a certain spicy character in all Latricières, and this Rémy 2002 is no exception: full-bodied, rich, and old-viney, but quite muscular and powerful. Latricières-Chambertin is a wine built for the long term. **CC**

🍷🍷🍷🍷 **Drink: to 2030**

Ridge
Monte Bello 2001

Origin USA, California, Santa Clara County
Style Dry red wine, 14% ABV
Grapes C. Sauvignon, Merlot, Petit Verdot

In 1959, a few scientists from Stanford University bought some land high in the Santa Cruz Mountains as a holiday retreat. They found some old Cabernet vines on the property, vinified them, and were surprised by the intensity of the wine. In the late 1960s they decided to reopen the winery that had been operating here in the late nineteenth century, and invited Paul Draper to run it. He is still there.

Draper initially produced a variety of wines, but soon realized that the old Cabernet vines produced the most exceptional fruit. The Monte Bello vineyard was expanded and some Bordeaux varieties other than Cabernet were planted. With an elevation of around 2,300 feet (700 m), it was exceptionally cool.

Draper aged Monte Bello mostly in new American air-dried oak. It is assembled from as many as thirty-four separate lots, and the blending process is done entirely by blind-tasting. Draper's aim is to produce a wine that is approachable young, but that will clearly benefit from age. Of recent vintages, the 2001 is particularly attractive. It is a dramatic wine, with spice and vigor and a fine acidic backbone that should guarantee a long life. **SBr**

🍷🍷🍷🍷 **Drink: to 2028**

Giuseppe Rinaldi
Barolo Brunate-Le Coste 1993

Origin Italy, Piedmont
Style Dry red wine, 13% ABV
Grape Nebbiolo

Chris Ringland
Three Rivers Shiraz 1999

Origin Australia, South Australia, Barossa Valley
Style Dry red wine, 15% ABV
Grape Shiraz

Until 1992, Giuseppe Rinaldi's Barolo production was (as tradition dictated) shared between two labels: a Barolo (*normale*) and a Riserva produced from the grapes of the Brunate vineyard. Since 1993, there have still been two labels, but the first is now a blend of the crus Brunate and Le Coste, and the second a blend of Ravera and Cannubi San Lorenzo.

Rinaldi did not mean to break with tradition: he merely noticed that grapes from cooler sites such as Le Coste and Ravera were perfect for balancing grapes from warmer vineyards such as Brunate and Cannubi. Production is still very traditional, including long maceration and fermentation, and maturation exclusively in large oak casks (*botti*).

Giuseppe's wines were never intended for early drinking: They need to be enjoyed in full maturity, when time has worked its magic. That magic is twofold: It softens the rough edges of youth, and it allows the wine to reveal itself in all its baroque beauty, with notes of cherries in alcohol, licorice, white pepper, tobacco, and even black truffle. Drink this 1993 partly to thank Rinaldi that changes have not been made for their own pointless sakes. **AS**

🍷🍷🍷🍷 **Drink: to 2020+**

Probably the most vaunted of the so-called "tin-shackistes" in the Barossa Valley, Chris Ringland produces less than 1,000 bottles of his Shiraz each year. In 1989 he named it "Three Rivers" after the Australian country singer Slim Dusty's song "Three Rivers Hotel." Ringland's wines soon caught the attention of wine critic Robert Parker, who awarded the 1996, 1998, and 2001 vintages a perfect score of 100 points. This launched Three Rivers on to the international market, and prices in Australia rose by 400 percent in a year. The market for "tin-shackistes" and other "cult" wines slumped dramatically by 2001, but this wine still commands astonishing prices.

Unlike most winemakers, Ringland does not top up his barrels. He closes them with silicon bungs and opens them only every six months to taste, claiming that oxygen stays out if the barrels are not opened frequently, and that with evaporation this concentrates the wines. His Shiraz has been likened to Screaming Eagle and Guigal's La-La bottlings because of its big, powerful, high-alcohol style. It seems prophetic that Slim Dusty sang: "And that's why we all worship Three Rivers Hotel." **SG**

🍷🍷🍷🍷🍷 **Drink: to 2017+**

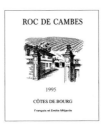

Rippon
Pinot Noir 2005

Origin New Zealand, Central Otago, Lake Wanaka
Style Dry red wine, 13% ABV
Grape Pinot Noir

Château Roc de Cambes
1995

Origin France, Bordeaux, Côtes de Bourg
Style Dry red wine, 13% ABV
Grapes Merlot 70%, C. Sauvignon 25%, Malbec 5%

Growing up in New Zealand between Dunedin and Wanaka, Rolfe Mills dreamed of one day moving back on to the family farm, at Wanaka Station, near Lake Wanaka, which had been bought by his grandfather Percy in 1912. In 1974, Rolfe and his wife Lois finally fulfilled this ambition. Inspired by a visit to the Douro Valley, they planted a few short rows of vines on a steep bank above their farmhouse. Despite mostly negative opinions from viticultural experts, the Mills' climate data encouraged them to plant their first commercial vineyard block in 1981.

Named after Percy's grandmother Emma Rippon, who had emigrated from England to Australia, Rippon is the most northerly vineyard in Central Otago, but that still makes it among the most southerly wineries in the world. It is at an altitude of 1,083 feet (330 m) on the shores of the stunning Lake Wanaka. The combination of the relatively high altitude with the cooling effect of the lake produces a vibrantly fruity Pinot Noir, with a relatively light color and structure. Rippon is run biodynamically—after all, who would want to spray chemicals in such beautiful and unspoiled surroundings? **SG**

🍷🍷🍷 Drink: to 2018+

It took the sharp eye of François Mitjavile, the owner of Château Tertre-Roteboeuf in St.-Emilion, to spot the potential of these vineyards in the then obscure Côtes de Bourg. The vineyards lie in two blocks near the estuary; the moderating influence of the Gironde helped many vines to escape the devastating frost of 1956, so Roc des Cambes was blessed with many old vines. They are also well exposed, facing almost due south. The winemaking is the same as for Tertre-Roteboeuf. The soils here are more generous than in St.-Emilion, but the age of the vines keeps yields in check. The wines are fermented in cement tanks with natural yeasts, and aged in 50 percent new oak.

Under Mitjavile's care, Roc des Cambes has become the leading wine of its appellation. It is made with such a fervent regard for the balance of the wine that the good vintages keep extremely well. That is why a relatively old vintage such as 1995 has been selected. The nose shows a residual opulence as well as charm, and pure red fruits soar on the palate, the texture is suave yet spicy, with richness and concentration being moderated by secondary flavors such as a hint of tobacco. **SBr**

🍷🍷🍷 Drink: to 2017

J. Rochioli
West Block Pinot Noir 1992

Origin USA, California, Sonoma Valley
Style Dry red wine, 14.5% ABV
Grape Pinot Noir

Unable to compete with Central Valley growers, the Rochiolis were not making any money in the 1960s when Joe Jr. decided to plant Pinot Noir. He crossed his father, who wanted grapes of quantity, and the academics at the University of California, who recommended Gamay Beaujolais. His resulting 4-acre (1.6 ha) West Block is the fount now feeding the area's reputation for rich, concentrated Pinot Noir. East facing, with deep soils, Joe Jr. planted it in 1969.

Son Tom has produced the wine since the mid-1980s. The inaugural West Block bottling was in 1992. After sorting in the vineyard and winery, the grapes are cold-soaked for three to five days. They ferment in 3-ton open-top tanks for eight to ten days; the cap is punched down thrice daily. The wines are inoculated for the malolactic fermentation in the fermentors, and then put into barrels without settling to retain as much of the yeast lees and sediment as possible. There is no postfermentation maceration. During the fifteen months in 100 percent new French barrels, Rochioli racks the wine only once and bottles it unfiltered to protect the fragile fruit and preserve its full character. **LGr**
🜚🜚🜚 **Drink: to 2017+**

Rockford
Basket Press Shiraz 2004

Origin Australia, South Australia, Barossa Valley
Style Dry red wine, 14.5% ABV
Grape Shiraz

In the 1980s, Robert "Rocky" O'Callaghan was one of a small group of farsighted winemakers who recognized the damage being caused in the Barossa Valley by the government-sponsored vine-pull scheme. Irreplaceable old-vine Shiraz was being uprooted, but O'Callaghan borrowed money to buy grapes at a price that would prevent growers from pulling out their vines. "Rocky" looks and acts like an old-style Barossa winemaker. His 1850s cottage on Krondorf Road, outside Tanunda, looks like a museum rather than a working winery. Basket Press Shiraz is presented in a brown 1950s-style bottle.

Although its reputation might suggest otherwise, Basket Press is not made in the Barossa blockbuster style. Typically, it is aged in oak, but there is rarely more than 15 percent new oak, which gives it a savory and mineral quality lacking in some other Barossa wines. And unlike most of its contemporaries, Basket Press ages extremely well, for up to ten years. The 2004 vintage is perhaps riper and more luscious than some previous examples, but Basket Press Shiraz remains Australia's quintessential handmade wine. **SG**
🜚🜚🜚 **Drink: to 2019+**

Bodegas Roda
Rioja Cirsión 2001

Origin Spain, Rioja
Style Dry red wine, 14.5% ABV
Grape Tempranillo

Dom. Rollin *Pernand-Vergelesses*
PC Ile-des-Vergelesses 1990

Origin France, Burgundy, Côte de Beaune
Style Dry red wine, 13% ABV
Grape Pinot Noir

Bodegas Roda was founded in 1987 by Mario Rottlant and Carmen Daurella. Their objective was to create red wines in the modern *Alta Expresión* (high expression) style, but also to reflect the classic character of Rioja. Maintained separately as single-vineyard cuvées until the blends are assembled, the casks destined for Roda I Reserva are selected from the firmer, more structured wines, whereas those for Roda Reserva are selected from more forward, expressive wines, each representing different vineyard selections and different varietal blends.

The flagship wine, Cirsión, was introduced in 1998. It follows a typical *Alta Expresión* recipe, with vinification of old-vine Tempranillo grapes followed by oak barrel aging for ten months. In 2005, Cirsión 2001 came top of a *World of Fine Wine* Rioja tasting, making it the very apotheosis of *Alta Expresión* Rioja. Deep, dark fruit aromas follow its bright purple color. The fruit flavors and oak tannins are immaculately balanced on the palate, and the finish is long, spicy, and warm. But like so many of the other so-called *Alta Expresión* wines, Cirsión remains controversial. It is certainly a terrific wine—but is it Rioja? **SG**

🍷🍷🍷🍷 **Drink: to 2020+**

Pernand-Vergelesses is the only village in Burgundy authorized to produce red and white wines at every level from regional AOC to grand cru. Domaine Rollins's Corton-Charlemagne shines so brightly that it sometimes eclipses unfairly not only its other excellent white wines—from Aligoté to Pernand-Vergelesses Premier Cru Sur Frétille—but the red wines as well. Among these, the most special is the Premier Cru Ile-des-Vergelesses, from the best of the village's red vineyards.

The current head of the family, Rémi, ably assisted by wife Agnès and son Simon, is meticulous in both vineyard and winery. The reds are cold-soaked, fermented with indigenous yeasts in large cement vats, and punched down twice daily. The Île-des-Vergelesses sees more new wood than the others, but still only 20–25 percent, and is bottled after sixteen months or so without fining or filtration wherever possible. The 1990 and other more recent warm vintages are at once reassuringly rustic and seductively stylish: a dark cherry, earthy, and floral nose ushers in a medium-bodied wine of gentle minerality, casual power, and silky refinement. **NB**

🍷🍷🍷 **Drink: to 2020**

Domaine de la Romanée-Conti *La Tâche GC* 1999

Origin France, Burgundy, Côte de Nuits
Style Dry red wine, 13.5% ABV
Grape Pinot Noir

When the de Croonembourg family elected to sell their vineyard holdings in Vosne and La Tâche in 1760, the wines already enjoyed a stellar reputation. That accounted for the ferocity of the bidding war, and the eventual price—an inconceivably vast sum of 8,000 *livres*—by which Louis François de Bourbon, prince de Conti, finally vanquished his sworn enemy, Madame de Pompadour. He added his title to the estate's name, Romanée, only to have the precious jewel seized thirty years later, in the Revolution.

One of the La Tâche vineyard's more remarkable abilities is to turn out great Pinot Noir even in the theoretically "off" vintages—quite some feat, given the notoriously unmalleable nature of Burgundian Pinot. The vineyard consists of little more than 15 acres (6 ha), and produces barely 1,900 cases a year, although this represents the largest production of all the estate's grands crus. Its stratospheric price is jointly explained by its scarcity, and the exalted reputation of the estate.

Production was down in 1999, and the wine is correspondingly even more concentrated. Tasted on release, it had an astonishingly complex bouquet of well-hung meat, strawberry essence, and smoke. On the palate, it displayed fairly severe tannin, but wrapped about with a sumptuous cloak of red and black fruits, lavish oak, and glints of cherrylike acidity, while the heavyweight finish played on black cherry, sandalwood, and Indian spice notes. **SW**

$$$$$ Drink: to 2040+

← A stone cross on the perimeter of Burgundy's most famous estate.

Domaine de la Romanée-Conti *Romanée-Conti GC* 2005

Origin France, Burgundy, Côte de Nuits
Style Dry red wine, 13% ABV
Grape Pinot Noir

René Rostaing *Côte-Rôtie La Landonne* 2003

Origin France, Northern Rhône
Style Dry red wine, 13% ABV
Grape Syrah

The greatest wine commune in Burgundy—indeed in the world, according to some—is Vosne-Romanée. Four of the six Vosne grands crus are monopolies: La Tâche, La Grande Rue, La Romanée, and Romanée-Conti itself. The sole owner of the last of these is the Domaine de la Romanée-Conti, whose antecedents included the Prince de Conti, a distant cousin of Louis XV, and, more immediately, the Duvault-Blochet family, ancestors of the de Villaines, half-owners today. Aubert de Villaine is a super-perfectionist in a region renowned for its perfectionism. Only one person is allowed to prune the 3.95-acre (1.6 ha) vineyard. The new cuttings come from the domaine's own nursery. Rare for the region, the juice is usually fermented with all the stems. And there is 100 percent new wood.

Romanée-Conti is feminine where La Tâche, its only rival in this cellar, is masculine. It is not always the better wine, despite selling at auction for several times more. But when it is at its best, as here in this 2005, it is quite sublime. One wonders how a wine could have more finesse, be more complex, more intensely flavored, more disarmingly perfect. **CC**
🆂🆂🆂🆂🆂 **Drink: 2020–2040**

A former property developer, René Rostaing entered winemaking in 1971 with a little land at La Landonne and some vines on the Côte Blonde. Then he married the daughter of Albert Dervieux-Thaize, which gave him another 8.5 acres (3.5 ha) of sites in Fongent, La Garde, and La Viaillière. Finally, he inherited a further 3 acres (1.2 ha) from his uncle, Marius Gentaz. Like Dervieux, he vinifies his Brunes and Blondes separately, and puts the less distinguished wine into a simple Côte-Rôtie bottling.

He has chosen the path of moderation—not too much new oak, and letting the fabulously old vines he inherited from Dervieux speak for themselves. His oldest vines are on the Côte Blonde. Some will soon be celebrating their centenary. They give concentrated juice, and the deep roots mean that they can deal with the austere climate.

His wines have been criticized, however, for their pallor and reliance on modern wizardry. Rostaing uses no Viognier in his wines from La Landonne, which are 100 percent Syrah. The 2003, a classic, will require a few more years to bring out all its aromas of cherry, earth, leather, coriander, and tobacco. **GM**
🆂🆂🆂🆂 **Drink: to 2025**

Domaine Georges Roumier
Bonnes Mares Grand Cru 1999

Origin France, Burgundy, Côte de Nuits
Style Dry red wine, 13.5% ABV
Grape Pinot Noir

Celler del Roure
Maduresa Valencia 2001

Origin Spain, Valencia
Style Dry red wine, 14% ABV
Grapes C. Sauvignon, Merlot, Tempranillo, Others

In 1924, Georges Roumier wed Genevieve Quanquin, who brought several choice vineyard sites into his young estate. In those days, vines had little intrinsic value, and to survive Georges earned a salary managing the neighboring Domaine Comte Georges de Vogüé, whose wines he made until 1955.

In 1952, when his son Jean-Marie was set to join the business, Georges bought several parcels of Bonnes Mares, both in the chalky white soils of the upper part of the site and the reddish, stony clay soils in the lower stretches. The Terres Blanches are marked by mineral spiciness; the Terres Rouges are richer and more succulent. Georges and Jean-Marie bottled the two separately. Since Christophe, the third generation, joined Jean-Marie in 1981, the entire production has been estate bottled and, beginning in 1987, he has blended the two parcels.

The 1999 is rich, without being heavy, sporting black chocolate, blood orange, and licorice in its aromatics; it is the unusual balance that makes the 1999 so impressive. Although less dense, the 2002 may be a touch more elegant; the 2005, tasted pre-bottle, appears to be a marriage of the two. **JP**
⊖⊖⊖⊖⊖ **Drink: to 2035**

Celler del Roure is a small, family-owned, quality-oriented winery, the brainchild of the young wine enthusiast Pablo Calatayud, in the province of Valencia, very close to Almansa. Pablo's personal quest is to recover an ancient variety from the region—Mandó. By the time he discovered it, there remained only a few old, forgotten vines, so he had to propagate from these plants and develop new vineyards, a process that takes years. The idea is that the proportion of Mandó will increase as the new plantings come into production.

In the meantime Pablo has experimented with other varieties. 2001 was only his second commercial release; the blend is still an experiment, and in the future Syrah and Monastrell are likely to have a more important role in his wines.

Maduresa is a powerful Mediterranean wine, dark in color, with plenty of dark, ripe fruit on the nose, as well as smoky, charcoal notes, spice, and leather. Medium to full-bodied in the mouth, with a fine acid spine, it is supple, with a good core of dense fruit and a long finish, although the tannins will be more polished after a few more years in bottle. **LG**
⊖⊖ **Drink: recent vintages for up to 12 years**

Domaine Armand Rousseau
Chambertin-Clos de Bèze GC 2005

Origin France, Burgundy, Côte de Nuits
Style Dry red wine, 13% ABV
Grape Pinot Noir

The Domaine Armand Rousseau is not only the largest landholder in Chambertin, but the second most important proprietor in neighboring Chambertin-Clos de Bèze. The estate includes no fewer than six grands crus, between them covering 20 acres (8 ha), built up in the 1950s and 1960s by Charles Rousseau and his father. The wine is produced in modern premises on the outskirts of Gevrey-Chambertin. The Chambertin and the Clos de Bèze are vinified using some of the stems, after which the wine is housed in one cellar to do its malolactic and to wait until the previous vintage is bottled. The barrels are then moved to a cooler, deeper cellar, racked once (it used to be twice), and bottled after twenty months or so.

Chambertin and Chambertin-Clos de Bèze are two of the few wines that can be ranked alongside the very best of Vosne-Romanée at the top of the Burgundian hierarchy. What is the difference between Chambertin and Clos de Bèze? In Rousseau's case, to quote Charles himself: "Chambertin is male and sturdy. It lacks a little finesse in its youth, but then it rounds off. Clos de Bèze is more complex, has more class, and is more delicate." Which you prefer is a question of taste. This Clos de Bèze comes from a magnificent vintage. It is profound, multi-dimensional, super-concentrated, rich, ample, and beautifully balanced. **CC**
🙂🙂🙂🙂 **Drink: 2018–2040+**

FURTHER RECOMMENDATIONS
Other great vintages
1988 • 1989 • 1990 • 1993 • 1995 • 1996 • 1999 • 2002
More Armand Rousseau Grands Crus
Chambertin • Charmes-Chambertin • Clos de la Roche
Clos des Ruchottes • Mazi-Chambertin

Domaine Armand Rousseau

Gevrey-Chambertin Premier Cru Clos St.-Jacques 1999

Origin France, Burgundy, Côte de Nuits
Style Dry red wine, 13% ABV
Grape Pinot Noir

Until 1954, the Clos St.-Jacques was a monopoly of the Comte de Moucheron, who failed to argue successfully for its inclusion among the many grands crus that were classified in the early years of Appellation Controlée. When he was obliged to sell, the vineyard was divided into five strips, each running from the top to the bottom of the slope. The southernmost of these belongs to Domaine Armand Rousseau, and it benefits, as do the other producers, from each of the three soil types: The whiter marlstone at the top of the slope generates power, the rocky middle section provides finesse, while the clay at the bottom of the slope adds flesh.

Though Clos St.-Jacques may be designated only as a premier cru, Domaine Rousseau rates and prices it higher than four grands crus where they have holdings (Charmes-Chambertin, Mazis-Chambertin, Ruchottes-Chambertin, and Clos de la Roche), with only Chambertin and Clos de Bèze taking precedence. The reason for this high regard is the exceptional aspect of Clos St.-Jacques, exposed to both the east and the south.

1999 was close to the ideal growing season in Burgundy. This wine is not the deepest colored Burgundy, but the bouquet is immediately evocative of great Pinot, with its intricate latticework of soft summer fruit, mid-palate intensity, and a stylish, savory finish that lingers magically. **JM**

🍷🍷🍷🍷 **Drink: to 2020**

FURTHER RECOMMENDATIONS
Other great vintages
1985 · 1988 · 1989 · 1990 · 1991 · 1996 · 2002 · 2005
More producers of Clos St.-Jacques
Bruno Clair · Michel Esmonin
Jean-Claude Fourrier · Louis Jadot

Rust en Vrede
Estate Wine 2009

Origin South Africa, Stellenbosch
Style Dry red wine, 15% ABV
Grapes C. Sauvignon 53%, Shiraz 35%, Merlot 12%

This fine estate, whose name means "rest and peace," has a history of decay and renewal as a wine producer going back to 1730, when the first vines were planted at the foot of the Helderberg Mountain. Rust en Vrede's modern history dates from 1978, when former Springbok rugby player Jannie Engelbrecht bought and started restoring it. Unusually for the Cape, the focus was on red wines.

The Estate Wine was born as a Cabernet/Merlot blend in 1986. From 1998 it became probably the first top wine in the Cape to have a significant Shiraz component, and one of the first to be matured in new oak. Innovation came again with the growing influence on the winemaking of Jannie's son Jean, who had lived in the United States and was influenced by top Californian reds.

Since around 1998 the wine has shown itself as a splendid example of the emphatically modern approach: Virus-free vineyards allow for greater ripeness; the tannins, while firm, are smooth and velvety; fine dark berry aromas and flavors are more apparent, along with spicy wood; and there is an approachably flavorsome succulence. **TJ**
🍷🍷🍷 **Drink: to 2020+**

Rustenberg
John X Merriman 2003

Origin South Africa, Stellenbosch
Style Dry red wine, 14.8% ABV
Grapes Merlot 52%, C. Sauvignon 42%, Others 6%

One of the Cape's most beautiful estates, Rustenberg has a wine-growing history dating to 1682, in the early decades of settlement. More unusually, wine has been bottled here in unbroken continuity since 1892, when John X. Merriman, later prime minister of the Cape Colony, participated in the property's revival after a time of vine disease and recession.

The John X Merriman is less touted than the single-vineyard Peter Barlow Cabernet Sauvignon. But the blend does show greater continuity, in its relative restraint and elegance, with the famous old varietal Cabernets and Dry Red—the fine Cabernet 1982, for example, is still drinking well. Although the blend varies with the vintage, the grapes for the 2003 were, as always now, from the predominantly decomposed granite soils of the southwestern slopes of the Simonsberg, the mountain towering above the estate. The wine combines a modern focus on ripe fruit with a classically oriented structure of natural acidity and firm, smooth tannins; there is, as British writer Jamie Goode says, a "lovely concentration on the palate … a fresh, well-defined style with a subtle, minerally edge to it." **TJ**
🍷🍷 **Drink: to 2019+**

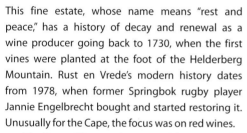

◀ Harvesters combine their pickings on the Rust en Vrede estate.

Sadie Family
Columella 2004

Origin South Africa, Swartland
Style Dry red wine, 14.5% ABV
Grapes Syrah 80%, Mourvèdre 20%

The decision to use Latin on the display label was a gesture less of preciousness than of Eben Sadie's awe at his own immense ambitions for this wine: Neither international English nor his own Afrikaans was commensurate. The idea for the wine (first vintage 2000) grew from Sadie's explorations of the terroir possibilities of the Swartland—a vast inland region of wheat fields, with mountainous granitic outcrops around which vineyards accrue.

Until nearly the end of the twentieth century, the area supplied only decent, overcropped grapes to the cooperatives. Meticulous attention to detail and natural winemaking methods—increasingly invoking biodynamic principles and procedures—mark Sadie's quest to express the Swartland in wine.

Columella is sourced from half-a-dozen widely scattered vineyards, all on long lease. The soils range from red clay-rich shale to slate to decomposed granite. Each parcel yields distinctive wine, vinified separately "according to its own demands" before blending. The wine is sleek, silkily rich, and fresh, sophisticated but characterful, with subtle supple tannins and characteristic Swartland minerality. **TJ**
🍷🍷🍷 **Drink: to 2019**

St. Hallett
Old Block Shiraz 2001

Origin Australia, South Australia, Barossa Valley
Style Dry red wine, 14% ABV
Grape Shiraz

Established by the Lindner family in 1944, St. Hallett had as its focus for many years the production of fortified wines. During the 1980s, Bob McLean—one of the Barossa's great characters—inspired St. Hallett to try premium table wines made from old Shiraz. Senior winemaker Stuart Blackwell first dabbled with Barossa winemaking in 1973, when he experimented with increased use of small-barrel fermentation for reds and new oak for maturation. His latter-day winemaking colleague was English-born Matt Gant, who was Australia's "Young Winemaker of the Year" only four years after settling down under.

Old Block is sourced from eight venerable Shiraz vineyards—six in the Barossa and two in the Eden Valley. The name comes from St. Hallett's own Old Block vineyard, next to the winery. 2001 was a warm vintage in the Barossa, hence this wine's 14 percent alcohol and slightly tough tannins. There is still much to enjoy here, though, with layers of flavors—smoke, chocolate, mocha, farmyard aromas—excellent mid-palate depth (from the old vines), and a fine, mellow finish. This is a benchmark Barossa Shiraz and it remains exceptional value for money. **SG**
🍷🍷 **Drink: to 2017+**

One of the St.Hallett vineyards at Tanunda in the Barossa Valley. ➡

Salvioni
Brunello di Montalcino 1985

Origin Italy, Tuscany, Montalcino
Style Dry red wine, 14% ABV
Grape Sangiovese

San Alejandro *Baltasar*
Gracián Garnacha Viñas Viejas 2011

Origin Spain, Aragón, Calatayud
Style Dry red wine, 14.5% ABV
Grape Grenache

Since his debut 1985 vintage, Giulio Salvioni's tiny but elite production has won a loyal following from around the world. For years, Salvioni's father made modest wine for family and friends from vineyards on the Salvioni's Cerbaiola farm. Realizing that the southeast-facing vineyards situated at 1,377 feet (420 m) held great potential, Giulio decided in the 1980s to dedicate his energies to winemaking, revamping the vineyards and expanding production.

Salvioni, assisted by consulting enologist Attilio Pagli, follows traditional methods in his small cellars in the center of Montalcino, fermenting his wines without using temperature-controlling equipment and aging his Brunello in Slavonian oak casks. He eschews selected yeasts and does not filter his wines.

The result is age-worthy Brunello of ample bouquet, with layers of violet, cherry, and tobacco, and complex flavors that are extraordinarily refined. Though the winery is relatively young, the oldest vintages are showing beautifully; the 1985, of which only 2,400 bottles were made, demonstrated itself to be extraordinarily youthful at a 2007 tasting, and should continue to age for years. **KO**
❺❺❺❺ **Drink: to 2020+**

Calatayud is Aragón's newest *denominación de origen*, and is situated in a geological basin rich in clay, marl, and chalk. Enormous differences in day and nighttime temperatures have an enormous influence in the ripening of the grapes, which are the last to be harvested in Aragón.

Bodegas San Alejandro was founded as a cooperative in 1962, and became a *bodega* in 1996. It now has 300 members, owning almost 3,000 acres (1,214 ha) of mostly garnacha vines. Importer Eric Solomon fell in love with these venerable garnachas, and created Las Rocas de San Alejandro, an exclusive cuvée for the American market. "Complex and rich, with great texture and a finish that goes on for forty seconds. The opaque purple color is followed by a phenomenally rich wine that is pure kirsch mixed with blackberries and minerals. Will we ever see another wine this extraordinary for this price?" wrote Robert Parker of the 2001 vintage. In a similar pattern, the resident enologist makes this wine for the European market. With 85 percent of sales outside Spain, San Alejandro exemplifies the old saying: "Nobody is a prophet in his own land." **JMB**
❺ **Drink: recent vintages for up to 10 years**

San Vicente

2000

Origin Spain, Rioja
Style Dry red wine, 13.5% ABV
Grape Tempranillo

Luciano Sandrone

Barolo Cannubi Boschis 1998

Origin Italy, Piedmont, Langhe
Style Dry red wine, 13% ABV
Grape Nebbiolo

Marcos Eguren is one of the stars of Rioja winemaking who rose in the 1980s and 1990s. He is a man with his feet firmly planted in the Riojan soil, but at the same time has had the courage needed to implement innovations. This formula has been the key to the Eguren family's winemaking success.

Of all Marcos's wines, San Vicente is his favorite—right from its very first vintage in 1991, this was the wine that marked the family transition from traditional to modern. San Vicente is sourced from La Canoca, a vineyard of 45 acres (18 ha) replanted in the 1980s with a selection of low-yielding vines from other parcels. All of these vines happened to share certain characteristics that set them apart from the rest: a peculiar shade of foliage, smaller berries, looser bunches, and a velvety feel to the leaves—hence the name of Tempranillo Peludo (Hairy Tempranillo) given to this subvariety.

It is hard to pick just one vintage of this wine. The level of other vintages is also very high, but in particular this round and elegant San Vicente 2000 exhibits a beautiful and rare balance of aromatic complexity, acidity, and tannin. **JB**

🍷🍷🍷 **Drink: to 2018+**

One of the leading producers in Barolo, Luciano Sandrone learned his art while working as enologist at Marchesi di Barolo. He began making wine from his own grapes in the late 1970s, and eventually his increasing fame induced him to leave Marchesi di Barolo to establish his own winery. Today, he produces about 8,000 cases of wine each year from his 54 acres (22 ha) of vineyards.

His finest wines are the single-vineyard Barolos—the opulent and perfumed Le Vigne, and denser, earthier, longer-lived Cannubi Boschis. Although his Barolo is made in the more modern style, with some use of new French oak barriques, he is not a modernizer as such. Using 10 percent new French oak makes his wines enjoyable in their youth, but they have the power and structure for long aging.

According to the Scottish wine merchant Zubair Mohamed, Barolo Le Vigne of the great 1998 vintage is "delicate, with perfumed red fruits and licorice on the nose; firm tannins underpinning lots of supple fresh red fruit on the palate; long and balanced." The Cannubi Boschis 1998 joins its distinguished stablemate as the very epitome of fine Barolo. **SG**

🍷🍷🍷🍷 **Drink: to 2018+**

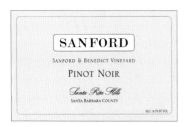

Sanford *Sanford & Benedict Vineyard Pinot Noir* 2002

Origin USA, California, Santa Rita Hills
Style Dry red wine, 14.8% ABV
Grape Pinot Noir

Viña Santa Rita *Casa Real Cabernet Sauvignon* 2003

Origin Chile, Maipo Valley
Style Dry red wine, 14% ABV
Grape Cabernet Sauvignon

The Sanford & Benedict vineyard was only the second planting of Pinot Noir in the Santa Rita Hills, and its first release was a sensation. But Richard Sanford and Michael Benedict ended their partnership in 1981, after only five vintages. Sanford then started his own venture, but without access to the vineyard's fruit, and it was not until the 1990s that Sanford regained access to his original vineyard.

The vineyard is a well-drained, north-facing hillside parcel only a few miles from the Pacific. The Santa Rita Hills cut a west-to-east channel through the region, open to morning fog and strong winds that maintain cool temperatures. These conditions lengthen the growing season and allow the grapes to gain full ripeness with firm acidity and structure.

The grapes are picked when the seeds turn brown. A relatively cool fermentation of 85 to 90°F (29–32°C) preserves delicate aromatics. Just before the fermentation is finished, the wine is pressed. Aging takes place in 100 percent new wood. There is no filtration, but the wines may be isinglass fined. The 2002 is a classic—intense, structured, and long, with a savory complexity of great persistence. **LGr**
🜂🜂 Drink: to 2015+

Viña Santa Rita's flagship red wine is named after the "royal house" (now hotel) built by the company's founder, Domingo Fernández-Concha, in 1880 at Buín in the Maipo Valley, 20 miles (35 km) south of Santiago. The Casa Real vineyard at Buín, replanted in the 1950s, forms the backbone of the Casa Real blend, one of the rare icon Chilean red wines that is really Chilean, not created as part of a foreign-backed joint venture. The fact that the brand has been overseen for nearly two decades by Cecilia Torres, Chile's first top female winemaker, has meant Casa Real's qualitative evolution has been steady, moving up a gear in terms of oak-aging from around 1993, and becoming more focused in terms of its fruit expression from 1997.

This wine is the essence of Chilean Cabernet Sauvignon: ripe, chewy, solid, full of menthol, black-currant, cigar-box, and pencil-shaving flavors, robust but not aggressive tannins, and an elegance that belies its concentration. Several Chilean winemakers admit that not only is Casa Real underrated as an icon red, but its modest price makes it a relative bargain, too. **MW**
🜂🜂🜂🜂 Drink: to 2020

Santadi *Terre Brune*
Carignano del Sulcis 1990

Origin Italy, Sardinia, Santadi (Cagliari)
Style Dry red wine, 13% ABV
Grapes Carignano 95%, Bovaleddu 5%

Most likely imported into Sardinia by the Spanish with the arrival of the conquistadors, the Carignano grape thrives in the southwestern corner of the island near Sulcis. It was long considered as a mere blending wine with few prospects.

Sardinian cooperative Santadi, one of the best cooperative cellars in Italy, has however proven the great potential of Carignano. In the 1980s, Santadi's growers began experimenting with the grape by lowering yields and employing more refined cellar practices. They also enlisted the help of Giacomo Tachis, one of Italy's most celebrated enologists.

In 1984 the Tachis-Santadi team created Terre Brune, named in honor of the dark soil around Sulcis, by adding a touch of local grape Bovaleddu to Carignano and aging in new French barriques. Grapes are carefully selected from bush-trained vines that are about fifty years old, with low yields that lend the wine its rich complexity. Terre Brune from top vintages also has surprising staying power thanks to its naturally high acidity and tannic structure—as the superb 1990, one of the most fabled vintages in Italy, aptly demonstrates. **KO**
☻☻☻ Drink: to 2017+

Viña Sastre
Pesus 2004

Origin Spain, Ribera del Duero
Style Dry red wine, 14.8% ABV
Grapes Tinta del País, Cabernet Sauvignon, Merlot

The Sastre family has been producing wine in La Horra (Burgos), the heartland of Ribera del Duero, for three generations. Rafael Sastre founded the bodega Hermanos Sastre in 1992 with the support of his father and two sons, Pedro and Jesús. The bodega owns 116 acres (47 ha) of old Tinta del País vineyards, on clay, limestone, and sandy soils, sheltered from the northerly winds by a dense pine forest.

Jesús works the vines in a sustainable, traditional way, while Pedro uses modern technology to achieve the highest expression of his grapes. The top wine is the spectacular Pesus, whose name is a contraction of Pedro and Jesús. This comes from selected plots of vines (Vadelayegua, Cañuelo, Carranguix, and Bercial) that are nearly 100 years old.

The 2004 is a beautiful deep purple color, with an aroma of cassis, prunes, coffee, slate, smoke, cinnamon, menthol, and sandalwood. On the palate it is dense, structured, and ripe, with a very long aftertaste of fruit compote, cocoa, spices, and herbs. Pesus became, from its very first vintage in 1999, one of the great new wines of the Ribera, equaling or even surpassing the legendary Pingus. **JMB**
☻☻☻☻☻ Drink: to 2020

Michele Satta
Piastraia 2001

Origin Italy, Tuscany, Bolgheri
Style Dry red wine, 13.5% ABV
Grapes Sangiovese, Merlot, C. Sauvignon, Syrah

Paolo Scavino
Barolo Bric dël Fiasc 1989

Origin Italy, Piedmont, Langhe
Style Dry red wine, 14.5% ABV
Grape Nebbiolo

When Michele Satta, as a young man on summer break from his agricultural studies at the University of Milan, first set eyes on the vineyards of the Tringali Casanuova winery, it was love at first sight. Michele transferred to the University of Pisa and, after graduating, decided to dedicate himself to viticulture, starting work at the same winery. In 1984, Satta made the move to become a winemaker and founded his own winery, starting with leased vineyards from Tringali Casanuova.

Michele has since bought his own vineyards in Castagneto Carducci, where he makes some of the area's best wines from Cabernet and Merlot, which excel in the area. Satta's 100 percent Sangiovese wine, Cavaliere, has demonstrated the great potential of Sangiovese if carefully cultivated. He also uses this native vine in his blends—including the superb Piastraia, which expresses the highest quality from Merlot and Cabernet, with Sangiovese for elegance and Syrah for roundness. His Piastraia 2001 is one of the best ever. Its combination of elegance and suppleness, while immensely enjoyable young, will also benefit from cellaring. **KO**
✺✺✺ Drink: to 2020

Lying at the foot of the Vignolo vineyard, the Scavino cellars lie equidistant between the villages of Barolo, La Morra, and Castiglione. Here, in Nebbiolo's spiritual homeland, the Scavino family has cultivated 49 acres (20 ha) of vineyards since 1921. They began bottling in 1958 and, by 1964, had stopped selling any wines in bulk. Enrico Scavino assumed the reins from his father Paolo in the late 1970s, and immediately decided to release the family's first cru wine from the Bric dël Fiasc vineyard.

This 15-acre (6 ha) vineyard enjoys perfect, southwest exposure and sports the region's famous blue-gray marl soil. The Scavinos' 3.9-acre (1.6 ha) parcel dates back to 1938, and the old vines contribute both aromatic complexity and a pronounced minerality. Yields are exceptionally low and the harvest is conducted entirely by hand.

The Bric dël Fiasc 1989 is only now shedding the unforgiving tannins of its youth and revealing Nebbiolo's astonishing complexity. Bric dël Fiasc played a crucial role in restoring the reputation of Barolo, and in so doing secured Enrico Scavino's superb world reputation as a winemaker. **MP**
✺✺✺✺ Drink: to 2019+

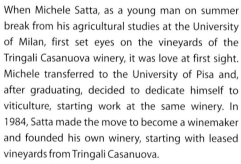

Screaming Eagle
1992

Origin USA, California, Napa Valley
Style Dry red wine, 13.5% ABV
Grape Cabernet Sauvignon

Seghesio
Home Ranch Zinfandel 2005

Origin USA, California, Sonoma County
Style Dry red wine, 15.3% ABV
Grape Zinfandel

The Screaming Eagle property was purchased by Jean Phillips in 1986; she changed the plantings from Riesling to Cabernet Sauvignon. The first vintage was in 1992, with just 225 cases produced. When Robert Parker awarded the wine a score of ninety-nine points, a phenomenon was born, and Screaming Eagle is by far the most expensive and sought-after Californian Cabernet. Although production is still miniscule, at about 500 cases a year, the wine costs a relatively modest $300 (£150; €220) a bottle for customers on its mailing list, although it fetches much more at auction; the Chicago auction house Hart Davis Hart sold a thirty-bottle vertical collection for $41,000 (£20,000; €30,000) in 2005.

Phillips sold Screaming Eagle to entrepreneurs Charles Banks and Stanley Kroenke in 2006, but Kroenke is now the sole owner. There was speculation about how the new owners might expand production by using more of the 60 acres (24 ha) already under vine, and increasing plantings elsewhere. Banks, however, stated: "You don't need to make more of it. Screaming Eagle's one of those special things. It's about keeping it special." **SG**

ϴϴϴϴϴ **Drink: to 2017+**

Edoardo Seghesio left Asti in 1886, and bought a home and vineyard land in Sonoma in 1895. Throughout the twentieth century the Seghesios were bulk wine producers, but production was cut in the 1990s, and viticulturalist Phil Freeze hired to help convert the estate to fine wine production.

The Home Ranch Zinfandel is grown next to the family home, on the original property planted in 1895. Located in an area of the Alexander Valley with no marine influence, the climate is warm, contributing to the juicy fruit and soft acidities in the wine. The soils are comprised of clay and clay loam over basalt, sandstone, and serpentine rock; the shallow topsoil and the clay's low nutrient level stress the vines to produce more concentrated fruit. Zinfandel is famous for its uneven ripening: Green grapes and raisins appear in every bunch; the Seghesios manage the vines to promote even ripening.

The 2005 season was relatively cool and long-growing, engendering a firmly structured wine with tremendous aromatic complexity, grip, and ripe—not raisiny—fruits, fully balancing Zinfandel's notoriously generous alcohol. **LGr**

ϴϴϴ **Drink: to 2017+**

Serafini e Vidotto
Rosso dell'Abazia 2003

Origin Italy, Veneto
Style Dry red wine, 13% ABV
Grapes C. Sauvignon, C. Franc, Merlot

Shafer *Cabernet*
Sauvignon Hillside Select 2002

Origin USA, California, Napa Valley
Style Dry red wine, 14.9% ABV
Grape Cabernet Sauvignon

Francesco Serafini and Antonello Vidotto started their company in 1987 with the intention of producing world-class wine—quite an unusual aspiration in the area at the time. Serafini and Vidotto have been replanting the centuries-old vineyards here at the rate of 2.5 acres (1 ha) per year.

The vineyards are south-facing; the soil is quite poor but rich in stones and pebbles—ideal for drainage. The climate is characterized by the cool air rising from the sea and from the River Piave valley; the resulting temperature variation helps the grapes maintain fresh aromas and good acidity levels.

The Rosso dell'Abazia 2003 shows the huge potential of the area. This wine retains its medium-bodied appeal and subtlety of aroma, despite the fierce heat of the vintage. The color is not particularly dense, and the nose enchants with black-currant and lead-pencil aromas, as well as the gentle greenness of Cabernet-based wines of northeast Italy. The entry is soft and round, with ripe fruits and subtle vegetal notes creating a very pleasant synergy. The wine has a warm mouthfeel and the finish is focused and long: a real pleasure. **AS**

❸❸❸ Drink: to 2018

In 1972 John Shafer left the publishing industry and moved his family to the Napa Valley, where he had bought an estate in the Stag's Leap District. Part of the property was vineyard land planted in the 1920s; the Shafers grubbed up existing vines, built terraces on the rocky hillsides, and replanted. They now cultivate 210 acres (85 ha) of vines. John Shafer evolved from grower to vintner in 1979; Doug Shafer, John's son, became winemaker in 1983, succeeded by his assistant, Elias Fernandez, in 1994.

The 54-acre (22 ha) estate vineyard from which Hillside Select grapes are sourced lies in the north of the district, with elevations up to 300 feet (90 m) and gradients up to 45 percent. Planted over rock, there is often no more than 18 inches (46 cm) of poor, rocky volcanic soil above weathered bedrock, offering ideal conditions for ripe, concentrated fruit—a hallmark of Shafer's consistent style.

Some thirty years from the estate's inception, the Hillside Select 2002 is a brilliant trophy of Napa fruit: intense and powerful, elegantly braided with supple tannins, a dynamic expression of black fruits, violets, spice, tobacco, and mineral. **LGr**

❸❸❸❸ Drink: to 2025

The weed charlock (*Sinapis arvensis*) grows among Napa vines. ➡

Cillar de Silos
Torresilo 2004

Origin Spain, Ribera del Duero
Style Dry red wine, 14% ABV
Grape Tinto Fino (Tempranillo)

Cillar de Silos is a young company in Ribera del Duero, founded in 1994 by the Aragón García brothers. They are located at Quintana de Pidio, a small village in the cold province of Burgos, where they own 125 acres (50 ha) of vineyards. This region, off the beaten track of Ribera, holds a real and now rare treasure in the form of very old vines.

The brothers began with the traditional set of wines—crianza and reserva, under the Cillar de Silos label—but soon created the Torresilo brand for their top wine. They are very focused on the quality of their wines, always somewhat unhappy with their results and looking for ways to improve. They take great care to adapt the maceration and oak regimes to the quality of the raw material from each harvest. The wine is creamy, focused, balanced, and supple.

The 2004 is very dark, almost black, with a glowing purple rim. The aroma is intense, with some toasted oak notes mixed with spicy tones, leather, licorice, ink, dried herbs, and a core of ripe, black fruit. Full-bodied in the mouth, very focused, clean, and pure, it is well balanced by the acidity, with solid fruit and a very long finish. **LG**
🝡🝡 **Drink: to 2019**

Château Simone
Palette Rosé 2012

Origin France, Palette
Style Dry rosé wine, 12.5% ABV
Grapes Grenache 45%, Mourvèdre 30%, Others 25%

This tiny, immaculate wine estate just east of Aix-en-Provence breaks many rules. The vineyard parcels all face north, and are surrounded by the tall trees of a calm forest; the River Arc and the traffic of the A8 motorway flow by, beneath an immaculately tended garden. The vineyard is planted with a small library of varieties (in addition to Grenache and Mourvèdre, this wine contains Cinsault, Syrah, Castet, Manosquin, Carignan, and various Muscats); the average age of the vines for this pink wine is, perhaps uniquely in the world, more than fifty years.

The result, according to the cultured and welcoming René Rougier and his son Jean-François, is a *rosé de repas*, a mealtime rosé. Brilliant bright pink, its fresh fruits are evident in both scent and flavor, underscored by the dramatic acidity of the site and the vinosity that comes from the slow ripening it imposes. The symphonic blend gives the wine an innate complexity rare with rosé.

Palette is a tiny 56-acre (23 ha) appellation brought into being by the tenacity of René's grandfather, Jean Rougier, in 1948, and still two-thirds owned by the Rougier family. **AJ**
🝡🝡 **Drink: recent vintages within 3 years**

Château Simone is the only property of the Palette appellation. ➡

Château Sociando-Mallet

2005

Origin France, Bordeaux, St.-Seurin
Style Dry red wine, 13% ABV
Grapes C. Sauvignon 55%, Merlot 40%, C. Franc 5%

In 1969 a *négociant* called Jean Gautreau bought a house north of St.-Estèphe as a holiday home. It came with 12 acres (4.8 ha) of vines and was located on a slope overlooking the estuary. Gautreau had no intention of planting more vineyards, but before long friends persuaded him of the potential of the terroir: The soils were essentially gravel over clay, like the best sites of St.-Estèphe, and Sociando's wine had been well regarded in the previous century.

Gautreau now has 182 acres (74 ha) under cultivation. He opted for a full-throttled style, with a good deal of press wine in the blend and, from the early 1990s, Sociando has been aged solely in new oak. The trade and customers were amazed by the quality of the wine, especially since Gautreau was adamantly opposed to the fashionable technique of green-harvesting to reduce yields. His yields were high, but he argued that high-density vineyards in good health should be able to produce a generous crop without dilution. After vinification he would declassify any lots below the required standard.

Jean Gautreau took no interest in the Cru Bourgeois classification of 2003, even though it seemed certain that Sociando would have been classified as Exceptionnel. The 2005 is shy in its aromas but explosive on the palate, with masses of rich, almost juicy black fruits, spice, and astonishing length. Like all good vintages of Sociando, it is structured to last. Gautreau may be a loner, happy to buck conventional wisdom, but the excellence of his wine and its popularity speak volumes. **SBr**

☉☉☉ Drink: to 2025

Soldera *Case Basse*

Brunello di Montalcino 1990

Origin Italy, Tuscany, Montalcino
Style Dry red wine, 14% ABV
Grape Sangiovese

Gianfranco Soldera is one of the great eccentrics of wine. A passionate biodynamist, he and his wife maintain a mini-ecological system, featuring birds, bats, and frogs, in the garden of their modest estate, which contains some 20 acres (8 ha) of vineyard.

A Milanese businessman, Soldera bought the estate in the early 1970s, well before the Montalcino boom began, and set himself to make the greatest wine in the world. He is not alone in thinking that he has succeeded brilliantly. The sometimes infuriating flip side of this lofty self-opinion is the negativity he heaps on almost all other winemakers of the world. Giovanni Conterno was exempt from his withering and near-universal contempt, for example, but another equally famous Barolo producer, according to Soldera, "never made a good wine in his life."

Soldera is a dyed-in-the-wool traditionalist, crafting his wines with lengthy maceration and no temperature control, followed by up to five-and-a-half years in large Slavonian oak barrels, the entire operation being overseen, as it has been for more than thirty years, by octogenarian *maestro-assaggiatore* Giulio Gambelli. The result is a wine light in color but multifaceted and remarkably ethereal, with fresh and dried fruits, herbs, and flowers registering tantalizingly, if fleetingly, on the nose and palate. This style, perhaps a bit short on depth and power, but long on subtlety and grace, has not always fared well with the points pundits. However, those who have not tasted Case Basse have not tasted Brunello di Montalcino. **NBel**

☉☉☉☉☉ Drink: to 2040+

Sangiovese grows near the Abbey of Sant'Antimo, Montalcino. ➡

Solms-Delta
Africana 2008

Origin South Africa, Paarl
Style Dry red wine, 13.5% ABV
Grape Syrah

Marc Sorrel
Hermitage Le Gréal 2004

Origin France, Northern Rhône, Hermitage
Style Dry red wine, 15% ABV
Grapes Syrah 92%, Marsanne 8%

Neuroscientist Mark Solms rediscovered ancient winemaking traditions after turning to farming in the lovely Franschhoek valley. Seeking the best way to make wine in a warm climate, he is bringing the Mediterranean past into the present, and he and his winemakers are successfully experimenting with grapes dried on the vine by crushing their stems.

Africana is made entirely from vine-dried Syrah, the whole bunches fermented and matured in new French oak. The wine is deep and rich, with drama, power, and complexity of flavors as it develops. There are 8 grams of residual sugar, but the palate scarcely shows sweetness. As Neil Beckett said of the 2005 vintage, while approving the conservative-radical thrust at Solms-Delta, "this pungently scented and powerfully tannic wine is unique."

Africana's name alludes to Solms-Delta's deeply humanistic commitment to the culture of Africa and to its people. The "painful history of dispossession, slavery, and apartheid" is both acknowledged (via a moving museum) and addressed (through shared ownership with the property's historically disadvantaged tenant-workers). **TJ**

🍷🍷 **Drink: to 2028+**

Marc Sorrel is the son of the local notary, but he was keener on wine than law, and it was a brother who took over his father's law practice. However, his father also had a small but valuable domaine on the great rock of Hermitage, and in 1982 Marc joined him in the winemaking. The latter died two years later. Marc came into his own after 1988, and has been one of the leaders since 1998. Now he makes around 8,000 bottles from his 5 acres (2 ha) of Hermitage.

Le Gréal is a blend of his vines in the crus of Greffieux and Méal. Robert Parker's discovery of Sorrel made his fortune. The wines were very much in his style, being big, tough, and tannic. With age, a feral note—not unusual in Syrah wines—creeps in.

Yields are notably small. In the late 1980s they were at around 25 hectoliters per hectare. The 2004 had 8 percent Marsanne in it to provide some extra aromas. It was not destemmed. In general the wines spend eighteen to twenty-four months in barrel before bottling and are never filtered. The wine is reminiscent of violets, black currants, and musk, and should easily last twenty years from the vintage. **GM**

🍷🍷🍷🍷🍷 **Drink: to 2025**

Sot
Lefriec 2004

Origin Spain, Penedès
Style Dry red wine, 13.5% ABV
Grapes C. Sauvignon, Merlot, Cariñena

Stag's Leap Wine Cellars
Cabernet Sauvignon 1973

Origin USA, California, Napa Valley
Style Dry red wine, 13% ABV
Grapes Cabernet Sauvignon 93%, Merlot 7%

Irene Alemany is from Vilafranca del Penedès, and her family has had vineyards in the region for generations, but not as their main business. Laurent Corrio is from Brittany and grew up in the Jura. Each bitten by the wine bug, they studied enology, then met in Burgundy and founded the Sot Lefriec project. The 1999 first vintage was the first garage wine from Penedès, literally fermented and raised in a small warehouse in Vilafranca. The founders even built their own stainless-steel fermentation tanks, and still do everything manually. The production is tiny. They own 20 acres (8 ha) of old Cariñena (planted in the 1940s), and of young Merlot and Cabernet Sauvignon (planted in the 1980s).

2004 may be the best balanced vintage for Sot Lefriec so far. The color is dark and opaque. It is initially closed on the nose, and needs some swirling in the glass, or even vigorous decanting if consumed young. It is a serious wine, quite reminiscent of Bordeaux, with black fruit, graphite mineral notes, ink, and smoke. Full in the mouth, it is balanced and fresh, with present but ripe tannins, very persistent and long. It will evolve slowly in the bottle. **LG**

🍷🍷🍷 **Drink: to 2019**

Warren Winiarski's Cabernet Sauvignon 1973 is arguably the most well-known and influential wine in U.S. history, having been judged "the best" at Steven Spurrier's 1976 Paris Tasting. Produced from vines only three years old, in Winiarski's first vintage, the wine beat top Bordeaux crus. Suddenly U.S. wines had the respect they lacked previously.

Winiarski's vision and winemaking philosophies differ from others in the region, which may account for how different the wines are, even if they all share the same soils. His foundation is grounded in classical ideals, balancing opposing elements to create wines that are dynamic, harmonious, even transcendent. This pursuit of the ideal is an exercise in restraint, nuance, and proportion.

He claims he glimpsed it, in 1969, when he tasted Nathan Fay's homemade wine, prompting him to purchase the adjoining plum orchard, replanting it to Cabernet Sauvignon and Merlot. He bought Fay's vineyard in 1986, and had to replant both in the late 1980s and 1990s. He sold Stag's Leap to a joint venture of Ste. Michelle Wine Estates and Marchesi Antinori in 2007, but the wines remain fine. **LGr**

🍷🍷🍷🍷 **Drink: to 2018+**

Stonier Estate *Reserve Pinot Noir* 2003

Origin Australia, Mornington Peninsula
Style Dry red wine, 13.5% ABV
Grape Pinot Noir

The first vines were planted in cool-climate Mornington Peninsula in the early 1970s. Stonier planted Pinot Noir in 1978, but they never expected to make red wine from it—the intention was to use it as a base wine for sparkling. But soon they realized they had hit upon a winner. Both the regular and Reserve Pinot Noir here are stunningly good. "The development of vineyards here was a bit of a steep learning curve," says winemaker Geraldine McFaul. "Pinot is so site sensitive, and we have had it in the wrong place before. We are at a stage now where we are happy with what is planted where."

McFaul did the 2002 vintage at Domaine de L'Arlot in Burgundy, and since then she has experimented with some whole-bunch ferments, using reserve-quality fruit. From 2003 the Reserve has about 5 percent whole-bunch fermented wine, and a little (fifty cases) was bottled separately. The Reserve Pinot Noir spends ten to fourteen days on its skins, hand-punched, in small open fermentors.

The result is an Australian interpretation of Pinot Noir that captures the complexity and elegance of which the grape is capable, but which is often lost. The 2003 Reserve is particularly successful, and with a Halliday rating of ninety-seven out of 100 is the equal highest rated Pinot Noir in Australia. The nose is bright and complex, with layers of dark spicy cherry and red berry fruit. The palate is concentrated yet elegant and fine. There is impressive balance between the fruit and the spicy structure. **JG**
🔊🔊 **Drink: to 2018**

FURTHER RECOMMENDATIONS
Other great vintages
1988 • 1989 • 1990 • 1995 • 1996
1998 • 1999 • 2000 • 2004 • 2005
More producers from Mornington Peninsula
Main Ridge • Moorooduc • Ten Minutes by Tractor

Stonier's vineyards face inland and are sheltered from sea winds. ➡

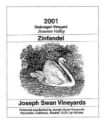

Stonyridge
Larose 2006

Origin New Zealand, Auckland, Waiheke Island
Style Dry red wine, 13.5% ABV
Grapes C. Sauvignon, Merlot, C. Franc, Others

Stonyridge is a true *garagiste*—the original winery and living accommodation of owner Stephen White was literally a large aluminum garage. White followed Goldwater to become Waiheke Island's second, and arguably its best, winemaker.

The first vintage of Larose was 1985, though it was the excellent 1987 vintage that really put this tiny producer on the map. Within a few years, Stonyridge had developed cult status, with sought-after vintages fetching several times their original cost on the secondary market. In a great vintage, such as 2006, the enthusiasm of investors and collectors is certainly justified. Weather conditions during the critical ripening period on Waiheke Island can, however, be wet with the risk of rot, exerting pressure to harvest before the grapes are ripe.

Larose is a Cabernet Sauvignon-dominant blend of five red Bordeaux grape varieties, which White believes bring complexity to the wine. The 2006 is an elegant rather than blockbuster red wine, with an aroma suggesting red berries, wild flowers, mixed spice, and fresh leather. This is a powerful wine, but the power is delivered with remarkable subtlety. **BC**
🍷🍷🍷 **Drink: to 2020**

Joseph Swan *Stellwagen*
Vineyard Zinfandel 2001

Origin USA, California, Sonoma Valley
Style Dry red wine, 15.2% ABV
Grape Zinfandel

Joseph Swan produced some of California's first cult wines. A pilot, he retired in 1967 near the town of Forestville in the Russian River Valley of Sonoma County, and planted vineyards on a site on Laguna Road with a heritage selection of Chardonnay, Cabernet Sauvignon, and Pinot Noir. While waiting for these vines to mature, he began making Zinfandel from bought-in grapes.

Swan's early Zinfandels were legendary in an era when respect for old-vine Zinfandel was rare. Joe's last vintage was 1987; he died in 1989 and was succeeded as winemaker by his son-in-law Rod Berglund. Rod's wines are aged in French oak barrels, and the style is atypical for California—less exuberantly fruity and oaky than many, with greater individuality and restraint, well balanced, and offering great transparency of fruit and site.

The Stellwagen vineyard is notable for its very old vines planted in the 1880s in deep, rich, volcanic soil. The 2001 is particularly elegant: very dry, with firm, taut structure and crisp acidity. The palate gives bright redcurrant, white pepper, savory, and spice flavors, with raisins on the finish. **SB**
🍷🍷🍷 **Drink: to 2017+**

◩ Stonyridge vineyard (center) in Waiheke's undulating landscape.

Château Talbot 2000

Origin France, Bordeaux, St.-Julien
Style Dry red wine, 13% ABV
Grapes C. Sauvignon 66%, Merlot 26%, Others 8%

Talbot is, at 250 acres (101 ha), one of the Médoc's largest vineyards and accounts for one-eighth of the St.-Julien appellation. The château and winery are tucked away in the center of the appellation and not easily visible to passersby. Talbot was bought by Désiré Cordier in 1917 and is owned at present by two sisters, Nancy Bignon and Lorraine Rustmann, who are directly descended from him. The vineyards are surprisingly homogenous, given their extent, with gravel of varying depths and some sand on the lesser sectors. The sisters invested heavily in Talbot in the 1990s, constructing new buildings, improving the drainage, and introducing stricter selection.

Ancient vintages such as 1934, 1945, 1949, and 1955 proved remarkably resilient and lively when tasted in the 1990s, suggesting that the potential of Talbot should not be underestimated. In its youth, the wine can be elegant and discreet, giving little hint of its potential. Indeed many wines from the 1960s and 1970s were somewhat undernourished, but the viticultural reforms of the past decade or so have revealed anew the stature of Talbot. The wine is also moderately priced for its status.

The 2000 is typical of Talbot at its best. Black fruits dominate the nose, with a discreet oakiness to give it some lift. There is no shortage of tannin on the palate, as one would expect, but the fruit, marked by black currants, is splendid and opulent and balanced by fine acidity that gives the wine excellent length. This wine combines energy with elegance. **SBr**
Θ Θ Θ **Drink: to 2035**

FURTHER RECOMMENDATIONS
Other great vintages
1961 • 1982 • 1986 • 1990 • 1996 • 2004 • 2005 • 2009
More producers from St.-Julien
Ducru-Beaucaillou • Lagrange • Léoville-Barton Léoville-Las Cases • Léoville-Poyferré

Château Talbot's elegant blend ages well for many years. ➜

Tapanappa Whalebone Vineyard *Cabernet/Shiraz* 2004

Origin Australia, Wrattonbully
Style Dry red wine, 14.3% ABV
Grapes C. Sauvignon, Shiraz, C. Franc

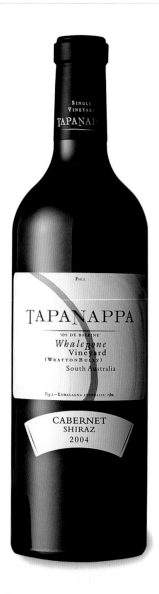

Brian Croser rose to prominence in the mid-1970s, when he left his position as chief winemaker with Hardys to begin the celebrated wine science course at Riverina College in New South Wales. At the same time he also founded an influential wine consultancy and his own winery, Petaluma. He lost control of Petaluma in 2001, and was left looking for a venture of his own. That venture is Tapanappa, a new super-premium label launched by Croser in collaboration with Bollinger and Jean-Michel Cazes.

The first wine released was the Whalebone Vineyard red, which comes from a vineyard just outside the Coonawarra appellation, in Wrattonbully. Croser first made a wine from this vineyard in 1980, and was so impressed by it that he has been trying to buy the vineyard ever since.

The vineyard now has thirty-year-old vines, with yields of a ton an acre (roughly 15 hectoliters per hectare). The Whalebone Red 2004 is the second vintage of this wine. It has a sweet, perfumed nose of red and black fruits with a bit of Coonawarralike minerality. There is really nice balance here, and it is smooth and complex. The palate has sweet rounded fruit countered by firm but silkily textured tannins. It comes across as quite New World in its sweetness, but there is good depth and complexity. The hallmark of this wine is superb balance; unlike many Coonawarra Cabernets, there is less of the minerally, gravelly greenness, and the extra ripeness makes this a more complete wine. **JG**

☉☉☉ **Drink: to 2020**

FURTHER RECOMMENDATIONS
Other great vintages
2003 · 2005
More Tapanappa wines
Tiers Vineyard Chardonnay
Whalebone Vineyard Merlot

A fossilized whalebone protrudes from the roof of a cave on the estate. ⏵

Dominio de Tares
Cepas Viejas Bierzo 2004

Origin Spain, Bierzo
Style Dry red wine, 13.5% ABV
Grape Mencía

Tasca d'Almerita
Rosso del Conte 2002

Origin Italy, Sicily
Style Dry red wine, 14% ABV
Grape Nero d'Avola

Dominio de Tares is a very young winery in the Bierzo DO in the northwest of Spain, founded at the turn of the century. There they combine tradition and the latest technology with the aim of producing high-quality wines, using only local grapes.

The first wine they put on the market was the Cepas Viejas (Old Vines) from 2000. It is produced from the fruit of head-pruned, sixty-year-old Mencía vines, the local red grape of the region, grown on argilo-calcareous soils with a high slate content. The boxes of hand-harvested grapes are put through a sorting table on their arrival at the winery to select only the perfect bunches. Alcoholic fermentation lasts for fifteen days and malolactic takes place in American oak barrels. The wine is later aged for nine months in a mixture of new and used barrels, of both French and American origin, and bottled unfiltered.

Cepas Viejas is normally very dark in color, almost opaque. It has good intensity of aroma, with dry straw, autumn leaves, and wild flowers covering a core of very mature red fruits. In the mouth it shows medium body, with good acidity, and is balanced, long, flavorful, and powerful. **LG**

🍷🍷 **Drink: recent vintages for up to 12 years**

Tasca d'Almerita, along with a handful of other wine producers on the island, have spearheaded the Sicilian winemaking revolution, bringing Nero d'Avola to unprecedented levels of quality.

The estate is still family owned and run by Lucio Tasca, son of Count Giuseppe Tasca, who first introduced the espalier training system to the area. The Regaleali Riserva del Conte, as it was originally named, came from grapes grown on bush-trained Nero d'Avola vines, and was left to age in large, chestnut casks. It was the first Sicilian example of a cru wine, because all its grapes came from the same vineyard, planted partly in 1959 (bush system) and partly in 1965 (spur-pruned cordon), at a high density of 9,850 plants per acre.

The Rosso del Conte 2002 is a wine that marks the end of a cycle. From 2003, the wine will benefit from the addition of a selection of the best red grapes of the estate. This is a beautifully crafted wine, able to change many minds about this unlucky, but far from unworthy, vintage. The powerful structure and fine yet firm tannins give way to an astonishing amount of luscious, sweet black-currant fruit. **AS**

🍷🍷🍷🍷 **Drink: to 2028**

Vineyards on the Regaleali estate, established by Count Giuseppe Tasca. ➡

Te Mata *Coleraine* 2005

Origin New Zealand, Hawke's Bay
Style Dry red wine, 13.5% ABV
Grapes Cabernet Sauvignon, Merlot, Cabernet Franc

Te Mata Estate first produced wine in 1896, making it one of New Zealand's oldest wineries. The present owners purchased and revitalized the rundown property in 1978, at a time when hybrid grape vines dominated the national vineyard and most of the wine produced was cheap "Port" and "Sherry." Owner-manager John Buck had returned to New Zealand with a passion for fine wine after a stint in the English wine trade. In 1981 Te Mata produced a miniscule amount of a Cabernet Sauvignon/Merlot blend that was vastly superior to any New Zealand red wine made at the time. The following year, a dense, ripe, and impressively stylish red made another quantum leap in quality. The wine was christened after the winery's home vineyard, Coleraine. It raised the bar for quality winemaking, particularly for red wine.

At first, the wine was made from grapes grown in a single vineyard, but the vagaries of vintage conditions resulted in a roller-coaster ride in quality and style. Coleraine has never missed a vintage since 1982. Then, in 1989, the company made the very wise decision to retain the vineyard name but to blend the wine from the best grapes grown in nine Hawke's Bay vineyards. Wine that does not make the cut may be bottled under two other labels. 2005 was a very good vintage in Hawke's Bay, the first time the region had experienced a really successful harvest in an odd year since 1991. The wine is dense but not heavy, showing concentrated dark berry, cedarwood, bramble, and spicy oak flavors. **BC**

ⓢⓢⓢ **Drink: to 2020**

FURTHER RECOMMENDATIONS
Other great vintages
1995 · 1998 · 2000 · 2002 · 2003 · 2004
More producers from Hawke's Bay
Craggy Range · CJ Pask
Sacred Hill · Stonecroft · Trinity Hill

John Buck's house, surrounded by Te Mata's Coleraine vineyard. ➜

Te Motu
Cabernet / Merlot 2000

Origin New Zealand, Waiheke Island
Style Dry red wine, 13% ABV
Grapes Cabernet Sauvignon 74%, Merlot 26%

Long resident on Waiheke Island, the Dunleavy family planted its first vines in 1989, and the first vintage of Te Motu was produced in 1993. Te Motu's blend varies from year to year. Each variety is aged separately and is tasted after a year to determine what goes into the second wine Dunleavy Cabernet/Merlot. The best of the rest is left to mature for six to nine months before being bottled as Te Motu.

When released in 2007, the 2000 was developing well. Ruby purple in color, with a rim tinged by garnet, the Cabernet character was particularly strong on the nose, suggesting the variety's typical cigar-box, smoke, and cassis flavors. The undergrowth aromas already apparent will become more pronounced with age; Te Motu always has a distinctively earthy and savory character. Medium-bodied, and still with plenty of tannin and juicy acidity, the 2000 may have attained its peak by 2010, but will stay there for several more years. Although Te Motu is usually ready to drink upon release, it also rewards patient cellaring: Terry Dunleavy reported in October 2007 that the 1993 was "absolutely stunning, with fresh sweet berry and currant." **SG**
🟢🟢🟢 **Drink: to 2018**

Domaine Tempier
Bandol Cuvée Cabassaou 1988

Origin France, Provence, Bandol
Style Dry red wine, 13% ABV
Grapes Mourvèdre, Syrah

The parcels of Tempier's domain, toward the north of Bandol's grand limestone amphitheatre, are scattered over three different communes. Cabassaou is the smallest of the three single-vineyard parcels whose wines are vinified separately.

Daniel Ravier, who has directed the domain since 2000, stresses its commitment to balance. The grapes are destemmed; extractions are carried out with a light touch, and the wines spend eighteen months in large, old wood casks.

The Cabassaou 1988 is still opaque red-black. Aromatically, the wine is hugely complex, suggesting burrows and hives, pine, tomato, and rosehip. With time in the glass it grows sweeter and more rounded. Later it casually tosses out more allusions—treacle, honey, malt. On the palate, it retains great weight, presence, intensity, and density; the tannins have the quality of fine leather, and its acidity is ripe, vivid, and rounded. There is a sumptuousness seeping into the flavor repertoire behind the leather and the earth. This fine Bandol is not just complex—but singular, too, as all great vins de terroir should be. **AJ**
🟢🟢🟢🟢 **Drink: to 2018**

Tenuta dell'Ornellaia
Masseto IGT Toscana 2001

Origin Italy, Tuscany, Bolgheri
Style Dry red wine, 14% ABV
Grape Merlot

Tenuta dell'Ornellaia
1988

Origin Italy, Tuscany, Bolgheri
Style Dry red wine, 12.5% ABV
Grapes C. Sauvignon 80%, Merlot 16%, C. Franc 4%

Having acquired a piece of prize Bolgheri real estate from his mother, Lodovico Antinori chose to turn it into a truly outstanding vineyard. Antinori recognized that high quality could be achieved by producing Bordeaux-style wines. In the early 1980s, he planted much virgin territory to vineyards, and built a space-age, Californian-style winery to accommodate everything needed to make top-quality wine. The first red wine released was the Ornellaia 1985, a blend of Cabernet Sauvignon, Cabernet Franc, and Merlot.

Masseto was born in 1986, when Tenuta dell' Ornellaia decided to bottle the Merlot from its Masseto vineyard by itself, because it was of such high quality. The first vintage was called simply Merlot, but from 1987 it was named after its 17-acre (7 ha) vineyard.

Since its first vintage, Masseto had been highly regarded and much sought-after internationally, but with the 2001's 100-point score from *Wine Spectator*, it began heading for the stars. By September 2007, Masseto 2001 was fetching the same price as the revered Sassicaia 1985. **SG**
ⓢⓢⓢⓢⓢ **Drink: to 2020+**

Cabernet Sauvignon has always dominated the varietal composition of Ornellaia, but the percentage of Merlot increased significantly in the late 1990s. Maturation takes place in barriques for twelve months before the final blending, and remains in barrique for a further six months. The wine spends a further twelve months in the bottle before being released from the winery.

Founded in 1981 by Lodovico Antinori, in 2005 the estate came into full ownership of the Frescobaldi family, who expressed firm commitment to continuity of practice and principle. Consultant Michel Rolland visits the estate around three times a year and is principally involved in blending.

The first Ornellaia was made in the stellar 1985 Tuscan vintage, but it was in 1988 that the estate hit its stride. Power and structure is evident in the wine, the texture is more solid, and the wine shows complexity and depth. There is aromatic intensity on the nose—almonds, Christmas cake, and cedarwood. Very firm on the palate—tannic structure is evident but there is enough fruit to cover it. Very classic, and could be cellared for longer. **SB**
ⓢⓢⓢⓢⓢ **Drink: to 2018+**

Tenuta delle Terre Nere
Etna Rosso Feudo di Mezzo 2004

Origin Italy, Sicily, Mt. Etna
Style Dry red wine, 14% ABV
Grapes Nerello Mascalese 95%, Nerello Cappuccio 5%

Tenuta di Valgiano
Rosso Colline Lucchesi 2003

Origin Italy, Tuscany
Style Dry red wine, 14% ABV
Grapes Sangiovese 60%, Syrah 30%, Merlot 10%

Although Etna DOC was the first controlled denomination in Sicily, its wines were bland and rustic until a small group of winemakers and entrepreneurs invested in the area in the early and mid-1990s. Their early efforts stunned critics and connoisseurs alike, since when Mount Etna's precipitous vineyards have witnessed one of the most impressive enological revolutions in all Italy.

Attracted by the dazzling potential of the wines, Italo-American artisanal wine broker Marc de Grazia began, in 2002, acquiring vineyards on Etna's northern slopes. He named his estate (where he is both agronomist and winemaker) Terre Nere in honor of the black, volcanic soil.

Produced from very old vines planted in 1927 and 1947, this wine is both rich and polished. The old vines generate concentrated flavors of red berries, herbs, and earth while the altitude causes wide diurnal temperature variation, contributing to the wine's complexity and elegance. The inaugural 2004 vintage of Feudo di Mezzo is both fresh and complex, with ample strawberry aromas reminiscent of Pinot Noir and a graceful but age-worthy structure. **KO**
♻♻♻ **Drink: to 2019+**

When Moreno Petrini bought this estate, his intention was merely to make enough money for him to keep the estate for the following year. A passionate collector and connoisseur who tastes widely, he soon realized that he had seriously underestimated the potential of his grapes.

While Petrini became confident that he could produce an expressive and original wine, he knew it could not happen before he fully understood how his vines "worked" with the soil—a quest that led him to adopt biodynamic viticulture.

Only in 1999 did he feel that he had sufficient understanding to release the first Rosso Colline Lucchesi. The estate wine was bound to be an important wine, and it is. The Tenuta di Valgiano 2003 has a sweet, spicy, dense appeal. The nose is both powerful and elegant. The oak, certainly present but never overwhelming, gives a first impression of sweetness that is quickly taken away by a very fine and tightly knit tannin, which also helps the fruit reach every corner of the mouth and to linger on the long finish. It is definitely a wine that will repay the most patient aficionados. **AS**
♻♻♻ **Drink: to 2025+**

Tenuta di San Guido
Sassicaia 1985

Origin Italy, Tuscany, Bolgheri
Style Dry red wine, 13% ABV
Grapes C. Sauvignon 85%, C. Franc 15%

Tenuta San Leonardo
San Leonardo 2004

Origin Italy, Trentino
Style Dry red wine, 14% ABV
Grapes C. Sauvignon 60%, Merlot 30%, and others

Sassicaia was a groundbreaker when the 1968 vintage came on the market in the early 1970s, created by Marchese Mario Incisa della Rocchetta, a Piedmontese vine-grower who in 1943 moved to the Tuscan estate inherited by his Gherardesca wife (sister of Piero Antinori's mother). Originally the wine was consumed by friends and family or sold privately, but in 1970 Mario's son Nicolò managed to persuade his father to offer it commercially with the professional assistance of the Antinori cousins.

Sassicaia was the first barrique-aged wine of Italy; the first great Italian Cabernet; and the first Italian wine (the 1985) to be awarded 100 points by Robert Parker. Recently Nicolas Belfrage MW declared the 1985 to be still remarkably youthful in color and in substance. "The classic blackcurrant aroma of Cabernet Sauvignon is there, together with the equally classic lead pencil of Cabernet aged in French oak, plus a wealth of herbs, spices, and leather. There is a remarkable liveliness to the palate, quantities of rich sweet fruit, and dense but smooth tannins." With great elegance but even greater youthfulness, the 1985 is an immortal wine. **SG**

☺☺☺☺☺ **Drink: to 2025+**

San Leonardo, from the eponymous estate nestling among the lower slopes of alpine southern Trentino, is probably the most prestigious wine of Italy, to judge by the stars, glasses, and points awarded over the past twenty years by guides, journalists, and online pundits. Then why is the Anglo-Saxon wine-world so ignorant of its existence?

Could it be because it is made not in the Italian way but in that of Bordeaux, from Bordeaux grapes, by a Bordeaux lover, Marchese Carlo Guerrieri Gonzaga, and his Bordeaux-loving son Anselmo, assisted by Italy's foremost contemporary expert in the making of Bordeaux-style wines, oenologist Carlo Ferrini? But then, something similar could be said of Marchese Niccolo Incisa della Rocchetta's Sassicaia, and there's no such lack of recognition there.

Whatever the reason, San Leonardo is a classy wine, and the 2004 is an excellent representative: deep and still youthfully bright of color; beautifully balanced in terms of fruit, firm acidity, and silky tannins; rich, ripe, and berrylike with the effect of fine oak rather than the aroma. A wine to be savored now or laid down for years. **NB**

☺☺☺ **Drink: to 2024+**

Tenuta Sette Ponti
Crognolo 2004

Origin Italy, Tuscany
Style Dry red wine, 14% ABV
Grapes Sangiovese 90%, Merlot 10%

Terrazas/Cheval Blanc
Cheval des Andes 2002

Origin Argentina, Mendoza
Style Dry red wine, 13.5% ABV
Grapes Cabernet Sauvignon 60%, Malbec 40%

Alberto Moretti, the father of present owner Antonio, bought this estate in 1957. At the end of the 1990s, his son wished to fulfill his dream of producing top-quality wines at his estate. He took on Carlo Ferrini as a consultant, and did not have to wait too long to read the first, flattering reviews of his wines.

The oldest vineyard on the property is the beautiful Vigna dell'Impero, initiated in 1935 to commemorate the end of the African campaign and the birth of the Italian empire. This vineyard, built with great difficulty, is planted with Sangiovese, and must be one of the oldest, still commercially productive Sangiovese vineyards in the region.

Crognolo was the first wine of the estate to be released on to the market, followed a year later by Oreno. Crognolo is mainly Sangiovese, with a small percentage of Merlot to soften the Tuscan grape's rustic side without changing its juicy appeal. The 2004 shows this structure particularly well, combining ripe, soft, cherry notes with more spicy, peppery ones. The well-judged tannins and refreshing acidity make this wine an ideal partner for a wide range of foods. **AS**

☻☻☻ **Drink: to 2017**

This estate is run by Frenchman Pierre Lurton of Château Cheval Blanc. Together with Roberto de la Mota (now winemaker at Mendel) they crafted a wine from Terrazas de los Andes's oldest vines, planted in the 1920s in the Vistalba subregion of Mendoza.

This area was targeted by Pierre Lurton when searching for Malbec—a key part of St.-Emilion vineyards before phylloxera struck. It fell from grace by dint of grafting poorly to phylloxera-tolerant U.S. rootstocks. Some argue that ungrafted vines, like those from which Cheval des Andes is partly blended, have a purer edge than their grafted peers.

What is unarguable is that this wine combines the ripe, plump, almost exotic but seductive character at which Argentina excels, with the restrained, smooth, but vitally crisp quality one hopes to find in the best Bordeaux. It shows the value of Lurton's urging restraint via slower ripening in the vineyard, and of de la Mota's refusal to overextract or to blast the wine with oak. It is the kind of joint-venture wine where you imagine both winemakers taking real pleasure in blending. **MW**

☻☻☻ **Drink: to 2017+**

Terrazas's Caicayen vineyard in the fall, in front of the Andes. ▷

LE TERTRE
ROTEBOEUF

Château Tertre-Roteboeuf
2001

Origin France, Bordeaux, St.-Emilion
Style Dry red wine, 13.5% ABV
Grapes Merlot 85%, Cabernet Franc 15%

François Mitjavile has transformed the rather rundown property of his in-laws into one of the leading estates of St.-Emilion. On taking on its management in 1978, he soon recognized that the 14 acres (5.6 ha) of vines in an amphitheater behind the house on the slopes facing the Dordogne valley were on a highly promising terroir, and from the outset his goal was to produce a single wine to the highest standards—and to a high price.

Mitjavile developed a kind of low-cordon pruning hardly ever encountered in St.-Emilion, because he believed it was best suited to his vines and soils. He aims for even maturation, high levels of ripeness, but no raisining. He scorns the current practice of green-harvesting, because he finds that high-yielding vines are balanced by those that, through age or disposition, produce little fruit. He ferments the wine in cement tanks and then ages it for at least eighteen months in new oak.

Tertre-Roteboeuf is a sensual wine, but with a good tannic structure, though some critics have argued that it does not age well. The 2001 is a highly typical vintage. As well as black fruits on the nose, there are aromas of black olives that are quite often found in Tertre-Roteboeuf. The palate is full-bodied and quite powerful, yet there is a sleekness and stylishness that keeps the wine from seeming overpowering, despite a relatively high level of alcohol. It is difficult to contest the quality of the wine here, though some might question whether it is worth the very high price demanded for it. **SBr**

❷❷❷❷ **Drink: to 2025**

Eric Texier *Côtes du Rhône*
Brézème Rouge 2010

Origin France, Rhône Valley
Style Dry red wine, 13% ABV
Grape Syrah

Falling just to the south of the cluster of Northern Rhône appellations, but some way north of the Southern Rhône, once-great Brézème was, until recently, somewhat overlooked in discussions of the Rhône Valley's greatest wines.

That may have been unjust, but it also provided a spur for the man who has done more than any other to forge its modern reputation. Former nuclear engineer Eric Texier had struggled to find affordable, suitable land when he was casting around for a site to begin his new career as a wine producer in the 1990s. In Brézème he found a great terroir hiding in plain sight, and available at a rock-bottom price.

Although he produces wine from the vineyards of his grower partners from Mâcon in southern Burgundy to the southern Rhône, and although he lives and keeps his cellar in the town of Charnay-en-Beaujolais near Lyon, it is for his work in Brézème that Texier has achieved his widest renown. Stylistically, the wines in this area owe more to the north than to the south, and Texier prefers restraint over maximum ripeness. He has a small area of around 1¼ acres (0.5 ha) of Roussanne that he uses to make a rich but taut apple-scented white, while this 100-percent Syrah is taken from a 7½-acre (3-ha) plot, including a 1¼-acre (0.5-ha) parcel of seventy-year-old vines. Unfiltered, and using natural yeasts, it is both succulent and supple in texture, with bright hedgerow fruit, savory meat, and pepper flavors. **DW**

❷❷ **Drink: to 2018**

◀ A boundary stone demarcates the edge of the Tertre-Roteboeuf estate.

Sean Thackrey
Orion 2001

Origin USA, California, Napa Valley
Style Dry red wine, 15% ABV
Grapes Syrah 80%, Others 20%

Thelema
Merlot Reserve 2010

Origin South Africa, Stellenbosch
Style Dry red wine, 14.1% ABV
Grape Merlot

Sean Thackrey, formerly an art dealer in San Francisco, now makes wine in Bolinas, overlooking the Pacific Ocean. It is too frigid and foggy for grape growing, so Thackrey sources his grapes from various parts of the state and vinifies them here in an open-air winery, where the fermenting is protected from the elements by a tarpaulin sheet, if at all. His blends are made by discarding unsatisfactory lots and components, and ending up, he hopes, with a seriously individual wine. There is little racking and no filtration.

The first Orion release was in 1981. Thackrey has a keen eye for old vineyards, such as Arthur Schmidt's in St. Helena, from which the Syrah grapes for Orion originally came. In 1991, the Orion grapes came from a field blend in the Rossi vineyard composed of old, dry-farmed Syrah as well as other varieties.

The Orion 2001 has very rich, dense, plummy aromas that are mirrored in the flavors. Despite the alcohol and opulence, the wine has splendid spice and pepperiness, and a very long finish. Like all Thackrey's wines, other than the deliberately easy-drinking Rhône-style blend called Pleiades, Orion has good structure that will allow it to age well. **SBr**

🍷🍷🍷🍷 Drink: to 2018

It is hard now—when the wines of Thelema Mountain Vineyards seem almost classical in their approach compared to some modern local blockbusters—to recall that when this winery was starting to offer its first wines, winemaker Gyles Webb seemed almost aggressively iconoclastic.

The estate developed from a ramshackle old fruit farm, with many of the vineyards carved from virgin mountainside. It is one of the highest situated properties in the Stellenbosch region.

Thelema is best known for its red wines—an irony, perhaps, because it was a bottle of Puligny-Montrachet that persuaded Webb to retrain as an enologist. His Merlot Reserve is made in tiny quantities in the best vintages, from a barrel selection of the very good standard Merlot. This is not, however, a wine made in the lush, sweet style of the Merlot disparaged by Miles in the film *Sideways*, but rather one with altogether more serious aspirations. Ripe and generous, indeed, but elegant rather than showy, complex rather than facile, with a black-currant concentration augmented by notes of fennel and a touch of herbaceousness. **TJ**

🍷🍷🍷 Drink: to 2019

Thelema Mountain Vineyards on the slopes of the Simonsberg. ➡

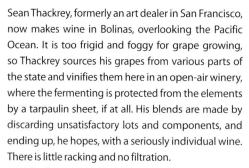

Torbreck *RunRig Shiraz* 1998

Origin Australia, South Australia, Barossa Valley
Style Dry red wine, 14.5% ABV
Grape Shiraz, Viognier

After studying economics, David Powell fell into a career in the South Australian wine industry. Having bought up some old, neglected vineyards in the Barossa, he began winemaking for himself in 1994 and, in 1997, the first Torbreck wines were released.

The wine's name harks back to Powell's work as a lumberjack in the Scottish Highlands. Torbreck is the name of the forest where he worked; and "runrig" was the land distribution system used by Highland clans. This system, with the emphasis on the communal rather than the individual farm, is in keeping with Powell's technique of blending grapes from a wide variety of sources in the Barossa Valley.

RunRig is based on old Shiraz vineyards, with a little bit of Viognier added. Torbreck's top wine is highly opulent, with super-ripe fruit expression. Despite such luscious fruit, RunRig retains surprising elegance, with a beautiful, velvety texture in its best vintages. It also ages well for up to ten years. In 2007, the 1998 was in superb condition, with intense black fruit and a smooth texture, though it needed decanting to show its best. RunRig appears to have turned toward a more extracted style in recent years—the 2004 was super-intense, with 60 percent new oak, compared to the 40 percent of previous years—and only time will tell if these wines will age as well as those from the late 1990s and early part of the century. Nonetheless, with just 1,500 cases made each year, RunRig is one of the few top Barossan wines to justify its ambitious price. **SG**

☻☻☻☻☻ **Drink: to 2018+**

FURTHER RECOMMENDATIONS
Other great vintages
1999 • 2003 • 2004 • 2006 • 2009
More Torbreck wines
Les Amis • Descendant • The Factor • Juveniles *The Pict • The Steading • The Struie*

David Powell noses the latest vintage of RunRig Shiraz. ➡

Torres
Gran Coronas Mas La Plana 1971

Origin Spain, Catalonia, Penedès
Style Dry red wine, 13.5% ABV
Grapes C. Sauvignon, Tempranillo, Monastrell

Domaine La Tour Vieille
Cuvée Puig Oriol 2005

Origin France, Roussillon, Collioure
Style Dry red wine, 14% ABV
Grapes Grenache Noir, Syrah

The revolutionary Gran Coronas Mas La Plana is the brainchild of Miguel A. Torres, the fifth-generation president of his family's firm and the best-known ambassador for Spanish wine around the world. In the 1960s, Miguel began experimental plantings of Cabernet Sauvignon. In areas where it is not indigenous, the introduction of the variety is frowned upon by traditionalists. But one of the subjects that most interests Miguel is the matching of site and variety, and few would now disagree that Cabernet is very much at home at Mas La Plana.

Vindication for his project came in 1979 when, in a blind tasting at *Gault Millau*'s "Wine Olympics," the Torres 1970 came top of the Cabernet class, ahead of Château Latour 1970 and other illustrious French wines. The 1971 is even more thrilling than its predecessor. The nose is complex and exciting, with the same fruit integrity and minerality as the 1970, but slightly wilder, with wet leaves, beef then game, juniper and tobacco. The palate still offers plenty of creamy black-currant fruit, is multi-layered, plush, and ravishingly smooth, with powerfully supportive suede tannins and excellent length. **NB**
⊖⊖⊖⊖ Drink: to 2021

Vincent Cantié's family were long-established traders who filled barrels with the typical salted anchovies of Collioure. When Vincent returned from traveling the world, he decided he wanted to fill his barrels with wine rather than anchovies. He was ably seconded in this by his wife, Christine, whose family was big in wine in neighboring Banyuls, and who brought with her a fine vineyard called La Salette.

Strictly traditional in everything they do, the Cantiés now cultivate more than 31 acres (76 ha) of land, on terraces of schist overlooking the Mediterranean. They make Collioures and some fascinating fortified wines using the traditional solera system, as well as modern-style vintage wines.

The Cuvée Puig Oriol 2005 is marked by a strong aroma of blackberries and a very soft palate, which has led the British philosopher Roger Scruton to compare it with the buttocks of a female nude by the sculptor Aristide Maillol, who lived and died in Banyuls, and whose art has a strong presence in the region. Wine trader Kermit Lynch has described it as "a little touch of Bandol, a little remembrance of Côte-Rôtie, but don't forget the Catalan accent." **GM**
⊖⊖⊖ Drink: to 2017+

◀ The family home of wine producer Miguel Torres in Penedès.

Domaine de Trévallon *Vin de Table des Bouches du Rhône* 2001

Origin France, Provence
Style Dry red wine, 13.5% ABV
Grapes Cabernet Sauvignon, Syrah

It was a refugee from Champagne and Bordeaux, Georges Brunet, who discovered the formula for a certain sort of wine that was eventually enshrined in the creation of the AOC Coteaux des Baux de Provence—a mainstay of Cabernet Sauvignon with a healthy dollop of Syrah. It was the nearest thing to the New World that France had ever seen. Some would say it still is.

In 1973, a young architect, Eloi Durrbach—whose parents had owned a domaine in the village since the 1960s—came to Les Baux to work with Brunet at Château Vignelaure. Durrbach released his first wine in 1978 and, by the early 1980s, he had achieved a reputation for his wines at places like Willi's Wine Bar in Paris; then came accolades from Robert Parker, and there was no looking back. The authorities tried to put a spanner in the works in 1994, when they changed the rules governing the appellation. Now only 20 percent Cabernet was permitted. However, Durrbach was easily able to sell Trévallon under the lesser appellation of Vin de Pays des Bouches du Rhône.

The wine is now half and half Cabernet and Syrah. The 2001 was a small, concentrated crop, where the Mistral wind played its role in drying out the grapes. The resulting wine has wonderful color and extract. The wine smells of black currants and strawberries, and has a faint whiff of tobacco and herbs. It finishes with a distinct mineral tang. **GM**
🍷🍷🍷🍷 **Drink: to 2020**

Domaine de Trévallon vines on the slopes of the Chaine des Alpilles. ➡

Trinity Hill *Homage Syrah* 2006

Origin New Zealand, Hawke's Bay, Gimblett Gravels
Style Dry red wine, 14% ABV
Grapes Syrah, Viognier

Homage is a tribute to the late Gérard Jaboulet who, according to Trinity Hill owner-winemaker John Hancock, was the inspiration for the wine. Hancock worked a vintage at Jaboulet and developed a great admiration for Gérard, who died in 1997. A portion of the grapes used in the wine were from grape vines that Jaboulet had provided.

Trinity Hill was one of the earliest New Zealand wineries to coferment a small proportion of Viognier with Syrah. Hancock believes that the addition of around 4 percent Viognier makes Syrah more feminine, by adding a floral note to the aroma and contributing toward a slipperier texture. Winemaking trials began in 1999 to determine the grape yield that would give optimum quality. The grapes for Homage are grown in a designated section of Trinity Hill's vineyard, where a more intensive viticultural regime is applied and fruit selection during harvest is more rigorous.

Traditional winemaking methods are applied, with fermentation in open tanks that are hand-plunged four times daily. After a short period of postfermentation maceration, the skins are pressed and the wine racked into new French oak barriques for eighteen months' maturation. Homage is a rich and powerful wine, displaying layers of dark berry, licorice, anise, and spicy oak flavors. It is a dense and firmly structured wine that is already accessible but shows great cellaring potential. **BC**

ⓢ ⓢ ⓢ **Drink: to 2020**

FURTHER RECOMMENDATIONS
Other great vintages
2002 · 2004
More Trinity Hill wines
Gimblett Gravels · Hawke's Bay
Homage Chardonnay · Homage The Gimblett

Trinity Hill vines on the Gimblett Gravels designation in Hawke's Bay. →

Château Troplong-Mondot

1998

Origin France, Bordeaux, St.-Emilion
Style Dry red wine, 13% ABV
Grapes Merlot 90%, C. Franc 5%, C. Sauvignon 5%

Since 1936 this superb property has been owned by the Valette family; the present incumbents are Christine Valette and her family. She has been guided for many years by Michel Rolland, who enjoined her to reduce yields and harvest later. Although in the 1960s and 1970s the property had been seriously underperforming, their joint efforts paid off when, to no one's surprise, Troplong-Mondot was promoted to Premier Cru Classé in 2006.

With its super-ripe Merlot fruit, its opulence and sensuality, Troplong is a quintessential St.-Emilion, with hedonism overriding rigor. A sheen of new oak smooths the edge of the wine and adds to the sweetness of the fruit. Yet Troplong is not without elegance, nor is it incapable of aging. 1998 was a superb year in St.-Emilion. Troplong from that vintage was impressive in its youth but very dense, but over the years its sensual appeal has become irresistible. On the palate it remains firm, tannic, and structured, but at the same time the wine has vigor and a sweet, silky finish. It will surely evolve positively over many years.

In the ripest years, Troplong-Mondot walks a tightrope of overripeness without quite falling off, though some might find the profusion of plummy, chocolaty aromas and flavors too much of a good thing. On the other hand, many wine lovers might single out Troplong-Mondot as a favorite wine from a much-prized appellation. **SBr**

🜹🜹🜹 **Drink: to 2020**

The Troplong-Mondot château sits atop the Mondot hill. ➡

Château Trotanoy 2005

Origin France, Bordeaux, Pomerol
Style Dry red wine, 13% ABV
Grapes Merlot 90%, Cabernet Franc 10%

This estate was known originally as "Trop Ennuie," a reflection of the tedious labors involved in working the poor gravelly clay soil. The name was changed to Trotanoy in the early nineteenth century. It occupies a high plateau less than a mile west of Pétrus, and has been in the ownership of the Moueix family since 1953. From being a little-known property producing modest quantities—the vineyard is only 20 acres (8 ha)—Trotanoy has shot into the Bordeaux firmament, becoming a reference wine for the unclassified Pomerol district. It now rejoices in the reputation of being the next greatest Pomerol after Pétrus, which is also a Moueix property.

The wine is fermented in concrete vats before being given a barrel maturation of up to twenty months, the proportion of new oak employed having risen steadily through recent decades. Its label is almost defiantly plain, eschewing all illustration in favor of a simple denotation of the name and district.

Early tastings of the glorious 2005 vintage confirmed what might easily have been suspected: Trotanoy has produced a gem. The wine has commanding structure, with plenty of beefy muscle, but is also showered with rose-petal perfume, which floats like a heat haze over the blackberry and black cherry fruit. Texturally, the wine has the silkiness of a super-ripe vintage, with gorgeous, echoing spicy tones on the majestic finish, but it will require long aging to begin to show its true paces. **SW**
😊😊😊😊 **Drink: to 2050+**

FURTHER RECOMMENDATIONS
Other great vintages
1982 · 1990 · 1993 · 1995 · 1998 · 2000 · 2001 · 2003
More Moueix wines
Bélair-Monange · Hosannah · La Fleur-Pétrus
Latour-à-Pomerol · Pétrus · Providence

Closely pruned vines border the Château Trotanoy winery. ➔

Tua Rita
Redigaffi IGT Toscana 2000

Origin Italy, Tuscany, Maremma
Style Dry red wine, 14.5% ABV
Grape Merlot

Redigaffi was not the first pure Merlot to attract attention in this part of the world, but it has been collecting *Gambero Rosso*'s top Tre Bicchieri award with monotonous regularity, and reached the apotheosis of 100 points in Robert Parker's *Wine Advocate* for the 2000 vintage.

Tua Rita is run today by Rita Tua, her husband Virgilio Bisti, and their son-in-law Stefano Frascolla. Since the wild success of the first few vintages, they have been busily planting more and more Merlot, together with Cabernet Sauvignon and Syrah. Now they produce an appreciably larger number of bottles of the precious liquid, but these are marketed as if the extreme shortage of the 1990s still pertained, and buyers have to get on their knees for their annual allocation.

The wine, however, remains its deep-hued, rich and velvety, berry-fruit-bomb self—as sumptuous and voluptuous as young Bordeaux Merlot can be structured and severe. But even if obtaining the wine and paying the price is pure masochism, so drinking Redigaffi is pure hedonism—and why not if you can afford it; is life not short enough? **NBel**

⊖⊖⊖⊖⊖ Drink: to 2017+

Turkey Flat
Shiraz 2004

Origin Australia, South Australia, Barossa Valley
Style Dry red wine, 14.5% ABV
Grape Shiraz

Turkey Flat can lay claim to owning the oldest vineyard land in the Barossa. The earliest documented vineyard was planted by Johann Fiedler in 1847 (although the current owner believes it was planted in 1844). The first winemakers in the Barossa are likely to have been the Fiedlers.

The vineyard was bought in 1865 by Gottlieb Ernst Schulz, who sold the grapes to local winemakers. With his wife Christie, Peter—a fourth-generation Schulz—made the transition in the early 1990s to bottling the product himself, finally turning this dynasty of grape growers into winemakers. Local artist Rod Schubert was commissioned for the Turkey Flat label: His depictions give bottles of Turkey Flat wine their distinctive elegance.

A dark, dense, opaque purple color, this Shiraz has flavors of chocolate, cocoa, and plum tart. Voluptuous and very intense, with a long finish, this is a sexy style of Barossa Shiraz, relatively restrained by the region's recent standards. And even more surprisingly (and pleasingly) for a wine made partly from a 150-year-old vineyard, it is still priced within the reach of mortals. **SG**

⊖⊖⊖ Drink: to 2019

Turley Wine Cellars
Dragon Vineyard Zinfandel 2005

Origin USA, California, Napa Valley
Style Dry red wine, 16.1% ABV
Grape Zinfandel

Umathum
Zweigelt Hallebühl 2004

Origin Austria, Burgenland, Neusiedlersee
Style Dry red wine, 13% ABV
Grapes Zweigelt, Blaufränkisch, C. Sauvignon

Turley Zinfandels, produced by Larry Turley and Ehren Jordan, do nothing if not incite controversy. What some might deride as sumo wines, overly extracted and exaggerated, others extol as the quintessence of the variety: expansive, spicy, and jammy, with well over 15 percent alcohol.

Larry Turley established his own winery in 1993, having left the partnership at Frog's Leap. Until 1995 his sister Helen was the winemaker; when she departed to focus on her own projects, her assistant Ehren Jordan stepped in. Apart from making the wines, Jordan exults in searching out old-vine Zinfandel vineyards in different terroirs, vines notoriously mistreated by a generation of growers committed to quantity over quality.

Turley Zinfandel shows surprising transparency in how each cuvée reveals its individual provenance. The Dragon Vineyard wine has a concentrated, stony core, bursting with fresh black pepper. The hefty alcohol levels and saturated ripe fruit leave quite a sweet impression on the palate. With their exuberance, Turley Zinfandels make compelling candidates for "The Great American Wine." **LGr**

🅂🅂🅂 **Drink: to 2017+**

A melancholy history is evoked by rows of Jewish headstones that abut the Umathum estate. Not far away, a sandy, gravelly rise (or "Bühl"), used as a watch post during the Turkish siege, looks out across a forlorn former internment camp.

What paradox! There is no more inspiring vintner, nor more joyous wine in Austria, than Josef Umathum and his Zweigelt from that very Hallebühl. Few vintners think Zweigelt capable of profundity, but as long as Umathum is one of them, this obscure grape will never lack for eloquent advocacy.

A sweet, ripe cherry essence and pungent orange zest rise exuberantly from the glass; tobacco, resin, pencil lead, and dark chocolate follow in their wake. Vigorous fruit and caressing creaminess comprise the contradictory appeal of this irresistible libation. Umathum gives it two years in barrels of mixed age, then further time in bottle before release. Is the unusual concentration of manganese in these soils a catalyst for Zweigelt's unusual layering of flavors? No one knows. But neither does anyone know a vintner more determined to let the wines he bottles "speak terroir" than Josef Umathum. **DS**

🅂🅂🅂 **Drink: to 2019**

Azienda Agricola G. D. Vajra

Barolo Bricco delle Viole 2001

Origin Italy, Piedmont, La Morra
Style Dry red wine, 14% ABV
Grape Nebbiolo

Dominating the ridge that runs between La Morra and Novello, Vergne, at 1,148 feet (350 m), is the highest village in the commune of Barolo. The grapes planted here on the famous white marl soils are always the last to ripen, and are particularly at risk from late autumn rains. In exceptional vintages, such as 2001, however, the windswept vineyards offer Nebbiolo of exceptional elegance.

Nebbiolo is a difficult grape at the best of times. Coaxing this obstinate grape into revealing its full aromatic complexity is the life's ambition of Aldo and Milena Vajra, who tend 25 acres (10 ha) of Nebbiolo in the communes of Barolo and La Morra. Aldo preserves his family traditions, favoring low yields and the time-honored use of large oak *botte*.

Nowhere is the merit of this approach more evident than in the 2001 Barolo Bricco delle Viole. Although officially lying within the Barolo parish boundary, Bricco delle Viole epitomizes the elegance of La Morra fruit. In 2001 the Nebbiolo ripened to perfection, and its telltale acidity and tannins underlie the wine's layered palate awash with red fruit, hay, tobacco, and licorice. **MP**

☻☻☻☻ Drink: to 2030

Château Valandraud

2005

Origin France, Bordeaux, St.-Emilion
Style Dry red wine, 14% ABV
Grapes Merlot, C. Franc, C. Sauvignon, Malbec

Château Valandraud is a collection of vineyards that has gradually expanded since its foundation in 1989. Its early reputation was made by resounding successes in the poor vintage of 1993, the decent vintage of 1994, and the good vintage of 1995, but it is really since the purchase of a plot close to Fleur-Cardinale on the St.-Emilion plateau that the wine has acquired authority as well as voluptuous charm.

Owner Jean-Luc Thunevin now has nearly 22 acres (9 ha) to call on, and the Valandraud "family" extends to a kosher version and a white wine, as well as the second wine Virginie and a Numéro 3, too.

The Valandraud secret, if secret there is, lies in the combination of the fastidious, low-yielding viticulture of Murielle Andraud, Thunevin's consort, combined with his own careful and intelligent winemaking. The dark, fresh-scented 2005 vintage (in which the original vineyards account for just 10 percent) combines classic Valandraud sweetness and fruit purity, but behind those comely charms lie almost statuesque levels of extract, vivacious acidity and perfumed tannins, all of which promise a more enduring beauty than the early successes. **AJ**

☻☻☻☻☻ Drink: to 2025

The sign at the entrance to the Château Valandraud estate. ➡

Valdipiatta *Vino Nobile di Montepulciano Vigna d'Alfiero* 1999

Origin Italy, Tuscany, Montepulciano
Style Dry red wine, 14% ABV
Grape Sangiovese

Valentini *Montepulciano d'Abruzzo* 1990

Origin Italy, Abruzzo
Style Dry red wine, 12% ABV
Grape Montepulciano

When Giulio Caporali took over this estate toward the end of the 1980s, his dream was to produce a wine so good that it would grace the tables of the world's most important restaurants. But the results have exceeded even that early ambition.

The Valdipiatta estate, which is now run by Caporali's daughter, Miriam, now encompasses not only wine production but hospitality, thanks to the addition of a beautiful farmhouse. The main focus, however, remains the wine. The Vino Nobile di Montepulciano Vigna d'Alfiero is from a single vineyard planted entirely with Sangiovese grapes. It is not a Riserva, and it is not produced only in exceptional years—but this is even better for us, because it means that we can enjoy it every year.

The 1999 oozes class and the rustic elegance of the great Tuscan grape. The nose shows ripe cherry and spicy notes with a floral, minty twist. The palate might seem rather taut to those not used to the real deal, but wine experts can vouch that this is it. Enjoy the long, elegant finish, and trust in the wine's ability to become even more complex, expressive, and seductive over the medium to long term. **AS**

Ⓢ Ⓢ Ⓢ **Drink: to 2020+**

Outside the vinous citadels of Piedmont and Tuscany lie many old denominations that are habitually passed over when surveys of notable wines are being made. One such is Montepulciano d'Abruzzo, and Edoardo Valentini was one of its superstars.

Now overseen by Edoardo's son, Francesco Paolo, Valentini will continue to be a name to watch. The old Montepulciano vines are harvested late to maximize color and flavor extraction. Low yields and bottling without filtration result in an ink-dark red of stunning intensity, fascinating, concentrated viscosity, and tremendous cellaring potential. It is aged in large old barrels of chestnut wood.

In 1990, glorious vintage conditions produced one of the finest Montepulcianos that Valentini senior ever bottled. It has an almost Pauillac-like cedariness on the nose, with cracked pepper sprinkled over the glutinous plum and damson fruit. The palate has taken on secondary notes of black truffles, which have insinuated their way into the plum-preserve fruit, while the tannic framework has remained relatively sturdy. It all leads to the kind of finish you will be dreaming about hours later. **SW**

Ⓢ Ⓢ Ⓢ **Drink: to 2020+**

Edoardo Valentini's home village of Loreto Aprutino. ➡

Vall Llach

2004

Origin Spain, Catalonia, Priorat
Style Dry red wine, 15.5% ABV
Grapes Cariñena, Merlot, Cabernet Sauvignon

Lluís Llach is one of the greatest Catalonian folk singers, as well as a politically involved author and, since the mid-1990s, a wine producer in Porrera, where he spent his childhood holidays. After helping to revitalize the local cooperative through the bodega Cims de Porrera, he founded with his childhood friend Enric Costa his own smaller winery in the same village, the Celler Vall Llach.

Both Cims de Porrera and Vall Llach have as their dominant grape variety not Granacha but Cariñena, which does better on the *costers* (non-terraced hillsides) of *licorella* (slate) surrounding the village. Today the bodega produces three wines. Above Embruix and Idus, the jewel in the crown is Vall Llach itself, two-thirds Cariñena from centenary vines, with one-third Merlot and Cabernet Sauvignon.

The Vall Llach 2004 is from an exceptional Priorat vintage, and is possibly its most spectacular wine to date. A very intense cherry red, it offers on the nose blackberry, graphite, and toast. On the palate it is well-nigh perfect, with amazing amplitude, power, elegance, harmony, and length. Almost addictive, it is among the great Priorat wines. **JMB**
🔵🔵🔵 **Drink: to 2019**

Valtuille

Cepas Centenarias 2007

Origin Spain, Bierzo
Style Dry red wine, 13.5% ABV
Grape Mencía

Young Raúl Pérez Pereira is a free spirit, and as such he is making highly idiosyncratic wines—one example is an incredible Albariño called Sketch, aged under water in the Atlantic. Raúl is a local *Berciano*, and was already there working in his family vineyards and winery, Bodegas y Viñedos Castro Ventosa, when the Bierzo revolution started in the late 1990s. He produces a wide range of wines, inside and outside the Bierzo DO. His experimentation is a reflection of his endlessly restless character.

As the name implies, Valtuille Cepas Centenarias comes from Mencía vines more than 100 years old. It has the power of a northern Rhône and the finesse of a top Côte de Nuits. It is aged for some fourteen months in French oak barrels, 80 percent of which are new. The wine is very dark and intense in color, almost opaque, and purple in its youth. The old-vine fruit intensity clearly comes through in this earthy and concentrated wine. Some toasty oak notes are present, intermixed with minerals (graphite), ink, and plenty of black fruit (blueberry). Very structured in the mouth, it has impressive fruit density, polished tannins, and a very long finish. **LG**
🔵🔵🔵 **Drink: to 2022**

Vasse Felix *Heytesbury*
Cabernet Sauvignon 2004

Origin Australia, Western Australia, Margaret River
Style Dry red wine, 14.5% ABV
Grapes Cabernet Sauvignon 95%, Shiraz 5%

Vasse Felix was the first commercial vineyard to be established in the Margaret River region. In 1965, Dr. John S. Gladstones confirmed the region's suitability for wine production; two years later, Dr. Tom Cullity planted vines, and Vasse Felix was born. Subsequently purchased in 1987 by businessman Robert Holmes à Court, the estate is now under the leadership of Robert's widow, Janet Holmes à Court.

The Heytesbury Cabernet combines parcels of fruit from various growers throughout the Margaret River subregions. Blending these allows Vasse Felix to create a house style that reflects its winemaking philosophy rather than the nuances of a single vineyard or region. A small portion of Cabernet Sauvignon from Franklin River and Mount Barker adds further complexity to the wine, and in some vintages Malbec, Merlot, and Cabernet Franc grapes have also been included.

Heytesbury Cabernet is plush, intensely flavored, and chocolaty, with a generous use of oak. The bird depicted on the label is a peregrine falcon—a reference to the trained falcons Dr. Cullity used to deter troublesome birds at harvest time. **SG**

⊖⊖⊖ Drink: to 2019

Vecchie Terre di Montefili
Bruno di Rocca 2002

Origin Italy, Tuscany
Style Dry red wine, 13.5% ABV
Grapes Cabernet Sauvignon 60%, Sangiovese 40%

In 1200, an important Florentine family donated this estate to an ancient monastic order. It was purchased in 1979 by the Acuto family, with the intention of producing quality wines.

The Acutos began from scratch, addressing the problems in the badly run vineyards and upgrading the winemaking facilities. Thanks to the advice of a good agronomist and a very competent winemaker, they soon hit their target. They believed in the huge potential that Sangiovese has in this stretch of the Chianti Classico, but they did not exclude the experimentation with other varieties that has led to their most important wine to date—Bruno di Rocca.

The Bruno di Rocca 2002 is a fantastic wine. And it is even more pleasurable when you remember that many "experts" dismissed this vintage altogether. But that means that there is all the more for those of us who are alert to its considerable charms. Stare into this wine's deep, bright, velvety purple color before inhaling the alluring black-currant and minty scents. On the palate, it is heavenly: an intense, caressing, cassis liqueur interwoven with young, soft leather, black pepper, and vanilla. Enjoy! **AS**

⊖⊖⊖⊖ Drink: to 2028

Vega de Toro
Numanthia 1998

Origin Spain, Toro
Style Dry red wine, 14.5% ABV
Grape Tinta de Toro (Tempranillo)

Vega Sicilia
Único 1970

Origin Spain, Ribera del Duero
Style Dry red wine, 13% ABV
Grapes Tinto Fino (Tempranillo), Merlot, Others

Numanthia Termesis is the Castilian venture of the Eguren brothers, who chose the name because the vines—seventy to 140 years old—have resisted the invasion of phylloxera, just as the historical city of Numancia fought its last battle after an exhausting siege by the Roman Legion in 133 bce.

The old Tinta de Toro vineyards are planted at 2,300 feet (701 m) above sea level. The soils are rich in clay and chalk, but with a high percentage of sand that makes it impossible for phylloxera to survive.

The first vintage for Numanthia was 1998, and it was an instant success. The wine fermented for a week, and was further macerated with the lees and skins for another twenty-one days. Aged for eighteen months in new French oak barrels, with malolactic in barrel, it was bottled without fining or filtration: dark cherry, completely opaque color and an intense aroma, showing a good dose of high-quality oak, graphite notes, and black fruit (mulberries, blueberries). It is rich and fruity in the mouth, full and powerful, with tannins in need of some bottle age, which should integrate well and make a long-lived wine. **LG**

🍷🍷🍷 **Drink: to 2020**

Vega Sicilia is without a doubt the most prestigious winery in Spain. But, however good a vintage 1970 was, expensive wines were not selling well in Spain at the time. These wines were bottled to order, so aging times and styles depended on how sales were doing.

Throughout its life, the Único 1970 was transferred a number of times, to cement, large oak containers, or barriques, depending on the needs of the winery or the different owners at the time. Great care, however, was taken by young enologist Mariano García to keep the barrels topped up, to avoid oxidation as much as possible, to preserve the fruit and minimize the volatile acidity and somewhat Porty style that was the signature of old Únicos.

The wine was released twenty-five years after the vintage, and the magnums were not sold until 2001, though some considered them still not ready to drink. On sight, smell, and taste it is impossible to guess its age, because it remains so youthful. Deep color, heady perfume, velvety texture, fresh, clean, smooth, intense, balanced, elegant, complex, pure, delineated, deep, long. Perfection. It is regarded by many as the best wine ever produced in Spain. **LG**

🍷🍷🍷🍷🍷 **Drink: to 2020**

Established in 1864, Vega Sicilia is considered "Spain's Château Latour". ➔

Venus
La Universal 2004

Origin Spain, Montsant
Style Dry red wine, 13% ABV
Grapes Cariñena 50%, Syrah 50%

Sara Pérez and René Barbier are the second generation at two pioneer wineries in Priorat— Clos Martinet and Clos Mogador respectively. In 1999, Sara started Venus La Universal in Falset as a personal project, now within the Montsant DO but originally Tarragona. When Sara and René got together, the winery became their joint project.

La Universal is the name of a 10-acre (4 ha) vineyard in Falset, planted with young Syrah on poor and acid granitic soil. They also purchase Cariñena from fifty to eighty-year-old vines from five local vineyards—one granite, two slate, and the other two clay-limestone. All are farmed organically.

The Venus 2004 is dark in color, the nose dominated by black fruit (black currant, mulberry, and blueberry), toasty notes in the form of *pain grillé*, black olives, and violets. Medium-bodied, well-balanced, and with good acidity, it is supple with plenty of fruit and great length. Sara is very clear about her image of the wine: "Venus is the result of our search for beauty. A trial to interpret femininity through a bottle of wine: mystery and seduction, articulacy and voluptuousness." **LG**

🌣🌣🌣 **Drink: to 2017+**

Vergelegen
2003

Origin South Africa, Stellenbosch
Style Dry red wine, 14% ABV
Grapes C. Sauvignon 80%, Merlot 18%, C. Franc 2%

Vines were first planted at Vergelegen in 1700, at the behest of its owner, Willem Adriaan van der Stel, the Cape's governor at the time.

The revitalization of South African wine in the years since the first democratic elections of 1994 has seen the estate's reemergence—and few argue against the claim by the U.S. critic Stephen Tanzer that "this is South Africa's single finest producer."

Any aspirations cellar master André van Rensburg might have toward a "cult wine" in the style of the celebrated Californians are focused primarily on the imposing, dramatically impressive Cabernet called simply "V." But the Vergelegen blend is the flagship red, and the one designed to express terroir (so that although "V" is produced only in the best vintages, this wine is invariably made).

2003 was a particularly fine vintage in the Cape, and the Vergelegen was beguiling and incipiently complex in youth, while promising long maturity. Rich and fully ripe, suavely tannic, with darkly bright fruit supported by plenty of oak needing a few years to integrate, it has also a restrained and elegant harmony. **TJ**

🌣🌣🌣 **Drink: to 2018**

A striking entrance to the winery at Vergelegen. ➔

Noël Verset

Cornas 1990

Origin France, Northern Rhône, Cornas
Style Dry red wine, 14% ABV
Grape Syrah

Noël Verset is to be remembered as a little old man in a cloth cap. He succeeded a father who died at more than 100 years old—about the same age as his vines. Noël started making wine in 1942 from three separate plots—Sabrottes, Les Chaillots, and Champelrose—and always united them in one wine.

Even just after the vintage, the 1990 was wonderfully seductive, seeming to exude aromas of tar and blackberries. One critic talked of smoldering charcoal, whereas another memorably described it as being like "a wild beast dragged from its lair." Robert Parker awarded it 100 of his points, thereby setting curtains twitching all over Cornas.

The charm of Noël Verset's wines was their old-fashioned nature. They were not destemmed; they were made in cement vats, and trodden down by foot. They went into old oak. This made some critics sniff—and one even uttered the damning words "bottle variation." The 1990 has also been called into question, with one or two people pronouncing that it was thinning out. During the 1990s, some of Verset's vines were taken over by the new broom, Thierry Allemand. **GM**
🍷🍷🍷🍷 Drink: to 2020+

Vieux Château Certan

2000

Origin France, Bordeaux, Pomerol
Style Dry red wine, 13.5% ABV
Grapes Merlot 70%, C. Franc 20%, C. Sauvignon 10%

Records date Château Certan back to the early sixteenth century, when it was established by a Scottish family, the Demays. In 1924 it was sold to Belgian wine merchant, Georges Thienpont.

Certan's holdings are all in one block on a plateau, where the topsoil is Bordeaux gravel, lying above a mixture of sandy clay with plenty of iron.

Hand-picking, followed by vinification in big wooden vats and a long maceration on the skins, is applied. The wine then undergoes oak-aging for between eighteen months and two years, with half the barrels renewed each vintage. Egg-white fining is followed by bottling without filtration.

After a tricky vintage, sunshine and harmony reigned through August and early September 2000. The result is a wine of immense aromatic complexity, with raspberry, black plum, and licorice jostling for attention. In the mouth, the wine is massive, built on elegant tannic foundations, with cloves, sandalwood, and cinnamon emerging through the dense, purple fruit. The finish is majestically long and intense, suggesting that this is yet another Bordeaux 2000 with a glittering future ahead of it. **SW**
🍷🍷🍷🍷 Drink: to 2030+

Domaine du Vieux Télégraphe
Châteauneuf-du-Pape 1998

Villa Ponciago
Fleurie Les Hauts de Py 2011

Origin France, Southern Rhône
Style Dry red wine, 14.5% ABV
Grapes Grenache 65%, Syrah 15%, Others 20%

Origin France, Beaujolais
Style Dry red wine, 13% ABV
Grape Gamay à Jus Blanc

The village of Châteauneuf-du-Pape is a magical place. The finest wines come from a handful of family-owned estates that have been tending vines here for generations. One of the best is Vieux Télégraphe, on the stony La Crau plateau on the southeastern fringe of the appellation.

The producers in Châteauneuf-du-Pape have given themselves draconian regulations. Permissible yields are much lower than elsewhere, and all grapes must be harvested by hand, with a natural alcohol content of at least 12.5 percent. A minimum of 5 percent of the crop must be eliminated to ensure that the wines are made from the healthiest grapes.

Although it began small, Vieux Télégraphe now has 173 acres (70 ha) under vine. Two-thirds of the crop is Grenache, which assures the estate's red wine its unctuous fleshiness, with another 15 percent each of Syrah and Mourvèdre adding warmth, structure, and spice. To improve quality, a second wine now known as Télégramme was introduced in 1994, and since 1998 an experimental bottling named Hippolyte, after the founder of the estate, is produced, but never released. **JP**

🍷🍷🍷 **Drink: to 2025**

An ancient wine domaine with a thousand-year history, Villa Ponciago was cultivated in the late tenth century by the Benedictine monks at nearby Cluny. By the 1890s, the best parcels of Fleurie, Ponciago prominent among them, were rated première classé and fetched prices as high as some villages in the Côte de Nuits. In 2008, the sleeping property was bought by the Henriot family of Champagne and Bouchard fame. They were quick to see the potential of Ponciago. The family has returned to classic methods of Burgundian winemaking, with open-topped vats and a judicious, careful use of oak.

The 121 acres (49 ha) of vineyards are gathered around a hillock northeast of Fleurie. Les Hauts de Py extends south, the vines rising to an altitude of 1,345 ft (410 m), the soils streaked with a unique vein of quartz. The 2011 is one of the best recent vintages, with a dash of raciness allied to its mineral depth and class. After three years, the violet hue cedes to ruby, and the high acidity is more integrated in the wine. It is still an energetic wine but with slowly developing adult wine flavors that have a life of several years. **ME**

🍷🍷🍷 **Drink: to 2020**

Viñedos Organicos Emiliana *Coyam* 2003

Origin Chile, Central Valley
Style Dry red wine, 14% ABV
Grapes Carmenère, Syrah, C. Sauvignon, Others

When the 2001 vintage of Coyam, the premium red wine from Chile's first large-scale biodynamic winery, Viñedos Orgánicos Emiliana (now Emiliana Orgánico), was crowned "Best of Show" at the inaugural Wines of Chile awards held in December 2003 in Santiago, it was hailed as a victory for biodynamics. Emiliana Orgánico was created as an offshoot of Santa Emiliana, whose owners, the Guilisasti family, used it primarily for bulk yields until director José Guilisasti embraced organic wine in the late 1990s. He brought in Alvaro Espinoza as biodynamic muse and winemaker, and converted the prime Finca Los Robles vineyard to biodynamics. Espinoza solved perennial hot-climate vineyard problems such as mites: "Mites like to attack the dustiest vines, so we covered the lanes around the vineyard with stones from the Colchagua River to prevent dust rising every time a tractor passed."

Merlot's "donut" tendency—to produce wines with a hollow center—was cured by cooling down the vines with organic compost spread over the parched soils. But the real achievement of Coyam is in its blend, which fused Bordeaux grapes such as Cabernet, Merlot, and Carmenère with Mediterranean ones like Syrah and Mourvèdre.

Coyam's combination of Bordeaux-like elegance and Mediterranean richness is a winning one. It allows the wine to remain identifiably Chilean in its tasty fruit, but also distinctively biodynamic, such is its intense minerality. **MW**

🟊🟊🟊 **Drink: to 2018**

FURTHER RECOMMENDATIONS
Other great vintages
2001 • 2002 • 2004 • 2005
More Viñedos Organicos Emiliana wines
Novas Cabernet Sauvignon
Novas Carmenère/Cabernet Sauvignon

The fertile valley floor and dry hillsides of Chile's Central Valley. ➡

Roberto Voerzio
Barolo Cerequio 1999

Origin Italy, Piedmont, La Morra
Style Dry red wine, 14% ABV
Grape Nebbiolo

Wendouree
Shiraz 2000

Origin Australia, Clare Valley
Style Dry red wine, 13.5% ABV
Grape Shiraz

Roberto Voerzio steers a middle path between the old and the new in his winemaking. His main priority is minute care in the vineyard. Each vine has only four bunches of grapes, resulting in very concentrated flavors. Fermentations continue for two weeks to thirty days, depending on soil, aspect, and microclimate of the vineyard in question.

There is the rub. At the end of the day, terroir is more important than the winemaker, and even the grape variety, as brilliantly illustrated in Roberto's Barbara d'Alba Riserva Pozzo dell'Annunziata—from one of La Morra's best sites but made from old-vine Barbera, a so-called second division grape variety. Nebbiolo is, of course, first division, and La Morra is celebrated as the home of the most succulent and supple Barolos, none more so than from Roberto's Cerequio cru in the ripe and suave 1999 vintage.

This lovely wine has a complexity of scents—at once leathery, meaty, yet with hints of old roses and truffles. On the palate, tastes of morello cherries merge naturally with those of oak, creating a sumptuously rich texture, and there is a glorious finale of burgeoning vinosity. **ME**
ʘʘʘʘʘ Drink: to 2020+

One of the cult legends of Australian wine, Wendouree can be purchased only through a mailing list that has been full for a long time, though odd bottles can be found on the secondary market. The vineyards were first planted in 1892. Current owner Tony Brady bought the property in 1974, but had no experience of winemaking. Fortunately, an existing employee stayed on for seven years, showing him the ropes. In the meantime, his wife did a wine science degree at Wagga.

Altogether, Wendouree has 28 acres (11 ha) of vines, all dry grown. The grapes are hand-picked super-ripe at around 13.5 percent alcohol. Herbicides are eschewed and vigor is controlled naturally by the vine age.

Of the range. it is the Shiraz that gets the most attention. All of them, however, are made in a tight, age-worthy style. The Shiraz 2000, tasted at age six, has a dark, spicy, tight nose. The palate shows fantastic concentration and lovely freshness to the bold ripe fruit, but with wonderful spicy structure and acidity. This is a massive wine with huge potential, and should age almost indefinitely. **JG**
ʘʘʘ Drink: to 2030+

The lyre training system in operation at Wendouree. ➡

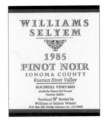

Wild Duck Creek
Duck Muck 2004

Origin Australia, Heathcote
Style Dry red wine, 17% ABV
Grape Shiraz

Duck Muck had its genesis in the 1994 vintage, when a few rows of Shiraz were left unpicked because there was no fermenter room left. Two weeks later, Anderson (whose nickname is Duck) and his friend and co-winemaker David McKee, stumbled across these vines, and the grapes tested 17.5° Baume and 8g/l of acid. McKee scrawled on the end of the barrel the words "Duck Muck." It was given away to friends but soon achieved mythic status.

This accidental hero is now one of the most unlikely top wines in Australia. What surprises people is the high alcohol level—up to 17 percent, without apparent loss of balance, because the fruit is so rich and concentrated. In fact, Wild Duck Creek's alcohol levels have been falling lately, and Anderson is keen to see them moderate further. The secret is that the grapes achieve extreme levels of sugar ripeness without any raisining. High acidity at high sugar levels is a feature of Heathcote grapes.

Duck Muck's style is lavishly rich and fleshy, with masses of sweet fruit but without portiness; ample, soft tannins; and freshness preserved by that all-important acidity. **HH**
🅢🅢🅢🅢 **Drink: to 2024**

Williams Selyem
Rochioli Vineyard Pinot Noir 1985

Origin USA, California, Sonoma County
Style Dry red wine, 13.5% ABV
Grape Pinot Noir

Burt Williams and Ed Selyem began making wine as a hobby in the late 1970s, and established the first U.S. "cult" Pinot Noir. Williams eventually developed his own modus operandi for winemaking.

Severe crop thinning was critical for concentration; a prefermentation cold soak, with ambient yeasts beginning the fermentation. A five- or six-day fermentation, punctuated by *pigeage* two to four times daily. At dryness, the must was pressed, inoculated for malolactic, and racked. Press juice was used to top up each free-run barrel.

Williams Selyem had access to Rochioli's West Block fruit only between 1985 and 1997. It was the first bottling that vaulted them into the spotlight, winning them the Winery of the Year award at the California State Fair. Each of the subsequent twelve vintages strengthened the West Block's reputation as one of California's finest vineyards for Pinot Noir. The 1985 vintage was one of the last vintages made in the old garage, in a style that came to be the benchmark for Russian River Valley Pinot Noir: concentrated and richly flavored, with luscious, sweet fruit flavors and velvety texture. **LGr**
🅢🅢🅢 **Drink: to 2017**

◄ Shiraz grapes ripen at Wild Duck Creek's Springflat vineyard.

Wynn's *Coonawarra Estate John Riddoch Cabernet Sauvignon* 2004

Origin Australia, South Australia, Coonawarra
Style Dry red wine, 14% ABV
Grape Cabernet Sauvignon

If any region in Australia can lay claim to instigating the drive toward terroir-based winemaking in the European fashion, it would be Coonawarra—a strip of singular vineyard land distinguished by a top layer of red loamy soil known as terra rossa. The preeminent variety in this region has always been Cabernet Sauvignon, which turns out wines that have Bordeaux-style purity of cassis fruit, but are surrounded by bizarre, sometimes slightly volatile, now-spicy, now-balsamic, aromatic compounds.

Wynn's John Riddoch bottling of Cabernet Sauvignon is a premium selection wine first produced in 1982. Only the top 1 percent of the Cabernet crush goes into it, and even then, only if vintage conditions are deemed suitably auspicious. Matured in French oak for around two years, it is a pitch-dark wine built for sedate evolution.

The 2004 is the product of a slow-ripening harvest, picked later than normal. The wine spent a total of twenty months in a mixture of new, one- and two-year-old barrels. In its youth, the color was as black as squid ink, and the nose only reluctantly hinted at the plum, blackberry, and black-currant richnesses to come. Its future development was naturally closely guarded behind an iron curtain of sturdy but ripe tannin. There are top notes of peppermint on the palate, supported by that heaving mass of purple fruit, and the finish hints at the chocolaty lushness that the wine will take on as it proceeds toward maturity. **SW**
☻☻☻ **Drink: to 2025**

FURTHER RECOMMENDATIONS
Other great vintages
1982 · 1990 · 1993 · 1997 · 1998 · 2005 · 2006
More Coonawarra Cabernets
Hollick Ravenswood · Hungerford Hill · Katnook Estate Parker Estate · Penley Estate · Yalumba The Menzies

New oak barrels and stainless steel tanks at Wynn's winery. ➔

Yacochuya de Michel Rolland
2000

Origin Argentina, Calchaquí Valley, Cafayate
Style Dry red wine, 16% ABV
Grapes Malbec 90%, Cabernet Sauvignon 10%

In 1988 Arnaldo Etchart's decision to hire Michel Rolland launched an enduring friendship. Even before the Etchart winery had attracted a lucrative bid from Pernod Ricard in 1996, the pair had embarked on a joint venture, San Pedro de Yacochuya. The 2000 vintage of Yacochuya and its lighter-textured second wine, called San Pedro de Yacochuya, were the first to be bottled here.

The vines on this estate are surrounded by gray, drystone walls, and are partially terraced, which allows furrow irrigation. Their elevated location, combined with mica-rich soils, gave Rolland the steady ripening and almost raisinlike fruit intensity necessary for wines fermented using his trademark month-long macerations of the grape skins in the fermented wine allied to around fifteen months' aging in new French oak barrels.

This kind of "extractive" winemaking finds its apotheosis in Argentina's high altitude vineyards. Here the heat and light intensity potentially provide tannins with the vividness and malleability lacking in Bordeaux, a shortfall that Rolland has challenged successfully to make his name. **MW**

⊖⊖⊖ Drink: to 2017+

Yalumba
The Octavius 1998

Origin Australia, South Australia, Barossa Valley
Style Dry red wine, 14.5% ABV
Grape Shiraz

Owned by the Hill-Smith family, Yalumba is one of the most successful of Australia's independent wine companies, with a portfolio stretching from the smash-hit Angas Brut sparkler to more serious stuff like The Octavius.

The first release of this wine was the 1990 vintage. Now made exclusively from a number of very old vineyards in the Barossa, it is matured in 80-liter American oak "octaves," with a higher than usual surface area to wine ratio. These unique barrels are made at Yalumba itself, which is one of very few wineries still to have its own cooperage. The Missouri timbers are left exposed to the elements for eight years to leech undesirable flavors from the oak; the wine is consequently less oak influenced than one might expect.

In 2005, the fourth Langton's Classification saw the inclusion of The Octavius for the first time, ranked as "Outstanding." The warmth of the 1998 vintage manifests itself in the generosity of that year's Octavius. It came first in a *World of Fine Wine* Barossa Shiraz tasting, held in 2007. Barossa at its flag-waving best. **SG**

⊖⊖⊖ Drink: to 2018+

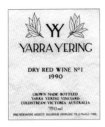

Yarra Yering
Dry Red Wine No. 1 1990

Origin Australia, Yarra Valley
Style Dry red wine, 13.5% ABV
Grapes C. Sauvignon, Merlot, Malbec, Petit Verdot

Alonso del Yerro
María 2004

Origin Spain, Ribera del Duero
Style Dry red wine, 14% ABV
Grape Tinta del país (Tempranillo)

Founder Dr. Bailey Carrodus, who died in 2008, was an eccentric and interesting man who rowed his boat outside the mainstream of the Australian wine industry, which is the way many of the country's greatest wines are produced. He was a man who knew what he wanted and how to set about achieving it.

Carrodus planted Yarra Yering in 1969, and the mature vines are hitting their peak. The wines are all estate grown on 74 acres (30 ha) of vines, the soils very deep, silty, clay-loam over clay with bands of gravel. They have always been dry grown on a north-facing slope, on a minimal single-wire trellis, with narrow spacings. Yields have been very low.

Why Dry Red Wine No. 1? (The top Shiraz is Dry Red Wine No. 2.) Said Carrodus: "It meant I didn't have to alter the labels as I developed the wine and the blend altered." The Dry Red Wine No. 1 1990 is a superbly elegant, finely textured and balanced Cabernet-based wine. The bouquet evokes cedar and cigar box. The palate is medium-bodied, elegant, and balanced, with great length and precision. At its best around eighteen years of age, this wine could go on for at least another ten. **HH**

🍷🍷🍷 **Drink: to 2018**

Along with Dominio de Atauta and a handful of others, Alonso del Yerro embodies the new concept of the "bodega-boutique"—family owned, with an exquisite, extremely limited production—that has developed along the Ribera del Duero. For Javier Alonso and María del Yerro, who abandoned their professional careers to begin winemaking in the village of Roa, in the province of Burgos, this is not an investment but a way of life. That is why they are building their house beside the bodega, why their top wine is called María (the name of one of their children), and why they decided to cross the Pyrenees to convince Stéphane Derenoncourt to become their consultant.

The winery has produced two wines since 2003: the basic Alonso del Yerro and the ambitious María, grown on two plots that add up to 12 acres (5 ha) in all, producing only 10,000 to 15,000 bottles. María 2004 may be the best wine so far. It is a powerful tinto, intense in aroma and taste, with a deep cherry color, a complex nose of ripe, dark fruits, noble wood, graphite, and peat, and a well-balanced palate, full, with smooth tannins and a long aftertaste. **JMB**

🍷🍷🍷 **Drink: to 2017+**

Fattoria Zerbina *Sangiovese di Romagna Pietramora* 2003

Origin Italy, Emilia Romagna, Faenza
Style Dry red wine, 15% ABV
Grapes Sangiovese 97%, Ancellotta 3%

Since 1987 Cristina Geminiani has run her grandfather's 99-acre (40 ha) estate in the foothills of the Apennines just east of Bologna. Armed with a brace of enology degrees and a healthy disregard for local tradition, Cristina set about producing serious Sangiovese in a region remarkably devoid of any viticultural legends. Using only the newest clones of Sangiovese—some sourced from the estate's own vineyards—Cristina replanted the vineyards in an effort to increase concentration and reduce yields. Such a severe measure was unprecedented here, but Cristina's decisions were quickly vindicated.

Her first vintage of Pietramora was in 1985. It is made only in the best vintages and sourced from the oldest vineyards, planted on a clay-and-limestone ridge that runs through the heart of the estate. Three weeks on the skins provides both depth of flavor and silky tannins, while a year in 70 percent new French oak adds the spicy complexity that only great Sangiovese can take in its stride.

Pietramora is a salient reminder of Italy's limitless viticultural potential. Even here, in an area more famous for prosciutto and parmigiano than for any vinous endeavor, it is possible to fashion wine of exceptional refinement. The old formula of high yields, unsuitable training systems, and clumsy winemaking ensured that Emilia-Romagna trailed behind Piedmont and Tuscany, but this fine Sangiovese looks set to change all that. **MP**
🜂🜂🜂🜂 **Drink: to 2018**

A vineyard in Emilia Romagna lies below Castell' Arquato. ➔

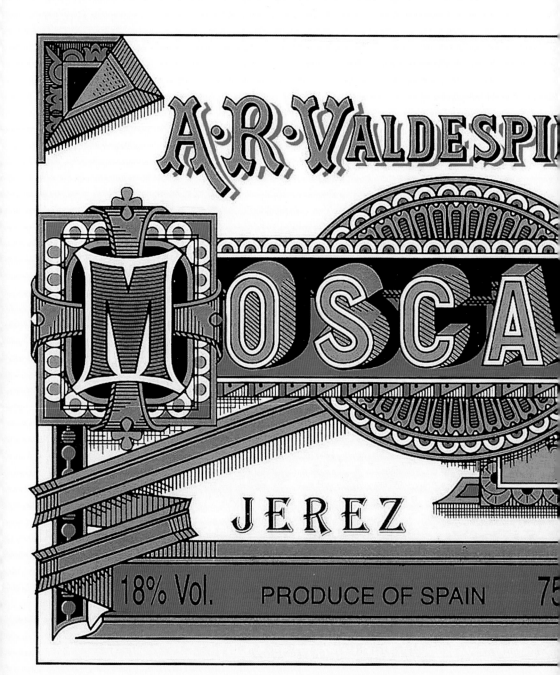

Fortified *Wines*

Alvear *Pedro Ximénez* 1830 *Solera Montilla*

Origin Spain, Montilla-Moriles, Montilla
Style Fortified sweet wine, 11.5% ABV
Grape Pedro Ximénez

Bodegas Alvear has its origins in the seventeenth century, when Diego de Alvear, whose family had come from Cantabria in the north of Spain, settled in Montilla. The oldest documents describing winemaking activities here date from 1729 and the house has remained a family business ever since, the family still owning 100 percent of the firm.

As with all the great Andalusian houses, the key to quality at Alvear lies in the balance between a brilliant tradition and competent winemaking. The team is led by Bernardo Lucena, who is deeply knowledgeable about traditional Andalusian wines.

Alvear 1830 Pedro Ximénez is a very old and rare wine; there are barely 400 gallons (1,500 liters) in the three butts that make up the solera. This noble wine enjoyed unprecedented success among consumers and critics when released at the end of the second millennium—so much so that sales had to be suspended for some time in order not to dilute the solera. Meanwhile, other old PX wines were released—Solera 1910 and Solera 1920—both of great quality but still without the depth and complexity of their elder brother, Solera 1830. **JB**

🜚🜚🜚🜚 **Drink: on release for at least 50 years**

Argüeso *San León* *Reserva de Familia Manzanilla*

Origin Spain, Sanlúcar de Barrameda
Style Fortified dry wine, 15% ABV
Grape Palomino Fino

The merchant León de Argüeso, born, like many other *bodegueros*, in the north of Spain, founded this house in 1822. He branded his Manzanilla after his own Christian name, and went on to produce one of the truly great wines of Sanlúcar de Barrameda.

Traditionally bottled as a Manzanilla pasada, San León is highly appreciated by the cognoscenti. That is why we should be grateful for Argüeso's parallel release of this genuine San León Reserva de Familia alongside a fresher, if less profound, version that was launched onto the market earlier this century.

Manzanilla San León Reserva de Familia comes from a single scale of forty-four butts, stored in the Bodega San Juan, a cool building in the heart of Sanlúcar. Only two withdrawals are performed each year—one in the spring, the other in the autumn. Each withdrawal is replaced by equivalent volumes from the solera of Manzanilla San León Clásica, formed by 877 butts arranged in six rows or scales. The clarification and filtration prior to bottling are very light, in order to respect the wine's true character. San León Reserva de Familia is, by age, body, and nose, a genuine Manzanilla pasada. **JB**

🜚 **Drink: current release for up to 3 years**

◨ Exposed to the air, wine ferments in *tinajas* at Bodegas Alvear.

Barbadillo
Palo Cortado VORS Sherry

Origin Spain, Sanlúcar de Barrameda
Style Fortified dry wine, 22% ABV
Grape Palomino Fino

Barbadillo was founded in 1821 by a group of businessmen who originated in the mountainous north of Spain. (Many other Andalusian bodegas such as Alvear, Hidalgo-La Gitana, Emilio Hidalgo, Argüeso, and La Guita, began in the same way.) The company's winemaking facilities occupy a large section of the Barrio Alto of Sanlúcar de Barrameda. It is partly thanks to the owners of Barbadillo that the historic area around the Castillo de San Diego is still fairly well preserved. Elsewhere in the town, many bodegas have disappeared over the past few decades, demolished to make way for a swathe of new buildings. For visitors to the town, it seems incredible that such losses are apparently tolerated by the very authorities that should protect the fine architectural heritage of the local wine cellars.

In the Barbadillo portfolio, four wines are officially classified as VORS, which signifies Very Old and Rare Sherry, aged for a minimum of thirty years: These are Amontillado, Oloroso Seco, Oloroso Dulce, and Palo Cortado. Although the first three wines certainly merit close attention, the Palo Cortado undoubtedly shines above the others for its authenticity and force of personality. Everything about it speaks of its long and careful nurture, from its deep-greenish rim to its classic, very old Palo Cortado nose, which is complex, clean, and intense, with a note of orange peel. The palate is full, with the pleasant acidity that comes from long years of concentration. Beyond that, it has the impressive finish of very old wine. **JB**

☻☻☻ **Drink: on release for at least 30 years**

Barbeito
20 Year Old Malmsey Madeira

Origin Portugal, Madeira
Style Fortified medium-sweet wine, 20% ABV
Grape Malvasia

Barbeito is the youngest of all the Madeira shippers still trading, and has recently been the most innovative. Like the other five shippers on the island, Barbeito's main business involved selling wine in bulk, until Ricardo Diogo, grandson of the founder, took over the helm in 1990. The company's turnover immediately fell by half, but Diogo was helped in his single-minded drive for quality by an injection of capital from the Kinoshita family of Japan, who became partners in Barbeito in 1991.

The company operates from three sites, each with its own distinct characteristics for aging wine. Their *adega* (winery) at Estreito de Camara de Lobos is the coolest, and produces the finest and gentlest of wines. The cliff-top wine lodge next to Reids Hotel in Funchal produces stronger, more concentrated wines. The strongest and richest wines come from the family quinta just above the center of Funchal.

Barbeito's 20 Year Old Malmsey is the ultimate exercise in finely tuned blending. After spending at least twenty years in cask, wines from a single year qualify for "vintage" status. As a result, few wines at this level end up in non-vintage blends, and all the other shippers overlook the 20 Year Old category. Bottled in tiny quantities, Barbeito's 20 Year Old is both brilliant and, currently, unique. Amber in color, with an olive-green tinge, high-toned, balsamic aromas, and a hint of vanilla, it is quite rich, complex yet delicate. Quincelike sweetness is offset by racy acidity leading to a fine, searing finish. This is a wine with supreme balance and poise. **RM**

☻☻☻ **Drink: to 2020+**

◀ The winery was built in 1821, the year of Barbadillo's foundation.

Barbeito
Single Cask Colheita Madeira

Origin Portugal, Madeira
Style Fortified sweet wine, 20% ABV
Grapes Malvasia, Boal (Bual)

The *colheita* has given a new lease of life to Madeira. Until 1998, only wines that had spent at least twenty years in wood could be bottled as "vintage," with the date on the label. These wines naturally command a high price and are made in very small quantities. Not to be confused with a *colheita* Port, a *colheita* Madeira is in effect an early bottled vintage, from a single grape, bottled after spending at least five years aging in wood.

All the shippers on the island have now embraced this style, but Barbeito has taken the *colheita* category a step further, bottling a specific number of bottles from a single, numbered cask. With around 1,000 50-cl bottles of each, Barbeito's Malvasia Cask 21c 1992, Malvasia Cask 18a 1994, Malvasia Cask 276 1994, Boal Cask 80a 1995, and Malvasia Cask 81a 1995 have followed on from each other in quick succession.

Although each wine has its own distinctive character, Barbeito's single-cask *colheitas* have much in common. Unusually pale in color (winemaker Ricardo Diogo eschews the use of caramel for coloring), these are wonderfully expressive wines, clean and fresh, with the incision of a fine Cognac—worlds away from the dark, soupy blends formerly passed off as Boal and Malmsey. Some have more than a hint of vanilla from being aged in new French oak. A back label explains the provenance of each wine, some of which are from single vineyards. Barbeito's Single Cask Colheitas already have a cult following: Look out for the latest release. **RM**
🍷🍷 **Drink: to 2025+**

Barbeito
Terrantez Madeira 1795

Origin Portugal, Madeira
Style Fortified dry wine, 21% ABV
Grape Terrantez

Vintage Madeira has more stamina than any other wine. Made at the end of the eighteenth century, this wine is still going strong and, incredibly, a few bottles are still available for sale. It predates the establishment of Barbeito, its owner, by 151 years, having originally belonged to the Hinton family who refined sugar cane on the island (and are credited with introducing soccer to Portugal). The wine then passed via the famous Madeira trader and collector Oscar Acciaioly to Mário Vasconcellos Barbeito, who founded his own shipping company in 1946. The wine was then in glass demijohns, but Barbeito returned it to wood before bottling it in the 1970s.

The wine's scarcity value is all the greater for having been made from Terrantez, the most highly prized of all Madeira's grape varieties. Introduced to the island from mainland Portugal in the eighteenth century, it was all but wiped out by the twin plagues of oidium and phylloxera in the mid-nineteenth century. By the 1920s, Terrantez was reported as being almost extinct, but it has recently made a modest but fortuitous comeback. Terrantez is capable of producing thrillingly ethereal wines—aromatic, at once both sweet and astringent, and with a capacity to age beautifully in cask.

Barbeito's Terrantez 1795 certainly lives up to its billing. Amber-mahogany in color with gentle smoky aromas, still beautifully fresh and redolent of green tea and jasmine, with a hint of lapsang; crisp, off-dry, with a penetrating flavor, amazing richness and texture, followed by a peacock's tail finish. **RM**
🍷🍷🍷🍷🍷 **Drink: to 2025+**

Three vintages of Barbeito Madeira, including the Terrantez 1795. ➡

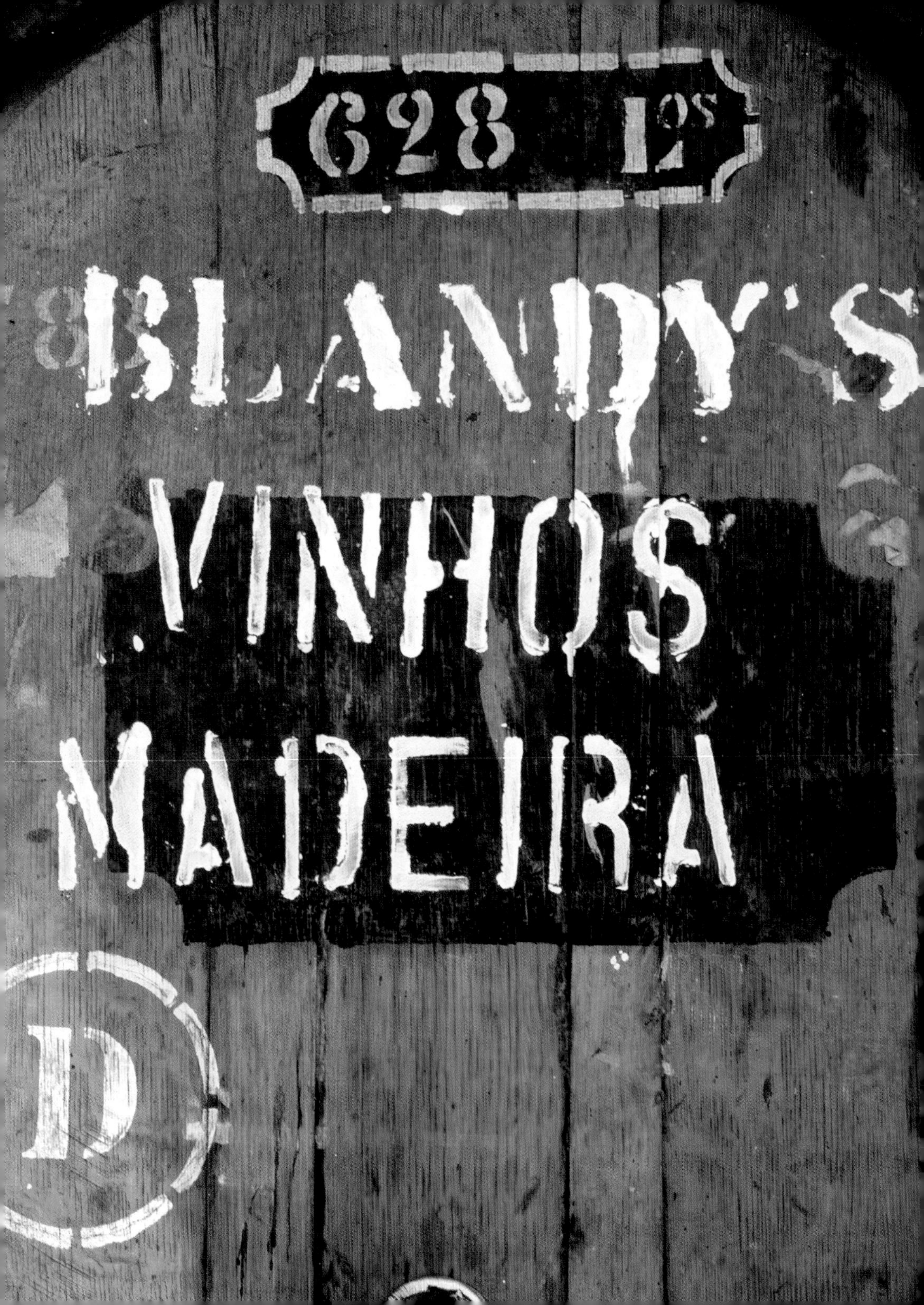
628
BLANDY'S
VINHOS
MADEIRA
D

Blandy's
1863 Bual Madeira

Origin Portugal, Madeira
Style Fortified medium-sweet wine, 20% ABV
Grape Bual

Bodegas Tradición
Oloroso VORS Sherry

Origin Spain, Jerez de la Frontera
Style Fortified dry wine, 20% ABV
Grape Palomino Fino

John Blandy, a quartermaster in the British Army, first landed on Madeira in 1807 during the Napoleonic Wars. He returned to the island four years later and set up the company that still bears his name. Steering a successful course through the early nineteenth century, the firm expanded into coaling, shipping, and banking. It was in a strong position during the twin plagues of oidium and phylloxera in the 1850s and 1870s, and John's son Charles had the foresight to buy up stocks of wine at a time when many other shippers were leaving the island.

Blandy's Bual 1863 just predates the phylloxera crisis, which broke out on Madeira in 1872. It was a small harvest, but is noted as an excellent year for Malmsey and Bual, the grapes producing the sweeter styles of wine from around Cama (now Câmara) de Lobos on the south side of the island. Red-mahogany in color with an olive-green tinge to the rim, this wine has fine, ethereal aromas and is still incredibly alive and fresh after almost a century and a half. With a bittersweet overtone, it has remarkable concentration redolent of molasses, butterscotch, and treacle toffee, and a powerful, lasting finish. **RM**
😊😊😊😊😊 **Drink: to 2020+**

Bodegas Tradición is the brainchild of businessman Joaquín Rivero, descendant of a great traditional winemaking family who owned the now legendary brand CZ more than 200 years ago. Between its foundation in 1998 and its first bottled release in 2003, this bodega acquired and assembled precious soleras as well as butts of remarkable quality and age from different bodegas. Some of the latter were disappearing, whereas others simply owned more old wine than they could release on to the market.

Bodegas Tradición exclusively ages and commercializes very old wines, all four recognized by the Consejo Regulador with one of its age certifications, be it VORS (more than thirty years of age) or VOS (more than twenty). The Oloroso VORS is archetypal in its category—spicy and expressive, round yet powerful, and well above the minimum of thirty years of age required for the VORS label.

The restored cellar buildings rise over the north quarters of the town of Jerez. The bodega facilities are home to more than 1,000 butts of old wines, and the Joaquín Rivero Collection of Spanish Painting from the fifteenth to nineteenth centuries. **JB**
😊😊😊 **Drink: on release for 15+ years**

Blandy's has produced Madeira wine for nearly 200 years.

Bredell's

Cape Vintage Reserve 1998

Origin South Africa, Stellenbosch
Style Fortified sweet wine, 20% ABV
Grapes Tinta Barroca 50%, Others 50%

Complicated negotiations with the European Union have led to the progressive phasing out of the word "Port" from the labels of South African fortified wine. The local product continues, however, to impress visitors from the Douro. Bruce Guimaraens once commented, "What I like is how the young wines here express their fruit—correct renditions of Touriga Nacional, of Tinta Barroca," whereas Johnny Graham, sniffing at a gently bubbling tank of Touriga at harvest time, said, "Unmistakable—just like the Douro." Whether the wines will have Port's power of lengthy evolution has still to be tested—and this wine, drinking superbly well and youthfully as it approached its decade, could be a suitable test.

The farm of J. P. Bredell Wines (in Stellenbosch's Helderberg basin, rather than the more inland Calizdorp) has been one of the leaders of a revolution in the Cape's Port-style wines that began in the early 1990s. Sweetness fell, alcohol levels rose, and other lessons were learned from Portuguese producers to make more classically styled wines. (Note that "Reserve" is a subjective quality indicator for wines made in exceptional years; a plain "Vintage" is also made, and more frequently.)

Bredell's Reserve 1998 has won many awards in South Africa for its quality. With notes of plums, dried fruit, leather, and nuts, it has an emerging complexity of flavor with a forceful tannin and alcohol grip, and a long, dry finish. **TJ**
🔵🔵🔵 **Drink: to 2018+**

Bredell wines come from the beautiful coastal Helderberg basin. ➡

Chambers *Rosewood Old Liqueur Tokay*

Origin Australia, Victoria, Rutherglen
Style Fortified sweet wine, 18.0% ABV
Grape Muscadelle

Rosewood has been passed down through six generations of the Chambers family since its foundation in 1858. Export-labeled as Chambers Rosewood Rare Muscadelle, this is truly one of Australia's rarest fortified wines.

Chambers and Morris are the two top exponents of Rutherglen Tokay, but there are a few key differences. One of Chambers's two blocks of Muscadelle is irrigated when necessary "to maintain growth, not promote it," says Stephen. The dry-grown block is straw-mulched to conserve soil moisture. One site, near the winery, is loam over clay, with quartz; the other straight clay, and they give quite different wines, both important in the blend. Chambers's Tokay style is what they call "mistella": an unfermented grape juice that is fortified and put directly into oak—starting with large vats and moving to smaller casks as the wine gets older. All are old casks, some more than 100 years old.

The Old Tokay, not blended every year, comes from a "modified solera." The oldest is from the start of the twentieth century: The Chambers do not know its average age. Stephen describes the Chambers style as lighter and finer than the Morris style, because there is no fermentation nor skin maceration. The style of both the Old and Special Tokays is unbelievably complex and concentrated, with *rancio*, malt, molasses, and butterscotch aromas. The Special has more young material in the blend, so has a slightly fruitier character. **HH**

😑😑😑😑 Drink: at least 20 years from release

FURTHER RECOMMENDATIONS
Other great Chambers wines
Rare Muscat • Rare Muscadelle (Tokay)
More Rutherglen Tokays/Muscadelles
Campbells • Morris Wines
Rutherglen Estates • Stanton and Killeen

Mixed barrels of Chambers' Rutherglen wines develop their unique flavors. ➡

Cockburn's
Vintage Port 2011

Origin Portugal, Douro Valley
Style Fortified sweet wine, 20% ABV
Grape Mixed traditional varieties

From the start of the twentieth century to the early 1960s, Cockburn's commanded the most respect (and the highest prices) of all Vintage Ports. Wines like the 1908, 1912, 1927, 1948, and 1963 were legendary, and if these wines share something, it is their supreme finesse rather than sheer power that marks them out.

Cockburn's had a rather quirky approach to which years it declared as vintages, missing out on other widely declared years like 1965, 1966, and 1977: they were emphatically not a shipper to be influenced by others! But under multinational ownership from the late 1960s, standards started to slip, and by the 1980s Cockburn's was something of a Vintage Port basket case. It all came back together in 2011, the first declared vintage with Cockburn's under the ownership of the Symington family (who also own Dow, Graham, and Warre).

The Symingtons are keen to rediscover the soul of Cockburn's. In this they are assisted by Quinta dos Canais, an outstanding vineyard in the Douro Superior that has long formed the backbone of Cockburns' Vintages and was bought by the Symington family in 2006. Replanted with a high percentage of Touriga Nacional, this fragrant, floral grape is very evident in Cockburn's 2011, where it makes up 55 percent of the blend. The wine is dense with sumptuous ripe, warm country fruit combining great purity, crucial finesse, and the structure to last. Cockburn's 2011 has all the makings of a very great Vintage Port. **RM**

⊖⊖⊖⊖ **Drink: to 2050+**

Cossart Gordon
Malmsey Madeira 1920

Origin Portugal, Madeira
Style Fortified sweet wine, 21% ABV
Grape Malvasia

The best-known of all Madeira's grapes, Malvasia (Malmsey in English) is an umbrella term covering a number of different varieties. By far the most highly prized is Malvasia Cândida, which almost certainly originated in Crete and was taken to Madeira in the fifteenth century. The grape is notoriously difficult to grow, and requires a sheltered, sunny position at or close to sea level, where the grapes shrivel, almost to raisins, before harvesting. During the second half of the eighteenth century, Francis Newton (erstwhile partner in the firm of Cossart Gordon) wrote frequently to his London partners lamenting the lack of Malvasia wine. Malvasia Cândida was subsequently decimated by oidium in the 1850s and not widely replanted after phylloxera thirty years later. By the early twentieth century, but for a few vines growing on Fajã dos Padres on the south side of the island, it had become extinct.

Cossart Gordon's Malmsey 1920 is said by Noel Cossart (partner in the family firm and author of *Madeira, the Island Vineyard*) to be the last vintage made from Malvasia Cândida, which he describes as the "true Malmsey." Subsequent Malmseys have been made from Malvasia Babosa (Lazy Malmsey), Malvasia Fina, Malvasia Roxa, and the so-called Malvasia de São Jorge, a productive grape that has never been officially identified as a Malvasia.

With a tawny-green color and a perfumed, floral exuberance that identifies it as genuine Malvasia, this wine is in near-perfect balance, its caramelized richness offset by characteristic searing acidity. **RM**

⊖⊖⊖⊖⊖ **Drink: to 2050+**

Cossart Gordon
Verdelho Madeira 1934

Origin Portugal, Madeira
Style Fortified medium-sweet wine, 21% ABV
Grape Verdelho

Founded by two Scotsmen, Francis Newton and William Gordon, in 1745, Cossart Gordon is the oldest shipper of Madeira still in business today. In 1808 William Cossart, an Irishman from a family of Hugenot origin, joined the firm, and in 1861 it took on its present name from its partners. By the mid-nineteenth century, Cossart Gordon had established a huge market in North America, and the firm was described at the time as being responsible for shipping "half the growth of the island." Despite this, the firm kept its British nationality, retaining a branch in London from 1748 until the late 1980s.

Cossart Gordon suffered more than most Madeira firms from the imposition of Prohibition in 1920, but retained its independence as a shipper until it became part of the Madeira Wine Company in 1953. Cossart Gordon is now the second largest brand in the Madeira Wine Company after Blandy. Its wines were always slightly drier in style than Blandy's, whose traditional market was the U.K., and this distinction has been maintained since the two houses were brought under one roof.

Recalling the days when the company was still run by members of the Cossart family, Noel Cossart noted that 1934 was an excellent year, especially for Verdelho. Gordon Verdelho 1934 (bottled in 1986) is an unusual wine, quite rich in style for a Verdelho. Mid-deep amber in color, it has aromas of kerosene and wood smoke, and great complexity with savory-spicy concentration balanced by nervy acidity. It dries off to a clean, vibrant finish. **RM**
◉◉◉◉ **Drink: to 2030+**

Croft
Vintage Port 2003

Origin Portugal, Douro Valley
Style Fortified sweet wine, 20.5% ABV
Grapes Tinta Roriz, T. Franca, T. Nacional, Others

Croft is one of the oldest surviving Port companies, having been founded by John Croft in 1678. Family-owned until the 1920s, it was then taken over by Gilbey's, later to become part of International Distillers and Vintners (IDV), and later still the multinational Diageo. As a result, for much of the latter part of the twentieth century the company suffered from underinvestment, so much so that Croft Ports of the 1970s and 1980s are really quite weak examples of their type. With the coming of the twenty-first century, however, Croft is back on track—the 2000 vintage was good, the 2003 excellent—the result of new ownership and great attention to detail.

Croft vintages have traditionally been based on the wines of Quinta da Roêda at Pinhão. This quinta, a relatively gentle amphitheater of vines, has been described as the jewel of the Douro. It became a Croft property in 1875 when it was acquired from John Fladgate of Taylor Fladgate and Yeatman. It was fitting, then, that when Diageo sold Croft and Delforce in 1999, they were bought by Taylor's. The Taylor's team improved the vineyard husbandry and rebuilt the winery. The old concrete autovinifiers were decapitated and mechanical plungers were installed; for the very best Port, a brand new granite *lagar* was built, round-cornered, as a replica of the one Croft had decommissioned in 1963. The result is a wine that truly deserves to be called Vintage Port—opaque purple in color, with vibrant, aromatic black fruit and stunning tannic backbone. **GS**
◉◉◉ **Drink: to 2050**

De Bartoli *Vecchio Samperi Ventennale Marsala*

Origin Italy, Sicily, Marsala
Style Fortified dry wine, 17.5% ABV
Grape Grillo

Delaforce *Curious and Ancient 20 Year Old Tawny Port*

Origin Portugal, Douro Valley
Style Fortified sweet wine, 20% ABV
Grapes Tinta Roriz, T. Franca, T. Nacional, Others

Appalled by the industrial-quality Marsala that had transformed this once glorious wine into a mere cooking ingredient, Marco De Bartoli began producing outstanding Sicilian wines in the late 1970s. He took over the old family farmhouse from his mother Josephine, and dissected the "local tradition," retaining only what he thought valuable. He died in 2011, but his work is ably continued by his sons, Renato and Sebastiano, and daughter Giuseppina.

He decided to work with varieties such as Grillo, arguably the best grape in the Marsala blend, but previously ditched by many producers because of its idiosyncratic personality and the fact that it only grows as bush vines, which do not lend themselves to production on a large scale.

De Bartoli's bid for excellence can be savored in the Vecchio Samperi Ventennale. The color is rich amber, while on the nose the aromas range from walnut to dark honey, from minty, almost balsamic tones to saffron and cinnamon notes. The wine is full and rich on the palate but never overpowering, the warmth from the naturally high alcohol keeping the flavors focused, well defined, and lingering. **AS**
🗙🗙🗙 **Drink: on release for up to 30 years**

The Delaforce family connection with the Port trade dates back to 1834, when John Delaforce established a Port company for Martinez Gassinot. His son, George Delaforce, established the Port company bearing his name in 1868.

Curious and Ancient, the twenty-year-old, wood-matured Port, and its younger sibling, His Eminence's Choice, were originally launched in the 1930s and are therefore perhaps the oldest existent brands of their kind in the Port trade.

Delaforce does not own vineyards in the Douro. Rather the company operates in the way that all Port firms did in the early days, buying grapes and wine from growers—in this case mostly from the spectacularly terraced vineyards of Quinta da Corte in the Rio Torto valley in the heart of the Cima Corgo.

Long wood-aging and deliberate oxidation have resulted in a mid amber-tawny color, quite pale compared to some; the aged nose is refined, with toffee and fudge notes, old wood showing through along with figs and raisins; sweet yet perfectly balanced by the acidity. This is not a wine to lay down, but to be enjoyed on release. **GS**
🗙🗙 **Drink: on release**

This *barcos rabelos* used to carry Port barrels down the Douro River. ➜

Delgado Zuleta
Quo Vadis? Amontillado Sherry

Origin Spain, Sanlúcar de Barrameda
Style Fortified dry wine, 20% ABV
Grape Palomino Fino

Pedro Domecq
La Ina Fino Sherry

Origin Spain, Jerez de la Frontera
Style Fortified dry wine, 15% ABV
Grape Palomino Fino

Founded in 1744, Delgado Zuleta is one of the oldest houses in the Marco de Jerez. Its vineyards are located in the Pago de Miraflores and provide almost all its wine—some 2,000 butts per year. The famed Manzanilla La Goya is their best-known bottling, but one should not forget that the soleras of the historical Manzanilla Barbiana, from Rodríguez Lacave, are also part of their holdings.

Although the greater part of its current production now takes place in modern facilities in the city outskirts, Delgado Zuleta also owns several old bodegas in the heart of Sanlúcar, whose future is in danger. In one of these, hidden among the narrow streets of the Barrio Alto, rest the 300 butts of Amontillado still owned by the house. One fraction nurses one of the true jewels of the local winemaking craft— Amontillado Quo Vadis?

At forty years of age, Quo Vadis? is a wine of great personality. Salty and reminiscent of its aging under *flor*, it has notes of noble wood, vanilla, mint, lemon, lavender, and licorice, on both nose and palate. Deep, mellow, and savory, with excellent acidity, length, and unique tannic character. **JB**

◊◊◊ **Drink: on release for up to 10 years**

Changes in ownership of the business during 2006 have led to a change in the name of this centuries-old Sherry house. Bodegas Pedro Domecq is now under Beam Global, which has grabbed the distribution of the best-selling Sherry label in the world: Harveys' Bristol Cream. But in the case of La Ina, to refer to this classic marque as Beam Global La Ina Fino would sound as bad as if Champagne Krug were suddenly to become LVMH. Fortunately, it seems that classic wines such as Botaina Amontillado, La Ina Fino, and Río Viejo Oloroso will retain the Pedro Domecq name on their labels.

La Ina has for many decades maintained an intense rivalry with Tío Pepe in terms of prestige and popularity. This healthy competition has been particularly pronounced within Andalusia itself, especially among local aficionados, who are often divided between followers of one or the other. Connoisseurs have traditionally valued La Ina Fino for its classic, uncompromising, and acetaldehydic character. La Ina receives, year in and year out, consistently outstanding ratings from Spain's most relevant wine guides. **JB**

◊ **Drink: most recent release within 1 year**

La Ina has been a popular Fino brand for decades. ▶

Fino La Ina
Pedro Domecq
JEREZ

Dow's *Quinta Senhora da Ribeira Single Quinta Port* 1998

Origin Portugal, Douro Valley
Style Fortified sweet wine, 20% ABV
Grapes Mixed traditional varieties

This wine embodies the late twentieth-century success of Port. Senhora da Ribeira is one of three properties bought for Silva and Cosens (producer of Dow's Port) by George Acheson Warre, and it remained with the company until the Symington family sold it in the mid-1950s. An entry in Dow's visitors book dated May 21, 1954, records the event: "Went to Senhora da Ribeira to conclude sale . . . It's been a most sad occasion but we leave the happiest memories and many good faithful friends here."

Senhora da Ribeira nonetheless continued to be an important component in Dow's Vintage Ports, and in 1998 (Silva and Cosens's bicentenary), it was bought back by the Symingtons. Although run down, it was eerily the same as when they had left it. 1998 proved to be a challenging growing season, producing small quantities of excellent wine. A warm start to the year was followed by mixed weather until hot, dry conditions finally arrived in July and continued through to early September.

Yields were some of the lowest on record, and by the middle of the month there was every prospect of a small but exceptional harvest. Picking began in the Douro Superior on September 14, but a week later the fine weather ended and most of the harvest took place amid heavy showers. A potentially great year became merely good in terms of quality. This wine, picked before the rain, is the most impressive wine of the vintage: Deep, dark, and dense, it has lovely, soft, multilayered fruit supported by a ripe, tannic backbone. It is a success story in every respect. **RM**
☻☻☻ Drink: to 2040+

Dow's *Vintage Port* 1955

Origin Portugal, Douro Valley
Style Fortified sweet wine, 20% ABV
Grapes Mixed from old, interplanted vineyards

The Symington family's involvement in Port began in 1863, when Andrew James Symington left his native Glasgow for Oporto. He was an astute businessman who was immediately attracted to the Port trade. "AJ" and his successors eventually took complete control of Warre & Co and Dow's, before adding Graham's to their portfolio in 1970. The Symingtons are now the second largest Port producers and the largest landowners in the Douro.

It is hard to credit now, but back in 1955, the Port trade was struggling for survival. World War II had hit business hard and the boom in sales that had followed World War I failed to materialize. In the 1950s, two of Dow's estates, Quinta do Zimbro and Quinta Senhora da Ribeira, were sold just to keep the company afloat.

Against this rather depressing backdrop came a wonderful vintage. As early as August 13, Ronald Symington wrote: "Vines looking wonderful . . . both bunches and grapes are much larger than last year . . . A few showers between now and the vintage should produce an excellent 1955." The rain materialized at the start of September and picking began on September 19. Ronald Symington noted: ". . . the color generally was good and [the wines] were all very nice on the nose and the palate."

With the Port trade now prospering, Dow's 1955 is still deep ruby in color, extraordinarily fresh, with youthful, minty concentration. The wine is full, firm, and rich but balanced, well focused with a huge tannic superstructure. It will go on and on. **RM**
☻☻☻☻☻ Drink: to 2050

Dow's vineyards opposite a citrus orchard on the Douro River. ➡

El Grifo
Canari 1997

Origin Spain, Canary Islands, Lanzarote
Style Fortified sweet wine, 17% ABV
Grape Malvasía

El Maestro Sierra
1830 Amontillado VORS Sherry

Origin Spain, Jerez de la Frontera
Style Fortified dry wine, 19% ABV
Grape Palomino Fino

The Malvasía for which Shakespeare's Falstaff offered his soul to the devil is no longer among the most planted grape varieties on the Canary Islands. But some 3,680 acres (1,490 ha) remain on Lanzarote, the easternmost island, where it arrived shortly after the 1730 eruption of the Timanfaya volcano.

Founded in 1775, El Grifo is the oldest bodega on the island. El Grifo can pride itself for having modernized the island's winemaking through the introduction of stainless steel vats and the switch to dry Malvasía and reds from the local Istán Negro grape. But it has not abandoned traditional solera sweet wines, which are still sold in small quantities.

Aside from the rare, Port-like G Glas 1997, or the Malvasía 1956, the bottling that comes closest to the revered sweet wines of yore is the Grifo Canari—a blend of the 1956, 1970, and 1997 vintages labeled, as demanded by law, according to the youngest. This sweet solera wine is made from very ripe grapes, partially dried and lightly fortified. Amber in color, it offers a nose of almonds, licorice, and orange peel. A mouth-filling wine with a complex, sweet aftertaste, it is charmingly *démodé*—a stroll back in time. **JMB**

🅢🅢 **Drink: to 2025**

Among the myriad different styles of traditional Andalusian wines, Amontillado is the true touchstone, the wine that best harmonizes character, finesse, and above all, complexity. Old Amontillados are fundamental wines, difficult and profound, and among the exclusive elite is this one from El Maestro Sierra, an old almacenista bodega that only started bottling Sherry under its own name in 1992. Until then the house of Emilio Lustau had successfully based part of its expansion into the Anglo-American market on one of El Maestro Sierra's wines—the memorable Oloroso Almacenista Vda. de Antonio Borrego.

El Maestro Sierra is an artisanal, traditional house where the feeding and the refreshing of the nurseries are carried out under the personal supervision of its expert *capataz*, Juan Clavijo, still using the traditional utensils and vessels of the craft—*jarra, canoa, sifón,* and *rociador*. The owner is Pilar Pla—still active at the helm but aided by her daughter, the historian Carmen Borrego. The bodega facilities are located on a beacon over the town of Jerez, welcoming the soothing sea breeze. **JB**

🅢🅢🅢 **Drink: on release for 15+ years**

◄ El Grifo's griffin flies over the bodega's entrance in arid Lanzarote.

Equipo Navazos *La Bota de Manzanilla No.50 Bota Punta*

Florio
Terre Arse Marsala 1998

Origin Spain, Sanlúcar de Barrameda
Style Dry fortified wine, 16% ABV
Grape Palomino Fino

Origin Italy, Sicily, Marsala
Style Fortified dry wine, 19% ABV
Grape Grillo

What began in 2005 as some enthusiasts attempting to secure private bottlings of the treasures lying in bodega cellars has blossomed into a micronegociant that is transforming the perception of traditional wines of Andalusia. Equipo Navazos selects specific casks from within soleras of outstanding personality and then bottles them with a minimum of handling in order best to express their intrinsic characteristics. Each release is numbered and dated, with an emphasis upon transparency for the consumer.

This fifteen-butt solera of Manzanilla Pasada is a perfect example of this approach. Rafael Rivas, at the time *capataz* at La Guita cellars, started this solera in 1986 to create a quality blending component to add some extra substance to the commercial releases of the house. Over time, the solera was pampered by Rivas, with just enough wine drawn off and refreshed to preserve it as a Manzanilla and prevent the *flor* dying completely. Taken from a single cask at the extreme end of the solera and with an average age of fifteen years, this wine has an unmatched biological character; a steely salinity paired by the delicate oxidative notes of a true Manzanilla Pasada. **FP**

☺☺☺☺ **Drink: on release for up to 30 years**

In 1773 Mr. John Woodhouse, a rich entrepreneur from Liverpool, was forced by a sudden storm to harbor his ship in Marsala. There he sampled a strong local wine called *Perpetuum*. He liked it so much that he decided to begin a large commercial operation based on it. He bought the wine, added alcohol in order to ensure its preservation during the voyage, and made his way back home. Marsala wine was an instant success in England, and Woodhouse moved to Sicily. The first Italian-owned Marsala cellar, however, was founded by Vincenzo Florio in 1832. Today, visiting the Florio cellars with their commemorative plaques is a rare step back in time.

Terre Arse (pronounced Terr-ay Ars-ay) is the perfect example of what an excellent Marsala should always be like. It is *vergine*, which means that only alcohol has been added to it, leaving the final wine perfectly dry. The color is old gold and the nose reminiscent of caramelized honey and toasted hazelnuts. On the palate, its dry, velvety richness and great complexity will leave you wondering why you have never thought to open a bottle of good Marsala on a more regular basis. **AS**

☺☺ **Drink: on release for up to 25 years**

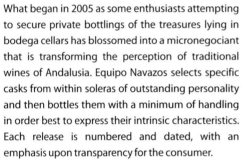

The Florio cellars contain many older vintages. ➡

José Maria da Fonseca
Setúbal Moscatel Roxo 20 Years

Origin Portugal, Setúbal
Style Fortified sweet wine, 18% ABV
Grape Moscatel Roxo

Fonseca
Vintage Port 1963

Origin Portugal, Douro Valley
Style Fortified sweet wine, 21% ABV
Grapes Mixed from old, interplanted vineyards

The Iberian Peninsula has more than its fair share of fine fortified wines. Port, Sherry, and Madeira are preeminent, but less well-known is Setúbal, from just south of Lisbon in Portugal. The largest and most important among its producers here is José Maria da Fonseca, a wine business now nearly 200 years old.

Setúbal Moscatel is made in much the same way as the *vins doux naturels* of southern France, fortifying the partially fermented Moscatel musts with high-strength neutral spirit to kill off the yeast and preserve a high level of natural grape sugar in the finished wine. Wines from the hot Setúbal Peninsula can lack acidity, and for this reason most Moscatels da Setúbal are blends, relabeled simply as "Setúbal." There remain, however, some pure Moscatels, including top-level wines from Fonseca.

The Moscatel Roxo 20 Years is the epitome of the style—quintessential Setúbal. Vivid mid-amber colored, with green hints from aging, it has a lovely, raisiny nose with caramel and singed peel hints. Sweet on the palate, but with a freshness from the balanced acidity, this is a wine to be enjoyed as an aperitif or an accompaniment to dessert. **GS**

🍷🍷🍷 **Drink: current release**

Perfect conditions made 1963 a once-in-a-lifetime Port vintage in which nearly every Port shipper produced an impressive wine. This outstanding example comes from Fonseca, a company with origins at the end of the eighteenth century, when Manuel Pedro Guimaraens began exporting cloth and comestibles from Portugal to Brazil. Despite vicissitudes of ownership, successive generations of the Guimaraens family have continued to steer the firm. Frank Guimaraens, followed briefly in the mid-1950s by Dorothy Guimaraens, and then Bruce Guimaraens were responsible for every one of Fonseca's remarkable vintages from 1896 to 1991.

Fonseca 1963, made by Bruce Guimaraens, is one of the great Ports of the twentieth century. Still looking youthful after spending more than forty years in bottle, it has developed the most wonderfully pure, floral aroma (crushed rose petals) that sings from the glass. Seemingly quite dry and delicate initially, it retains great purity of fruit and combines finesse with a long, powerfully assertive, yet elegant finish. Anyone born in 1963 probably has a wine to accompany them for life. **RM**

🍷🍷🍷🍷🍷 **Drink: to 2050**

◄ Ingenious lighting identifies the cellar at José Maria da Fonseca.

Garvey
San Patricio Fino Sherry

Origin Spain, Jerez de la Frontera
Style Fortified dry wine, 15% ABV
Grape Palomino Fino

William Garvey went to Spain in the second half of the eighteenth century to buy sheep for crossbreeding with those his family owned in the green pastures of Ireland. But the sweet eyes of a local girl (daughter to a Spanish captain who rescued him from a shipwreck) proved even more unforgettable than memories of home, so he established himself as a wine merchant, a business of which he knew nothing.

It is little coincidence, then, that San Patricio—the Spanish name for St. Patrick—is the most important brand name in Bodegas Garvey (owned by the Ruiz Mateos family for the past few decades), or that San Patricio was the name given to its most important cellar building, one of the most awe-inspiring surviving Sherry cathedrals. Unlike other memorable buildings lost to heedless urbanization, the Bodega San Patricio, right in the heart of Jerez de la Frontera, still stands, even though Garvey has moved to new facilities in the Complejo Bellavista. It is sad, however, that the building's current use is completely unrelated to its original raison d'être.

One of the peculiarities of Fino San Patricio is that, right before bottling, and overseen by enologist Luis Arroyo, it undergoes a second—brief but intense—phase of biological aging under *flor* to emphasize its aromatic properties. Like some other Fino Sherries, San Patricio stuns consumers with its exceptional quality at an affordable price. **JB**

🕒 **Drink: current release within 1 year**

Dry conditions for Palomino vines near Jerez de la Frontera. ➡

González Byass
Cuatro Palmas Amontillado Sherry

Origin Spain, Jerez de la Frontera
Style Fortified dry wine, 21% ABV
Grape Palomino Fino

González Byass
Tío Pepe Fino Sherry

Origin Spain, Jerez de la Frontera
Style Fortified dry wine, 15% ABV
Grape Palomino Fino

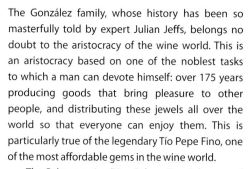

The González family, whose history has been so masterfully told by expert Julian Jeffs, belongs no doubt to the aristocracy of the wine world. This is an aristocracy based on one of the noblest tasks to which a man can devote himself: over 175 years producing goods that bring pleasure to other people, and distributing these jewels all over the world so that everyone can enjoy them. This is particularly true of the legendary Tío Pepe Fino, one of the most affordable gems in the wine world.

The Palmas series (Una Palma, Dos Palmas, and Tres Palmas Finos, and Cuatro Palmas Amontillado) was first bottled in 2011, following the success of Tío Pepe Fino En Rama in 2010. This was a movement toward authenticity inspired by Equipo Navazos' relaunching of unfiltered, raw Finos and Manzanillas as the purest expression of true Sherry heritage. Since then, a small quantity of each of these wines has been released by González Byass every year.

The average age of this outstanding wine is more than forty years. Deep amber, its aromas are fine and delicate, with fresh herbs and a hint of dried fruit. The palate is clean, long, well-defined, and expressive. **JB**
🜚🜚🜚🜚 **Drink: on release and up to 30+ years**

In the mid-1830s, Sanlúcar-born Manuel María González Ángel founded what today is González Byass with the help of his uncle, José Ángel de la Peña. After his uncle he gave the name Tío Pepe (Uncle Joe) to a wine that through the years has become the most important label in the Sherry region. Perhaps some brand of Manzanilla, such as La Guita or La Gitana, could now challenge this supremacy in terms of marketing; perhaps another Fino, maybe La Ina or Inocente, might deserve—for history and quality—a similar status in the hearts of connoisseurs; perhaps some other trademark, such as Osborne's bull, has a similar visual power. But no fewer than 170 years in the market with a wine of consistently top quality is a feat that very few, in Jerez or elsewhere in the world, have achieved.

Actually, Tío Pepe is one of the most important labels in the world, and there are few, if any, names that could rival it in terms of consistent quality and tradition. Not to mention price, of course, but this is perhaps rather a handicap for the brand, in a marketplace where fashion and image too often dictate consumption trends. **JB**
🜚 **Drink: most recent release within 1 year**

The monumental archway of the González Byass bodega at Jerez. ➡

Graham's
Malvedos Single Quinta Port 1996

Origin Portugal, Douro Valley
Style Fortified sweet wine, 20% ABV
Grapes T. Nacional, T. Franca, Tinta Roriz, Others

Graham, one of the great names of Port, began as a Glasgow-based textile manufacturer and entered the wine trade by accident in 1820 when it accepted pipes of Port in lieu of a bad debt. Wines from the Malvedos estate overlooking the Douro at Tua in the Cima Corgo have been a component in Graham's Vintage Ports for more than a century. Graham's Malvedos is one of the first of the modern generation of single estate Ports, having been produced in good years between full vintage declarations since the 1950s.

In general, 1996 proved to be a good year for replenishing stocks of premium Ruby and Late Bottled Vintage (LBV) Port—but it also produced some really lovely Single Quinta wines. 1996 was not a year for blockbuster wines for long-term keeping, yet Graham's Malvedos 1996 blossomed into a fine, fruit-driven Port in less than ten years (compared with a true vintage that can need twenty years or more). With its fine, fragrant, floral aroma, redolent of violets, and lovely, pure, berry fruit flavors, Malvedos 1996 is the classic expression of Single Quinta Vintage Port. **RM**
🍷🍷🍷 **Drink: to 2020+**

Graham's *The Stone Terraces*
Vintage Port 2011

Origin Portugal, Douro Valley
Style Fortified sweet wine, 20% ABV
Grapes T. Nacional and other traditional varieties

In the twenty-first century, a number of leading Port shippers have begun to make small quantities of site-specific Port released in parallel to their classic Vintage declarations. Graham's The Stone Terraces is just such a wine and made its debut in 2011.

Drawn from two parcels of steep, traditional terraced vineyards at Quinta dos Malvedos, Graham's flagship estate, just 250 cases of this wine were made. You might have expected these to be some of the oldest vines on the property, but these vineyards have been replanted with a high percentage of Touriga Nacional, the leading grape variety in the Douro. Between them, the two parcels—Port Arthur and Vinha dos Cardenhos—account for just 4½ acres (1.8 ha) of the Malvedos vineyard's 220 acres (89 ha), and they are predominantly east-facing and north-facing (whereas Malvedos is mostly south facing). These cooler aspects mean the grapes ripen gradually and evenly, being shielded from the July and August Douro afternoon sun.

The Stone Terraces 2011 is a wonderfully deep and dense debut, with lovely rich fleshy fruit, minty ripeness, and a touch of eucalypt. **RM**
🍷🍷🍷 **Drink: to 2060+**

◧ Traditional grape baskets stacked at Graham's Quinta dos Malvedos.

Graham's
Vintage Port 1970

Origin Portugal, Douro Valley
Style Fortified sweet wine, 20% ABV
Grapes Mixed traditional varieties

The Graham family built up such a strong presence in Oporto that there is even an area of the city still known as Graham. The firm remained in family hands until 1970 when the business fell on hard times and was sold to the Symington family.

The old vines of Quinta dos Malvedos have always been at the core of Graham's Vintage Ports. The year 1970 may have marked the end of an era for the Graham family, but it coincided with an outstanding vintage. Picking began around the normal time of the September equinox, when temperatures were unusually high.

Early tastings played down the 1970s, the best of which have taken thirty years to come around. The overall quality is not as high as 1963, but Graham's 1970 undoubtedly deserves to be among the twentieth century's great Vintage Ports. Still deep and youthful in color, it has tremendous intensity, with black cherry and dark chocolate aromas and big, broad-shouldered tannins still disguising the underlying richness and elegance. With a peacock's tail of a finish, this wine combines power and finesse in equal measure, and still has a long way to go. **RM**

🔅🔅🔅🔅🔅 **Drink: to 2020+**

Gutiérrez Colosía
Palo Cortado Viejísimo Sherry

Origin Spain, Andalusia, El Puerto de Santa María
Style Fortified dry wine, 22% ABV
Grape Palomino Fino

Members of the Gutiérrez Colosía family have owned this old firm since José Gutiérrez Dosal bought it in the early twentieth century. To the main bodega, built in 1838 according to the efficient plans of the Sherry "cathedrals," they added new cellar wings, on the ruins of the palace of the Count of Cumbrehermosa, a former *cargador de Indias* (shipper to and from the Spanish Americas).

The facilities are close to the mouth of the River Guadalete, near the Bay of Cádiz. The great industrial expansion of Puerto de Santamaría took place here from the mid-1830s, and it is here that most of the winemaking buildings are still found. Gutiérrez Colosía is the only firm whose bodegas rise on the very banks of the River Guadalete, with the added benefit that the higher humidity provides for the proper biological aging under *flor*.

Although the house of Gutiérrez Colosía has in its portfolio all the different styles of Sherry, the Palo Cortado Viejísimo is its greatest jewel, as precious as it is scarce. In this complex and intense wine, the two souls of Palo Cortado—those of Amontillado and Oloroso—contend for dominance. **JB**

🔅🔅🔅 **Drink: on release for at least 10 years**

Gutiérrez de la Vega *Casta Diva*
Cosecha Miel / Reserva Real 1970

Henriques & Henriques
Century Malmsey 1900 Solera

Origin Spain, Alicante
Style Fortified sweet wine, 14% ABV
Grape Moscatel Romano (Muscat of Alexandria)

Origin Portugal, Madeira
Style Fortified sweet wine, 21% ABV
Grape Malvasia

Gutiérrez de la Vega is a family winery in the Marina Alta subzone of the Alicante DO where Felipe, his wife Pilar, and their three children work in two charming, old houses in the village of Parcent. The wines come from 37 acres (15 ha) dotted around nearby villages. Felipe, a sailor, has been a winemaker since 1973, but did not begin marketing his wine until 1984. Now he offers fourteen wines, some named for William Blake, María Callas, Donizetti, and James Joyce, and alluding to literary or operatic themes: Viña Ulises, Rojo y Negro, Furtiva Lágrima, Casta Diva.

As Victor de la Serna has written, Gutiérrez de la Vega "has modernized in an exquisite manner the tradition of Spanish Moscatels." The Casta Diva, in its Cosecha Miel variant, is the jewel in the crown, and this extraordinary Moscatel, labeled as Reserva Real, has become a collector's item. An attractive golden color, it offers scents of honey, citrus fruits, spices, and figs. On the palate, the wine is very sweet, rich, and velvety, with a long, powerful, seductive finish. This is a world-class dessert wine or, as its creator likes to say, "a wine made for happiness." **JMB**

💲💲 **Drink: to 2020**

According to the local pun, "There are only two names in Madeira." The Henriques family were originally large landowners on Madeira, planting vineyards on the island at Pico de Torre in the mid-fifteenth century, only a few years after it was discovered and colonized by the Portuguese.

When Portugal joined the European Union in 1986, Madeira's soleras—ill-defined and open to fraud—were effectively abolished. However, since 1998, the solera has been reintroduced and defined much more tightly by the authorities. The basis for any solera bottled today must be wine from a single year, of which not more than 10 percent can be withdrawn for bottling in any one year.

Henriques & Henriques took advantage of the new legislation, bottling a solera that had been laid down in 1899 just in time for the millennium. The wine is extraordinary: mahogany in color with a thin olive-green rim; pungent, high-toned aromas, redolent of green tea leaves and flowers; incredibly rich, verging on unctuous figgy fruit, balanced by powerful, ravishing acidity that keeps the wine fresh and alive. A powerful, sinewy finish follows. **RM**

💲💲💲💲 **Drink: to 2050+**

Emilio Hidalgo *1860 Privilegio Palo Cortado VORS Sherry*

Origin Spain, Jerez de la Frontera
Style Fortified dry wine, 20% ABV
Grape Palomino Fino

Privilegio Palo Cortado 1860 is, together with Santa Ana Pedro Ximénez 1861, the jewel in the crown of Bodegas Emilio Hidalgo. This small Sherry bodega is nowadays run by fourth and fifth-generation descendants of its founder, who owned vineyards and wine soleras dating back to 1860 and 1861.

Sometimes the labels of traditional Andalusian wines include references to specific dates that consumers might believe to be vintage dates. It is very rarely so, and with very few exceptions these wines are produced following the traditional solera system, whereby wines progress from the youngest row of butts (criadera) to others containing older wine, and so on until they reach the solera.

Once inside the solera butts, wines of different vintages are blended and homogenized, and so the residual proportion of old vintages decreases proportionately. In the case of Privilegio Palo Cortado, "1860" makes reference to the date of the solera's foundation, which precedes even the formal constitution of the bodega as such, and therefore it is likely that a minuscule percentage of the wine bottled nowadays comes from that year. **JB**

🚫🚫🚫🚫🚫 **Drink: on release for up to 5 years**

Emilio Hidalgo *1861 Santa Ana Pedro Ximénez VORS Sherry*

Origin Spain, Jerez de la Frontera
Style Fortified sweet wine, 15% ABV
Grape Pedro Ximénez

Emilio Hidalgo is one of the few Sherry houses still under family management by descendants of the founder, in this case Emilio Hidalgo, who founded the bodega in 1874. The starting point was a series of soleras chosen personally by the founder.

The solera of Santa Ana Pedro Ximénez, one of the mythical sweet wines of Jerez, was founded in 1861. Emilio Hidalgo thrives on the reputations of this wine and the Privilegio Palo Cortado 1860, whereas wine lovers soon discover the excellence of the Fino Especial La Panesa. Virtually unfiltered Fino is likely to hold the key to the future of this wine region, combining distinction, complexity, affordability, and feasible commercial production.

Santa Ana Pedro Ximénez 1861 is a relic of the Hidalgo family. It originates in Pedro Ximénez vineyards—now disappeared—in the Pagos de Añina, one of the top four terroirs in the Sherry region (together with Macharnudo, Carrascal, and Balbaína). The wine is opaque, extremely dense, extraordinarily fresh, light, and even fruit-driven for its age. A real joy, released in limited lots in order not to dilute the age and depth of its solera. **JB**

🚫🚫🚫🚫🚫 **Drink: on release for up to 30 years**

Hidalgo-La Gitana
Palo Cortado Viejo VORS Sherry

Origin Spain, Sanlúcar de Barrameda
Style Fortified dry wine, 19% ABV
Grape Palomino Fino

Hidalgo-La Gitana
Pastrana Manzanilla Pasada

Origin Spain, Sanlúcar de Barrameda
Style Fortified dry wine, 15.5% ABV
Grape Palomino Fino

Hidalgo-La Gitana, owner of one of today's best-selling Manzanilla labels, is one of the many Sanlúcar-based houses founded by merchants originally from Cantabria, in northern Spain. Its old wines are stored in a semi-subterranean cellar that works wonders for the aging of Manzanillas, because the reduced availability of oxygen is compensated for by proper ventilation, while the proximity of the River Guadalquivir estuary provides an optimum degree of humidity at this depth for the development of *flor*, essential for a Manzanilla.

Losses through evaporation in the butts of old wines are also smaller because of this high humidity, and this in turn limits the natural rise in alcohol. This is likely one of the distinctive features that characterize the organoleptic profile of the old wines at Hidalgo-La Gitana, sometimes initially marked by a reductive nose that eventually dissipates after meticulous aeration in the glass or decanter.

Exceptionally, as part of the Matador series, in 2000 a Palo Cortado Scully was released, a veritable jewel of a Sherry that no true aficionado should miss for its sheer quality and rarity. **JB**

🚫🚫🚫🚫 **Drink: on release for up to 10+ years**

Any aficionado who has visited the Sherry district and tried wines directly from the butt knows that Amontillados, Olorosos, and Pedro Ximénez from cask differ only marginally from their bottled versions. There are, however, perceptible differences in terms of color, nose, and palate between Finos and Manzanillas in cask and those in bottle.

The reason for this difference is the intense filtration process carried out on wines that have been subject to biological aging, which is justified on two grounds. Firstly, by the consumer's preference for pale Finos and Manzanillas, to the point that many will reject any wine of slightly deeper hue. And secondly, by the greater stability of these ultra-filtered wines, which can then be shipped and stored without loss of freshness for a year or two.

In contrast to these almost universal practices, Hidalgo has undertaken a bold, groundbreaking experiment with its Pastrana Manzanilla Pasada—a wine possessing a beautiful golden color, with an age and structure that allow it to ship virtually unfiltered, proving that there is room in the market for true Manzanillas Pasadas. **JB**

🚫 **Drink: most recent release for several years**

KWV
Muscadel Jerepigo 1953

Origin South Africa, Boberg
Style Fortified sweet wine, 18.2% ABV
Grape Muscadel (Muscat Blanc à Petits Grains)

Until its new breed of Port-style wines emerged in the early 1990s, the Cape's greatest contribution to fortified wines was its sweet jerepigos—though "wine" (or *vin doux naturel*) does not quite account for these luscious *mistelles*, made by heavy alcohol additions to unfermented juice. As a class, jerepigo is now languishing, unfairly unfashionable.

KWV, then a national cooperative also with statutory powers, produced some of the best. The 1953 was made before KWV established its own cellar for such wines, and it blended a number of jerepigos. The area of origin, Boberg, exists in the Wine of Origin system only for fortified wines.

Since its bottling in 1981, this 1953 Jerepigo has enjoyed near-mythical status among nostalgic cognoscenti, who snap it up when it occasionally comes on to the secondary market. The rich, massive sweetness resists cloy, braced by a moderate acidity, a little tannin, and the substantial alcohol. There are notes reminiscent of old Madeira, some of molasses (rather than raisin), and genuine complexity of flavor. Development has darkened the color to deep tawny, but the wine shows no sign of tiring. **TJ**

🜨🜨 **Drink: to 2050+**

Domaine de La Rectorie
Cuvée Leon Parcé Banyuls 2000

Origin France, Banyuls
Style Fortified sweet wine, 16% ABV
Grapes Grenache Noir, occasional Mourvèdre

Marc and Thierry Parcé are *petits cousins* of the Parcés at Mas Blanc and part of the *noblesse du bouchon* of the little port of Banyuls. Marc is a schoolmaster by training, and began dabbling in wine on their 49-acre (20 ha) family domaine in 1984. The brothers are self-taught, but Thierry received some expert guidance from the heroic local enologist André Brugirard, who played a major role in modernizing the wines of the Roussillon. The Parcés possess an old Wehrmacht bunker, which provides them with excellent cool cellaring in this hot corner of France. They abandoned filtration from the first, embraced organic farming, and continue to be luminaries of the Slow Food movement.

The best Banyuls from the domaine is the Cuvée Léon Parcé. The 2000 is ruby colored with violet lights. The wine is well structured and redolent of cherries and sweet strawberries. Former World's Best Sommelier Olivier Poussier finds "soft spices" on the palate and recommends serving the wine at 57°F (14°C). The Cuvée Léon Parcé may be enjoyed with a blue cheese like Roquefort, or with certain desserts. Poussier recommends a red fruit crumble. **GM**

🜨🜨🜨 **Drink: to 2025**

Leacock's
Serial Madeira 1963

Origin Portugal, Madeira
Style Fortified dry wine, 20.5% ABV
Grape Sercial

M. Gil Luque *De Bandera*
Palo Cortado VORS Sherry

Origin Spain, Jerez de la Frontera
Style Fortified dry wine, 19% ABV
Grape Palomino Fino

Leacock is one of the great names in Madeira, having been established as a wine shipper by John Leacock in the mid-eighteenth century. The most famous member of the family is Thomas Slapp Leacock, grandson of the founder, who owned vineyards at São João on the outskirts of Funchal. When his vineyard was attacked by phylloxera in 1873, he went to great lengths to protect his vines, treating their roots with resin, essence of turpentine, and tar. By 1883, he had the disease under control, and it is thanks to him that many of the traditional grape varieties remain on the island today.

Sercial is perhaps the most underappreciated of these varieties, producing a searingly dry style of Madeira that is not an easily acquired taste. Leacock's Sercial 1963 (bottled in 1994) is still a relative youngster, but it is one of the most expressive examples of the grape. Mid-amber in color, with characteristically delicate, green-leaf aromas, slightly smoky and floral, it is searingly austere, yet delicate, clean as a whistle, very finely poised with a lovely steely finish. This wine will be around for many, many years to come. **RM**

🕙🕙🕙🕙 **Drink: to 2050+**

In the small circles of true Sherry aficionados, the old wines of Fernando Carrasco Sagastizábal are fondly missed. Those soleras, aged in his old cellar in the Rincón Malillo and Cordobeses streets, were bought by the firm of M. Gil Luque in 1995 and moved to the Viña El Telégrafo of the Pago Carrascal. Twelve years later, the Estévez group bought M. Gil Luque, and this has opened a new era for these old wines in the De Bandera series. Another move to a new residence has been necessary, something never welcomed by these wines, but the Estévez team, under the direction of Eduardo Ojeda, has already succeeded in moving, reorganizing, and restoring the many butts of the legendary Valdespino house.

A very limited special release was made in 2007: 300 half-bottles selected from the best of the seven butts that form the solera of this Palo Cortado. This finest butt, or *Bota Punta*, is the one in each solera of Sherry wines that outclasses the rest for its superior age, depth, and balance. Consequently, the *Bota Punta* traditionally undergoes the strictest regime of withdrawals and refreshment, accentuating its age and distinction over the years. **JB**

🕙🕙🕙 **Drink: on release for up to 30+ years**

Lustau *Almacenista Cuevas Jurado Manzanilla Amontillada*

Lustau *Almacenista García Jarana Pata de Gallina Oloroso Sherry*

Origin Spain, Sanlúcar de Barrameda
Style Fortified dry wine, 17.5% ABV
Grape Palomino Fino

Origin Spain, Jerez de la Frontera
Style Fortified dry wine, 20% ABV
Grape Palomino Fino

Almacenistas are stockholders who buy wine or must from producers, then age them in their own bodegas. Sometimes, as in the case of Manuel Cuevas Jurado, they also have their own vineyards. But if they do not register themselves with the Regulatory Council as shippers, they cannot sell their bottled wines directly. Instead, their stocks are usually bought by larger houses that include them in the final blend of their main brands.

In the 1980s, while still under the direction of Rafael Balao (a big name in the recent history of Sherry), Bodegas Lustau recognized the huge potential stored in the soleras of many stockholders, and in a bold and successful operation released choice wines selected according to its own criteria.

Although the general level of the several dozen Almacenista wines bottled by Lustau is remarkably high, some are outstanding, like this Manzanilla Amontillada. Beyond its intrinsic quality is the exclusiveness of being one of the few Manzanilla Amontilladas—if not the only one—commercially available. The figure 1/21 on the label indicates that the solera comprises twenty-one butts. **JB**

⊖⊖ Drink: on release for 5+ years

Luis Caballero Florido, a businessman with a powerful personality, is the main stockholder of the house of Luis Caballero, a bodega in El Puerto de Santa María that produces, among other wines, Pavón Puerto Fino Sherry, Don Luis Amontillado, and Padre Lerchundi Moscatel. But the jewel of his portfolio in terms of Sherry is Lustau, which he bought in 1990 and whose technical direction is the responsibility of Manuel Arcila.

The elegant and spicy Pata de Gallina Oloroso 1/38 is sourced from a century-old bodega with 300 butts that Juan García Jarana owns in the popular barrio de Santiago. This owner of a motorbike company is a great Sherry lover; Current economic conditions dictate that he maintains this bodega mostly as a hobby, because the Sherry trade is still embroiled in the crisis that started in the 1970s.

Pata de Gallina means "hen's foot," referring to the shape of the chalk marks drawn by the *capataces* to classify the butts of wine. After the original stick, successive branching curves were added to classify the wine as having a particular aromatic profile— the resulting shape indeed recalling a hen's foot. **JB**

⊖⊖ Drink: on release for 10+ years

Harvesting Palomino Fino grapes in Jerez. ➡

Marqués del Real Tesoro
Covadonga Oloroso VORS Sherry

Origin Spain, Jerez de la Frontera
Style Fortified dry wine, 19.5% ABV
Grape Palomino Fino

Mas Amiel
Maury 2003

Origin France, Maury
Style Fortified red wine, 16% ABV
Grape Grenache Noir

Marqués del Real Tesoro was in 1984 the first of the major acquisitions by José Estévez. Since then, the Grupo Estévez, already managed by the second generation, has consolidated its position as one of the most important companies in the sector, both by turnover and volume. In 2006/2007 it acquired Rainera Pérez Marín (La Guita) and M. Gil Luque.

As well as producing the Grupo Estévez's range of affordable and mass-produced wines, the winemaking team (under Eduardo Ojeda and Maribel Estévez) is in charge of an impressive selection of rare gems of world class, among which we find this Covadonga Oloroso VORS.

The traditional label of this wine ranks as the most indecent of those from the Sherry district. On it we see an old Noah, drunk under a vine tree, exposing himself (as related in the Book of Genesis), much to the scandal of his children. Apparently the image was borrowed from a sixteenth-century Central European engraving. Additionally, some claim that the typography of the label is vaguely reminiscent of the part of the body so shamefully revealed by Noah. **JB**

☯☯☯☯ **Drink: on release for up to 20+ years**

At the end of the arid, rocky Maury Valley is a great cathedral-like building dedicated to fortified wine, constructed at the start of the twentieth century. The Roussillon is France's warmest region and this estate is in its hottest corner, with the sun shining an average of 260 days a year. The estate is old, dating from 1816, but it was the Dupuy family who built it up. Latterly the family showed less interest in the large estate, and in 1997 sold out to Olivier Decelle.

There are 372 acres (155 ha) of chiefly Grenache vines here, with an average age of thirty-five years. Most of the wines are fortified, but not to the degree of Port, and then lodged in huge oak tuns or glass demijohns. The "vintage" wine dates only from the 1990s, but it has more concentration and sappy fruit than the more traditional wines that are wood aged and bottled at six or ten years.

The 2003 vintage Maury is 100 percent Grenache. The color is as deep as you would expect from wines that bake in such a fierce sun. The wine has an aroma of chocolate and figs, on the palate the texture is creamy, and the taste is reminiscent of pepper and raspberries. **GM**

☯☯☯ **Drink: to 2020+**

◀ The Jerez bodega of Marqués del Real Tesoro.

Mas Blanc

La Coume Banyuls 2003

Origin France, Banyuls
Style Fortified sweet wine, 16.5% ABV
Grape Grenache Noir

Banyuls, a small, sleepy port on the Spanish border, has a long tradition of making fortified red and white wines from grapes culled from the schistose soils of the Pyrenean foothills. The founder of Mas Blanc, Dr. André Parcé, was the head of the local cooperative until a small scandal drove him out: Revenues were so low that they were unable to pay the members. But Parcé's reputation transcended Banyuls: He was also on lots of national committees. People might grumble now, but André Parcé deserves praise: Not only did he revive the production of the Portlike fortified wine, but he pretty well invented the unfortified wine of Collioure. His standing with the Institut National des Appellations d'Origine in Paris meant that no one was in a position to resist him.

The wines at the 50-acre (20 ha) domaine of Mas Blanc are now ably made by André's sons, Jean-Michel and Bernard. Mas Blanc is still bubbling with innovation. There are excellent, unfortified Collioures, a solera-style wine, and the top Banyuls La Coume, made from 90 percent Grenache Noir with a little Syrah and Mourvèdre. The vintage wines are often labeled *rimatge*, which is the Catalan word for the age of the grape.

The La Coume 2003 is beautifully balanced, noble, and elegant, and will make a marvelous dessert wine by its tenth birthday. It wears its 80 g/l residual sugar lightly, and is wonderful with a plate of blue cheese and local black figs. **GM**

$$$ Drink: to 2025

Banyuls's vineyards overlook the Gulf de Lion. ➔

Massandra Collection
Ayu-Dag Aleatico 1945

Origin Ukraine, Massandra, Ayu-Dag
Style Fortified sweet wine, 15.5% ABV
Grape Aleatico

A winery at Massandra, near Yalta on the Black Sea, has existed since the mid-nineteenth century. It was built to supply wines for the tsar's summer palace, Livadia, also near Yalta, and catered for every conceivable vinous need of the tsar. In order to ensure high standards, the tsar employed Prince Lev Sergervich Golitzin to oversee production. Golitzin established the Massandra Collection by retaining bottles of every wine made. Wine is still made by the Massandra Collective, where a number of member estates farm 4,400 acres (1,780 ha) of vines.

The library retains a minimum of one bottle of every wine, but limited numbers of these are released for sale periodically. On November 27, 2007, the London auction house Bonhams held a specialized wine sale in London, before which a 1945 Massandra Collection Ayu-Dag Aleatico was tasted. Ayu-Dag, or "Bear Mountain", overlooks the winery, and Aleatico is an Italian red variety with a close relationship to Muscat Blanc à Petits Grains. The nose was not especially pungent, but these wines have a remarkable balance of sugar and acidity, so they are never cloying or unctuous. **SG**
⊖⊖⊖⊖⊖ **Drink: to 2040**

Morris Wines
Old Premium Liqueur Muscat

Origin Australia, Victoria, Rutherglen
Style Fortified sweet wine, 18% ABV
Grape Muscat à Petits Grains (Brown Muscat)

A wine style unique to Australia, this "stickie" is an example of the fortified dessert wines made from Brown Muscat grapes grown in the hot Rutherglen area of northeast Victoria. The late Mick Morris was something of a legend in these parts; his son David now makes the wines.

To make these hedonistic liquids, the grapes are left on the vine as long as possible to obtain the maximum sugar level, almost turning them into raisins. On arrival at the winery, the grapes are crushed and allowed to partially undergo fermentation before a high-strength neutral spirit is added to arrest the fermentation and fortify to 18 percent alcohol. The wine is then transferred into oak casks and barrels to mature slowly for many years in furnacelike sheds. During blending, older wines give intensely concentrated flavors of burned sugar syrup and rum, while younger wines impart a fresh fruit character.

This wine is guaranteed to put a smile on your face, with its herbal nose leading into a super-sweet palate that evokes raisins and baked apples. It is unctuous, and certainly not for everyone. **SG**
⊖⊖ **Drink: current release**

Morris Wines
Old Premium Liqueur Tokay

Origin Australia, Victoria, Rutherglen
Style Fortified sweet wine, 18% ABV
Grape Muscadelle

Founded in 1859, Morris is owned by Pernod Ricard, but newly placed on the market at the time of writing. It has always been run by a member of the Morris family. Old Premium is the oldest commercially distributed Morris label for Tokay and Muscat, and is in very limited production each year. The Muscadelle grapes are entirely estate grown on red loam over red and yellow clays, which have good water-holding ability, enabling Morris to be unusual in the region for not irrigating at all. Also unusually, the grapes ferment a little, which, David Morris (winemaker since the mid-1990s) believes, alters the flavor in a subtle but important way.

Old Premium Tokay, blended once a year, has an average age of twenty years, with the oldest wine being about sixty years old. Tokay, although made with the ripest grapes, tends to be less sweet than Muscat, but very complex and mellow. Old Premium is blended to achieve a balance between malty, honeyed, fruity, young-wine flavors and butterscotch, toffee-aged characters, with a low-note of ultra-complex *rancio*. "The wine has to lead with fruit," adds Morris: "Age alone is not beauty." **HH**
🜍🜍🜍 **Drink: on release for up to 20+ years**

Niepoort
Colheita Port 1987

Origin Portugal, Douro Valley
Style Fortified sweet wine, 20% ABV
Grapes Mixed from old, interplanted vineyards

Colheita is one of the most misunderstood and misrepresented categories of Port. The Portuguese word *colheita* (pronounced col-yate-a) means "harvest," and is sometimes confused with "vintage" as a result. Two dates appear on the label of a *colheita*: the year of harvest and the year of bottling. The latter is also significant because, unlike a Vintage Port, which might need thirty years to develop in bottle, *colheitas* are bottled ready to drink.

Niepoort holds stocks of *colheita* dating back to 1935. While these older single-vintage wines are undeniably impressive and tend to be bottled to order, Niepoort also releases more accessible wines that combine the freshness of youth with the complexity of maturation in wood. Although fully ready to drink, younger *colheitas* will continue to develop slowly in bottle. Niepoort's 1987 Colheita (bottled 2005) is a relative youngster, having spent eighteen years in wood. Pale amber-tawny in color, it is still very fresh and fragrant, with refined aromas and flavors. It is beautifully poised and complete, soft, suave, and silky, with great delicacy and a deliciously zesty finish. **RM**
🜍🜍🜍 **Drink: to 2017+**

Niepoort
30 Years Old Tawny Port

Origin Portugal, Douro Valley
Style Fortified sweet wine, 20% ABV
Grapes Mixed from old, interplanted vineyards

Niepoort
Vintage Port 2005

Origin Portugal, Douro Valley
Style Fortified sweet wine, 20% ABV
Grapes Mixed from old, interplanted vineyards

Although Niepoort has made some very fine Vintage Ports, its long-standing reputation has been for its fine array of Tawnies, graduating from the so-called Junior and Senior to the 10, 20, and 30 Years Old blends, all of them among the finest in their class.

As the components in a Tawny blend age in cask they become increasingly concentrated, gaining sweetness through evaporation. Much depends on how and where the wines have been aged. A wine that has been stored inland in the Douro Valley, where temperatures (and therefore evaporation levels) are higher, will mature at a faster rate than a wine aged in the cooler, more humid conditions of Vila Nova de Gaia, close to the coast.

Niepoort's 30 Years Old Tawny is made of component wines that range from eight to 100 years old. It is pale amber-tawny in color, with a telltale olive-green tinge to the rim that speaks of the wine's high average age. The aroma is fine, delicate, and lifted, with flavors of freshly roasted almonds and dried apricots and tawny marmalade. Overall it is sweet, silky, and refined, finishing with a beauty and flair that reflect its masterful blending. **RM**

☻☻☻ **Drink: current release for 10+ years**

Portugal suffered the most severe drought in living memory in 2005. Younger vineyards, unable to withstand the extreme conditions, produced raisined grapes and burned, unbalanced wines. But with yields down significantly on average, small quantities of concentrated, rich wine were produced from old, deep-rooted vines that were able to withstand the drought. For most Port shippers, 2005 was a "non-classic," single quinta year, and some powerful, tight-knit wines were declared in the spring of 2007. A number of shippers, however, opted for a full vintage declaration.

Dirk Niepoort could not contain his enthusiam: "2005 is for me the best wine that I have made and probably the best Niepoort has done since 1945." Niepoort describes the brilliance of his 2005 as being its "harmony and balance"—unusual traits from such extreme conditions. The wine is just at the start of a long life: deep and opaque in color, still closed and raw, its amazing underlying density and intensity are already evident. It is by no means the biggest Niepoort vintage, but it has remarkable purity of fruit backed by a firm tannic backbone. **RM**

☻☻☻ **Drink: to 2050+**

Demijohns of Port age in Niepoort's lodge at Vila Nova de Gaia. ➡

Quinta do Noval *Vintage Port* 1997

Origin Portugal, Douro Valley
Style Fortified sweet wine, 19.5% ABV
Grapes Mixed traditional varieties

There can be no finer estate in the Douro than Quinta do Noval with its commanding view over the Pinhão and Douro Valleys. The property first appeared in land registries in 1715, and passed through the hands of the Rebello Valente family and Visconde de Vilar d'Allen until it was sold, ravaged by phylloxera, to Port shipper António José da Silva in 1894. Noval was thoroughly renovated, and the major part of the vineyard replanted on phylloxera-resistant American rootstock.

In 1981 Noval suffered a disastrous fire that destroyed much of the company's stock as well as its archives. This, combined with a long-running family dispute, eventually brought the company to its knees, and brother and sister Cristiano and Teresa van Zeller were forced to sell Noval in 1993 to AXA Millésimes. Since then, nearly half of the vineyard has been replanted and the famous terraces have all been retained. Onward from 1994, the first vintage under the new ownership, declarations have been much smaller than in the past, often amounting to fewer than 1,000 cases.

In 1997, Noval produced one of the very best wines of this widely declared vintage. However, the wines were by no means as immediately appealing as the 1994s that preceded them. Noval is opulent, with dense fruit, bitter chocolate intensity, and ripe tannins rising to an explosive finish. Needing twenty years to show at its best, Noval 1997 marks the start of a new era for this landmark estate. **RM**
◒◒◒◒ **Drink: to 2050+**

FURTHER RECOMMENDATIONS
Other great vintages
1931 • 1963 • 1966 • 1970 • 1994 • 2000 • 2003 • 2011
More Quinta do Noval Ports
Aged Tawny • Colheita
Late Bottled Vintage • Nacional • Silval

Pruning in one of Quinta do Noval's stone-walled vineyards. ➡

Quinta do Noval *Nacional Vintage Port* 1963

Origin Portugal, Douro Valley
Style Fortified sweet wine, 20.5% ABV
Grapes Touriga Nacional, Tinta Francisca, Souzão

The 1963 Ports are remarkable for excellence across the board, with nearly every shipper producing an impressive Vintage Port in this year. One of the weaker wines of the vintage was Quinta do Noval, but this disappointment is more than compensated for by Quinta do Noval Nacional, which is without doubt one of the greatest Vintage Ports ever made.

"Nacional" denotes a plot of some 6,000 ungrafted vines situated on either side of the main driveway to Quinta do Noval. Planted in the 1920s, the vines are on their own roots, and thus deemed to be attached to the soil of the nation. The Nacional vineyard is on the so-called *meia encosta* (halfway up the slope), at an altitude of 1,150 feet (350 m) and, facing southwest, has a perfect exposure. Yields are low, averaging around 15 hectoliters per hectare, compared to an average of 30 to 35 hectoliters per hectare on the rest of the Noval estate.

Port expert Richard Mayson has sampled (and drunk) the Nacional 1963 four times over the past decade, and calls the wine "one of the most perfect Ports ever produced." His note from a vertical tasting of Nacional held in Portugal in March 2001, when the wine was in its thirty-eighth year, reads: "Incredibly deep color, purple-pink rim with only the merest hint of brown. Tight but intense, black cherry aromas on the nose; incredible concentration and focus, bitter chocolate fruit. Of the highest quality. Very, very, very fine. Lovely length—lost for words— finish that goes on forever." **SG**

☺☺☺☺☺ **Drink: to 2050+**

FURTHER RECOMMENDATIONS
Other great vintages
1931 • 1934 • 1945 • 1966 • 1970 • 1994 • 2000 • 2011
More 1963 Ports
Cockburn's • Croft • Delaforce
Fonseca • Graham • Taylor • Warre

Quinta do Noval's terraced vineyards above the Pinhão River. ➔

Olivares Dulce
Monastrell Jumilla 2003

Origin Spain, Jumilla
Style Fortified sweet wine, 16% ABV
Grape Monastrell

Bodegas Olivares is a family operation founded in 1930. It owns more than 500 acres (202 ha) of vineyards planted with Monastrell, Syrah, and Tempranillo in Jumilla, the Mediterranean appellation in the province of Murcia. The winery does not, however, belong to the Denominación de Origen, because its main business is bulk wine.

Among its vineyards, Bodegas Olivares owns a parcel with very old and ungrafted vines of Monastrell, planted among olive trees (*olivares* means olive groves) at an altitude of more than 2,600 feet (792 m). From these grapes it produces Olivares, a sweet red dessert wine. By some unknown means, perhaps by some kind of infusion, notes of olives do find their way into the wine.

2003, a very warm vintage, produced overripe grapes ideal for sweet wine. The color is very dark, due to the long maceration. A distinctive note of olives and tomato juice makes the wine instantly recognizable, even when served blind. There are flowery notes and plenty of dried fruit, such as figs and dates. Rich and tannic in its youth, with a thick texture, the wine has a very persistent finish. **LG**

🍷🍷 Drink: to 2020

Osborne
Pedro Ximénez Viejo VORS Sherry

Origin Spain, Andalusia, El Puerto de Santa María
Style Fortified sweet wine, 17% ABV
Grape Pedro Ximénez

Viejo Pedro Ximénez Rare Sherry is one of the stars in the much-treasured firmament of extremely old sweet PX wines. Almost black, it is so dense that it coats the glass, and on both nose and palate offers sweetness, complexity, and persistence, with notes of raisins, dates, iodine, salt, toast, and incense.

The house of Osborne's wines are generally very good, with a basic entry-level range with an excellent quality–price ratio, and then the world-famous Sacristía reserves—the Rare Sherries of which this Viejo Pedro Ximénez VORS is one.

The Rare Sherries lineup comes from extremely old soleras, most of which rest in the bodega La Honda. These wines used to be reserved for the private enjoyment of the Osborne family until they were commercially released in the 1990s. Initially the series included other equally magnificent wines now no longer for sale (Very Old Dry Oloroso, Alonso el Sabio Oloroso, La Honda Fino Amontillado, El Cid Amontillado). But these soleras are still maintained and can be tasted if one is lucky enough to share a quiet walk among the venerable oak vessels with the house enologist Ignacio Lozano. **JB**

🍷🍷🍷🍷 Drink: on release for up to 50 years

Osborne
Solera PΔP Palo Cortado Sherry

Origin Spain, Andalusia, El Puerto de Santa María
Style Fortified medium-sweet wine, 22% ABV
Grape Palomino Fino

Solera PΔP Palo Cortado is an off-dry old Sherry that blends concentration, smoothness, and aromatic richness like almost no other. Local tradition tends to preserve wines destined to undergo oxidative aging in soleras that are either dry (Amontillado, Oloroso, Palo Cortado) or sweet (Pedro Ximénez mostly, but also Moscatel), so these off-dry wines are obtained by blending in different proportions.

This blending softens the high astringency and austerity of old wines, to make them more attractive to delicate palates. However, the addition of even small amounts of PX to an old dry wine often results in a dumbing down of the fragrance of a great Palo Cortado or Oloroso, robbing it of character on the nose as well as raciness on the palate.

The secret to the delicious nose of Solera PΔP Palo Cortado lies in the moment when the blending takes place; it is not immediately prior to bottling, but rather as early as its origin. Right from the start, in the criaderas, this Palo Cortado already contains a dollop of PX, which gradually blends in harmoniously over decades, resulting in a wine that is old and expressive yet mellow on the palate. **JB**

ⓈⓈⓈⓈ **Drink: on release for up to 10 years**

Paternina *Fino Imperial*
Amontillado VORS Sherry

Origin Spain, Jerez de la Frontera
Style Fortified dry wine, 18% ABV
Grape Palomino Fino

If there is one Sherry entitled, by its own singularity, to so strict a selection as this uniqueness implies, Paternina's Fino Imperial Amontillado Sherry would be a strong candidate. The arguments supporting its case are many, and all of weight.

It is a living relic of the historic house of Díez Hermanos (1876), which experienced several changes of ownership during the second half of the twentieth century until it was absorbed by the Paternina Group of Rioja. Moreover, it is, like another legendary Amontillado—Valdespino's Coliseo—an Amontillado from Jerez but refreshed with Manzanilla from Sanlúcar. So one could say that it spends its childhood and adolescence by the River Guadalquivir, then moves inland in its maturity, where it enjoys the loving care of Paternina's experienced enologist Enrique Pérez.

It is also a "natural" Amontillado—that is, a wine that results from a Fino's natural consumption of the veil of *flor* (without the addition of alcohol), and its progress to a second phase of oxidative aging. Hence its name Fino Imperial, which underlines the markedly biological character of the wine. **JB**

ⓈⓈⓈ **Drink: on release for 10+ years**

Carlo Pellegrino
Marsala Vergine Vintage 1980

Origin Italy, Sicily, Marsala
Style Fortified sweet wine, 18% ABV
Grape Grillo

For more than a century until the 1960s, Marsala was the most widely exported wine from Sicily and the popular equal of Sherry and Madeira in the U.K. It was an Englishman, Port shipper John Wodehouse of Liverpool, who "invented" Marsala, named for a town on the west coast of the island, where he built a wine lodge or *baglio*. As a protective measure on long sea voyages, Woodhouse added alcohol to Marsala wine, thus making it a popular drink in the Royal Navy: Horatio Nelson was its greatest devotee.

By the end of the nineteenth century, the Sicilian houses of Vincenzo Florio and Carlo Pellegrino in particular had won reputations for top-quality Marsala—though in line with Victorian tastes for a strong, warming drink, these houses were obliged to make the wine reach 20 percent ABV. However, the truly fine and complex natural wine of Marsala is the *vergine*, which rarely exceeds 16 percent ABV. Regrettably, in a well-intentioned move of 1986, the Italian wine authorities revised the DOC laws to impose stricter production regulations. By decreeing that all Marsala must attain 18 percent ABV, they excluded the best wine from official DOC status.

Luckily, we still have this glorious Pellegrino Vergine Vintage 1980. The color is pale amber, the exquisite nose combining nuttiness with a touch of gently oxidative *rancio* from twenty-two years of cask aging. The palate is silky, perfectly balanced, and long. A true *vino di meditazione*. **ME**
🌣🌣🌣🌣 Drink: to 2050+

A traditional Sicilian Marsala barrel cart in Carlo Pellegrino's cellar. ➡

Penfolds
50 Year Old Rare Tawny

Origin Australia, South Australia
Style Fortified sweet wine, 20% ABV
Grape Shiraz, Mataro, C. Sauvignon, Grenache

Pérez Barquero
1905 Amontillado Montilla

Origin Spain, Montilla-Moriles, Montilla
Style Fortified dry wine, 21% ABV
Grape Pedro Ximénez

To celebrate its 170th anniversary in 2014, Penfolds created from some of its oldest and rarest wines an exquisite Tawny at the top of its fortified range. Among the wines in the blend is the last of the precious glass stock reserves from 1915, the year Max Schubert, the creator of Penfolds Grange, was born.

Penfolds has been producing fortified wines from its beginning. But the blending skills of the Penfolds team under chief winemaker, Peter Gago, can never have been deployed more successfully than here. The wine has a beautiful color, a rich amber-tawny of fiery intensity like great old Cognac, and the exquisite nose is exceptionally fine, fresh, and stable; not fragile but subtle, with no heady rancio but pure light walnut, tea, rose, mock orange, rowan, sandalwood. A gloriously layered silken texture, effortless intensity, exhilarating freshness, and vitality; harmonious, seamless, with a fabulous, flourishing finish.

While the wine appears timeless, Gago is right to insist that it is "not for the cellar, trophy cabinet, or mantelpiece. Open, share, and indulge." The initial release ran to only 330 bottles, though Penfolds hopes to release the same number each year. **NB**
⊖⊖⊖⊖⊖ **Drink: to 2020+**

The Pedro Ximénez variety is often associated in consumers' minds with the dense and sweet wines made with raisins in the Sherry and Montilla-Moriles regions. These wines are often designated "PX" to refer to the sweet wine category, but the variety PX is not necessarily synonymous with sweet wine. It is most widely planted grape variety in Montilla-Moriles, and is responsible for all the different local styles of wine (Fino, Amontillado, Oloroso, young dry whites, and so on), including this Solera Fundacional Amontillado 1905.

As in most other bodegas in Andalusia, the very existence of this Amontillado is the result of the accumulated knowledge and expertise of generations of winemakers, who pass the legacy of these soleras from one generation to the next. The musts come invariably from the excellent chalky soils of the Sierra de Montilla.

In the case of Pérez Barquero, 1905 marks both the foundation of the solera and the birth date of the bodega, so the solera from which this wine emerges (like the sweet PX in the same lineup) is one of those established by the very founders of the firm. **JB**
⊖⊖⊖⊖⊖ **Drink: on release for up to 10 years**

Pedro Ximénez vineyards surround the town of Montilla. ➡

Pérez Marín
La Guita Manzanilla

Origin Spain, Sanlúcar de Barrameda
Style Fortified dry wine, 15% ABV
Grape Palomino Fino

In the early nineteenth century—when the wines of Jerez sprung up commercially—many of the main entrepreneurs in the area came from Britain or the north of Spain, more specifically the highlands around Santander. These mountain men settled mostly as shop owners in Sanlúcar de Barrameda and Cádiz; in fact to them is rightly attributed the discovery of biological aging under *flor*—and with it the discovery of Manzanilla and Fino. Domingo Pérez Marín, founder of the bodega in 1852, was one of these mountain people. His was the happy invention of the brand name La Guita, which originated from his demand for cash rather than credit (*guita* means "cash" in the popular dialect of the Baja Andalusia).

La Guita is the best-selling Manzanilla in the market, having enjoyed remarkable commercial success in the second half of the 1990s. Now the winemaking team of José Estévez S.A., led by the prestigious enologist Eduardo Ojeda, must preserve its popular light and easy character while trying to recover the levels of cleanliness and complexity that once made this Manzanilla one of the favorites of local aficionados and connoisseurs. **JB**

⊖ Drink: current release within one year

Quinta do Portal
20 Year Old Tawny Port

Origin Portugal, Douro Valley
Style Fortified sweet wine, 20% ABV
Grapes Tinta Roriz, T. Franca, T. Nacional, Others

Quinta do Portal is one of the leading lights of the revolution that has swept through the Douro. For centuries the trade here has been clearly split in two, with the small number of Oporto-based shipping firms buying in either wines or grapes from the thousands of growers to supplement the production of their own quintas. But now, instead of just selling the raw material and watching others add value, more growers are going it alone, making their own wines and selling the finished product.

Portal itself is at the top of the Pinhão valley, in the Cima Corgo. The family also owns three other neighboring properties totaling 230 acres (95 ha). Much of Portal is flat, by Douro standards, and all four properties include some fairly high-altitude vineyards. The wines have a freshness and lightness of touch, most pleasant of all in an aged Tawny.

Long aging has given this vibrant orange-tawny wine a beautifully nutty nose of marzipan and toasted almonds, with hints of dried orange peel and old Cognac. It is sweet on the palate, but lighter and less clumsy than many single quinta Tawnies, with a long, complex finish. **GS**

⊖⊖ Drink: on release

Vineyards fringe the Douro Valley, homeland of Port production. ◾

Quady *Essensia* 2005

Origin USA, California, Madera County
Style Fortified sweet wine, 15% ABV
Grape Orange Muscat

Andrew Quady had the misfortune of being an aspiring winemaker based in California's Central Valley—misfortune, because this was the source of almost all the state's most wretched bulk wine. However, the valley was capable of producing some oddities, such as creditable Port-style wines and inky Alicante Bouschet. Although based in sweltering Madera County, Quady bought Zinfandel grapes from Amador County in the Sierra foothills and produced some very decent Port-style wine.

Unfortunately, the Port did not sell. He recalled tasting some attractive Orange Muscat during his days as a wine student at the University of California, Davis, so he bought some local grapes and tried his hand. The grapes ripen by mid-August; acidity is adjusted when the grapes are crushed. After a few days, Quady arrests fermentation with alcohol; the brief period of skin contact is essential for extracting the delicate Muscat flavors. Once fermentation is arrested, about 120 g/l of residual sugar remains. Quady gives Essensia a final polish by aging it for three months in French oak.

Quady packaged the wine in half-bottles with very stylish labels, and the wine was an immediate hit, perhaps because it is so versatile, serving as an aperitif or dessert wine or even as a mixer. The delicate orange and mandarin aromas of Essensia are hard to resist, and ample acidity keeps it from being cloying. Although Essensia is a vintage wine, there is little variation from year to year. **SBr**
☉☉ Drink: on release for up to 5 years

FURTHER RECOMMENDATIONS
Other great vintages
2000 • 2001 • 2002 • 2003 • 2004
More wines from the same producer
Electra • Red Electra • Elysium • Palomino Fino Starboard Batch 88 • Starboard Vintage

Quady's labels are commissioned from local artists in a variety of styles. ➡

Ramos Pinto
20 Year Old Tawny Port

Origin Portugal, Douro Valley
Style Fortified sweet wine, 20% ABV
Grapes T. Nacional, T. Franca, Tinta Roriz, Others

Rey Fernando de Castilla
Antique Palo Cortado Sherry

Origin Spain, Jerez de la Frontera
Style Fortified dry wine, 20% ABV
Grape Palomino Fino

This house, established by Adriano Ramos Pinto in 1880, has long been better known for its wood Ports (those aged in wood and bottled ready to drink) than its bottle-matured Vintages. Whereas Ramos Pinto's Vintage Ports tend to be quite soft and early maturing, its aged Tawnies are the very finest of the genre. The number of years on the label is only an indication of age, for an aged Tawny may be made from anything between ten and fifty different components, with younger, fruit-driven wines balancing older, mature wines that have gained in complexity and sweetness from aging in cask.

Few wines are more finely tuned than a 20 Year Old Tawny, a complex blend of some of the finest and most elegant of all Ports usually set aside and put into cask after making up potential vintage *lotes* (blends). Ramos Pinto's 20 Year Old has a delicacy and deftness of touch that eludes so many aged Tawnies. Pale tawny-pink in hue, with an aroma akin to good fruit cake, it is rich yet supremely refined. On the palate, it is smooth and seductive, sweet yet with a delicate, savory, toasted almond and Brazil nut character; the finish is surprisingly dry. **RM**

🝮🝮🝮 **Drink: current release within 3 years**

Terroir can amount to very little if it is not properly understood and interpreted by insightful craftsmen. In the case of Antique Palo Cortado from Bodegas Rey Fernando de Castilla, the necessary insight is provided by a Scandinavian (Jan Pettersen) and a native Jerezano (Andrés Soto). Greatly experienced after long years at two of the big houses in Jerez (Osborne and González Byass, respectively), they have assumed the leadership of this small bodega founded by Fernando Andrada-Vanderwilde in 1972 and now owned by a group of four investors that includes Pettersen himself.

Antique Palo Cortado shows finesse and balance, and is probably the most remarkable of wines halfway along the age curve; it is old, no doubt, but not to the extreme extent of some other Sherries. It is bottled necessarily in limited quantities, from a solera of only fourteen butts, and just one equivalent criadera. The wine bought to refresh this criadera comes—after merciless selection—from a venerable almacenista house, the same since the bodega's foundation, as well as from the odd butt of Fino Antique that strays from the "right" path. **JB**

🝮🝮🝮 **Drink: on release for up to 10+ years**

Pedro Romero
Aurora en Rama Manzanilla

Origin Spain, Sanlúcar de Barrameda
Style Fortified dry wine, 15% ABV
Grape Palomino Fino

The house of Pedro Romero, still under the management of his descendants, boasts as its flagship product its best-known label: Manzanilla Aurora, a wine of splendid biologically aged character and personality. The regular bottling of this Manzanilla has long been one of Sanlúcar's classic wines, but its somewhat fragile *en rama* ("as is" or "unfiltered") version, bottled exclusively upon demand and sadly extremely difficult to obtain other than directly from the bodega, truly deserves to be included among the chosen few for its delicacy and subtlety, as well as for its complexity and depth.

Pedro Romero, defiantly running contrary to the current regrettable trend, has not only preserved its old cellars in the heart of Sanlúcar, but expanded them through the acquisition of the neighboring bodega, Müller-Ambrosse. The strategic location of the cellars in the lower district of Sanlúcar offers ideal conditions for the development and growth of the fragile veil of *flor*, aided by the higher humidity nearer the Guadalquivir estuary, and benefiting from a favorable orientation that allows it to receive the sea breeze from the west. **JB**

🕑 **Drink: most recent release within one year**

Quinta de la Rosa
Vale do Inferno Vintage Port 1999

Origin Portugal, Douro Valley
Style Fortified sweet wine, 20% ABV
Grapes Mixed from old, interplanted vineyards

The Quinta de la Rosa vineyards span an altitude of nearly 1,000 feet (300 m), giving winemaker Jorge Moreira a wide range of microclimates for different styles of wine. The most hallowed corner of the estate is a sheltered hollow immediately above the River Douro. Planted with old vines on traditional stone terraces, it is also the hottest part of the vineyard, known as Vale do Inferno (Hell Valley).

In 1999 the owners, the Bergqvist family, decided to keep the wine from Vale do Inferno separate from the rest of the estate. It was a potentially outstanding year for Vintage Port. A cold, dry winter was followed by an intensely hot summer. Wells dried up all over the region and many properties were without water. By early September the Douro had high hopes of a small but very high-quality harvest. Picking began on September 15, and there was just enough time to gather the grapes from the oldest vineyards before Hurricane Floyd blew in. From this small crop, this wine is deep, dense, intensely ripe, and powerful, reflecting the naturally low yields and the heat of the summer months. It is now a rare taste of what might have been a thrilling vintage. **RM**

🕑🕑🕑 **Drink: to 2050**

The Douro Valley's vineyards have long been elaborately terraced. ➡

Sánchez Ayala
Navazos Amontillado Sherry

Origin Spain, Sanlúcar de Barrameda
Style Fortified dry wine, 20% ABV
Grape Palomino Fino

Sánchez Ayala, a house of good repute among connoisseurs for the quality of its Manzanillas, owns bodegas in the old district of La Balsa in Sanlúcar de Barrameda, an area that has been reclaimed through the years from the estuary of the River Guadalquivir. Until recently, its bodegas were surrounded by *navazos*, wetlands excavated by farmers in order to extract the humidity of the subsoil layer.

In the second half of the eighteenth century, a naval disaster forced the Marqués de Arizón to sell off the Bodega San Pedro to a priest from Cádiz. It is in this old cellar building that Sánchez Ayala stores several dozen butts of old Amontillado, untouched for the past twenty years. These are wines of uncommon freshness and Manzanilla character, in spite of their advanced age. Periodically from among these butts, one is selected by the *Equipo Navazos* to become the Amontillado of the same name.

The *capataz*, Luis Gallego, is currently in charge of maintaining authenticity in the wines of this small and secret bodega. He is one of the young names in the Sherry district, in whose hands lies the future of these hugely important wines. **JB**

🝔🝔🝔 Drink: on release for up to 20+ years

Sánchez Romate *La Sacristía*
de Romate Oloroso VORS Sherry

Origin Spain, Jerez de la Frontera
Style Fortified dry wine, 20% ABV
Grape Palomino Fino

Among the prominent men in the history of the Sherry district, there are two named Juan Sánchez. One is the mythical, Santander-born, flying winemaker who assessed the most important bodegas in the first half of the nineteenth century. The other is Juan Sánchez de la Torre, philanthropist and founder of Sánchez Romate in 1781.

The brilliant era of this house started only in the mid-1950s, when it was sold to a group of five friends, the descendents of whom own the business today. Sánchez Romate is among the few big houses that still maintains its facilities in the heart of Jerez, despite the ensuing logistic difficulties. They almost moved at the turn of the twenty-first century, but the purchase of the old cellars of Wisdom & Warter next door afforded them the necessary additional space to remain functional within the city limits.

This wine boasts a neat Oloroso character, with typical volatile notes and a palate of great structure, body, and persistence. Several other wines shine in the Sánchez Romate portfolio—not only the VOS and VORS, but also the classy Marismeño Fino and Cardenal Cisneros Pedro Ximénez. **JB**

🝔🝔🝔 Drink: on release for up to 10+ years

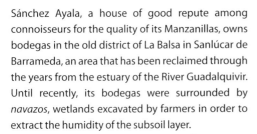

◀ Sánchez Ayala stores old Amontillado in this historic bodega's cellar.

Sandeman *40 Years Old Tawny Port*

Origin Portugal, Douro Valley
Style Fortified sweet wine, 20% ABV
Grapes Mixed from old, interplanted vineyards

The Sandeman don is one of the most instantly recognizable of all wine logos. It was devised in 1928 by George Massiot Brown, and helped to turn Sandeman into one of the largest Port brands. The company was established 138 years earlier by Scotsman George Sandeman, who began selling Port from Tom's Coffee House in the City of London. Under his grandson, the House of Sandeman was the first Port shipper to export wine bottled and labeled in Oporto. There followed a high-profile advertising campaign, with the Sandeman don, dressed in a Portuguese student's cape and wide-brimmed hat, embellishing London's famous red buses.

The Sandeman family lost control of their business in 1952; finally, in 2001, the company was sold to Portugal's largest wine producer, Sogrape. But throughout decades of changing ownership, the one style of wine that never seemed to suffer was aged Tawny. The company produces a good Reserve Tawny named Imperial, and some outstanding 10, 20, 30, and 40 Year Olds. While other 40 Year Olds are often unbalanced by excess sweetness, and show more than a touch of *rancio* and volatility, Sandeman's retains remarkable freshness and poise. Pale amber-tawny in color, the wine is clean and delicate, only slightly high-toned and much less rich and unctuous in style than most of its peers. The sweetness is restrained, and the flavors unusually delicate, with a long, smooth, candied-peel finish, still combining vibrancy with elegance. **RM**

⊖⊖⊖⊖ **Drink: current release within 3 years**

FURTHER RECOMMENDATIONS
Other great Sandeman Tawny Ports
Imperial • *10 Years Old* • *20 Years Old* • *30 Years Old*
More 40 Years Old Tawny Ports
Calém • *Dow* • *Feist* • *Fonseca* *Graham* • *Kopke* • *Noval* • *Taylor*

Sandeman's mysterious don and Tawny Port in a 1934 advertisement. ➡

G. Massiot

PORTO
SANDEMAN

Smith Woodhouse
Vintage Port 1977

Origin Portugal, Douro Valley
Style Fortified sweet wine, 20% ABV
Grapes Tinta Roriz, T. Franca, T. Nacional, Others

Smith Woodhouse is an enigma of a Port. It is a second-tier label, formerly used by the brand owners, the Symington family, for cheap own-label Ports, but at the same time a capable top-quality Vintage Port, often at a very reasonable price.

Originally established in 1784 by Christopher Smith, onetime Member of the British Parliament and Lord Mayor of London, Smith Woodhouse is now one of the three lesser Port shipping brands owned by the Symington family. Their top three brands are Graham, Warre, and Dow, with Smith Woodhouse alongside Gould Campbell and Quarles Harris at the second level. But despite its relatively lowly position in the company, Smith Woodhouse often punches above its weight in blind tastings and competitions.

1977 was a very good vintage in the Douro, very highly rated when released, though more recently some tasters have downgraded their original scores. While many are fully mature now, paling in color, and delicate on the nose, the Smith Woodhouse, from low yields, still has a deep ruby hue, remarkably still with purple hints. Rich and full on both nose and palate, despite being more than thirty years old. **GS**

🚫🚫🚫 Drink: to 2020+

Stanton & Killeen
Rare Muscat

Origin Australia, Victoria, Rutherglen
Style Fortified sweet wine, 19% ABV
Grapes Red Frontignan (Rutherglen Brown Muscat)

Of the twin Rutherglen fortified specialties, liqueur Muscat and liqueur Tokay (Muscadelle), Stanton & Killeen has a strong leaning toward Muscat, covering all four classes (basic Rutherglen, Classic, Grand, and Rare) with highest quality. Founded in 1875 and still a family business, it has a belligerently anti-economic bent for Vintage Port and also makes superb dry reds. Its Muscat style is subtly different to that of other makers: Slightly lower sweetness levels and subtly higher wood tannins from the younger average barrel age mean the wines have a drier finish than, say, Chambers or Morris.

The wines are classified as soon as possible after fortification, and key indicators for the top grades are a bright crimson color with no orange or brown tints, a rose-petal aroma, and a high degree of sweetness. They use a "bastardized" solera system for maturation. Classic averages twelve years of age; Grand, twenty-five; and Rare, thirty to thirty-five years. The basic Rutherglen Muscat runs out at 2,000 dozen, 500-ml bottles a year, Classic 1,000, Grand 100, and Rare, just 350 half-bottles. When they say Rare, they mean it. **HH**

🚫🚫🚫🚫 Drink: on release for 20+ years

Stanton & Killeen's nineteenth-century winery in Rutherglen. ➡

Taylor's *Quinta de Vargellas Vinha Velha* 1995

Origin Portugal, Douro Valley
Style Fortified sweet wine, 20% ABV
Grapes Mixed from old, interplanted vineyards

For more than a century, Quinta de Vargellas has formed the backbone of Taylor's Vintage Ports. This remote estate, high in the Douro Superior, was established in the 1800s and by the 1830s had already gained a reputation for quality. Between 1893 and 1896, three quintas bearing the name Vargellas were merged into one by Taylor, Fladgate, and Yeatman, to be joined a century later by Quinta do São Xisto (St. Schist), which lies alongside. Vargellas now extends to cover 383 acres (155 ha).

Taylor's was one of the first shippers to release a single-estate Vintage Port, and in 1995 it broke the mold again by bottling a wine from the oldest vines on the estate. Known as Quinta de Vargellas Vinha Velha (old vines), the wine comes from vines planted in the 1920s by Dick Yeatman, great-uncle of Taylor's current chairman, Alistair Robertson. Yields from these old terraced vineyards are astonishingly low, just 9 ounces (200 g) per vine. As a result, these grapes produce wines with natural intensity.

Taylor's Quinta de Vargellas Vinha Velha 1995 is a wine on a monumental scale, still deep and opaque, quite withdrawn on the nose but with the wonderful underlying floral perfume that is so characteristic of Vargellas. On the palate it is more impressive still, with big, rich, multilayered, fat, ripe fruit and licoricelike intensity; yet despite the undeniable concentration and power, it is supremely fine and elegant, the very essence of a fine Douro estate. **RM**
ΘΘΘΘΘ Drink: to 2100

The quinta's own station in a fanciful William Rushton cartoon. ➜

the Empire Nº 207 — VARGELLAS Station.

R. 85

Taylor's
Vintage Port 1970

Origin Portugal, Douro Valley
Style Fortified sweet wine, 20% ABV
Grapes Tinta Roriz, T. Franca, T. Nacional, Others

If Latour and Margaux are the first growths of Bordeaux, then Taylor (Taylor Fladgate in the United States) is one of the first growths of Vintage Port, consistently fetching higher prices than most of its rivals at auction. The company, formerly called Taylor, Fladgate and Yeatman, is now known officially as the Fladgate Partnership.

The backbone of Taylor Vintage Ports is the foot-trodden wine from the spectacular Quinta da Vargellas in the Douro Superior. The mostly north-facing quinta lies near where this subregion meets the Cima Corgo, experiencing a climate that is hot but not too baked. Massive concentration caused by the heat is offset by judicious blending with wines from Terra Feita, in the Pinhão valley. Vintage Port, like the best Champagne, is always a blend, the combination of two or more different terroirs.

1970 saw classic Vintage Port weather—above-average winter rain, dry weather at flowering, and a long, dry ripening period right through to October. This, along with foot-treading in the granite *lagares* still in use at Vargellas, led to a deep, very rich wine that still has years to go. The color, though fading a little, is still a deep brick red; the wine certainly does not look some forty years old. It is perfumed on the nose, with some dried fruit characters, but still a lot of red fruit and a lovely floral top note. The palate is complex and balanced, with soft tannins and some spicy licorice and chocolate notes. **GS**
🍷🍷🍷🍷 Drink: to 2020+

Foot-treading grapes in the traditional manner at Vargellas. ➜

Toro Albalá
1922 Solera Amontillado Montilla

Origin Spain, Montilla-Moriles, Aguilar de la Frontera
Style Fortified dry wine, 21% ABV
Grape Palomino Fino

Valdespino *Cardenal*
Palo Cortado VORS Sherry

Origin Spain, Jerez de la Frontera
Style Fortified dry wine, 20% ABV
Grape Palomino Fino

The remote origins of the house of Toro Albalá date back to 1844, when Antonio Sánchez founded a small bodega in La Noria, at the foot of the Castillo de Aguilar. However, the uninterrupted ownership of the present bodega in the current era begins in 1922, when José María Toro Albalá purchased the facilities and outbuildings belonging to the old electric plant in Aguilar.

Antonio Sánchez Romero, present owner and enologist, is a relative of both, being a direct descendant to the Antonio who founded La Noria, as well as nephew and heir to José María; Antonio was orphaned as a child, and subsequently adopted by his uncle. Deep at heart, this man of endless intellectual curiosity considers Fino the true glory of Andalusian viticulture, well above the Amontillados and Pedro Ximénez that have made him famous.

As with most wines from this house, the date on the label does not express a vintage date, but appears rather as a form of homage to some personally relevant event. What really matters is their level of quality, and that of the 1922 Solera Amontillado is amazing indeed. **JB**
🍷🍷 **Drink: on release for 10+ years**

The age and depth of Cardenal Palo Cortado VORS can be guessed from its profoundly greenish rim and marvelously complex nose, which draws the taster into a seemingly endless feast of incense and spice. The palate is powerful, salty, extremely old but cleanly focused. Although difficult for the non-initiated because of its density and profundity, for Sherry lovers it is the stuff that dreams are made of.

When the Estévez Group bought Valdespino at the turn of the millennium, there was some concern on the part of aficionados regarding the fate of these venerated wines. It would not have been the first time that a unique range of soleras had been lost as a result of the fusion of companies. Happily, no such thing has happened in this case, because José Estévez decided to preserve the character of the bodega and establish a superb winemaking team. The result is a hugely impressive portfolio of authentic Sherries, including Cardenal Palo Cortado VORS—a characterful wine that is now matured to perfection in the new facilities on the outskirts of Jerez. The sad but single trade-off is the charm of the original Valdespino bodegas in the town center. **JB**
🍷🍷🍷🍷 **Drink: on release for up to 30 years**

Valdespino
Coliseo Amontillado VORS Sherry

Origin Spain, Jerez de la Frontera
Style Fortified dry wine, 22% ABV
Grape Palomino Fino

Coliseo Amontillado VORS may be the most remarkable of the world-class wines that destiny has placed in the hands of the Estévez family and its winemaking director, Eduardo Ojeda: Cardenal Palo Cortado, Niños PX, Real Tesoro Covadonga Oloroso, Soleras de su Majestad Oloroso, Toneles Moscatel Viejísimo, and the recently acquired De Bandera VORS lineup from M. Gil Luque.

The extremely low availability of this wine is governed by its incredibly old age. In the case of Coliseo, scarcely 1 percent of the total is bottled every year, whereas another 2 or 3 percent must be replaced due to evaporation ("the angels' share"). Therefore the average age of the final butt is a great deal older than the minimum of thirty years required for the VORS certification.

One of the defining peculiarities of Coliseo, the one that accounts for its saline and sharp character, is that its youngest criaderas (nurseries) are refreshed with Manzanilla Pasada selected from the best almacenistas in Sanlúcar, rather than with the equally excellent but fuller-bodied old Finos from the Pago Macharnudo owned by Valdespino. **JB**
🥂🥂🥂🥂 **Drink: on release for up to 30 years**

Valdespino
Inocente Fino Sherry

Origin Spain, Jerez de la Frontera
Style Fortified dry wine, 15% ABV
Grape Palomino Fino

Inocente Fino (not "Ynocente," as many mistakenly believe, thanks to the peculiar capital "I" on the label) is one of the greatest Spanish whites and for many connoisseurs the most genuine and characterful Fino on the market. Its magnificent solera comes at the end of a series of twelve scales (one *sobretabla*, ten criaderas, and one solera, each of them comprising seventy butts), where it undergoes prolonged aging for an average of ten years, protected from oxygen by the layer of *flor*.

Valdespino is among the few Sherry houses that still follow the traditional methods of Fino production. But Inocente is also a wine marked by terroir, a single-vineyard Fino. Its scales are refreshed only with the fruit of the Pago Macharnudo, more specifically the chalky soil of the Macharnudo Alto vineyard, located in a privileged area north of the town of Jerez, long the property of Valdespino.

Inocente is a wine for connoisseurs, bottled at maturity to emphasize its character. It can be enjoyed upon release, fresh from the solera. But if properly stored it can provide enormous pleasure even decades after bottling. **JB**
🥂 **Drink: on release for up to 3 years**

Valdespino

Moscatel Toneles Sherry

Origin Spain, Jerez de la Frontera
Style Fortified sweet wine, 18% ABV
Grape Muscat

Moscatel Toneles is one of the great wines of the world, a precious and extremely scarce jewel that invariably seduces every taster, no matter how demanding, with its rare class, smooth power, and magic acidity. It is the ideal choice to crown a tasting of world-class wines, be it the most exclusive crus of the Côte d'Or, the most prestigious Bordelais châteaux, or even venerable Port vintages.

The production of this wine consists of merely half a dozen butts culminating in a single solera butt. Its average age cannot be established with precision, but its organoleptic qualities and the history of the solera suggest that the wine could easily be more than seventy-five years old.

Although it is against the current norm to bottle these fortified wines at less than 15 percent ABV, the alcohol level of Moscatel Toneles in the solera butt is a relatively modest 12 percent ABV. One hundred bottles are extracted from this solera every year. Wines of this degree of density and sweetness are low in water content (they often contain more than 50 percent sugar), so the wooden butts do not soak up much liquid. As a consequence, unlike dry wines exposed to oxidative aging, the loss in ethanol due to evaporation is greater than the loss of water through osmosis (through the wooden staves). The result of this process is that, perhaps contrary to expection, the alcohol percentage falls rather than rises with time until it reaches a natural balance. **JB**

Ⓢ Ⓢ Ⓢ Ⓢ Ⓢ **Drink: on release for up to 100 years**

Valdespino has produced Sherry for more than 600 years. ➡

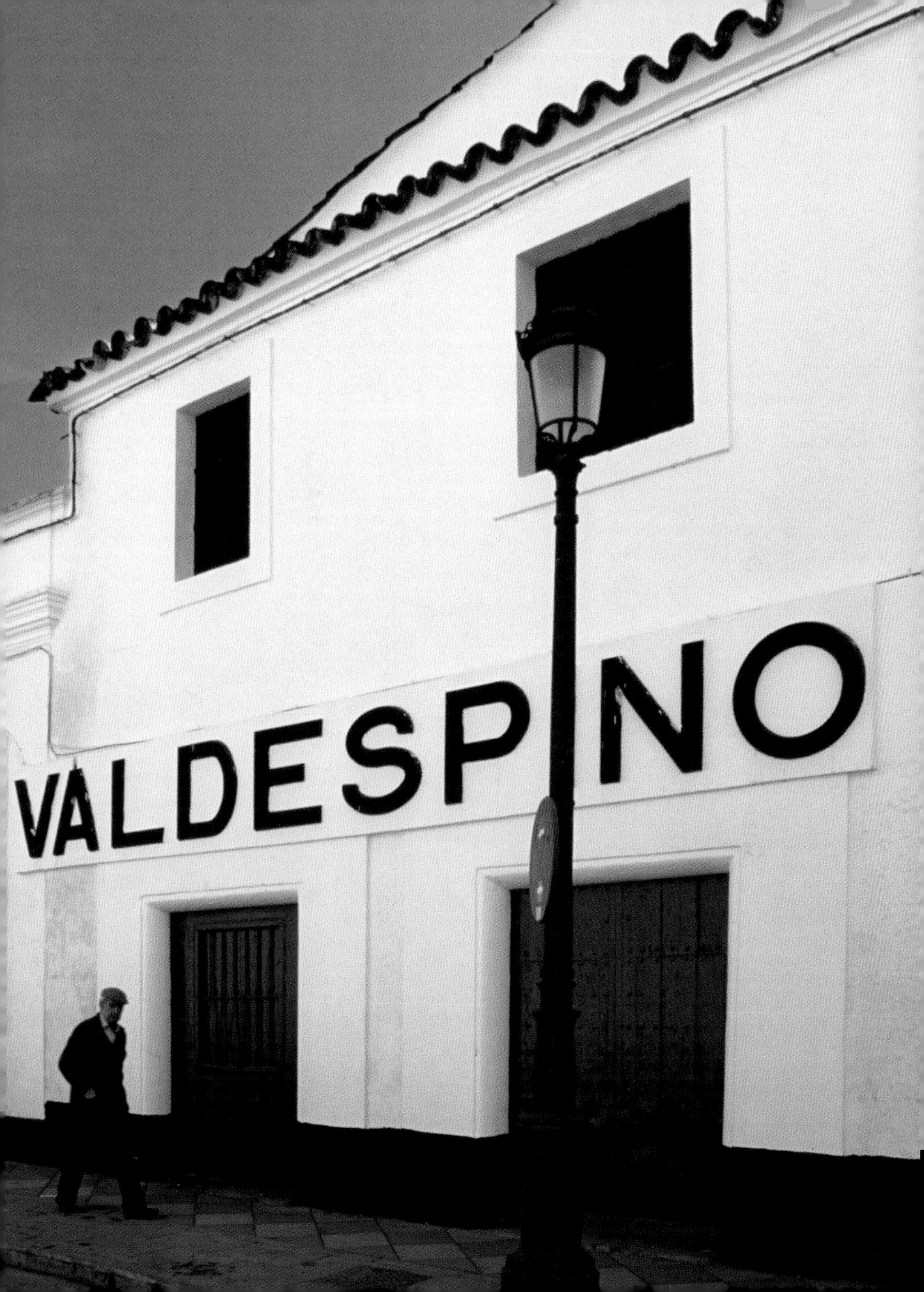
VALDESP NO

Quinta do Vesuvio
Vintage Port 1994

Origin Portugal, Douro Valley
Style Fortified sweet wine, 20% ABV
Grapes Mixed traditional varieties

Warre's
Late Bottled Vintage Port 1995

Origin Portugal, Douro Valley
Style Fortified sweet wine, 20% ABV
Grapes Tinta Roriz, T. Franca, T. Nacional, Others

Quinta do Vesuvio is without doubt the most stately and impressive estate in the Douro. The estate is located in the remote Douro Superior and was created in the early nineteenth century by António Bernado Ferreira. It remained with the Ferreira family until it was sold to the Symington family in 1989.

At the time it was acquired by the Symingtons, Vesuvio was in a poor state of repair. Much has been done since to revive and restore the estate, which is predominantly north facing, covering 1,008 acres (408 ha), of which just a quarter are now under vine. The grapes are trodden in eight *lagares* equipped with their own temperature control.

Unlike shipper's Vintage Ports, usually declared three times a decade, Quinta do Vesuvio produces Vintage Port nearly every year. It was clear from the start that 1994 would be a great vintage. It was universally declared, and Vesuvio is one of the top wines of the vintage. The wines were surprisingly approachable from an early stage, but have gained in gravitas. Quinta do Vesuvio 1994 is gloriously rich and fleshy, slightly jammy on the nose, but with fine sinewy fruit backed by broad, ripe tannins. **RM**
🟢🟢🟢 **Drink: to 2050+**

Late Bottled Vintage (LBV) Port should be exactly what it says on the label: high-quality Port of one vintage, bottled later than normal. The implication is that the wine in the bottle is at least similar in style to Vintage Port. Most LBV today, however, is more in the style of a premium ruby. Yes, legally it has to be of one vintage, but the wines are far lighter in style and far less complex than true Vintage Port.

The most notable exception, and one that has won almost every competition into which it has been entered, is Warre's. Unlike most big-selling LBVs, Warre's matures in wood, in the lodges of Vila Nova de Gaia, for just four years (the rules require a minimum of four and a maximum of six years in wood) before being bottled unfiltered. It is then bottle-matured before release. This allows the wine to develop the complexity and elegance expected of a true Vintage Port, and because it is unfiltered it will continue to improve in the cellar, unlike its peers.

The resultant wine is massively deep in color. A fresh black-currant jam nose has delicate floral top notes, and the palate has great finesse but at the same time retains a firm tannic backbone. **GS**
🟢🟢 **Drink: to 2020+**

Williams & Humbert *Dos Cortados Palo Cortado VOS Sherry*

Origin Spain, Jerez de la Frontera
Style Fortified dry wine, 19.5% ABV
Grape Palomino Fino

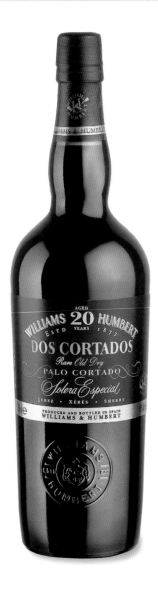

Williams & Humbert is a good example of the paradoxical situation that more than thirty years of crisis have caused in the Sherry district. This historic house has everything that one would expect of a Sherry house in an enviable market situation—wines of excellent quality, labels of international prestige (Dry Sack, Don Zoilo, Jalifa), and a meticulous and able *capataz* in the figure of Antonio Fernández-Vázquez. And yet it is nevertheless subject—like most other houses—to the dictatorship of large volume sales, price wars, and the own labels of the great European distribution firms.

It was this house that first attracted to Jerez one of its most important writers—the venerable Julian Jeffs, who recounts the detailed history of this house in his seminal book on Sherry. Its origins date back to the romance between Alexander Williams, a clerk at Wisdom & Warter during the second half of the nineteenth century, and Amy Humbert. Now a highly influential wine, it contributed to the creation of the Jerez-Xérès-Brandy Quality Demarcation.

This Palo Cortado has a profile of particular finesse: clean and expressive, with spirited notes of fresh herbs and egg yolk. Although it is no doubt a real Palo Cortado, at some point in its long history it has been bottled as Oloroso. Such uncertainty should not amaze anyone, because Palo Cortado is defined as a wine that combines the delicacy and refinement of aroma of an Amontillado with the structure and the roundness of an Oloroso. **JB**
☻☻☻ Drink: on release for up to 10+ years

FURTHER RECOMMENDATIONS

Other great Williams & Humbert wines

*Jalifa Amontillado VORS Sherry • Don Guido
Pedro Ximénez VOS Sherry • Don Zoilo Fino Sherry*

More producers of Palo Cortado

Barbadillo • Emilio Hidalgo • Bodegas Tradición

Sherry drinking at the wheel—Spanish motoring in a more relaxed era. ▸

Glossary

Acidity
Component of wine felt as sharpness in the mouth. Too much makes a wine tart; too little makes it flabby. Measured by grams per liter.

Alta Expresión
Spanish for "High expression." The intense, high-alcohol, modern style of some Rioja red wines.

American Viticultural Area (AVA)
U.S. system of permitted wine geographical designations.

Amontillado
Style of Sherry in which the *flor* yeast of a Fino dies, leading to oxidization and a richer, nuttier style of wine. See **Fino** and **Flor**

Appellation d'Origine Contrôlée (AOC)
French system of naming wines. To qualify, a wine must be produced from grapes grown within a defined geographical area, and conform to regulations on grape varieties, yields, alcohol content. Not a guarantee of quality.

Assemblage
French term for the blending of several component wines to make a single grand vin.

Aszú
Hungarian for "dried." Botrytized grapes used to make Tokaji.

Ausbruch
Austrian wine style, made in a similar fashion to Tokaji.

Auslese
German for "selected harvest." A category of German wine made from very ripe grapes. In Austria, it is made from even riper grapes.

Autolysis
The destruction of dead yeast cells after the second fermentation of sparkling wine has taken place. It leads to biscuit and bread aromas and flavors.

Azienda Agricola
An Italian wine estate that makes wine only from grapes grown on its own land.

Barrel fermentation
Alcoholic fermentation that takes place in barrels rather than steel or concrete tanks, often imparting a strong oak flavor.

Barrique
The most common type of barrel, 225 liters (60 gal) in capacity.

Bâtonnage
French term for lees stirring. *See* **Lees stirring**

Beerenauslese
German for "selected berries." German or Austrian sweet wine made from botrytized grapes. *See* **Botrytis**

Biodynamic
An enhanced form of organic grape-growing based on the theories of Rudolf Steiner. *See* **Organic**

Blanc de Blancs
French for "white of whites." A white wine, especially Champagne, made only from white grapes.

Blanc de Noirs
French for "white of blacks." A white wine, especially Champagne, made only from black grapes.

Blind tasting
Tasting wine without knowing what the wine is or, sometimes, which producer it is from.

Bodega
Spanish for "winery."

Botrytis
Fungal disease that, if conditions are right, concentrates the sugars and acids in grapes and enables the production of some of the world's finest sweet wines. Also known as Noble Rot.

Brettanomyces (Brett)
A fungal infection. In small amounts it contributes to the aroma of a wine. In excess, it creates unappealing farmyard smells and flavors.

Brut
French for "dry." Usually applied to Champagne.

Cantina
Italian for "winery."

Carbonic maceration
Winemaking technique in which uncrushed grapes are fermented whole in a sealed container under a blanket of carbon dioxide. The finished wine is typically fruity.

Chaptalization
Process that adds sugar to the fermenting grape juice to increase its potential alcohol.

Château
French for "castle." A winemaking estate, especially in Bordeaux.

Climat
French for "climate." A Burgundian term for a specific vineyard site.

Clone
A vine derived from a "mother vine," selected for a particular attribute.

Clos
French for "enclosure." A walled vineyard, especially in Burgundy and Champagne.

Colheita
Single vintage Tawny Port.

Corked
Wine spoiled by a cork contaminated by Trichloroanisole. A wine is not corked if it has bits of cork floating in it. *See* **Trichloroanisole**

Côte
French for "slope" or "hill." Usually refers to hillside vineyard sites.

Crémant
French for "creaming." Sparkling wine made outside of Champagne using the Méthode Traditionelle.

Crianza
Spanish term for a red wine that has been aged for two years, with at least six months in barrel. *See* **Reserva** and **Gran Reserva**

Cru
French for "growth." In wine terms a specific vineyard, most often in Burgundy or Bordeaux.

Cru Bourgeois
Category of Bordeaux red wine below Cru Classé.

Cru Classé
Category of Bordeaux red wine, established in 1855 and sub-divided into five divisions.

Cryo-extraction
Winemaking process in which grapes are frozen to concentrate the sugars and acids.

Cult wine
Californian (not exclusively) red wines made in small quantities and sold at very high prices.

Cuvée
French term for "blend."

Dégorgement
French for "disgorgement." Traditional process for sparkling wines in which frozen sediment is removed from the bottle.
See **Méthode Traditionelle**

Demi-Sec
French for "medium-dry."

Denominación de Origen (DO)
Spanish equivalent of Appellation d'Origine Contrôlée.

Denominação de Origem Controlada (DOC)
Portuguese equivalent of Appellation d'Origine Contrôlée.

Denominación de Origen Calificada
Spanish equivalent of Denominazione di Origine Controlata e Garantita.

Denominazione di Origine Controllata (DOC)
Italian equivalent of Appellation d'Origine Contrôlée.

Denominazione di Origine Controllata e Garantita (DOCG)
The highest quality level for Italian wine. Only thirty-six wines have been promoted to this level.

Destemming
Removing stems from grape berries.

Dolce
Italian for "sweet."

Domaine
French for "estate."

Dosage
Sugar added to a sparkling wine after dégorgement to determine the final level of sweetness.

Doux
French for "sweet."

Dulce
Spanish for "sweet."

Échelle des crus
French for "scale of growths." The rating system of Champagne-producing villages.

Edes
Hungarian for "sweet."

Eiswein
Very sweet German or Austrian wine made from frozen grapes. *See* **Icewine**

En primeur
French term for "wine futures." A method of buying wine before it is bottled, mainly for Bordeaux.

Essencia
The free-run wine of Aszú berries. *See* **Aszú** and **Free-run wine**

Estufagem
Portuguese for "hothouse." Heating Madeira to accelerate development.

Extraction
Process in which compounds are extracted from the skin of grapes to impart tannin and color.

Fino
A light and dry style of Sherry, strongly influenced by *flor*. *See* **Flor** and **Manzanilla**

First Growth
One of five Left Bank Bordeaux châteaux classified as "premier cru" in 1855 and 1973. *See* **Left Bank** and **Premier Cru**

Flor
A yeast that forms a thick film on the surface of a wine, especially in the production of Fino and Manzanilla Sherry.

Flying winemaker
Term coined in the 1980s to describe a winemaker, usually but not always Australian, who flies around the world to make wine in different countries.

Fortification
Winemaking process in which spirit is added to a wine to increase the alcohol and/or stop fermentation to increase sugar levels.

Free-run wine
Juice or wine that drains without pressing; usually of superior quality.

Garagiste
Term coined for some of the tiny and very expensive wine estates in Bordeaux's Right Bank, supposedly so small that their wine could be made in a garage. *See* **Right Bank**

Geographical Indication (GI)
Australian equivalent of Appellation d'Origine Contrôlée.

Gran Reserva
Spanish term for a red wine that has been aged for five years before release, with at least two years in cask and three years in bottle.

Grand Cru
French for "great growth." In Burgundy, one of thirty-four top vineyards. In Alsace, one of fifty-one. In Bordeaux, the second tier of the St.-Emilion classification. In Champagne, a village rated at 100 percent on the *échelle des crus*. *See* **Échelle des crus** and **Premier Cru**

Grand Vin
French term for the main wine produced by a Bordeaux château, as opposed to a second wine. *See* **Second wine**

Grandes Marques
French for "big brand." Term applied to some of Champagne's major firms.

Green harvest
Viticultural process of removing bunches of grapes in mid-summer to reduce the yield and increase quality. *See* **Yield**

Halbtrocken
German for "half-dry." *See* **Trocken**

Hogshead
A 300-liter (80 gal) Australian barrel. *See* **Barrique**

Icewine
Very sweet Canadian wine made from frozen grapes. *See* **Eiswein**

Indicazione di Geografica Tipica (IGT)
Italian equivalent of Vin de Pays.

Jerepigo
South African equivalent of *vin doux naturel.*

Jerez
Spanish for "Sherry."

Kabinett
Category of German wine made from ripe grapes picked before Spätlese grapes.

Lagar (pl. Lagares)
Portuguese for the low-sided stone troughs in which grapes are trodden and fermented, now used mainly in the production of Port.

Late Bottled Vintage (LBV)
Port of a single vintage that is aged in wood for up to six years.

Lees stirring
Winemaking process of stirring the lees, or sediment, to impart extra flavor. *See* **Bâtonnage**

Left Bank
Collective term for the part of Bordeaux that lies on the left bank of the River Garonne, and which

includes Margaux and Pauillac. *See* **Right Bank**

Length
How long the flavor of a wine persists after it has been swallowed or spat.

Lieu-dit
French for "named place." Term used in reference to a specific, named vineyard within a larger area, especially in Burgundy.

Maceration
Process in which the materials of the grape (e.g., tannins and flavor compounds) are leeched from the grape skins, seeds, and stems.

Malolactic fermentation
Process that follows alcoholic fermentation and softens harsh malic acid into softer lactic acid.

Manzanilla
In Spain, dry style of Sherry, similar to Fino. *See* **Fino**

Master of Wine (MW)
A person who has passed the examinations held by the Institute of Masters of Wine.

Mesoclimate
Term used to describe the climate of an individual vineyard or hillside. *See* **Microclimate**

Méthode Traditionelle
Sparkling winemaking process in which bubbles are formed during the second fermentation that takes place in the bottle. In Champagne, France, it is called Méthode Champenoise.

Microclimate
Term used to describe the climatic conditions surrounding a vine. *See* **Mesoclimate**

Moelleux
French for "mellow." Medium sweet.

New World
Term used to describe wine regions outside the traditional wine-growing areas of Europe, particularly from Australia,

Argentina, Canada, Chile, New Zealand, South Africa, and the United States. *See* **Old World**

Noble Rot
See **Botrytis**

Non-vintage (NV)
A wine, particularly Champagne or sparkling wine, blended from several vintages.

Oechsle
Scale of measuring grape sugars (for ripeness). In Germany it is used to determine a wine's classification.

Old World
Term used to describe the traditional winemaking regions of Europe. *See* **New World**

Oloroso
Dry, nutty style of Sherry in which the *flor* is suppressed by fortification. *See* **Fino** and **Flor**

Organic
Viticultural process that eschews fertilizers, pesticides, and other chemicals. *See* **Biodynamic**

Palo Cortado
Sherry based on a fluke of nature in which the *flor* fails to develop.

Parker, Robert
Hugely influential U.S. wine critic who developed the 100-point scoring system for wine.

Passito
Winemaking process in Italy, especially for Amarone and Recioto di Valpolicella, in which grapes are dried prior to fermentation.

Pedro Ximénez (PX)
Spanish grape variety that makes intensely sweet fortified wine of the same name.

Pétillant
French for "sparkling."

Phylloxera
Vine louse of American origin that devastated European vineyards in the late eighteenth century.

Premier Cru
French for "first growth." In Burgundy,

one of hundreds of top vineyards classified below grand cru. In Bordeaux, one of five Left Bank châteaux classified as "premier cru" in 1855 and 1973, or one of eleven Sauternes châteaux also classified as such. In Champagne, a village rated at 90 to 99 percent on the *échelle des crus. See* **Cru, échelle des crus, Grand Cru** and **Left Bank**

Premiers Grands Crus Classé A/B
The top tier of the St.-Emilion wine classification in Bordeaux.

Pumping over
Winemaking process that circulates fermenting red wine.

Puttonyos
Term used to describe the sweetness of Tokaji wine, ranging from three to six puttonyos, with six being the sweetest.

Quinta
Portuguese for "farm." Portuguese equivalent of French château or domaine.

Racking
Winemaking process of transferring wine from one container to another.

Recioto
Style of Italian dried grape wine, particularly Recioto di Valpolicella. *See* **Passito**

Remuage
French for "riddling." Part of the Méthode Traditionelle process for sparkling wines, in which bottles are gradually turned to bring the lees into the neck prior to dégorgement. *See* **Dégorgement** and **Méthode Traditionelle**

Reserva
Spanish term for a red wine that has been aged for three years, with at least one year in cask and two years in bottle, before release. *See* **Crianza** and **Gran Reserva**

Residual sugar
The amount of unfermented sugar left in the wine after alcoholic fermentation.

Right Bank
Collective term for the part of Bordeaux that lies on the right bank of the River Garonne, including St.-Emilion and Pomerol. *See* **Left Bank**

Saignée
French for "bled." Winemaking process involving "bleeding" off a portion of red wine after only a short period of contact with the grape skins to make a rosé wine.

Sec
French for "dry."

Second wine
Wine made from juice or grapes not considered worthy of an estate's main wine, particularly in Bordeaux.

Sélection de Grains Nobles (SGN)
Richest and ripest style of Alsace wine.

Solera
Winemaking process of fractional blending, especially for Sherry, in which barrels of wine are arranged in a vertical system.

Spätlese
Category of German or Austrian wine made from late-harvested grapes, above Kabinett and below Auslese in terms of ripeness.

Spumante
Italian for "foaming." Term for sparkling wine.

Sur lie
French for "on the lees." Wine, usually white, that has been left in contact with its lees to add more flavor. *See* **Lees stirring**

Tawny Port
Wood-aged Port usually blended at either ten, twenty, thirty, or forty years of age, comprising a blend of wines that average the age declared on the label. *See* **Colheita**

Terroir
French term for the natural environment of a vineyard site, encompassing soil, mesoclimate, and microclimate.

Tête de Cuvée
French term for top bottlings, especially in Champagne.

Trichloroanisole (TCA)
Chemical compound that causes corked (dirty, musty-smelling) wines. *See* **Corked**

Trocken
German for "dry."

Trockenbeerenauslese (TBA)
German for "dry berry selected." The ripest and rarest style of German or Austrian white wine.

Vendange tardive
French for "late harvest." Style of Alsace wine, less sweet than Sélection de Grains Nobles.

Vieilles vignes
French for "old vines."

Vin de garde
French term for a wine that is made to be aged.

Vin de Pays
Category of French wine below Appellation d'Origine Contrôlée.

Vin doux naturel
French for "sweet natural wine." Sweet, strong wine made by adding spirit to unfermented grape juice.

Vitis vinifera
Species of grape vine from which most wine is made.

Volatile acidity
Aromas of acetic acid or ethyl acetate. In small amounts it can enhance a wine's character, but too much makes a wine smell of vinegar or nail-polish remover.

Weingut
German for "wine estate."

Wine of Origin (WO)
South African equivalent of the French Appellation d'Origine Contrôlée.

Yield
The amount of wine produced in a vineyard, usually expressed in hectoliters per hectare.

Index of producers

Aalto, Bodegas 412
Abbazia di Novacella 125
Accornero 414
Achával Ferrer 416
Adami 22
Agrapart 22
Alaverdi Monastery 416
Alheit Vineyards 125
Allegrini 417
Allende 417
Alta Vista 418
Altare, Elio 418
Altos Las Hormigas 419
Alvear 851
Angélus, Château 419
Angerville,
    Domaine Marquis d' 420
Angludet, Château d' 420
Ànima Negra 422
Anselmi, Roberto 126
Antinori 422, 423
Antiyal 424
Anwilka Estate/
    Klein Constantia 427
Araujo 427
Argiano 429
Argiolas 429
Argüeso 851
Arlay, Château d' 129
Armand, Domaine du Comte 430
Arnot-Roberts 126
Artadi 430
Ata Rangi 432
Atauta, Dominio de 434
Au Bon Climat 434
Ausone, Château 436
Auvenay, Domaine d' 129
Avignonesi 131
Azelia 438
Bachelet, Domaine
    Denis 438
A. A. Badenhorst Family
    Wines 131

Balnaves 439
Banfi 439
Barbadillo 853
Barbeito 853–4
Barca Velha 440
Barry, Jim 440
Barthod, Domaine
    Ghislaine 441
Bass Phillip 441
Bassermann-Jordan, Dr. von 132
Battle of Bosworth 442
Baudouin, Domaine
    Patrick 134
Baumard,
    Domaine des 134
Beaucastel,
    Château de 135, 442
Beaulieu Vineyards 443
Beaumont des Crayères 24
Beauséjour Duffau-Lagarrosse,
    Ch. 443
Beau-Séjour Bécot,
    Château 444
Beaux Frères 446
Bélair-Monange, Château 446
Bellavista 24
Belondrade y Lurton 135
Beringer 447
Berliquet, Château 447
Billecart-Salmon 26, 28
Billiot, Henri 28
Biondi Santi 448
Bisol 30
Blanck, Paul 136
Blandy's 857
Blue Nun 136
Bodegas Tradición 857
Boekenhoutskloof 450
Boillot,
    Domaine Jean-Marc 138
Bollinger 32, 35
Bon Pasteur, Château Le 452
Bonneau du Martray,
    Domaine 141
Bonneau, Henri 454
Bonny Doon 141, 143, 456
Borgo del Tiglio 143
Borie de Maurel 457
Borsao 457

Boscarelli 458
Bott Geyl, Domaine 144
Bouchard, Cédric 35
Bouchard Père & Fils
    146, 458
Bouchard-Finlayson 460
Bourgeois,
    Domaine Henri 148
Braida 460
Branaire-Ducru,
    Château 462
Brane-Cantenac,
    Château 462
Bredell's 858
Breuer, Georg 148
Brokenwood 465
Brown, Château 465
Bruce, David 466
Brun, Roger 36
Bründlmayer 149
Bucci 149
Buhl, Reichsrat von 150
Bürklin-Wolf, Dr. 150
Busch, Clemens 151
Bussaco Palace Hotel 151, 466
Bussola, Tommaso 467
Cà del Bosco 36
Calon-Ségur, Château 468
Calvente 152
Ca'Marcanda 467
Can Ràfols dels Caus 152
Candido 469
Canon, Château 469
Canon-La-Gaffelière,
    Château 471
Canopy 471
Capçanes, Celler de 472
Cape Point Vineyards 153
Capezzana, Villa di 472
Capichera 153
Caprai, Arnaldo 473
Carillon, Domaine 154
Carnasciale, Podere Il 473
Carrau, Bodegas 474
Casa Castillo 474
Casa Gualda 475
Casa Lapostolle 475
Casablanca, Viña 476
Cascina Corte 476

Castaño 477
Castel de Paolis 154
Castello dei Rampolla 477
Castello del Terriccio 479
Castello di Ama 480
Castelluccio 480
Castillo de Perelada 481
Catena Alta 481
Cathiard,
    Domaine Sylvain 482
Cattier 38
Cauhapé, Domaine 155
Cavalleri 38
Cavallotto 482
Ca'Viola 468
Cayron, Domaine du 483
Cazals, Claude 40
Cèdre, Château du 484
Cesani, Vincenzo 155
Chambers 860
Chamirey, Château de 483
Chamonix 157
Champalou, Didier et
    Catherine 157
Chandon, Domaine 40
Channing Daughters 158
Chapoutier,
    Domaine 158, 159
Chapoutier, M. 484, 486
Chappellet 486
Chateau Montelena 159
Chateau Ste. Michelle 161
Chave, Domaine 487
Chave, Domaine J.-L. 161
Cheval Blanc, Château 487
Chevalier, Domaine de
    162, 488
Chidaine, Domaine
    François 162
Chimney Rock 491
Chivite 163
Christmann 163
Christoffel 164
Chryseia 491
Clape, Domaine Auguste 492
Clerico, Domenico 492
Climens, Château 166
Clonakilla 493
Clos de l'Oratoire 493

Clos de la Coulée de
    Serrant 169
Clos de Los Siete 494
Clos de Tart 494
Clos des Papes 495
Clos du Tue-Boeuf Touraine 170
Clos Erasmus 495
Clos Floridène 169
Clos Mogador 496
Clos Naudin,
    Domaine du 170
Clos Uroulat 171
Cluver, Paul 171
Coates & Seely 42
Coche-Dury, Domaine 172
Cockburn's 862
Codorníu, Jaume 42
Col Vetoraz 44
Coldstream Hills 498
Colet–Navazos 44
Colgin Cellars 501
Collard, René 45
Colle Duga 172
Colli di Lapio 173
Concha y Toro 501, 502
Conseillante,
    Château La 502
Contador 504
Conterno Fantino 505
Conterno, Giacomo 504
Còntini, Attilio 173
Contino 505
Coppo 506
Coriole Lloyd 506
Corison 507
Correggia, Matteo 507
Cortes de Cima 508
COS 508
Cos d'Estournel,
    Château 509
Cossart Gordon 862, 863
Costanti, Andrea 509
Costers del Siurana 510
Cotat François 174
Couly-Dutheil 510
Cousiño Macul, Viña 511
Coutet, Château 174
Craggy Range 511
Crochet, Lucien 176

Croft 863
Cullen 512
Cuomo, Marisa 176
CVNE 178, 514
Dal Forno, Romano 516
Dalla Valle 516
Dampierre,
    Comte Audoin de 45
Dard et Ribo 517
D'Arenberg 517
Darviot-Perrin,
    Domaine 180
Dauvissat, Domaine
    René & Vincent 180
De Bartoli 181, 864
De Bortoli 181
De Meric 47
De Sousa 47
De Trafford 518
Deiss, Domaine
    Marcel 182
Delaforce 864
Delamotte 48
Delgado Zuleta 866
DeLille Cellars 518
Dettori,
    Azienda Agricola 520
Deutz 51
Diamond Creek 520
Diebolt-Vallois 51
Diel, Schlossgut 182
Disznókö 185
Dogliotti, Romano 52
Doisy-Daëne, Château 185
Dom Pérignon 52, 54
Dom Ruinart 56–7
Domaine A 522
Domaine de l'A 522
Dominus 523
Donnafugata 186
Dönnhoff, Hermann 188
Dow's 868
Drappier 59
Droin, Domaine 188
Drouhin, Domaine 523
Drouhin,
    Domaine Joseph 189, 525
Druet, Pierre-Jacques 525
Dry River 190, 526

Duas Quintas 528
Duboeuf, Georges 530
Duckhorn Vineyards 532
Ducru-Beaucaillou,
    Château 532
Dugat,
    Domaine Claude 534
Dugat-Pÿ, Domaine 534
Duhr, Mme. Aly, et Fils 193
Dujac, Domaine 535
Dunn Vineyards 535
Dupasquier, Domaine 194
Durfort-Vivens,
    Château 536
Dutton Goldfield 194
Ecu, Domaine de l' 194
Eglise-Clinet,
    Château L' 536
Egly-Ouriet 59
El Grifo 871
El Maestro Sierra 871
El Nido 538
El Principal, Viña 538
Els, Ernie 539
Emrich-Schönleber 197
Engel, Domaine René 539
Equipo Navazos 872
Esmonin, Domaine Sylvie 540
Evangile, Château L' 540
Eyrie Vineyards 542
Fable Mountain Vineyards 542
Faiveley, Domaine 544
Falfas, Château 544
Far Niente 546
Fargues, Château de 197
Fattoria La Massa 548
Feiler-Artinger 198
Felluga, Livio 198
Fèlsina Berardenga 548
Felton Road 549
Ferrara, Benito 201
Ferrari, Giulio 60
Ferreiro, Do 201
Feudi di San Gregorio 202
Fèvre, William 202
Fiddlehead 549
Figeac, Château 550
Filhot, Château 204
Fillaboa Seléccion 207

Finca Luzón 550
Finca Sandoval 551
Fiorano 207
Florio 872
Flowers 208, 551
Fonseca 875
Fonseca, José Maria da 875
Fontodi 552
Foradori 552
Fourcas-Hosten,
    Château 553
Fourrier,
    Domaine Jean-Claude 553
Framingham 211
Frank, Dr. Konstantin 211
Freemark Abbey 554
Freie Weingärtner
    Wachau 212
Frog's Leap 554
Fromm Winery 556
Fucci, Elena 556
Fuissé, Château de 212
Gago Pago La Jara 557
Gaia Estate 557
Gaja 558
Ganevat, Jean-François 213
Garvey 876
Gauby, Domaine 559
Gazin, Château 561
Cave Geisse 60
Germanier, Jean-René 561
Gerovassiliou 562
Giaconda 213, 564
Giacosa, Bruno 564
Gilette, Château 214
Gimonnet, Pierre 62
Giraud, Henri 64
Giscours, Château 566
Gloria Ferrer 66
Goldwater 569
González Byass 878
Gosset 68
Gouges, Domaine Henri 569
Gourt de Mautens,
    Domaine 214
Grace Family Vineyards 570
Grace Winery 215
Graillot, Alain 573

Gramona 70
Grand-Puy-Lacoste,
    Château 574
Grange des Pères 576
Grans-Fassian 215
Grasso, Elio 576
Grasso, Silvio 577
Gratien & Meyer 71
Gratien, Alfred 70
Grattamacco 577
Gravner, Josko 216
Greenock Creek 578
Grgić, Miljenko 578
Grillet, Château 216
Grivot, Domaine Jean 579
Gróf Dégenfeld 219
Gros, Domaine Anne 579
Grosset 219
Gruaud-Larose, Château 581
GS 581
Guelbenzu, Bodegas 582
Guffens-Heynen,
    Domaine 220
Guigal 582
Guiraud, Château 220
Guitián 222
Gunderloch 224
Gutiérrez Colosía 882
Gutiérrez de la Vega 883
Haag, Fritz 224
Hacienda Monasterio 583
Hamilton Russell
    Vineyards 226
Hanzell 228
Haras de Pirque, Viña 583
Hardys 584
Harlan Estate 586
Haut-Bailly, Château 588
Haut-Brion,
    Château 230, 590
Haut-Marbuzet,
    Château 592
Heidsieck, Charles 71
Heitz Wine Cellars 592
Henriot 72
Henschke 593
Herdade de Cartuxa 593
Herdade de Mouchão 594
Herdade do Esporão 594

Herzog 595
Hétsölö 233
Heyl zu Herrnsheim,
   Freiherr 233
Heymann-Löwenstein 235
Hidalgo, Emilio 884
Hidalgo-La Gitana 885
Hiedler 235
Hirsch Vineyards 595
Hirtzberger 236
Hosanna, Château 596
Hövel, Weingut von 236
Howard Park 237
Huet, Domaine 72, 237
Hugel 239
Idylle, Domaine de l' 239
Inama, Stefana 240
Inniskillin 240
Iron Horse 74
Isabel 242
Isole e Olena 596
Itsasmendi 242
Izadi, Viña 597
Jaboulet Aîné, Paul 597
Jackson Estate 243
Jacqueson, Domaine 243
Jacquesson 77
Jade Mountain 598
Jasper Hill 598
Jayer, Domaine Henri 599
Jobard,
   Domaine François 244
Josmeyer 244
K Vintners 599
Kalin Cellars 246
Kanonkop 601
Karthäuserhof 246
Katnook Estate 602
Kefraya, Château 604
Keller, Weingut 249
Kesselstatt, Reichsgraf
   von 249
Királyudvar 250
Kistler 252
Klein Constantia 252
Kloster Eberbach
   Staatsweingüter 253, 606
Knoll 253
Koehler-Ruprecht, Weingut 254

Kogl Estate 256
Kracher 256
Kreydenweiss, Marc 258
Krug 78–83
Ksara, Château 608
Kumeu River 258
Künstler, Franz 260
KWV 886
La Dominique,
   Château 611
La Fleur-Pétrus,
   Château 611
La Gomerie, Château 613
La Jota Vineyard
   Company 613
La Louvière, Château 260
La Mission-Haut-Brion,
   Château 615
La Monacesca 263
La Mondote 615
La Morandina 84
La Rame, Château 263
La Rectorie,
   Domaine de 886
La Rioja Alta 616
La Spinetta 616
Labet, Domaine 264
Lafarge,
   Domaine Michel 617
Lafaurie-Peyraguey, Château 266
Lafite Rothschild,
   Château 617
Lafleur, Château 618
Lafon, Domaine des Comtes
   268–9, 618
Lafon,
   Héritiers du Comte 268
Lagrange, Château 621
Lagrézette, Château 621
Lake's Folly 269
Lamarche, Domaine 623
Lambrays,
   Domaine des 624
Landmark 624
Langlois Château 84
Lassaigne, Jacques 86
Larmandier-Bernier 86
Laroche, Domaine 270
Latour, Château 626

Latour-à-Pomerol,
   Château 628
Laurent-Perrier 88
Laville Haut-Brion,
   Château 270
Le Dôme 628
Le Due Terre 629
Le Macchiole 629
Le Pin 631
Le Riche 632
Le Soula 271
Leacock's 887
L'Ecole No. 41 634
Leeuwin Estate 271
Leflaive, Domaine 273
Lehmann, Peter 637
Lenz 273
Leonetti Cellars 637
Léoville-Barton,
   Château 638
Léoville-Las Cases,
   Château 640
Léoville-Poyferré,
   Château 640
Leroy, Domaine 642
Lezongars,
   L'Enclos de Château 642
Liger-Belair,
   Domaine du Vicomte 274, 644
Lilbert-Fils 88
Lisini 644
Littorai Wines 646
Livio Felluga 198
Loimer 277
Long-Depaquit,
   Domaine 277
Loosen, Dr. 279
López de Heredia 279, 646
L'Origan 96
Luque, M. Gil 887
Lusco do Miño 280
Lustau 888
Lynch-Bages, Château 647
Macari Vineyard 647
Macle, Jean 280
Maculan 282
McWilliam's 282
Magdelaine, Château 648
Majella 648

Malartic-Lagravière, Château 284
Malle, Château de 284
Malvirà 89, 286, 649
Marcarini 649
Marcassin 286
Margaux, Château 289, 651
Marqués de Griñón 652
Marqués de Murrieta 290, 652
Marqués de Riscal 653
Marqués del Real
   Tesoro 891
Martínez-Bujanda 653
Mas Amiel 891
Mas Blanc 892
Mas de Daumas
   Gassac 654
Mas Doix 654
Mas Martinet 655
Más Que Vinos 655
Mascarello, Bartolo 656
Mascarello, Giuseppe 656
Massandra Collection 894
Mastroberardino 659
Matassa, Domaine 293
Matetic 659
Mathieu, Serge 89
Maume, Domaine 660
Mauro 660
Maurodos 661
Maximin Grünhauser 293
Mayacamas 661
Mayr, Josephus 662
Medici Ermete 90
Meerlust 664
Meín, Viña 294
Mellot, Alphonse 294
Melton, Charles 666
Mendoza, Abel 668
Mendoza, E. 668
Méo-Camuzet,
   Domaine 669
Mercier, Denis 669
Meyer-Näkel 670
Miani 296, 670
Michael, Peter 296, 671
Michel, Bruno 90
Millton Vineyard 298
Mission Hill 300
Mitchelton 300

Moccagatta 671
Molettieri, Salvatore 672
Mondavi, Robert 301, 672
Montaiguillon,
   Château 675
Montana 91
Montelena, Château 675
Montes 676
Montevertine 679
Montevetrano 679
Montille, Domaine Hubert de 680
Montrose, Château 682
Montus, Château 682
Mordorée,
   Domaine de la 683
Moric 683
Moris Farms 684
Moro, Bodegas Emilio 687
Morris Wines 894–5
Moss Wood 687
Moulin-à-Vent, Château du 688
Mount Difficulty 688
Mount Eden 301
Mount Horrocks 302
Mount Langi Ghiran 691
Mount Mary 691
Mountadam 305
Moutard 91
Mouton Rothschild, Château 693
Muga 693
Mugnier, Domaine J.-F. 695
Müller, Egon 306
Müller-Catoir 306
Mullineux Family Wines 695
Mumm 92
Murana, Salvatore 307
Muré, René 307, 695
Murietta, Marqués de 290
Musar, Château 696
Nada, Fiorenzo 698
Nairac, Château 308
Nardello, Daniele 308
Navazos Niepoort 309
Négly, Château de la 698
Negri, Nino 699
Neudorf 309
Newton Vineyards 310
Niebaum-Coppola
   Estate 699

Niedrist, Ignaz 700
Niepoort 310, 700, 702, 895–6
Nigl 311
Nikolaihof 311
Noemía de Patagonia,
   Bodega 702
Noval, Quinta do 898, 900
Nyetimber 95
Oak Valley 313
Oberto, Andrea 703
Ojai Vineyard 703
Olivares Dulce 902
Omar Khayyam 95
Opitz, Willi 704
Opus One 704
Ordoñez, Jorge, & Co 313
Oremus 314
Osborne 902–3
Ossian 314
Ostertag, André 315
Pacenti, Siro 706
Pagos de los
   Capellanes 706
Pahlmeyer 707
Paitin 707
Palacio de Bornos 315
Palacio de Fefiñanes,
   Bodega del 316
Palacios, Alvaro 709
Palacios, Descendientes
   de J. 709
Palacios, Rafa 316
Palari Faro 710
Palmer, Château 710
Pape-Clément,
   Château 712
Parker 714
Parusso 716
Pataille, Domaine Sylvain 716
Paternina 903
Paternoster 717
Pato, Filipa 717
Pato, Luís 718
Pavie, Château 718
Pavie-Macquin,
   Château 720
Pazo de Señoras 317
Peay Vineyards 723
Pelissero, Giorgio 723

Pellé, Domaine Henry 317
Pellegrino, Carlo 904
Penfolds 724–5, 726, 906
Peregrine 319
Pérez Barquero 906
Péres Marín 908
Perret, André 319
Perrier-Jouët 96
Pesquera, Tinto 726
Peters, Pierre 98
Petit-Village, Château 729
Petrolo 729
Pétrus 730
Pez, Château de 732
Pfaffl, R & A 320
Phelps, Joseph 734
Philipponnat 98
Piaggia 734
Pichler, F.X. 320
Pichon-Longueville,
   Château 735
Pieropan 323
Pierre-Bise, Château 323
Pierro 324
Pieve di Santa
   Restituta 737
Pinard, Vincent 324
Pingus, Dominio del 737
Pintia 738
Pithon, Domaine Jo 326
Plageoles, Robert & Bernard 326
Podere 738
Pol Roger 101
Poliziano 739
Polz, E & W 327
Pommery 103
Ponsot, Domaine 327, 739
Pontet-Canet, Château 740
Portal, Quinta do 908
Pouillon, Roger 103
Poujeaux, Château 740
Prager 328
Prévost, Jérôme 104
Pride Mountain 742
Prieler 742
Prieuré de St.-Jean de
   Bébian 743
Prieuré St.-Christophe,
   Domaine 743

Produttori del
   Barbaresco 745
Providence, Château 745
Prüm, J.J. 328–9
Puffeney, Jacques 329
Quady 910
Quenard, André
   et Michel 330
Querciabella, Agricola 747
Quilceda Creek 748
Quinta das Bágeiras 106
Quinta do Côtto 748
Quinta do Mouro 749
Quinta do Vale Meão 749
Quinta dos Roques 750
Quintarelli 752
Quintessa 752
Qupé 330, 753
Rabaud-Promis,
   Château 332
Radio-Coteau 753
Ramey Hyde Vineyard 334
Ramonet, Domaine 334
Ramos Pinto 913
Rauzan-Ségla, Château 754
Raveneau, Domaine 335
Ravenswood 756
Raventós i Blanc 108
Rayas, Château 758
Rayne-Vigneau,
   Château 335
Rebholz, Ökonomierat 336
Remelluri 338
Remirez de Ganuza 758
Rémy, Louis 759
Rey Fernando de
   Castilla 913
Richter, Max Ferd. 341
Ridge 759
Riessec, Château 341
Rinaldi, Giuseppe 760
Ringland, Chris 760
Rippon 761
Roc de Cambes,
   Château 761
Rochioli, J. 762
Rockford 762
Roda, Bodegas 763
Rodríguez, Telmo 343

Roederer, Louis 108
Rojo, Emilio 343
Rollin Père & Fils,
   Domaine 763
Rolly-Gassmann 344
Romanée-Conti,
   Domaine de la 347, 765–6
Romero, Pedro 914
Rosa, Quinta de la 914
Rostaing, René 766
Roulot, Domaine 347
Roumier,
   Domaine Georges 767
Roure, Celler del 767
Rousseau,
   Domaine Armand 768–9
Royal Tokaji Wine Co. 348
Rudera 350
Rust en Vrede 771
Rustenberg 771
Sadie Family 350, 772
St. Hallett 772
Salomon-Undhof 351
Salon 111
Salvioni 774
San Alejandro 774
San Vicente 775
Sánchez Ayala 917
Sánchez Romate 917
Sandeman 918
Sandrone, Luciano 775
Sanford 776
Santa Rita, Viña 776
Santadi 777
Sastre, Viña 777
Satta, Michele 778
Sauer 351
Sauzet, Domaine
   Etienne 352
Scavino, Paolo 778
Schaefer, Willi 352
Schiopetto 355
Schloss
   Gobelsburg 355
Schloss Lieser 356
Schloss Vollrads 356
Schlumberger 359
Schram, J. 111
Schröck, Heidi 359

Screaming Eagle 779
Seghesio 779
Sekthaus Raumland 106
Selbach-Oster 360
Selosse, Jacques 112
Seppelt Great Western 112
Serafini e Vidotto 780
Seresin 362
Shafer 780
Shaw + Smith 362
Silos, Cillar de 782
Simčič, Edi 363
Simone, Château 782
Smith Woodhouse 920
Smith-Haut-Lafitte,
    Château 363
Soalheiro 364
Sociando-Mallet,
    Château 784
Soldera 784
Solms-Delta 786
Sorrel, Marc 786
Sot 787
Stadlmann, Johann 364
Stag's Leap Wine
    Cellars 787
Stanton & Killeen 920
Steenberg 367
Stonier Estate 367, 788
Stony Hill 368
Stonyridge 791
Suduiraut, Château
    368–70
Swan, Joseph 791
Szepsy 372
Tahbilk 374
Taille aux Loups,
    Domaine de la 114, 376
Taittinger 114
Talbot, Château 792
Tamellini 376
Tapanappa Whalebone
    Vineyard 794
Tares, Dominio de 796
Tarlant 117
Tasca d'Almerita 796
Taylor's 922, 924
Te Mata 798
Te Motu 800

Tempier, Domaine 800
Tenuta di Valgiano 802
Tenuta delle Terre Nere 802
Tenuta dell'Ornellaia 801
Tenuta San Guido 803
Tenuta San Leonardo 803
Tenuta Sette Ponti 804
Terlano, Cantina di 377
Terrazas/Cheval Blanc 804
Tertre-Roteboeuf,
    Château 807
Testalonga 378
Texier, Eric 807
Thackrey, Sean 808
Thelema 808
Thévenet, Jean 378
Tirecul, Château 379
Tissot, André &
    Mireille 379
Torbreck 810
Torelló, Agustí 117
Toro Albalá 926
Torres 813
Torres Estate, Marimar 380
Tour Vieille,
    Domaine La 813
Tour Blanche,
    Château La 382
Traeger, David 384
Trévallon,
    Domaine de 814
Trinity Hill 816
Troplong-Mondot,
    Château 818
Trotanoy, Château 820
Tschida, Angerhof 387
Tua Rita 822
Turkey Flat 822
Turley Wine Cellars 823
Tyrrell's 389
Umathum 823
Vajra, Azienda Agricola
    G.D. 824
Valandraud, Château 824
Valdespino 926–8
Valdipiatta 826
Valentini 389, 826
Vall Llach 828
Valtuille 828

Vasse Felix 829
Vecchie Terre di
    Montefili 829
Vega de Toro 830
Vega Sicilia 830
Venus 832
Vergelegen 392, 832
Verget 392
Vernay, Georges 393
Verset, Noël 834
Vesúvio, Quinta do 931
Veuve Clicquot 118
Veuve Fourny 120
Vie di Romans 393
Vieux Château Certan 834
Vieux Télégraphe,
    Domaine du 835
Vigneti Massa 394
Villa Ponciago 835
Villaine,
    Domaine A. et P. de 394
Vilmart 120
Viñedos Orgánicos
    Emiliana 836
Voerzio, Roberto 838
Vogüé, Domaine Comte Georges
    de 397
Vollenweider 397
Volxem, Weingut
    van 390
Warre's 931
Weil, Robert 398
Weinbach, Domaine 400
Wendouree 838
Wild Duck Creek 841
Williams & Humbert 932
Williams Selyem 841
Wittmann, Weingut 402
Wynn's 842
Yacochuya de Michel
    Rolland 844
Yalumba 404, 844
Yarra Yering 845
Yerro, Alonso del 845
Yquem, Chateau d' 404
Zerbina, Fattoria 846
Zilliken 406
Zind-Humbrecht,
    Domaine 406–8

Index by price

⑨

Adami
  Prosecco di Valdobbiadene 22
Argüeso
  *San León Reserva de Familia
  Manzanilla* 851
Blue Nun 136
Borsao *Tres Picos* 457
Calvente
  *Guindalera Vendimia
  Seleccionada Moscatel* 152
Canopy *Malpaso* 471
Casa Gualda *Selección C&J* 475
Casa Lapostolle *Clos Apalta* 475
Castaño *Hécula Monastrell* 477
Col Vetoraz *Prosecco Extra Dry* 44
Dogliotti, Romano
  Moscato d'Asti La Galesia 52
Domecq, Pedro
  La Ina Fino Sherry 866
Dupasquier, Domaine
  Marestel Roussette de Savoie 194
El Principal *Cabernet Sauvignon* 538
Finca Luzón *Altos de Luzón* 550
Frank, Dr. Konstantin
  Dry Riesling 211
Garvey *San Patricio Fino Sherry* 876
González Byass
  Tío Pepe Fino Sherry 878
Guitián *Valdeorras Godello* 222
Haras de Pirque
  Haras Style Syrah 583
Hidalgo-La Gitana
  Pastrana Manzanilla Pasada 885
Idylle, Domaine de l' *Vin de Savoie
  Cuvée Orangerie* 239
Itsasmendi *Txakolí* 242
Lenz *Gewürztraminer* 273
Malvirà *Birbét Brachetto* 89
Medici Ermete
  *Lambrusco Reggiano
  Concerto* 90
Meín, Viña 294
Michel, Bruno *Cuvée Blanche* 90
Millton *Te Arai Vineyard Chenin
  Blanc* 298

Palacio de Bornos
  *Verdejo Fermentado en
  Barrica Rueda* 315
Palacio de Fefiñanes, Bodega del
  Rías Baixas Albariño 316
Péres Marín
  La Guita Manzanilla 908
Quenard, André et Michel
  *Chignin-Bergeron Les
  Terrasses* 330
Romero, Pedro
  Aurora en Rama Manzanilla 914
San Alejandro *Baltasar Gracián
  Garnacha Viñas Viejas* 774
Tamellini *Soave Classico Le Bine
  de Costiola* 376
Valdespino
  Inocente Fino Sherry 927

⑨⑨

Abbazia di Novacella
  Praepositus Kerner 125
Alaverdi Monastery *Saperavi* 416
Antiyal 424
A. A. Badenhorst Family Wines
  White Blend 131
Barbeito *Single Cask
  Colheita Madeira* 854
Bassermann-Jordan, Dr. von
  Forster Pechstein Riesling 132
Belondrade y Lurton *Rueda* 135
Bisol *Cartizze Prosecco* 30
Bonny Doon
  Vin Gris de Cigare 456
Borie de Maurel *Cuvée Sylla* 457
Bourgeois, Domaine Henri
  Sancerre d'Antan 148
Bründlmayer
  *Zöbinger Heiligenstein
  Riesling Alte Reben* 149
Bucci
  *Verdicchio dei Castelli di Jesi
  Riserva Villa Bucci* 149
Buhl, Reichsrat von
  *Forster Ungeheuer
  Riesling ST* 150
Can Ràfols dels Caus
  Vinya La Calma 152
Cape Point Vineyards *Semillon* 153
Carrau, Bodegas *Amat* 474
Casa Castillo *Pie Franco* 474
Casablanca, Viña *Neblus* 476

Castel de Paolis *Muffa Nobile* 154
Catena Alta *Malbec* 481
Cesani, Vincenzo
  *Vernaccia di San Gimignano
  Sanice* 155
Chamonix *Chardonnay Reserve* 157
Chandon, Domaine *Green Point* 40
Channing Daughters
  Tocai Friulano 158
Chateau Ste. Michelle
  Eroica Riesling 161
Chidaine, Domaine François
  Montlouis-sur-Loire Les Lys 162
Clos de l'Oratoire 493
Clos de Los Siete 494
Clos du Tue-Boeuf *Touraine
  Le Brin de Chèvre* 170
Clos Floridène 169
Clos Uroulat
  Jurançon Cuvée Marie 171
Cluver, Paul
  *Noble Late Harvest Weisser
  Riesling* 171
Codorníu, Jaume *Brut* 42
Colet *Assemblage Extra Brut* 44
Colle Duga *Tocai Friulano* 172
Colli di Lapio *Fiano di Avellino* 173
Cortes de Cima *Incógnito* 508
COS *Cerasuolo di Vittoria* 508
Cousiño Macul, Viña
  *Antiguas Reservas Cabernet
  Sauvignon* 511
Cullen *Diana Madeline Cabernet
  Sauvignon Merlot* 512
Dard et Ribo *C'est le Printemps* 517
De Bartoli *Grappoli del Grillo* 181
Delaforce
  *Curious and Ancient 20 Years
  Old Tawny Port* 864
Donnafugata *Ben Ryé* 186
Duboeuf, Georges
  Fleurie La Madone 530
Duhr, Mme. Aly, et Fils
  Ahn Palmberg Riesling 192
Dutton Goldfield
  Rued Vineyard Chardonnay 194
Ecu, Domaine de l'
  *S. & M. Expression
  d'Orthogneiss* 195
El Grifo *Canari* 871
El Nido *Clio Jumilla* 538

Fable Mountain Vineyards
  Syrah 542
Falfas, Château 544
Ferrara, Benito
  Greco di Tufo Vigna Cicogna 201
Ferreiro, Do
  Cepas Vellas Albariño 201
Fillaboa Seléccion
  Finca Monte Alto 207
Florio *Terre Arse Marsala* 872
Fourcas-Hosten, Château 553
Framingham *Select Riesling* 211
Freie Weingärtner Wachau
  Achleiten G. Veltliner
  Smaragd 212
Gerovassiliou *Avaton* 562
Gloria Ferrer *Royal Cuvée* 66
Grace Winery
  Koshu Kayagatake 215
Gramona *III Lustros Gran Reserva* 70
Grosset *Watervale Riesling* 219
Gutiérrez de la Vega *Casta Diva*
  Cosecha Miel / Reserva
  Real 883
Herdade do Esporão
  Esporão Reserva 594
Heyl zu Herrnsheim, Freiherr
  Niersteiner Pettental Riesling 233
Hiedler
  Riesling Von Blauem Schiefer 235
Howard Park *Riesling* 237
Inama, Stefana *Vulcaia Fumé*
  Sauvignon Blanc 240
Iron Horse *Vrais Amis* 74
Isabel *Sauvignon Blanc* 242
Jackson Estate
  Sauvignon Blanc 243
Jacqueson, Domaine *Bouzeron*
  "Les Cordères" Aligoté 243
K Vintners *Milbrandt Syrah* 599
Kalin Cellars *Semillon* 247
Kanonkop *Pinotage* 601
Királyudvar *Furmint* 250
Kogl Estate *Traminic* 256
Künstler, Franz
  Hochheimer Kirchenstück Riesling
  Spätlese 260
KWV *Muscadel Jerepigo* 886
La Louvière, Château 260
La Morandina *Moscato d'Asti* 84
La Rame, Château *Réserve* 263

Lafon, Héritiers du Comte
  Mâcon-Milly-Lamartine 268
Le Riche
  Cabernet Sauvignon Reserve 632
Lehmann, Peter *Stonewell Shiraz* 637
Lezongars, L'Enclos de Château 642
Lilbert-Fils
  Cramant GC Brut Perle 88
Loimer *Steinmassl Riesling* 277
L'Origan *L'O Cava Brut Nature* 96
Lusco do Miño
  Pazo Piñeiro Albariño 280
Lustau *Almacenista Cuevas Jurado*
  Manzanilla Amontillada, 888
  Almacenista García Jarana Pata
  de Gallina Oloroso Sherry 888
Macari Vineyard *Merlot Reserve* 647
McWilliam's *Mount Pleasant*
  Lovedale Semillon 282
Malvira' *Roero Arneis Saglietto* 286
Marqués de Griñón
  Dominio de Valdepusa Syrah 652
Matassa, Domaine
  Blanc Vin de Pays des Côtes
  Catalanes 293
Matetic *EQ Pinot Noir* 659
Mathieu, Serge
  Cuvée Tradition Blanc de Noirs
  Brut 89
Mendoza, Abel
  Tempranillo Grano a Grano 668
Mendoza, E. *Estrecho* 668
Montaiguillon, Château 675
Montana
  Deutz Marlborough Cuvée
  Blanc de Blancs 91
Morris Wines
  Old Premium Liqueur
  Muscat 894
Mount Horrocks
  Cordon Cut Riesling 302
Navazos Niepoort *Vino Blanco* 309
Newton Vineyards
  Unfiltered Chardonnay 310
Niedrist, Ignaz
  Lagrein Berger Gei 700
Oak Valley *Mountain Reserve*
  Sauvignon Blanc 313
Olivares Dulce
  Monastrell Jumilla 902
Omar Khayyam 95

Ossian 314
Palacios, Rafa *As Sortes* 316
Pataille, Domaine Sylvain
  Marsannay Fleur du Pinot 716
Peregrine *Ratasburn Riesling* 319
Pfaffl, R & A
  Grüner Veltliner Hundsleiten 320
Piaggia *Carmignano Riserva* 734
Pierre-Bise
  Quarts-de-Chaume 323
Pintia *Toro* 738
Pithon, Domaine Jo *Coteaux du*
  Layon Les Bonnes Blanches 326
Polz, E & W *Hochgrassnitzberg*
  Sauvignon Blanc 327
Pouillon, Roger
  Cuvée de Réserve Brut 103
Poujeaux, Château 740
Prüm, J.J.
  Wehlener Sonnenuhr Riesling
  Spätlese No. 16 329
Quady *Essensia* 910
Quinta do Côtto
  Grande Escolha 748
Quinta do Mouro *Alentjo* 749
Quinta do Portal
  20 Year Old Tawny Port 908
Quinta do Vale Meão 749
Quinta dos Roques
  Dão Touriga Nacional 750
Qupé
  Marsanne Santa Ynez Valley 330
Raventós i Blanc
  Gran Reserva de la Finca
  Brut Nature 108
Remelluri *Blanco* 338
Rojo, Emilio *Ribeiro* 343
Roure, Celler del
  Maduresa Valencia 767
Rudera *Robusto Chenin Blanc* 350
Rustenberg John X Merriman 771
St. Hallett *Old Block Shiraz* 772
Salomon-Undhof
  Riesling Kögl 351
Sanford *Sanford & Benedict*
  Vineyard Pinot Noir 776
Seresin
  Marama Sauvignon Blanc 362
Silos, Cillar de *Torresilo* 782
Simone, Château
  Palette Rosé 782

Soalheiro
  *Alvarinho Primeiras
  Vinhas* 364
Solms-Delta *Africana* 786
Stadlmann, Johann
  Ziefandler Mandel-Höh 364
Steenberg
  Sauvignon Blanc Reserve 367
Stonier Estate
  Reserve Pinot Noir 788
  Reserve Chardonnay 367
Suduiraut, Château
  S de Suduiraut 368
Tahbilk *Marsanne* 374
Taille aux Loups, Domaine de la
  Triple Zéro 114
Tares, Dominio de
  Cepas Viejas Bierzo 796
Testalonga *El Bandito*
  Chenin Blanc 378
Texier, Eric *Côtes du Rhône*
  Brézème Rouge 807
Tissot, André & Mireille *Arbois*
  Chardonnay Le Mailloche 379
Toro Albalá *1922 Solera Amontillado*
  Montilla 926
Torres Estate, Marimar
  Chardonnay Dobles Lias 380
Tyrrell's *Vat 1 Semillon* 389
Vergelegen *White* 392
Verget
  St.-Véran Les Terres Noires 392
Vie di Romans
  Chardonnay 393
Vogüé, Domaine Comte Georges
  de *Bourgogne Blanc* 397
Warre's
  Late Bottled Vintage Port 931

❸❸❸
Accornero *Barbera del Monferrato*
  Superiore Bricco Battista 414
Achával Ferrer
  Finca Altamira Malbec 416
Agrapart *L'Avizeoise* 22
Alheit Vineyards *Cartology* 125
Allegrini *La Poja* 417
Alta Vista *Alto* 418
Altos Las Hormigas
  Malbec Reserva Viña
  Hormigas 419

Angludet, Château d' 420
Ànima Negra
  Vinyes de Son Negre 422
Anselmi, Roberto
  I Capitelli Veneto Passito
  Bianco 126
Antinori *Guado al Tasso* 422
  Tignanello 423
Anwilka Estate/Klein Constantia
  Anwilka 427
Argiano *Barolo di Montalcino* 429
Argiolas *Turriga* 429
Arlay, Château d'
  Côtes du Jura Vin Jaune 129
Armand, Domaine du Comte
  Pommard Clos des Epeneaux 430
Arnot-Roberts *Ribolla Gialla Vare
  Vineyard "A"* 126
Ata Rangi *Pinot Noir* 432
Atauta, Dominio de
  Ribera del Duero 434
Au Bon Climat *Pinot Noir* 434
Azelia *Barolo San Rocco* 438
Balnaves
  Tally Cabernet Sauvignon 439
Barbadillo
  Palo Cortado VORS Sherry 853
Barbeito
  *20 Years Old Malmsey
  Madeira* 853
Barry, Jim *The Armagh Shiraz* 440
Barthod, Domaine Ghislaine
  *Chambolle-Musigny PC
  Les Cras* 441
Battle of Bosworth *White Boar* 442
Baudouin, Domaine Patrick
  *Après Minuit Coteaux du
  Layon* 134
Baumard, Domaine des
  Quarts-de-Chaume 134
Beaumont des Crayères
  Fleur de Prestige 24
Beaux Frères *Pinot Noir* 446
Bellavista *Gran Cuvée Brut* 24
Berliquet, Château 447
Blanck, Paul
  *Schlossberg Grand Cru
  Riesling* 136
Bodegas Tradición
  Olorosos VORS Sherry 857
Boekenhoutskloof *Syrah* 450

Bonny Doon
  Le Cigare Blanc 141
  Le Cigare Volant 456
  Muscat Vin de Glacière 143
Borgo del Tiglio
  Malvasia Selezioni 143
Boscarelli *Vino Nobile Nocio dei
  Boscarelli* 458
Bott Geyl, Domaine
  *Sonnenglanz GC Tokay
  Pinot Gris VT* 144
Bouchard-Finlayson
  *Galpin Peak Tête de Cuvée
  Pinot Noir* 460
Braida *Bricco dell'Uccellone
  Barbera d'Asti* 460
Brane-Cantenac, Château 462
Bredell's *Cape Vintage Reserve* 858
Breuer, Georg
  *Rüdesheimer Berg Schlossberg
  Riesling Trocken* 148
Brun, Roger *Grand Cru Aÿ
  La Pelle* 36
Brokenwood *Graveyard Shiraz* 465
Brown, Château
  Château Brown 2004 465
Bruce, David
  *Santa Cruz Mountains
  Pinot Noir* 466
Bürklin-Wolf, Dr.
  *Forster Kirchenstück Riesling
  Trocken* 150
Bussaco Palace Hotel *Buçaco Tinto
  Reservado* 466
Ca'Marcanda *IGT Toscana* 467
Candido *Capello di Prete* 469
Canon, Château 469
Canon-La-Gaffelière, Château 471
Capçanes, Celler de
  Montsant Cabrida 472
Capezzana, Villa di
  Carmignano 472
Capichera *Vermentino di Gallura
  Vendemmia Tardiva* 153
Caprai, Arnaldo *Sagrantino di
  Montefalco* 473
Cascina Corte
  *Dolcetto di Dogliani Vigna
  Pirochetta* 476
Castelluccio *Ronco dei
  Ciliegi* 480

Castillo de Perelada
Gran Claustro 481
Cauhapé, Domaine Quintessence du
Petit Manseng 155
Cavalleri
Brut Satèn Blanc de Blancs
Franciacorta 38
Cavallotto
Barolo Riserva Bricco Boschis
Vigna San Giuseppe 482
Ca'Viola Bric du Luv 468
Cayron, Domaine du
Gigondas 483
Cazals, Claude Clos Cazals 40
Cèdre, Château du Le
Cèdre 484
Chappellet Signature Cabernet
Sauvignon 486
Chateau Montelena
Chardonnay 159
Chevalier, Domaine de 488
Chimney Rock
Stags Leap Cabernet Sauvignon
Reserve 491
Chivite Blanco Fermentado en
Barrica Colección 163
Christmann Königsbacher Idig
Riesling Grosses Gewächs 163
Christoffel
Ürziger Würzgarten Riesling
Auslese 164
Chryseia 491
Clonakilla Shiraz/Viognier 493
Clos de la Coulée de Serrant
Savennières 169
Clos Mogador 496
Clos Naudin, Domaine du
Vouvray Goutte d'Or 170
Clos des Papes 495
Coates & Seely Rosé 42
Coldstream Hills
Reserve Pinot Noir 498
Colet–Navazos Extra Brut 44
Collard, René
Cuvée Réservée Brut 45
Concha y Toro Don Melchor 502
Conseillante, Château La 502
Conterno Fantino
Barolo Parussi 505
Còntini, Attilio
Antico Gregori 173

Coppo
Barbera d'Asti Pomorosso 506
Coriole Lloyd Reserve Shiraz 506
Cos d'Estournel, Château 509
Costanti, Andrea
Brunello di Montalcino 509
Cotat François
Sancerre La Grande Côte 174
Couly-Dutheil
Chinon Clos de l'Echo 510
Coutet, Château Sauternes 174
Craggy Range
Syrah Block 14 Gimblett
Gravels Vineyard 511
Crochet, Lucien
Sancerre Cuvée Prestige 176
Croft Vintage Port 863
Cuomo, Marisa
Costi d'Amalfi Furore Bianco
Fiorduva 176
CVNE
Real De Asúa Rioja Reserva 514
Dampierre, Comte Audoin de
Family Reserve GC Blanc
de Blancs 45
De Bartoli Vecchio Samperi
Ventennale Marsala 864
De Meric Cuvée Catherine 47
De Sousa
Cuvée des Caudalies 47
De Trafford Elevation 518
Deiss, Domaine Marcel
Altenberg de Bergheim 182
Delamotte Blanc des Blancs 48
Delgado Zuleta
Quo Vadis? Amontillado
Sherry 866
DeLille Cellars Chaleur Estate 518
Diel, Schlossgut Dorsheimer
Goldloch Riesling Spätlese 182
Doisy-Daëne, Château 185
Domaine A
Cabernet Sauvignon 522
Domaine de l'A 522
Dow's
Quinta Senhora da Ribeira
Single Quinta Port 868
Droin, Domaine
Chablis Grand Cru Le Clos 188
Drouhin, Domaine Oregon Pinot
Noir Cuvée Laurène 523

Dry River
Pinot Gris 190
Pinot Noir 526
Duas Quintas Reserva Especial 528
Durfort-Vivens, Château 536
El Maestro Sierra
1830 Amontillado VORS
Sherry 871
Esmonin, Domaine Sylvie Gevrey-
Chambertin VV 540
Feiler-Artinger
Ruster Ausbruch Pinot
Cuvée 198
Felton Road
Block 3 Pinot Noir 549
Feudi di San Gregorio
Fiano di Avellino 202
Fiddlehead
Lollapalooza Pinot Noir 549
Figeac, Château 550
Filhot, Château 204
Finca Sandoval 551
Flowers
Camp Meeting Ridge
Chardonnay 208
Sonoma Coast Pinot Noir 551
Fonseca, José Maria da
Serúbal Moscatel Roxo
20 Years 875
Freemark Abbey
Sycamore Cabernet
Sauvignon 554
Frog's Leap Rutherford 554
Fromm Winery
Clayvin Vineyard Pinot Noir 556
Fucci, Elena
Aglianico del Vulture Titolo 556
Fuissé, Château de Le Clos 212
Gago Pago La Jara 557
Ganevat, Jean-François Les Grands
Teppes Vieilles Vignes 213
Gazin, Château 561
Cave Geisse Terroir Nature 60
Germanier, Jean-René
Cayas Syrah du Valais
Réserve 561
Giaconda Chardonnay 213
Warner Vineyard Shiraz 564
Goldwater Goldie 568
Gourt de Mautens, Domaine
Rasteau Blanc 214

Graham's
  Malvedos Single Quinta Port 881
  The Stone Terraces
  Vintage Port 881
Graillot, Alain
  Crozes-Hermitage 573
Grand-Puy-Lacoste, Château 574
Grange des Pères 576
Gratien & Meyer
  Cuvée Flamme Brut 71
Gravner, Josko *Breg* 216
Grgić, Miljenko *Plavac Mali* 578
Gruaud-Larose, Château 581
GS *Cabernet* 581
Guelbenzu, Bodegas
  Lautus Navarra 582
Guffens-Heynen, Domaine
  Pouilly-Fuissé La Roche 220
Guiraud, Château 220
Gutiérrez Colosía
  Palo Cortado Viehísimo
  Sherry 882
Hacienda Monasterio
  Ribera del Duero Reserva 583
Hamilton Russell *Chardonnay* 226
Hanzell *Chardonnay* 228
Hardys *Eileen Hardy Shiraz* 584
Haut-Bailly, Château 588
Haut-Marbuzet, Château 592
Heidsieck, Charles
  Brut Réserve Mis en Cave 71
Herdade de Mouchão 594
Herzog *Montepulciano* 595
Hirsch Vineyards *Pinot Noir* 595
Hirtzberger
  Singerriedel Riesling
  Smaragd 236
Jacquesson *Cuvée 730* 77
Jade Mountain
  Paras Vineyard Syrah 598
Jasper Hill
  Emily's Paddock Shiraz 598
Josmeyer
  Grand Cru Hengst Riesling 244
Kanonkop
  Paul Sauer 601
Karthäuserhof
  Eitelsbacher Karthäuserhofberg
  Riesling ALG 246
Katnook Estate
  Odyssey Cabernet Sauvignon 602

Kefraya, Château *Comte de M* 604
Knoll
  Kellerberg Riesling Smaragd 253
Kreydenweiss, Marc *Les Charmes*
  Gewurztraminer 258
Ksara, Château
  Cuvée du Troisième
  Millénaire 608
Kumeu River
  Mate's Vineyard Chardonnay 258
La Dominique, Château 611
La Monacesca
  Verdicchio di Matelica Riserva
  Mirum 263
La Rectorie, Domaine de
  Cuvée Leon Parcé Banyuls 886
Labet, Domaine
  Côtes du Jura Vin de Paille 264
Lafaurie-Peyraguey, Château 266
Lagrange, Château 621
Lake's Folly *Chardonnay* 269
Landmark
  Kastania Vineyard Sonoma
  Pinot Noir 624
Langlois Château
  Crémant de Loire Brut 84
Lassaigne, Jacques *Les Vignes de*
  Montgueux Blanc de Blancs 86
Laroche, Domaine *Réserve de*
  l'Obédience 270
Le Due Terre *Sacrisassi* 629
L'Ecole No. 41
  Walla Walla Seven Hills Vineyard
  Syrah 634
Le Macchiole *Paleo Rosso* 629
Leonetti Cellars *Merlot* 637
Léoville-Poyferré, Château 640
Lisini *Brunello di Montalcino*
  Ugolaia 644
Loosen, Dr.
  Ürzinger Würzgarten Riesling
  Auslese Goldkapsel 279
Luque, M. Gil
  De Bandera Palo Cortado
  VORS Sherry 887
Macle, Jean *Château-Chalon* 280
Maculan *Torcolato* 282
Majella
  Malleea Cabernet/Shiraz 648
Malartic-Lagravière, Château 284
Malle, Château de 284

Malvirà
  Roeo Superiore Mombeltrano 649
Marcarini *Barolo Brunate* 649
Marcassin *Chardonnay* 286
Martínez-Bujanda *Finca Valpiedra*
  Rioja Reserva 653
Mas Amiel *Maury* 891
Mas Blanc *La Coume Banyuls* 892
Mas de Daumas Gassac 654
Mas Doix
  Costers de Vinyes Velles 654
Mas Martinet
  Clos Martinet Priorat 655
Más Que Vinos
  Más Que Vinos 655
Mascarello, Giuseppe
  Barolo Monprivato 656
Mastroberardino
  Taurasi Riserva Radici 659
Maurodos *San Román Toro* 661
Maximin Grünhauser *Abtsberg*
  Riesling Auslese 293
Mayr, Josephus
  Maso Unterganzner
  Lamarein 662
Meerlust *Rubicon* 664
Mellot, Alphonse
  Sancerre Cuvée Edmond 294
Melton, Charles *Nine Popes* 666
Mercier, Denis *Cornalin* 669
Michael, Peter *L'Après-Midi*
  Sauvignon Blanc 296
Mitchelton *Airstrip Marsanne*
  Roussanne Viognier 300
Molettieri, Salvatore
  Taurasi Riserva Vigna Cinque
  Querce 672
Mondavi, Robert
  Fumé Blanc I Block Reserve 301
Montille, Domaine Hubert de
  Volnay PC Les Taillepieds 680
Montus, Château *Cuvée Prestige* 682
Moris Farms *Avvoltore* 684
Morris Wines
  Old Premium Liqueur Tokay 895
Moro, Emilio
  Malleolus 687
Moss Wood
  Cabernet Sauvignon 687
Moulin-à-Vent, Château du
  Croix des Vérillats 688

Mount Difficulty
  Long Gully Pinot Noir 688
Mount Langi Ghiran *Shiraz* 691
Mount Mary *Quintet Cabernet* 691
Mountadam *Chardonnay* 305
Moutard *Cuvée des 6 Cépages* 91
Muga *Prado Enea Gran Reserva*
  Rioja 693
Mullineux Family Wines
  Schist Syrah 695
Mumm *De Cramant* 92
Muré, René *Pinot Noir Cuvée "V"* 695
Musar, Château 696
Nairac, Château 308
Nardello, Daniele
  Recioto di Soave Suavissimus 308
Négly, Château de la
  La Porte du Ciel 698
Neudorf *Moutere Chardonnay* 309
Niepoort
  30 Year Old Tawny Port 896
  Batuta 700 *Charme* 702
  Colheita 895
  Redoma Branco Reserva 310
  Vintage Port 896
Nigl *Riesling Privat* 311
Nikolaihof
  Vom Stein Riesling Smaragd 311
Nyetimber
  Tillington Single Vineyard 95
Ojai Vineyard *Thompson Syrah* 703
Ordoñez, Jorge, & Co *No. 3* 313
Ostertag, André
  Muenchberg Grand Cru
  Riesling 315
Pacenti, Siro
  Brunello di Montalcino 706
Palacios, Descendientes de J.
  Corullón 709
Palari *Faro* 710
Parker *Coonawarra Estate Terra*
  Rossa First Growth 714
Paternina
  Fino Imperial Amontillado
  VORS Sherry 903
Paternoster
  Aglianico del Vulture Don
  Anselmo 717
Pato, Filipa *Nossa Tinto Calcario* 717
Pato, Luís *Quinto do Ribeirinho Pé*
  Franco Bairrada 718

Pavie-Macquin, Château 720
Pazo de Señoras
  Albariño Selección de Añada 317
Peay Vineyards *Pinot Noir* 723
Pelissero, Giorgio
  Barbaresco Vanuto 723
Pellé, Domaine Henry
  Menetou-Salon Clos des
  Blanchais 317
Perret, André *Condrieu Chéry* 319
Petit-Village, Château 729
Pez, Château de 732
Pichler, F.X.
  Grüner Veltliner Smaragd M 320
Pieropan *Vigneto La Rocca* 323
Pierro *Chardonnay* 324
Pinard, Vincent *Harmonie* 325
Plageoles, Robert & Bernard
  Gaillac Vin d'Autan 326
Pol Roger *Blanc de Blancs* 101
Poliziano *Vino Nobile di*
  Montepulciano Asinone 739
Ponsot, Domaine
  Moray St.-Denis PC 327
Pontet-Canet, Château 740
Prager
  Achleiten Riesling Smaragd 328
Prévost, Jérôme
  La Closerie Cuvée
  Les Béguines 104
Prieuré de St.-Jean de Bébian
  Mondeuse Prestige 743
Prieuré St.-Christophe,
  Domaine 743
Produttori del Barbaresco
  Barbaresco Riserva Rabajà 745
Providence, Château La 745
Puffeney, Jacques
  Arbois Vin Jaune 329
Querciabella, Agricola
  Chianti Classico 747
Quinta das Bágeiras *Espumante*
  Grande Reserva 106
Qupé *20th Anniversary Syrah* 753
Rabaud-Promis, Château 332
Radio-Coteau
  Cherry Camp Syrah 753
Ramey Hyde Vineyard
  Carneros Chardonnay 334
Ramos Pinto
  20 Year Old Tawny Port 913

Ravenswood *County Old Hill*
  Vineyard Zinfandel 756
Rayne-Vigneau, Château 335
Rebholz, Ökonomierat
  Birkweiler Kastanienbusch
  Riesling Spätlese Trocken
  Grosses Gewächs 336
Remírez de Ganuza
  Tioja Reserva 758
Rey Fernando de Castilla
  Antique Palo Cortado Sherry 913
Riessec, Château 341
Rippon *Pinot Noir* 761
Roc de Cambes, Château 761
Rochioli, J.
  West Block Pinot Noir 762
Rockford *Basket Press Shiraz* 762
Rodríguez, Telmo
  Molino Real Mountain Wine 343
Rollin, Domaine
  Pernand-Vergelesses PC
  Ile-des-Vergelesses 763
Rolly-Gassmann
  Muscat Moenchreben 344
  Riesling de Rorschwihr Cuvée
  Yves 344
Rosa, Quinta de la
  Vale do Inferno Vintage Port 914
Roulot, Domaine *Meursault Tessons*
  Le Clos de Mon Plaisir 347
Rust en Vrede *Estate Wine* 771
Sadie Family
  Columella 772
  Palladius 350
San Vicente 775
Sánchez Ayala
  Navazos Amontillado Sherry 917
Sánchez Romate
  La Sacristía de Romate Oloroso
  VORS Sherry 917
Santadi
  Terre Brune Carignano
  del Sulcis 777
Satta, Michele *Piastraia* 778
Sauer
  Escherndorfer Lump Silvaner
  TBA 351
Schiopetto *Pinot Grigio* 355
Schlumberger
  Gewurztraminer SGN
  Cuvée Anne 359

Schram, J. 111
Schröck, Heidi *Ruster Ausbruch Auf den Flügeln der Morgenröte* 359
Seghesio
Home Ranch Zinfandel 779
Seppelt Great Western
Show Sparkling Shiraz 112
Serafini e Vidotto
Rosso dell'Abazia 780
Shaw + Smith
M3 Chardonnay 362
Simčič, Edi *Sauvignon Blanc* 363
Smith Woodhouse
Vintage Port 920
Sociando-Mallet, Château 784
Sot *Lefriec* 787
Stony Hill *Chardonnay* 368
Stonyridge *Larose* 791
Suduiraut, Château 370
Swan, Joseph
Stellwagen Vineyard Zinfandel 791
Taille aux Loups, Domaine de la
Romulus Plus 376
Talbot, Château 792
Tapanappa Whalebone Vineyard
Cabernet/Shiraz 794
Tarlant *Cuvée Louis* 117
Te Mata *Coleraine* 798
Te Motu *Cabernet/Merlot* 800
Tenuta di Valgiano
Rosso Colline Lucchesi 802
Tenuta delle Terre Nere *Etna Rosso Feudo di Mezzo* 802
Tenuta San Leonardo
San Leonardo 803
Tenuta Sette Ponti
Crognolo 804
Terlano, Cantina di
Sauvignon Blanc Quarz 377
Terrazas/Cheval Blanc
Cheval des Andes 804
Thelema *Merlot Reserve* 808
Thévenet, Jean
Domaine de la BonGran Cuvée EJ Thévenet 378
Tirecul, Château
La Gravière Cuvée Madame 379
Torelló, Agustí *Kripta* 117
Tour Vieille, Domaine La
Cuvée Puig Oriol 813

Tour Blanche, Château La
Sauternes 382
Traeger, David *Verdelho* 384
Trinity Hill *Homage Syrah* 816
Troplong-Mondot, Château 818
Tschida, Angerhof
Trockenbeerenauslese Sämling 387
Turkey Flat *Shiraz* 822
Turley Wine Cellars
Dragon Vineyard Zinfandel 823
Umathum *Zweigelt Hallebühl* 823
Valdipiatta
Vino Nobile di Montepulciano Vigna d'Alfiero 826
Valentini
di Montepulciano d'Abruzzo 826
Vall Llach 828
Valtuille *Cep Centenarias* 828
Vasse Felix
Heytesbury Cabernet Sauvignon 829
Vega de Toro *Numanthia* 830
Venus *La Universal* 832
Vergelegen 832
Vernay, Georges
Coteaux de Vernon 393
Vesúvio, Quinta do *Vintage Port* 931
Veuve Fourny *Cuvée du Clos Faubourg Notre Dame* 120
Vieux Télégraphe, Domaine du
Châteauneuf-du-Pape 835
Vigneti Massa
Timorasso Costa del Vento 394
Villa Ponciago *Fleurie Les Hauts de Py* 835
Villaine, Domaine A. et P. de
Bouzeron 394
Viñedos Orgánicos Emiliana
Coyam 836
Volxem, Weingut van
Scharzhofberger Pergentsknopp Riesling 390
Wendouree *Shiraz* 838
Williams & Humbert
Dos Cortados Palo Cortado VOS Sherry 932
Williams Selyem
Rochioli Vineyard Pinot Noir 841
Wittmann, Weingut
Westhofener Morstein Riesling Trocken 402

Wynn's
Coonawarra Estate John Riddoch Cabernet Sauvignon 842
Yacochuya de Michel Rolland 844
Yalumba *The Octavius* 844
The Virgilius Viognier 404
Yarra Yering *Dry Red No. 1 Shiraz* 845
Yerro, Alonso del *María* 845

ⓢⓢⓢⓢ
D'Arenberg *Dead Arm Shiraz* 517
Allende *Aurus* 417
Altare, Elio *Barolo* 418
Alvear *Pedro Ximénez 1830 Solera Montilla* 851
Angerville, Domaine Marquis d'
Volnay PC Clos des Ducs 420
Antinori *Solaia* 423
Artadi *Viña El Pisón* 430
Banfi *Brunello di Montalcino Poggio all'Oro* 439
Bass Phillip *Premium Pinot Noir* 441
Beaucastel, Château de
Châteauneuf-du-Pape Roussanne 135
Beaulieu Vineyards *Georges de Latour Cabernet Sauvignon* 443
Beau-Séjour Bécot, Château 444
Bélair-Monange, Château 446
Beringer *Private Reserve Cabernet Sauvignon* 447
Billecart-Salmon *Cuvée Nicolas François Billecart* 28
Billiot, Henri *Cuvée Laetitia* 28
Boillot, Domaine Jean-Marc *Puligny-Montrachet PC La Truffière* 138
Bon Pasteur, Château Le 452
Bonneau du Martray, Domaine
Corton-Charlemagne GC 141
Bouchard Père & Fils
Clos de Vougeot Grand Cru 458
Bouchard Père et Fils *Corton-Charlemagne Grand Cru* 146
Branaire-Ducru, Château 462
Bussaco Palace Hotel *Buçaco Branco Reservado* 151
Cà del Bosco
Annamaria Clementi 36
Calon-Ségur, Château 468
Castello di Ama *Chianti Classico Vigneto Bellavista* 480

Cathiard, Domaine Sylvain
  Romanée-St.-Vivant GC 482
Cattier Clos du Moulin 38
Chamirey, Château de Mercurey
  Premier Cru Les Cinq 483
Chapoutier, Domaine
  Ermitage Vin de Paille 159
Chevalier, Domaine de 162
Clerico, Domenico
  Barolo Percristina 492
Clos de Tart 494
Clos Erasmus 495
Cockburn's Vintage Port 862
Concha y Toro Almaviva 502
Contino Viña del Olivo 505
Corison Cabernet Sauvignon
  Kronos Vineyard 507
Correggia, Matteo
  Roero Ròche d'Ampsèj 507
Costers del Siurana
  Clos de l'Obac Priorat 510
CVNE Corona
  Reserva Blanco Semi Dulce 178
Darviot-Perrin, Domaine
  Chassagne-Montrachet PC
  Blanchots-Dessus 180
Dauvissat, Domaine René & Vincent
  Chablis GC Le Clos 180
De Bortoli Noble One 181
Dettori, Azienda Agricola
  Cannonau Dettori Romangia 520
Deutz Cuvée William Deutz 51
Diamond Creek Vineyards
  Gravelly Meadow 520
Diebolt-Vallois Fleur de Passion 51
Disznókő Tokaji Aszú 6 Puttonyos 185
Dom Pérignon 52
Dominus 523
Drappier Grande Sendée 59
Drouhin, Joseph
  Beaune PC Clos des Mouches 189
Druet, Pierre-Jacques
  Bourgueil Vaumoreau 524
Duckhorn Vineyards
  Three Palms Merlot 532
Ducru-Beaucaillou, Château 532
Eglise-Clinet, Château L' 536
Egly-Ouriet
  Les Crayères Blanc de Noirs Vieilles
  Vignes 59
Els, Ernie 539

Equipo Navazos La Bota de
  Manzanilla No.50 Bota Punta 872
Evangile, Château L' 540
Far Niente Cabernet Sauvignon 546
Fattoria La Massa Chianti Classico
  Giorgio Primo 548
Fèlsina Berardenga
  Chianti Classico Riserva Rancia
  548
Fèvre, William
  Chablis GC Bougros Côte
  Bouguerots 202
Fiorano Semillon Vino da Tavola 207
Fontodi Flaccianello delle Pieve 552
Foradori Granato 552
Gaia Estate Agiorghitiko 557
Gauby, Domaine
  Côtes de Roussillon Villages
  Rouge Muntada 559
Gimonnet, Pierre
  Millésime de Collection Blanc
  des Blancs 62
Gonzáles Byass Cuatro Palmas
  Amontillado Sherry 878
Gosset Célébris 68
Gouges, Domaine Henri
  Nuits-St.-Georges PC Les
  St.-Georges 569
Grasso, Elio Barolo Runcot 576
Grasso, Silvio
  Barolo Bricco Luciani 577
Gratien, Alfred 70
Grattamacco 577
Grillet, Château
  Cuvée Renaissance 216
Gróf Dégenfeld
  Tokaji Aszú 6 Puttonyos 219
Gunderloch Nackenheimer
  Rothenberg Riesling 224
Haag, Fritz
  Brauneberger Juffer-Sonnenuhr
  Riesling ALG #15 224
Henriot Cuvée des Enchanteleurs 72
Hétsölö Tokaji Aszú 6 Puttonyos 233
Hidalgo-La Gitana Palo Cortado Viejo
  VORS Sherry 885
Huet, Domaine Vouvray Brut 72
Inniskillin Okanagan Valley
  Vidal Icewine 240
Isole e Olena
  Cepparello Toscana IGT 596

Izadi, Viña Rioja Expresión 597
Jobard, Domaine François
  Meursault PC Les Poruzots 244
Keller, Weingut
  Riesling Trocken G Max 249
Kesselstatt, Reichsgraf von
  Josephshöfer Riesling
  AG 249
Kistler Chardonnay 252
Klein Constantia
  Vin de Constance 252
Koehler-Ruprecht, Weingut
  Kallstadter Saumagen Riesling
  Auslese Trocken "R" 254
Kracher Nouvelle Vague
  Welschriesling 256
Krug Grande Cuvée 83
La Gomerie, Château 613
La Jota 20th Anniversary 613
La Rioja Alta
  Rioja Gran Reserva 890 616
La Spinetta
  Barbaresco Vigneto Starderi 616
Lafarge, Domaine Michel
  Volnay PC Clos des Chênes 617
Lafon, Domaine des Comtes Volnay
  PC Santenots-du-Milieu 618
Lambrays, Domaine des
  Clos des Lambrays 624
Larmandier-Bernier
  Cramant GC Extra Brut 86
Laurent-Perrier
  Grand Siècle La Cuvée 88
Leacock's Sercial Madeira 887
Leeuwin Estate
  Art Series Chardonnay 271
Léoville-Barton, Château 638
Liger-Belair, Domaine du Comte
  Clos des Grandes Vignes 274
Littorai Wines
  The Haven Pinot Noir 646
Livio Felluga Picolit 198
Long-Depaquit, Domaine
  Chablis GC La Moutonne 277
López de Heredia
  Viña Tondonia 279
Magdelaine, Château 648
Margaux, Château
  Pavillon Blanc 289
Marionnet, Henri Provignage
  Romorantin Vin de Pays 289

Marqués de Murrieta
  *Castiloo Ygay Rioja GR
  Especial* 652
Marqués del Real Tesoro
  *Covadonga Oloroso
  VORS Sherry* 891
Maume, Domaine
  Chambertin GC 660
Mauro
  Terreus Pago de Cueva Baja 660
Mayacamas
  Cabernet Sauvignon 661
Meyer-Näkel
  *Dernau Pfarrwingert
  Spätburgunder ATG* 670
Miana *Tocai* 296
Michael, Peter, Winery
  Les Pavots 671
Mission Hill
  S.L.C. Riesling Icewine 300
Moccagatta
  Barbaresco Basarin 671
Montelena, Château
  Cabernet Sauvignon 675
Montes *Folly* 676
Montevetrano 679
Moric *Lutzmannsburg Blaufränkisch
  Alte Reben* 683
Mount Eden *Chardonnay* 301
Mumm *Cuvée R. Lalou* 92
Murana, Salvatore *Passito di
  Pantellaria Martingana* 307
Muré, René *Vorbourg Grand Cru
  Clos St.-Landelin Riesling* 307
Nada, Fiorenzo
  Barbaresco Rombone 698
Negri, Nino *Sfursat 5 Stelle* 699
Noemía de Patagonia *Noemía* 702
Noval, Quinta do *Vintage Port* 898
Oberto, Andrea *Barbera Giada* 703
Opitz, Willi *Optiz One* 704
Oremus *Tokaji Aszú 6 Puttonyos* 314
Osborne
  *Pedro Ximénez Viejo VORS
  Sherry* 902
  *Solera PΔP Palo Cortado
  Sherry* 903
Pagos de los Capellanes *El Picón
  Ribera del Duero* 706
Paitin *Barbaresco Sorè Paitin* 707
Pape-Clément, Château 712

Parusso *Barolo Bussia* 716
Pellegrino, Carlo
  Marsala Vergine Vintage 904
Pesquera, Tinto
  Janus Gran Reserva 726
Peters, Pierre
  *Cuvée Speciale Grand Cru
  Blanc de Blancs* 98
Phelps, Joseph *Insignia* 734
Pichon-Longueville, Château 735
Pieve di Santa Restituta
  *Brunello di Montalcini
  Sugarille* 737
Podere *Salicutti Brunello di
  Montalcino Piaggione* 738
Pol Roger
  Cuvée Sir Winston Churchill 101
Pommery *Cuvée Louise* 103
Pride Mountain
  Reserve Cabernet Sauvignon 742
Prieler *Blaufränkisch Goldberg* 742
Quilceda Creek
  Cabernet Sauvignon 748
Quintessa 752
Rauzan-Ségla, Château 754
Raveneau, Domaine
  *Chablis PC Montée de
  Tonnerre* 335
Remy, Louis
  Latricières-Chambertin 759
Ridge *Monte Bello* 759
Rinaldi, Giuseppe
  Barolo Brunate-Le Coste 760
Roda, Bodegas *Rioja Cirsión* 763
Rostaing, René
  Côte-Rôtie La Landonne 766
Royal Tokaji Wine Co. *Mézes Mály
  Tokaji Aszú 6 Puttonyos* 348
Salvioni *Brunello di Montalcino* 774
Sandeman
  40 Year Old Tawny Port 918
Sandrone, Luciano
  Barolo Cannubi Boschis 775
Santa Rita, Viña *Casa Real Cabernet
  Sauvignon* 776
Schloss Gobelsburg
  Ried Lamm Grüner Veltliner 355
Schloss Lieser *Lieser Nederberg
  Helden Riesling Auslese Gold* 356
Sekthaus Raumland
  MonRose Brut 106

Selbach-Oster *Zeltinger Schlossberg
  Riesling Auslese Schmitt* 360
Selosse, Jacques
  Cuvée Substance 112
Smith-Haut-Lafitte, Château
  Pessac-Léognan 363
Stanton & Killeen *Rare Muscat* 920
Tasca d'Almerita
  Rosso del Conte 796
Taylor's *Vintage Port* 924
Tempier, Domaine
  Bandol Cuvée Cabassaou 800
Terlano, Cantina di
  Chardonnay Rarità 377
Tertre-Roteboeuf, Château 807
Thackrey, Sean *Orion* 808
Torres *Gran Coronas Mas La
  Plana* 813
Trévallon, Domaine de
  *Vin de Table des Bouches du
  Rhône* 814
Trimbach
  Clos Ste.-Hune Riesling 387
Vajra, Azienda Agricola G.D.
  Barolo Bricco delle Viole 824
Valdespino
  *Cardenal Palo Cortado VORS
  Sherry* 926
  *Coliseo Amontillado VORS
  Sherry* 927
Valentini *Trebbiano d'Arbruzzo* 389
Vecchie Terre di Montefili
  Bruno di Rocca 829
Vieux Château Certan 834
Vollenweider *Wolfer Goldgrube
  Riesling ALG* 397
Weinbach, Domaine
  Cuvée Théo Gewurztraminer 400
  Schlossberg GC Riesling 400
Wild Duck Creek *Duck Muck* 841
Zerbina, Fattoria *Sangiovese di
  Romagna Pietramora* 846
Zind-Humbrecht, Domaine
  Clos Jebsal Pinot Gris 406
  Rangel Clos St-Urbain Riesling 408

$ $ $ $ $
Aalto, Bodegas *PS* 412
Angélus, Château 419
Araujo *Eisele State Vineyard* 427
Ausone, Château 436

Auvenay, Domaine d'
    Chevalier-Montrachet 129
Avignonesi *Occio di Pernice Vin
    Santo di Montepulciano* 131
Bachelet, Domaine Denis
    Charmes-Chambertin GC 438
Barbeito *Terrantez Madeira* 854
Barca Velha 440
Beaucastel, Château de
    Hommage à Jacques Perrin 442
Beauséjour Duffau-Lagarrosse 443
Billecart-Salmon *Clos S.-Hilaire* 26
Biondi Santi
    *Tenuta Greppo Brunello
    di Montalcino DOCG Riserva* 448
Blandy's *1863 Bual Madeira* 857
Bollinger *R.D. 32 Vieilles Vignes* 35
Bonneau, Henri *Châteauneuf-du-
    Pape Reserve des Célestins* 454
Bouchard, Cédric *Le Creux d'Enfer* 35
Busch, Clemens *Pünderichter
    Marienburg Riesling* 151
Bussola, Tommaso *Recioto della
    Valpolicella Classico* 467
Carillon, Domaine *Bienvenues-
    Bâtard-Montrachet GC* 154
Carnasciale, Podere Il *Il Caberlot* 473
Castello dei Rampolla
    Vigna d'Alceo 477
Castello del Terriccio *Lupicaia* 478
Chambers
    Rosewood Old Liqueur Tokay 860
Champalou, Didier et Catherine
    Vouvray Cuvée CC Moelleux 157
Chapoutier, Domaine
    Ermitage L'Ermite Blanc 158
    Ermitage Vin de Paille 159
Chapoutier, M. *Châteauneuf-du-
    Pape, Barbe Rac* 484
    Ermitage Le Pavillon 486
Chave, Domaine
    Hermitage Cuvée Cathelin 487
Chave, Domaine J.-L.
    Hermitage Blanc 161
Cheval Blanc, Château 487
Clape, Domaine Auguste *Cornas* 492
Climens, Château 166
Coche-Dury, Domaine
    Corton-Charlemagne GC 172
Colgin Cellars *Herb Lamb Vineyard
    Cabernet Sauvignon* 501

Contador 504
Conterno, Giacomo
    Barolo Monfortino Riserva 504
Cossart Gordon
    Malmsey Madeira 862
    Verdelho Madeira 863
Dal Forno, Romano
    Amarone della Valpolicella 516
Dalla Valle *Maya* 516
Dom Pérignon *Rosé* 54
Dom Ruinart 56 *Rosé* 57
Dönnhoff, Hermann
    Oberhäuser Brücke Riesling AG 188
Dow's
    1908 Vintage Port 868
Drouhin, Domaine Joseph
    Musigny Grand Cru 524
Drouhin, Joseph/Marquis de
    Laguiche *Montrachet* 189
Dugat, Domaine Claude
    Griottes-Chambertin GC 534
Dugat-Pÿ, Domaine *Mazis-
    Chambertin Grand Cru* 534
Dujac, Domaine
    *Gevrey-Chambertin
    PC Aux Combottes* 535
Dunn Vineyards
    *Howell Mountain Cabernet
    Sauvignon* 535
Emrich-Schönleber *Monzinger
    Halenberg Riesling Eiswein* 197
Engel, Domaine René *Clos de
    Vougeot Grand Cru* 539
Eyrie Vineyards *South Block
    Reserve Pinot Noir* 542
Faiveley, Domaine *Chambertin-
    Clos de Bèze Les Ouvrées Rodin* 544
Fargues, Château de *Sauternes* 197
Ferrari, Giulio
    Riserva del Fondatore 60
Fonseca *Vintage Port* 875
Fourrier, Domaine Jean-Claude
    Charmes-Chambertin GC 553
Gaja *Barbaresco* 558
Giacosa, Bruno *Asili di Barbaresco* 564
Gilette, Château *Crème de Tête* 214
Giraud, Henri *Cru Aÿ Fût de Chêne* 64
Giscours, Château 566
Gosset *Cuvée Célébris Blanc* 68
Grace Family
    Cabernet Sauvignon 570

Graham's *Vintage Port* 882
Grans-Fassian
    Leiwener Riesling Eiswein 215
Greenock Creek
    Roenenfeldt Road Shiraz 578
Grivot, Domaine Jean
    Richebourg Grand Cru 579
Gros, Domaine Anne
    Richebourg 579
Guigal *Côte-Rôtie La Mouline* 582
Harlan Estate
    Proprietary Red Wine 586
Haut-Brion, Château 590
    Blanc 230
Heitz Wine Cellars *Martha's Vineyard
    Cabernet Sauvignon* 592
Henriques & Henriques
    W.S. Boal Madeira 883
Henschke *Hill of Grace* 593
Herdade de Cartuxa *Pera Manca* 593
Heymann-Löwenstein
    Riesling Gaisberg 235
Hidalgo, Emilio
    *1860 Privilegio Palo Cortado VORS
    Sherry* 884
    *1861 Santa Ana Pedro Ximénez
    VORS Sherry* 884
Hosanna, Château 596
Hövel, Weingut von
    Oberemmeler Hütte Riesling 236
Huet, Domaine
    Le Haut Lieu Moelleux 237
Hugel *Riesling Sélection de
    Grains Nobles* 239
Jaboulet Aîné, Paul
    Hermitage La Chapelle 597
Jacquesson
    Grand Cru Aÿ Vauzelle Terme 77
Jayer, Domaine Henri *Vosne-
    Romanée PC Cros Parentoux* 599
Kloster Eberbach Assmannshäuser,
    Staatsweingüter *Höllenberg
    Spätburgunder Cabinet* 606
    Steinburger Riesling 253
Krug
    Clos d'Ambonnay 78
    Clos du Mesnil 81
    Collection 82
La Fleur-Pétrus, Château 611
La Mission-Haut-Brion, Château 615
La Mondote 615

Lafite Rothschild, Château 617
Lafleur, Château 618
Lafon, Domaine des Comtes
    Le Montrachet Grand Cru 269
    Meursault PC Genevrières 268
Lagrézette, Château
    Cuvée Pigeonnier 621
Lamarche, Domaine
    La Grande Rue GC 622
Latour, Château 626
Latour-à-Pomerol, Château 628
Laville Haut-Brion, Château 270
Le Dôme 628
Le Pin 631
Le Soula *Vin de Pays de Côtes*
    Catalanes Blanc 271
Leflaive, Domaine *Puligny-*
    Montrachet PC Les Pucelles 273
Léoville-Las Cases, Château 640
Leroy, Domaine *Romanée-St.-Vivant*
    Grand Cru 642
Liger-Belair, Domaine du Vicomte
    La Romanée 644
López de Heredia
    Viña Tondonia Rioja GR 646
Lynch-Bages, Château 647
Margaux, Château 651
Marqués de Riscal
    Rioja RM (Reserva Médoc) 653
Mascarello, Bartolo *Barolo* 656
Massandra Collection
    Ayu Dag Aleatico 898
Méo-Camuzet, Domaine
    Richebourg Grand Cru 669
Miani *Merlot* 670
Mondavi, Robert
    Cabernet Sauvignon Reserve 672
Montevertine *Le Pergole Torte Vino*
    da Tavola 679
Montrose, Château 682
Mordorée, Domaine de la
    Cuvée de la Reine des Bois 683
Mouton Rothschild, Château 693
Mugnier, Domaine Jacques-Frédéric
    Le Musigny 695
Müller, Egon
    Scharzhofberger Riesling
    Auslese 306
Müller-Catoir
    Mussbacher Eselshaut
    Rieslaner 306

Murietta, Marqués de
    Castillo Ygay Blanco Gran
    Reserva 290
Niebaum-Coppola Estate
    Rubicon 699
Noval, Quinta do
    Nacional Vintage Port 900
Opus One 704
Pahlmeyer *Proprietary Red* 707
Palacios, Alvaro *L'Ermita* 709
Palmer, Château 710
Pavie, Château 718
Penfolds *Bin 95 Grange* 724
    50 Year Old Rare Tawny 906
    Bin 707 Cabernet Sauvignon 725
    Block 42 Kalimna Cabernet
    Sauvignon 726
Pérez Barquero
    1905 Amontillado Montilla 906
Perrier-Jouët *La Belle Epoque* 96
Petrolo *Galatrona* 729
Pétrus 730
Philipponnat *Clos des Goisses* 98
Pichon-Longueville, Château
    Comtesse de Lalande 735
Pingus, Dominio del 737
Ponsot, Domaine
    Clos de la Roche Vieilles
    Vignes 739
Prüm, J. J.
    Wehlener Sonnenuhr
    Riesling AG 328
Quintarelli
    Amarone della Valpolicella 752
Ramonet, Domaine
    Bâtard-Montrache GC 334
Rayas, Château 758
Richter, Max Ferd.
    Helenenkloster Riesling
    Eiswein 341
Ringland, Chris *Three Rivers Shiraz* 760
Roederer, Louis *Cristal* 108
Romanée-Conti, Domaine de la
    La Tâche 765–6
    Le Montrachet GC 347
Roumier, Domaine Georges
    Bonnes Mares Grand Cru 767
Rousseau, Domaine Armand
    Chambertin-Clos de Bèze 768
    Gevery-Chambertin Premier Cru Clos
    St.-Jacques 769

Royal Tokaji Wine Co. *Szent Tamás*
    Tokaji Aszú Esszencia 348
Salon 111
Sastre, Viña *Pesus* 777
Sauzet, Domaine Etienne
    Bâtard-Montrachet GC 352
Scavino, Paolo
    Barolo Bric dël Fiasc 778
Schaefer, Willi *Graacher*
    Domprobst Riesling BA 352
Schloss Vollrads *Riesling*
    TBA 356
Screaming Eagle 779
Shafer *Cabernet Sauvignon*
    Hillside Select 780
Soldera *Case Basse Brunello*
    di Montalcino 784
Sorrel, Marc
    Hermitage Le Gréal 786
Stag's Leap Wine Cellars
    Cabernet Sauvignon 787
Szepsy *Tokaji Esszencia* 372
Taittinger
    Comtes de Champagne 114
Taylor's *Quinta de Vargellas*
    Vinha Velha 922
Tenuta dell'Ornellaia
    Masseto IGT Toscana 801
Tenuta di San Guido
    Sassicaia 803
Torbreck *Runrig Shiraz* 810
Trotanoy, Château 820
Tua Rita
    Redigaffi IGT Toscana 822
Valandraud, Château 824
Valdespino *Moscatel Viejísimo*
    Toneles Sherry 928
Vega Sicilia *Único* 830
Verset, Noël *Cornas* 834
Veuve Clicquot
    La Grande Dame 118
    La Grande Dame Rosé 118
Vilmart *Coeur de Cuvée* 120
Voerzio, Roberto
    Barolo Cerequio 838
Weil, Robert
    Kiedricher Gräfenberg Riesling
    TBA G 316 398
Yquem, Château d' 404
Zilliken *Saarburger Rausch*
    Riesling TBA A.P. #2 406

Contributors

Sarah Ahmed (SA) is an independent London-based wine writer, educator, and judge with a particular interest in the wines of Portugal and Australia. She was awarded the Vintners Cup in 2003, the Portuguese Annual Wine Awards'Wine Writer of the Year 2009, and was short-listed for the International Wine & Spirit Competition Communicator of the Year in 2009 and 2010. In addition to publishing thewinedetective.co.uk, she writes for several respected titles.

Katrina Alloway (KA) has written on wine and food with a particular interest in the Loire Valley. When she needs to stretch her legs she does long distance trekking and mountaineering, particularly in the Alps, the Himalayas, and her native Yorkshire.

Jesús Barquin (JB) has loved wine since being given a spoonful of sweet Malaga by his grandmother at the tender age of four. He writes regularly on wine and food matters at Elmundovino.com and *Metrópoli*. He is a professor of criminal law and director of the Institute of Criminology of the University of Granada.

Juan Manuel Bellver (JMB) is Chief Editor of the newspaper *El Mundo*, where he currently directs the weekend magazine *Metrópoli*. He is member of the Academia Española de Gastronomía and Vice President of its Madrid chapter. In 1999, he won the Arzak Gastronomic Journalism Prize and in 2001 he won Spain's National Gastronomy Award, the youngest winner in its history.

Sara Basra (SB) is currently Deputy Editor of *The World of Fine Wine* magazine. She studied Modern History at Oxford, and subsequently worked in the wine trade and as a freelance writer for *Harpers* and *Decanter* magazines. In 2003, she won the Rouyer Guillet Cup as top trade graduate in the Wine & Spirit Education Trust Diploma, as well as the Geoffrey Jameson Memorial award and The Vintners' Scholarship.

Neil Beckett (NB) took a first class honors degree in English and Medieval History (St. Andrews), a doctorate in Medieval History (Magdalen College, Oxford) and a fellowship of the Royal Historical Society (University of London). Always equally interested in wine, he worked at UK shippers Richards Walford and then Lay & Wheeler wine merchants, where he graduated with distinction in the WSET Diploma before going on to *Harpers Wine & Spirit Weekly*, of which he was contributing editor and for which he wrote a regular column. In 2004, he became the first editor of *The World of Fine Wine*. He is one of the two UK tasters on the Grand Jury Européen.

Nicolas Belfrage MW (NBel) is an Anglo-American Master of Wine (vintage 1980) who has made a speciality of Italian wines and is particularly inspired by the great Nebbiolos of Alba. He has written several books on Italian wine.

Stephen Brook (SBr) has won numerous awards for his writing, including the André Simon, Glenfiddich, Lanson, and Veuve Clicquot. He has written several books, including the perennial British obsession with *Class*, and a study of the Salvation Army, *God's Army*. In what spare time is left, he enjoys travel, opera, and theater-going.

Bob Campbell MW (BC) was the second New Zealander to hold the Master of Wine qualification. He is group wine editor of ACP Publications and wine editor of for five magazines within ACP. He contributes to wine publications in seven countries. Since 1986, more than 20,000 people have attended his wine diploma courses in New Zealand, Asia, and Europe.

Clive Coates MW (CC) published *The Vine*, his independent fine wine magazine, for twenty years and has published several books. Prior to being an author, he spent twenty years as a wine merchant, serving as Executive Director of the wines division of British Transport Hotels and establishing the Malmaison Wine Club.

Daniel Duane (DD) holds a Ph.D. in American Literature and is the author of five books, including the novel *A Mouth Like Yours*. He has written about food and wine for *The World of Fine Wine, Bon Appetit, Outside Magazine*, the *Los Angeles Times*, and *Men's Journal*.

Anastasia Edwards (AE) is the Tastings Editor at *The World of Fine Wine* magazine. She has also written about food and food history for several publications, including the *Financial Times*, and has appeared as a food historian on *The Great British Bake-Off*. Her forthcoming book about the history of the Biscuit/Cookie (Reaktion Press) was published in 2014.

Michael Edwards (ME) joined Laytons, the London wine shippers, in 1968. In 1984, Michael became a restaurant critic, rising to be Chief inspector of the Egon Ronay Guides. He is a regular contributor on Champagne and Burgundy to a wide range of publications including *The World of Fine Wine* and *Wine Kingdom* (Japan). In 2005, he was elected *Ambassadeur d'Angleterre* by the *Archiconfrerie St Vincent des Vignerons de Champagne*.

Ken Gargett (KG) was born and bred in Brisbane, Queensland, and studied law at Queensland University. On a break from fishing on the Great Barrier Reef, someone opened a good bottle of Port, and so commenced a serious obsession. Further studies and work followed in London; Washington, D.C.; and Sydney—but a return to Queensland led him to work as a wine writer.

Stuart George (SG) studied English and European Literature at Warwick University and subsequently worked at wine merchants Haynes Hanson & Clark. In 2003 he was awarded the Websters Young Wine Writer of the Year Award. He has worked harvests in Friuli and Provence and traveled extensively in the wine regions of Europe, South Africa, Australia, and New Zealand.

Jamie Goode (JG) did a PhD in plant biology and spent several years working as a book editor. He is now wine correspondent of *The Sunday Express*, in addition to writing regularly for several publications including *The World of Fine Wine, Harpers Wine & Spirit Weekly, Hong Kong Tatler*, and the *Western Mail*. Jamie's first book, *Wine Science*, was published in 2005, and in 2007 he was named Glenfiddich Wine Writer of the Year. His website is www.wineanorak.com

Lisa Granik MW (LGr) works in New York City as a wine consultant and educator. Lisa gained her doctorate from Yale Law

School and was a Fulbright Scholar in Russia until she decided that the wines were better elsewhere. She teaches candidates for the Wine and Spirit Education Trust Advanced Certificate and Diploma in New York.

Luis Gutiérrez (LG) writes and tastes regularly for Elmundovino.com and other *El Mundo* newspaper publications in Spain, and is a columnist for *blueWine* magazine in Portugal. He also contributes to other wine and gastronomy journals in Spain, Puerto Rico, and the UK.

Huon Hooke (HH) is a leading independent wine writer, who makes his living writing, judging, lecturing, and educating about wine. Currently he writes two weekly columns in the *Sydney Morning Herald* "Good Living" section and *Good Weekend* magazine, and regular articles in *Australian Gourmet Traveller Wine* Magazine, for which he is contributing editor.

Tim James (TJ), who lives in Cape Town, has a PhD in English Literature but has never had proper ambitions or a proper job. The latter factors leave him time to write about wine and to edit the quixotic project called *Grape* and the similarly non–advertising and fiercely independent website about Cape wine www.grape.co.za.

Andrew Jefford (AJ) studied English at the University of Reading and pursued postgraduate studies on the short fiction of Robert Louis Stevenson with Malcolm Bradbury at the University of East Anglia. In the 1980s he combined a passion for wine and for writing, and since then has worked as a freelance drinks journalist and broadcaster. He has won a plethora of awards for his work including the 2006 and 2007 Louis Roederer International Wine Writer of the Year.

Hugh Johnson's (HJ) first book, *Wine*, published in 1966, established him as one of the foremost English writers on the subject. In the late 1960s research for *The World Atlas of Wine* took him all over the world; the result was a bestseller, currently on its sixth edition. He was awarded the Order of the British Empire for "services to horticulture and winemaking" in the 2007 New Year's Honors, and is Editorial adviser to *The World of Fine Wine*.

Frank Kämmer MS (FK) has worked for many years as sommelier for the Michelin-stared restaurant Délice in Stuttgart. In 1996 he passed the Master Sommelier Diploma and later became a member of the board of directors of the UK Court of Master Sommeliers. He has published several wines and spirits books. Beside wine, his other great passion is the music of Richard Wagner.

Chandra Kurt (CK) is a freelance wine writer based in Switzerland. She contributes to books and websites by Hugh Johnson, Jancis Robinson, Tom Stevenson, and Stuart Pigott. As a wine consultant she works for Swiss International Airlines and several Swiss retail institutions. Her website is www.chandrakurt.com

Gareth Lawrence (GL) has made many visits to the vineyards of Croatia, Slovenia, and Greece, as well as to other countries in that region. In addition to his work at the WSET London Wine and Spirit School, Gareth has been technical adviser on central and southeastern Europe to numerous publications.

Helen Gabriella Lenarduzzi (HL) owes her love of wine to her Italian upbringing. Born in Como and raised in Lombardy, her affinity with Italy remains strong, despite having moved to England. She is at her happiest when sitting on the terrace at her grandparents' house, with Montasio cheese, San Daniele ham, and unlabeled bottiglione on the table.

Ella Lister (EL) is a full-time wine writer and consultant, the experience she gained as an investment banker at Lazard in London bringing a unique and sophisticated insight to her take on fine-wine investment. She lives in London and was recognized as Emerging Wine Writer of the Year in the 2013 Louis Roederer International Wine Writers' Awards.

John Livingstone-Learmonth (JL-L) is the leading writer on the wines of France's Rhône Valley. This region was little known when he first assembled material for *The Wines of the Rhône* in 1973, now on its third edition. In 2005 the University of California Press published *The Wines of the Northern Rhône*, to be followed by *The Wines of the Southern Rhône*. John has also written on

wines of the Loire, Beaujolais, and Bordeaux, and published articles in UK magazines. He is an Honorary Citizen of the Rhône village of Châteauneuf-du-Pape.

Wink Lorch (WL), a wine writer, educator, and editor divides her time between London and Haute Savoie, France. She writes on Jura and Savoie for Tom Stevenson's annual *Wine Report*. In 2007 she launched www.winetravelguides.com for independent wine travelers, initially covering France.

Giles MacDonogh (GM) was born in London and educated there and in Suffolk before attending university at Oxford and Paris. He began writing about wine more than twenty years ago and is the author of four books on the subject, as well as contributing articles on wine to newspapers and magazines in Britain and abroad.

Patrick Matthews (PM) is a freelance writer and journalist and has contributed to newspapers and magazines including the *Independent*, the *Guardian*, and *Time Out*. His two books on wine, *Real Wine* and *The Wild Bunch: Great Wines from Small Producers*, have both won awards.

Richard Mayson (RM) is one of the world's most respected authorities on Port, Sherry, and Madeira. After working at The Wine Society for five years, he wrote *Portugal's Wines and Winemakers, Port and the Douro*, and *The Story of Dow's Port*. His latest book, *The Wines and Vineyards of Portugal*, won the André Simon Award. He makes wine at the Pedra Basta estate in Alentejo, Portugal.

Jasper Morris MW (JM) became involved in the world of wine while at Oxford University. He founded noted Burgundy experts Morris & Verdin Ltd in 1981. In 2003 Morris & Verdin was sold to Berry Bros & Rudd, for whom Morris is now buying director, based in his home town of Basingstoke. He became a Master of Wine in 1985, is the author of books on White Burgundy, the Loire, and a contributor of Burgundy articles to *The Oxford Companion to Wine*, and was elected Chevalier de l'Ordre du Merite Agricole in 2005.

Bill Nanson (BN) is a chemist by profession, with no connection to the wine trade. For more than eighteen years, he has made frequent visits to Burgundy, where he regularly works the vintage. He publishes the Burgundy-Report website, a respected source of independent comment.

Kerin O'Keefe (KO) graduated with an honors degree in English Literature from the University of Massachusetts in Amherst. In 1989 she moved to Italy and began traveling around the country to meet the winemakers and walk the vineyards. Her first book, *Franco Biondi Santi–The Gentleman of Brunello*, was published in 2005.

Michael Palij MW (MP) was born in Toronto and read English and Philosophy at the University of Toronto before emigrating to the UK in 1989. He founded the independent wine importers Winetraders in 1995. In the same year he became a Master of Wine, winning the J. Sainsbury award for best dissertation in the examination. He lectures for the Wine and Spirit Education Trust and writes for several magazines and books.

Joel B. Payne (JP) was born in the United States but has spent most of his adult life in Europe. After living in France, where he did seven harvests with Marcel Guigal, he finally settled in Germany in 1982. He began writing about wine and has been a regular contributor to both of Germany's leading wine consumer magazines, *Alles–Über–Wein* and *Vinum*, and numerous other publications.

Francis Percival (FP) read history at Christ's College, Cambridge, before embarking on a career in professional food. After stints as a chef and fishmonger, he now dedicates his time to writing on food and gastronomy. He lives in London and was recognized as Columnist of the Year in the 2013 Louis Roederer International Wine Writers' Awards.

Margaret Rand (MR) tried to escape from wine some 15 years ago by running away to edit *Opera Now* magazine but wine reclaimed her and she now writes for several publications, as well as serving as general editor of Mitchell Beazley's *Classic Wine Library*.

Stephan Reinhardt (SR) discovered wine as a student in Munich, where he worked in a wine shop and became a self-confessed "wine maniac." Since 2002 he has worked as a journalist in Hamburg. He was editor of the monthly German/Swiss review *Weinwisser*, contributes regularly to *The World of Fine Wine*, and runs his own website, stephanreinhardt.de.

David Schildknecht (DS), affiliated with Cincinnati, Ohio–based Vintner Select, trained in philosophy and worked as a restaurateur before entering the wine trade. His annual reports from Austria and Germany have appeared in Stephen Tanzer's *International Wine Cellar* and, more recently, in Robert Parker's *Wine Advocate*.

Michael Schuster (MS) is a wine writer and independent lecturer who runs his own wine school in London. He lived and worked in Bordeaux for two years and holds the Tasting Diploma from Bordeaux University. Among his own books is *Essential Winetasting*, which won both the Glenfiddich and Lanson Awards in 2001.

Barry C Smith (BS) is director of the Institute of Philosophy at the School of Advanced Study in the University of London. He has written on philosophy and wine and is the editor of *Questions of Taste: The Philosophy of Wine* and contributed the entry on "Wine and Philosophy" to the third edition of *The Oxford Companion to Wine*.

Godfrey Spence (GS) has been involved in the wine trade since 1983, initially starting in the retail sector in London and Kent. He is the author of the *Port Companion* (Apple Press) and is a Cavaleiro do Confraria do Vinho do Porto. He regularly writes for on Port for the wine trade press.

Tom Stevenson (TS) has been writing about wine, and particularly Champagne and Alsace, for more than thirty years. He is the author of twenty-three books and winner of thirty-one literary awards, including The Wine Literary Award, America's only lifetime achievement award for wine writers. In addition to his own books, Tom conceived the annual *Wine Report*.

Andrea Sturniolo (AS) is an Italian wine journalist, living and working in London. He now has a regular weekly wine column in an Italian newspaper and contributes to many other wine publications in Italy and other countries.

Kazumi Suzuki (KS) advocates the distinctive, exquisite beauty of Japan's national drink, Sake, and of course, Japanese wine. She holds the WSET Level 4 Diploma in Wines and Spirits, and is a certified Sake Sommelier. She has worked for wine merchant Berry Brothers & Rudd and currently works for *The World of Fine Wine* magazine.

Jonathan Swinchatt (JS) is co-author, with David Howell, of *The Winemaker's Dance: Exploring Terroir in the Napa Valley*. Trained in geology at Yale and Harvard, he conducts detailed geologic studies of unique vineyard properties. His clients include Stag's Leap Wine Cellars, Opus One, and Harlan Estate.

Terry Theise (TT) is an American wine merchant who specializes in Germany, Austria, and Champagne. His accolades include *Food & Wine* magazine Importer of the Year 2005; *Wine & Spirits* magazine Man of the Year; and inclusion in *The Wine Advocate's* "Most Important Wine Personalities of the Last 25 years."

Monty Waldin (MW) realized while working on a Bordeaux château as a teenager, that the more chemicals were applied to a vineyard, the more corrective treatments became necessary in the winery. His books include *Discovering Wine Country–Bordeaux*, *Discovering Wine Country–Tuscany*, *Wines of South America*, and *Biodynamic Wines*. In 2007, Monty produced his own French wine from biodynamic grapes, in an eighteen-month project filmed by British television.

Stuart Walton (SW) has been writing on wine and gastronomic issues, as well as aspects of cultural history, since 1991, having been successively wine writer on *The Observer*, *The European*, *BBC Magazines*, and *Food and Travel*. He has been a senior contributing writer on Britain's *Good Food Guide* since 1994.

Jeremy Wilkinson (JW) studied Chemistry at University College, London and Emmanuel College, Cambridge before teaching. He worked for Shell for eighteen years before taking the WSET Diploma in 2007, gaining the IWSC/Waitrose scholarship. After working for *The World of Fine Wine*, he entered the wine trade with London wine merchant Jeroboams.

Picture credits

2 © Danita Delimont/Alamy 23 Comité Interprofessionnel du Vin de Champagne 25 Cephas/Mick Rock 26-27 courtesy of Billecart-Salmon 29 Comité Interprofessionnel du Vin de Champagne 31 www.bisol.it 33 Cephas/Mick Rock 34 Panoramic Images/Getty Images 37 Cephas/Mick Rock 39 © Cephas Picture Library/Alamy 41 © Cephas Picture Library/Alamy 43 © Cephas Picture Library/Alamy 46 Comité Interprofessionnel du Vin de Champagne 48 © Lordprice Collection/Alamy 49 © Lordprice Collection/Alamy 53 © Cephas Picture Library/Alamy 55 © Corbis 58 © WinePix/Alamy 61 © Flickr Vision/Getty Images 63 Comité Interprofessionnel du Vin de Champagne 65 © Lordprice Collection/Alamy 67 Cephas/Bruce Fleming 69 Champagne Gosset 73 Domaine Huet 75 Cephas/Mick Rock 76 © Corbis 79 Champagne Krug 80-81 Champagne Krug 85 © Lordprice Collection/Alamy 87 © Cephas/Mick Rock 93 Champagne Mumm 94 © Cephas Picture Library/Alamy 97 © Lordprice Collection/Alamy 99 Pekka Nuikki 100 © Corbis 102 © Lordprice Collection/Alamy 105 Comité Interprofessionnel du Vin de Champagne 107 Hendrik Holler/ Getty Images 109 akg-images 110 Cephas/Clay McLachlan 113 The Art Archive/Global Book Publishing 115 Cephas/Mick Rock 116 © Greg Balfour Evans/Alamy 119 Art Archive/Château de Brissac/Gianni Dagli Orti 121 Cephas/Mick Rock 124 Cephas/Mick Rock 127 © Aerial Archives/Alamy 128 Cephas Picture Library/Alamy/Mick Rock 130 Cephas/Mick Rock 137 Cephas/Mick Rock 139 Cephas/Ian Shaw 140 Photolibrary/Cephas Picture Library/Mick Rock 142 Photolibrary/Cephas Picture Library/R & K Muschenetz 145 © JLImages/Alamy 147 Cephas/Mick Rock 156 © Robert Hollingworth/Alamy 160 Cephas/Mick Rock 165 Photolibrary/Cephas Picture Library/Mick Rock 167 Cephas/Nigel Blythe 168 © Per Karlsson–BKWine.com/Alamy 175 Château Coutet 177 Cephas/Herbert Lehmann 179 Cephas Picture Library/Alamy/Mick Rock 183 Schlossgut Diel 184 © Per Karlsson–BKWine.com/Alamy 187 Cephas/R.A.Beatty 191 Dry River 192 Mme. Aly Duhr et Fils 195 Cephas/Mick Rock 196 © StockFood.com/Armin Faber 200 © CuboImages srl/Alamy/Alfio Giannotti 203 William Fèvre 205 Cephas/Mick Rock 206 Cephas/Mick Rock 209 Cephas/Mick Rock 210 © WinePix/Alamy 217 Cephas Picture Library/Alamy/Mick Rock 218 © Per Karlsson–BKWine.com/Alamy 221 Cephas/Mick Rock 223 Cephas Picture Library/Alamy/Mick Rock 225 Cephas/Nigel Blythe 227 © Cephas Picture Library/Alamy/Alain Proust 229 © Corbis All Right Reserved 231 Cephas/Mick Rock 232 © Bon Appetit/Alamy/Armin Faber 234 © Bon Appetit/Alamy/Feig/Feig 238 Cephas/Mick Rock 241 Cephas Picture Library/Alamy/Kevin Argue 245 © Cephas Picture Library/Alamy/Nigel Blythe 247 Karthäuserhof 248 © Bildarchiv Monheim GmbH/Alamy/Florian Monheim 251 © Per Karlsson–BKWine.com/Alamy 255 Cephas/Nigel Blyth 257 Cephas/Herbert Lehmann 259 Cephas/Kevin Judd 261 © Cephas Picture Library/Alamy/Mick Rock 262 Azienda Agricola La Monacesca 265 © isifa Image Service s.r.o./Alamy/PHB 267 Château Lafaurie-Peyraguey 272 © Cephas Picture Library/Alamy/Ian Shaw 276 Loimer 279 Panoramic Images/Getty Images 281 Cephas/Mick Rock283 McWilliam's 285 Cephas/Mick Rock 287 Photolibrary/Steven Morris Photography 288 Cephas/Nigel Blythe 291 © Cephas Picture Library/Alamy/Nigel Blythe 295 © Cephas Picture Library/Alamy/Ian Shaw 297 © Cephas Picture Library/Alamy/Jerry Alexander 299 © D. H. Webster/Robert Harding World Imagery/Corbis 303 Cephas/Mick Rock 304 © Cephas Picture Library/Alamy/Kevin Judd 312 © Peter Titmuss/Alamy 318 Cephas/Kevin Judd 321 © StockFood.com/Armin Faber 325 Cephas Picture Library/Alamy/Mick Rock 331 © Cephas Picture Library/Alamy/Mick Rock 333 Château Rabaud-Promis 337 © Cephas Picture Library/Alamy/Mick Rock 339 Cephas/Mick Rock 340 Cephas/Andy Christodolo 342 © Michael Busselle/CORBIS 345 Cephas/Mick Rock 346 Cephas/Ian Shaw 349 © Per Karlsson –BKWine.com/Alamy 353 © Cephas Picture Library/Alamy/Nigel Blythe 354 Cephas/Mick Rock 357 © Cephas Picture Library/Alamy/Mick Rock 358 © Corbis All Right Reserved 361 Cephas/Nigel Blythe 365 Cephas/Mick Rock 366 Cephas/Peter Titmuss 369 Château Suduiraut 371 Cephas/Mick Rock 373 © Cephas Picture Library/Alamy 375 Cephas/Mick Rock 381 Cephas/Ted Stefanski 383 Cephas/Mick Rock 385 © Bill Bachman/Alamy 386 Cephas/Mick Rock 388 © StockFood.com/Hendrik Holler 391 Van Volxem 395 Cephas/Clay McLachlan 396 © Cephas/Mick Rock 399 © Cephas Picture Library/Alamy/Nigel Blythe 401 Cephas/Nigel Blythe 403 Weingut Wittmann 405 © Cephas Picture Library/Alamy/Mick Rock 407 © Cephas Picture Library/Alamy/Kevin Judd 409 Cephas/Mick Rock 412 Cephas Picture Library/Alamy 415 © CuboImages srl/Alamy 420 Cephas/Mick Rock 423 Cephas/Mick Rock 424 © Corbis 427 Cephas/Ted Stefanski 428 © Cephas Picture Library/Alamy 431 Artadi 433 Cephas/Bruce Jenkins 435 © Cephas Picture Library/Alamy 437 Pekka Nuikki 445 © AM Corporation/Alamy 449 Pekka Nuikki 451 Photolibrary/Cephas Picture Library/Graeme Robinson 453 © Per Karlsson–BKWine.com/Alamy 455 Cephas/Mick Rock 459 Photolibrary/Cephas Picture Library/Mick Rock 461 © CuboImages srl/Alamy 463 Cephas/Ian Shaw 464 Brokenwood 470 Cephas/Ian Shaw 478 Cephas/Mick Rock 485 Cephas/Mick Rock 489 Pekka Nuikki 490 Chimney Rock 497 Cephas/Mick Rock 499 Cephas Picture Library/Alamy 500 © Corbis 503 Château La Conseillante 513 Cephas/Kevin Judd 515 CVNE 519 © Bon Appetit/Alamy 521 Cephas/Ted Stefanski 524 Domaine Drouhin 527 Cephas/Kevin Judd 529 © LOOK Die Bildagentur der Fotografen GmbH/Alamy 531 © David Hansford/Alamy 533 Cephas/Stephen Wolfenden 537 David Eley 541 Cephas/Stephen Wolfenden 543 Fable Mountain Vineyards 545 Cephas/Mick Rock 547 © Brad Perks Lightscapes/Alamy 555 Cephas/Ted Stefanski 560 Château Gazin 563 Cephas/Herbert Lehmann 565 © imagebroker/Alamy 567 Cephas/Mick Rock 568 Cephas/Kevin Judd 571 Cephas/Bruce Fleming 572 Cephas/Kjell Karlsson 575 Château

Grand-Puy-Lacoste 580 © Cephas Picture Library/Alamy 585 Hardys 587 Cephas/Clay McLachlan 589 Château Haut-Bailly 591 Pekka Nuikki 600 © Bon Appetit/Alamy 603 © Cephas Picture Library/Alamy 605 © Cephas Picture Library/Alamy 607 Klein Constantia 614 Cephas/Kjell Karlsson 619 Cephas/Mick Rock 620 Cephas/Mick Rock 622 © Per Karlsson–BKWine.com/Alamy 625 Cephas/Steve Elphick 627 Pekka Nuikki 630 Pekka Nuikki 635 © Joseph Becker/Alamy 636 Cephas/Mick Rock 639 David Eley 641 © Cephas Picture Library/Alamy/Mick Rock 643 Château Lezongars 645 Consorzio del Vino Brunello di Montalcino 650 Cephas/Kjell Karlsson 657 Consorzio Tutela Barolo Barbaresco Alba Langhe e Roero 658 Cephas/Ian Shaw 665 Meerlust 667 Cephas/Andy Christodolo 673 Cephas/Mick Rock 674 Cephas/Nigel Blythe 678 Cephas/Mick Rock 681 Cephas/Mick Rock 685 Cephas/Herbert Lehmann 686 Cephas/Mick Rock 688 Cephas/Kevin Judd 690 © Cephas Picture Library/Alamy/Andy Christodolo 692 Christie's 694 Cephas/Mick Rock 697 Cephas/Char Abu Mansoor 701 Cephas/Pierre Mosca 705 Opus One 708 © Stock Food.com/Hans-Peter Siffert 711 Cephas/Mick Rock 713 Cephas/Mick Rock 715 Cephas/Kevin Judd 719 © Cephas Picture Library/Alamy/Mick Rock 721 Château Pavie Macquin/ANAKA 722 Cephas/Herbert Lehmann 727 Cephas/Mick Rock 728 Cephas/Mick Rock 733 © Corbis All Right Reserved 736 © Cephas Picture Library/Alamy/Mick Rock 741 Château Poujeaux 744 Cephas/Mick Rock 746 Cephas/Mick Rock 751 Cephas/Mick Rock 755 Cephas/Stephen Wolfenden 757 Ravenswood 764 Cephas/Mick Rock 770 © Chad Ehlers/Alamy 773 Cephas/Andy Christodolo 781 © Bon Appetit/Alamy/Hendrik Holler 783 Cephas/Andy Christodolo 785 Consorzio del Vino Brunello di Montalcino 789 © James Osmond/ Alamy 790 © Cephas Picture Library/Alamy/Kevin Judd 793 © Bon Appetit/Alamy/Joerg Lehmann 795 Tapanappa 797 Cephas/Mick Rock 799 Cephas/Mick Rock 805 Cephas/Kevin Judd 806 © Per Karlsson–BKWine.com/Alamy 809 Cephas/Alain Proust 811 Torbreck 812 Cephas/Matt Wilson 815 Cephas/Mick Rock 817 Trinity Hill Wines 819 Cephas/Ian Shaw 821 Cephas Picture Library/Alamy/Stephen Wolfenden 825 Pekka Nuikki 827 Cephas/Mick Rock 831 Pekka Nuikki 833 Cephas/Alain Proust 837 © David R. Frazier Photolibrary, Inc./Alamy 839 Cephas/Kevin Judd 840 Cephas/Ian Shaw 843 Cephas/Andy Christodolo 847 Cephas/Mick Rock 849 Cephas/Mick Rock 852 © Gordon Sinclair/Alamy 855 © Bon Appetit/Alamy 856 © Ian Dagnall/Alamy 861 Chambers 865 The Fladgate Partner-ship 867 © Peter Horree/Alamy 869 The Fladgate Partnership 870 Cephas/Ian Shaw 873 © CuboImages srl/Alamy 874 © Bon Appetit/Alamy 877 Cephas/Mick Rock 879 © Cephas Picture Library/Alamy/Roy Stedall-Humphryes 880 © Cephas Picture Library/Alamy/Mick Rock 889 Cephas/Mick Rock 890 Cephas/Ian Shaw 893 Cephas/Mick Rock 897 Cephas/Herbert Lehmann 899 David Eley 901 © Cephas Picture Library/Alamy 903 David Eley 905 © Cephas Picture Library/Alamy 907 © Cephas Picture Library/Alamy 909 © Cephas Picture Library/Alamy 910 Quady 912 Ramos Pinto 915 Quinta de la Rosa 916 © Mirjam Letsch/Alamy 919 © Mary Evans Picture Library/Alamy 921 Cephas/Mick Rock 923 The Fladgate Partnership 925 Cephas/Mick Rock 929 © Cephas Picture Library/Alamy/Ian Shaw 933 Corbis 934 The Symington Group 937 © Corbis

Acknowledgments

Quintessence would like to thank the following:

Editing Rob Dimery, Irene Lyford, Fiona Plowman, Jane Simmonds; Proofreading Anne Plume; Indexing Ann Barrett; Additional Picture Research Helena Baser; Design Assistance Emma Wood; Image Retouching Chris Taylor; Additional Photography Simon Pask

From Neil Beckett, General Editor

I am deeply grateful to the many people who have helped with this book. My special thanks to Piers Spence, the Director of Publishing at Quarto; Sara Basra and Stuart George, my colleagues at The World of Fine Wine; Tristan de Lancey, Jane Laing, Jodie Gaudet, Frank Ritter, and Akihiro Nakayama at Quintessence; Pekka Nuikki for his brilliant photography; and my family for all their support.

Stuart George would also like to thank all the producers cited in the book; the staff of Astrum Wine Cellars, Berkmann Wine Cellars, Caves de Pyrene, Justerini & Brooks, Mille Gusti, Portland Media, Raymond Reynolds, and Emma Wellings PR; also Sarah Chadwick, Patricia Parnell, Dacotah Renneau, Sue Glasgow, Sally Bishop, Lorraine Carrigan, Petra Kulisic, Margaret Harvey MW, Helen Lenarduzzi, John Michael, Thomas Winterstetter, Ben Smith at Bibendum, Isabelle Philippe at Bouchard Père & Fils, Rachel Thompson at Corney & Barrow, Sylvain Boivert at Conseil des Grands Crus Classés en 1855, Tamara Grischy at Langtons, Simon Larkin MW at Lay & Wheeler, Nicola Lawrence at Liberty Wines, Joanna Locke MW at The Wine Society, Johana Loubet at Château Margaux, Louise Du Bosky at McKinley Vintners, Elizabeth Ferguson at Mentzendorff, Kristy Parker and Genavieve Alexander at Moët Hennessy UK, Corine Karroum at Ets Jean-Pierre Moueix, Verena Niepoort at Niepoort Vinhos S.A., Chantal Gillard at Le Pin, Marita Heil at VDP Die Prädikatsweingüter, Zubair Mohamed at Raeburn Fine Wines, Audrey Domenach and Karen Jenkins at Richards Walford, Antonella Lotti at Thurner PR, Akos Forczek and David Smith at Top Selection, Tim Johns at Wines of Argentina, Karen Sutton and Lauren Laubser at Wines of Chile, and David Motion at The Winery.